A PRELIMINARY GUIDE TO PRE-1904 COUNTY RECORDS

IN THE

VIRGINIA STATE LIBRARY AND ARCHIVES

Compiled by

Suzanne Smith Ray
Lyndon H. Hart III
J. Christian Kolbe

Virginia State Library and Archives
Richmond • 1994

Printed in the United States of America.

This book is printed on acid-free paper meeting the
requirements of the American National Standard for Permanence
of Paper for Printed Library Materials.

Standard Book Number 0–88490–179–3

Contents

PREFACE

In order to make its holdings accessible, the Virginia State Library and Archives adopted a program of inventorying its collections. This program has resulted in greater administrative control over the official records and private manuscripts in the Archives, as well as better public access to the collections through a series of published inventories, guides, and an online database.

A large proportion of the public records in the Archives were produced or received by county and superior courts and by constitutional officers at the local level. These records reflect the relationship between Virginia's citizens and their government at the level at which it most often touched their daily lives. Because of the vital importance of the records, this guide has been published to improve understanding of Virginia's local history, as well as to increase administrative control and provide better access to the records.

This volume is the first of two preliminary guides to the Archives' holdings of pre-1904 local records. It contains entries for Virginia's counties, and a companion volume includes holdings for municipalities. The guide also includes information about the history and development of local government in Virginia as well as information concerning the Archives and Records Division's local records programs.

Guide entries reflect holdings and processing status as of June 30, 1985. With the creation of the Circuit Court Clerks Record Program in 1992 and the hiring of additional staff to process the court records housed in the Archives, additional materials have been found, date ranges have been refined, and the volume of records has expanded significantly. As records are arranged and described, additional information has been made available in the Archives Manuscript Search Room. New acquisitions and additions to the collection can be found in the *Annual Reports of Archival Accessions*. Researchers should contact the Archives concerning access to local records because many were transferred under court orders restricting public access pending the completion of arrangement and security microfilming. Access to restricted records may be granted by written permission from the clerk of court. Researchers should also note that additional records may be found in the courthouses.

This guide was prepared to increase researchers' awareness and understanding of local government records. It is our intention that the information contained herein will aid them in identifying materials overlooked at times by even the most experienced researcher.

Louis H. Manarin
State Archivist

INTRODUCTION

The Archives and Records Division traditionally has considered all court records, and most other local records as well, to be historically valuable and archival if they were created prior to February 1, 1904. That date is used because on January 31, 1904 the county courts ceased to exist, and their functions passed to the circuit courts. Records created by the defunct county court system, and by other contemporary offices, comprise the irreplaceable documentation of Virginia's earliest local government.

The Preliminary Guide to County Records therefore includes records, created in the commonwealth's counties and cities prior to February 1, 1904, which are now held in the Virginia State Library and Archives in Richmond. Volumes and certain short series may extend beyond that date, but 1904 is in general the cutoff point for records included in this guide. Records created subsequent to that date, and stored in the Archives, are included in unpublished finding aids in the Archives Manuscript Search Room.

The guide is arranged alphabetically by county. Since the great majority of records were transferred to the State Library and Archives from offices of clerks of court, most entries are under the major heading Circuit Court Clerk. These include Board of Supervisors Records, Bonds/Commissions/Oaths, etc. Four other major headings follow, to cover the offices of Commissioner of Revenue, Commonwealth's Attorney, Sheriff, and Treasurer. A list of headings and subheadings follows the introduction on page xiv.

Entries under each subheading are alphabetical with two exceptions. The first exception is that when there are entries for both a bound volume and its separately bound index, the index follows the record to which it refers, regardless of alphabetization. The second exception is that when titles of an obviously consecutive series vary, they are listed chronologically, regardless of alphabetization; e.g., Deed, Will, and Order Books, 1663-1697, would be entered before Deed Books, 1746-1770.

The guide contains listings for two broad categories of records. The first is original records, which includes the bound volumes and loose papers of the localities, as well as typescript, photostatic, or other paper copies of original records. The second category is microfilmed records, which includes both the records filmed during the 1950s by the Church of Jesus Christ of Latter Day Saints, and those filmed since 1974 by the Records Branch of the Archives and Records Division. No original records are circulated outside the Archives Manuscript Search Room, regardless of medium, but certain microfilm copies of records may be borrowed through interlibrary loan. Availability can be determined by submitting requests through local libraries.

There are also two categories of pre-1904 records that are not included in the guide. The first, obviously, is the unfortunate number of records that have been lost. Visitors to the Virginia State Library and Archives may hear references to "burned" or "burned out" counties; th is means that the locality suffered an extensive loss of records, usually in a courthouse fire.

The other group of records not included in this guide are those of counties formerly in Virginia but that now comprise West Virginia, or are now in Illinois, Kentucky, or Pennsylvania. Parts of three counties (Monongalia, Ohio, and Yohogania) were added to Pennsylvania between 1776 and 1785; Illinois County was ceded to Congress and ceased to be part of Virginia on March 1, 1784. Kentucky's nine counties became a state on June 1, 1792. When West Virginia became a separate state on June 23, 1863, its counties' records remained in the localities of origin, and are now either in the county seats or at the West Virginia Archives in Charleston. The Virginia State Library and Archives does, however, have personal property tax records and legislative petitions created prior to 1792 for Kentucky and prior to 1863 for West Virginia, as well as a very small number of West Virginia local records. These records are described in finding aids available in the Archives reading room.

Several other former Virginia counties are now extinct. Several were divided or incorporated into present-day counties, and in the twentieth century several tidewater counties have merged with their principal cities and thereby have ceased to exist. The records of those counties are included in the second volume of this guide under the names of the cities of which they are now part; there is, however, a cross-reference under the name of the extinct county name, which refers the researcher to the proper place. For example, in this volume there is an entry for Elizabeth City County, giving date of formation and other information, with a note to see records listed under City of Hampton.

For those wishing to use the local records stored in the Virginia State Library and Archives, a final caveat concerns closed or restricted records. The Virginia Public Records Act mandates the Virginia State Library and Archives to preserve, arrange, and microfilm security copies of permanently valuable records. Subsequent to formation of the local records program in 1972, most county and municipal records transferred to the Virginia State Library and Archives were under a court order closing them to public access and photoduplication pending completion of security microfilming. This measure was taken to assure that the records remained in their original order until a security microfilm copy was obtained.

When records are closed by court order, access to them may be gained only with written permission from the clerk or judge of the relevant court. Researchers should contact the Virginia State Library and Archives to determine whether there are restrictions on records in which they are interested, and, if so, obtain the necessary written permission prior to visiting the Archives.

Origins of Local Government

The Virginia colony was established in 1607 by a trading corporation known as the Virginia Company of London, under whose charter a president and council, responsible to the company authorities in England, governed the colony. A later charter (1609) placed control of the company in its own council, centralizing power in a governor who could appoint advisors and other officers; Lord De La Warr, a member of the company's council, was the first governor. In 1612 a third charter increased the powers of the company, giving more of its members a voice in government.

Under this system, communal possession of land was the rule in Virginia. As settlement stabilized, and the population increased, private ownership was suggested by the large amount of available land. In 1619, Sir Thomas Smith, first treasurer of the Virginia Company, was succeeded by Sir Edwin Sandys, whose liberal, ambitious plans regarding land, laid the base of Virginia's political institutions. Under Sandys, grants of land were to be made to stockholders, some tracts were to be designated for public use, and the "headright" system (by which private individuals might obtain a fifty-acre grant for each person transported to the colony) was instituted.

To accelerate colonization, the company, assigned large estates or plantations to associations of private individuals. They were to be self-sustaining, with limited lawmaking powers. Although more than forty of these quasi-independent plantations received patents, only a few materialized. The oldest was Smith's Hundred, an 18,000-acre grant between the James and Chickahominy rivers, which was patented in 1617. The first one actually to be organized was Martin's Hundred, patented in 1618. These hundreds antedate counties, and it was from them and the associations that burgesses were sent in 1619 to the first legislative assembly in North America.

Prior to establishment of formal plantation colonies, groups of one hundred men had been stationed at certain points on the rivers for settlement and military purposes. In 1611 the governor laid off several hundreds near the mouth of the Appomattox River. They became early models for local government when a system was devised by which several plantations, or hundreds, formed precincts with monthly courts.

Another developmental step was taken when the colony was divided into four corporations (James City, Charles City, Henrico, and Kiccowtan), that existed when the first assembly met in 1619. The Virginia Company was dissolved in 1624, and the present structure of local government was begun in 1634 with the formation of eight shires,[1] or counties, which became the units of representation in the colonial legislature.

The monthly courts, whose members were first called commissioners, were established in 1619 and were central to the judicial system. In March 1643 members were restyled commissioners of the county court, and individual magistrates were empowered to hear cases involving less than twenty shillings sterling. After 1662 the commissioners of the court were known as justices of the peace.

During the English Commonwealth, the justices recommended to the governor persons to be appointed to their court; under this system, and with lifetime appointments, they became a self-perpetuating body. The clerk of the court, appointed by the secretary of state, also customarily had long terms in office, and this position became hereditary, in fact, if not by law, in many cases.

The county lieutenant, or commander, was chief of militia in the shires. The sheriff was also important, for it was he who executed court orders, collected taxes and other moneys, and performed numerous additional duties. Other officers included constables appointed by the county court commissioners, and surveyors appointed by the surveyor general. All others were commissioned by the governor after nomination by the county court.

Another division of local government that predated the county was the parish. The Anglican church followed the advancing settlements. Since formation of the shires removed parish representatives from the legislature, the parishes became more concerned with local problems and were empowered by the colonial government to make bylaws. In 1679 that authority was passed entirely to the county courts, to which each parish could then send two representatives to have a voice in making county rules. The parish vestry concerned itself with civil matters such as land processioning and care of the indigent as well as clerical matters.

Colonial government was hierarchical, operating from the top down. The governor was responsible to the king and was the center of power. He and the Council appointed the local court justices. The "gentlemen justices" were the ruling class. They served only in the court of their own county and maintained a sense of local pride, responsibility, and independence. The office of justice was nonsalaried with few perquisites, and it became customary for the governor to fill vacancies from a list provided by the justices themselves.

Justices' court procedures evolved slowly. It was originally planned to have a member of the Council assist at each monthly court, but the increasing number of counties made that impractical. Circuit courts consisting of the governor and councillors, to sit in each county, also proved unfeasible and lasted only one year, 1662-1663. These and other factors strengthened the justices' county courts, and by the time of the American Revolution they decided most law and

---

[1]   The original shires were Accawmack, Charles City, Charles River, Elizabeth City, Henrico, James City, Warrosquyoake, and Warwick River.

chancery cases and had extensive fiduciary duties.

The Revolution left the court system virtually unchanged, except that clerks henceforth were appointed by the courts rather than by the secretary of state. An act passed in 1785 and amended in 1788 called for quarterly sessions for all common-law and chancery cases and petitions for debt, and monthly sessions for all other matters. A revision in 1792 reduced all the courts to one.

As the county courts became more stable, the established church was being undermined by a growing dissenter movement. Some vestries were dissolved during the American Revolution and replaced by elected overseers of the poor. Salaries of the clergy were suspended in 1777 and the Church of England was effectively disestablished. The final blow came in 1787 when the act reserving the glebe and other church property for the Protestant Episcopal church was repealed. The overseers were empowered in 1802 to sell the glebe lands when they became vacant; by 1830 most were gone.

Under the Constitution of 1776 the governor, Council of State, and superior court judges were all chosen by the legislature. While a county court was not specified in the constitution, the tradition was so strong that despite criticism from numerous sources it continued, liberalized only by broadening the suffrage.

The courts had several weaknesses, however. The only elected officials were the overseers of the poor and, after 1846, the school commissioners. Since the colonial period the sheriff, coroner, and militia officers were commissioned by the governor after court nomination; by custom a senior justice was then selected to be sheriff and was recommissioned each year. The clerk, commissioner of revenue, commonwealth's attorney, road surveyor, commissioner of roads, and constables were appointed by the court. The court itself was self-perpetuating, as noted, and inefficiency and declining quality were the gradual results.

In an effort to mitigate these problems, the 1830-1831 session of the General Assembly divided the state into districts, and a circuit superior court of law and chancery was thereafter held twice annually in each county. A judge of the General Court, chosen by the General Assembly, presided. This system replaced the superior courts of law, that had met since 1809 in each county, and the superior courts of chancery, that were district courts established in 1802. The new courts had civil and criminal jurisdiction, overlapping in some areas with the county courts, and limited appellate jurisdiction in mill, road, and fiduciary matters.

The circuit courts proved to be efficient. Additional liberal gains were made in the constitutional convention of 1850-1851, when all county officers except the road surveyor, superintendent of schools, deputy clerks of court, deputy sheriffs, and coroner were made elective. County courts were retained, but the state was redistricted, to have ten district courts with appellate jurisdiction only, and circuit courts similar to the old circuit superior courts of law and chancery were established.

The Civil War interrupted local government functions, and many court records were lost or destroyed as a result of military action. After the war, Virginia became part of Military District Number One, the government was taken over by radicals, and many former Confederates were disfranchised. The Constitution of 1869, which made important changes in county government, was framed under those conditions. Under it, salaried judges, chosen by the General Assembly, were placed over the county courts. A statewide system of public schools was formed, controlled by a superintendent of public instruction and a state board of education, which appointed a superintendent of schools for each county.

The most significant change, however, was creation of boards of supervisors that assumed the administrative duties formerly performed by the county courts. Counties were divided into townships similar to those in New England, and supervisors were elected from each one. Although the postwar townships were abandoned by 1875 in favor of magisterial districts, the boards of supervisors were retained. From then until 1904 most county officials were elected by the people, with judges and school commissioners appointed by various county or state officials.

The county court system was again debated in the 1901-1902 constitutional convention and this time its opponents' views prevailed. No provisions were made for the court in the new constitution, and its powers and duties were transferred to the circuit courts effective February 1, 1904.[2]

The 1902 constitution remained in effect until 1971, when Virginia's most recent constitution was adopted. The new constitution made few changes in local government. Today Virginia's counties operate on two levels: 1) they serve as agents of the state, administering justice and assessing and collecting taxes, and 2) as local units of government, passing and enforcing local laws and operating their own local education systems.[3] There are today ninety-five counties in the commonwealth.

Virginia's Independent Cities

Virginia's government is unique in that cities and counties have separate areas of political power. Residents of a Virginia city vote for only one set of officials, pay taxes to one locality, and are subject to one set of ordinances and regulations. Residents of towns, however, are subject to the county or counties in which the towns are located, vote for officials of two localities, and use the services of the county's officials and agencies.[4]

Status as a city depends on population, and, as a result, most cities are of recent origin. Many were settled and established in the eighteenth and nineteenth centuries, but more than half were incorporated as cities after 1904. Today there are forty-one independent cities in Virginia. The Archives and Records Division deals with counties and independent cities as equivalent entities.

Records Keeping

The actual records keeping practices of the various county court clerks varied little. The types of records that each created and retained are uniform and based upon English record keeping precedents. Variety occurs in the naming patterns of large series - i.e., judgments may be variously labelled and included among dead papers, court papers, or promiscuous papers. The labelling in no way affects the materials that are kept.

A number of factors have, however, resulted in very different rates of survival for records

---

[2]   Historical data is excerpted from: Lester J. Cappon, "The Evolution of County Government in Virginia," *Inventory of the County Archives of Virginia: No. 21 Chesterfield County (Chesterfield Court House)* Charlottesville: The University of Virginia, 1938), 4-33.

[3]   George W. Jennings, *Virginia's Government: The Structure and Functions of the State and Local Governments of the Commonwealth of Virginia*, 16th ed., Rev. (Richmond: Virginia State Chamber of Commerce, 1982), 52.

[4]   Ibid.

among the various counties. Dates of settlement and county formation, geographic size and population, historical background, and economic development and prosperity are all factors. Records loss by fire and natural disaster, the efficiency of various clerks, and years of use and abuse by the public have also influenced the status of Virginia's extant records.

Some uniformity has been achieved by use of standard forms distributed by state agencies to the offices reporting to them. For example, the auditor of public accounts began supplying land and personal property tax books to local commissioners of revenue prior to 1860, and the 1919 and subsequent editions of the Code of Virginia required much greater uniformity of modern records than had previously existed.

Records maintenance facilities also vary. The records of some localities are still stored in the original courthouse, while others have been moved into new, modern storage facilities. Environmental controls, fireproofing, and security precautions vary widely depending on the age and condition of the storage place, and improvements depend on the economic resources and other factors within the locality.

The importance of records keeping and maintenance is illustrated by the fact that more than 40 percent of Virginia's county courts have suffered records losses by fire, war, floods, or other causes. About half of those have lost all or almost all of their records; the others have had less extensive but still significant losses. While Appomattox County was the last to suffer a major records loss, over a century ago, there have been three known cases of vandalism and one attempted arson in the last twenty years, as well as known or suspected thefts, and two courthouse fires and a flood since 1970.

The vulnerability of records gained legislative attention when the Botetourt County Courthouse was destroyed by fire in December 1970. A measure was then introduced in the General Assembly, and in 1972 House Bill 308 was passed, providing for the inventorying, scheduling, and microfilming of official records of permanent value, and calling for safe storage for microfilm copies of such records.

The primary goal of the resulting local records program has been to microfilm vital and historical records, the majority of which originate in the offices of clerks of the circuit court and its predecessor courts. The state was divided into five districts, and localities within each district were ranked for priority treatment, based on three general criteria: value of the records in terms of age and content, condition of the records and storage facilities, and whether or not security microfilming of any records had already been done by any other group.

The security microfilm aspect of the local records program is handled by the Information Imaging Branch of the Archives and Records Division. The Archives Appraisal and Description Branch is responsible for transfer of original records. The Code of Virginia and general schedules give firm guidelines on disposition of records, so that even if permanent records have been filmed, they cannot be destroyed. Localities lacking adequate storage facilities are encouraged to transfer records to the Archives. Once transferred, the records will eventually be flat filed, arranged, stored in acid-free containers, and scheduled for microfilming. After filming, the original records usually remain in the Archives; as a result, the Virginia State Library's holdings of local records are the single largest source of local history documentation in Virginia.

Conclusion

This guide describes the Archives' local records holdings as of June 30, 1985. At that time there were approximately 18,000 cubic feet of permanently valuable county and municipal records housed in the Archives. They contain an enormous amount of information of value to researchers. In addition to preservation, arrangement, and security, it is the duty of archivists to make public records available for examination and study, and it is hoped that this preliminary guide will facilitate access to the local records.

ADDITIONAL SUGGESTED READING

Bain, Chester W. *"A Body Incorporate": The Evolution of City-County Separation in Virginia.* Charlottesville: University Press of Virginia, 1967.

Curtis, George Martin, III. "The Virginia Courts During the Revolution." Ph. D. diss., University of Wisconsin, 1970.

Hiden, Martha W. *How Justice Grew: Virginia Counties, An Abstract of Their Formation.* Virginia 350th Anniversary Celebration Corporation, no. 19. Williamsburg, 1957.

Jennings, George W. *Virginia's Government: The Structure and Functions of the State and Local Governments of the Commonwealth of Virginia.* 16th ed., rev. Richmond: Virginia State Chamber of Commerce, 1982.

Kuroda, Tadahisa. "The County Court System of Virginia from the Revolution to the Civil War." Ph. D. diss., Columbia University, 1970.

Salmon, Emily J., ed. *A Hornbook of Virginia History.* 3d ed. Richmond: Virginia State Library, 1983.

Wertenbaker, Thomas J. *The Government of Virginia in the Seventeenth Century.* Virginia 350th Anniversary Celebration Corporation, no. 16. Williamsburg, 1957.

HEADINGS USED IN THIS GUIDE

Circuit Court Clerk
    Board of Supervisors Records
    Bonds/Commissions/Oaths
    Business Records/Corporations/Partnerships
    Census Records
    Court Records
        County Court
        District Court
        Superior Court of Chancery
        Superior Court of Law
        Circuit Superior Court of Law and Chancery
        Circuit Court
        District Court
        [Other courts, out-of-state, etc.]
        County and Superior Courts
        Unspecified Court
    Election Records
    Fiduciary Records
    Free Negro and Slave Records
    Justice of the Peace Records
    Land Records
    Marriage Records and Vital Statistics
    Military and Pension Records
    Organization Records
    Road and Bridge Records
    School Records
    Tax and Fiscal Records
    Wills
    Miscellaneous Records

Commissioner of Revenue

Commonwealth's Attorney

Sheriff

Treasurer

GLOSSARY

This glossary reflects the status of Virginia records and records keeping prior to 1 February 1904.

ADMINISTRATOR: A person appointed by the court to manage the assets and liabilities of a person who dies without having written a valid will. An administrator may also be appointed if the testator leaves an incomplete will naming no executor, or if the named executor cannot or will not serve. See also Fiduciary.

APPEARANCE DOCKET: A docket for appearances in court, usually for preliminary pleading, containing a brief abstract of the successive steps in each action.

APPRENTICE INDENTURES: Bonds and contracts of apprenticeship, showing the names of master and apprentice, the trade to be taught, details of the contract, amount of the bond, and names of sureties.

ARGUMENT DOCKET: A list of cases to come before the court at each term for arguments of motions and demurrers (objections); it names the parties to the action, their attorneys, and suit styles.

ASSESSOR: A county official has assessed taxes since 1634, but county courts were first authorized to appoint specific land assessors in 1870. The office was abolished in 1926, and its duties conferred on the commissioners of revenue. Assessors were reinstated in 1930. See also Commissioner of Revenue.

BANNS: See Marriage Banns.

BENCH DOCKET: The judge's copy of the Memorandum Docket.

BOARD OF SUPERVISORS: The board of supervisors has been the chief administrative body of the county since its establishment in 1869. Board members were originally elected by township voters; since abolition of the township system they have been elected from districts. The board's duties are fixed by statute and are primarily concerned with maintenance and construction of county buildings and fiscal matters. See also Townships.

BONDS: Obligations or covenants between persons, made binding by a money guarantee. Bonds are given for various causes, and show the names of the principal and sureties, the date, amount and condition of the obligation, and signatures.

BOUNTY LAND: Land awarded as a bonus to attract soldiers to enlist, or as payment in addition to or instead of wages for military service.

CHANCERY: The forms and principles of judicial equity; that is, justice according to fairness rather than according to strictly formulated common law.

CHATTEL: See Crop Liens.

COMMISSIONER OF REVENUE: The title commissioner of revenue appeared in 1792, although tax assessing agents have existed since the establishment of shires in 1634. Commissioners were at first required to take a list of taxable property, licenses granted, and free Negroes or mulattoes in their districts, and they provided the escheators with lists of lands left by persons who died intestate and without heirs. Later they were required to list white males eligible to vote and to register births and deaths. During the township period they were designated assessors of the tax. Today the commissioner is the taxation official at the local level, with the main function of assessing land and personal property. See also Assessor.

COMMITTEE: The person(s) to whom a duty or trust is committed, especially persons invested by court authority with guardianship of someone adjudged to be a lunatic. This person is also referred to as curator. See also Fiduciary.

COMMON LAW: In Virginia common law is "English law" based on usages and customs of antiquity, as practiced in colonial America.

COMMONWEALTH'S ATTORNEY: First appointed by statute in 1788 for the district courts, and in 1800 for the county courts, this has been an elected office since 1850. Its general duty is to defend the commonwealth and to prosecute in its behalf.

CONSERVATOR: A guardian, protector, or preserver appointed by the court to manage the affairs of an incompetent person or to liquidate a business. See also Fiduciary.

CONSTABLE: The appointed office of constable was established by 1637. Duties are similar to those of a sheriff, but constables are less powerful and have a smaller jurisdiction.

CORONER: The separate office of coroner appeared in Virginia about 1660. The judicial duty of the office is to hold inquisitions in cases when persons meet violent or unnatural deaths, to establish the cause of death, to deliver the guilty person to the sheriff, and to act as administrator of the deceased's estate. The coroner also performs the sheriff's duties when there is a vacancy in that office. The office of coroner is appointive.

COUNTY CLERK: From the records-keeping point of view, the county clerk has always been the most important local official, since he recorded both the administrative and judicial activities of the court and of other officers of the county. The five general historical duties of the clerk are: 1) county clerk, 2) clerk of the court, 3) probate officer, 4) county recorder, and 5) clerk of the board of supervisors.

CROP LIENS: Crop liens, or encumbrances, exist in favor of persons expending labor, skill, or materials on any chattel or furnishing storage thereof at request of the owner, reputed owner, or lawful possessor. Chattel is personal property, either animate or inanimate, as opposed to real property. See also Judgment Docket, Lien, and Real [property].

CURTESY: The future potential interest (usually one-third) that a husband has in the real property of his wife as the result of the birth to them of a living child capable of inheriting from her. It is a freehold estate for the term of the husband's natural life. See also Dower.

DEAD PAPERS: Suits in common law or equity that have been brought to some conclusion (either dismissal, settlement, or decree). Such a series may also contain papers from suits that were continued through many terms of court without resolution and were therefore removed from current files. Dead papers are also called determined papers, ended causes, or other titles, depending on the practices of individual clerks.

DEED: An instrument, signed and usually sealed by the grantor, containing some legal transfer, bargain, or contract from one person to another. During the seventeenth and eighteenth centuries conveyances were sometimes made by a combination of deeds of lease and release, which taken together had the effect of a single conveyance; this was a common practice in the Northern Neck.

DEED INDENTED (INDENTURE): An indented deed is executed in two or more parts, and takes its name from the fact that the top or side edge formerly was cut, or indented, to resemble the teeth of a saw. The cutting is now more commonly either a waving line or notching at the edge of the instrument. See also Indenture.

DEED POLL: A deed poll is made by one party, who binds himself by it. The name comes from the fact that the edge of the paper was polled, or cut, in a straight line.

DEPOSITION: Written testimony taken under oath, authenticated, and used in trials of actions in court.

DETERMINED PAPERS: See Dead Papers.

DIVORCE: Until the nineteenth century divorces were granted in Virginia by the General Assembly; on 17 March 1841 a law was passed giving jurisdiction over divorce suits, which are heard in chancery, to the circuit superior court of law and chancery (now the circuit court) in each county.

DOCKET: A brief formal record of proceedings in a court of justice; an entry of all acts in the conduct of a case, from inception to conclusion. See also specific dockets.

DOWER: The part or interest (usually one-third) in the real estate of a deceased husband that is given by law to his widow for her support and the nurture of her children during her life. See also Curtesy.

ELECTORAL BOARD: Special officers have been appointed specifically to oversee general elections since 1831; these have included registrars, commissioners of elections, election judges, and clerks. The election law of 1884 created electoral boards, which have since appointed all other election officials. The electoral boards and registrars are the recording agents of the election machinery.

ENDED CASES: See Dead Papers.

ENTAILED: Entailed lands automatically descend to a specific person and his or her lineal descendants.

EQUITY: See Chancery.

ESCHEAT: Reversion of property to the state when there are no legal heirs to inherit it.

ESTABLISHED CHURCH: A specific denomination officially supported by local taxes or government funds. During the colonial period the Anglican church was the established church in Virginia. Disestablishment occurred in 1786.

ESTRAY: In common law an (e)stray is a wandering animal whose owner is unknown. Records of strays are notices of discovery of lost livestock, with reports of commissioners appointed to determine proper reimbursement of the finder for caring for the animals.

EXECUTION DOCKET: Lists executions sued out or pending in the sheriff's office. It shows notices of process, names of all parties, amount of judgment, date of execution, return date, and sheriff's return; it is not a record of instances of capital punishment. See also Fieri Facias.

EXECUTOR: The person appointed by the testator to carry out the directions and requests in his will.

EXHIBIT: A document or object produced and identified in court or before an examiner for use as evidence. Exhibit papers are often referred to in, and filed with, a deposition or with the bill, answer, or petition in an equity suit.

FEE BOOK: A volume showing the date of a duty performed by the clerk, the name of the person paying the fees, and the amount. It includes fees charged attorneys, cash accounts, and the clerk's fees in common law and chancery suits.

FEE SIMPLE: Absolute ownership.

FIDUCIARY: A confidential and legal relationship which binds one person to act on behalf of another. A fiduciary is also the person who acts as trustee for another.

FIERI FACIAS (FI FA): From the Latin phrase meaning "cause it to be done," a Fi Fa is a writ of execution commanding the sheriff to levy and take the amount of a judgment from the goods and chattels of the judgment debtor.

FORM BOOK: Before statewide standard court forms were used, clerks of court used form books to insure correctness. The books contained models of forms used, showing the principal necessary information, correct technical terms or phrases, and other information that was required.

GRANTOR/GRANTEE: The grantor is the person conveying land by deed (the seller). The grantee is the person to whom the land is conveyed (the buyer).

GUARDIAN: A person legally invested to take care of another person, and of the property and rights of that person. Since ca. 1660 guardians have been required to file a yearly account with the clerk of court. These accounts are sometimes called orphans' accounts.

HEIR AT LAW: Next of kin by blood. The term is used in intestacy cases, and is interchangeable with the phrase "heir by intestacy."

INDENTURE: A deed to which two or more persons are parties, in which they enter into reciprocal and corresponding grants or obligations to each other; such a deed is cut, or indented, along the top or side edge. An indenture is also a contract binding one person to work for another for a specified period of time. See also Apprentice Indentures.

INQUISITION: In the broadest sense, an inquisition is any judicial inquiry or hearing. More specifically, it is an examination, usually before a jury, as well as the finding of the jury. Also it is called an inquest.

INSOLVENTS: Those who cannot pay their debts as they fall due in the normal course of business. Alternatively, they are persons who can pay, but whose property is so situated that it cannot be reached by process of law and subjected to payment without consent.

INTESTATE: Someone who dies without having made a valid will. Property not disposed of by a will is described as being intestate, as well. The word is also commonly used to describe the condition of dying without a valid will.

ISSUE DOCKET: An issue is the act of issuing or promulgating; e.g., to issue an order or writ. An issue docket is the record of issuance, showing parties' names, actions, and remarks.

JOURNAL: A book of daily entries made for each available fund. Less frequently in public records, a journal is an account of day-to-day events. See also Ledger.

JUDGE'S DOCKET: See Bench Docket.

JUDGMENT DOCKET: Lists judgments and other liens entered in all courts; it is a register of liens on all owners of property.

JUSTICE OF THE PEACE: First known as commissions, this office originated with the county quarterly court in 1623. Commanders of Plantations (1607-1629) were predecessors of the commissioners, who since 1662 have been called justices of the peace. They have traditionally had both civil and criminal jurisdiction, and have served other functions, including performing coroners' and lunacy inquisitions. Until 1869 justices served both as judges of the county court and as individual justices; since then they have had only the latter function.

LAND ENTRIES: Original entries of claims to vacant land, giving a description of the land, the name of the claimant, the number of acres, and an endorsement.

LEDGER: Often called a book of final entry, a ledger is a record of transaction data classified by account and summarized from a journal; it is arranged by fund, showing daily receipts or disbursements thereunder. See also Journal.

LIEN: A charge or claim against property for payment of an obligation, duty, or debt, including taxes. Lien dockets list the nature and amount of the lien and services or materials supplied upon which it is based.

LUNACY INQUISITION: Detailed records of hearings for commitment of the insane and inebriates, including orders of commitment. See also Inquisitions.

MARRIAGE BANNS: Prior to 1848, banns were a legal substitute for a marriage license. Banns were published, or announced, during the church service on three successive Sundays or worship days prior to the marriage. Marriages by banns were recorded only in the church or parish register.

MARRIAGE BONDS: The first law requiring a bond was enacted in 1660/1661. It required the prospective groom to give bond at the courthouse in the bride's county of residence. A license was then prepared by the clerk and presented to the minister who performed the ceremony. The only alternative to marriage by bond was marriage by banns.

MARRIAGE CERTIFICATES: This term most frequently describes the ministers' returns of marriages they performed. It is also used to describe the consent given by parents, masters, or guardians of underage persons seeking to marry. A third use of the term is that if a parish was without a minister, the person who published the banns was required to issue a certificate of publication. Finally, after 1858 licenses required issuance of a certificate of names and other information for recordation in a marriage register.

MARRIAGE LICENSE: Permission granted by public authority to persons who intend to marry. See also Marriage Bonds.

MECHANICS LIENS: Records of statutory liens held by mechanics and laborers and those furnishing materials for construction. It includes the number of the lien, names of parties, the nature and amount of the lien, and a description of the labor or materials upon which the lien is based. See also Crop Liens, and Liens.

MEMORANDUM BOOK: Used for notations of entries to be made in other books.

MINISTER'S RETURN: Prior to 1780 marriages could only be performed legally in Virginia by ministers of the established church, who were required to record marriages in the parish register. After 1780 dissenting ministers were also permitted to conduct marriages, and in order to have a record of all marriages ministers were required to sign a certificate to be filed with the county clerk. These are commonly called ministers' returns. See also Marriage Certificates.

MINUTE BOOK: Contains the clerk's rough notes of court proceedings, which were later transcribed into an order book. Court order books were usually indexed and neat in appearance, while minute books were not.

MULATTO: A person of mixed Caucasian and Negro ancestry. The Virginia law of 1792 defined a mulatto as one with one-fourth or more Negro blood.

NEXT FRIEND: A person admitted to or appointed by a court to act for the benefit of a person lacking full legal capacity to act for himself. See also Guardian.

OFFICE JUDGMENT: After the end of any court rule, if required notice had been given and the defendant failed to appear, judgments by default and nonsuits were signed by the clerk in his office, as of the preceding court. Office judgments were final in actions of debt, and the defendant was obligated to pay the amount of the debt, interest on the amount of the debt, and court costs. The term is sometimes used in reference to the clerk's recovery of court costs.

ORDERS: The directions of a court made in writing and not included in a judgment. An order book is the formal, corrected transcription of the clerk's notes of the proceedings of court. See also Minute Book.

ORPHANS' ACCOUNTS: See Guardian.

OVERSEERS OF THE POOR: Prior to 1785 the parish vestry administered poor relief; in that year counties were divided into districts from which overseers of the poor were elected. The office existed into the twentieth century, although by then other officials shared responsibility for the poor. The Constitution of 1869 provided for election of a superintendent of the poor, and he shared with the overseers responsibility for the almshouse, beggars, vagrants, and other welfare concerns.

OYER AND TERMINER: Courts of oyer and terminer (hear and determine) are English in origin. In Virginia they were convened to try slaves who committed capital offenses, persons accused of committing capital offenses at sea, and other special situations concerning capital offenses.

PARISH: The local unit of the Episcopal church, consisting of a population living within definite bounds. Parishes were established for the administration of religious affairs. See also Vestry.

PATROLS: In an effort to control slaves, eighteenth century laws were passed to provide for a militia officer and up to four men per district to patrol and visit Negro quarters and other places suspected of housing unlawful assemblies. They had authority to take anyone unlawfully assembled, or slaves roaming the countryside without a valid pass, and present them to justices of the peace. These patrollers were required to enter reports to their militia captain, who then filed a return to the court. This system was continued into the nineteenth century.

PETITION DOCKET: Lists petitions and other ex parte proceedings to be heard by the court at each term. It includes the names of petitioners, the nature of proceedings, and notes of actions taken.

POLLS: Lists of persons who voted in each election in each precinct; they may be recorded on a single sheet of paper or in poll books, which is the modern practice. Polls are also heads of household, usually free white males, responsible for payment of taxes, or eligible to vote. See also Tithable.

POWER OF ATTORNEY: An instrument conferring authority to act as attorney in fact of another person. Powers of attorney are commonly related to land conveyances, and are often recorded in deed books.

PRESENTMENT: May be any presentation of a formal statement of a matter to be dealt with, but is usually a notice taken or statement made by a grand jury. Presentments are in the latter sense statements of crime based on first hand knowledge, or accusations of a crime.

PRIMOGENITURE: First born among several children of the same parents; seniority by birth in the same family. The word also refers to the right to inherit on the basis of that seniority, and to the common-law concept that the oldest son inherits one's landed estate.

PROCESS: Any means used by the court to acquire or exercise jurisdiction over a person or a specific property.

PROCESSIONING (PERAMBULATION): Two freeholders were appointed on order of the county court to procession (review) the bounds of farms or tracts of land in each precinct, in order to renew or replace old landmarks. This was originally a function of the church vestry, but was continued by the court after disestablishment. Persons who walked the boundaries were called processioners.

PROMISCUOUS PAPERS: Another name for Miscellaneous Papers, which include many kinds of records produced by the court.

REAL: Real relates in civil law to a thing, movable or immovable, as opposed to a person; i.e., lands, tenements, and hereditaments, as opposed to personal property.

RECOGNIZANCE: An obligation undertaken by a person, usually the defendant in a criminal case, to appear in court or to keep the peace.

REFERENCE DOCKET: The exact use of this docket is uncertain, but it may include only cases referred to a commissioner in chancery. The docket shows parties to action, a summary of the history of the case, and a note of the proceedings.

REFUNDING BONDS: Bonds used to replace or pay off outstanding bonds that the holder surrenders in exchange for new security.

REGISTER OF FREE NEGROES: An act passed in 1803 required every free Negro or mulatto to be registered and numbered in a book to be kept by the county clerk. The register listed the age, name, color, stature, marks or scars, in what court the person was emancipated, or whether he was born free. Some clerks recorded additional information not required by the law.

REPLEVIN BOND: A bond filed by a person to recover goods or chattels that he claims were wrongfully taken from him or detained. The matter is then tried in court, and the goods returned if the claimant is defeated.

RESERVATIONS OF PERSONALTY: Also called conditional contracts of sale, these are verbatim copies of contracts of sale under which title to personal or movable property is retained by the vendor until payment is completed.

ROAD COMMISSIONERS: Until 1869 the county court controlled construction, alteration of, and maintenance of roads. Surveyors and viewers were appointed to carry out those duties, although after 1835 the courts had the option of appointing commissioners The constitution of 1869 created overseers of the roads, whose duties passed in the twentieth century to superintendents of roads.

RULES: Orders or directions made by a court regulating court practices or the actions of parties; also, a session of the court.

SCHOOL BOARD: The state literary fund was established in 1811, and was assigned the next year to the education of the poor. After 1818 the county court appointed school commissioners to direct the education of indigent children; these commissioners were the active ancestors of the county school board. In 1869 a uniform system of free schools was made compulsory, and the new system was administered by a county superintendent and by school trustees whose general duties were administration of school matters and construction and maintenance of school buildings.

SHERIFF: Sheriffs appeared in Virginia when the original shires were formed in 1634. They originally had three functions: 1) law enforcement, 2) conduct of elections, and 3) financial officer. The sheriff's duties have been curtailed over the years, but he is still the major law enforcing agent in a county.

STRAYS: See Estrays.

SUBPOENA: Official written order to appear in court under penalty.

SUPERINTENDENT OF THE POOR: See Overseer of the Poor.

SURVEYOR: The office of surveyor dates to the seventeenth century in Virginia. Duties have changed little and include: 1) surveying land that has reverted to the state; 2) marking boundaries and platting new counties; 3) surveying delinquent land sold and not redeemed; and, 4) making plats of any land by court order.

TESTATOR: A person who dies leaving a will or testament in force.

TITHABLE: A person subject to pay a tithe, which is traditionally a tenth part of one's income, to support a church. In ordinary usage, a tithable is a person subject to be taxed. See also Polls.

TOWNSHIPS: The Constitution of 1869 set up township offices of record in Virginia counties. Residents of townships elected a supervisor, clerk, assessor, collector, commissioner of roads, and overseer of the poor, as well as justices of the peace and constables. Legislation further provided for a township board of supervisors and clerk. The system was abolished in 1875, although the county divisions have been carried forward as magisterial districts, and as such still exist today.

TREASURER: The Constitution of 1869 placed the sheriff's tax collection function in the new office of treasurer, who was both the cashier and the bookkeeper of the county. During the township period (1870-1875) the township collector and clerk also had treasurer's functions; later the county treasurer's duties were expanded to include the township officer's activities.

TRIAL DOCKET: A list of civil cases to appear before the court for trial. It includes the names of parties, the nature of the action, a summary of pleadings, and a note of proceedings had.

TRUSTEE: A person holding property in trust, to be administered to the benefit of a beneficiary. See also Fiduciary.

VESTRY: Administration of parish affairs by the vestry probably dates to the first church at Jamestown. The vestry was composed of the minister, two or more churchwardens and a number of men chosen by parishioners. Their functions included: 1) administering the church; 2) guarding public morality; 3) laying the parish levy; 4) caring for the poor; and, 5) registering vital statistics and appointing processioners. Since 1785, when overseers of the poor appeared, the vestry has been solely a church body.

WARD: A person under guardianship. A ward is also an administrative division of a city.

WARRANT: A written authorization to receive or pay money to one who is entitled to it. In the courts, a warrant is a precept or writ issued by a competent magistrate to perform acts incident to administration of justice; e.g., an arrest warrant.

CHRONOLOGY

This chronology lists dates of formation of Virginia's original shires, and contains other information relevant to development of local government and records keeping.

1607	First permanent English settlement established at Jamestown
1611	Plantations, or hundreds, established
1619	All residents of Virginia declared members of Church of England
	Meeting of first representative legislature in North America
	Arrival of first recorded black colonists (probably indentured servants)
1624	County quarterly courts established
1631	First law requiring license or banns to legalize marriage
1634	Eight original shires (counties) established: Accawmack, Charles City Charles River, Elizabeth River, Henrico, James City, Warrosquyoake (Isle of Wight), and Warwick River
1660	First law requiring marriage bonds to legalize marriage
1699	Capital moved from Jamestown to Williamsburg
1705	Consents first required for marriages of underage persons
	First slave codes formulated
1776	Court of Admiralty established, sitting at the state capital
	First Virginia state constitution adopted
1777	High Court of Chancery established, sitting at the state capital
	General Court, an appellate court, established
1779	Supreme Court of Appeals established
1780	Certain dissenting ministers allowed to perform marriages
1782	State capital moved from Williamsburg to Richmond
1783	Justices of the Peace first allowed to perform marriages
1784	All ordained ministers allowed to perform marriages and Quakers and Mennonites permitted to marry under their own customs
1786	Disestablishment of the Church of England
1789	Portion of Fairfax County ceded to Congress for use as site of the new national capital
	District Courts established
1792	Kentucky counties became a separate state
1801	Alexandria County became part of the District of Columbia
1802	Superior Courts of Chancery superseded High Court of Chancery
1803	Law passed requiring registration of free Negroes
1808	Superior Courts of Law established in each county
1831	Circuit Superior Courts of Law and Chancery established in each county, superseding both the Superior Courts of Chancery and Superior Courts of Law
1846	Alexandria County retroceded to Virginia by Congress
1851	Constitution of 1851 adopted, providing for counties to be divided into districts
1852	Circuit Courts established in each county, superseding the Superior Courts of Chancery and Superior Courts of Law
	Another district court system established (see 1789)
1861	Virginia seceded from the Union on 17 April
1863	West Virginia counties admitted to the Union as a separate state
1865	Richmond burned as Confederate troops evacuated the city on 3 April
1867	Virginia became part of Military District No. 1 on 13 March

1869	Underwood Constitution of 1869 adopted, creating boards of supervisors, township divisions, state supported schools, and other changes in local government
1870	Military government removed; District Courts established in 1852 were abolished
1875	Townships abolished, but dividing lines retained as districts boundaries
1902	Constitution of 1902 adopted, with no provisions for continuing the county court system
1904	County courts ceased to exist on 1 February

A Preliminary Guide to

Pre-1904 County Records

in the Archives Branch

Virginia State Library and Archives

ACCOMACK COUNTY

Formed in 1663 from Northampton County.
For records of the entire Eastern Shore, 1632-1663,
including Accawmak, see Northampton County.

Original Records

Circuit Court Clerk

Bonds/Commissions/Oaths
[Apprenticeship] Indentures, 1786-95, ca. .25 cu. ft.
Bail Bonds, 1791-96, ca. .25 cu. ft.
Bonds [various types], 1790-96, ca. .1 cu. ft.
Commissions, 1785, 5 items
Officials' Bonds, 1809, 1815, 8 items
Ordinary License Bonds, 1786-88, 1797-1806, 1810-12, 3 vols.

Census Records
U.S. Census Enumeration, 1800, 1 vol.

Court Records

County Court
[Clerk] John W. Gillett's Papers, 1834-72, n.d., 16 items
Court Books [rough dockets], 1766-68, 1785-86, 1801-04, 1808-10, 4 vols.;
  and, 1808, 1811, 2 items (fragments)
Court Papers, 1681-ca. 1860, n.d., 20 cu. ft.
Executions, 1767-ca. 1800, 2.45 cu. ft.
Memorandum Book, 1836-40, 1 vol.
Minutes, 1729-30, 1752-58, 2 vols. (copies)
Office Judgments, ca. 1785-1830, ca. 1.25 cu. ft.
Orders Books, 1666-70, 1676-78, 1690-1703, 1710-31, 1737-63, 1765-67,
  21 vols. (copies). See also Land Records.
Summons, 1804-1839, 2 cu. ft.
Trial Docket, 1806-12, 1 vol.

District Court
Fee Book, 1803-05, 1 vol.
Witness Book, 1793-1820 (includes Superior Court of Law, 1809-1920), 1 vol.

Superior Court of Law
Minutes, 1809-11, 1 vol.
Witness Book, see District Court

Unspecified Court
[Deputy Clerk?] Edmund Bayley's Fee Book, 1797-98, 1 vol.
Fee Books, 1795, 1812, 2 vols.
Schedules, ca. 1805-20, ca. .1 cu. ft.

Election Records
Ballots, 1836, 1840-56, 1860, ca. 1 cu. ft.
Congressional Poll, 1815, 1 vol.

Fiduciary Records
Administrators' Bonds, 1738, 1740-43, 1757-68, 1773-85, 1792-99, 13 vols.
Estate Papers [including wills and guardians' accounts], ca. 1710-1850, ca. 10 cu.
  ft. See also Wills.
Executors' Bonds, 1757-60, 1762-64, 1766-76, 1778-90, 1792-98, 21 vols.
Guardians' Bonds [also titled Orphans' Bonds], 1755-60, 1767-69, 1772-86, 1791-
  92, 1794-97, 15 vols.
Orphans' Accounts, ca. 1745-1805, 2.45 cu. ft. See also Estate Papers.

Free Negro and Slave Records
    Affidavits and Certificates, ca. 1795-1815, 11 items
    List of Free Negroes, 1804, 1 item
    Manumissions, ca. 1785-1815, ca. .25 cu. ft.
    Registration of Free Negro, 1805, 1 item
Land Records
    Common Law Land Causes, 1831 [1832]-50, 1 vol.
    Deed, Will, and Order Books [titles vary], 1663-97, 1717-29, 8 vols. (copies)
    Deeds, 1727-ca. 1825, 7.2 cu. ft.
    Deeds, 1746-70, 2 vols. (copies)
    Deeds Admitted to Record, 1821-23, 1 vol.
    Land Causes, 1727-63, 1773, 1 vol. (copy)
    Plats, 1800-01, 7 items
    Processioners' Returns, ca. 1795-1820, ca. .25 cu. ft.
Marriage Records and Vital Statistics
    Marriage Bonds, 1774-1806 (Stratton Nottingham compilation), 1 vol. (Ms.)
    Marriage Bonds [and Records], 1733, 1798-1832, 1.45 cu. ft.
    Marriage Consents, 1817-27, ca. 100 items
    Ministers' Returns, 1798, 1800-01, 4 items
    Register of Births and Deaths, 1871, 1 item
    Registers of Deaths, 1869-93, .7 cu. ft.
Tax and Fiscal Records
    Accomack Parish Ticket Book, 1806, 1 vol.
    Land and Personal Property Tax Lists, 1787, 1 vol.
    Lists of Tithables, 1676-95, 4 items (copies)
    Parish Levy Papers, 1805, ca. 1830-55, 1 cu. ft.
    Personal Property Tax Lists, 1783, 1784, 1788, 1792, n.d., 5 vols.
    Tax List, [1778?], 1 vol.
    Tithables, 1778, 1 vol.
Wills
    Wills, 1757-61, 1 vol. (copy). See also Land Records.
    Wills [and inventories], ca.1695-1830, ca. 15 cu. ft. See also Fiduciary Records.
Miscellaneous Records
    Inquisitions, 1799-1801, 7 items
    Inventories of Property Belonging to the Poor House, 1840, 1845, 2 items
    Miscellaneous, M-R and S-T, ca. 1850, ca. .1 cu. ft.
    Overseer of the Poor Records, 1838-39, ca. .1 cu. ft.
    Port of Accomack Entry Book, 1783-93, 1 vol.
    Shipping Records [accounts, sales, wreck records, etc.], 1847-50, ca. .1 cu. ft.
    Unidentified Cash Book, 1762-63, 1 vol.
    Unidentified List of Names [by district], n.d., 1 item
    Unidentified [William Taylor's?] Account [Memorandum] Book, 1766 [1766-69],
        1 vol.

Commissioner of Revenue
    Land and Personal Property Tax Lists, 1795, 1796, 2 vols.
    See also Tax and Fiscal Records

Microfilm Records

Circuit Court Clerk
    Bonds/Commissions/Oaths
        [Apprenticeship] Indentures, 1798-1835, 1 reel

Court Records
County Court
Minutes, 1729-30, 1 reel
Orders, 1666-70, 1676-78, 1690-1860, 31 reels. See also Land Records.
District Court
Orders, 1789-1816 (includes Superior Court of Law, 1809-16), 1 reel
Superior Court of Law
Common Law Order Book, 1822-31, 1 reel (part)
Orders, see District Court
Circuit Superior Court of Law and Chancery
Chancery Orders, 1831-55 (includes Circuit Court, 1852-55), 1 reel (part)
Common Law Order Books, 1850-66 (includes Circuit Court, 1852-66), 1 reel
Circuit Court
Chancery Orders, 1859-69, 1 reel (part). See also Circuit Superior Court of Law and Chancery.
Common Law Order Book, see Circuit Superior Court of Law and Chancery
Fiduciary Records
Inventories, etc., 1828-65, 7 reels
Orphans' and Fiduciary Accounts, 1741-1850, 4 reels
Land Records
[County Court] Land Cases [also titled Complete Records], 1727-63 [1773], 1773-1805, 1812-37, 1840-72, 4 reels
District Court Land Causes, Complete Records [titles vary], 1789-1809 [1789-1804, 1809], 1806-27 (includes Superior Court of Law, 1809-27), 3 reels
Superior Court of Law Complete Record, 1827-30, 2 reels (parts)
Circuit Superior Court of Law and Chancery Complete Records, 1831-91, 1835-44 (includes Circuit Court, [1852]-91), 2 reels
Deed, Will, and Orders Books [titles vary], 1663-1746, 11 reels
Deeds, 1746-1865, 37 reels
Indexes to Deeds, Grantor-Grantee, 1663-1799, 1 reel; and, A-Z, 1800-77, 1 reel
Processioners' Returns [titles vary], 1723-84, 1787-1832, 1836-44, 1848-65, 3 reels
Surveyors' Records Nos. 1-6, 1784-1873, 2 reels
Marriage Records and Vital Statistics
Marriage Bonds, 1774-1806 (Stratton Nottingham compilation), 1 reel (part)
Marriage Records Nos. 1-2, 1805-53, 1 reel (part)
Marriage Registers Nos. 3-4, 1853-1925, 1 reel (part)
Register of Deaths, 1853-[70], 1 reel (part)
Registers of Births, 1854-96, 1 reel (part)
Wills
[County Court] Wills, 1737-1882, 23 reels. See also Land Records.
District Court Wills, 1789-1830 (includes Superior Court of Law, 1809-30), 1 reel
Circuit Superior Court of Law and Chancery Wills, 1831-55 (includes Circuit Court, 1852-55), 1 reel
Circuit Court Wills, 1855-92, 1 reel
General Indexes to Wills, A-Z, 1663-1922, 1 reel
Miscellaneous Records
Naval Officer's Book of Entries and Clearances, [1780] 1785-87, 1 reel

ALBEMARLE COUNTY

Formed in 1744 from Goochland County.
Part of Louisa County was added in 1761, and
certain James River islands in 1769.

Original Records

Circuit Court Clerk
Bonds/Commissions/Oaths
Register of Amnesty Oaths, 1865-66, 1 vol.
Circuit Court Bond Books, 1879-1902, 4 vols.
County Court Bond Books, 1874-1904, 1892-1903, 7 vols.
Orphans' [Apprenticeship] Indentures, 1817-87, 1 vol.
Sheriffs' Bonds, 1806-42, 1 vol.
See also Court Records, Circuit Court and County and Superior Courts
Business Records/Corporations/Partnerships
A. P. B. & Co. Ledgers A-[B], 1871-72, 1874, 2 vols.
Charlottesville Chronicle Account Book and Subscriber List, 1860-68, 1 vol.
Price Phares & Randolph Real Estate Listings, n.d., 1 vol.
Unidentified Account Books, 1857-90, 1897-98, 1902-04, 3 vols.
Unidentified Dentist's Book, 1830 (also Warrants for Sheep Claims, 1891-92, and List of Claims on Auditor from County Court, 1887-1904), 1 vol.
Unidentified [General Store] Ledger, 1879-80, 1 vol.
[Unidentified] Lawyer's Receipt Books, 1869-77, 1872-1902, 2 vols.
Unidentified Tavern Day Book, 1876-77, 1 vol.
Woods & Co. [Grocers] Order Book No. 4, 1897-98, 1 vol.
Court Records
County Court
Account Book, 1839-72, 1 vol.
Account of Sheriff with the County Court and the Court with Commissioners, 1813-53, 1 vol.
Blotter, 1884-88, 1 vol.
Causes Ended, 1780-1904, ca. 72 cu. ft. [inventory available]
Chancery Fees, 1846-49, 1872-73, 2 vols.
Chancery Motion Docket, 1832-42, 1 vol.
Chancery Rules No. 2, 1837-52, 1 vol.
Clerk's Fees Received, 1887-92, and Taxes Received, 1887-90, 1 vol.
Clerk's Memorandum of Cash Received, 1887-88, 1 vol.
[Clerk's] Tax Book, 1898-1903, 1 vol.
Commonwealth Law and Chancery Issue Docket, 1868 (also Orders for Appraisal of Strays, 1872-91), 1 vol.
Court Scratch [Memorandum Docket], 1893-97, 1 vol.
Day Book of Fees Charged, 1869-70, 1 vol.
Docket, 1872-1903, 1 vol.
Execution Books, 1798-1855, 16 vols.; and, Execution Book, 1828 (also Law Rules and Law References, 1866-68), 1 vol.
Fee Books, 1804-07, 1813-40, 1843-69, 16 vols.
Index to Fees, 1832, 1 vol.
Indexes to Judgment Dockets, 1854-79, 1854-1904, 2 vols.
Issue Dockets, 1825-27, 1851-72, 6 vols.
Jailer's Accounts, see List of Fines Imposed
Judge A. L. Cochran's Docket, 1872-74, 1 vol.

Jury Book, 1867-70 (also list of fees due Sheriff from other localities, 1856-66), 1 vol.

Law and Chancery Rule Docket, 1869-73, 1 vol.

Law Docket, 1878-84, 1 vol.

Law Executions, 1855-70, 3 vols.

Law Fees, 1869-1901, 4 vols.

Law Rules, 1852-65, 1 vol. See also Execution Books.

List of Claims, see Business and Organization Records

List of Fees Due from St. Anne's Parish, 1832-40, 1 vol.; and, Fees Due from Fredericksville Parish, 1846-52, 1 vol. See also Jury Book; and, Sheriff.

List of Fees Received, 1889-91, 1 vol.

List of Fines Imposed, 1820-32 (also Jailer's Accounts 1856-58), 1 vol.

List of Licenses, etc. [lists of justices, various licenses, fines, etc.], 1786-1887, 3 vols.

Memorandum Books, 1816-23, 1826-29, 1841-43, 1845-98, 17 vols. See also Court Scratch.

Order Book, 1791-93, 1 vol. (copy)

Process Book, 1869-19[04], 1 vol.

Receipt Book [for records charged out and returned], 1853-63, 1 vol.

Record of Fees Received, 1889-91, 1 vol.

Record of Receipts of the Clerk of Court, 1887-91, 1 vol.

Suits [old suits] A-Z, 1791-1872, 9.5 cu. ft.

Warrants, 1831-96, 5 vols.

Witness Attendance Books, 1849-1901, 2 vols.

District Court

Superior Court Old Chancery Papers, ca. 1795-1900 (includes Superior Court of Chancery, 1802-31; Circuit Superior Court of Law and Chancery, 1831-51; and, Circuit Court, 1852-1900), 1.35 cu. ft. See also County and Superior Courts.

Superior Court of Chancery

Superior Court Old Chancery Papers, see District Court

Superior Court of Law

Common Law Causes Ended, 1821, 1823-99 (includes Circuit Superior Court of Law and Chancery, 1831-51, and Circuit Court, 1852-99), 41 cu. ft.

Executions A-Z, 1822-91, 1899 (includes Circuit Superior Court of Law and Chancery, 1831-51, and Circuit Court, 1852-99), 6.3 cu. ft.

Law Execution Book, 1812-31, 1 vol.

Law Rules, 1826-29, 1 vol.

Circuit Superior Court of Law and Chancery

Chancery Court Docket No. 1, 1831-38, 1831-41, 2 vols. [both labeled No. 1]

Chancery Executions, 1832-69 (includes Circuit Court, 1852-69), 1 vol.

Chancery Fees No. 1, 1832-33, 1 vol.; and, Chancery Fees, 1832-51, 1 vol.

Chancery Process Docket No. 1, 1831-48, 1 vol.

Chancery Rough Rule Docket No. 1, 1832-34, 1 vol.

Chancery Rules No. 2, 1837-65 (includes Circuit Court, 1852-65), 1 vol.

Commissioner's Report, Sampson v. George, 1844, 1 vol.

Common Law Causes Ended, see Superior Court of Law

Common Law Fees No. 1, 1831-33, 1 vol.

Common Law Rules No. 1, 1844-54 (includes Circuit Court, 1852-54), 1 vol.

Docket Book, 1831-32, 1 vol.

Ended Chancery Nos. 1-1966, 1831-99 (includes Circuit Court, 1852-99), ca. 75 cu. ft. See also County and Superior Courts.

Executions, see Superior Court of Law

Issue Docket, 1831-35, 1 vol.

Judgment Docket No. 1, 1843-55 (includes Circuit Court, 1852-55), 1 vol.

Law Executions, 1831-55 (includes Circuit Court, 1852-55), 5 vols.

Law Fees, 1832-52 (includes Circuit Court, 1852), 2 vols.

Law Process Docket No. 1, 1831-42, 1 vol.; and, Process Docket, 1842-60 (includes Circuit Court, 1852-60), 1 vol.

Law Rules, 1831-42, 2 vols.

Memorandum Book, 1831-32, 1 vol.

Superior Court Old Chancery Papers, see District Court

Witness Attendance Books, 1832-37, 1849-60 (includes Circuit Court, 1852-60), 2 vols.

Circuit Court

Chancery Blotter [Memorandum], 1878-88, 1 vol.

Chancery Dockets, 1873-86, 1885-86, 2 vols.

Index to Chancery Docket, 1873, 1 vol.

Chancery Executions, 1870-1904, 1 vol. See also Circuit Superior Court of Law and Chancery.

Chancery Fees, 1852-1917, 4 vols.

Chancery Rules, see Circuit Superior Court of Law and Chancery

Common Law Causes Ended, see Superior Court of Law

Common Law Rules, see Circuit Superior Court of Law and Chancery

Ended Chancery, see Circuit Superior Court of Law and Chancery

Executions, see Superior Court of Law

Heath v. Chesapeake & Ohio Railway Co., transcript, 1902, 1 vol. (Ts.)

Index to Chancery Causes, n.d., 1 vol.

Index to Execution Book, 1870, 1 vol.

Index to Fees, 1880, 1 vol.

[Index] to Law Executions, 1855-59, 1 vol.

Issue Docket S[uperior] Court, 1852-59, 2 vols.

Issue Dockets, 1873-1902, 5 vols.

Judges' Law Dockets, 1887-1916, 2 vols.

Judgment Docket, see Circuit Superior Court of Law and Chancery

Jury Books, 1853-1903, 2 vols.

Law Docket, 1902-16, 1 vol.

Law Execution Books, 1855-1904, 4 vols. See also Circuit Superior Court of Law and Chancery.

Law Fees, 1853-1904, 2 vols. See also Circuit Superior Court of Law and Chancery.

Law Minutes, 1857 [1856-60], 1 vol.; and, Clerk's Blotters [Law Minute Books?], 1860-73, 1866-78, 1881-84, 1888-93, 5 vols.

List of Convicts, see Corporation Court

Memorandum Books, 1853-96, 10 vols. See also Chancery Blotter.

Powers et ux v. Powers et al., transcript, 1895, 1 vol. (Ts.)

Process Book, 1869-98, 1 vol. See also Circuit Superior Court of Law and Chancery.

Subpoenas, 1854, 1857, 1859-61, 1866-83, 1891, 2.7 cu. ft.

Superior Court Old Chancery Papers, see District Court

Witness Attendance Books, see Circuit Superior Court of Law and Chancery

County and Superior Courts

Chancery Papers (Old Series), Nos. 1-58 and 62-3209, ca. 1855-1940, 22 cu. ft.; and, Brunn v. Brunn and other suits filed separately, but included in this series, various dates [1871-1938], 1 cu. ft. See also District Court and Circuit Superior Court of Law and Chancery.

Commonwealth Cases Ended [including oaths, bonds, etc.], 1801, 1812-1936, 4.5 cu. ft.

[Court Papers], ca. 1780-1910, n.d., ca. 50 cu. ft.; and, Miscellaneous Court Papers (including tax lists), 1833-80, ca. .25 cu. ft.

Day Book [Circuit and County Courts' fines and taxes, and other fee records], 1866-72, 1 vol.

Ended Chancery Nos. 1967-2522 and 2525-2550, ca. 1890-1940, 16 cu. ft. See also Circuit Superior Court of Law and Chancery.

Miscellaneous Chancery Papers, 1840-94, ca. 6 cu. ft.

[Old] Chancery, 1820-1931, 1 cu. ft. See also County Court.

Old Papers [including bonds, fiduciary papers, etc.], 1780-1916, ca. 25 cu. ft. [inventory available]; and, Old Papers in W. L. M.'s desk, 1822-1901, .5 cu. ft.

Corporation Court, City of Charlottesville

Corporation and Police courts, and Albemarle County Circuit Court, List of Convicts, 1888-1909 [also a list of marriages, 1888-1903], 1 vol.

Unspecified Court

[Clerk's] Account Book [Ledger], 1872-73, 1 vol.

Convict Day Book, 1878-1905, 1 vol.

Fee Books, 1804-07 [with index to Fee Book, 1820], 1817-29, 3 vols.; and, 1799-1802, 1 vol. (fragment)

Indexes to Fees, 1828, 1829, 2 vols.

Index to Judgment Docket No. 3, 1872-86, 1 vol.

Indexes [to suits?], ca. 1850, n.d., 2 vols.

Issue Docket for the Judge, 1868, 1 vol.

Memorandum Book, 1877-81, 1 vol.

Miscellaneous Papers [declarations, writs, etc.], A-Z, 1873-93, .45 cu. ft.

Election Records

General Register, 1902-03, 1 vol.

Lists of Voters Registered, 1902-44 [overlapping date ranges], 34 vols.

Lists of Voters Registered, Colored, 1902-47 [overlapping date ranges], 59 vols.; and, White, 1902-47 [overlapping date ranges], 71 vols.

Fiduciary Records

Circuit Court Fiduciary Bonds, 1888, 1 vol.

County Court Executors' and Administrators' Bonds, 1831-52, 3 vols.

County Court Fiduciary [Bond] Books, 1853-68, 1870-73, 10 vols.

Guardians' Bonds, 1797-1853, 1839-52, 3 vols.

Index to Fiduciaries, 1857-1932, 1 vol.

List of Fiduciaries, 1870-1937, 1 vol.

See also Court Records, County and Superior Courts

Free Negro and Slave Records

Registrations of Free Negroes, ca. 1825-63, ca. 100 items

Justice of the Peace Records

[Constable] Samuel O. Moon's Receipt Book, 1824-32, 1834, 1840-41, 1 vol.

Constable W. H. Burnley's Record Book, 1899-1900, 1 vol.

Justices' Judgments, 1897-1903, 1 vol.

List of Justices, see Court Records, County Court

Records of Judgments, A. R. McKee, J. P., 1877-85, 2 vols.

Land Records

Deed Books Nos. 2-5, 7-12, 14, 19, 1758-72, 1776-98, 1802-04, 1814-15, 14 vols. (copies). See also Wills.

Index to Deed Book 26, 1855, 1 vol.; and, Indexes to Deed Books 16, 18, 23, and 27, n.d., 4 vols. (fragments)

Deeds, 1745, 1757-58, 1761-1905, 23 cu. ft.

[Old] Deeds for Further Proof, A-Y, [ca. 1785]-1863, 1868-96, 1909, n.d., 1.35 cu. ft.

Indexes to Deeds, A-Z, 1748-86, 5 vols.; and, Indexes to Deeds Nos. 1-6, 1820-1903, 6 vols.

List of Lands in Charlottesville Township, 1871, 1 vol.; and, List of Lots and Owners in Charlottesville and Scottsville Townships, n.d., 1 vol.

Processioners' Books, 1795-1824, 2 vols.

Registers of Deeds, 1858-1907, 8 vols.

Reports and Plats of Land, James River and Kanawha Canal Co., 1836, 1 vol.

Surveyors' Books Nos. 1-2, 1744-1892, 2 vols. (copies)

Marriage Records and Vital Statistics

Marriage Certificates and Returns, ca. 1800-56, ca. 60 items

Record of Marriage Bonds No. 1, 1780-1805, 1 vol. (copy)

Marriage Register, 1806-68, 1 vol. (copy); and, Marriage License Register, 1868-94, 1 vol.

Indexes to Marriage Registers Nos. 2-3, 1903-[40], 2 vols.; and, Index to Register of Marriages, n.d., 1 vol.

Index to Marriage Records, 1853-[89], 1 vol.

Register of Births, 1853-61, 1 vol.

Register of Deaths, 1853-61, 1 vol.

Registers of Births and Deaths [titles vary], 1853-68, 4 vols.

See also Court Records, Corporation Court

Military and Pension Records

Confederate Pension Board Minutes, 1900-02, 1 vol.

Pension Papers, 1902-06, .35 cu. ft.

Organization Records

City of Charlottesville Democratic Executive Committee Minutes, 1888-91, 1 vol.

Road and Bridge Records

Road Book [List of Surveyors], 1806-70, 1 vol.

Road [Receipt Book], 1866-87, 1 vol.

Tax and Fiscal Records

Docket of Insolvent Debtors since 1806 [to 1850], 1 vol.

Insolvent Capitations and Personal Property Tax, 1881, 1 vol.

Land and Property Tax Books, 1841-42, 1845-62, 1865-71, 24 vols.

Personal Property Tax Books, 1872-1904, 33 vols.

Record of Delinquent Lands, 1884-1905, 4 vols.

General Index to Delinquent Lands, 1902-31, 1 vol.

[Register of Warrants Paid and Settlement of Accounts with Supervisor of County Home], 1901-25, 1 vol.

Tax Books, 1893-99, 1896-97, 2 vols.

Tax Lists, see Court Records, County and Superior Courts

Warrants, see Business Records/Corporations/Partnerships

Township Records

Charlottesville Township Board Minutes, 1871-75, 1 vol.

Samuel Miller Township Account Book, 1871, 1 vol.

See also Land Records; and, Treasurer

Wills

Wills [and estate papers], 1774-1900, 8.4 cu. ft.

[Old] Circuit Court Wills, 1798-1898, .35 cu. ft.

Will Book No. 2, 1752-85, 1 vol. (copy)

General Index to Wills No. 1, 1744-1930, 1 vol.; and, Index to Wills, 1749-1904, 1 vol.

Miscellaneous Records

    Contracts for Personal Property, 1890-1902, 1 vol.

    Mechanics' Lien Records No. 1, 1890-1914, 1 vol.

    Orders for Appraisal of Strays, see Court Records, County Court

    Unidentified Indexes, n.d. [ca. 1850], 2 vols.

Sheriff

    Sheriffs' Receipt Books, 1807-22, 1835-46, 2 vols.; and, Receipt Book, 1863-66 (includes List of Fees Due to the Clerk from Fredericksville Parish, 1842-46, 1863-66), 1 vol.

    See also Bonds/Commissions/Oaths; and, Court Records, County Court

Treasurer

    [County] Account Books [Ledgers], 1886-91, 1 vol.

    Journal [Estimates of County Levy and Settlement of Treasurer's Account], 1871-81, 1 vol.

    Registers of School Warrants, 1871-91, 2 vols.

    Treasurer's Tax Collection Books, Samuel Miller Township, 1871-81, 1885-90, 2 vols.; Charlottesville District, 1885-90, 1 vol.; Scottsville District, 1871-80, 1885-90, 2 vols.; Rivanna Township, 1871-81, 1885-90, 2 vols.; and, Whitehall Township and Scottsville, 1871-81, 1 vol.

    See also Tax and Fiscal Records

Microfilm Records

Circuit Court Clerk

  Court Records

    County Court

      Minute Books, 1830-66, 5 reels

      Order Books, 1744-48, 1783-85, 1791-1804, 1806-31, 11 reels

  Land Records

    [County Court] Deed Books Nos. 2-61, 1758-1866, 29 reels. See also Wills.

    District Court Deed Book No. 1, 1790-1806, 1 reel (part)

    Superior Court of Chancery Deed Book, 1807-32, 1 reel (part)

    General Indexes to Deeds Nos. 1-3, 1748-1884 (not including Superior Court Deed Books), 2 reels

    [Old] Deeds for further proof, A-Y, [ca. 1785]-1863, 1868-69, n.d., 3 reels

  Marriage Records and Vital Statistics

    Marriage Bonds, Consents, etc. [titles vary], 1780-1913, 47 reels

    Record of Marriage Bonds No. 1, 1780-1805, 1 reel (part)

    Marriage Register, 1806-68, 1 reel (part); and, Marriage Register No. 1, 1854-1903, 1 reel (part)

    General Index to Marriage Registers Nos. 1-3, 1854-1940, 1 reel (part)

    Register of Births, 1853-61, 1 reel (part)

    Register of Deaths, 1853-61, 1 reel (part)

  Wills

    Wills and Deeds No. 1, 1748-52, 1 reel. See also Land Records.

    Will Books Nos. 2-27, 1752-1867, 11 reels

    [Superior Court] Will Book No. 1, 1798-1904, 1 reel (part)

    General Index to Wills No. 1, 1744-1930 (not including Superior Court Will Book), 1 reel

ALEXANDRIA COUNTY

Formed in 1789 from a portion of Fairfax County,
it became part of the District of Columbia
in 1801, and was named Alexandria County.
It was returned to Virginia in 1846,
and the name was changed to
Arlington County in 1920.

For listing of records, see Arlington County.

ALLEGHANY COUNTY

Formed in 1822 from Bath, Botetourt, and
Monroe (West Virginia) counties. Parts of Monroe
and Bath were added later.

Original Records

Circuit Court Clerk
 Board of Supervisors Records
  An Act to issue bonds, n.d., 1 item (2 copies)
  Papers relating to the condition of the Alleghany County Courthouse, 1878, 1888,
   1902, 8 items
 Town Records
 Clifton Forge
  Payrolls, 1901-03, 69 items
  Taxes Collected, 1901-02, 1 item
  Treasurer W. R. Duerson's Papers, 1859-1939, n.d., 145 items
 Covington
  Rolls of Colored Voters Registered in the 2nd Ward, 1903-46, 1 vol.

Microfilm Records

Circuit Court Clerk
 Court Records
 County Court
  Order Books Nos. 1-6, 1822-73, 3 reels
  General Index to Minute [Order] Books, 1822-1904, 1 reel
 Circuit Superior Court of Law and Chancery
  Chancery Order Book No. 1, 1831-52, 1 reel (part)
 Circuit Court
  Chancery Order Book No. 2, 1853-83, 1 reel (part)
 Fiduciary Records
  Guardians' Bonds, 1825-71, 1 reel
  Settlement of Estates Nos. 1-2, 1833-92, 1 reel. See also Wills.

Land Records
    Deed Books Nos. 1-6, 1822-73, 4 reels
    General Index to Deeds No. 1, 1822-89, 1 reel
    Surveyors' Books Nos. 1-2, 1822-1946, 1 reel
Marriage Records and Vital Statistics
    Marriage Registers, 1822-1916, 1 reel
Wills
    Wills and Inventories Nos. 1-2, 1833-76, 1 reel. See also Fiduciary Records.
    General Index to Wills, 1822-1953, 1 reel

AMELIA COUNTY

Formed in 1734 from Prince George and Brunswick counties.

Original Records

Circuit Court Clerk
  Bonds/Commissions/Oaths
    Bond Register, 1861-69, 1 vol.
    Bridge Bonds, ca. 1740-90, ca. 2 cu. ft.
    Commissions, 1736-1777, 3 items (copies)
    Delivery Bonds, 1854-55, ca. 100 items
    Execution Bond Book, 1809-10, 1 vol.
    [List of] Oaths of Allegiance, 1777, 1 item (copy)
    Ordinary Bonds, 1810-30, ca. .1 cu. ft. See also Court Records, County Court; and, Road and Bridge Records.
    See also Land Records; and, Wills
  Business Records/Corporations/Partnerships
    Unidentified Account Books, 1809-11, 2 items (fragments); and, 1854, 1 vol.
  Census Records
    U. S. Census Enumerations, 1850, 1860, 1880, 12 items
    Schedule II [slaves], 1850, 1 item
  Court Records
  County Court
    Appearance Docket, 1784-85, 1 vol.
    [Clerk] John T. Leigh's Account Book, 1800-01, 1 vol.; and Memorandum Books, 1805-35, 2 vols.
    Docket Books, 1750-58, 1768-72, 1826-28, 1845, 5 vols.
    Execution Books, 1755, 1768-97, 1799-1833, 1835-56, 26 vols.
    Fee Books, 1742-50, 1762-91, 1794-1861, 41 vols.
    Form Books, 1741, 1788, n.d., 5 vols.
    Grand Jury Book, 1827 (also list of ordinary keepers and road surveyors), 1 vol.
    Issue Dockets [titles vary], 1792-[1814], 1802-06, 1816-23, 1827-34, 1836-40, 1844-62 [1868], 19 vols. See also Superior Court of Law.
    Judgments and Executions, see Fiduciary Records
    Judgments on Warrants, 1754-66, 1 vol.
    Memorandum Books, 1740-1818, 1823-38, 1843-47, 45 vols.
    Minute Books, 1735-37, 1744-46, 1751-54, 1758-66, 1778-1800, 1804-55, 1871, 37 vols.; and, 1763-65, 1 vol. (fragment)

Minutes, 1739, 1 p.

Office Judgments, 1794-99, 1810-61 [1866], 6 vols.

Order Book, 1791-92, 1 vol.

Index to Order Book No. 43, [1851-55], 1 vol.

Process Books, 1835-46 [1852], 1848-69, 3 vols.

Reference Docket, 1743-45, 1 vol.

[Rough] Minutes, 1824-25, 1832, 3 items

Rule Dockets, 1739-95, 1797, 1807-11, 1815-43, 16 vols.

Scratch Memorandum Book, 1816-22, 1 vol.

Suit Papers, 1744 [1737-46], 1753, 1757, 1759, .45 cu. ft.

Trial Docket, 1768, 1 item

Witness Attendance Books, 1809-33, 1835-1904, 6 vols.

See also Goochland County Court Records, County and Superior Courts

Superior Court of Law

Execution Book, 1823-31, 1 vol.

Fee Books, 1809-35 (includes Circuit Superior Court of Law and Chancery, 1831-35), 3 vols.

Issue Dockets, 1809-38 (includes Circuit Superior Court of Law and Chancery, 1831-38 [and County Court, 1823-26?]), 5 vols.

Judgment Book, 1809-22, 1 vol.

Memorandum Books, 1819-21, 1823-31, 3 vols.

Minute Books, 1809-15, 1819-23, 1825-35 (includes Circuit Superior Court of Law and Chancery, 1831-35), 6 vols.

Records on Appeal, 1823 (also Deeds, 1810-14, 1816), 1 vol.

[Rough] Minutes, 1823, 1 item

Circuit Superior Court of Law and Chancery

Chancery Execution Docket No. 1, 1831-1904 (includes Circuit Court, 1852-1904), 1 vol.

Chancery Issue Docket, 1832-47 (also Process Book, 1831-41), 1 vol.

Common Law Execution Books, 1831-52 [1854] (includes Circuit Court, 1852-[1854]), 2 vols.

Common Law Process, see Witness Attendance Book

Fee Books, 1836-54 (includes Circuit Court, 1852-54), 4 vols. See also Superior Court of Law.

Issue Dockets, 1842-44 (includes Office Judgments), 1844-52 (includes Circuit Court, 1852), 1 vol. See also Superior Court of Law.

Minute Books, 1836-69 (includes Circuit Court, 1852-69), 2 vols. See also Superior Court of Law.

Office Judgments, 1844-60 (includes Circuit Court, 1852-60), 1 vol. See also Issue Dockets.

Process Book, see Chancery Issue Docket and Witness Attendance Book

Witness Attendance Book, 1832-50 (also Common Law Process Book, 1831-50), 1 vol.

Circuit Court

Chancery Execution Docket, see Circuit Superior Court of Law and Chancery

Common Law Execution Books, see Circuit Superior Court of Law and Chancery

Fee Books, see Circuit Superior Court of Law and Chancery

Index to Fee Book, 1854, 1 vol.

Issue Dockets, 1852-60, 1868-72, 4 vols. See also Circuit Superior Court of Law and Chancery.

Minutes, see Circuit Superior Court of Law and Chancery

Office Judgments see Circuit Superior Court of Law and Chancery

Witness Book, 1851-60, 1863, 1866-94, 1 vol.

County and Superior Courts

Court Papers, 1734-1905, 28.75 cu. ft.

Fee Books and Fees Due the Clerk, 1821, 1826-27, 1830-31, 1836, 7 vols.

Judgments and Executions [including bonds, etc.], 1736-1860, 6.25 cu. ft.; and, Judgments, etc., 1853-69, ca. 1.5 cu. ft. See also Fiduciary Records.

Unspecified Court

Fee Book, 1833, 1 vol.

Indexes [to fee books?], 1784, 3pp. (fragments); and, n.d., 2 items

Indexes [to minutes?], n.d., 2 items

Judge's Docket, 1827, 1 item

Old Papers [including court papers and correspondence], 1830-1914, ca. .5 cu. ft.

Process Book, n.d., 1 vol.

Election Records

Election Records, 1792-1877, 1 cu. ft.

Poll Books, 1851, 1852, 2 vols.

Polls, 1758, 1768, 2 items (copies); and, 1795, 1850-54, n.d., 10 items

Voter Registration Books for Giles, Jackson, and Leigh districts, 1903, 39 vols.

Fiduciary Records

Accounts of the estates of Anne Jones, 1805-23, and John Tabb, 1818, 2 vols.

Estate Accounts, 1756-89 (also Judgments and Executions, 1743-54), 1 vol.

Guardians' Bond, 1787, 1 item

Inventories and Accounts [including Guardians' Accounts], ca. 1800-50, 5.9 cu. ft.

List of Certificates for Obtaining Probates and Administrations, 1754-55, 1 item

Free Negro and Slave Records

Register of Free Negroes, 1835, 1855 (also Surveyors of Roads, 1836-55), 1 vol.; and, Free Negro Register, 1855-65 (also Freedmen's Marriage License Book, 1865-69), 1 vol.

See also Census Records; and, Miscellaneous Records

Justices of the Peace Records

List of Commissioners of the Peace, 1777-1809, 1 item

Land Records

Beaver Pond Precinct [processioner's] Report, 1881, 1 vol.

Deed Books Nos. 1 (includes Bonds, 1734-43), 2, 3, 6-7, 10 and 12, 1734-47, 1750-54, 1759-62, 1768-69, 1773-74, 7 vols. (copies). See also Court Records, Superior Court of Law.

Index [to Deed Book No. 5, 1749-57], 1 vol.

Deed Receipts, 1894-96, ca. 30 items

Land Causes, 1744-69, 1 vol. (original and copy)

Plat [Osborne's, Prince George County?], n.d., 1 item

Processioners' Books, 1795-1824 (includes Delinquent Lands, 1797-1816), 1824-32, 2 vols.

Processioners' Reports, 1812, 1824-26, 1828, 1845, ca. 60 items

Returns of Surveys, 1750 [1736-37], 1 vol. See also Tax and Fiscal Records (Mf.).

Marriage Records and Vital Statistics

Birth, Death, and Marriage Register sheets, 1853-64, 21 items

Freedmen's Marriage Licenses, see Free Negro and Slave Records

Lists of Births and Deaths, 1874, 1 vol.

Marriage Bonds and Ministers' Returns, 1744-85, 16 pp. (copies). See also Tax and Fiscal Records (Mf.).

Military and Pension Records

Courts Martial Book, 1st Battalion, 1822, 1 vol.; 2nd Battalion, 1810, 1 vol., and, 1st and 2nd Battalions, 1811, 1 item

List of Persons 18 to 45 liable to be enrolled in the Militia, . . . 1855, 1 vol. (printed; Ms. notations added)

Militia Fines, 1808, 1 vol.

[Militia] Orders (also Courts of Inquiry records, rosters, etc.), 1794-1809, 1 vol.

See also Miscellaneous Records

Road and Bridge Records

Appointments of Road Surveyors, 1809, ca. 25 items

List of Surveyors of Roads and Ordinary Keepers, 1793-1807, 1 vol.

Surveyors of Roads, see Court Records, County Court; and, Free Negro and Slave Records

See also Bonds/Commissions/Oaths

Tax and Fiscal Records

County Levies [titles vary], 1743, 1746-48, n.d., 9 items; and, 1794, ca. 25 items; See also Tax and Fiscal Records (Mf.).

County Levy, 1864, 1 vol. See also Tax and Fiscal Records (Mf.).

Delinquent Land, see Land Records; and, Sheriff

Insolvent Land, 1787-1813, 12 items; and, 1797-1811, 1 vol.

Insolvents, 1746, 1763, 1811, 3 items

Land and Personal Tax Books, 1825-78, ca. .2 cu. ft. (fragments)

Personal Property Tax Lists, 1797, 1805, 2 vols. See also Tax and Fiscal Records (Mf.).

Tithables, 1736-71, 1778-82, n.d., 1 cu. ft.; and, 1746, 1 item. See also Tax and Fiscal Records (Mf.).

Township Records

Leigh Township Records, 1871-75, 1 vol.

Wills

Will Books Nos. 1 (includes Bonds, 1739-54), 2X-2, and 4-6, 1736-80, 1786-99, 6 vols. (copies)

Wills, 1734, 1753, 2 items

Miscellaneous Records

Ben Bragg's Ledger, 1816-17 [used as Home Guard Memorandum Book, 1864], 1 vol.

E. B. Seay's Arthmetic Book, 1817, 1 vol. (Ms.)

Estray Book, 1797, 1819 (also Free Negro Register, 1804-35), 1 vol.

Inquisitions, 1810-30, 30 items

Overseer of the Poor Returns, 1786, 1787, 2 items. See also Tax and Fiscal Records (Mf.).

Petition for location of the courthouse, 1746, 1 item (copy)

Post Office Book, 1832-34, 1 vol.; and, P. R. Leigh's Post Office Book, 1837, 1 vol.

Commissioner of Revenue

Land Tax Book, 1812, 1 vol.

List of Delinquent Capitations and Personal Property Tax, 1877, 1 item (printed)

See also Tax and Fiscal Records

Sheriff
Proceedings of the Sheriff on Delinquent Land, 1815, 1 vol.

Treasurer
[Tax] Coupon Register, 18[?], 1 vol.
See also Tax and Fiscal Records

Microfilm Records

Circuit Court Clerk
Court Records
County Court
Order Books Nos. 1-45 (No. 1 includes Sheriff's Book, 1735-48), 1735-82, 1784-1866 (No. 16 [1782-84] is missing, as are court proceedings, 1804-10), 15 reels
Land Records
Deed Books Nos. 1-40, 1734-1869, 18 reels
General Index to Deeds, Grantors-Grantees A-Z, 1734-1947, 9 reels
See also Tax and Fiscal Records
Marriage Records and Vital Statistics
Register of Births, 1853-71, 1 reel (part)
Register of Deaths, 1853-71, 1 reel (part)
Register of Marriages, 1853-1918, 1 reel (part)
Index to Marriage Bonds, 1735-1854 (Ts.), 1 reel (part)
See also Tax and Fiscal Records
Military and Pension Records
Muster Roll in the War of Defense of Virginia, 1861-65, 1 reel (part)
Tax and Fiscal Records
Tithables, 1736-71, 1778-82, n.d. (also Overseers of the Poor, 1786-87; County Levy, 1743, 1746-48; Returns of Surveys, 1750; Insolvents, 1746-63, 1787-1813, 1797-1811; Personal [Property] Tax, 1797; and, marriage bond, Booker to Clarke, 1755), 1 reel
Wills
Will Books No. 1-19, 1734-1865, 10 reels
General Index to Wills No. 1, 1734-1926, 1 reel

AMHERST COUNTY

Formed in 1761 from Albemarle County.

Original Records

Circuit Court Clerk
Bonds/Commissions/Oaths
Apprenticeship Indentures, 1793-1823, ca. 50 items
Replevin Bonds, 1789, ca. 50 items
Business Records/Corporations/Partnerships
Amherst Savings Bank Account Book B, 1879-81, 1 vol.
[B. Miller's?] Ledger, 1820-26, 1 vol.

Brown and Whitehead [attorneys] Ledger, 1849-55, 1 vol.

Central Savings Bank Day Book [board minutes and notes], 1859-60, 1 vol.

Higginbotham Company Journals and Ledgers, 1804-60, 69 vols.:

    Journal (Bedford County), September 1818-August 1819, 1 vol.

    Journals A-D (New Glasgow, Amherst County), June 1818-April 1822, 4 vols. See also D[aniel] & D[avid] H[igginbotham] Journals.

    T[homas] & D[aniel?] H[igginbotham] Journals A-C, E, and G, (Lynchburg), 1815-19, 1819-21, 1821-22, 5 vols.

    T[homas] & D[aniel?] H[igginbotham] Journals B-E (Richmond) 1817-23, 4 vols. See also D[aniel] & D[avid] H[igginbotham] Journals.

    D[aniel] & D[avid] H[igginbotham] Journals F-H (New Glasgow, Amherst County), 1824-43, 3 vols.

    J[ohn] & R[ichard] S. E[llis] Journals C-H, L-M, and O (Wheeling), 1804-10, 1812-14, 1815-23, 9 vols.

    Pedlar's Mill Journals C-D (Amherst County), 1818-23 [1821?], 2 vols.; and, 1821-22, 1828-30 and 1831-32, 2 vols.

    [Personal Journal?] B, Soldier's Joy (Nelson County), 1832-39, 1 vol.; and, Account Book, 1846-51, 1 vol.

    J[ohn] & R[ichard] S. E[llis] Ledgers C-D, F-[J], 1804-06, 1807-12, 7 vols.

    R[ichard] S. E[llis] Ledger B, 1817-18, 1 vol.

    T[homas] & D[aniel?] H[igginbotham] Ledgers A-B and D-E, 1815-17, 1819-36, 4 vols.; and, Ledgers B, [D], and [F]-H, 1815-17, 1818-19, 1820-27, 5 vols.

    [N. G.]/D[aniel] & D[avid] H[igginbotham] Ledgers A-D and F-H, 1818-22, 1824-43, 7 vols.

    Ledgers A-B and D, 1816-18, 1818-19, 3 vols.

    Ledgers A-[C], 1819-45, 3 vols.

    Ledgers D-E and H, 1814-18, 1818-1819, 3 vols.

    Ledger B, 1852-60, 1 vol.

    Ledger E, 1831-41, 1 vol.

    Ledgers, 1832-46, 1836-40, 2 vols.

J[ohn] T[homas] E[llis] Day Book 1885-87, 1 vol.; and, Ledgers, 1885-88, 2 vols.

Jones and Morris [ice house] Ledger, 1848-79, 1 vol.

McPennalton &c. [tanyard] Ledger, New Glasgow, 1831-32, 1 vol.; and, unidentified [McPennalton?] tanyard ledger, 1826-28, 1 vol.

[R. M. Brown's?] Attorney's Account Book, 1837-57, 1 vol.; and, 1853-78, 1 vol.

[S. A. Day's?] Sales Ledger D, 1900-03, 1 vol.

T. H. [merchant's] Ledger E, 1831-39, 1 vol.

Unidentified [contractor's] A[ccount] B[ook], 1833-40, 1 vol.

Unidentified [general] Store Day Book, New Glasgow, 1821, 1 vol.

Unidentified [general] Store Journal, Lynchburg, 1818-19, 1 vol.

Unidentified Liquor Merchant's Ledger [D], 1814-15, 1 vol.

Unidentified Merchant's Journal, 1819-24, 1 vol.

Unidentified Printer's Account Book [Ledger], 1836-38, 1 vol.

Unidentified Store Ledgers, 1881-82, 1882-85, 2 vols.

Unidentified [Tobacco?] Ledger, 1886-87, 1 vol.

Court Records

County Court

    Account Book, 1869-70, 1 vol.

    Accounts Current, 1775-1862, ca. 50 items

    Chancery Rules, 1823-28, 1 vol.; and, No. 2, 1842-60, 1 vol.

    Claims Against the County, 1811, ca. 50 items

    Court Docket [Issues, Office Judgments, Commonwealth Docket], 1859-69, 1 vol.

Determined Causes, 1775-1843, ca. 1 cu. ft.

Ended Papers, 1802, 1805, 1819, 1823-27, 1830, ca. .35 cu. ft.

Executions Books, 1771-90, 1800-05, 1808-24, 1829-38, 1842-45, 13 vols.

Fee Books, 1779-80, 1783-84, 1799, 1801-06, 1808-14, 1819, 1824-32, 1834-49, 1851-55, 1858-66, 1873-74, 1888, 54 vols.

Indictments, 1796-1871, ca. 75 items

Issue Docket, 1825-26,1 vol. See also Court Docket.

Judgments and Executions, etc., 1761-1857, ca. 2 cu. ft.

Law Memorandum Books, 1837-41, 1845-49, 3 vols.

Law Process Books Nos. [1]-2, 1831-45, 2 vols.

Law Rules, 1837-53, 2 vols.

Memorandum Books, 1824-28, 1831-44, 1847-55 1893-97, 8 vols.

Order Books, 1776-69, 1773-82, 2 vols. (copies); and, 1886-92, 1 vol.

Process Books, 1835-69, 3 vols.

Record of Proceedings responding to requisitions made by the Governor . . . . [labeled Justice Docket], 1862-65, 1 vol. See also Free Negro and Slave Records.

Rule Dockets [titles vary], 1819-25, 2 vols.

Witness Attendance Book, 1838-66, 1 vol.

Superior Court of Law

Docket Book, 1807-10, 1 vol.

Fee Books, 1809-16, 2 vols.

Issue Dockets [titles vary], 1813-19, 1826-31, 2 vols.

Memorandum Book, 1826-27, 1 vol.

Minute Book, 1825-31, 1 vol.

Office Judgments, 1818-23, 1 vol.

Witness Attendance, 1825-38 (includes Circuit Superior Court of Law and Chancery, 1831-38), 1 vol.

Circuit Superior Court of Law and Chancery

Chancery Dockets [titles vary] Nos. [1]-3, 1832-63 (includes Circuit Court, 1852-63), 3 vols.

Chancery Executions, 1839-55 (includes Circuit Court, 1852-55), ca. .35 cu. ft.

Chancery Memorandum Book, 1844-55 (includes Circuit Court, 1852-55), 1 vol.

Clerk's Memorandum Book, 1831-32, 1 vol.

Common Law Minute Book, 1831-39, 1 vol.

Commonwealth Docket, Issues, and Office Judgments [labeled Docket], 1847-53 (includes Circuit Court, 1852-53), 1 vol.

Executions, 1839, ca. 50 items

Issue Docket, 1836-41, 1 vol.

Law Docket, 1841-47, 1 vol.; and, No. 4, 1848-53 (includes Circuit Court, 1852-53), 1 vol.

Law Memorandum Book 6, 1849-56 (includes Circuit Court, 1852-56), 1 vol.

Memorandum Book, 1849-56 (includes Circuit Court, 1852-56), 1 vol.

Minute Book, 1839-46, 1 vol.

Witness Attendance Book, 1831-41, 1 vol. See also Superior Court of Law.

Circuit Court

Chancery Docket, see Circuit Court of Law and Chancery

Chancery Executions, see Circuit Superior Court of Law and Chancery

Chancery Fee Books, 1855-58, 1866-69, 2 vols.

Chancery Memorandum Book, see Circuit Superior Court of Law and Chancery

Commonwealth Docket, etc., see Circuit Superior Court of Law and Chancery

Fee Books, 1869-76, 2 vols.

Law Docket, see Circuit Superior Court of Law and Chancery

Law Fee Books, 1855-56, 1859-62, 1878, 3 vols.

Law Memorandum Book, see Circuit Superior Court of Law and Chancery

Memorandum Books, 1856-68, 1859-89, 2 vols. See also Circuit Superior Court of Law and Chancery.

Witness Attendance Books, 1852-66, 1889-1912, 2 vols.

County and Superior Courts

Court Papers [judgments, executions, bonds, etc.], ca. 1780-1910, 32 cu. ft.

Executions, 1809-24, ca. 50 items

Fiduciary Records

John A. Rowon's Plantation Overseer's Book, Washington County, Mississippi [estate inventory, etc.], 1843-54, 1 vol.

Record of Fiduciary [a record of personal representatives authorized to act as such], 1850-68, 1 vol.

Free Negro and Slave Records

Record of Proceedings responding to requisitions made by the Governor upon the county for slave labor to work upon public defenses [labeled Justice Docket], 1862-65, 1 vol.

See also Fiduciary Records; Land Records; and, Miscellaneous Records

Justice of the Peace Records

Docket of Justices' Executions Returned, 1822-42, 1 vol.

Land Records

County Surveys [land entry book], 1781-1802 (also Miscellaneous Papers, 1786-91, 1793-98, 1802-05, 1807-08, 1810, 1814, 1816-20, 1822-24, 1849, 1864), 1 vol. (copy)

Deed Books A-B, 1761-69, 2 vols. (copies)

[Liber Index to Deed Books, A-Z], 1761-1846, 1 vol.

Delinquent Land and County Levy, 1795-1873, ca. 50 items

Delinquent Real Estate Books Nos. 1-2, 1883-1926, 2 vols.

[List of Deeds Recorded in the Clerk's Office], 1845-50 (also Register of Free Negroes, 1822-64), 1 vol.

Unrecorded Deeds, 1771-96, 1800-39, ca. 50 items

Marriage Records and Vital Statistics

Marriage Consents, 1787-1895, ca. 100 items

Marriage Register, 1763-1852 [1853], 1 vol. (copy); and, 1792-1852, 2 vols.

Index to Marriage Registers, 1763-1853, 1 vol. (Ts. and copy)

Road and Bridge Records

Road Records, 1790-1830, 1793-1871, ca. 100 items

Road Tax Book, 1902-1903, 1 vol.

School Records

Public School Register, 1886-1903, 1 vol.

School Board Account Book, 1897-98, 1 vol.

Tax and Fiscal Records

Capitation, Land, and Personal Property Tax Forms [unsigned], 1865-85, ca. 50 items

Wills

Will Books Nos. 1-2, 1761-86, 2 vols. (copies)

Miscellaneous Records

Building Plans (including plans for the Clerk's Office), 1808-23, ca. 50 items

Coroners' Inquests, 1803-57, ca. 100 items

Indexes to Ledger D and Unidentified Ledger, n.d., 2 vols.

John Cabell's [personal] Account Book [lists of Negroes and rent], 1813-24, 1 vol.

Unidentified Account Books, 1846-51, 1880-83, 1886-88, 3 vols.

Unidentified Journal for Ledger C, 1785-88, 1 vol.

Sheriff

Sheriff's Poll and Land Tax Bills, 1867, ca. 50 items

Treasurer

Treasurer's Warrant Books, 1893-1910, 4 vols.

Microfilm Records

Circuit Court Clerk

Court Records

County Court

Order Books, 1766-69, 1773-94, 1799-1802, 1811-24, 1826-31, 1836-40, 1844-68, 8 reels

Circuit Superior Court of Law and Chancery

Chancery Orders Nos. 1-3, 1831-55 (includes Circuit Court, 1852-55), 2 reels

Circuit Court

Chancery Orders No. 4, 1856-66, 1 reel (part). See also Circuit Superior Court of Law and Chancery.

Land Records

Deed Books A-Z and AA-FF, 1761-1865, 14 reels

General Indexes to Deeds Nos. 1-3, 1761-1885, 2 reels

Land Warrants [Entry Book of Warrants to Survey], 1783-1906, 1 reel (part)

Plot [Plat] Books Nos. 1-2, 1761-1930, 1 reel (part)

Marriage Records and Vital Statistics

Marriage Register, 1763-1852 (Ts. compilation), 1 reel (part)

Marriage Register Index, 1763-1852 (Ts. compilation), 1 reel (part)

Marriage Registers Nos. 2-3, 1854-1900, 1 reel

Index to Marriages, Males-Females A-Z, 1854-1949, 1 reel

Wills

[County Court] Will Books Nos. 1-17, 1761-1870, 8 reels

[Circuit] Court Will Book A-1, 1810-31, 1 reel (part)

Circuit Superior Court of Law and Chancery Will Book B-2, 1832-97 (includes Circuit Court, 1852-97), 1 reel (part)

General Index to Wills, 1761-1920, 1 reel

APPOMATTOX COUNTY

Formed in 1845 from Buckingham, Prince Edward, Charlotte, and Campbell counties. Another part of Campbell was added in 1848.

Original Record

Circuit Court Clerk

School Record

Oakland School Register, 1887-98, 1 vol.

ARLINGTON COUNTY

**Formed from the part of Fairfax County that was ceded
to the United States in 1789, it became part of the
District of Columbia in 1801, and was named Alexandria County. The area was returned to Virginia
in 1846, and the name was changed to Arlington
County in 1920. See also City of
Alexandria and Fairfax County.**

Development of Arlington County Courts

Because it was for a short time part of the District of Columbia, the court system of Arlington (Alexandria) County is unique among Virginia counties. A brief outline of the history of its courts follows.

Fairfax County, 1789-1801

1789	General Assembly offered to cede land to the federal government for a permanent seat of government
1791	District of Columbia surveyed and set aside
1801	Federal offices moved from Philadelphia to the District of Columbia

District of Columbia Period, 1801-1846

1801	Alexandria County and the Circuit Court, District of Columbia formed; also, Admiralty Court (1801-1802) and Orphans' Court formed
1802	U.S. District Court restored, absorbing the Admiralty Court
1824	Levy Court established
1838	Criminal Court created

Retrocession, 1846

1846	Alexandria County retroceded to Virginia
1847	Alexandria County Court organized (assumed Levy and Orphans' courts' functions)
	Circuit Superior Court of Law and Chancery formed (District of Columbia Circuit and Criminal courts' functions passed to it)
1852	Circuit Superior Court of Law and Chancery superseded by Circuit Courts
1904	County Court ceased to exist; jurisdiction passed to the Circuit Court
1920	Name changed to Arlington County

City of Alexandria, 1748-1870

1748	Town of Alexandria chartered in Fairfax County
1779	Rechartered as a City and Hustings Court established

1801	Hustings Court abolished, its jurisdiction passing to the Circuit Court, District of Columbia
1846	Retrocession
1863-65	Alexandria the capitol of the Restored Government of Virginia
1870	Became a city independent of Alexandria County; Corporation Court organized, equivalent to a county Circuit Court

Arlington County

Original Records

Circuit Court Clerk
Board of Supervisors Records
Accounts Allowed, 1874-88, ca. .1 cu. ft.

Correspondence, 1875-76, 2 cu. ft.

Index, 1875, 1 vol.

Records [Minutes] Nos. 1-3, 1870-1907, 3 vols.; and, Record, 1874-77, 1 vol.

Index to Minute Books Nos. 1-5 , [1870-1922] 1 vol.; and, Index to Minute Book, 1899-1900, 1 vol.

Selection of Officers, 1879-81, 1893, 6 items

Bonds/Commissions/Oaths
Appointments [of Officials], 1805-81, ca. .1 cu. ft.

Bonds, 1798-1881, ca. 50 items

Bonds to Keep the Peace, 1863-70, ca. 50 items

Certificate of Ordination, 1802, 1 item

Circuit Court Bonds, 1894-1904, 1 vol.

Circuit Court Ordinary Bond and License Books, 1802-11, 1820-50, 6 vols.

County Court General Bond Book, 1850-55, 1 vol.

Indentures, 1796-1843, 5 items; and, Apprenticeship Indentures, A-Z, 1797-1869, ca. .2 cu. ft.

Officials' Bonds and Oaths, 1798-1899, n.d., ca. .1 cu. ft.; and, Oaths, 1798, 1820, 1823, 1830, 4 items

Orders to Execute Officials' Bonds, 1880, 5 items

Petitions for Appointments of Officials, 1801-47, n.d., ca. .1 cu. ft.

Register of Persons Who Have Taken the Oath of Allegiance, 1862-65, 1 vol.

U.S. District Court [Marshals'] Bond Book, 1801-46, 1 vol.

Business Records/Corporations/Partnerships
Charles Alexander's Ledger, 1801-17, 1 vol.

Ezra Kinsey & Co. [tanyard] Memorandum, 1796-1812, 1 vol.

Massie & Co. Day Book, 1824-39, 1 vol.

Unidentified Ledgers, 1819, 1862-64, 2 vols.

Unidentified Merchant's Day Book, 1859, 1 vol.

Unidentified Rent Book, 1864-70, 1 vol.

William Hodgson's Day Book, 1796-1810, 1 vol.

Court Records
Hustings Court, Town of Alexandria
Accounts and Notes upon which Suits have not been Brought, 1782-96, n.d., ca. 30 items

Attorney's Memorandums, 1786-89, ca. .1 cu. ft.

Complete Records (Wills, Deeds, etc.), A-P, 1786-1846 (includes Circuit Court, District of Columbia, 1801-46), 15 vols.

Dismissals at Rules, 1790-1844, 1864 (includes Circuit Court, District of Columbia, 1801-44, and Alexandria Circuit Court, 1864), 10 cu. ft.

Execution Books, 1782-90, 1795-1801, 4 vols.

Executions on Judgments, 1783-1878 (includes Circuit Court, District of Columbia, 1801-46, and Alexandria County Circuit Court, 1847-78), 16 cu. ft.

Fee Books, 1783-85, 1797, 1799-1801, n.d., 7 vols.

Grand Jury Presentments, 1796-1834 (includes Circuit Court, District of Columbia, 1801-34), ca. 25 items

Judgments, 1783-1867 (includes Circuit Court, District of Columbia, 1801-46, and Alexandria County Circuit Court, 1847-67), 80.4 cu. ft.

Minute Books, 1785-88, 1791-1801, 11 vols.

Order Books, 1780-91, 1797-99, 4 vols.

Pleas of the Commonwealth, 1799-1800, 1 vol.

Record of Common Law Chancery Cases, 1791-93, 1 vol.

Rule Books, 1788-1800, 4 vols.

Subpoenas, 1787-1845 (includes Circuit Court, District of Columbia, 1801-45), ca. 50 items

Suit Papers, 1780-1877, n.d. (includes Circuit Court, District of Columbia, 1801-46, and Alexandria County Circuit Court, 1847-77), ca. 50 items

See also Circuit Court, District of Columbia; and, Alexandria County Superior Courts

Court of Oyer and Terminer, Town of Alexandria

Opinions, 1794-1800, 1 vol.

Record of Trials and Examinations of Criminals, 1794-1800, 1 vol.

Circuit Court, District of Columbia

Appearance Dockets, 1807-08, 1811, 1818, 1828-31, 4 vols.

Attachments, 1811-69 (includes Alexandria County Circuit Court, 1847-69), 20 items

[Clerk's Tax Book?], 1822, 1 vol.

Complaints, 1811-42, n. d., 7 items

Complete Records, see Hustings Court

Court Papers, 1801-54, n.d. (includes Alexandria County Circuit Court Papers, 1846-54), ca. .1 cu. ft.; and, Court Papers related to the Glebe Land, 1837, ca. 25 items

Decrees, 1801-46, 6 items

Dismissals at Rules, see Hustings Court

Docket of Witness Attendance, 1801-17, 1 vol.

Execution Books A-F, 1801-52 (includes Alexandria County Circuit Court, 1847-52), 6 vols.

Executions on Judgments, see Hustings Court

Fee Books, 1801-46, n.d., 48 vols.

Grand Jury Presentments, see Hustings Court

Index to Liber K No. 4, [ca. 1800?], 1 vol.

Judgments, see Hustings Court

Indexes to Judgments, 1801-73 (includes Alexandria County Circuit Superior Court of Law and Chancery, 1847-51, and Circuit Court, 1852-73), 4 vols.

Land Suits A, 1835-42, 1 vol.

Liber A (Pleas), 1801-02, 1 vol.

List of Fines, Penalties, and Forfeitures in the Circuit and Criminal Courts, 1801-46, 1 vol.

Minute Books, 1801-66 (includes Alexandria County Circuit Superior Court of Law and Chancery, 1847-51, and Circuit Court, 1852-66), 28 vols.

Order Books Nos. 1-21, 1801-27, 21 vols.

Petitions for Relief Under Insolvent Law, 1820-42, ca. .1 cu. ft.; and, Petitions, 1822, 1825, 1830, n.d., 4 items

Recognizances, see Hustings Court

Record of Actions, U.S. Government as Plaintiff, 1839-46, 1 vol.

Record of Executions on Judgments, 1801-02, 1 vol.

Rule Dockets A-I and K-L, 1800-49 (includes Alexandria County Circuit Court, 1847-49), 11 vols.

Stewart-McCall suit papers, 1804-17, ca. .1 cu. ft.

Subpoenas, see Hustings Court

Suit Papers, see Hustings Court

Trial Dockets, 1801-02, 1805-46, 68 vols.

Warrants, Greenleaf v. Cozens, 1821, ca. .1 cu. ft. See also Hustings Court.

Witness Attendance Docket No. 1, 1818-36, 1 vol.

Writs of Error, 1810-22, ca. .5 cu. ft.

Writs of Habeas Corpus, 1817-84 (includes Alexandria County and Superior courts, 1847-84), ca. 50 items

Levy Court

Ledger, 1815-46, 1 vol.

Minutes, 1811-27, 1 vol.

Orphans' Court

Account Books Nos. 1-9, 1810-50 (includes Alexandria County Court, 1847-50), 9 vols.

Cases at Law, see County Court

[Indentures], 1811-17, 1 vol.

Records [Minute Books], 1801-05, 1822-34, 1842-47, 4 vols.

Criminal Court

Dockets, 1838-46, 2 vols.

Judgments, 1839-42, ca. .5 cu. ft.

Minute Book, 1838-46, 1 vol.

See also Circuit Court, District of Columbia

U.S. District Court, District of Columbia

Admiralty Court Orders, 1802-27, 1 vol.

Admiralty Court Records, 1806-30, 1 vol.

Admiralty Court Rules A, 1807-46, 1 vol.

Admiralty Judgments, 1803-45, 1.45 cu. ft.

Bankruptcy Proceedings, 1802-21, 1 vol.

Exemplifications, 1799-1810 (includes Fairfax County and Superior Court records), .5 cu. ft.

Fee Books, 1809-31, 1810-12, 1814, 1824-29, 4 vols.

Trial Dockets, 1805-32, 2 vols.

County Court

Account Book, see Orphans' Court

Account vouchers and miscellaneous, 1862-1900, ca. 1 cu. ft.

Cancelled Checks, bank deposits, etc., 1882-1900, ca. 1 cu. ft.

Cases at Law, 1838-1903, n.d. (includes Orphans' Court, 1838-46), 3.5 cu. ft.; and, Cases at Law and Related Papers, 1847-1903, n.d., 3.5 cu. ft.

Cases Delivered to Attorney, 1884-1900, 1 vol.

Chancery Court Dockets, 1848-73, 2 vols.

Chancery Rule Book, 1847-72, 1 vol.

Clerk's Accounts for Claims Allowed, 1803-56, 12 items

[Clerk's] Tax Books, 1864-70, 1898-1904, 2 vols.

Common Law Rule Book, 1862-72, 1 vol.

Dockets, 1871-76, 1879, 1888, 1890, 6 vols.

Execution Books Nos. 1-3, 1847-98, 3 vols.

Fee Books, 1852-53, 1857-58, 1902-03, 3 vols.

Index and Amount of Fee Bills, 1858-60, 1 item

Judgments, see Hustings Court

Jury Lists, 1864-85, n.d. (includes Circuit Court lists), ca. .1 cu. ft.; and, Jury Papers, 1867, 1870, 1878, 3 items

Law Rule Books, 1847-61, 2 vols.

Lists of Fines Imposed and Paid into Court, 1863-69, ca. 25 items

Memorandum for Suits, 1854-57, 1860-71, 3 vols.

Memorandums for Suits, 1862-64, ca. 25 items

Minute Books Nos. 7-15, 1866-1904, 10 vols.; and, Supplemental Minute Book No. [11], 1888, 1 vol.

Index to Minute Books, 1875-79, 1898, 2 vols.

Old Motions, Appeals, Road Causes, Justices' Attachments, and Other Monthly Causes, 1863, ca. 50 items

Petition, 1850, 1 item

Process Books, 1847-1901, 3 vols.

Witness Books, 1847-80, 1886-90 and 1899, 2 vols.

Circuit Superior Court of Law and Chancery

Chancery Rules, 1847, 1 item; and, 1850-68 (includes Circuit Court, 1852-68), 1 vol.

Common Law Fee Books, 1848-52 (includes Circuit Court, 1852), 2 vols.

Court Appearance Docket, 1847-50, 1 vol.

Dockets for Motion and Monthly Causes, 1848-67 (includes Circuit Court, 1852-67), 1 vol.

Fee Books, 1847-53 (includes Circuit Court, 1852-53), 2 vols.

Index to Judgments see Circuit Court, District of Columbia

Law Rule Book, 1850-90 (includes Circuit Court, 1852-90), 1 vol.

Minutes, see Circuit Court, District of Columbia

Index to Minute Books Vol. 1, 1847, 1 vol.

Process Book No. 1, 1847-69 (includes Circuit Court, 1852-69), 1 vol.

Trial Dockets, 1847-51, 9 vols.

Circuit Court

A. &. W. R. R. Co. v. Fowle Snowden et al., exhibit [ledger], n.d., 1 vol.

Attachments, see Circuit Court, District of Columbia

Chancery Docket, 1857-59, 1 vol.

Chancery Execution Book No. 1, 1853-1903, 1 vol.

[Chancery] Fee Books, 1853-68, 1871-86, 1899-1909, 3 vols.

Chancery Rule Book No. 1, 1868-1909, 1 vol. See also Circuit Superior Court of Law and Chancery.

Clerk George H. Rucker's Correspondence Files, 1901-05, 2.8 cu. ft.

Common Law Execution Book H, 1869-1907, 1 vol.

Common Law Fee Books, 1852-70, 2 vols. See also Circuit Superior Court of Law and Chancery.

Commonwealth and Chancery Causes [Judges' Dockets], 1868-69, 1871-74, 3 vols.

[Commonwealth Witness Attendance Book], 1894-95, 1 vol. (partial)

Complaint, 1882, 1 item

Court Papers, see Circuit Court, District of Columbia

Dismissals at Rules, see Hustings Court

Docket for Motion and Monthly Causes, 1867-1900, 1 vol. See also Circuit Superior Court of Law and Chancery.

Dockets, 1859-1904, 2 vols. See also Circuit Superior Court of Law and Chancery.

Execution Book [G], 1852-70, 1 vol. See also Circuit Court, District of Columbia.

Index to Execution Book G, n.d. [1852-70], 1 vol.

Executions on Judgments, see Hustings Court

Fee Books, 1854-60, 2 vols.; and, Fee Books [labeled Cash Ledgers], 1866-68, 1871-74, 2 vols. See also Circuit Superior Court of Law and Chancery.

Grand Jury [Stub Book], 1899-1904, 1 vol.

Index to Chancery Order Books A-D, n.d., 2 vols.

Index to Common Law Order Books Nos. 1-4, n.d., 1 vol.

Index to Minute Books Vol. 3, 1852, 1 vol.

Irwin et al. v. McKnight et al., exhibits, 1851 (includes Butcher and Paton Cash Book, 1825-31, 1 vol.; Copy of Accounts, 1812-25, 1 vol.; Day Books, 1815-26, 1821-37, 4 vols.; Expense Books, 1803-25, 2 vols.; Invoice Book, 1811-25, 1 vol.; and, Ledgers A-B, 1811-26, 1819-37, 2 vols.), 10 vols.; and, Exhibits, 1776-1915, n.d., 1 cu. ft.

Judge's Copy of Court Docket, n.d., 1 vol.

Judgments, see Hustings Court

Indexes to Judgments, see Circuit Court, District of Columbia

Jury Lists, see County Court

Law Rule Book, 1878-1926, 1 vol. See also Circuit Superior Court of Law and Chancery.

Memorandum Books, 1852-54, 1859-63, 1860-68, 3 vols.

Memorandum of Copies, 1859-79, 1 vol.

Minutes, see Circuit Court, District of Columbia

Moneys Deposited by Order of Court, 1895-1900, 1 vol.

Petit Jurors' [Stub Book], 1893-1906, 1 vol.

Phillips v. Washington, Arlington and Falls Church Railway Co., exhibit [cash book], 1900-01, 1 vol.

Pleas of the Commonwealth, 1865-70, n.d., 5 vols.

Process Books No. 2, 1869-1901, 1 vol. See also Circuit Superior Court of Law and Chancery.

Rule Dockets, see Circuit Court, District of Columbia

Stet Docket, Chancery and Law Cases, 1900-17, 1 vol.

Suit Papers, see Hustings Court

Trial Dockets, 1852-60, 1864-70, 1872-73, 33 vols. See also Circuit Superior Court of Law and Chancery.

Venire Jurors, 1893-1900, 1 vol.

Witness Attendance Docket, 1851-77, 1 vol.

County and Superior Courts

Arlington County Records [including Washington estate papers, commissions, land records, etc.; also Town of Alexandria and District of Columbia records], 1772-1867, . 5 cu. ft.

General Judgments, [1862-66], 1 vol.

Index to General Judgments, n.d. [1862-66], 1 vol.

List of Papers Taken from or Returned to Clerk's Office, 1879-1904, 1 vol.

Writs of Habeas Corpus, see Circuit Court, District of Columbia

Unspecified Court

Clerk's Correspondence, 1797-1892, ca. 35 items; and, [Clerk's] Papers, 1835-36, 1863, 1868-69, 1881, 8 items

Index to Actions, n.d., 1 vol.

[Index to Minute Book?], n.d., 1 vol.

[Index to Suits], n.d., 1 vol.

Election Records

Certificates of Election, 1883, ca. 25 items

Election Records, 1847-1901, n.d., 1 cu. ft.

General Registration, 1902-03, 1 vol.

List of Voters Registered, 1865, 1 vol.

Lists of Registered Voters, 1874, 1878, 2 items

Poll Books, 1865, 1901, 2 vols.

Polls, 1852-61, n.d., ca. .5 cu. ft.

Qualifications for Office, 1801-74, n.d., ca. 40 items

Rolls of Registered Voters, Colored, 1902-04, 4 vols.; and, White, 1902-04, 9 vols.

Fiduciary Records

Circuit Court Commissioners' Bond Book, 1850-99, 1 vol.

Circuit Court Fiduciary Bond Book, 1851-77, 1 vol.

County Court Accounts Books Nos. 1-2, 1871-84, 2 vols.; and, Circuit Court Account Book No. 3, 1876-99, 1 vol.

Index to County Court Account Book Journal C, 1883, 1 vol.

County Court Administrators' Bond Book, 1847-50, 1 vol.

County Court Executors' Bond Book, 1847-50, 1 vol.

County Court Fiduciary Bond Books, 1866-1902, 3 vols.

County Court Guardians' Bond Book, 1848-50, 1 vol.

Estate Accounts (and Wills), 1801-97, 24 cu. ft.; Estate Accounts and Wills, Alexander-Zimmerman, 1786-1897, 2 cu. ft.; and, Account of John Brown's estate, 1814, 2 items. See also Wills.

Executors' and Administrators' Bonds, 1803-44, 1.5 cu. ft.

Fiduciary Accounts, 1871-1903, 1 vol.

Fiduciary Register, 1850-78, 1 vol.

Index to Fiduciary Register, 1875-18[?], 1 vol.

Guardians' Bonds, 1804-43, .5 cu. ft.

Inventories and Appraisements, 1795-1848, 3 cu. ft.

Petitions, 1832-47, ca. .2 cu. ft.

Record of Fiduciaries, 1851, 1 vol.

Sales, 1802-40, 1 cu. ft.

Free Negro and Slave Records

Bills of Sale for Negroes, 1801, 1815, 2 items

Certificates of Importation of Slaves, ca. 1795-1845, 9 items

Deeds of Manumission, 1794-1843, 16 items

Free Negroes Delinquent for Nonpayment of Capitation Tax, 1859, 1 item

Indentures [of free Negroes], 1788, 1835, 1864, 1866, 4 items

Register of Free Negroes in Alexandria County, 1858, 1 vol.

Registrations of Free Negroes, 1794-1823, ca. 25 items

Justice of the Peace Records

Constables' Execution Books, 1811-16, 1819-21, 2 vols.

Constables' Executions, 1803-26, 4 cu. ft.

Executions on Magistrates' Judgments, 1806-13, 1 cu. ft.

Executions Returned by Constables, 1882-83, 1 vol.

Justices' Docket, 1846-47, 1 vol.

Justices' Judgment and Execution Books, 1828-32, 1877-82, 1903, 5 vols.

Justices' Judgments, 1899-1912, 2 vols.

Lists of Justices' Fines, 1888-91, ca. 25 items

Magistrates' Docket, 1839-42, 1 vol.

Magistrates' Docket A, Executions, 1836-39, ca. .5 cu. ft.

Magistrates' Judgments, ca. 1788-1903, ca. 19.5 cu. ft.

[Monthly Reports], 1879-88, 1 vol.

Records of Executions Issued on Judgments, 1802-07, 1816-19, 2 vols.

Records of Judgments Rendered, 1823-27, 2 vols.

Warrants Returned, 1836-37, 1841, 2 vols.

Land Records

Copies of Deeds, 1669-1867, ca. .1 cu. ft.

Daily Index to Receipt of Deeds, 1902-03, 1 vol.

Deeds, 1785-1894, ca. 6 cu. ft.

Indexes to Deeds Vols. 118-119, 121-128, 130-134, 136, and 143-167, 1867, 1870, n.d., 31 vols.; Indexes to Deed Book 4, A-Z, n.d., 22 vols.; Index to Liber A No. 5, 1902-03, 1 vol.; and, Cross Index [to Deeds], n.d., 1 vol.

Land Suits, see Circuit Court, District of Columbia

[List of Transfers], 1871-72, 1 vol.

Lists of Deeds Recorded, 1785-89, 1847, 8 items

Miscellaneous Deeds, 1846-93, ca. .2 cu. ft.

Plat Book No. 1, 1869-84, 1 vol. See also Road and Bridge Records.

Plats, 1865-1912, n.d., ca. .6 cu. ft.

Index to Plats, n.d., [1928?], 1 vol.

Surveyors' Book, 1852-54, 1 vol.

Surveys and Plats, 1817, 1823, 1826, 3 items

Unrecorded Deeds, 1784, ca. .5 cu. ft.

See also Court Records, Hustings Court, Town of Alexandria

Marriage Records and Vital Statistics

Book of Records Containing the Marriages and Deaths that have Occurred within the Official Jurisdiction of Rev. A. Gladwin, 1863-68, 1 vol.

Card Index [to marriages, by brides?], ca. 1801-52, ca. 1 cu. ft.

Marriage Bonds, 1801-52, ca. 4.2 cu. ft.

Marriage Licenses, 1876, 5 items

Marriage Records, 1850-81, 2 vols.

Ministers' Returns, 1801-50, 1 vol.

Ministers' Returns, 1801-52, ca. .2 cu. ft.

Persons who Died in 1870, Alexandria City, 1 item

Register of Deaths, 1888, 1 item

Register of Marriages, 1853-79, 1 vol.

Registers of Births, 1872-89, ca. .1 cu. ft.

Registers of Births and Deaths, 1853-69, 14 items

Index to Register of Births, Deaths, and Marriages, 1853-68, 1 vol.

Military and Pension Records

Courts Martial, Military District of Alexandria, 1864-65, 1 vol.

Militia Roll, 1834, 1 item

Road and Bridge Records

Correspondence and Reports of the Middle Turnpike Co., 1827-40, 1 cu. ft.

County Roads and Plats Liber No. 1, 1888-90, 1 vol.

Road Book, 1890-1909, 1 vol.

Road Commission Minutes, Arlington District, 1877-84, 1 vol.

Road Warrants, Arlington, Jefferson, and Washington Districts, 1887-99, 3 vols.

School Records

Free School Papers, 1829-35, ca. 50 items

[Jefferson District School Record], 1871-80, 1 vol.

Superintendent of Schools Correspondence, 1851-84, n.d., 1 cu. ft.

Teachers' Registers [titles vary], 1887-1907, 21 vols.

Tax and Fiscal Records

Accounts against the Commonwealth and the County, 1825-79, n.d., ca. 50 items; Accounts against the Commonwealth, 1870-71, ca. 25 items; and, Accounts and Notes, 1780-1865, ca. .1 cu. ft.

Applications to Purchase Delinquent Lands, 1898, ca .1 cu. ft.

Assessments, 1847, 1 vol.

[County Fund] Ledger, 1899-1905, 1 vol.

[Delinquent Land Sold for Taxes], 1884-1912, 1 vol.
Delinquent Real Estate, 1805-1903, ca. 25 items
Delinquent Real Estate, ca. 1865-1905, ca. 40 vols. (including fragments)
[Delinquent Tax Lists?], n.d., 2 vols.
Delinquent Tithables, 1854-70, 6 items
Index [to delinquent taxes?], n.d., 1 vol.
Expenditures for Ft. Washington, 1814-15, 1 vol.
Insolvent Debtors, 1803-10, 1819-46, 5 vols.
Lists of Lands Sold for Taxes, 1855, 2 items
Lists of Personal Property Taxes Delinquent, 1856-58, 7 items
Lists of Taxable Property, A-Z, 1787, ca. .2 cu. ft.
Lists of Tithables, 1817, 1 vol.
Persons Who Paid Direct Taxes, 1863-64 [compiled 1892], 1 item
Real Estate to be Sold for Taxes, 1901, 1903, 2 items
Schedules of Insolvent Debtors under Bankruptcy Act, 1803-44, 2.5 cu. ft.
Tithables, 1788-[89], 1803-05, 15 items
Tithables Insolvent, 1843, 1 item
See also Free Negro and Slave Records

Town Records

See Court Records, Hustings Court and Court of Oyer and Terminer; and, Tax and Fiscal Records

Township Records

[Washington Township Board Minutes], 1871-75, 1 vol.
See also School Records

Wills

Will Book No. 10, 1880-1903, 1 vol. See also Court Records, Hustings Court.
Indexes to Will Books Nos. 9 and 12-13, n.d., 2 vols.
Wills, 1803-04, ca. .1 cu. ft.
Wills, Accounts, etc., 1847-97, 5 cu. ft.
General Index to Wills, 1778-1905, 1 vol.
See also Fiduciary Records

Miscellaneous Records

Advertisements and related items, 1790-1839, 9 items
Circuit Court, District of Columbia, Reports of Aliens, 1801-32, 1 vol.; and, Declarations of Intention and other Naturalization Papers, 1802-96, n.d., ca. 50 items
Coroners' Inquisitions, 1799-1885, ca. .5 cu. ft.
District Court Copyrights Secured, 1803-45, 1 vol.
[Estray Book], 1822-70, 1 vol.
Estrays, 1802-21, 6 items; and, Estray Reports, 1825-86, ca. 30 items
Flour Inspector's Accounts [and papers], 1803-23, ca. 25 items
Goods and Chattels Sold upon Condition, 1894-1919, 1 vol.
Lists of Prisoners in the Jail, 1802-35, ca. 25 items
Log of the Schooner Enterprise, 1803-04, 1 vol.
Mechanics' Liens Liber A No. 1, 1898-1910, 1 vol.
Index to Mechanics' Liens Liber A, n.d., [1898-1910?], 1 vol.
Notices, 1810, 1853, 1863, 3 items
Overseer of the Poor Appointments, 1808, 2 items; Accounts, 1880-84, ca. 50 items; and, Superintendent of the Poor Annual Report, 1878, 1 item
Powers of Attorney, 1812, 1847, 2 items
Unidentified Index Book, n.d., 1 vol.

Commissioner of Revenue

Insolvent Capitations and Property, 1865, 1877-78, 4 items
Land Taxes [titles vary], ca. 1845-1920, ca. 90 vols. (including fragments)
Lists of Persons Assessed with License Taxes, 1891-1911, ca. .1 cu. ft.
Moffett Law Returns, 1873-83, 1901, ca. .1 cu. ft.
Personal Property Interrogatories, 1879-88, 1.8 cu. ft.
Personal Property Taxes, [titles vary], 1843-1920, n.d., 113 vols.
Tithables, Town of Alexandria, 1829, 1 vol.
See also Tax and Fiscal Records

Treasurer

Ledger, V. P. Corbett in Account with Auditor, 1871-80, 1 vol.
List of Delinquent Town Lots Resold, 1886-1912, 1 vol.
Report of Land not Sold . . . in 1903, 1 item
Report of Sale of Land for Nonpayment of Taxes, 1903, 1 item
Treasurer's Warrant Book No. 1, 1898-1916, 1 vol.
See also Tax and Fiscal Records

Microfilm Records

Circuit Court Clerk

Bonds/Commissions/Oaths

General Bond Book, 1850-55, 1 reel (part)
Ordinary Bond [and license] Books, 1802-11, 1820-50, 2 reels
Persons Who Have Taken the Oath of Allegiance Vol. A, 1862-63, 1 reel (part)
See also Court Records, Circuit Court, District of Columbia

Court Records

County Court

Chancery Orders A-B, 1847-71, 1 reel
Common Law Orders Nos. 1-2, 1847-68, 1 reel

County Court, Fairfax County

Minute Book, 1822-23, 1 reel

Hustings Court, Town of Alexandria

Common Law Chancery Cases Vol. C, 1791-93, 1 reel (part)
Complete Records, see Circuit Court, District of Columbia
Minute Books A-B, 1785-87, 1 reel (part); and, 1787-1801, 2 reels
Order Books, 1780-99, 2 reels

Court of Oyer and Terminer, City of Alexandria

Opinions, 1794-1800, 1 reel (part)
[Records of Trials and Examinations of Criminals] Vol. D, 1794-1800, 1 reel (part)

Circuit Court, District of Columbia

Butcher and Paton Expense Book Vol. G, 1803-11, 1 reel (part)
Complete Records A-P [wills, bonds, inventories, etc.], 1786-1846 (includes Town of Alexandria Hustings Court, 1786-1800), 7 reels
Docket of Witnesses Vol. K, 1801-17, 1 reel (part)
Fee Books Vols. P-S, 1807, 1846, 3 reels (parts)
Indexes to Judgments, 1801-13, 1854-73 (includes Circuit Court, 1852-73), 1 reel (part); and, Index to Judgments, Plaintiffs-Defendants, 1814-54 (includes Circuit Superior Court of Law and Chancery, 1847-51, and Circuit Court, 1852-54), 1 reel (part)
Liber A, 1801-02, 2 reels (parts)
Minute Books, 1801-43, 7 reels

Order Books [1]-21, 1801-27, 7 reels
Record of Executions Issued on Judgment Vol. A, 1801-02, 1 reel (part)
Rule Book F, 1817-19, 1 reel (part)
Trial Dockets Vols. A-I, 1802, 1810-11, 1813, 1816, 1818, 1820, 1822, 1 reel (part)
U.S. Government Plaintiff Vol. E, 1836-46, 1 reel (part)

Criminal Court

Minute Book, 1838-46, 1 reel

Criminal and Circuit Courts

Fines, Penalties, and Forfeitures Vol. O, 1801-46, 1 reel (part)

U. S. District Court, District of Columbia

Orders, 1801-27, 1 reel (part)
Records, 1806-30, 1 reel (part)

Levy Court, District of Columbia, Alexandria County

Minute Books, 1801-27, 1 reel (part)

Orphans' Court

Minute Books, 1842-47, 2 reels
Records, 1801-05, 1811-17, 1822-30, 1 reel

Circuit Superior Court of Law and Chancery

Index to Judgments, see Circuit Court, District of Columbia

Circuit Court

Commonwealth Dockets Vols. A and C-E, 1871-73, 1879-80, 2 reels (parts)
Docket Vol. C, 1874-76, 1 reel (part)
Index to Judgments, see Circuit Court, District of Columbia
Index to Liber K, 1880, 1 reel (part)

Fiduciary Records

Administrators' Bond Book, 1847-50, 1 reel (part)
Commissioners' Bond Book, 1850-99, 1 reel (part)
Fiduciary Bond Book, 1851-77, 1 reel (part)
Fiduciary Register, 1850-78, 1 reel (part)
Guardians' Bond Book, 1848-50, 1 reel (part)
[Guardians', etc.] Account Books Nos. 1-9, 1810-50, 4 reels
See also Court Records, Circuit Court, District of Columbia

Free Negro and Slave Records

Free Negroes Vol. A, 1858, 1 reel (part)
Registers of Free Negroes, 1797-1861, 1 reel

Justice of the Peace Records

Judgments by Justices of the Peace Vols. T-U, 1823, 1825-27, 1 reel (part)
Records of Executions Issued on Judgment Vols. B-C, 1802-07, 1816-19, 1 reel (part)

Land Records

Deed Books Nos. 1-8, 1801-65 (Ts.), 4 reels
General Index to Deeds O, 1800-69, 1 reel
Land Suits A, 1834-43, 1 reel

Marriage Records and Vital Statistics

Marriage Bonds, 1801-52, 10 reels
Marriage Records, 1850-81, 1 reel
Ministers' Returns, 1801-50, 1 reel (part); and, 1801-53, 1 reel (part)
Register of Births, 1853-96, 1 reel (part)
Register of Deaths, 1853-96, 1 reel (part)
Register of Marriages, 1853-79, 1 reel (part)

Military and Pension Records

Courts Martial, Military District of Alexandria, 1864-65, 1 reel (part)

Tax and Fiscal Records
> Assessments, Town and County of Alexandria, 1847, 1 reel (part)
> Bankruptcy Proceedings, 1802-21, 1 reel (part)
> Expenditures for Ft. Washington Vol. M, 1814-15, 1 reel (part)
> Insolvent Debtors, 1803-10, 1819-46, 3 reels
> Record Book of Schedules of Insolvent Debtors Vol. A, 1810-19, 2 reels (part)

Town Records
> See Tax and Fiscal Records

Wills
> Will Book No. 9, 1858 [1867]-1878, 1 reel (part)
> General Index to Wills, 1800-1951, 1 reel (part). See also City of Alexandria records.
> See also Court Records, Circuit Court, District of Columbia

Miscellaneous Records
> Log of the Schooner Enterprise Vol. A, 1803-04, 1 reel (part)
> Report of Aliens, 1801-32, 1 reel
> Unidentified Index, n.d., 1 reel (part)

Commissioner of Revenue
> Tithables, 1829, 1 reel (part)
> See also Tax and Fiscal Records

AUGUSTA COUNTY

Formed in 1738 from Orange County, government established in 1745.

Original Records

Circuit Court Clerk
  Bonds/Commissions/Oaths
    Ordinary Bonds, 1745-75, 1 vol. (copy)
  Census Records
    Enumeration, [1840], 1 vol. (printed)
  Court Records
  County Court
    Court Papers, 1745-76, 1 vol. (copy)
    Minute Books, 1745-64, 4 vols. (copies)
    Order Book No. 1, 1745-47, 1 vol. (copy)
  High Court of Chancery, Richmond
    McMeechen v. Rumsey, suit papers, 1799-1802, 14 items
  Superior Court of Chancery
    Peachy v. Henderson, exhibits (wills of John Blair, Jr., 1800; Mary Blair
      Andrews, 1820; and, Rev. James Henderson, 1820), 1821, 3 items (copies
      and Ts.)
  Fiduciary Records
    James Patton Estate Papers, see Giles County Fiduciary Records
  Land Records
    Deed Book No. 2, 1748-50, 1 vol. (copy)
    Deeds, 1760, 1768, 1769, 4 items
    Land Partitions, 1787, 1 item
  Marriage Records and Vital Statistics
    Marriage Bonds Vols. 1-13, 1785-1812, 13 vols. (copies)
    Marriage License, Snyder to Wheeler, 1842, 1 item
    Marriage Licenses and Ministers' Returns Vols. 1-4, 1785-1853, 4 vols. (copies)
    Marriage Record, 1813-46, 1 vol. (copy)
  Military and Pension Records
    Court Martial Records, 1756-96, 1 vol. (copy)
    Public Service Claims, 1782-84, 1 vol. (copy)
  Tax and Fiscal Records
    Land Tax Lists, 1839, 4 items
    Tithables, 1777-78, n.d., 19 pp.
  Town Records
    Day Book [Monthly Statement of Financial Condition of the Town of Staunton],
      1858-74, 1 vol.
    See also Miscellaneous Records
  Wills
    Will Books Nos. 1-2, 1745-60, 2 vols. (copies)
    Superior Court Will Book No. 1-A, 1778-1828, 1 vol. (copy)
    Will, see Court Records, Superior Court of Chancery
  Miscellaneous Records
    Augusta County/Corporation of Staunton Overseer of the Poor Records, 1769-
      1807, .9 cu. ft. See also Franklin County Miscellaneous Records.

Microfilm Records

Circuit Court Clerk
  Court Records
    County Court
      File Index to Loose Papers, 1745-1952 (includes Circuit Court, 1904-52), 1 reel
      Minute Books, 1745-49, 1 reel
      Order Books Nos. 1-60, 1745-1867, 23 reels
    District Court
      Order Books, 1789-1804, 3 reels
    Superior Court of Chancery
      Order Books, 1801-42 (includes Circuit Superior Court of Law and Chancery, 1831-42), 5 reels
    Circuit Superior Court of Law and Chancery
      Chancery Order Books Nos. 1-8, 1831-67 (includes Circuit Court Chancery, 1852-67), 3 reels
      Common Law Order Books Nos. 1-7, 1831-66 (includes Circuit Court, 1852-66), 3 reels
      Orders, see Superior Court of Chancery
    Circuit Court
      Chancery Orders, see Circuit Superior Court of Law and Chancery
      Common Law Orders, see Circuit Superior Court of Law and Chancery
      File Index, see County Court
      See also Military and Pension Records
  Fiduciary Records
    Executors' and Administrators' Bonds, 1787-1804, 1809-50, 1854-65, 3 reels
    Guardians' Bonds, 1809-50, 2 reels. See also Executors' and Administrators' Bonds.
  Land Records
    Deed Books Nos. 1-82, 1745-1866, 33 reels
    [District] Court Deed Books Nos. 1-A and 2-A, 1789-1813 (includes Superior Court of Law, 1808-13), 2 reels (parts)
    General Index to Deeds, Grantors-Grantees A-Z, 1745-1930, 7 reels
    Surveyors' Records Nos. 1-6, 1744-1906, 2 reels
  Marriage Records and Vital Statistics
    Marriage Records, 1785-1846, 1842-53, 1850-87, 1 reel
    Marriage Register No. 1, 1854-1900, 1 reel
    Register of Births, 1853-74, 1 reel (part)
    Register of Deaths, 1853-96, 1 reel (part)
  Military and Pension Records
    Court Martial Records, 1756-96, 1 reel (part)
    Militia Court [Court of Inquiry] Records, 1807-12, 1 reel (part)
    Muster Roll, 1861-65, 1 reel
  Tax and Fiscal Records
    Tithables, 1777, 1 reel
  Wills
    Will Books Nos. 1-40, 1745-1865, 20 reels
    Superior Court Will Books 1-A and 2-A, 1778-1828, 1831-71, 1 reel (part)
    Index to Wills No. 1, 1745-1903, 1 reel

BATH COUNTY

Formed in 1790 from Augusta, Botetourt, and Greenbrier (West Virginia) counties.

Original Records

Sheriff
Sheriff's Papers, 1840-46, 30 items

Microfilm Records

Circuit Court Clerk
Court Records
County Court
Order Books, 1791-1873, 4 reels
Circuit Superior Court of Law and Chancery
Chancery Order Book No. 1, 1831-58 (includes Circuit Court Orders, 1852-58), 1 reel (part)
Circuit Court
Chancery Order Book No. 2, 1858-79, 1 reel (part). See also Circuit Superior Court of Law and Chancery.
Election Records
See Land Records
Fiduciary Records
Administrators' Bonds, 1808-71, 1 reel
Executors' Bonds, 1793-1861, 1 reel
Land Records
Deed Books Nos. 1-12 [No. 2 includes voter list], 1791-1874, 5 reels
General Index to Deeds No. 1, Grantor-Grantee, 1791-1903, 1 reel
Surveyors' Records Nos. 1-3, 1791-1897, 1 reel
See also Wills; and, Botetourt County Land Records
Marriage Records and Vital Statistics
Marriage Bonds, 1791-1860 (Ts.), 1 reel (part)
Register of Births, 1853-70, 1 reel (part)
Register of Deaths, 1853-70, 1 reel (part)
Register of Marriages, 1853-95, 1 reel (part); and, Marriage Registers Nos. 1-3, 1861-89, 1883-97, 1896-1906, 2 reels (parts)
Wills
Will Books Nos. 1-6, 1791-1876, 3 reels
Circuit Court Wills, Deeds, etc., 1809-71 (includes Superior Court of Law, 1809-31, and Circuit Superior Court of Law and Chancery, 1831-51), 1 reel

BEDFORD COUNTY

**Formed in 1753 from Lunenburg County.
Parts of Albemarle and Lunenburg
counties were added later.**

Original Records

Circuit Court Clerk
Board of Supervisors Records
Accounts Allowed by the Board, 1876, 11 items
Papers, 1883-89, ca. .9 cu. ft.
Bonds/Commissions/Oaths
Bonds, ca. 1820-90, ca. 2 cu. ft.
Declaration Bonds, ca. 1820-60, ca. .1 cu. ft.
Delivery Bonds, ca. 1820-60, ca. .25 cu. ft.
Injunction Bonds, ca. 1820-60, ca. .2 cu. ft.
Oaths of Office, 1865-95, .35 cu. ft.
Officials' Bonds, 1839-74, 1891-1901, ca. 1 cu. ft.
Orphans' Indentures, ca. 1790-1860, .45 cu. ft.
Replevy Bonds, ca. 1790-1865, .45 cu. ft.
Salt Bonds, 1862, ca. 50 items
Business Records/Corporations/Partnerships
Farmers Mutual Fire Insurance Co., cancelled checks, ca. 1900-20, .35 cu. ft.
Shanklin Campbell & Co. Cash Book, 1884-87, 1 vol.
Census Records
Enumeration Sheets, 1850, 5 pp.
Court Records
County Court
Attachments, Injunctions, etc., ca. 1770-1860, ca. .35 cu. ft.
Attendance Books, 1790-1834, 1837-46, 1851-80, 1895-1904, 11 vols.
Chancery Docket, 1870-73, 1 vol.
Chancery Fee Book, 1870-73, 1 vol.
Chancery Memorandum, 1870-73, 1 vol.
Chancery Rules, 1844-73, 1 vol.
Common Law Rule Books, 1851-1904, 3 vols.
Commonwealth Papers, 1777-1904, .45 cu. ft.
Commonwealth Recognizances, ca. 1795-1904, ca. .45 cu. ft.
Commonwealth Rules, 1879-80, ca. 50 items
Commonwealth Warrants, 1822, 1865-87, ca. 50 items
Determined Causes, 1764-99. ca. 7.65 cu. ft.
Docket, 1759-61, 1 item (fragment)
Docket Books, 1761-62, 1764-65, 1767, 3 vols.; Nos. 1-[2], 1772-82, 2 vols.;
    and, Dockets, 1783-92, 1794, 1799-1850, 1860-74, 1895-1904, 149 vols.
Escape Warrants, 1814-21, 11 items
Execution Books, 1769-73, 3 vols.; and, Nos. 1-23, 1774-1905, 22 vols. [there
    is no No. 21]
Executions to Warrants, 1817-61, 1.05 cu. ft.
Indexes to Execution Books, 1843, 1874, 1889, n.d., 4 vols.
Index to Common Law Execution Book, 1887, 1 vol.
Fee Books, 1754, 1764-79, 1783-1870, 1875, 1879-1902, 111 vols.
Grand Jury Presentments, Commonwealth Cases, 1792-ca. 1880, .45 cu. ft.
Injunction Dockets [titles vary], [1808-42], 4 vols.

Jury Books, 1865-1904, 3 vols.

Law Dockets, 1846-50, 1880-90, 2 vols.

Law Fee Books, 1871-74, 1876-78, 5 vols.

Law Memorandum Book, 1761-64, 1872-80, 3 vols.

Memorandum Books, 1755-56, 1760-66, 1770-82, 1784-85, 1787-1872, 1874-86, 1892-95, 1898-1904, 45 vols.

Minutes, 1869-73, 1880-91, 6 vols.

Miscellaneous Papers, ca. 1790-1904, ca. 1 cu. ft.

Motion Docket, 1824, 1 vol.

Order Books Nos. 1-A, 1-B, 2, 4 [Minute Book], 5-B, and 6, 1754-62, 1772, 1774-82, 6 vols. (copies)

Process Books, 1835-49, 1869-88, 2 vols.

Rule Books, 1787-1806, 1828-42, 1860-82, 7 vols.

Superior Court of Law

Attendance Books, 1814-30, 2 vols.

Dockets, 1809-26, ca. .15 cu. ft.

Fee Books, 1809-30, 5 vols.

Law Memorandum Book, 1809-13, 1 vol.

Law Rule Book, 1828-31, 1 vol.

Memorandum Books, 1819-31, 2 vols.

Minutes, 1809-31, 4 vols.

Rule Book, 1820-29, 1 vol.

Circuit Superior Court of Law and Chancery

Attendance Books, 1831-54 (includes Circuit Court, 1852-54), 3 vols.

Chancery Court Process Book, 1831-79, 1 vol.

Chancery Court Rule Books [Nos. 1-2], 1831-52 (includes Circuit Court, 1852), 2 vols.

Chancery Dockets, 1832-64 (includes Circuit Court, 1852-64), 2 vols.

Chancery Executions, A-Z, 1832-54 (includes Circuit Court, 1852-54), ca. .2 cu. ft.

Chancery Fee Books, 1831-51, 7 vols.

Chancery Memorandum Books, 1831-64 (includes Circuit Court, 1852-64), 4 vols.

Chancery Minute Books, 1831-67 (includes Circuit Court, 1852-67), 2 vols.

Chancery Motion Docket, 1831-54 (includes Circuit Court, 1852-54), 1 vol.

Common Law Dockets, 1831-56 (includes Circuit Court, 1852-56), 3 vols.

Common Law Process Books, 1831-60 (includes Circuit Court, 1852-60), 3 vols.

Common Law Rule Books, 1831-60 (includes Circuit Court, 1852-60), 3 vols.

Fee Books, 1831-37, 2 vols.

Law Fee Books, 1833-53 (includes Circuit Court, 1852-53), 11 vols.

Law Memorandum Books, 1834-51, 4 vols.

Law Minutes, 1831-52 (includes Circuit Court, 1852), 4 vols.

Motion and Appeal Docket, 1832, 1 vol.

Orders, 1828-30, 1838-39, 2 vols.

Circuit Court

Attendance Books, 1855-87, 1896-97, 3 vols. See also Circuit Superior Court of Law and Chancery.

Chancery Docket Books, 1864-79, 1885-93, 3 vols. See also Circuit Superior Court of Law and Chancery.

Chancery Dockets, 1893, 2 items

Chancery Executions, A-Z, 1855-1905, ca. .45 cu. ft. See also Circuit Superior Court of Law and Chancery.

Chancery Fee Books, 1852-93, 21 vols.

Index to Chancery Fee Book, 1894-[?], 1 vol.

Chancery Memorandum Books, 1864-1935, 5 vols. See also Circuit Superior Court of Law and Chancery.

Chancery Minute Books, 1869-93, 5 vols. See also Circuit Superior Court of Law and Chancery.

Chancery Motion Dockets, see Circuit Superior Court of Law and Chancery

Chancery Rule Books [Nos. 3-4], 1852-73, 2 vols. See also Circuit Superior Court of Law and Chancery.

Common Law Dockets, see Circuit Superior Court of Law and Chancery

Common Law Memorandum Books, 1851-80, 1886-1905, 11 vols.

Common Law Minutes, 1852-85, 7 vols.

Common Law Process, see Circuit Superior Court of Law and Chancery

Common Law Rules, see Circuit Superior Court of Law and Chancery

Fee Books, 1895-1905, 2 vols.

Jury Book, 1868-92, 1 vol.

Law Dockets, 1857-83, 2 vols.

Law Fee Books, 1854-1905, 19 vols. See also Circuit Superior Court of Law and Chancery.

Law Memorandum Book, [1876] 1877-84, 1 vol.

Law Minutes, see Circuit Superior Court of Law and Chancery

Papers in Hands of Counsel, 1881-84, 1887-92, 2 vols.

Process Book, 1860-76, 1 vol.

Suits at Law, 1881-87, and in Chancery, 1881-86, 1 vol.

County and Superior Courts

Abstracts of Judgments, 1861-68, 1880-1905, ca. 1 cu. ft.

Executions, 1754-1904, ca. 18.1 cu. ft.

Fee Bills, ca. 1800-1907, ca. .8 cu. ft.

Judgments Docketed, 1855-79, ca. .75 cu. ft.

Lists of Fee Bills, ca. 1870, n.d., 7 items

Miscellaneous Papers, 1754-1910, 2.8 cu. ft.

Orders, ca. 1800-90, 1 cu. ft.

Subpoenas, 1783-1906, 11 cu. ft.

Unspecified Court

Form Book, n.d., 1 vol.

Registers of Persons Convicted of Felony [title vary], 1870-71, 1893-1948, 2 vols.

Venire Facias, 1868-1903, .35 cu. ft.

Election Records

Abstracts of Votes, Election Returns, etc., ca. 1810-1900, .45 cu. ft.

Congressional Poll, 1793, 1 item

Lists of Voters, 1853-54, 1857 (includes Militia List), 1858 (includes Militia List, 1854), 4 vols.

Rolls of [white and colored] Voters, 1902-64 [overlapping date ranges], 9 vols.

Fiduciary Records

Executors' and Administrators' Bonds, 1756-1844, ca. 1 cu. ft.

Fiduciary Accounts and Vouchers, ca. 1825-85, .35 cu. ft

Fiduciary Bonds, ca. 1830-1900, ca. .8 cu. ft.

Guardians' Bonds, 1770-1844, .45 cu. ft.

Index to Fiduciary Register, 1861-1919, 1 vol.

Free Negro and Slave Records

Free [Negro] Papers (registrations, etc.), ca. 1850, ca. 50 items

Lists of Slaves, etc., 1814-57, 13 items

Registers of Free Negroes, 1803-60, 2 vols.

Justice of the Peace Records

    Justices' and Magistrates' Executions, 1819-1914, n.d., 2 cu. ft.

    Justices' Certificates, 1899-1903, ca. 50 items

    Justices' Judgment and Execution Books, 1872-88, 1892-1903, 1893-99, 1897-1902, 5 vols.

    Justices' Judgment Dockets, 1885-97 (John A. Hunt), 1895-96 (W. R. Abbot), 2 vols.

    Justices' Reports, 1889-99, ca. 1.35 cu. ft.

    Justices' Warrants and Judgments, 1851-1904, ca. .5 cu. ft.

    Magistrates' Judgments, etc., Satisfied, 1865-68, ca. .15 cu. ft.

    Magistrates' Returns [on Executions], 1827-50, 1 vol.

    Reports of Criminal Cases Disposed of by Justices, 1888-1903, 1 vol.

Land Records

    Deeds and Plats, ca. 1770-1900, ca. .35 cu. ft.; Deeds (including Deeds Partly Proved), 1806-70, 1905, .35 cu. ft.; and, Miscellaneous Deeds, etc., ca. 1860-70, ca. 50 items

    Deeds of Trust, A-W, ca. 1895-1925, .7 cu. ft.; and, Deeds of Trust [and miscellaneous papers], A-Z, ca. 1890-1925, .7 cu. ft.

    Indexes to Deed Books, 1754-1841, 2 vols.; and, Index to Deed Book 78, 1899-1900, 1 vol.

    Maps and Surveys, 1840, n.d., 15 items (and fragments)

    Processioners' Book, 1796-1812, 1 vol.; and, Processioners' Returns, 1812-24, 1 vol.

    Processioners' Returns, 1800-16, 1820-24, 1844, .7 cu. ft.

Marriage Records and Vital Statistics

    Registers of Births, ca. 1865-95, 6 items

    Registers of Deaths, ca. 1855-95, 6 items (and fragments)

Military and Pension Records

    [Civil War Pensioners], 1886-1904, 1900-05, 3 vols.

    Exemptions from Military Service, 1862, 1 item

    List of Non-Commissioned Officers and Soldiers of the Virginia State Line, 1835, 1 item

    List of Persons Liable to be Enrolled in the Militia, 1855, 1 item

    List of Wounded Confederate Soldiers, 1862-64, 1 item

    Militia Lists, see Election Records

Road and Bridge Records

    Bridge Papers, ca. 1800-95, ca. .35 cu. ft.

    Lists of Road Surveyors, 1789-1804, 1812, 1826, 3 items

    Lists of Surveyors of Roads, 1789-1800, 1789-1807, 1795-1812, 1836, 4 vols.

    Overseer's Account Book, Forest Township, 1872-75, 1 vol.; and, Staunton Township, [1874?], n.d., 3 vols.

    Overseers' and Commissioners' Reports, ca. 1860-1900, ca. .3 cu. ft.

    Petitions, ca. 1780-1920, .9 cu. ft.

    Plats, 1909-11, n.d., 8 items

    Reports of Viewers, ca. 1790-1915, .35 cu. ft.

    Road Bonds, see Micellaneous Records

    [Road Papers], ca. 1775-1920, .45 cu. ft.

    Road Surveyors' Papers, ca. 1830-90, .35 cu. ft.

    Road Warrants, 1888, ca. 100 items

    Transit Books [titles vary], 1875-76, n.d., 8 vols.

School Records

    Trustees' [Oaths], 1891-1921, 1 vol.

Tax and Fiscal Records

    Applications to Purchase Lands for Taxes, filed 1898-1903, ca. 1.5 cu. ft.

    [County] Cash Book, 1899, 1 vol.

County Claims, 1770, 1796-1892, ca. 3.5 cu. ft.
County Levy, 1828, 1 item; and, Vouchers for County Levy, 1757, ca. 25 items
Levies, 1889 [1881-94], 1880-88, 2 vols. (and fragments)
List of Insolvent Lands, 1784-1813, 1 vol.
List of Lands Exonerated, 1814, 1 vol.
List of Tax Tickets, 1871-74, 1 item
List of Tithables, n.d., 1 item
Lists of Insolvents, 1784-1880, 1892-96, ca. 2.5 cu. ft.
Lists of Land Sold for Delinquent Taxes, 1784-1816, 2 items
Parish Levies, 1840-56, 9 items
Tax Vouchers, 1790, 1792, 1794, 3 items

Township Records
Chamblissburg Township Financial Book, 1871-75, 1 vol.; and, Minutes, 1871-75, 1 vol.
Charlemont Township Minutes, 1871-74, 1 vol.
Forest Township Records Book, 1871-75, 1 vol.
Staunton Township Account Book, 1872-75, 1 vol.
See also Road and Bridge Records; and, Miscellaneous Records

Wills
Will Book No. 1 [A-1], 1763-87, 1 vol. (copy)

Miscellaneous Records
Calohill Minnis' Fee Book, 1818-24, 1 vol.
Estray Notices, 1783-1902, ca. 1 cu. ft.
Inquisitions, 1813-99, .35 cu. ft.
John M. Speece, Notary Public, Account Book, 1879-90, 1 vol.
List of County Seals, 1823-39, 1 vol.
Lunacy Papers, etc. (also Road Bonds), 1871-72, .35 cu. ft.
Mill Papers, 1790-1861, ca. 25 items
Old Courthouse Plans, etc., 1784-1840, n.d., 10 items
Overseer of the Poor Orders (Staunton District), 1873-75, ca. 50 items; and, Vouchers, 1881, ca. 50 items
Overseer of the Poor Record Book, 1816-30, 1 vol.
Reply to Editorial, [ca. 1900], 2 items
Stray Books, 1773-1828, 2 vols.
Superintendent of the Poor Annual Reports, 1871, 1878-79, 1881-84, 1886, 8 items; and, Settlements, 1879, ca. 25 items
William A. Creasy's Fee Book, 1855-59, 1 vol.

Commissioner of Revenue
Land Taxes, ca. 1790-1855, 1 cu. ft.
Lands Improperly Assessed or not Ascertainable, 1885, 1 vol.
License Reports, 1866, 1873-1908, 1.5 cu. ft.
Lists of Taxable Property, 1782-1853, n.d., 2 cu. ft.
See also Tax and Fiscal Records

Sheriff
Sheriff's Bonds and Tax Receipts, 1755-1851, .35 cu. ft.

Treasurer
County Warrants, 1891, ca. 100 items
Delinquent Land Records, ca. 1880-1900, ca. 1 cu. ft.
Lists of County Warrants, 1895-97, 2 items
Memorandums of County Levy, 1894-95, 4 items
See also Tax and Fiscal Records

Microfilm Records

Circuit Court Clerk
  Court Records
    County Court
      Order Books Nos. 1-34, 1754-1865, 11 reels
      General Index to County Court Order Books, A-Z, 1754-1904, 5 reels
    Circuit Superior Court of Law and Chancery
      Chancery Order Books Nos. 1-2, 1831-51, 1 reel
    Circuit Court
      Chancery Order Books Nos. 3-4, 1851-68, 1 reel
  Land Records
    Deed Books Nos. 1-42, 1754-1865, 18 reels. See also Wills.
    General Index to Deeds, Grantors-Grantees A-Z, 1754-1930, 6 reels
    Processioner's Book, 1796-1812 (also Marriage Returns, 1785-1811), 1 reel (part)
    Surveyors' Records Nos. 1-3, 1754-95, and No. 4, 1811-81 (includes Land Entries, 1877), 1 reel
  Marriage Records and Vital Statistics
    Index to Marriage Bonds, Husbands-Wives A-Z, 1754-1870, 1 reel
    Marriage Registers Nos. 1-2, 1854-1909, 1 reel
    General Index to Marriage Registers, Husbands-Wives A-Z, 1854-1949, 4 reels
    Marriage Returns, 1812-52, 1 reel (part). See also Land Records.
    Register of Births, 1853-97, 1 reel
    Index to Births, A-Z, 1853-97, 1 reel
    Register of Deaths No. 1, 1853-97, 1 reel (part)
    Index to Deaths, A-Z, 1853-1917, 1 reel (part)
  Military and Pension Records
    Muster Roll, War Between the States, 1861-65, 1 reel (part)
  Wills
    Will Books Nos. 1-20, 1763-1866, 9 reels
    Superior Court of Law [Deed] & Will Book A, 1810-63 (includes Circuit Superior Court of Law and Chancery, 1831-51, and Circuit Court, 1851-63), 1 reel (part)
    Circuit Court Will Book B, 1863-88, 1 reel (part)
    General Index to Will Book, Decedents, Trusts, or Wards, A-Z, 1754-1949, 4 reels

BLAND COUNTY

**Formed in 1861 from Giles, Wythe, and
Tazewell counties. Another part
of Giles was added later.**

Original Records

Circuit Court Clerk
  Board of Supervisors Records
    Papers, 1889-1904, 1 cu. ft.
    See also Court Records, County Court
  Bonds/Commissions/Oaths
    [Appeal, bail, and officials'] Bonds, 1899-1944, .25 cu. ft.
    Circuit Court Bond Book, 1889-1903, 1 vol.
    County Court Bond Books, 1861-1919 (includes Circuit Court, 1904-19), 4 vols.

Business Records/Corporations/Partnerships

Barclay Dodd [general merchandise] Ledger, 1880-90, 1 vol.; and, B. Dodd [charge account] Book No. 1, 1889-90, 1 vol.

[Charter Book], 1889-1903, 1 vol.

[John W. Early Co. Day Book], 1890-93, 1 vol.

Miscellaneous Contracts, 1893-1932, 1 vol.

Unidentified Merchant's Ledger, 1899-1904, 1 vol.

Unidentified Ledger, 1886-91, 1 vol.

Court Records

County Court

Accounts Allowed by County Court, 1894, .25 cu. ft.

Clerk of Court, Correspondence, 1889-1904, ca. 1 cu. ft.

Common Law Rule Docket, 1863-97 (includes Circuit Court, 1897-1903), 1 vol.

Court Cases on Sleeping Docket, etc., 1889-1917, .25 cu. ft.

Court Papers, 1888-1903, 2.25 cu. ft.

Current Court Papers, 1903-04, .25 cu. ft.

Fee Book, 1893-1913 (includes Circuit Court, 1904-13), 1 vol.

G. R. Repass, Clerk of Court, [private papers], 1895-1946, .5 cu. ft.

Hoge v. Chumbley, exhibit books, 1898-99, n.d., 2 vols.

Issue Docket, 1871-81, 1 vol.

Judgment Dockets, 1875-1900, 2 vols.; and, County and Circuit Courts Judgment Docket No. 4, 1901-16, 1 vol.

List of Fines Paid into Court, 1874-88, 1 vol.

Memorandum Book, 1871-1903, 1 vol.

Minute Book, 1900-01, 1 vol.

Old Papers Disposed of Before the Burning of the Courthouse, 1886-90, .25 cu. ft.

Pleas, 1861-62 (also Board of Supervisors' Minutes, 1870-96), 1 vol.

Witness Attendance Books, 1882-93, 1892-1903, 2 vols.

Circuit Court

Chancery Decrees, 1889-1919, .5 cu. ft.

[Chancery] Docket, 1894-1903, 1 vol.

Chancery Fee Book, 1899-1921, 1 vol.

Chancery Issue Docket, 1871-81, 1 vol.

Chancery Memorandum Book 1888-1932, 1 vol.

Chancery Papers Nos. 1-190 and unnumbered, 1889-1924, 9.25 cu. ft.

Chancery Rule Dockets Nos. [1]-2, 1863-1904, 2 vols.

Clerk's Tax Books, 1898-1909, 2 vols.

Common Law Issue Docket, 1871-81, 1 vol.

Common Law Memorandum Book, 1888-1932, 1 vol.

Common Law Papers, 1889-1928, 6.75 cu. ft.

Common Law Rule Dockets, 1863-92, 1 vol. See also County Court.

Execution Books, 1867-1925, 2 vols.

Executions Returned, 1888-1957, .25 cu. ft.

Fee Books, 1873-79, 1893-99, 2 vols. See also County Court.

Journal [file docket of Chancery cases Nos. 1-181], n.d., 1 vol.

Judgments Confessed, 1889-1923, .25 cu. ft. See also County Court.

Law Process Book, 1894-1939, 1 vol.

Old Law Papers, etc., Disposed of Before the Courthouse was Burned, 1884-88, .25 cu. ft.

Orders for Claims, 1902-13, ca. .1 cu. ft.

Witness Attendance Books, 1889-1936, 2 vols.

See also Miscellaneous Records

Election Records
General Registration, 1902-03 [1906], 1 vol.
List of Voters Registered,1902-09, 1 vol.
Poll Books, 1890-1904, 1.75 cu. ft.
Rolls of Registered Voters, 1902-67, 2 vols.
Fiduciary Records
Fiduciary Settlements, 1888-1927, 2.25 cu. ft.
Lists of Heirs, see Land Records
Record of Fiduciaries, 1877-1903, 1 vol.; and, Record of Fiduciaries No. 1, 1899-
1909, 1 vol.
Sale of Appraisement Bills Recorded, 1896-1914, .25 cu. ft.
Justice of the Peace Records
Abram N. Miller's [Judgment] Book, 1888-94, 1 vol.
Civil Judgment and Execution Books, 1890-1916, 1893-1903, 1895-1915, 3 vols.
Constables' Returns, 1881-1905, .5 cu. ft.
Constables' Returns Docketed, 1889-97, .25 cu. ft.
Land Records
Deed Book No. 5, 1886-1923, 1 vol.
Deeds (also Lists of Heirs and Deeds of Trust), 1889-1957, 3 cu. ft.
General Index to Deeds, Grantee, 1900, 1 vol.
Marriage Records and Vital Statistics
Lists of Births and Deaths, 1867-79, 1888-95, .25 cu. ft.
Military and Pension Records
Lists of Pensioners, 1903, 1 vol.
Pension Papers, 1901-10, ca. .25 cu. ft.
Tax and Fiscal Records
[County Fund Ledger], 1895-1904, 1 vol.
Old License Reports, 1888-1921, .25 cu. ft.
See also Miscellaneous Records
Wills
Wills, 1889-1977, 2 cu. ft.
Miscellaneous Records
Miscellaneous Papers [receipts, tax lists, and court papers], 1901-05, .25 cu. ft.
Records of Persons Adjudged Insane, 1902-27, 1 vol.
Register of Physicians and Surgeons, 1898-1949, 1 vol.

Sheriff
Sheriff's Receipt Book, 1875-88, 1 vol.

Microfilm Records

Circuit Court Clerk
Bonds/Commissions/Oaths
Bonds, 1861-90, 1 reel
Court Records
County Court
Order Book No. 1, 1861-69, 1 reel
Land Records
Deeds No. 1, 1861-70, 1 reel
General Index to Deeds, Grantor-Grantee, 1861-1907, 1 reel
Marriage Records and Vital Statistics
Register of Marriages, 1861-1929, 1 reel
Wills
Will Book No. 1, 1861-1904, 1 reel

BOTETOURT COUNTY

Formed in 1769 from Augusta County. Part
of Rockbridge County was added later.

Original Records

Circuit Court Clerk
Bonds/Commissions/Oaths
Clergymen's Bonds, 1801-05, ca. 25 items
Commissions, 1800-60, ca. .1 cu. ft.
Constables' Bonds, ca. 1805-50, ca. .2 cu. ft.
Delivery and Appeal Bonds, etc. 1788-ca. 1820, 1852-57, ca. .3 cu. ft.
Indentures, 1772, 1791-1856, .35 cu. ft.
Officials' Bonds, 1770, ca. 50 items
Ordinary Bonds, ca. 1750-1850, ca. .35 cu. ft.
Replevin Bonds, ca. 1775-1810, .35 cu. ft.; and, Replevin and Judgment Bonds,
    etc., ca. 1785-1810, ca. .25 cu. ft.
Business Records/Corporations/Partnerships
Beckley & Bro. Account Book, [ca. 1875], 1 vol.
Benford and Wilson Account Ledger B, 1866-67, 1 vol.
Burgess Steel and Iron Works to Board of Supervisors, 1896, 1 item
Clintons Savings Bank Ledger, 1853-60, 1 vol.
Farmers Bank of Fincastle Stock Ledger, 1856-1919, 1 vol.
Jno. McDowell's Ledger No. 3, 1872-75, 1 vol.
[Lybrook, Beckley & Co.] Day Book, 1866-93, 1 vol.
Madison Waskey's [Account] Book, 1840-45, 1 vol.
McKnight and Galbraith's [Ledger], Buchanan, 1836-46, 1 vol.
Quarterly Return of Manufacture of Iron by Joseph Hannah, 1815, 1 item
Smith and Briggs Brass Works Capital Stock, 1892, 1 vol.; Exhibit B.E.S. No. 35,
    1895-96, 1 vol.; Ledger, 1896-97, 1 vol.; Letter Books, 1893-95, 2 vols.;
    Minute Book, 1891-97, 1 vol.; Payroll Book, 1893-96, 1 vol.; and, Sale Book,
    1891-92, 1 vol.
Smith and Briggs Suit Papers, 1891-98, ca. .1 cu. ft.
The Iron Belt Building and Loan Papers, 1891, 2 items
Unidentified Account Books, 1849-52, 1854, 1870, 1875-76, 1884-87, n.d., 8 vols.
Unidentified Accounts, 1840-42, 1852-57, 2 items (fragments)
Unidentified Cash Book, 1844-45, 1 vol.
Unidentified Day Book, 1856-57, 1 item
Unidentified Merchant's Account Books, 1870, 1882, 2 vols.
Unidentified Ledgers, [1872-73], 1873-74, 2 vols.
Unidentified Mill Account Book, 1851-52, 1 vol.
Unidentified Store Account Books, 1803-06, 1882, 2 vols.
Western Hotel Ledger, 1856-57, 1 vol.
White and Robinson Wool Carding Book, 1851-52, 1 vol.
Williams and Woodville [doctors] Account Books, 1849, 1852, 1861-64, 3 vols.
Zimmerman and Thrasher [Livery Stable] Account Books, 1843-50 (fragment),
    1851, 1858-59, 3 vols.
Census Records
Enumerations, 1850-80, 4 vols.
List of Souls, 1782, 1 item

Court Records

County Court

Chancery Memorandum Book, 1860-73, 1 vol.

Chancery Rule Book, 1870-73, 1 vol.

[Clerk's] Tax Book, 1898-1912, 1 vol.

Commonwealth Cases, 1777-94, ca. 75 items

Commonwealth Pleas, 1791-1814, .35 cu. ft.

Decrees and Dismissions in Chancery, 1789-92, 1808, .35 cu. ft.

Docket Book, 1808-11, 1 vol.

Execution Books, 1785-1821, 1831-38, 1899-1903, 7 vols.

Fee Books, 1778, 1784, 1795-99, 1802-06, 1808-11, 1816-17, 1819-22, 1825-29, 1832-36, 1839-42, 1844, 1846-49, 1858-61, 1863-71, 1881-85, 1894-1903, 43 vols.

Issue Dockets, 1773-89, 1804-05, 1820-24, 1838-47, 1856-1903, 9 vols.

Memorandum and Minute Book, 1890-93, 1 vol.

Memorandum Books, 1773-74, 1793, 1823-30, 1842-50, 1866-73, 1890-1904, n.d., 9 vols. See also Memorandum and Minute Book.

Minute Books, 1773-83, 1788-99, 4 vols. (copies); and, [1812]-28, 1814-16, 1858, 3 vols. See also Memorandum and Minute Book.

Office Judgments, 1789-1829, 3 cu. ft.

Order and Account Book, 1797-1801, 1 vol.

Order Books, 1770-1800, 11 vols. (copies); and, [1860], 1 vol.

Orders of the Court, 1813-57, .35 cu. ft.

Petitions Ended, 1797-1801, 1804, .35 cu. ft.

Process Book, 1850-98, 1 vol.

[Rough Minutes?], 1819-22, 1833-37, 1834-40, 3 vols.

Rule Books, 1786-91, 1796-1805, 1809-19, 1821-73, 8 vols.

Witness Attendance Book, 1895-1903, 1 vol.

Superior Court of Law

Execution Book, 1809-30, 1 vol.

Executions, 1809-17, 1823-26, ca. .15 cu. ft.

Fee Books, 1810-13, 1816-30, 4 vols.

Minute Book, 1809, 1 vol.

Rule Docket, 1809-31, 1 vol.

Superior Court Judgments, 1809-28, 1.25 cu. ft.

Circuit Superior Court of Law and Chancery

Chancery Court Docket, 1847-48, 1 vol.

Chancery Court Rule Book, 1831-45, 1 vol.; and, Chancery Rule Book, 1846-69 (includes Circuit Court, 1852-69), 1 vol.

Chancery Minute Docket, 1833-46, 1 vol.

Common Law Execution Book, 1831-45, 1 vol.

Common Law Fee Books, 1832-38, 1842-52 (includes Circuit Court, 1852), 2 vols.

Common Law Minute Docket, 1846-57 (includes Circuit Court, 1852-57), 1 vol.

Common Law Rule Book, 1831-68 (includes Circuit Court, 1852-68), 1 vol.

Executions in Chancery, 1843-52 (includes Circuit Court, 1852), ca. 100 items

Fee Books, 1832-47, 4 vols.

Issue Docket, 1834-46, 1 vol.

Minutes, 1841-42 (also Memorandum of Cases Removed from Office, 1842), 1 vol.

Process Book, 1831-83 (includes Circuit Court, 1852-83), 1 vol.

Superior Court Executions, 1834, 1837-41, ca. .1 cu. ft.

Superior Court Judgments, 1831-35, ca. .75 cu. ft.

Witness Book, 1822, 1 vol.; and, Vol. [A], 1831-55 (includes Circuit Court, 1852-55), 1 vol.

Circuit Court

Chancery Dockets, 1891-1911, 3 vols.
Chancery Fee Books, 1866-76, 3 vols.
Chancery Issue Docket, 1858-71, 1 vol.
Chancery Memorandum Book, 1890-1903, 1 vol.
Chancery Rules, see Circuit Superior Court of Law and Chancery
[Circuit Court of Common Law?] Issues, 1869-83, 1 vol.
Clerk's Book for Papers Taken Out of Office, 1887-1900, 1 vol.
Common Law Fee Books, 1855-62 1865-67, 1870-76, 9 vols. See also Circuit Superior Court of Law and Chancery.
Common Law Minute Book, see Circuit Superior Court of Law and Chancery
Common Law Rule Book, see Circuit Superior Court of Law and Chancery
Execution Docket, 1891-1907, 1 vol.
Executions, 1871-87, ca. .25 cu. ft.
Executions in Chancery, 1875-84, ca. .1 cu. ft. See also Circuit Superior Court of Law and Chancery.
Fee Books, 1852, 1854-58, 1874-79, 1883-95, 4 vols.
Guggenheimer et al. v. Zimmerman et al., suit papers, 1885-90, 1 item
Letters from the Supreme Court of Appeals, 1894-95, 3 items
List of Papers Taken from the Clerk's Office, 1866-73, 1 vol.
Lucade v. Tyler, transcript, 1888, 1 vol.
Process Book, 1883-1903, 1 vol. See also Circuit Superior Court of Law and Chancery.
Superior Court Executions, 1852-55, 1860, 1870, 1885-86, ca. .2 cu. ft.
Witness Attendance Book B, 1855-95, 1 vol. See also Circuit Superior Court of Law and Chancery.

County and Superior Courts

Criminal Papers, 1824, ca. 50 items
Criminal Trials, 1871-92, 1 vol.
Dismissals and injunctions,1843, and suit papers, 1795-1838, ca. .5 cu. ft.
Executions, 1770-1876, 13.5 cu. ft.
Indictments, 1862-67, ca. 50 items
Judgments, ca. 1770-1860, ca. 26.25 cu. ft.; Judgments and Dismissions, 1788-1841, 5 cu. ft.; Judgments and Executions, 1770-1852, 3 cu. ft.; and Judgments on Petitions, ca. 1770-1805, ca. .8 cu. ft.
Suit Papers, ca. 1800-95, ca. .85 cu. ft.
Suits Ended, ca. 1795-1805, 1 cu. ft.
Summons, 1770-75, 1850-60, 1864, ca. .25 cu. ft.

Unspecified Court

Court Papers (and Teachers' Warrants), 1773-1892, ca. .6 cu. ft.
[Grand Jury] Presentment, 1776, 1 item
Lists of Clerk's Tickets Returned, 1889, 2 items
Unidentified Index [to suits], n.d., 1 vol.

Election Records

Election Board Minutes, 1884-1940, 1 vol.
Election of Trustees, Salem, 1828, 1 item
Lists of Voters and Muster Rolls, 1854-58 (also List of Free Negroes, 1855), ca. 25 items
Lists of Registered Voters, [18]87-1900, 1892-1901, 1902-09, 4 vols.
Polls, ca. 1785-1870, .35 cu. ft.; and, Poll for General Assembly, 1792, 7 pp. (copies)
Qualifications, 1864-66, n.d., ca. .1 cu. ft.

Fiduciary Records

[Clerk's Estate Sale Book?], n.d., 1 vol.; [Clerk's Estate Sale?] Collection Book, n.d., 1 vol.; and, [Clerk's Sale Book, Bean Bros. Store?], n.d., 1 vol.

Estate Vouchers, 1780-1868, n.d., ca. 8 cu. ft.

Fiduciary Bonds, 1816-24, 1855-60, ca. .1 cu. ft.

Figgatt's Estate Papers, 1883-1905, ca. .1 cu. ft.

Guardians', Administrators', and Executors' Bonds, 1779-1851, ca. 1 cu. ft.

James Tapscott's Estate Accounts, 1801-06, ca. .1 cu. ft.

List of Sales from Philip Gartner's Estate, 1813, 1 item

Sales of Personal Property of William R. Rowland, 1853 (also accounts, 1851-52), 1 vol.

Schedules, ca. 1815-50, ca. .7 cu. ft.

Free Negro and Slave Records

Certificates of Non-importation, 1794, 1796, 2 items

Emancipation Papers, 1790, 1792, 1798, ca. 25 items

Letter from Governor Henry Horatio Wells to County Clerks about Keeping Records of Colored People, 1868, 1 item

Lists of Free Negroes and Mulattoes, ca. 1800-50, ca. .1 cu. ft.

See also Election Records

Justice of the Peace Records

Executions Rendered and Judgments, 1852-68, 1852-72, 2 vols.

Judgment and Execution Book, 1900-03, 1 vol.

Lists of Magistrates, 1803-05, 2 pp.

Magistrates' Executions, 1846-74, 1 vol.

Magistrates' Executions, ca. 1835-60, ca. .25 cu. ft.

Magistrates' Judgment Docket [and Execution Book], 1876-94, 1 vol.

Magistrates' Judgments, 1827-35, 1838-40, ca. .2 cu. ft.

Land Records

Commissioners' Report on the Boundary Line between Bath and Botetourt Counties, 1804, 4 pp. (copies)

Deed Books Nos. 1-2, 1770-80, 2 vols. (copies)

Deeds and Maps ca. 1700[?]-1920, ca. .5 cu. ft.

General Indexes to Deeds, 1770-1881, 1854-57, n.d., 3 vols.; and, Grantor-Grantee A-Z, 1890-1924, 4 vols.

Kanawha Canal Maps, 1848, 90 items

Marriage Records and Vital Statistics

Marriage Consents, 1881, 1888-93, ca. .25 cu. ft.

Marriage Register, 1770-1853, 1 vol. (Ms. compilation)

Index to Marriage Register, 1770-1853, 1 vol. (Ts.)

Marriage Register, n.d., 2 pp.

Register of Births and Deaths, [ca. 1855], 1 vol.

Registers of Births, 1865-67, 1881, n.d., 11 items

Registers of Births and Deaths, 1854-62, 1870-96, n.d., ca. .1 cu. ft.

Registers of Deaths, 1865-68, 1870, 1873-76, 1879-80, 1889, 1896, 20 items

Military and Pension Records

Certificate of Election of the 27th Regiment of Virginia Volunteers, 1861, 1 item

Civil War Matters, 1864, ca. .1 cu. ft. See also Montgomery County Military and Pension Records.

Military Judgment, Pitzer v. Welch, 1867, 1 item

Military Roll, 1857, 1 item

Militia Lists, 1843, 2 items

Minute Book, Court Exemption from Military Draft, 1862-65, 1 vol.

Muster Fines, 1819, 1 item

Qualifications of Militia Officers, 1830-50, ca. .1 cu. ft.

Revolutionary War Pensions, etc., 1820-38, ca. .1 cu. ft.

Revolutionary War Supplies Certificates, 1780, ca. 50 items

<u>See also</u> Election Records

Organization Records

[Masonic Lodge dues and fee?] book, 1824-30, 1 vol.

Road and Bridge Records

Circuit Court Road Book, 1865-75, 1 vol.

Field Book, n.d., 1 vol.

Florence Railroad and Improvement Co. Stocks, 1888, 2 pp.

[Junctions?] Valley Turnpike Co. Minutes, 1849-[?], 1 vol.

Road Commissioner's Book, Buchanan District, 1900-05, 1 vol.; and, Fincastle and Amsterdam districts, 1901, 2 vols.

Road Papers and Reports, ca. 1767-1920, .35 cu. ft.

Road Surveys, Reports, etc., ca. 1820-80, ca. .5 cu. ft.

Statement Showing the Assessed Value of Railroad and Canal Property . . . 1894, 1 item

Valley Co. Papers, n.d., ca. 50 items

School Records

School Fund Account Book, 1880-83, 1 vol.

School Fund Book, 1880-83, 1 vol.

School Papers, 1834, 1854-55, ca. 50 items

<u>See also</u> Court Records, Unspecified Court

Tax and Fiscal Records

Amsterdam District Tax Books, 1892-94, 1896, 5 vols.

Buchanan District Tax Books, 1891-94, 1898, 8 vols.

Catawba District Tax Book, 1855-67, 1 vol.

Claims Allowed, 1771-1897, ca. 1 cu. ft.

Claims Levied, 1799-1819, 1845, ca. .25 cu. ft.

Delinquent Land, 1892 and 1894, 1897-1907, 2 vols.

Delinquent Land Sales, 1889, 1 vol.

Delinquent Taxes, 1786-1835, 1844-62, ca. .25 cu. ft.

Direct Taxes, n.d., 4 vols.

Fincastle District Tax Books, 1891-95, 1897, 1899-1905, n.d., 10 vols.

Insolvent Schedules, ca. 1830-40, ca. .1 cu. ft.; and, Insolvent Taxes, 1834, 1836-39, 1840-45, 1847-49, 1850-60, 1862-63, ca. .2 cu. ft.

Land Books, 1871-81, 1883-86, 1888-1904, 72 vols.; and, 1872, 1876, 1885, 1895-96, 1901, 9 pp. (fragments)

Land Sold and Purchased by the Commonwealth, 1889, 5 pp.

Land Sold for Taxes, 1816, 1 item; and, Report of Sales of Delinquent Land, 1875, 5 pp.

Liquor License Returns, 1878, 1880, 1882-1900, 1902, 1904, n.d., ca. .15 cu. ft.

List of All Persons Assessed with a License Tax, 1866, 1873, 1875, 1899, 1901, 7 pp. (including fragments); and, 1880-1910, ca. 50 items

List of Delinquent Lands, 1842, 1 item

List of Insolvents, 1885, 1 vol.

[List of Land Left Off of Book], 1876, 1 vol.

List of Lands Upon Which the Central Land Co. is to Pay Taxes, 1891, 1 item

List of Lots [Land Tax], 1892-96, 1 vol.

Lists of Delinquent Land, 1870-1923, 1 vol.

Lists of Licenses Issued to Merchants and Owners of Stallions, 1851-52, ca. 50 items

Personal Property Books, 1850, 1852-62, 1865-1904, n.d., 113 vols.

Personal Property Taxes, 1786-1822, n.d., ca. 1 cu. ft.

Real Property Maps, n.d., 1 vol.

Reassessment of Lands, 1885, 1900, 2 vols.

Receipts for Land Redeemed Which had been Sold for Taxes, 1816, ca. .1 cu. ft.; and, Receipts and Purchases of Delinquent Land, 1853, ca. 50 items

Records of All Real Estate Delinquent for Non-payment of Taxes, 1779, 1865-83, 2 vols.

Tax Books, 1885-90, 1897, n.d., 5 vols.; and, G. W. Bowyer's Tax Books, [ca. 1895], 1896, 2 vols.

Tax Collection Books, 1883-86, 1897, 3 vols.

Tax Vouchers, 1782, ca. 50 items; and, Tithable Tax Vouchers, 1782-86, ca. 50 items

Tithables, 1770-90, 2 vols. (copies)

Town Records

Town of Fincastle Minute Book, 1821-57, 1 vol.

Town of Fincastle Papers, 1857-66, ca. 50 items

Township Records

Buchanan Township Board Minutes, 1870-75, 1 vol.

Town[ship?] of Fincastle Minute Books, 1870-75, 2 vols.

Wills

Will of Christian France, 1821, 1 item

Will of James Shanks, 1834, 1 item

Miscellaneous Records

Charles Williams' Journal, 1854, 1 vol.

Contracts and Specifications for Construction of the Prison and County Buildings, 1896-98, ca. 50 items

Estray Book, 1890-1903, 1 vol.

Estrays, ca. 1770-1835, ca. .5 cu. ft.

Inquests, 1836-37, ca. .1 cu. ft.

John Barger's Papers, 1870-87, ca. .1 cu. ft.

Miscellaneous Papers, ca. 1775, ca. .1 cu. ft.

Old Letters, 1845, ca. .1 cu. ft.

Receipts for Houses of Private Entertainment, 1861-64, ca. 50 items

Reports of the Investigating Committee, 1839-45, ca. 25 items

Commissioner of Revenue

Record of Improper Assessments, 1885, 1 vol.

See also Tax and Fiscal Records

Sheriff

Sheriff's Receipts, 1830-32, ca. .1 cu. ft.

Treasurer

Treasurer's District Tax List, 1892, 1 vol.

Treasurer's Papers, 1861-64, ca. .1 cu. ft.

Treasurer's Settlements, 1902-12, 1 vol.

Wolf Scalp Warrants and Miscellaneous Papers, 1770-ca. 1860, .35 cu. ft.

See also Tax and Fiscal Records

Microfilm Records

Circuit Court Clerk
  Court Records
    County Court
      Order Books, 1770-1813, 1815-17, 1820-25, 1828-46, 1851-67, 7 reels
    Circuit Superior Court of Law and Chancery
      Chancery Order Books, 1831-52 (includes Circuit Court, 1852), 1 reel (part)
    Circuit Court
      Chancery Order Books, 1853-69, 1 reel (part). See also Circuit Superior Court of Law and Chancery.
  Fiduciary Records
    Guardians' Accounts, 1799-1839, 1 reel
  Land Records
    Deed Books Nos. 1-35, 1770-1869, 17 reels
    Circuit Court Deed Book No. 1, 1810-13, 1 reel
    General Index to Deeds, Grantor-Grantee A-Z, 1770-1889, 1 reel
    Surveyors' Records, 1774-1914, 2 reels
  Marriage Records and Vital Statistics
    Marriage Registers, 1770-1913, 2 reels; and, Marriage Registers Nos. 1-2, 1787-1853, 2 reels (parts)
    Index to Marriage Register, 1770-1853 (Ts.), 1 reel; and, Index to Marriage Register No. 1, 1787-1844, 1 reel (part)
    Register of Births, 1853-70, 1 reel (part)
    Register of Deaths, 1853-70, 1 reel (part)
    Index to Register of Births, Marriages, and Deaths, 1853-1913, 1 reel
  Wills
    Circuit Court Will Books Nos. 1-2, 1835-1903 (includes Circuit Superior Court of Law and Chancery, 1835-51), 1 reel
    Will Books [A]-L, 1770-1869, 5 reels
    Wills, 1770-1875, 21 reels
    General Index to Wills No. 1, 1770-1952, 1 reel

BRUNSWICK COUNTY

**Formed in 1720 from Prince George County.
Parts of Surry and Isle of Wight
counties were added later.**

Original Records

Circuit Court Clerk
  Board of Supervisors Records
    Board of Supervisors' Papers, 1870-1905, ca. 2 cu. ft.
    Claims Allowed by the Board, 1891-1902, 1 cu. ft.
    Warrants, 1871-76, 1 vol.
  Bonds/Commissions/Oaths
    Attachment Bonds, 1851, ca. 25 items
    Bastardy Bonds, see Ordinary Bonds
    Bonds, etc., 1799-1827, ca. .5 cu. ft.

Bonds Executed by Merchants and Keepers of Ordinaries and Houses of Private Entertainment, 1858, ca. 25 items

Bonds Listed by Commissioner of Revenue for Districts Nos. 1-2, 1898-99, ca. .2 cu. ft.

Bridge Bonds, 1785, 1828-57, ca. .1 cu. ft. See also Ordinary Bonds.

Commissions, 1865-66, ca. 100 items

Constables' Bonds, 1815-74, ca. .1 cu. ft.

County Court Bond Book No. 1, 1897-1903, 1 vol.; and, County and Circuit Court Bond Book [No. 2], 1903-07, 1 vol.

Indexes to County and Circuit Court Bond Books, 1897-1907, n.d., 3 vols.

Delivery Bonds, 1808-35, ca. .2 cu. ft.

Indentures, 1789-1878, n.d., .45 cu. ft.

Lists of Licenses Returned by the Commissioner, 1880-1927, 1.25 cu. ft.

Officials' Bonds, 1833-1903, ca. .45 cu. ft.

Orders Appointing Surveyors of Roads, 1826-86, ca. .6 cu. ft.

Ordinary Bonds (also Bridge and Bastardy Bonds), 1765, 1786-1851, ca. .45 cu. ft.

Ordination Bond, n.d., 1 item

Refunding Bonds, 1845-82, ca. .1 cu. ft.

Registrars' Oaths, 1884, 1902, 1917, ca. .1 cu. ft.

Replevin Bonds, 1765-1817, ca. .5 cu. ft.

Sheriffs' Bonds, 1763, 1766, 1768, 1786-1851, ca. .2 cu. ft.

Stay Bonds, 1800-18, ca. .25 cu. ft.

See also Court Records, County Court; Land Records; and, Wills

Business Records/Corporations/Partnerships

Anna P. Harrison's [I. Harrison's?] Receipt Book, 1855, 1 item

Bank of Lawrenceville General Ledger No. 3, 1899-1903, 1 vol.; Individual Ledger G, 1901-02, 1 vol.; and, Individual Scratcher B, 1892-94, 1 vol.

[Blacksmith?] Shop Book, 1813-14, 1 item

I. & P. Harrison Memorandum [Cash] Book, 1852, 1 item

Index to [unidentified] Ledger D, 1809, 1 vol.

Thomas C. Proctor's [blacksmith or livery] Ledger, 1871-76, 1 vol.; and, Account Book, 1850-70, 1 vol.

Trotter & Quarles, see Tax and Fiscal Records

[William Turnbull's?] Ledger, 1824-46, 1 vol.

Court Records

County Court

Cases in Bankruptcy, 1868-71, ca. .6 cu. ft.

Chancery Fee Book, 1804-05, 1 vol.

Chancery Rule Docket No. 1, 1860-73, 1 vol.

Chancery Suits Issued, Referred, and Dismissed (also Chancery Causes Undecided), 1806-75, 2.8 cu. ft.

[Clerk's] Tax Book, 1898-1910 (includes Circuit Court, 1904-10), 1 vol.

Directions of Clerk to Pay Witnesses (Orders), 1809-33, ca. 100 items

Docket Books, 1786-89, 1841-1904, 4 vols.

Execution Books, 1740-54, 1766-84, 1787-1805, 1809-16, 1824-29, 11 vols.; Execution Book No. 3, 1887-1904, 1 vol.; and, 1747-51 and 1756, 1 vol. (fragment)

Index to Execution Book No. 3, 1887-1904, 1 vol.

Fee Books, 1764, 1771-78, 1772-78, 1782-85, 1787, 1790-91, 1793-99, 1801-07, 1809-12, 1814-22, 1825-28, 1830-33, 32 vols.

Indexes to Fee Books, 1819-22, 1824, 1828, 3 vols.

Hicks v. Lewis, exhibit, 1819-27, 1 vol.

Judgments, 1854-94, 1898-1903, 9.5 cu. ft.

Minute Books, 1800, 1802-03, 1807-10, 1812, 1820-24, 1835-42, 6 vols.; and, 1794-96, 1794-1814, 3 vols. (fragments?)

Notices, Dead for Want of Continuance [also bonds and tax lists], 1789-1817, ca. .1 cu. ft.; and, Notices Dismissed for Want of Prosecution, 1823-28, ca. 50 items

Office Judgments No. 10, 1840-55, 1 vol.

Order Books Nos. 2-3, 7, and 13, 1741-42, 1745-49, 1757-59, 1774-82, 7 vols. (copies [2 copies each of 3, 7, and 13]); and, Order Books, 1827, 1828 and 1834, 2 vols. (fragments)

Pardons, 1891-1903, 6 items

Process Book, 1816-17, 1 vol.; and, Letter [Process] Book, 1826-31, 1 vol.

Recognizances to Keep the Peace, 1871-92, ca. .1 cu. ft.

Record [Form] Book (Herbert Hill's Book, Private), n.d., 1 vol.

Record [Minute?] Book, 1817-20, 1 vol.; and, Record [Minutes] and Account Book, 1888-94, 1 vol.

Rough Alphabet to Execution Docket, 1801-05, 1 vol.

Rule Book, 1749-81, 1 vol.; and, Rule Books Nos. 1-[11], 1783-1809, 1816-73, 11 vols.

Indexes to Rule Books Nos. 8-9, 1816-40, 2 vols.

Witness Attendance Books, 1807-1904, 3 vols.

District Court

Judgment Book, 1789-92, 1 vol.

Miscellaneous Papers [writs, executions, accounts, etc.], 1805-27 (includes Superior Court of Law, 1808-27), .45 cu. ft.

[Plea Book], 1803-05, 1 vol.

Rule Docket, 1789-1814 (includes Superior Court of Law, 1809-14), 1 vol.

Witness Book, 1804-13 (includes Superior Court of Law, 1809-13), 1 vol.

Superior Court of Law

Execution Books, 1809-30, 3 vols.

Fee Books, 1815-31, 3 vols.

Letter Book [Office Judgments], 1814-22, 1 vol.

Memorandum Book, 1812-14, 1 vol.

Minutes, 1819-23, 1 vol.

Miscellaneous Papers, see District Court

Rule Books, 1814-17, 1822-31, 2 vols. See also District Court.

Witness Book, see District Court

Witness Claims, 1811-12, ca. 50 items

Circuit Superior Court of Law and Chancery

Chancery Court Docket No. 1, 1832-38, 1 vol.

Chancery Court Execution Docket Book No. 3, 1832-1916 (includes Circuit Court, 1852-1916), 1 vol.

Index to Chancery Court Execution Docket No. 3, 1832-1916, 1 vol.

Chancery Fee Book [No. 1], 1831-56 (includes Circuit Court, 1852-56), 1 vol.

Index to Chancery Fee Book, 1831-56, 1 vol.

Chancery Rule Docket No. 2, 1848-1903 (includes Circuit Court, 1852-1903), 1 vol.

[Clerk's] Record [Fee] Book, 1847-71 (includes Circuit Court, 1852-71), 1 vol.

Common Law Execution Docket No. 1, 1831-43, 1 vol.

Court Papers, 1847-1931, 1 vol.

Execution Book No. 2, 1843-70 (includes Circuit Court, 1852-70), 1 vol.

Index to Execution Book No. 2, 1843-70, 1 vol.

Fee Books, 1831-68 (includes Circuit Court, 1852-68), 3 vols.

Judgment Docket, 1843-47 and 1866-86 (includes Circuit Court, 1866-86), 1 vol.

Office Judgments, 1831-57 (includes Circuit Court, 1852-57), 1 vol.

Parties to Actions [Witness] Attendance, 1814-50, 1 vol.

Rule Docket No. 2, 1840-41, 1 vol.

Superior Court Docket No. 3, 1845-62 (includes Circuit Court, 1852-62), 1 vol.

Witness Attendance Book, 1850-1914 (includes Circuit Court, 1852-1914), 1 vol.

Circuit Court

Chancery Court Execution Docket and Index, see Circuit Superior Court of Law and Chancery

Chancery Fees Nos. 2-[4], 1856-1909, 3 vols. See also Circuit Superior Court of Law and Chancery.

Chancery Rule Docket, see Circuit Superior Court of Law and Chancery

Clerk's Correspondence, 1903-04, 1.25 cu. ft.

Clerk's Record [Fee?] Books, 1871-85, 1 vol. See also Circuit Superior Court of Law and Chancery.

[Clerk's] Tax Book, see County Court

Copies of Judgments from Circuit Court and Entered on Judgment Docket, 1885-90, ca. .1 cu. ft.; Copies of Judgments Granted in Other Counties Which have been Entered on Judgment Docket, 1857-1903, ca. .1 cu. ft.; and, Certificates of the Clerk of the Circuit Court as to Judgments that have been Satisfied in Whole or in Part, 1886-1901, ca. .1 cu. ft.

Court Papers, see Circuit Superior Court of Law and Chancery

Docket Books, 1881-1905, 2 vols.

Index to Docket Book, 1881-95, 1 vol.

Execution Book No. 3, 1870-1911, 1 vol. See also Circuit Superior Court of Law and Chancery.

Executions, 1892-1944, ca. 2 cu. ft.; and, Fifas, Bonds for Court Appearances, Petit Juror Lists, etc., 1894-97, ca. 50 items

Extracts and Copies of Decrees, 1890-93, ca. .2 cu. ft.

Fee Books, 1868-1905, 2 vols. See also Circuit Superior Court of Law and Chancery.

Judgment Docket, see Circuit Superior Court of Law and Chancery

Judgments, 1851-1916, ca. 9 cu. ft.

[Law?] Fee Book, 1885-1909, 1 vol.

Moneys Deposited by Order of Court, 1900-26, 1 vol.

Office Judgments, see Circuit Superior Court of Law and Chancery

Statement of Case of Prosecution No. 2, 1888-1923, 1 vol.

Superior Court Docket, see Circuit Superior Court of Law and Chancery

Witness Attendance Book, see Circuit Superior Court of Law and Chancery

County and Superior Courts

Arrest Warrants, 1816-17, ca. 50 items

Capiases, 1788-1805, 1812, .25 cu. ft.

Commonwealth Subpoenas, 1830-42, 1 cu. ft.

Court Papers, 1782-1930 ca. 4 cu. ft.; and, Miscellaneous Court Papers, 1788-1893, 1 cu. ft.

Executions, 1760-1895, ca. 9 cu. ft.

Inquisitions and Pardons (including slave trade), 1800-79, ca. .2 cu. ft.

Judgments, 1782-1853, 45 cu. ft.

Register of Convicts, 1871-1954, 1 vol.

Index to Register of Convicts, 1871-1954, 1 vol.

Schedules (including Schedules Delivered by Insolvent Debtors, 1818-44), ca. 1820-50, ca. .3 cu. ft.

Subpoenas, 1790-1847, 4.75 cu. ft.

Suit Papers, ca. 1800-1900, ca. .5 cu. ft.; and, Law Suits, etc., 1809-22, .45 cu. ft.

Unspecified Court

Unidentified [suit] Indexes, n.d., 6 vols.

Election Records

Abstracts of Votes, 1870-1932, .8 cu. ft.

Ballots, 1868, 1871, 1893, ca. .3 cu. ft.

Electoral Board Commission Papers, 1884-85, ca. 25 items

Lists of Voters, 1853-66, ca. .1 cu. ft.

Notices of Candidacy, 1895-99, ca. .1 cu. ft.

Permanent Roll of Voters, 1902-03, 1 vol.

Polls, 1787-1868, 1882, n.d., ca. 1.8 cu. ft.

Fiduciary Records

Accounts Current, 1732-1895, 3.25 cu. ft.; and, Old Accounts Current, Not Confirmed, 1822-36, ca. 25 items

Accounts of Sales, 1751-1820, ca. .2 cu. ft.

Index to Fiduciary Accounts No. 1, n.d., 1 vol.

Administrators' Bonds, 1732-1890, 1.8 cu. ft.; Administrators', Executors', Guardians', [etc.], Bonds and Declarations, ca. 1825-1904, ca. 1 cu. ft.; Executors' Bonds, 1760-1870, 1.35 cu. ft.; and, Guardians' Bonds, 1750-1860, 1.35 cu. ft.

Estate Papers, ca. 1795-1875, ca. 300 items

Estates of Insane, 1805-06, 3 items

Guardians' Accounts, 1850-1890, 1.4 cu. ft.; and, Reports, 1837-39, .5 cu. ft.

Index to Guardians' Account Book No. 7, n.d., 1 vol.

Inventories and Appraisements, 1732-1895, 3.2 cu. ft.

Orders of Orphans' Court to William Dunlap, 1741, 1 item

Report of Audit by W. W. Tally Estate, 1874-1912, 1 vol.

Stith Estate Papers, 1829, ca. 25 items

Vouchers and Receipts from estates, 1775-97, ca. 75 items

Free Negro and Slave Records

Contracts with Freedman Returned by Agents of the Freedmen's Bureau, 1866-68, ca. .2 cu. ft.

Lists of Free Negroes Returned by Commissioner of Revenue, 1851-62, List of Free Negroes in St. Andrew's Parish, 1851, and List of Free Negroes in Meherrin Parish, 1851, ca. .25 cu. ft.

Patrol Returns and Claims, 1822-32, ca. 50 items

Registrations of Free Blacks, 1830-50, ca. 50 items

See also Court Records, County and Superior Courts

Justice of the Peace Records

Certificates of Trials of Misdemeanor Cases by Justices No. 1, 1878-88, 1 vol.

Executions Returned by Constables, 1860-70, ca. 1885-1930, ca. 3 cu. ft.

Executions Returned by Constables No. 1, 1880-1917, 1 vol.

Index to Executions Returned No. 1, n.d., 1 vol.

Fee Book, N. S. Turnbull, JP, 1885-1909, 1 vol.

Judgments, 1895-1923, 1 cu. ft.

Papers Returned by Justices in Cases Other than for Larceny, 1880-98, ca. .6 cu. ft.

Reports, 1889-1910, 1.5 cu. ft.

Warrants, 1818, 1877-1925, ca. .1 cu. ft.

Land Records

Deed Books Nos. 3-6, 10-13, and 15, 1744-62, 1770-80, 1790-94, 15 vols. (copies [2 copies each of 3, 5-6, 12-13, and 15]). See also Wills.

Deeds, 1734-1910, 15.65, cu. ft.; Deeds Partly Proved, ca. 1760-70, 1807-29, ca. .4 cu. ft.; Deeds, Bonds and Notices, 1801-08, ca. .1 cu. ft.; Deeds, Wills and Bills of Sale, 1809, ca. 50 items; and, Lodged Deeds, 1761-1806, .1 cu. ft.

Deeds, Wills, etc., No. 1, 1732-40, 1 vol. (copy)

Daily Receipt Index to Deeds for Recordation, 1902-11, 1 vol.

Indexes to Deeds Nos. 45-51, 55, 59, 68, 73, 79, 83, 90, 93-95, 97, 101, n.d., 19 vols.

Entry Book, 1771-1816, 1 vol.

Indexes to Deeds of Trust Nos. 14, 32, 35, n.d., 3 vols.

Index to Release Deeds No. 3, n.d., 1 vol.

Lists of Alterations in Land, prior to 1860, ca. 75 items; and, 1860-1928, .75 cu. ft.

Lists of Mortgages, 1900, 2 items

Lists of Surveys, 1762-65, 4 items

Map of the Town of Lawrenceville, n.d., and Plot of Meherrin, 1886, 2 items; and, unidentified maps, n.d., 18 items

Processioners' Book, 1826-31, 1 vol.; and, County Court Processioners' Returns, 1819-55, 1870, 3 vols.

Processioners' Returns, 1795-1871, ca. .5 cu. ft. See also Miscellaneous Records.

W. B. Price's notebook [land descriptions, etc.], 1843-50, 1 item; and, unidentified notebook [land descriptions, etc.], 1854-87, 1 item

Marriage Records and Vital Statistics

Card Index to Marriages, A-Z, n.d., 2 cu. ft.

Marriage Bonds and Consents, 1751-1849, ca. 4.15 cu. ft.; Bonds for Obtaining Licenses to Solemnize Matrimony, 1824-26, ca. 25 items; and, Consents, 1880-81, 8 items

Marriage Certificates, 1855-61, .45 cu. ft.; Certificates Granting Marriage Licenses before 1885 (also Marriage Consents), 1879-84, .45 cu. ft.; and, Certificates and Licenses, 1860-66, .45 cu. ft.

Marriage Licenses, 1866-84, 3.15, cu. ft.; and, Licenses and Consents, 1885-89, 2.25 cu. ft.

Marriage Registers, 1751-1853 (Ms. compilation), 2 vols. (copies)

Indexes to Marriage Register, 1751-1853, (Ms. compilation), 2 vols. (copies)

Ministers' Returns, ca. 1785-1855, ca. .35 cu. ft.; and, Marriage Bonds and Ministers' Returns, n.d. (fragments)

Register of Births, 1853-57, 1 vol.

Register of Deaths, 1853-55, 1 vol.

Register of Marriages, 1854-60, 1 vol.

Registers of Births and Deaths, 1854, 1864-69, 1871-85, 1887-89, 1894-96, 1.35 cu. ft.

Index to Registers of Births, Marriages, and Deaths, 1853, 1 vol.

Military and Pension Records

Applications for Exemption from Military Duty, 1862, ca. 100 items

Confederate Pension Papers, 1902-25, .35 cu. ft.

Militia Rolls, 1854-57, 7 items

Organization Records

Sons of Temperance, Lawrenceville Division [expense notation book], 1851, 1 vol.

Road and Bridge Records

Overseer of Roads, District 1, Red Oak Township, 1871-74, 1872-75, 2 vols.; District 2, Red Oak Township, 1871-74, 1 vol.; and, District 4, Red Oak Township, 1874-1911, 1 vol.

Reports of Surveyors of Roads, 1876-85, ca. .5 cu. ft.

Road Construction Papers, 1767, ca. 50 items

Warrants on [Road] Levy, 1890-1902, 1 vol.

See also Bonds/Commissions/Oaths

School Records

School Commissioners' Reports, 1825-63, ca. .2 cu. ft.

Tax and Fiscal Records

Applications to Purchase Land Sold for Delinquent Taxes and Purchased by the Commonwealth, 1896-99, ca. .15 cu. ft.

Claims, 1750-99, 1805-27, and Claims Allowed, 1782-1825 (also Procession of Boundaries, 1816-17; Thomas Clayborn's Papers, 1792; and, Trotter and Quarles [merchants] Account Receipts, 1799), .45 cu. ft.; and, Claims Allowed, 1780-1890, 3 cu. ft.

Copies of Returns to Auditors, 1831-1903, ca. .45 cu. ft.

Delinquent Capitation and Personal Property Taxes, 1890-91, 1896-1904, ca. .6 cu. ft.

Delinquent Land, ca. 1820-1904, ca. .6 cu. ft.

Delinquent Real Estate Sold, 1876-1926, 1886-1927, 2 vols.

Delinquent Taxes Collected on Persons and Property, 1903-12, 1 vol.

Insolvent Capitation and Property Taxes, and Delinquent Lands, 1882-89, 1898-1903, ca. .45 cu. ft.; and, Insolvents, Land and Property, 1882, ca. 25 items

Insolvent Tax Accounts, 1816, 1822-28, ca. .2 cu. ft.

List of Real Estate Returned Delinquent for Non-payment of Taxes Assessed Thereon, 1890-1926, 1 vol.

Lists of Insolvents, 1840-81, ca. .8 cu. ft.

Personal Property Taxes, 1782-96, 1800, 1835, ca. .1 cu. ft; List of Taxable Property, 1787, 1 item

Receipts from Auditors, 1813-36, ca. 50 items; and, Receipts, 1817-25, 1846-53, ca. 100 items

Record of Commissioner of Accounts, 1870-1909, 1 vol.

Record of Delinquent Lands, 1884-89, 1 vol.

Record of Delinquent Taxes Paid to County Court Clerk No. 1, 1888-1917, 1 vol.

Redeemed Coupons, 1890-91, 1896, ca. 100 items

Reports of Collectors of the County Levies, 1801-07, ca. 30 items

Settlements of the County Levy, 1862, 1901 ca. .1 cu. ft.

Tax Assessment, 1806, 1 item

Tax Lists and Delinquent Land, 1773-1831, ca. .1 cu. ft.; and, Tax List, n.d., 1 item. See also Court Records, County Court.

Tax Returns, 1807, c. .1 cu. ft.

Town Records

Town of Lawrenceville Receipts and Disbursements Journal, 1891-1906, 1 vol.

See also Land Records

Township Records

Meherrin Township Board Checkbook, 1870, 1 vol.; and, Meherrin Township Record, 1872-75, 1 vol.

Totaro Township Board Records, 1870-1920 (includes Magisterial District Records, 1875-1920), and Mechanics' Liens, 1881-1916, 1 vol.

See also Road and Bridge Records

Wills

Will Books Nos. 2 (includes Deeds, 1783-85) and 3, 1739-69, 2 vols. (copies [2 copies of each])

Index to Will Book No. 22, 1887, 1 vol.

Wills, 1755-1870, 1881, n.d., ca. 1.15 cu. ft.

Superior Court Wills, Bonds, etc., 1789-1861, ca. .15 cu. ft.; and, Circuit Court
Wills and Bonds, 1871-1904, .35 cu. ft.
Index to Circuit Court Wills [also deeds, bonds, etc.] No. 2, n.d., 1 vol.
See also Land Records

Miscellaneous Records
Crop Lien Docket [No. 1], 1892-1916, 1 vol.
Crop Liens and Contracts for Personal Property, 1895-1900, ca. .1 cu. ft.
[Debt Book], 1806-09, 1 vol.
Estrays, ca. 1790-1875, ca. .35 cu. ft.
Inquisitions, 1883-1940, .35 cu. ft.
Letters, 1800, ca. 50 items
Mechanics' Liens, see Township Records
Overseer of the Poor Proceedings, 1824-70, ca. 100 items; Superintendent of the
Poor Reports, 1871-79, 1880-1900, and Reports and Warrants, 1899-1903,
ca. 1.6 cu. ft.; and, Receipts of the Superintendent of the Poor, 1884, ca.
50 items
Papers Found [misfiled] in Deeds, [1760-70], ca. 25 items
Reports of Commissioners on Insane Persons to Circuit Court, 1901-54, 1.25 cu.
ft.
Reservation of Title to Personalty No. 2, 1902-11, 1 vol.
Index to Reservation of Title to Personalty No. 2, 1902-11, 1 vol.
Stray Book, 1772-1810, 1 vol.; and, [Certificates of Stray Horses, Bulls, etc.],
1773-1820, 1 vol.

Commissioner of Revenue
Commissioner's Books, 1843-50, ca. .35 cu. ft.
Commissioner's List of Land Taxes, 1801, ca. 15 items
Commissioners' Returns, ca. 1805-40, ca. 2 cu. ft.
Land Book, St. Andrew's Parish, 1837, 1 vol.
Land Tax, 1839, 1 item
Record of Improper Assessment of Lands, 1893-1913, 1 vol.
Record of Insolvent Capitation and Property Tax, 1885-86, 1 vol.
See also Tax and Fiscal Records

Sheriff
Account of Jury Tickets of F. W. Jones, Sheriff, 1871-73, ca. 50 items
Jail or Sheriff File, 1818-24, ca. 25 items
Sheriff's List of Insolvents, 1835-39, 1 item
Sheriff's Process [Execution] Books, 1804-05, 1829-30, 2 vols.
Sheriff's Receipts, 1838-50, ca. .1 cu. ft.
Tax Receipts Addressed to Sheriff, 1868, ca. .1 cu. ft.

Treasurer
Reports of Settlements of County Levy with the Treasurer, 1871-99, ca. .35 cu. ft.;
Reports of Settlement, 1885-1901, 1 cu. ft.; and, Settlement of Treasurer's
Accounts, 1902, ca. .1 cu. ft.
Returns made by the County Treasurer, 1879-1900, ca. 50 items
Treasurer's Recapitulation for Delinquent Land Tax Paid to Clerk, 1887-1900, ca.
50 items
Treasurer's Warrants, 1871-75, 1 vol.
See also Tax and Fiscal Records

Microfilm Records

Circuit Court Clerk
  Court Records
    County Court
      Minute Books, 1824-35, 1842-52, 1 reel
      Order Books Nos. 1-38 [No. 2 includes wills], 1732-42, 1745-1864, 16 reels
    County and Superior Courts
      Index to Ended Chancery Clauses, 1830-1901, 1 reel (part)
  Fiduciary Records
    Fiduciary Accounts, 1904-11, 1 reel (part)
    Guardians' Accounts Nos. 2-4 [No. 1 is missing]. 1828-60, 2 reels (parts). <u>See</u> <u>also</u> Land Records.
    General Index to Guardians' Accounts No. 1, 1732-1948, 1 reel (part)
    Orphans' Book No. 1, 1740-81, 1 reel (part)
  Land Records
    Deeds, Wills, etc., No. 1, 1732-04, 1 reel
    Deed Books Nos. 2-38, 1740-1869 (Vol. 4 includes Guardians' Accounts, 1780-1808), 17 reels. <u>See also</u> Court Records, County Court.
    General Index to Deeds Vol. A, 1732-1881, 1 reel
    Processioners' Returns, 1795-1816, 1 reel (part)
  Marriage Records and Vital Statistics
    Certificates of Marriage, 1834-48, 1 reel; Marriage Licenses and Certificates, 1850-91, n.d., 10 reels; and, Original Marriage Licenses, 1891-1912, 12 reels
    Marriage Bonds, 1751-1849, 3 reels
    Marriage Licenses Nos. 1-7, 1850-1901, 3 reels; and, Abstract of Marriage Licenses Issued Nos. 8-17, 1901-67, 4 reels
    Marriage Records, 1750-1850, 1 reel (part)
    Marriage Register and Index, Parts 1-2, 1751-1853 (Ms. compilation), 1 reel
    Index to Marriages, Male-Female, 1850-1948, 1 reel; and, 1850-1974, 3 reels
    Register of Births, 1853-57, 1 reel (part)
    Register of Deaths, 1853-55, 1 reel (part)
  Military and Pension Records
    List of Revolutionary War Patriots, n.d., 1 reel (part)
  Wills
    Will Books Nos. 2-18, 1739-1865, 8 reels. <u>See also</u> Land Records; and, Court Records, County Court.
    General Index to Wills Vol. A, 1732-1948, 1 reel
  Miscellaneous Records
    St. Andrew's Parish Vestry Book, 1732-98, 1 reel (part)

BUCHANAN COUNTY

Formed in 1858 from Tazewell and Russell counties.

Original Records

Circuit Court Clerk
  Bonds/Commissions/Oaths
    Record of Forfeited Forthcoming Bonds, 1902, 1 vol.

Corporations and Partnerships
Contracts, 1902-46, 1 vol.
Court Records
County Court
Judgment Lien Dockets Nos. 1-2, 1885-94, 1892-1902, 2 vols.
Minute Book, 1893-1901, 1 vol.
Witness Attendance Book, 1880-95, 1 vol.
County and Circuit Courts
Appraisement of Estrays, 1893-1907, 1 vol.
Common Law Executions No. 2, 1893-1914, 1 vol.
Executions, 1891-1913, .7 cu. ft.
Judgment Lien Docket No. 3, 1901-16, 1 vol.
Law Execution Book No. 3, 1899-1919, 1 vol.
Process Book, 1902-15, 1 vol.
Unspecified Court
Clerk's Fee Book, 1899-1902 (also Road Book, 1928-32), 1 vol.
Election Records
General Registration, 1902-03, 1 vol.
List of Voters Registered, 1902-35, 1 vol.
Fiduciary Records
Fiduciary Settlements, 1896-1930, 1 vol.
Index to Fiduciary Settlements, n.d., 1 vol.
Justice of the Peace Records
Civil Judgment and Execution Book, 1895-1910, 1 vol.
Criminal Judgments Nos. 1-2, 1899-1902, 2 vols.
Executions Returned by Constables on Judgments of the Justices of the Peace, 1889-95, 1 vol.
Record of Judgments, 1877-90, 1 vol.
Land Records
Entry Book, 1853-65, 1 vol.
Indexes to Deed Books C, F-I, L and N, n.d. 7 vols. (Ts.); and, Index to Deed Book, n.d., 1 vol. (Ts.)
Road and Bridge Records
[Board of Supervisors] Road Book, 1896-98, 1 vol.
See also Court Papers, Unspecified Court
Tax and Fiscal Records
Real Estate Sold for Non-payment of Taxes Purchased by Other than the Commonwealth No. 1, 1886-1933, 1 vol.

BUCKINGHAM COUNTY

Formed in 1761 from Albemarle County.

Original Records

Circuit Court Clerk
Election Records
Polls, 1788, 2 items; and, 1788, 1 item (copy)
Land Records
Surveyors' Book, 1762-1814, 1872-1908, 1 vol. (copy)
Surveyors' Plat Books, 1762-1814, 1783-99, 2 vols. (copies)

Marriage Records and Vital Statistics
Marriage Bonds, 1784-87, 1791-92, 1794, 35 items (copies)
Military and Pension Records
Courts Martial, 24th Regiment, Virginia Militia, 1832-43, 1 vol. (copy)
Tax and Fiscal Records
Lists of Tithables, 1773-74, 2 items (originals and copies)

CAMPBELL COUNTY

Formed in 1781 from Bedford County.

Original Records

Circuit Court Clerk
  Bonds/Commissions/Oaths
    Bond to Perform Marriages, 1792, 1 item
  Court Records
    County Court
      Order Book [Minutes] No. 4 & 5, 1791-97, 1 vol. (copy)
      Warrant, 1789, 1 item
  Free Negro and Slave Records
    Register of Negroes and Mulattoes, 1801-50, 1 vol. (copy)
  Marriage Records and Vital Statistics
    Marriage Records, A-Z, 1782-1853, 5.4 cu. ft.; and, Marriage Records [Bonds and
      Consents], A-D, 1782-1853, .75 cu. ft. (copies)
  Wills
    Will Book No. 1, 1782-1800, 1 vol. (copy)

Microfilm Records

Circuit Court Clerk
  Court Records
    County Court
      Order Books Nos. 1-29, 1782-1869, 9 reels
      General Index to Order Books, 1782-1904, 1 reel
    Circuit Superior Court of Law and Chancery
      Chancery Order Books, 1831-64 (includes Circuit Court, 1852-64), 1 reel
    Circuit Court
      Chancery Order Book, see Circuit Superior Court of Law and Chancery
  Land Records
    Deed Books Nos. 1-34, 1782-1869, 16 reels
    Circuit Court Deed Book No. 1, 1809-86 (includes Superior Court of Law, 1808-
      31, and Circuit Superior Court of Law and Chancery, 1831-51), 1 reel (part)
    General Index to Deeds, Grantor-Grantee A-Z, 1782-1896, 2 reels
    Processioners' Returns, 1804-20, 1842, 1 reel
    Surveyors' Books Nos. 1-[2], 1783-1924, 1 reel
  Marriage Records and Vital Statistics
    Marriage Bonds and Consents, A-Z, 1782-1853, 11 reels
    Marriage Registers Nos. 1-3, 1782-1936, 1 reel (part)
    General Index to Marriages, 1782-1930, 1 reel (part)
  Wills
    Will Books Nos. 1-13, 1782-1869, 9 reels

Circuit Court Will Book, 1816-78 (includes Superior Court of Law, 1808-31, and
    Circuit Superior Court of Law and Chancery, 1831-51), 1 reel (part)
General Index to Will Books Vol. 1, 1782-1947, 1 reel

CAROLINE COUNTY

**Formed in 1727 from Essex, King and Queen, and
King William counties. Additional parts of
King and Queen were added later.**

Original Records

Circuit Court Clerk
Board of Supervisors Records
Minutes, 1870-86, 1890-1914, 3 vols.
Stump [stub] Book, 1885-86, 1 vol.
Bonds/Commissions/Oaths
Circuit Court Record of F[orth] C[oming] Bonds, 1887-1901, 1 vol.
County Court Record of F[orth] C[oming] Bonds, 1888-97, 1 vol.
County and Circuit Court Bonds No. 1, 1888-1904, 1 vol.
Officials' Bonds, 1870-1901, .7 cu. ft.
Ordinary Bond Book, 1804-14, 1 vol.
Business Records/Corporations/Partnerships
L. C. Sale's Ledgers, 1902-04, 1903-06, 2 vols.
Solomon and Davidson Dry Goods Store Ledgers, 1885-87, n.d., 4 vols
Unidentified Merchant's Day Book, 1826-30, 1 vol.
W. W. D. Ledger B [William and Henry Dickenson's Ledger A], 1804-05, 1 vol.;
    and, [W. H. D.?] Ledger 3, 1805-07, 1 vol.
Census Records
U.S. Census Enumeration, 1870, 1 item
Court Records
County Court
Chancery and Common Law Docket and Judgment Book, 1806-08, 1 vol.
Chancery Issues, 1790-1873, 1 vol.
Chancery Suits, A-Z [by plaintiffs], ca. 1780-1850, 3.5. cu. ft.
Clerk's Correspondence, ca. 1800-50, .5 cu. ft.
[Clerk's] Tax Book, 1898-1908 (includes Circuit Court, 1904-08), 1 vol.
Commonwealth Papers, 1886-1900, 1.75 cu. ft.
County Court Papers, 1724-1904, n.d., ca. 28 cu. ft.; and, ca. 1665-1850,
    n.d., 128 items (copies)
Docket, 1829-41, 1 vol.
Dudley v. Pickett, writ, [1736], 1 item
Execution Books, 1788-97, 1801-15, 1803-20, 1806-20, 9 vols.; and Nos. 17-18
    and 20-21, 1822-33, 1849-1904, 4 vols. See also Court Records, County
    Court.
Executions, 1851-98, 1.25 cu. ft.
Fee Books, 1790, 1792, 1796-97, 1804-05, 1809-14, 1818, 1820-21, 1823,
    1825-27, 1832-40, 1844-46, 1853-58 (includes Executions, 1797), 1858-63,
    1865-92, 1876-1904, 20 vols.
Fees, see Fiduciary Records
Issue Dockets, 1819-23 [1790-1828], 1838-78, 3 vols.
Judge's Docket, 1889-93, 1 vol.

Law Actions, 1808-11, ca. .1 cu. ft.

Law and Chancery Rule Dockets, 1860-73, 2 vols.

Memorandum Books, 1787-90, 1891-1904, 3 vols.

Memorandums, 1873-86, .45 cu. ft.

Minute Books, 1785-87, 1797-1800, 1810-12, 1824-27, 1838-41, 1844-51, 1861-70, 1885-89, 1899-1904, 11 vols.; and, 1770-81, 1787-91, 1794-96, 5 vols. (copies)

Minutes, 1773, 1784, 2 items (fragments)

Order Books, 1732-54, 1765-76, 1781-89, 11 vols.; and, 1732-89, 1799-1804, 1807-09, 20 vols. (copies)

Rule Books [Dockets], 1786-96, 1804-06, 1821-34, 7 vols.; and, 1792-96, 1 vol. (copy)

Thornton v. Kingland, ledger, 1870-71 (also Delinquent Land Tax, 1898), 1 vol.

Witness Attendance, 1870-1904, 1 vol.

Superior Court of Law

Execution Book, 1818-24, 1 vol.

Fee Book, 1813-14, 1 vol.

Issues, 1828-46 (includes Circuit Superior Court of Law and Chancery, 1831-46), 1 vol.

Order Book No. 3, 1821-26, 1 vol. See also Land Records.

Circuit Superior Court of Law and Chancery

Chancery Docket, 1831-90 (includes Circuit Court, 1852-90), 1 vol.

Chancery Execution Book, 1833-1909 (includes Circuit Court, 1852-1909), 1 vol.

Chancery Issues, 1832-66 (includes Circuit Court, 1852-66), 1 vol.

Issues, see Superior Court of Law

Law Execution Books Nos. 1-3, 1831-64 (includes Circuit Court, 1852-64), 3 vols.

Law Issue Docket, 1847-67 (includes Circuit Court, 1852-67), 1 vol.

Law Process Book, 1850-70 (includes Circuit Court, 1852-70), 1 vol.

Rule Docket, 1835-42, 1 vol.; and, Law Rule Docket No. 2, 1842-52 (includes Circuit Court, 1852), 1 vol.

Witness Attendance Book, 1840-67 (includes Circuit Court, 1852-67), 1 vol.

Circuit Court

Attorney's Memorandum, 1901-08, 1 vol.

Chancery Court Dockets, 1867-1904, 2 vols.

Chancery Court Process Books, 1866-1902, 1867-75, 2 vols.

Chancery Docket, see Circuit Superior Court of Law and Chancery

Chancery Executions, see Circuit Superior Court of Law and Chancery

Chancery Issues, see Circuit Superior Court of Law and Chancery

Chancery Rule Docket, 1890-1917, 1 vol.

[Clerk's] Tax Book, see County Court

Executions, 1859-1930, 1.4 cu. ft.

Fee Books, 1855-75, 1892-1922, 3 vols.

Judge's Docket, Law and Chancery, 1876-1907, 1 vol.

Law Court Process Book, see Circuit Superior Court of Law and Chancery

Law Execution Books Nos. 3-4, 1866-1911, 2 vols. See also Circuit Superior Court of Law and Chancery.

Law Issue Dockets, 1867-1907, 2 vols. See also Circuit Superior Court of Law and Chancery.

Law Process, see Circuit Superior Court of Law and Chancery

Law Rule Dockets Nos. 3-4, 1853-1909, 2 vols.

Memorandum Book, 1897-1907, 1 vol.

Process Books, 1870-91, 1890-1936, 2 vols.

Witness Attendance, 1867-1903, 1 vol. See also Circuit Superior Court of Law and Chancery.

County and Superior Courts

Accounts and Schedules, ca. 1800-50 (also Fees, ca. 1790-1810), ca. .75 cu. ft.

Court Papers, 1896-1916, ca. .7 cu. ft.

Criminal Suits, ca. 1800-50, .5 cu. ft.

Fee Books, 1819-21, 1826-37, 1830-31, 5 vols.

Judgment Docket No. 1, 1843-88, 1 vol.; and, Judgment Lien Docket No. 2, 1888-1916, 1 vol.

Indexes to Judgment Dockets Nos. [1]-2, n.d., 2 vols.

Witness Attendance, 1827-69, 1 vol.

Unspecified Court

E. G. Allen's Exhibit Books Nos. 2-3, 1897-99, 2 vols.

Fox v. Doggett and Page v. Doggett, exhibit, 1849-70, 1 vol.

Jurors, Registrars, and Judges [Attendance Book], 1893-94, 1 vol.

Election Records

Abstract of Votes, see Justice of the Peace Records

Ballots, 1895, ca. 100 items

Certificates of Election, 1895, 2 items

Lists of Registered Voters, 1884-95, 1884-98, 1902-03, 3 vols.

Lists of Registered Voters and related correspondence, [1867], 9 items

Notices of Candidacy, 1901, ca. 75 items.

See also Miscellaneous Records

Fiduciary Records

Administrators' Bonds, 1806-24, 1822-58, 1887-1908, 4 vols.; and, 1806-24, 1 vol. (copy)

Estate Papers, 1783-1841, .25 cu. ft.

Executors' Bond Books, 1824-58, 1866-1916, 4 vols.; and, Executors' and Administrators' Bonds, 1806-24, 2 vols. (original and copy)

Fiduciaries Registry, 1863-77, 1 vol.; and, Register of Fiduciaries, 1898, 1 vol.

Fiducuary Accounts, 1888-1904, 2 vols.; and, Fiduciary Accounts No. 2, 1901-07, 1 vol.

Fiduciary Bonds, 1866-86, 1 vol.

[Fiduciary?] Indexes, n.d., 2 vols.

Guardians' Bond Books, 1806-64, 1866-1911, 5 vols.; and, 1806-44, 4 vols. (copies)

Guardians' Papers, 1807-39, .25 cu. ft.

Index [to Fiduciaries, or Bonds?], n.d., 1 vol.

Orders of Probate in Order Books [Index to Wills, etc.], 1732-1802, 1 vol. (copy)

Justice of the Peace Records

Civil Judgments and Executions, 1893-1915, 1 vol.

Criminal Record, 1888-1903, 1 vol.

Criminal Reports, ca. 1800-1905, .35 cu. ft.

Indexes to Trial Justice Civil Warrants, n.d., 2 vol.

Judgment and Execution Books, 1886-89, 1886-1923, 2 vol.

Judgments, 1888-98, .35 cu. ft.

Judgments and Executions, 1866-75, 1900-09, .5 cu. ft.

Warrants, 1876-1883 (also Abstracts of Votes, 1901), 1 vol.

Land Records

Appeals and Land Causes, 1777-1807, 2 vols. (copies)

Circuit Court Land Causes No. 1, 1835-72 and 1881-1913, 1 vol.

Deeds, 1758-1904, ca. .5 cu. ft.

Deeds, 1815-59 [1889], 2 vols.; and, Deeds [from Chancery Suits], 1758-1845, 1 vol. (copy). See also Wills.

Daily Index of Receipt of Deeds for Recordation, 1902-04, 1 vol.

Indexes to Deed Books Nos. 30-135, 1861-[ca. 1950], 82 vols.; and, Indexes to Deed Books Nos. 29-56, 1836-76, 1 vol.

General Index to Deeds, A-Z, 1728-1838, 2 vols.; and, General Indexes to Deeds Nos. 2-4, n.d., 3 vols.

Land Causes, 1787-1807, 1 vol.

Lists of Real Estate Sold for the Years, 1876-84, 1887, 6 items

Plats, 1777-1847, 54 items; Plat, Bowling Green Estate, 1824, 1 item; and, Plat, Brame v. Brame, 1822, 1 item. See also Wills.

Processioners' Returns, 1846-65, 1 vol.

Superior Court Deed Book, 1809-14 (also Superior Court of Law Order Book, 1820-21), 1 vol.

Surveys, 1729-1863, 1 vol. (copy)

Marriage Records and Vital Statistics

Marriage Bonds, 1810-16, 1845-51, 2 vols.; and, 1810-16, 2 vols. (copies)

Marriage Bonds and Consents No. 3, 1819-57, 1 vol.

Marriage License, 1838, 1 item

Marriage Register, 1787-1853, 1 vol. (copy); and, 1852-57, 1 vol.

Marriage Register, 1787-1853 (Ts.), 58 pp.

Minister's Return, 1791, 1 item

Ministers' Returns, 1796-1852, 1 vol.

Register of Births, 1864-67, 1 vol. See also Miscellaneous Records.

Register of Deaths, 1865-67, 1 vol.

Register of Marriages, 1893-1932, 1 vol.

Registers of Births and Deaths, ca. 1855-95, ca. 1 cu. ft.

Organization Records

Human [Humane?] Association Minutes, see Tax and Fiscal Records

Masonic Lodge Ledger, 1902-10, 1 vol.

Road and Bridge Records

County Court Road Books, 1824-30, 1881, 2 vols.; and, Road Books, 1833-63, 1882-93, 2 vols.

Road Surveys, 1875-80, ca. .1 cu. ft.

School Records

Educational Census, n.d., 1 vol.

Tax and Fiscal Records

Applications to Purchase Delinquent Land, 1896-98 (also Poll Taxes, 1904-07, and Minutes of the Human Association, 1902-03), 1 vol.

Accounts against the County, ca. 1900-10, .35 cu. ft.

County Claims, 1866-70, ca. .15 cu. ft.

Delinquent Land, ca. 1870-85, ca. .25 cu. ft. See also Court Records, County Court.

General Licenses, 1872-1904, ca. .1 cu. ft.

Land Taxes, ca. 1890-1922, ca. 25 items (fragments)

List of Real Estate Sold, 1887-1931 (also List of Real Estate Redeemed before Sale, 1886-1930), 1 vol.

Moffett Registers, 1878-80, ca. .1 cu. ft.

Poll Taxes, see Applications to Purchase Delinquent Land

Record of Delinquent Lands, 1884-1908, 1 vol.

Record of Lands Purchased by the Commonwealth, 1886-1933, 1 vol.

Record of Warrants, 1885-86, 1 vol.

Wills

Wills, 1742, 1762-1830, 1851, n.d., 80 items

Wills, 1794-1897, 1 vol.; and, Wills, 1742 and 1762-1830 (includes Plats, 1777-1840) [from Chancery Suits], 1 vol. (copy)

Wills and Deeds, 1794-1863, 1 vol. (copy)
Indexes to Will Books Nos. 29-30 and 33-37, 1858, 1870-71, 1881-88, 7 vols.
General Index to Wills, A-Z, n.d., 1 vol.

Miscellaneous Records

Board of Overseer of the Poor Minutes, 1845-71, 2 vols.
Crop Lien Docket, 1893-1931, 1 vol.
Historical Papers [removed from other series?] (includes birth, lunacy, Overseers of the Poor records, polls, military papers, etc.; inventory available), 1771-1864, 1 cu. ft.
Proceedings of the Committee of Safety, 1774-76, 2 vols. (copies)
Register of Medical Examiners, 1894-1928, 1 vol.
Reports of Overseers of the Poor, 1871-84, 1897-98, ca. .15 cu. ft. See also Historical Papers.
Reservation of Title to Personalty, 1892-1920, 1 vol.

Commissioner of Revenue

Personal Property Tax, Second District 1896, 1 vol.
Record of Improper Assessment of Lands, 1886-1917, 1 vol.
Record of Insolvent Capitation and Property Tax, 1885-88, 1 vol.
See also Tax and Fiscal Records

Treasurer

Tax and License Book, 1894, 1 vol.
Treasurer's Settlements No. 1, 1886-1904, 1 vol.
See also Tax and Fiscal Records

Microfilm Records

Circuit Court Clerk

Court Records

County Court

Minute Books, 1770-81, 1787-91, 1794-96, 1815-19, 1847-51, 1858-66, 4 reels
Order Books, 1732-89, 1799-1824, 1862-63 (includes Board of Exemption Minutes, 1862), 14 reels
Rule Book, 1792-96, 1 reel (part)

Superior Court of Law

Order Book, 1820-26 (also Deeds, 1809-14), 1 reel

Circuit Superior Court of Law and Chancery

Order Book, 1836-66 (includes Circuit Court, 1852-66), 1 reel

Circuit Court

Order Book, see Circuit Superior Court of Law and Chancery

Fiduciary Records

Guardians' and Will Book No. 32, 1857-66, 1 reel
Guardians' Bonds, 1806-58, 2 reels
Index to Inventories and Administrations, see Wills

Land Records

Appeals and Land Causes, 1777-1807, 1 reel
Deed Books Nos. 39-40, 45-51, 1836-40, 1846-65, 4 reels
Deeds [from Chancery Papers], 1758-1845, 1 reel
Index to Deeds No. 1, 1836-72, 1 reel
Land Causes Vol. 1, 1835-1913, 1 reel (part)
Plats, see Wills
Processioners' Returns, 1846-65, 1 reel (part)

Surveys, 1729-62, 1 reel (part)
See also Court Records, Superior Court of Law
Marriage Records and Vital Statistics
Marriage Bonds, 1795, 1802-60, 1 reel
Marriage Records, 1864-1932, 1 reel (part)
Marriage Register, 1787-1853, 1 reel
Index to Marriage Register, 1787-1853, 1 reel
Register of Births, 1864-67, 1 reel (part)
Register of Deaths, 1865-67, 1 reel (part
Military and Pension Records
Board of Exemptions Minutes, see Court Records, County Court
Wills
Will Books Nos. 19 and 29-31, 1814-18, 1853-63, 2 reels
Wills and Plats [from Chancery Papers], 1742-1830, 1 reel
General Index to Wills, 1814-1950, 1 reel
Index to Wills, Inventories and Administrations from Caroline County Order Books, 1732-1800, 1 reel
See also Fiduciary Records
Miscellaneous Records
Proceedings of Committee of Safety, 1774-76 (also unidentified account book, n.d.), 1 reel (part)

CARROLL COUNTY

Formed in 1842 from Grayson County. Part of Patrick County was added later.

Microfilm Records

Circuit Court Clerk
Court Records
County Court
Order Books, 1842-67 (also Judgments, 1842-60), 3 reels
Land Records
Deed Books Nos. 1-8, 1842-67, 4 reels
General Index to Deeds, Grantors-Grantees A-Z, 1842-1927, 2 reels
Surveyors' Records, 1842-1910, 1 reel
Marriage Records and Vital Statistics
Register of Births, 1853-91, 1 reel (part)
Register of Deaths, 1853-70, 1 reel (part)
Register of Marriages, 1854-1913, 1 reel (part)
Index to Births, Deaths, and Marriages, 1853-1913, 1 reel
Wills
Will Books Nos. 1-2, 1842-75, 1 reel
General Index to Wills No. 1, 1842-1953, 1 reel

CHARLES CITY COUNTY

Original shire established in 1634.

Original Records

Circuit Court Clerk
Board of Supervisors Records
Minutes, 1870-95, 1 vol.
Papers, 1871-82, 14 items
Bonds/Commissions/Oaths
Apprenticeship Indentures, 1837-63, 25 items
Attachment, Appeal, and Indemnifying Bonds, 1768-1869, 25 items
Bond Books, 1873-99, 2 vols.
Bonds, 1762-69, 130 items (originals and copies)
Commissioners' Appointments, 1810-86, 46 items
Election [and loyalty] Oaths, 1866, 1869-83, 184 items
Fishing Rights and Licenses, 1885-97, 17 items
Injunction Bonds, see Marriage Records and Vital Statistics
Justice of the Peace Commissions, 1854-69, 46 items
Liquor License Bonds, 1877-86, ca. 150 items
Ministers', Ordinary, and Miscellaneous Bonds, 1754-ca. 1880, ca. 25 items; and, Ordinary Bonds, 1762-64, 3 items (copies)
Officials' Bond, 1763, 1 item (copy)
Refunding Bonds, 1760-1834, ca. 100 items
Replevy and Stay Bonds, 1767-1844, 49 items
Sheriff's Bonds, Commissions, etc., 1760-1889, 17 items
Business Records/Corporations/Partnerships
M. D. Coalter, Weyanoke Farm, Accounts of Sales, 1894-98 (also Time Book, 1894-98), 1 vol.
Neston Store Account Book, 1874-75, 1 vol.; Day Books, 1870, 1872, 1876-78, 5 vols.; and, Ledger, 1875-78, 1 vol.
R. L. Adams' Ledger, 1866-76, 1 vol.
Willcox and Graves Ledgers, Union Hall, 1871-75, 1873-74, 2 vols. See also Fiduciary Records.
Court Records
County Court
Chancery Order Book Vol. 1, 1872-73, 1 vol.
Chancery Rules, 1814-27, 1 vol.
Common Law Process Book, 1865-95, 1 vol.
Docket Book No. 2, 1868-95, 1 vol.
Execution Books, 1821-53, 1849-61, 2 vols.
Fee Book, 1856-63, 1 vol.
Judgment Docket Book, 1850-79, 1 vol.
Minute Books, 1769, 1788-89, 1872-79, 4 vols. (originals, and copy of 1769, 3 vols.); Minute Books Nos. [1]-3, 1823-60 [1862], 3 vols.; and, 1696 and 1762, 6 pp. (fragments)
Order Books, 1672-73 (original and copy), 1677-79, 1737-51, 1758-62, 4 vols.; and, 1650 (original and copy), 1680, 1682, 1685, 1722-23, 34 pp. (fragments). See also Land Records.
Process Book, 1867-1900, 1 vol.
Subpoena Docket, 1861-68, 1 vol.; and, Subpoena Docket and Witness Attendance Book, 1868-95, 1 vol.

Superior Court of Law
    Royster v. Tyler, order 1827, 1 item (original and copy)
Circuit Superior Court of Law and Chancery
    Orders, 1831-52 (includes Circuit Court, 1852), 1 vol.
Circuit Court
    Chancery Docket Book, 1865-95, 1 vol.
    Chancery Order Book, 1866-94, 1 vol.
    Chancery Process Book, 1865-96, 1 vol.
    Chancery Rules, 1865-95, 1 vol.
    Common Law and Chancery Docket, 1881-82, 1 vol.
    Common Law Docket Book, 1865-95, 1 vol.
    Common Law Minutes, 1853-63, 1 vol.
    Index to Common Law Minute Book, 1853-63, 1 vol.
    Common Law Rules, 1865-95, 1 vol.
    Orders, see Circuit Superior Court of Law and Chancery
    Subpoena Docket Book, 1870-95 (also Jurors, 1874-89), 1 vol.
County and Superior Courts
    Abstracts of Judgment and Miscellaneous, 1858-71, n.d., c. 450 items
    Cases [suits], 1760-1897, n.d., 4.4 cu. ft.
    Indexes to Cases [suits], n.d., ca. .15 cu. ft.
    Clerk's Papers, 1788-1889, 38 items
    Grand Jury Summons and Presentments, 1785-1896, ca. 110 items
    Jury Lists, Summons, etc., ca. 1845-95, ca. .25 cu. ft.
Unspecified Court
    Jones v. Jones, decree, n.d., 1 item
    Judges' Papers, 1852-97, 1901, 9 items
    Miscellaneous Court Papers, 1821-80, 28 items (including fragments)
Election Records
    Election Papers, 1795-1896, ca. .1 cu. ft.
Fiduciary Records
    Administrators' Accounts and Papers, 1787-1793, 1828-87, ca. 110 items
    Administrators' Bonds, 1783-1877, 42 items
    Estate of James M. Willcox, Union Hall, Ledger, 1875-78, 1 vol. See also
        Business and Organization Records.
    Executors' Accounts, 1805-70, 80 items
    Executors' Bonds, 1785-1877, 31 items; and, 1763, 1 item (copy)
    Fiduciary Bond, 1763, 1 item (copy)
    [Fiduciary] Bond Book, 1886-1907, 1 vol.
    Guardians' Accounts and Papers, 1782-1893, ca. 175 items
    Guardians' Bonds, 1772-1877, 43 items
    Homestead Papers, 1871-79, 10 items
    Inventories, Appraisements, and Audits, 1782-1859, 25 items
    Sales, 1789-1855, 19 items
    Schedules, etc., 1794-1887, 17 items
Free Negroes and Slave Records
    Papers concerning Free Negroes, 1821-52, 11 items
    Patrols' and Guards' Papers, 1804-52, 16 items
    Register of Free Negroes, 1856-64, 1 vol.
Justice of the Peace Records
    Constables' Papers, 1854-88, 6 items
    Justices' Papers, 1865-92, 19 items
    Summons, 1827-70, 63 items

Land Records

Deeds and related papers, 1784-1897, ca. 100 items

Deeds, Wills, Orders, etc., 1655-65, 1 vol. (copy)

General Index to Deeds Vol. 1, 1790-1911, 1 vol.

See also Court Records, County Court

Marriage Records and Vital Statistics

Lists of Births, 1892-96, 6 items

Lists of Deaths, 1865-96, 22 items

Marriage Bonds [and Records] and Injunction Bonds, 1784-1878, 40 items

Military and Pension Records

Exemptions, pensions, etc., 1815-90, ca. 200 items

Road and Bridge Records

Bridge Papers, 1851-83, n.d., 66 items

Public Works, Turkey Island, Soanes, and Long bridges, 1823-95, ca. 100 items

Road Books, 1865-70, 1875-81, 2 vols.

Road Papers, 1821-95, ca. 150 items

Surveyor of the Roads Appointments and Papers, 1853-96, ca. .15 cu. ft.

Wharfs and Landings, 1795-1865, n.d., 8 items

School Records

Chickahominy Township School Journal, 1870-86, 1 vol.; and, Chickahominy District, Public Schools Nos. 1-2, Daily Records [of Attendance], 1887-98, 1 vol.

County School Fund Book, 1899-1902, 1 vol.

Medical College of Virginia Medical Examinations, 1901-02, 40 items

School Board Correspondence, 1872-1900, 18 items; and, Papers, 1884-99, 44 items

School Census, etc., 1889-99, 8 items

School Commissioners' Papers, 1853-66, 9 items

School Receipts, 1816-17, 7 items

Teachers' Applications and Certificates, 1901-02, 21 items; and, Contracts, 1899-1900, 20 items

Warrants, 1898-1902, 192 items

Tax and Fiscal Records

Accounts of the Commonwealth, 1796-1856, and Commonwealth [Accounts] Allowed, 1857-97, .25 cu. ft.

Accounts of the County, 1794-1860, and [County Accounts] Allowed, 1861-1902, .5 cu. ft.

Assessors' Papers and Accounts, 1870-84, 8 items

Auditors' Papers, 1823-97, 56 items

Collectors' Appointments and Papers, 1872-74, 5 items

Delinquent Tax Lists, 1797-1873, ca. .1 cu. ft.

Land Tax and Tithables, 1812-13, 2 vols.

Reports of Fines, Taxes, etc., 1844-89, 31 items

Tax Papers, ca. 1850-95, ca. .15 cu. ft.

Township Records

Tyler Township Board Minute Book, 1870-74, 1 vol.

See also School Records

Wills

Record of Wills, etc., 1724/5-31, 1 vol. (original and copy)

Will Book, 1789-1808, 1 vol.

Wills, etc., 1788-1868, ca. 50 items; and, Will of Barnard Major, 1777, 2 pp. (original and copy)

See also Court Records, County Court; and, Land Records

Miscellaneous Records

    Agreements, 1780-1870, 19 items
    Coroners' Inquests and Papers, 1771-1893, ca. 100 items
    Estray Bills, 1802-78, 18 items
    Food and Salt Agents' Reports, 1862-64, 31 items
    Index to Miscellaneous, n.d., 1 item
    Jail Keepers' Records, 1824-96, 8 items. See also Road Records.
    Letters and Papers from the Governor's Office, 1851-83, 22 items
    Lunacy Papers, 1813-91, 48 items
    Memorial Resolutions, 1855-86, 13 items
    Miscellaneous Letters, 1772, 1815, 1819, 1854, 4 items
    Overseer of the Poor Papers and Reports, 1816-95, ca. 40 items
    Personal Accounts, 1759-[1880?], .25 cu. ft.
    Promissory Notes, 1752-1897, ca. .15 cu. ft.
    Public Works (construction of the couthouse, clerk's office, etc.), 1832-98, n.d., 81 items
    Virginia Grand Assembly Acts 22-30, 1641/2, 1 item (original and Ts.)
    Water and Grist Mill Papers, 1772-1817, 19 items

Commissioner of Revenue

    Commissioner of the Revenue Papers, 1831-78, 8 items
    Insolvent Capitations and Property Taxes, 1885-89, 1 vol.
    See also Tax and Fiscal Records

Commonwealth's Attorney

    Commonwealth Attorney's Papers, 1867, 1869, 2 items

Sheriff

    Warrants, [1770]-1820, 11 items

Treasurer

    Tax Affidavits, n.d., 7 items
    Treasurer's Office Check Book, 1871-73, 1 vol.; and, Ledger, 1874-91, 1 vol.
    Treasurer's Papers and Warrants, 1871-93, ca. .25 cu. ft.
    See also Tax and Fiscal Records

Microfilm Records

Circuit Court Clerk
Court Records
County Court
    Order Books, 1650, 1672-73, 1677-80, 1685, 1687-96, 1737-62, 3 reels
    Minutes, 1762, 1769, 1788-89, 1 reel (part); and, Minute Books [Orders] Nos. 1-6, 1823-79, 4 reels
Circuit Superior Court of Law and Chancery
    Order Book, 1831-52 (includes Circuit Court, 1852), 1 reel (part)
Circuit Court
    Order Book (Minutes), 1853-63, 1 reel (part). See also Circuit Superior Court of Law and Chancery.
Land Records
    Deeds, Wills, Orders, etc., 1655-65, 1 reel (part); and, Deeds and Wills, 1689-90, 1692/3-94, 1766-74, 2 reels
    Deed Books Nos. 4-11, 1789-1867, 4 reels
    General Index to Deeds, Grantor-Grantee A-Z, 1789-1913, 1 reel; and, General Index to Deeds, 1790-1911, 1 reel

Marriage Records and Vital Statistics
Miscellaneous Marriage Bonds and Loose Papers, 1762-1855, 1 reel (part)
Register of Births, 1865-96, 1 reel (part)
Register of Deaths, 1865-96, 1 reel (part)
Registers of Marriages Nos. 1-2, 1850-73, 1861-1931, 1 reel (part)
Military and Pension Records
Muster Roll, 1861-65, 1 reel (part)
Wills
Will Books Nos. [1]-6, 1789-1878, 3 reels
Circuit Court Will Book, 1862-1920, 1 reel
General Index to Wills and Fiduciary Accounts No. 1, 1789-1954, 1 reel

CHARLES RIVER COUNTY

**Original shire formed in 1634;
see York County.**

CHARLOTTE COUNTY

Formed in 1764 from Lunenburg County

Original Records

Circuit Court Clerk
Bonds/Commissions/Oaths
Bonds and Suit Papers, 1763-1860, n.d., ca. .15 cu. ft.
Commissions of Justices of Oyer and Terminer, 1766-84, 7 items
Election Oaths, etc., 1841, n.d. [ca. 1867], 12 items
Justice of the Peace Commissions and Appointments, 1764-1869, ca. .15 cu. ft.
Oaths Prescribed by Acts of 1862, 1868-69, 9 items
Officials' Appointments and Commissions, ca. 1770-1870, 10 items; and, [Officials'] Bonds and Oaths, 1853, 1871, 6 items
Ordinary Bonds and Licenses [titles vary], 1765-1803, 1812-30, ca. .3 cu. ft.
Poll Commissioner's Appointment, 1831, 1 item
Recognizances and Peace Bonds, 1847-72, ca. .2 cu. ft.
Replevy Bonds, 1788-96, ca. .75 cu. ft.
Sheriff's Appointments, Commissions, and Bonds, ca. 1770-1850, n.d., ca. .25 cu. ft.
Business Records/Corporations/Partnerships
C. & Co. Ledgers A-1 and B, 1865-68, 2 vols.; and, Index [to C. & Co. Ledger?], n.d., 1 vol.
C & M Ledger, ca. 1860, 1 vol.
C. H. & Co. Journal, ca. 1860-75, 1 vol.
C[harlotte] B[anking] & I[nsurance] Co. Bills [Receivable], 1883-99, 2 vols.; Blotters and Ticklers, 1872-88, 1891-98, 1902-03, 9 vols.; Cashiers' Books, 1898, 1900, 1902, 3 vols.; Check Books, 1890, 1898, 2 vols.; Day Books, 1896-99, 2 vols.; Journals A-B and F-G, 1893-1907, 10 vols.; and, Ledgers A and C-D, 1872-84, 1893-1905, 3 vols.
C. H. M[orton] Journal B, 1861-[64], 1 vol.

D. H. Morton Day Book, 1861-63, 1 vol.
M. B. & E. Ledger A, 1856-58, 1 vol.; and, Journal B, 1857-58, 1 vol.
R. W. C. Ledger A, 1869-71, 1 vol.
Spencer & Co. Day Books, 1860-62, 2 vols.
S[pencer?] & Co. Day Book, 1860, 1 vol.; Journal, 1861-62, 1 vol.; and, Ledger, 1852-57, 1 vol.
Unidentified Ledger, 1856-60, 1 vol.
Watkins and Jones Day and Account Book, 1876-80, 1 vol.

Court Records
County Court
Attachments, Distress Warrants, and Peace Warrants, [1764]-1847, ca. .1 cu. ft.
[Court] Correspondence, 1852-75, n.d., 6 items
Court Receipts, fees collected, 1846-51, 5 items
Criminal Forms, 1855-61, ca. .1 cu. ft.
Executions [titles vary], 1764-1867, n.d., ca. 11 cu. ft.
Extradition, 1770, 1 items
Fee Books, 1852, 1897-1901, 2 vols.
Jury Lists (and witness attendance?), 1866-70, n.d., ca. .15 cu. ft.
Single Bills, Hairston v. Roberts, etc., 1822, 2 items
Suit Papers, see Bonds/Commissions/Oaths
Summons, 1766, 8 items

County and Circuit Courts
Judgments, etc. [titles vary], 1765-1878, 1910, n.d., ca. .1 cu. ft.
Lists of All Fines, 1860, 5 items

Election Records
Polls and Election Records, 1837-80, n.d., ca. .85 cu. ft.

Fiduciary Records
Estate of Dr. George Cabell, 1823, 1 item
Estate of John Randolph of Roanoke, 1845, 1857, 2 items
Fiduciary Bond, 1774, 1 item
Record of Fiduciaries, 1893-1914, 1 vol.
Index [to Fiduciaries?], n.d., 1 vol.

Justice of the Peace Records
Constables' Executions and Magistrates' Judgments, 1866-67, ca. .15 cu. ft.
Justice of the Peace Executions Paid Off, 1853-55, ca. 25 items
Justices' Returns, 1801, 1806, 2 items
Letters to the Several Magistrates, etc. [titles vary], 1784, 4 items
Lists of Justices Attending Court, 1773-74, 2 items
Request for Transmission of List of Magistrates, 1784, 1 item

Land Records
Deed Book No. 3, 1771-77, 1 vol. (copy)
Land Processioner Reports, 1837, 1854, 2 items

Marriage Records and Vital Statistics
Marriage Licenses, 1870, 19 items

Military and Pension Records
Militia Lists and Commissions, 1806, 1821, 1855-57, 5 items
Proceedings of the Court of Enquiry, 26th Regiment, Virginia Militia, 1811-22, 1 vol. (copy)
"Return of the Militia" Form, 1854, 1 item

Road and Bridge Records
Road Commissioner's Report with Map, 1853, 1 item
Road Papers, Bacon Township, ca. 1873-74, ca. 50 items; Roanoke District, 1861-64, and Township, 1871-74, ca. .1 cu. ft.; Walton Township, ca. 1871-74, 10 items; and, unspecified township, 1871, n.d., 10 items

Road Receipts Allowed, 1872-83, ca. 50 items
Road Taxes, 1872-75, ca. 25 items
Surveyors' Appointments and Papers, 1803-70, n.d., ca. .5 cu. ft.
Tax and Fiscal Records
Claims and Accounts, 1816-35, 1873-75, n.d., ca. .1 cu. ft.
Land and Property Tax Books, 1846, 2 vols.
Tax Records (including lists of insolvents, receipts, and delinquent lists), 1824-27, 1867-75, n.d., ca. .2 cu. ft.
Township Records
Receipts, Bacon Township, 1871-75, ca. .2 cu. ft.; Roanoke Township, 1871-75, ca. .1 cu. ft.; and, Walton Township, 1871-75, ca. 150 items
<u>See also</u> Road and Bridge Records
Wills
Will, Patrick Henry, 1799, 6 pp. (copies)
Will Book No. 1, 1765-91, 1 vol. (copy)
Miscellaneous Records
Circular, 1801, 1 item
Coroners' Inquests, ca. 1785-1865, ca. .1 cu. ft.
Estray Papers [titles vary], 1744-1864, n.d., ca. 1 cu. ft.
Jury Allowances, 1868, ca. 150 items
Letter Verifying Age, 1858, 1 item
Miscellaneous Papers, 1771-[19?]26, 25 items
Notary Public Appointments, 1852-70, 6 items
Overseer of the Poor Indentures and Papers, 1787-1871, ca. .15 cu. ft.
Personal Claims and Accounts, 1848-66, ca. 40 items
Salt Distribution Register, 1862-64, 1 vol.

Commissioner of Revenue
Memorandum Book of S. Bedford, Commissioner, 1841, 1 vol.
Tax Lists [personal property interrogatories], 1866-69, 1880, 9.45 cu. ft.
<u>See also</u> Tax and Fiscal Records

Microfilm Records

Circuit Court Clerk
Court Records
County Court
Cases, 1765-74, 30 reels
Orders Books Nos. 1-36, 1765-1868, 15 reels
General Indexes to Minute [Order] Books Nos. 1-2, 1765-1904, 1 reel
Fiduciary Records
Guardians' Accounts Nos. 1-7, 1765-1880, 2 reels
Land Records
Deed Books Nos. 1-32, 1765-1870, 14 reels
General Indexes to Deeds Nos. 1-2, 1765-1881, 1 reel
Land Causes, 1818, 1 reel
Marriage Records and Vital Statistics
Marriage Bonds [and records], 1765-1912, 32 reels
Marriage Registers Nos. 1-3, 1782-1900, 1 reel
Wills
Will Books Nos. 1-14, 1765-1867, 5 reels
General Index to Wills, 1765-1904, 1 reel

CHESTERFIELD COUNTY

Formed in 1749 from Henrico County.

Original Records

Circuit Court Clerk
Board of Supervisors Records
Dead Papers, 1870-1904, 5.6 cu. ft.
Bonds/Commissions/Oaths
Bonds and Executions, 1751-63, ca. .2 cu. ft.
Bonds, Appointments, etc., 1809-74, ca. .1 cu. ft.
Bonds in Chancery Suits, 1872-90, ca. .15 cu. ft.
County and Circuit Court Records of Bonds, 1889-1904, 2 vols.
Delinquent Superior Court Bonds, 1817-22, 1827-33, ca. 50 items
Delivery Bonds, 1795-1831, 1861, ca. .2 cu. ft.
Forthcoming Bond Book, 1896-1925, 1 vol.
Injunction Bonds upon which Injunctions were granted by the Superior Court of
    Chancery, 1804-35, ca. .1 cu. ft.
Inspection Bonds, 1791-1819, ca. 100 items; and, Inspection of Tobacco Bonds,
    1790-1820, ca. .1 cu. ft. See also Fiduciary Records.
Officials' Bonds, 1873-89, 1 vol.
Old Sheriff's Bonds, 1778-1841, ca. 25 items
Ordinary Bonds, 1772-1805, ca. 50 items; and, Ordinary Keepers' Bonds since
    1803, [1804-20], ca. .15 cu. ft. See also Fiduciary Records.
Recognizances to Keep the Peace, 1804-19, ca. .2 cu. ft.
Superior Court Bonds, 1809-15, ca. 25 items
Whiskey Bonds, 1883, ca. 25 items
See also Election Records
Business Records/Corporations/Partnerships
Southern Coal and Iron Co., cancelled bonds, 1891, .35 cu. ft.
Census Records
Enumeration, 1870, 169 pp.
Court Records
County Court
Chancery and Common Law Rule Dockets, 1805-12, 1816-41, 10 vols.
Claims of Grand Jurors, 1861-63, ca. 25 items
Common Law and Chancery Executions upon which the Returns have been
    Recorded, 1832, ca. .1 cu. ft.
Common Law and Chancery Issue Dockets, 1805-37, 9 vols.
Common Law Fee Book, 1868-73, 1 vol.
Common Law Issue Docket, 1869-99, 1 vol.
Common Law Rule Papers, 1842-60, ca. .1 cu. ft.
Commonwealth Warrant, 1820, 1 item
Condemnation Papers, Richmond and Petersburg Electric Railway and Co.,
    and Richmond Petersburg & Carolina Railroad Co., 1881, 1889, .7 cu. ft.
Copies of Court Orders, Decrees, etc., 1820-41, ca. 100 items
Court Papers, 1814-62, ca. .3 cu. ft.
Execution Dockets, 1799-1831, 1842-60, 1867-95, 10 vols.
Executions, ca. 1770-1840, ca. .5 cu. ft.
Fee Books, 1783-89, 1794-1803, 1808-17, 1823-42, 1845-55, 1857-60, 17 vols.
Grand Jury Presentments, Appeals, etc., 1806-18, ca. .15 cu. ft.
Judgment Papers, ca. 1790-1855, ca. .3 cu. ft.

Judgments Docketed, 1840, 1865, ca. .1 cu. ft.
Minutes, 1811-13, 1819-29, 1833-36, 5 vols.
Office Judgments, 1824, ca. .15 cu. ft.
Old Miscellaneous County Court Dead Papers Mutilated during the War by
    Federal Troops, 1840-57, ca. .1 cu. ft.
Order Book No. 1, 1749-54, 1 vol. (copy)
Orders Entered in Vacation Term, 1873-76, ca. 100 items
Orders of Attendance, 1800-60, ca. .15 cu. ft.
Orders of Pay, 1812-37, ca. .25 cu. ft.
Orders of Witness Attendance, 1811-44, 2 vols.
Recognizances and Criminal Prosecutions, 1797-1805, ca. .1 cu. ft.
[Record of Taxes Collected in the Office of the County Clerk], 1870-88,
    1 vol.
Statements of Prince Edward, Goochland, and Powhatan Fees due the Clerk
    of Chesterfield, 1815-39, ca. .1 cu. ft.
Subpoenas, ca. 1820-60, ca. .85 cu. ft.
Suit Papers (summons, executions, etc.), 1790-1805, ca. .15 cu. ft.
Warrants, ca. 1755-1805, 1874-94, 1902-03, ca. .6 cu. ft.

District Court
Office Judgments, declarations, etc., 1806-1907 (includes Superior Court of
    Law, 1808-31; Circuit Superior Court of Law and Chancery, 1831-51;
    and, Circuit Court, 1852-1907), ca. 1.25 cu. ft.
Superior Court Dead Papers, 1802-43 (includes Superior Court of Law, 1808-
    31, and Circuit Superior Court of Law and Chancery, 1831-43), 4.55
    cu. ft.

Superior Court of Law
Chancery Execution Dockets, 1826-72 (includes Circuit Superior Court of
    Law and Chancery, 1831-51, and Circuit Court, 1852-72), 2 vols.
Common Law Ended Causes, 1817, ca. .1 cu. ft.
Executions, 1809-57 (includes Circuit Superior Court of Law and Chancery,
    1831-51, and Circuit Court, 1852-57), ca. .6 cu. ft.
Fee Book, 1816-22, 1 vol.
Office Judgments, 1824, ca. .15 cu. ft.
Office Judgments [and Rules], 1809-27, 1 vol.; and, Office Judgments, 1827-
    48 (also Chancery Rule Docket, 1809-48), 1 vol. See also District Court.
Orders of Attendance, 1809-44 (includes Circuit Superior Court of Law and
    Chancery, 1831-44), 1 vol.
Subpoenas, ca. 1815-40 (includes Circuit Superior Court of Law and
    Chancery, 1831-40), ca. .2 cu. ft.
Superior Court Dead Papers, see District Court
Warrants, 1810-73, .75 cu. ft.

Circuit Superior Court of Law and Chancery
Chancery Execution Docket, see Superior Court of Law
Chancery Process Book, 1831-82 (includes Circuit Court, 1852-82), 1 vol.
Chancery Rule Dockets Nos. 1-2, 1831-67 (includes Circuit Court, 1852-67),
    2 vols.
Common Law Execution Docket, 1831-42, 1 vol.
Common Law Process Books Nos. 1-[2], 1831-70 (includes Circuit Court,
    1852-70), 2 vol.
Common Law Rule Dockets Nos. 1-2, 1831-57 (includes Circuit Court, 1852-
    57), 2 vols.
Court Papers of Edward B. Boisseau, 1833-36, ca. .15 cu. ft.
Declarations, Bonds, etc., 1833-35, ca. 50 items
Executions, 1831-69 (includes Circuit Court, 1852-69), ca. .15 cu. ft. See
    also Superior Court of Law.

Miscellaneous Papers, 1837-71 [1836-1913], ca. 100 items

Office Judgments, see Superior Court of Law

Orders of Attendance, see Superior Court of Law

Rule Docket, 1847-93 (includes Circuit Court, 1852-93), 1 vol.

Subpoenas, A-F, 1838-41, ca. 100 items; and, Subpoenas, 1846-50, .35 cu. ft. See also Superior Court of Law.

Superior Court Dead Papers, see District Court

Circuit Court

Argument Docket, 1853-1908, 1 vol.

Chancery Docket, 1873-75, 1 vol. (fragment)

Chancery [Executions], 1870, ca. .15 cu. ft. See also Superior Court of Law.

Chancery Process Book, 1883-1922, 1 vol. See also Circuit Superior Court of Law and Chancery.

Chancery Rules, 1874-1931, 2 vols.; and, Chancery Rule Docket, 1853-58, 1 vol. (fragment). See also Circuit Superior Court of Law and Chancery.

Common Law Docket, 1893-1911, 1 vol.

Common Law Fee Book, 1868-73, 1 vol.

Common Law Process Books [titles vary], 1871-1952, 1 vol. See also Circuit Superior Court of Law and Chancery.

Common Law Rules, 1874-1916, 1 vol. See also Circuit Superior Court of Law and Chancery.

Commonwealth v. Sarah Morris, suit papers, 1898, ca. .15 cu. ft.

Executions, see Superior Court of Law, and Circuit Superior Court of Law, and Chancery

Fee Books, 1870-80, 1884-1923, 5 vols.

Indictments, 1859-60, ca. .1 cu. ft.

List of Jury Allowances, 1896, 1 item

Miscellaneous Papers, see Circuit Superior Court of Law and Chancery

Office Judgments, see District Court

Receipt Books, 1870-95, 1885-87, 3 vols.

Record [Clerk's Tax Account Book], 1876-1918, 1 vol.

Rule Docket, see Circuit Superior Court of Law and Chancery

Summons and Jury Receipts, 1853, 1864, 3 items

Warrants, see Superior Court of Law

County and Superior Courts

Common Law Papers, 1746-1904, 16.65 cu. ft.

Court Papers Found in Chancery Suits, 1823-74, ca. .1 cu. ft.

Dead Papers, 1749-1907, 80.85 cu. ft.; Dead Papers in Criminal Prosecutions, 1804-08, 1815-20, .45 cu. ft.; and, Miscellaneous Dead Papers, [1772]-1927, ca. 2.65 cu. ft.

Docket of Executions Issued and Returned by Officers No. 1, 1871-1927, 1 vol.

Ended Chancery Causes, 1750-1914, 52.2 cu. ft.

Executions, 1828-60, ca. .1 cu. ft.

Homestead Papers, 1871-72, ca. 25 items

Miscellaneous Papers, 1779-1917, ca. .75 cu. ft.

Record of all Taxes and other Money belonging to the Commonwealth of Virginia [collected by the Clerk], 1898-1903, 1 vol.

Rule Docket, 1856-74, 1 vol.

Scattering Fee Bills, F-Z, 1809-21, ca. .2 cu. ft.

S. W. Carter's Correspondence (also jury lists, etc.), 1808-1912, ca. .1 cu. ft.

Warrants, see Treasurer

Unspecified Court

Jury List, 1873, 1 item

Lists of Fines, 1826-40, 16 items

Reports of Suits and Fines, 1852-55, 8 items

Election Records

    Affidavits of Ownership of Land, 1832-35, ca. 75 items

    Lists of Registered Voters, Dale District, 1892, 1899, 3 vols.

    Index to Registered Voters, by districts, 1902-12, 1 vol.

    Petitions, 1855, 6 items

    Poll Books, Ballots, and Oaths, 1872, 1885-88, ca. .5 cu. ft.

    Polls, 1828-56, ca. .45 cu. ft.

    Record [Certificates by Clerk of Registration of Voters Acts], 1902-04, [1885-1951], 1 vol.

Fiduciary Records

    Administrators' and Executors' Accounts to which there are Exceptions, 1808-35, ca. .2 cu. ft.

    Administrators', Executors', Guardians', Curators', Committee, and Trustees' Bonds, [1749]-1851, 1875-1900, ca. 3.5 cu. ft.

    Administrators', Inspection, and Ordinary Bonds, 1749-1849, ca. .25 cu. ft.

    Estate Papers (estates of John Baker, Edward Burnett, John R. Cogbill, John Johnson, and Benjamin Thweatt), ca. 1800-80, ca. .5 cu. ft.; and, Appraisement of Estate of Francis B. Clopton, 1865, 1 item

    Fiduciary Bond Books, 1850-1909, 1870-73, 11 vols.

    Guardians' Bonds and Accounts, 1755-1850, n.d., ca. 3 cu. ft. See also Administrators' Bonds.

    Inventories, Appraisements, and Reports, 1794-1856, n.d., ca. 11 cu. ft. See also Wills.

    Miscellaneous Papers of Estates (bills, etc.), 1829-61, ca. .1 cu. ft.

    Record of Fiduciaries Vol. 1, 1850-64, 1 vol.

Free Negro and Slave Records

    Registers of Free Negroes Nos. [1]-3, 1804-53 (also Estrays, 1805-63), 3 vols.

    Registrations and Papers, 1797-1833, ca. 75 items

    See also Court Records, County and Superior Courts

Justice of the Peace Records

    Justices' Civil Warrants and Executions, 1886-92, 1895-1905, .7 cu. ft.

    Justices' Judgment and Execution Book, 1878-1907, 1 vol.

    Justices Qualified since May, 1852, [1852-56], ca. 25 items

    Papers relative to Warrants Returned by Constables, 1811, ca. 25 items

    Reports of Criminal Cases Disposed of by Justices of the Peace, 1888-1905, 1 vol.

Land Records

    Daily Index of Receipt of Deeds for Recordation, Grantor-Grantee, 1902-04, 1 vol.

    Deed Books Nos. 1-2, 1749-55, 2 vols. (copies)

    Index to Deed Book No. 41, Grantor-Grantee, 1854-59, 1 vol.

    Deeds, 1764-1904, n.d., ca. 31 cu. ft.

    Processioners' Reports, 1796-1800, ca. .1 cu. ft.

    Surveyors' Book, 1801-11, 1 vol. (copy)

    See also Tax and Fiscal Records

Marriage Records and Vital Statistics

    Marriage Bonds, 1771-1853, n.d., 3.15 cu. ft.

    Marriage Licenses, 1836, 1838, 1850-1912, 8.55 cu. ft.

    Marriage Registers, 1771-1853, 2 vols. (Ms. compilation and copy)

    Indexes to Marriage Register, 1771-1853, 2 vols. (Ms. compilation and copy)

    Ministers' Returns, 1780-1853, .35 cu. ft.

    Register of Deaths, Lower and Upper Districts, 1855-70, 1 vol.

Military and Pension Records

    Courts Martial Minutes, 1760, 1 item

    Militia Muster Rolls, Fines, and Minutes, 1843-55, ca. .2 cu. ft.

    Qualification of William Dyson as Lieutenant, 1812, 1 item

Organization Records

Magna Carta of the Chesterfield Bar [a list of fees agreed to be charged], 1807-30, 2 items

Chesterfield Grange No. 184, Roll Call List, n.d., 1 vol.

Church and Lodge Papers [removed from other series?], 1892-1937, .35 cu. ft.

Patrons of Husbandry withdrawal card, 1874, 1 item

Virginia State Farmers' Alliance Minutes, Secretary's Book, 1889-94, 1 vol.

Road and Bridge Records

Delinquent Road Fines Returned by Ambrose Bassets, 1814 [1874?], ca. 50 items

Overseer of Roads Bonds, Oaths, and Accounts, 1871-74, ca. .1 cu. ft.

Road Accounts, 1870, ca. 50 items

Road District No. 2 Papers, 1864, ca. .1 cu. ft.

Road Petitions and Final Orders, 1874-78, and Road Petitions, 1881-1900, ca. .35 cu. ft.

Road Reports, 1806-20, ca. 50 items

Road Warrants (also poor and jury warrants), 1860-1904, ca. 1 cu. ft. See also Tax and Fiscal Records.

School Records

Report of School Superintendent, 1861, 10 pp.

School Board Clerk's Correspondence, etc., 1900-12, 1 cu. ft.

School Commissioner's Account, 1822, 1 item

School Commissioner's Report, 1823, 1 item

School Superintendents' Bonds, 1849, 1852, 2 items

Tax and Fiscal Records

Applications for Purchase of Delinquent Lands, Deeds, and Release Deeds, 1872-1907, ca. 50 items

Claims see Miscellaneous Records

Delinquent Capitation and Personal Property Taxes [Nos. 1-2], 1896-1908, 2 vols. See also Warrant Book.

Delinquent Lands and Sales for Taxes, 1886-1904, 3 vols.

Delinquent Tax Lists, 1791-1819, ca. .1 cu. ft.

Land Taxes, 1889-1902, 4 pp.

Land Tax Receipts, 1895-98, ca. .1 cu. ft.

Land Transfer Book, 1896-1906, 1 vol.

Lists of Delinquent Land, 1832-33, 1851, 4 items

Lists of Delinquent Personal Property for 1863, [1864], 5 items

Lists of Taxable Property, 1846, 1850-53, 1 cu. ft.

Lists of Tithables, 1747-1821, n.d., ca. .25 cu. ft.; and, 1776-78, 3 items (copies)

Personal Property Book, 1823, 1 vol.

Personal Property Tax Receipts, Manchester, 1903-15, ca. .1 cu. ft

Reports of writ taxes, 1851-63, 7 items

Sundry Accounts [against the County], 1839-40, ca. .1 cu. ft.

Tithables, 1756, 1758, 1776-78, n.d., 7 vols.

Warrant Book (includes delinquent taxes), 1873-82, 1 vol.

See also Miscellaneous Records

Township Records

Bermuda Township Records [Minutes], 1871-78 (includes Magisterial District, 1875-78), 1 vol.

Dale Township Board Minutes, 1870-75, 1 vol.

Manchester Township Board Minutes, 1870-76 (includes Magisterial District, 1875-76), 1 vol.

Matoaca Township Board Record [Minutes], 1870-75, 1 vol.

Midlothian Township Records [Minutes], 1870-76 (includes Magisterial District, 1875-76), 1 vol.; and, Accounts, 1871-75, 1 vol.

Township Warrant, 1875, 1 item

Wills

    Will Books Nos. 1-4, 1749-1800, 4 vols. (copies)

    Wills, 1740-54, 3.6 cu. ft.

    Wills, Inventories, Appraisements, Accounts, etc., 1855-1904, n.d., ca. 9.75 cu. ft.

Miscellaneous Records

    Claims, Estrays, and Miscellaneous Papers, (including tax and fiscal records), 1757-1853, ca. .1 cu. ft.

    Conditional Sales of Personal Property No. 7, and Miscellaneous Lien Book No. 1, 1890-1902, 1 vol.

    Estray Notices, 1800-44, 1861, .35 cu. ft. See also Free Negro and Slave Records.

    Inquests, 1783-1853, ca. .1 cu. ft. See also Court Records, County and Superior Courts.

    Jail Record List of Prisoners and Jailer's Accounts, 1868-79, 1 vol.

    Jury Warrants, see Road and Bridge Records

    Mechanics' Liens No. 1, 1870-1920, 1 vol.

    Petition (ardent spirits), n.d., 1 item

    Phillip V. Cogbill, attorney, correspondence (includes Cooperative Extension Work in Agriculture and Home Economics), 1890-1930, ca. .25 cu. ft.

    Poor Warrants, 1899-1905, ca. .5 cu. ft. See also Road and Bridge Records.

    Receipts, 1833, 5 items

    Record of Estrays, 1869-1905, 1 vol. See also Free Negro and Slave Records.

    Reports of Overseers of the Poor, 1804-49, ca. .1 cu. ft.

    [Washington A. Brown's?] Memorandum Book, 1892, 1 vol. (fragment)

    William E. Winfree Family Papers, 1830-40, ca. .25 cu. ft.

Commissioner of Revenue

    Land Books [titles vary], 1813-56, 1870, 1875, 1885-86, 1888-89, 11 vols.

    List of Lands and Lots Placed on Commissioners' Book, 1832, 1 item

    Personal Property Interrogatories, 1892-1904, 2 cu. ft.

    See also Tax and Fiscal Records

Sheriff

    Sheriff W. C. Gill's Papers, 1901-21, 2.1 cu. ft.

    Sheriff's Accounts, 1804-10, ca. .15 cu. ft.

    Sheriffs' Lists of Insolvents, 1782-1802, ca. .1 cu. ft.

    Sheriffs' Receipts for Fees, 1820-35, ca. .1 cu. ft.

Treasurer

    County Warrants [includes court warrants], 1741-70, 1804-1905, ca. 1.75 cu. ft.

    Treasurers' Accounts, Receipts, and County Court Orders, 1810-41, 1.7 cu. ft.

    Treasurers' Correspondence, etc., 1813-1938, ca. 2 cu. ft.

    Treasurers' Reports to the Board of Supervisors, 1874-1917, 1 vol.

    See also Tax and Fiscal Records

Microfilm Records

Circuit Court Clerk
Court Records
County Court
Order Books Nos. 1-33 and 37-39 [there are no Order Books 34-36], 1749-1865, 18 reels
Land Records
Deed Books Nos. 1-47, 1749-1866, 21 reels
General Index to Deeds, Grantors-Grantees A-Z, 1749-1913, 4 reels
Marriage Records and Vital Statistics
Marriage Bonds, 1770-1854, 19 reels
Marriage Records No. 3, 1772-1854, 1 reel (part); and, Marriage Records, 1836-1912, 12 reels
Marriage Register, 1771-1853 (Ms. compilation), 1 reel (part); and, Marriage Register No. 1, [1853]-96, 1 reel (part)
Index to Marriage Register, 1771-1853 (Ts. compilation), 1 reel (part)
Ministers' Returns, 1780-1860, 4 reels (part)
Military and Pension Records
Muster Roll, 1812-65, 1 reel (part)
Tax and Fiscal Records
Land Books, 1864, 1888, 1914, 1927-31, 1942, 1956, 1965, 9 reels
Wills
Will Books Nos. 1-23, 1749-1865, 11 reels

CLARKE COUNTY

Formed in 1836 from Frederick County.
Part of Warren County was added later.

Microfilm Records

Circuit Court Clerk
Court Records
County Court
Order Books A-B, 1836-58, 1 reel; and, Minute Book C, 1858-62, 1 reel
Circuit Superior Court of Law and Chancery
Chancery Order Book A, 1836-57 (includes Circuit Court, 1852-57), 1 reel (part)
Circuit Court
Chancery Order Book B, 1857-60, 1 reel (part). See also Circuit Superior Court of Law and Chancery.
Fiduciary Records
[Administrators'] Bonds, 1836-50, 1 reel (part)
[Executors'] Bonds, 1836-50, 1 reel (part)
Guardians' Bonds, 1836-1904, 1 reel (part)
Land Records
Deed Books A-G, 1836-66, 4 reels
General Index to Deeds, Grantors-Grantees A-Z, 1836-1934, 2 reels

Marriage Records and Vital Statistics
    Marriage Bonds [and records], 1836-50, 1 reel (part)
    Index to Marriage Licenses, Certificates, etc., 1836-65, 1 reel (part)
    Marriage Registers Nos. 1-3, 1865-1933, 1 reel (part)
Military and Pension Records
    Muster Roll, 1861-65 (also World War I [1917-18]), 1 reel (part)
Wills
    Will Books A-E (includes inventories, accounts, etc.), 1836-67, 2 reels
    General Index to Wills, 1836-1904, 1 reel (part)
    Circuit Court Will Book A, 1841-78 (includes Circuit Superior Court of Law and
        Chancery, 1841-51), 1 reel (part)
    General Index to Circuit Court Wills, A-Z, 1841-52, 1 reel (part)

CRAIG COUNTY

**Formed in 1851 from Botetourt, Roanoke, Giles,
and Monroe (West Virginia) counties. Parts of
Alleghany, Giles, Monroe, and Montgomery
counties were added later.**

Original Records

Circuit Court Clerk
  Land Records
    List of Deeds Recorded, 1893, 1 item

Microfilm Records

Circuit Court Clerk
  Court Records
    County Court
      Order Books Nos. 1-2, 1851-63, 1 reel
  Land Records
    Deed Books B-C, 1851-84, 2 reels
    General Index to Deeds, Grantor-Grantee, 1851-1912, 1 reel
    Platt [sic] Book, 1851-1932, 1 reel
  Marriage Records and Vital Statistics
    Register of Births, 1864-96, 1 reel (part)
    Register of Marriages No. 1, 1865-1937, 1 reel (part)
  Military and Pension Records
    Muster Roll, 1861-65, 1 reel
    See also Montgomery County Military and Pension Records
  Wills
    Will Book A, 1851-67, 1 reel

CULPEPER COUNTY

Formed in 1749 from Orange County.

Original Records

Circuit Court Clerk
Land Records
Deed Books A-G, R, and No. 14, 1749-75, 1791-94, 1858-64, 9 vols. (copies)
Marriage Records and Vital Statistics
Marriage Registers, 1781-1853, 2 vols. (Ms. compilation and copy)
Indexes to Marriage Registers, 1781-1853, 2 vols. (Ts. and copy)
Tax and Fiscal Records
Accounts Current [of rents], 1764, 10 pp. (copies)
Quitrent Accounts, 1773, 3 pp. (copies)
Rentals, 1764, 33 pp. (copies)
Wills
Will Books [A]-C, 1749-91, 3 vols. (copies)

Microfilm Records

Circuit Court Clerk
Court Records
County Court
Minute Books, 1763-64, 1 reel (part); and, Minute Books Nos. 1-6, 8, 10-16, and 18-25 [Nos. 7, 9, and 17 are missing], 1798-1869, 8 reels
Land Records
Deed Books A-ZZ and Nos. 1-14, 1749-1864, 28 reels
Index to Deeds, Grantors-Grantees A-Z, 1749-1913, 3 reels
Land Causes Nos. 1-2, 1810-26, 1831-[n.d.], 1 reel (part)
Marriage Records and Vital Statistics
Birth Records, 1864-96, 1 reel (part)
Death Records, 1864-96, 1 reel (part)
Marriage Register, 1781-1853 (Ms. compilation), 1 reel (part)
Index to Marriage Register, 1781-1853 (Ms. compilation), 1 reel (part)
Marriage Registers Nos. 2-3, 1850-97, 1 reel
Index to Marriage Records, Male-Female A-Z, [1781-1948], 1 reel
Military and Pension Records
Fifth Regiment, Militia Proceedings, 1815, 1 reel (part)
Wills
Will Books A-V, 1749-1868, 7 reels
Superior Court Will Books Nos. 1-2, 1811-27, 1831-70, 1 reel
General Index to Wills No. 1, 1749-1930, 1 reel

CUMBERLAND COUNTY

Formed in 1749 from Goochland County.

Original Records

Circuit Court Clerk
Board of Supervisors Records
Warrant Receipt Stub Books, 1876-86, 1889-1904, 5 vols.
Bonds/Commissions/Oaths
[Apprenticeship] Indentures, 1800-83, ca. .2 cu. ft.
Bonds, Captain Carter Harrison's Cavalry Troop, 1861, ca. 50 items
Circuit Court Bond Books, 1875-98, 1887-1904, 2 vols.
Constables' Bonds, 1830-60, ca. .1 cu. ft.
County Court Bond Books, 1887-1902, 2 vols.
County Court Officers' Bond Book, 1879-1905, 1 vol. See also Fiduciary Records.
Delivery Bonds, 1790-1831, n.d., ca. .3 cu. ft.
General Index to Bonds, n.d., 1 vol.
Injunction Bonds, 1820-30, ca. .15 cu. ft.
[Justices'] Commissions, 1807-65, 20 items
Miscellaneous Bonds (including officials' and other bonds), 1795-1825, 1865, .45 cu. ft.
Officials' Bonds, see Fiduciary Records
Ordinary License Bonds, [A-W], ca. 1800-60, .45 cu. ft. See also Tax and Fiscal Records.
Recognizance Bonds, 1853-68, ca. 100 items
Refunding Bonds, 1858-59, 1863-64, 1867, 10 items
Replevy Bonds, 1784-96, 1829, ca. .2 cu. ft.
Sheriffs' Bonds, A-W, 1748-ca. 1860, .45 cu. ft.
See also Court Records, County and Superior Courts
Business Records/Organization/Partnerships
A. &. D. S[mith] Letter Book, 1829-41, 1 vol.
A. C. S. Ledgers C-D, 1836-43, 2 vols.
Alexis M. Davenport Journal to Ledger A, 1816, 1 vol.
A[rmistead] & M[cAshan] Ledger, 1836-38, 1 vol.
B. B. I. Journal C, 1824-25, 1 vol.; and, Ledger C, 1824-25, 1 vol.
B[enjamin] H. Powell, Muddy Creek Mill Account Book, 1847-49, 1 vol.; and, Day Book, 1852-54, 1 vol.
[Charles R. Carrington's?] Day Book, 1842-43, 1 vol.
C. R. Palmore, M.D., Account Book, 1870-76, 1 vol.
Eubank & Dunaway, Lancaster C. H., Journal, 1855-56, 1 vol.
F. Woodson's Account Book, 1795-1800, 1 vol.
James & Samuel Boyd Account Books, 1798 (includes inventories), 1800, 2 vols.
[James Smith's?] Account Book, 1840-43, 1 vol.
Robert M. Moore's Account Book, 1833-42, 1 vol.
S. & M. Ledger, 1856-68, 1 vol.
Unidentified [doctor's?] Account Book, 1844, 1 vol.
[William D. Austin's?] Ledgers, 1831, 2 vols.
Census Records
Enumerations, 1850, 1880, 2 vols.
Court Records
County Court
Causes Determined, 1773-1800, 1828, 6 cu. ft. See also Suit Papers.
Chancery Causes Struck from Docket at May Court, 1853, .5 cu. ft.

Chancery Dismissions and Abatements, 1815-20, ca. .1 cu. ft.

Chancery Issue Docket, 1822-71, 1 vol.

Chancery Rule Dockets, 1810-21 and 1826-72, 1822, 2 vols.

Clerk's Reports [of probate, licenses, etc.], 1814-58, ca. 50 items

[Clerk's] Tax Book, 1898-1904, 1 vol.

Common Law Issue Dockets, 1846-84, 2 vols.

Copies of Court Orders, 1839-62, ca. 100 items

Dead Papers (and Miscellaneous), ca. 1770-1830, ca. .25 cu. ft.

Execution Books, 1783-88, 1799-1826, 1830-38, 1851-1919 (includes Circuit Court, 1904-19), 11 vols.

Indexes to Execution Books Nos. [1?]-2, 1846-[?], n.d., 2 vols.

Executions (and Executions on Warrants), 1765-1873, 7.85 cu. ft. See also Suit Papers.

Fee Books, 1752-58, 1761-62, 1769-70, 1773-74, 1786-94, 1797-1860, 1873-83, 47 vols.

Index to Fee Book, n.d., 1 vol.

Grand Jury Presentments, 1799-1820, ca. .15 cu. ft.

Injunctions at Issue, 1796-1842, ca. .5 cu. ft.

Issue Dockets, 1797, 1800, 1805, 1809-12, 1814-16, 1818-32, 1835-43, 35 vols.

Indexes to Issue Dockets, 1812-13, 2 vols.

Judgments, 1800-66, 25.6 cu. ft.; and, Judgments on Petition, 1794-95, ca. 150 items. See also Suit Papers.

Law Docket, 1884-99, 1 vol.

List of Writings Committed to Records, 1891, 1 item

Memorandum Books, 1806-09, 1813-14, 1816-17, 1820-21, 1824, 1826-35, 8 vols.

Minute Books, 1749-50, 1783-94, 1799-1815, 1812, 1817-19, 1821-36, 1850-69, 26 vols.; and, 1752-79, 2 vols. (copies)

Office Judgments, 1811-21, 1824-73, 3 vols.

Old Appeals on Warrants, ca. 1815-65, ca. 150 items

Orders, 1749-51, 1762-64, 1779-84, 4 vols. (copies)

Rule Dockets, 1798, 1807-09, 1812-15, 1817, 1821-36, 16 vols.

Subpoenas, 1825-63, 1 cu. ft.

Suit Papers, ca. 1750-1800, 13.9 cu. ft. See also Causes Determined, Judgments, and Executions.

Witness Attendance Books, 1809-84, 2 vols.

Superior Court of Law

Chancery Causes Determined, [1773], 1817-67 (includes Circuit Superior Court of Law and Chancery, 1831-51, and Circuit Court, 1852-67), 7.35 cu. ft.

Common Law and Office Judgments, 1829-64 (includes Circuit Superior Court of Law and Chancery, 1831-51, and Circuit Court, 1852-64), 7.35 cu. ft.

Dead Papers (and Miscellaneous), 1809-63 (includes Circuit Superior Court of Law and Chancery, 1831-51, and Circuit Court, 1852-63), .25 cu. ft.

Execution [Process] Books, 1809-31, 2 vols.

Executions, 1809-64 (includes Circuit Superior Court of Law and Chancery, 1831-51, and Circuit Court, 1852-64), 2 cu. ft.

Fee Books, 1809-31, 6 vols.

Issue Dockets, 1810-31, 7 vols.

Judgments, 1810-29, 3 cu. ft.

Memorandum Books, 1814-18, 1821-25, 2 vols.

Minute Books, 1809-30, 3 vols.

Rule Books, 1809-31, 3 vols.

Subpoenas, 1809-57 (includes Circuit Superior Court of Law and Chancery, 1831-51, and Circuit Court, 1852-57), ca. .35 cu. ft.

Witness Attendance Book, 1809-30, 1 vol.

Circuit Superior Court of Law and Chancery

Chancery Causes Determined, see Superior Court of Law

Chancery Issue Docket, 1832-50, 1 vol.

Chancery Rules No. 1, 1831-51, 1 vol.

Common Law and Office Judgments, see Superior Court of Law

Common Law Issue Docket, 1831-41, 1 vol.; and, Common Law Docket, 1842-46, 1 vol.

Common Law Rule Dockets, 1831-84 (includes Circuit Court, 1852-84), 2 vols.

Dead Papers, see Superior Court of Law

Execution Books Nos. 1-3, 1831-67 (includes Circuit Court, 1852-67), 3 vols. See also Superior Court of Law.

Fee Books, 1831-52, 7 vols.

Memorandum Book, 1845-54 (includes Circuit Court, 1852-54), 1 vol.

Minute Books, 1831-82 (includes Circuit Court, 1852-82), 2 vols.

Miscellaneous Papers, 1831-51, ca. 200 items

Office Judgments Nos. 1-[3], 1831-1907 (includes Circuit Court, 1852-1907), 3 vols. See also Superior Court of Law.

Process Book, 1831-53 (includes Circuit Court, 1852-53), 1 vol.

Rule Book, 1836-73 (includes Circuit Court, 1852-73), 1 vol.

Subpoena Docket, 1831, 1 vol.

Subpoenas, 1832, ca. 50 items. See also Superior Court of Law.

Witness Attendance Books [titles vary], 1831-48, 1850-81 (includes Circuit Court, 1852-81), 2 vols.

Circuit Court

Chancery Causes Determined, see Superior Court of Law

Chancery Docket, 1886-98, 1 vol.

Chancery Issue Dockets, 1851, 1870-86, 2 vols.

Chancery Rules [No. 2], 1852-1904, 1 vol.

[Clerk's] Tax Book, 1898-1905, 1 vol.

Common Law and Office Judgments, see Superior Court of Law

Common Law Issue Dockets, 1857-1924, 2 vols.

Common Law Rule Docket, 1884-1922, 1 vol. See also Circuit Superior Court of Law and Chancery.

Dead Papers, see Superior Court of Law

Execution Books Nos. 1-2, 1867-1917, 2 vols. See also County Court and Circuit Superior Court of Law and Chancery.

Executions, see Superior Court of Law

Fee Books, 1852-63, 1869-75, 1900-07, 3 vols.

Memorandum Books, 1854-74, 1883-1908, 2 vols. See also Circuit Superior Court of Law and Chancery.

Minute Book, see Superior Court of Law

Office Judgments, see Superior Court of Law and Circuit Superior Court of Law and Chancery

Receipt [Process] Book, 1853-98, 1 vol. See also Circuit Superior Court of Law and Chancery.

Rule Book, see Circuit Superior Court of Law and Chancery

Subpoenas, 1856-57, ca. 100 items, see also Superior Court of Law and Circuit Superior Court of Law and Chancery.

Witness Attendance Book, see Circuit Superior Court of Law and Chancery

County and Superior Courts

Judgment Docket No. 1, 1842-77, 1 vol.

Judgment Lien Docket, 1884-92, 1 vol.

General Indexes to Judgment Lien Docket, 1843-1916, 2 vols.

Miscellaneous Papers (including bonds, road papers, court papers, etc.), ca. 1760-1850, ca. 1 cu. ft.

Register of Convicts, 1871-98, 1 vol.

Subpoenas (also bonds, insolvent lists, declarations, decrees, etc.), 1773-1867, ca. 150 items

Unspecified Court

Indexes [to executions or orders?], n.d., 4 vols.

Election Records

Election and Convention Polls, 1802-62, .9 cu. ft.; and, Oak Forest Poll, 1856, 1 item

Lists of Voters, 1853-56, 1861, 1866, 5 items

Lists of Voters, 4th District, 1856, 1858, 1867, 3 vols.

Poll Books, 1850-53, 1855-56, 1858-65, 16 vols.

Report of Commissioners Districting County, 1852, 1 item

Rolls of Registered Voters, 1902-55 [overlapping dates], 27 vols.

Fiduciary Records

Administrators' Bonds, [A-Y], 1749-1862, 4.5 cu. ft.

Estate Records [inventories, accounts, etc.], [A-Y], 1749-1865, ca. 10 cu. ft. See also Land Records.

Executors' and Administrators' Accounts, see Estate Records

Executors' Bonds, [A-Y], 1749-1860, 2.7 cu. ft.

Fiduciary [and Officials] Bond Book, 1850-81, 1 vol.

Fiduciary Settlements No. 1, 1900-28, 1 vol.

Guardians' Bonds (and Accounts), 1749-ca. 1870, 1.9 cu. ft.; and, Guardians' Committee, and Curators' Accounts, 1790-1872, .9 cu. ft.

Index to Guardians' Account Book, n.d., 1 vol.

Inventory, Estate of Benjamin Johnson, 1826, 1 vol.; and, Sale Book, 1826, 1 vol.

Lists of Fiduciaries, 1850-1903, 2 vols.

Reports of Charles Ballow, Committee of Jessee Ballow, 1808-44, ca. 50 items

Tait v. DeEnde's admr. (of Cumberland County), suit in Second District Court, New Orleans, 1841-45, 1 item

Free Negro and Slave Records

List of Free Negroes Detailed for Hospital Service at Farmville, 1862, 1 item

Lists of Negroes to Work on Fortifications, 1864-65, 5 items

Lists of Registers of Free Negroes, 1821-61, ca. .2 cu. ft.

Justice of the Peace Records

Appointments, 1769, 8 items

Executions and Warrants, 1885-1934, 1 vol.

Judgment Book, 1833-36 and 1852-68, 1 vol.

Land Records

Deed Books Nos. 1-3 and 5-6, 1749-65, 1771-90, 6 vols. (copies)

Deeds, 1749-1878, n.d., ca. 8 cu. ft.; and, Deeds, Wills, and Inventories Recorded in Superior Court, ca. 1810-70, 30 items

Deeds, [A-W], and Wills not Fully Proven, 1780-1850, .9 cu. ft.

Deeds of Release and Trust, 1831-47, ca. 50 items

[Index to Deeds, n.d.], 1 vol.

General Indexes to Deeds, 1749-1912, 2 vols. (Ts.)

Plats, 1793-1855, ca. 150 items

Processioners' Reports, ca. 1805-60, .45 cu. ft.

Processioners' Reports, 1808, 1824-41, 2 vols.

Marriage Records and Vital Statistics

Marriage Bonds and Consents, 1749-1866, n.d., and Ministers' Returns, 1854-65, 1.75 cu. ft.

Marriage Register, 1850-61, 1 vol.

Registers of Births, 1859, 1867-68, 3 vols.

Registers of Births and Deaths, 1854-55, 1857, 1860, 1862, 1879, 6 vols.

Registers of Deaths, 1858, 1865-66, 3 vols.

Military and Pension Records

List of Persons Between the Ages of 18 and 45 Liable to be Enrolled in the Militia, 1857, 1 vol.

Militia Appointments, 1839, 4 items

Minutes and Accounts, Cumberland Dragoons, 1857-62, 1 vol.

Muster Rolls and Payrolls, Captain Allen Wilson's Company, Militia, 1814-15, 1 vol.

Order Book, 1st Brigade, Virginia Militia, 1814 [labeled Execution Book], 1 vol.

Roll Book, Cumberland Troops, 1861-65 (includes Minutes, Reunions of Cumberland Troops, 1889-1912), 1 vol.

Road and Bridge Records

Bridge and Road Viewers' Reports, 1822-36, ca. 100 items

Madison District Road Board Correspondence (and Overseer of the Poor indentures), 1829-83, ca. 50 items

Road Books, 1803-70, 4 vols.

See also Court Records, County and Superior Courts

School Records

Madison District Accounts, 1871-80, 1 vol.; School Fund Receipt Book, 1871-79, 1 vol.; School Rolls, n.d., 2 items; Teachers [accounts with teachers, school census], 1875-85, 1 vol; and, Teachers' Pocket Records [of attendance, etc.], 1871-86, 13 vols.

School Commissioners' Reports, 1822-60, .45 cu. ft.

Tax and Fiscal Records

[Applications to Purchase Delinquent Land], 1884-1900, 1 vol.

Claims Against the County, 1845, ca. 50 items

County Levy Accounts and Settlements, ca. 1825-75, 40 items

D[elinquent] L[and] Sold to others than Com[monwealth] 1884-1934, 1 vol.

Inactive Vouchers, 1795-1825, ca. 150 items

Land Sold by Com[monwealth], 1886-1934, 1 vol.

Lists of Insolvents, see Court Records, County and Superior Courts

Merchants' (and Ordinary) Licenses, 1858-61, 1864-65, ca. 50 items

Old Insolvent Fees, 1830-39, ca. 100 items

Personal Property Books, 1783, 1785, 1787, 1792-93, 1798, 1804-07, 1810, 1812-13, 1815-17, 1820-26, 1830, 1833, 1836, 1839, 1841-43, 1846, 1850, 1854-55, 1857, [1864], 1892, 42 vols.

Reassessment of Lands, 1900, 1 vol.

Records of Delinquent Lands, 1884-91, 1896-1908, 2 vols.

Superior Court Schedules of Insolvent Debtors, 1843, 1845-58, 25 items

Tithables, 1758-59, 1763-66, 1772, n.d., 21 items

Unsettled Accounts, ca. 1830-1850, ca. 150 items

William H. Ranson's Tax Book, 1826, 1 vol.

Township Records

Madison Township Board Stub Book, 1875, 1 vol.

Wills

Will Books Nos. 1-3, 1749-1864, 5 reels

Wills, [A-Y], 1749-1865, ca. 4 cu. ft.; Will and Papers of Martha William, 1799-1845, ca. 50 items; and, Will of Benjamin Wilson, 1814, 1 item (copy)

General Index to Wills, 1749-1905, 1 vol. (Ts.)

Unrecorded Wills, 1834, 1836, 3 items

Wills not Fully Proven, see Land Records

Miscellaneous Records

Contract for Erection of the Courthouse, 1818, 7 pp. (copies)

Crop Lien Dockets Nos. 1-2, 1897-1910, 2 vols.

Estray Books, 1773-1850, 2 vols.

Estrays, 1808-09, ca. 50 items

Index to Federal Farm Credit Lien Book, n.d., 1 vol.

Inquisitions, 1811-66, 1872-1933, ca. .2 cu. ft.

Notes on Tucker's Blackstone's Commentaries, by John Daniel, 1824-25, 1 vol. (Ms.)

Overseers of the Poor Reports, 1850-64, ca. 50 items. See also Road and Bridge Records.

Petitions, 1749-1811, ca. 100 items

Proceedings of the Committee of Safety, 1775-76 (also Goochland County form book), 1 vol.

Reservation to Title to Personalty, 1891-1924, 1 vol.

Unidentified Indexes, 1831, n.d., 5 vols.

Commissioner of Revenue

Land Books, 1787-1846, 1850-78, 1884-96, 35 vols.

See also Tax and Fiscal Records

Sheriff

Sheriffs' Fee Book, 1835-81, 1 vol.

Treasurer

Record of Capitation Taxes, 1903-12, 1 vol.

Upper District Receipt Stub Book, n.d. [18?], 1 vol.

Microfilm Records

Circuit Court Clerk
Court Records
County Court

Order Books, 1749-1869, 14 reels

Fiduciary Records

Guardians' Accounts, 1769-1860, 1 reel

Land Records

Deed Books Nos. 1-29, 1749-1868, 14 reels

Superior Court Deed Book No. 1-A, 1809-27, 1 reel (part)

Index to Deeds, Grantor-Grantee A-Z, 1749-1918, 2 reels

Marriage Records and Vital Statistics

Marriage Bonds, 1749-1866, 7 reels

Marriage Licenses, 1908-12, 1 reel

Register of Births, 1853-70, 1 reel (part)

Register of Deaths, 1853-70, 1 reel (part)

Register of Marriages, 1854-1919, 1 reel (part)

Index to Registers of Births, Marriages, and Deaths, 1853-1919, 1 reel

Wills
> Will Books Nos. 1-13, 1749-1864, 5 reels
> Superior Court Will Book No. 1, 1820-87, 1 reel (part)
> General Index to Wills, 1749-1949, 1 reel

DICKENSON COUNTY

Formed in 1880 from Russell, Wise, and Buchanan counties.

As of 1 July 1985 there were no Dickenson County records in the Virginia State Library.

DINWIDDIE COUNTY

Formed in 1752 from Prince George County.

Original Records

Circuit Court Clerk
Business Records/Corporations/Partnerships
> Keeler and Scott Ledger, 1857-73, 1 vol.

Census Records
> Lists of Persons, Dinwiddie County and Petersburg, 1880, 17 vols.

Court Records
County Court
> Accounts of the Clerk [also labeled Record of Estrays], 1881-89, 1 vol.
> Chancery and Common Law Docket Book, 1859-88, 1 vol.
> Chancery Execution Docket No. 1, 1832-1904, 1 vol.
> [Clerk's] Tax Book, 1898-1911 (includes Circuit Court, 1904-11), 1 vol. See also Circuit Court.
> Court Papers, 1856-74, ca. .25 cu. ft.
> Execution Docket No. 3, 1846-1903, 1 vol.
> Order Book, 1789-91, 1 vol. (copy)
> Rule Docket, 1856-73, 1 vol.

Circuit Superior Court of Law and Chancery
> Chancery Issue Docket, 1847-63 (includes Circuit Court, 1852-63), 1 vol.
> Common Law Execution Docket No. 1, 1831-41, 1 vol.
> Execution Book No. 3, 1841-56 (includes Circuit Court, 1852-56), 1 vol.

Circuit Court
> Chancery Issue Docket, 1891-1941, 1 vol. See also Circuit Superior Court of Law and Chancery.
> Clerk's Account Book, 1897-1909 [County Court prior to 1904?], 1 vol.
> [Clerk's] Tax Book, 1899-1903, 1 vol. See also County Court.
> Common Law Docket, 1872-97, 1 vol.
> Execution Book No. 3, 1856-1905, 1 vol.; and, Execution Book No. 1, 1903-16, 1 vol. See also Circuit Superior Court of Law and Chancery.

Fee Books, 1891-1900, 1891-1909, 2 vols.
Old Cases in Appeals, 1902-26, ca. .1 cu. ft.
Process Books, 1875-1944, 2 vols.
Rule Docket, 1845-1902, 1 vol.
Subpoena and Witness Docket, 1871-79, 1 vol.

County and Superior Courts

Chancery Papers, 1832-1938, ca. 3.35 cu. ft.
Miscellaneous Court Papers, 1873-88, ca. .1 cu. ft.
Register of Convicts, 1871-1927, 1 vol.

Election Records

Poll, 1838, 1 item
Rolls of Registered Voters, White and Colored, 1902-49 [overlapping date ranges], 68 vols.

Fiduciary Records

Accounts, 1880-89, ca. .1 cu. ft.
Special Commissioners' Bonds, 1900-49, ca. .25 cu. ft.
See also Wills

Justice of the Peace Records

Criminal Cases, Trial Justice Court, 1901-30, 1 vol.
Justices' Judgments, 1866-1904, ca. .65 cu. ft.
Index to Judgments, Trial Justice Court, n.d., 1 vol.
Justices' Reports of Fines, 1898-1904, 1 vol.

Land Records

Deed Book No. 1, 1833-37, 1 vol. (copy)
Deeds, 1755-56, 1774, 1865-1922, 3 cu. ft.
General Index to Deeds No. 1, 1833-89, 1 vol.
[List of Deeds and Conveyances], 1900-04, 1 vol.
Surveyors' Plat Book, 1755-1865, 1 vol. (copy)
Index to Plat Books Nos. 1-2, n.d., 1 vol.
See also Wills

Marriage Records and Vital Statistics

Card Index [to Births?], 1873-76 [1853-96?], ca. .5 cu. ft.

Tax and Fiscal Records

Assessment Book, n.d., 1 vol.
Delinquent Land, 1885, 1897, ca. .85 cu. ft.
Delinquent Land Books, 1883-1903, 1885-1903, 3 vols.
Erroneous Assessment of Lands, 1897, ca. .25 cu. ft.
Insolvent Capitation and Property Taxes 1891, ca. .5 cu. ft.
Personal Property Books, 1875-1900, ca. 70 vols. (including fragments)
Tax Assessed, Namezine, Darvills, Rowanty, and Sapony Districts, 1901-02, 4 vols.

Wills

Wills, ca. 1755-1865, 35 items (copies); and, Miscellaneous Papers [mostly wills; also estate papers, deeds, etc.], 1704-1869, 36 items (copies)

Miscellaneous Records

Crop Lien Docket No. 1, 1892-1915, 1 vol.
Mechanics' Liens, 1874-1924, 1 vol.
Records of Meetings of Overseers of the Poor, 1831-70, 1 vol.

Commissioner of Revenue

Records of Improper Assessment, 1886-1923, 1 vol.
See also Tax and Fiscal Records

Treasurer
> Disbursements of County Levy by Treasurer, 1894-99, 1 vol.
> Land Books, 1885-1905, ca. 15 vols. (including fragments)
> See also Tax and Fiscal Records

Microfilm Records

Circuit Court Clerk
> **Court Records**
> > **County Court**
> > > Minute Books Nos. 1-4, 1855-73, 2 reels
> > > Order Book, 1789-91, 1 reel
> > **Superior Court of Law**
> > > Record Book [Rules and Office Judgments], 1819-41 (includes Circuit Superior Court of Law and Chancery, 1831-41), 1 reel (part)
> > **Circuit Superior Court of Law and Chancery**
> > > Chancery Order Book No. 1, 1832-52 (includes Circuit Court, 1852), 1 reel (part). See also Circuit Court.
> > > Record Book, see Superior Court of Law
> > **Circuit Court**
> > > Chancery Order Book No. 2, 1852-73, 1 reel (part). See also Circuit Superior Court of Law and Chancery.
> **Fiduciary Records**
> > Fiduciary Bonds, 1850-97, 1 reel (part)
> > Fiduciary Book, 1850-69, 1 reel (part)
> > Guardians' Accounts, 1844-1906, 1 reel
> **Land Records**
> > Deed Books Nos. 1-12, 1833-71, 7 reels
> > General Index to Deeds No. 1, 1833-89, 1 reel
> > Surveyors' Plat Book, 1755-1865, 1 reel
> **Marriage Records and Vital Statistics**
> > Marriage Registers, 1850-1916, 2 reels
> **Wills**
> > Will Books Nos. 1-8, 1830-75, 5 reels
> > Superior Court Will Book No. 1-A, 1830-97, 1 reel (part)
> > General Index to Wills, 1833-1949, 1 reel

Sheriff
> Sheriff's Execution Book, 1841-56, 1 reel (part)

DUNMORE COUNTY

**Formed in 1772 from Frederick County.
The name was changed in 1778 to
Shanando (now Shenandoah).**

For listing of records, see Shenandoah County.

ELIZABETH CITY COUNTY

**Original shire established in 1634.
It became extinct in 1952, when
it was incorporated into
the City of Hampton.**

For listing of records, see <u>A Preliminary Guide to Pre-1904 Municipal Records</u>, City of Hampton entry.

ESSEX COUNTY

Formed in 1692 from old Rappahannock County.

Original Records

Circuit Court Clerk
Board of Supervisors Records
Papers, [1870]-1933, ca. .25 cu. ft.
<u>See also</u> Court Records, County Court
Bonds/Commissions/Oaths
Bond Book, 1816-17 and 1820-25, 1 vol.
<u>See also</u> Court Records, County Court; and Wills
Business Records/Corporations/Partnerships
Rixberg & Battery Co., inventory, 1894, 1 item
Court Records
County Court, [Old] Rappahannock County
Order Books, 1683-92, 2 vols. (Ts. and copies)
County Court
Chancery Reference, 1815-21, 1 vol.
Court Papers, 1717-52 and 1798-1924 (including Board of Supervisors' Papers and land records), ca. .25 cu. ft.; and, Court Papers (including wills, deeds, bonds, etc.), [1652] 1677-1848, n.d., 40 items (copies)
Execution Books, 1793-98, 1820-31, 1834-74, 4 vols.; and, Execution Books Nos. [5]-9, 1802-16, 5 vols.
Index to Execution Book, n.d., 1 vol.
Executions, Judgments, etc., 1752-ca. 1865, 4.5 cu. ft.
Judgment [Rule] Books [Nos. 3-5?], 1794-1810, 3 vols.; and, Rule Book, 1822-28, 1 vol.
List of Fees due William B. Matthews, Clerk, 1817, 4 pp.
McCall Suit Papers, ca. 1770-1800, ca. .5 cu. ft., and 39 items (copies)
Orders, 1665-99, 2 vols. (copies); Orders [titles vary] Nos. 3-7, 9-24, and 27-32, 1703-14, 1716-29, 1733-43, 1745-63, 1767-82, 1784-94, 31 vols.; and, Order Books, 1834-38 (includes List of Acting Magistrates), 1838-41, 1845-51, 3 vols. <u>See also</u> Records.
Records [Orders, etc., No. 1, and Deeds, Wills, etc.], 1692-95, 1 vol. (copy). <u>See also</u> Orders.
Summons, [ca. 1740], 1791-1804, ca. 200 items
Superior Court of Law
Order Book, 1825-31, 1 vol.
Rule Book, 1809-31, 1 vol.

Circuit Superior Court of Law and Chancery

    Chancery Dockets Vols. 1-2, 1831-47, 2 vols.; and, No. 2, 1848-62 (includes Circuit Court, 1852-62), 1 vol.

    Chancery Rule Docket, 1831-88 (includes Circuit Court, 1852-88), 1 vol.

Circuit Court

    Chancery Docket, <u>see</u> Circuit Superior Court of Law and Chancery

    Chancery Rule Docket, <u>see</u> Circuit Superior Court of Law and Chancery

    Law Issue Docket, 1856-70, 1 vol.

County and Superior Courts

    Executions, ca. 1765-1850, 1 cu. ft.

    Judgments, 1785-1885, ca. .5 cu. ft.

    Papers, 1751-1924, ca. 2 cu. ft.

    Reports of Fines, 1886-1911, ca. .1 cu. ft.

    Suit Papers (also Wills and Deeds), 1801-1806, ca. 14.5 cu. ft.

Fiduciary Records

    Accounts of Orphans' Estates, 1731-60, 1 vol. (copy)

    Guardians' Book, 1829, 1 vol.; and, Orphans' Accounts [Guardians' Books], 1731-1811, 4 vols. (copies)

    List of Guardians, 1804-23, 1 vol. (copy)

    Record of Guardians' Bonds, 1850-71, 1 vol.

    <u>See also</u> Free Negro and Slave Records

Free Negro and Slave Records

    List of Negroes Belonging to those under a Guardian and Unsettled Estates, 1821-24, 1 vol.

Land Records

    [Old] Rappahannock County Records [deeds, wills, etc.], 1656-64, 1 vol, (Ts. and copy); Deeds, etc., Nos. 3-6, 1663-82, 4 vols. (Ts. and copies); and, Deed Books Nos. 7-8, 1682-88, 2 vols. (Ts. and copies). <u>See also</u> Wills.

    Deeds, etc. [titles vary], Nos. 9-11, 13-16, 18-21, 23-27 and 33, 1695-1704, 1707-21, 1724-38, 1742-57, 1786-93, 17 vols. (copies); and, Deed Book, 1809-30, 1 vol.

    Indexes to Records of [Old] Rappahannock, 1654-92, and Essex, 1692-1700, Grantors-Grantees, by Alvin T. Embrey, 11 vols. (copies)

    Land Trials [titles vary], 1711-60, 4 vols. (copies)

    Processioners' Returns, 1837, 1843, ca. .25 cu. ft.

    Survey Book, 1792-97, 1 item (copy)

    <u>See also</u> Court Records, County Court and County and Superior Courts; and, Wills

Marriage Records and Vital Statistics

    Marriage Bonds, 1804-50, 1853, 1.75 cu. ft.

    Ministers' Returns, 1850-53, 1 vol. (original and copy)

Road and Bridge Records

    Road Papers, 1886-1918, ca. .1 cu. ft.

    Road Surveyors' and Overseers' Appointments, 1838, ca. 100 items

    <u>See also</u> School Records

School Records

    [School and Road] Warrants, 1877-1900, ca. .2 cu. ft.

    School Board Papers, 1823-1915, .7 cu. ft.

    School Funds, Receipts, etc., 1873-91, ca. .15 cu. ft.

Tax and Fiscal Records

    Arrears of Quitrents, 1714, and Quitrent Roll, 1715, 4 pp. (copies); and, Quitrent Rolls, 1714-15, 2 items

    County Levy Papers, ca. 1830-50, ca. .25 cu. ft.

    Erroneous Assessments of Land, 1888-1906, and of Personal Property, 1886-1909, ca. .1 cu. ft.

Insolvent Lists, 1873, 1889-1904, ca. .2 cu. ft.
Memorandum of Warrants, etc., Levy of 1897, 2 items
See also Court Records, County Court

Wills

[Old] Rappahannock County Wills, Deeds, etc., No. 1, 1665-77, 1 vol. (Ts. and copy); and, Will Book No. 2, 1677-82, 1 vol. (Ts. and copy). See also Land Records.
Index to [Old] Rappahannock County Wills, see Land Records
Wills, Inventories, etc., Nos. 3-4, 1717-30, 2 vols. (copies); and, Will Books Nos. 5 and 7-14, 1730-35, 1743-92, 9 vols. (copies)
See also Court Records, County Court and County and Superior Courts; and, Land Records

Miscellaneous Records

Oyster Inspection Reports, 1887-92, ca. .15 cu. ft.
Personal Letters [various writers], 1847-78, 6 items

Sheriff

Sheriffs' Commissions, 1795, 1849, 2 items
Sheriff's Memorandum [Fees Due Clerks of Courts], 1817, 3 pp.

Treasurer

Lands Redeemed before Sale, 1876-1905, 22 items
Sale of Delinquent Land, 1897-1915, ca. .1 cu. ft.
Treasurers' Reports and Correspondence (includes delinquent land), 1817-1919, ca. .5 cu. ft.
See also Tax and Fiscal Records

Microfilm Records

Circuit Court Clerk
Court Records
County Court, [Old] Rappahannock County

Order Books [Nos. 1-2], 1683-92, 1 reel

County Court

Orders, etc. [Deeds, Wills, etc.] No. 1, 1692-95, 2 reels
Orders, 1695-99, 1 reel; and, Orders [Nos. 3-51], 1703-1858, 36 reels

Circuit Superior Court of Law and Chancery

Office Judgments No. 1, 1834-43, 1 reel

Circuit Court

Order Book No. 1, 1853-63, 1 reel

Fiduciary Records

Orphans' Accounts, 1731-60, 1 reel (part); and, Guardians' Books, 1761-1821, 1825-29, 1831-67, 4 reels
See also Wills

Land Records

[Old] Rappahannock County Records [deeds, wills, etc.; titles vary] Nos. [1] and 3-8, 1656-92, 9 reels. See also Wills.
Deeds, etc. [titles vary] Nos. 9-28, 1695-1761, 14 reels; and, Deed Books Nos. 29-51, 1761-1867, 21 reels. See also Court Records, County Court.
General Indexes to Deeds Vols. C and 1, 1722-1867, 1 reel
Index to Records of [Old] Rappahannock, 1654-92, and Essex, 1692-1700, Grantors-Grantees, by Alvin T. Embrey, 5 reels. See also Wills.
Land Trials, 1711-60, 1790-1818, 2 reels
Processioners' Returns, 1796-1814, 1816-37, 1843-56, 1 reel

Marriage Records and Vital Statistics
    Marriage Bonds, 1804–50, 6 reels
    Marriage Register, 1804–1921, 1 reel (part)
    Register of Births, 1856–1916, 1 reel (part)
    Register of Deaths, 1856–1916, 1 reel (part)
Military and Pension Records
    Record of Confederate Veterans, 1861–65, 1 reel (part)
Organization Records
    [United] Daughters of the Confederacy Records, 1898–1948, 1 reel (part)
Wills
    [Old] Rappahannock County Wills, Deeds, etc., Nos. 1–2, 1665–82, 2 reels. See also Land Records.
    General Index to Wills and Deeds Vol. A, 1654–91, 1 reel. See also Land Records.
    Circuit Court Wills, Bonds, Inventories, and Accounts, 1834–1902, 1 reel
    Wills, Inventories, etc., Nos. 3–28, 1717–1868, 23 reels
    General Index to Wills No. 1, 1717–1903, 1 reel
    See also Court Records, County Court; and Land Records

FAIRFAX COUNTY

Formed in 1742 from Prince William County.
See also Arlington County.

Original Records

Circuit Court Clerk
  Court Records
    County Court
      Court Papers [Records], 1731–1854, 20 items
      Order Book, 1772–74, 1 vol. (original and copy)
      Petition to the Court, 1746, 1 item (copy)
      Rule Docket, 1793, 1 vol. (copy)
      Washington v. Owens, answer in Chancery, 1789, 3 pp. (copies)
    County and Superior Courts
      Executions, 1851–52, 1857, 7 items
  Fiduciary Records
    Executors' Bond Book, 1773–87, 1 vol.
  Road and Bridge Records
    Road Petition, 1746, 1 item
  Tax and Fiscal Records
    Rent Rolls for Fairfax and Loudoun counties, 1761, 27 pp. (copies); and, Rent Rolls, Fairfax County, 1764, 1770, 1772, 1774, 68 pp. (copies)
    Tithables, 1749, 5 pp. (copies)

Sheriff
  Sheriff's Fee Book, 1817–18, 1 vol.

Microfilm Records

Circuit Court Clerk
Bonds/Commissions/Oaths
Bond Book, 1752-82, 1 reel (part)
Court Records
County Court
Order [Minute] Books, 1749-65, 1768-74, 1783-93, 1799-1800, 1807-08, 1824-27, 1829-31, 1835-60, 1863-67, 11 reels
Surname and Subject Index to County Court Records, 1749-1865, 618 microfiche cards
Land Records
Deed Books [Land Records], Libers A-1 through E-4, 1742-1865, 25 reels; and, Land Records (of long standing), 1742-70, 1 reel (part)
General Indexes to Deeds Nos. 1-3, 1742-1866, 1 reel
Land Causes No. 1, 1788-1824, 1812-32, 1 reel (part)
Record of Surveys, 1742-1856, 1 reel (part)
Marriage Records and Vital Statistics
Marriage Register No. 1, 1853-1906, 1 reel (part); and, Register of Marriages, 1853-1933, 1 reel (part)
Register of Births, 1853-69, 1 reel (part)
Register of Deaths, 1853-69, 1 reel (part)
Index to Births, Marriages, and Deaths, 1853-1933, 1 reel (part)
Military and Pension Records
Muster Roll, 1861-65, 1 reel (part)
Wills
Copies of Wills of George and Martha Washington, and other . . . records of Fairfax, Virginia, published by E. Richardson Holbrook, 1904, 1 reel (part)
Will Books, Libers A-1 through Z-1, 1742-1866, 9 reels
Superior Court Will Book, 1809-64, 1 reel (part)
General Index to Wills No. 1, 1742-1855, 1 reel (part); and, Index to Wills, etc., 1855-1951, 1 reel (part)
Miscellaneous Records
Miscellaneous Loose Papers (including wills; inventory available), 1742-1861, 1 reel (part)

FAUQUIER COUNTY

Formed in 1759 from Prince William County.

Original Records

Circuit Court Clerk
Bonds/Commissions/Oaths
Officers Bond Book No. 1, 1899-1927, 1 vol.
Business Records/Corporations/Partnerships
Charters No. 2, 1890-1924, 1 vol.
Depot House [Hotel] Daily Register, 1866-70, 1 vol.
E. A. W. Hore's [Store?] Account Book, 1871-73, 1 vol.
J. W. Bailey's Sawmill Account Book, 1897-98, 1 vol.

Marshall & Joseph Smith's [Store] Journal, Elk Run Church, 1816-20, 1 vol.

Partnership Matters of Brooke and Scott, 1843-87, 1 vol.

Unidentified Account Book, 1871-73, 1 vol.; and, Account Books A-[B], 1871-90, 2 vols.

Unidentified Store Day Book, Oak Hill, 1833-34, 1 vol.

Unidentified [Store] Ledger C, 1887-93, 1 vol.

Census Records

Enumeration Books, 1880, 10 vols.

Court Records

County Court

Chancery [Rule] Docket, 1871-73, 1 vol.

[Clerk's Fees for Copies], 1800-01, 1 vol.

Execution Books Nos. [2]-43, 1770-1910 (includes Circuit Court, 1904-10), 42 vols.; and, Executions, 1805-06, 1 vol.

Fee Books, 1770-83, 1787-88, 1794-95, 1822-29, 1831, 1859-60, 1873-1903, 15 vols. See also Rough Chargers.

Felony Register, 1891-96, 1 vol.

Issue Docket, 1860-68, 1 vol.

Law Execution Books A-E, 1809-41, 5 vols.

Law Issue Dockets [titles vary], 1820-24, 1833-98, 7 vols.

Memorandum Books, 1821-92, 2 vols.

Minutes, 1759-64, 1788-91 [Orders, Judgments, and Decrees], 1795-97, 4 vols. (copies); and, Minutes, 1797-99, 1812-19, 2 vols.

Motion Docket, 1869-1903, 1 vol.

Robert Brent & Co. v. Mooney, bond and notice of judgment, 1823-24, 2 items

Rough Chargers [fee accounts], 1842-45, 1856-58, 1869-80, 1873-96, 1895-1903, 1902-17 (includes Circuit Court, 1904-17), 13 vols.

Rough Docket of Chancery Causes, 1837-52, 1 vol.

Rule Books, 1789-92, 1806-07, 1814-26, 1837-40, 1843-51, 1860-72, 11 vols.

Subpoenas in Chancery, 1829-51, 4 vols.

Suggestion Docket, 1869-1902, 1 vol.

Summons, 1795, 1 item

Witness Books, 1880-1903, 2 vols.

Superior Court of Law

Fee Books, 1809-21, 2 vols.

Law Issue Docket, 1809-26, 1 vol.; and, Issue Docket, 1826-33 (includes Circuit Superior Court of Law and Chancery, 1831-33), 1 vol.

Rule Books, 1809-40 (includes Circuit Superior Court of Law and Chancery, 1831-40), 2 vols.

Witness Books, 1809-16, 1820-44 (includes Circuit Superior Court of Law and Chancery, 1831-44), 3 vols.

Circuit Superior Court of Law and Chancery

Chancery Court Dockets, 1831-52 (includes Circuit Court, 1852), 3 vols.

[Chancery] Executions, 1833-1917 (includes Circuit Court, 1852-1917), 1 vol.

Chancery Fee Books, 1831-54 (includes Circuit Court, 1852-54), 3 vols.

[Chancery] Process Book, 1831-59 (includes Circuit Court, 1852-59), 1 vol.

Chancery Rule Dockets Nos. 1-3 [titles vary], 1831-55 (includes Circuit Court, 1852-55), 3 vols.

Commonwealth Cases [Law Issues?], 1831-44, 1 vol.

Fee Books, 1831-38, 1843-48, 3 vols.

Issue Docket, 1848-51, 1 vol. See also Superior Court of Law.

John Marr, Commissioner in Chancery, Account Book, 1844-47, 1 vol.

[Law] Execution Books Nos. 1-9, 1831-1916 (includes Circuit Court, 1852-1916), 9 vols.

Law Fee Books, 1839-42, 1849-56 (includes Circuit Court, 1852-56), 2 vols.

[Law] Process Books, 1831-69 (includes Circuit Court, 1852-69), 3 vols.

Law Rule Dockets, 1840-77 (includes Circuit Court, 1852-77), 3 vols. See also Superior Court of Law.

Memorandum Books, 1831-58 (includes Circuit Court, 1852-58), 3 vols.

Witness Books, 1845-95 (includes Circuit Court, 1852-95), 1 vol. See also Superior Court of Law.

Circuit Court

Accounts of Court Cases, 1853-81, 1 vol.

Caffrey & Carpenter v. Gordon, exhibit, 1852, 1 vol.

Chancery Argument and Motion Dockets [titles vary], 1869-95, 4 vols.

Chancery Court Dockets, 1853-1913, 6 vols. See also Circuit Superior Court of Law and Chancery.

Chancery Executions, see Circuit Superior Court of Law and Chancery

Chancery Fee Books, 1855-1917, 5 vols. See also Circuit Superior Court of Law and Chancery.

Chancery Memorandum Books, 1873-1903, 1876-1910, 3 vols.

Chancery Process Book, 1860-1926, 1 vol. See also Circuit Superior Court of Law and Chancery.

Chancery Rule Dockets, 1856-77, 1869-1910, 1895-1918, 4 vols. See also Circuit Superior Court of Law and Chancery.

[Clerk's] Tax Books, 1898-1907, n.d., 2 vols.

Commissioners' [in Chancery] Dockets, 1889-1916, 2 vols.

Common Law Rule Dockets, 1878-1909, 2 vols. See also Circuit Superior Court of Law and Chancery.

Commonwealth Cases [Law Issues?], 1861-79, 1 vol.

Execution Book, 1857-74, 1 vol. See also County Court.

Fee Book, 1859-60, 1 vol.

Law Executions, see Circuit Superior Court of Law and Chancery

Law Fee Books, 1857-1907, 4 vols. See also Circuit Superior Court of Law and Chancery.

Law Issue Docket, 1901-18, 1 vol.

Law Memorandum, 1876-90, 1 vol.

Law Process Books, [1856] 1870-1905, 2 vols. See also Circuit Superior Court of Law and Chancery.

Law Rules, see Circuit Superior Court of Law and Chancery

Memorandum Books, 1858-75, 5 vols. See also Circuit Superior Court of Law and Chancery.

Rough Chargers, see County Court

Scott v. Scott, farm account book, 1867, 1 vol.

Witness Book, 1896-1916, 1 vol. See also Circuit Superior Court of Law and Chancery.

County and Superior Courts

Clerk's Tax Book, 1898-1912, 1 vol.

General Indexes to Judgment Lien Dockets, Plaintiff-Defendant A-Z, 1841-1916, 4 vols.

Unspecified Court

Indexes to Chancery Causes Ended Nos. 1-2, n.d., 2 vols.; and, Index to Chancery Causes, n.d., 1 vol.

Jett v. Jett, Account Book [Z], 1856-61, 1 vol.

Porter v. Ward, H. C. Ward's Account Book, 1852-60, 1 vol.

Sinclair v. Reardon, Trial Balance, 1868-70, 1 vol.

U. S. Bank v. Steenberger, B. P. Noland's [accounts of Indiana lands], 1843-44, 1 vol.

Election Records

General Registration, 1902-03, 1 vol.

Fiduciary Records

Account Book, John S. Byrne, executor of William Byrne, 1861-81, 1 vol.

Administrators' Bonds, 1793-96, 1822-50, 7 vols.

A. D. Payne's Fiduciary Accounts, 1870-92, 1 vol.

Commissioners' Bonds, 1902-08, 1 vol.

Executors' Bonds, 1787-93, 1797-1805, 1822-50, 8 vols.

Fiduciary Bond Book, 1887-1902, 1 vol.; and, Fiduciary Bonds, 1850-1904, 4 vols.

Fiduciary Registers, 1850-1903, [1850] 1854-1940, 4 vols.

Guardians' Bond Books, 1818-33, 1850-1903, 6 vols.

[Inventories and Appraisements], 1840-41, 1 vol.

Justice of the Peace Records

Justices' Dockets, 1897-1903, 1900-04, 1902-08, 3 vols.

Land Records

Deed, 1788, 1 item (copy)

Deed Books Nos. 1-2, 4, 8, and 11, 1759-67, 1770-72, 1784-85, 1792-94, 5 vols. (copies)

General Indexes to Deeds, 1759-1898, n.d., 6 vols.

Processioners' Reports, 1795-1814, 1 vol.

Superior Court Land Causes Nos. 1-3, 1809-50, 3 vols.

Military and Pension Records

Muster Roll, Captain William H. Payne's Company, 1861, and Black Horse Camp, 1890-1905, 1 vol.

Record Books, 8th Regiment, Militia, 1807-51, 2 vols.

Records of the B. M. Randolph Camp, Confederate Veterans, 1896-1916, 1 vol.

Road and Bridge Records

Road Applications, 1875-97, 1 vol.

Tax and Fiscal Records

Account of Warrants, 1871-72, 1 vol.

Delinquent Tax Memorandums, 1876-97, 1 vol.

Land Sold for Taxes and Purchased by Other than the Commonwealth, 1890-1908, 1 vol.

List of Persons Credited for the Payment of Revenue Tax Due in 1785, 1 item (copy)

Rent Rolls, 1770-1777, 87 pp. (copies)

Tithables, 1759-1800, n.d., 1 vol. (2 copies)

Township Records

Cedar Run Township Records, 1871-75, 1 vol.

Centre Township Board Minutes and Accounts, 1871-75, 1 vol.

Wills

General Index to Wills, 1759-1900, 1 vol.

Miscellaneous Records

Crop Liens, 1893-1924, 1 vol.

Docket on Goods and Chattels, 1891-1910, 1 vol.

Lien Dockets Nos. 1-4, 1841-1915, 4 vols.

Indexes to Lien Dockets Nos. 1-5, n.d., 5 vols.

List of Insurance Policies [various companies], n.d., [ca. 1890], 1 vol.

Minutes, Overseers of the Poor, 1804-45, 1 vol.

[Naturalization] Petition and Record, 1890-1912, 1 vol.

Records of Estrays, 1800-31, 2 vols.

Commissioner of Revenue
   Personal Property Books, 1857-59, 1877-79, 4 vols.
   See also Tax and Fiscal Records

Sheriff
   Sheriffs' Execution Books, 1856-60, 1857-74, 3 vols.

Microfilm Records

Circuit Court Clerk
   Court Records
      County Court
         Minute [Order] Books, 1759-1865, 17 reels
      Circuit Superior Court of Law and Chancery
         Chancery Order Books Nos. 1-3, 1831-56 (includes Circuit Court, 1852-56), 2 reels
      Circuit Court
         Chancery Order Book No. 4, 1857-67, 1 reel (part). See also Circuit Superior Court of Law and Chancery.
   Land Records
      Deed Books Nos. 1-59, 1759-1866, 26 reels
      [Superior Court of Law] Deeds, Wills, etc., 1809-29, 1 reel (part).
      Index to Deeds, Grantors-Grantees A-Z, 1759-1914, 4 reels
      Land Causes Nos. 1-3, 1809-1850, and Miscellaneous Records [Land Causes?], 1759-1807, 2 reels
      See also Wills
   Marriage Records and Vital Statistics
      Marriage Bonds and Returns Vols. 1-6, 1759-1854, 3 reels; and, Marriage Register Vol. 7, 1854-1906, 1 reel (part)
      Index to Marriage Bonds and Returns Vols. 1-6, 1759-1853 [1854], 1 reel (part)
      Register of Births, 1853-96, 1 reel (part)
      [Register of] Births and Deaths, 1853-60, 1 reel (part)
      Register of Deaths, 1853-96, 1 reel (part)
   Military and Pension Records
      Muster Roll, etc. 1861-65, 1 reel (part)
   Wills
      Will Books Nos. 1-29, 1759-1865, 13 reels
      [Superior Court] Records at Large (Wills, etc., Vol. A), 1821-82, 1 reel (part)
      Index to Wills, A-Z, 1759-1920, 1 reel
      See also Land Records

FINCASTLE COUNTY

Formed in 1772 from Botetourt County.
It became extinct in 1776 when
it was divided to form Mont-
gomery, Washington, and
Kentucky counties.

For listing of records, see Montgomery County.

FLOYD COUNTY

Formed in 1831 from Montgomery County.
Part of Franklin County
was added later.

Original Records

Circuit Court Clerk
  Marriage Records and Vital Statistics
    Marriage Bonds, 1831-43, 2 vols. (copies)
    Marriage Register No. 2, 1843-62, 1 vol. (copy)
    Index to Marriage Bonds and Marriage Register, 1831-53, 1 vol. (Ts. and copy)
  Military and Pension Records
    See Montgomery County Military and Pension Records

Microfilm Records

Circuit Court Clerk
  Court Records
    County Court
      Order Books, 1831-64, 2 reels
    Circuit Superior Court of Law and Chancery
      Chancery Order Book No. 1, 1831-66 (includes Circuit Court, 1852-66), 1 reel
    Ciruit Court
      Chancery Order Books, see Circuit Superior Court of Law and Chancery
  Land Records
    Deed Books A-L, 1831-70, 4 reels
    General Index to Deeds No. 1, Grantor-Grantee, 1831-92, 1 reel
  Marriage, Records and Vital Statistics
    Marriage Registers Nos. 2-4 [there is no No. 1], 1843-1925, 1 reel
    Register of Births, 1853-72, 1 reel (part)
    Register of Deaths, 1853-72, 1 reel (part)
  Wills
    Will Books A-D, 1831-73, 2 reels
    General Index to Wills, 1831-1953, 1 reel

FLUVANNA COUNTY

Formed in 1777 from Albemarle County.

Original Records

Circuit Court Clerk
  Board of Supervisors Records
    Warrants and Vouchers Filed, see Tax and Fiscal Records
    Warrants Issued by Order of the Board, 1871-1922, 1 vol.

Bonds/Commissions/Oaths

Bail Bonds, 1887–ca. 1905, ca. 75 items

Bonds, 1777–1861, ca. 250 items

Circuit Court Indemnifying Bonds, 1855–67, 21 items

Circuit Court Supersedeas and Injunction Bonds, 1830–77, 1894–96, ca. .15 cu. ft.

Commissions Issued to Justices by Military Commander, 1869, ca. 50 items

Execution Bonds, 1777–ca. 1825, ca. .1 cu. ft.

Forthcoming Bonds, 1801–17, ca. 100 items

Indemnifying Bonds Returned by Constables, 1834–65, ca. 50 items

Indentures of Apprenticeship, 1797–1828, 1834–48, 1864, ca. .25 cu. ft.

Injunction Bonds, 1802–44, ca. 75 items

Lists of Ordinary Licenses and Tavern Keepers, 1787–1836, ca. 40 items

Officials' Oaths [titles vary], ca. 1880–1910, ca. 125 items

Old Attachment Bonds and Receipts not Acted on, ca. 1825–75, ca. .1 cu. ft.

Ordinary Bonds, ca. 1780–1825, ca. .2 cu. ft.

Refunding Bonds, ca. 1835–75, ca. 75 items

Replevy Bonds, 1785–88, ca. 150 items

See also Court Records, County and Superior Courts

Business Records/Corporations/Partnerships

[Accounts on A & D McRae's Books], 1844–55, 1 vol.

[Benjamin A. Minter's?] Farm Ledger, 1847–50, 1 vol.; and, private ledger, 1847–51, 1 vol.

D. S. B. [merchant's] Journal No. 1, 1860–64, 1 vol.

D. W. B. Journal, 1838–70, 1 vol.

Edmond W. Crutchfield's Ledger, 1880–88, 1 vol.

Fluvanna Telephone Co. Account Book, 1899–1902, 1 vol.

[George F. Tisdale and Co.?] Ledger [with deposition], 1851, 1 vol.

Hopkins & Harris [merchant's] Day Book No. 3, 1851–52, 1 vol.; Ledger No. 1, 1852, 1 vol.

Mason, Walker & Richardson [merchants] Day Books, 1860–61, 1860–75, 2 vols.; and, Ledger A, 1860–61, 1 vol.

N. Evans' Rent Book, 1873–1922, 1 vol.

[R. S. Holland's Farm] Account Book, 1868–78, 1 vol.

[R. W. Ashlin's?] Ledger, 1870–74, 1 vol.

T. A. Davis' [carpenter's] Account Book, 1882–1932, 1 vol.

Unidentified Account Book, 1872–74, 1 vol.

Unidentified Cooper's Shop [and house and store?] Account Book, 1871–73, 1 vol.

Unidentified [merchant's?] Cash Book, Palmyra, 1864–65, 1 vol.

William B. Payne's [shoe shop record book], 1842–50, 1 vol.

Census Records

Lists of People [white and black] and Sundry Vouchers, 1782, 1785, 13 items

Court Records

County Court

Affidavits of Non-payment of Interest [on Executions], 1869, ca. 25 items

Attachment, 1832, 1 item; and, Attachments Not Acted on, 1786–1843, ca. 50 items

Cases of Unlawful Detainer, 1825–1849, ca. 50 items

Chancery References, 1832–56, 1 vol.

Chancery Rule Dockets, 1808–13, 1838–73, 1848–51, 3 vols.

[Clerk's] Tax Book, 1898–1904, 1 vol.

Common Law Issue Dockets, 1815–19, 1828–1904, 5 vols.

Common Law Process Book, 1803–08, 1 vol.

Common Law Rule Dockets, 1815–23, 2 vols.

Commonwealth Trial Papers, 1864–65, 11 items

Copies of Judgments in Attachments and Orders for Sale, etc., 1833-48, ca. 50 items

Depositions, 1788, 4 items

Ended Causes, 1777-1904, ca. 21.9 cu. ft.

Escape Warrants, 1789-1833, 18 items

Execution Books, 1786-87, 1800-67, 10 vols.

Executions, 1831-62, 1866-72, 3.8. cu. ft.; and, Executions on Warrants, 1830-52, 1 vol.

Fee Books, 1786, 1802, 1806-07, 1811-12, 1814-15, 1829-1901, 1888-1905 [1904], 26 vols.

Indictments, Warrants, and Recognizances against Disturbers of the Peace, 1778-1810, ca. .1 cu. ft.

Judgments wherein Executions have been Issued, 1809-11, ca. .1 cu. ft.

List of Executions Returned Insolvent, 1818, 1 item

Memorandum Books, 1805-06, 1817-19, 1827-30, 1833-34, 1850-68, 1875-1903, 21 vols. (and fragments)

Minute Books, 1777-79, 1785-1802, 1805-43, 1836-49, 1868-75, 27 vols.

Indexes to Minutes [or Orders], n.d. [ca. 1830], 2 vols.

Notices, 1815, 3 items

Order Book, 1777-82, 1 vol. (copy)

Process Books [Rough Dockets], 1797-1802, 1808-45, 2 vols. See also Circuit Superior Court of Law and Chancery.

Rule [Reference] Dockets [titles vary], 1786-1832, 1827-87, 1858-73, 18 vols.

Schedules of [Insolvents and Debtors'] Estates in County Court No. 2, 1843-48, ca. .1 cu. ft.

Witness Books, 1812-1903, 4 vols.

Superior Court of Law

Fee Book, 1810, 1 vol.

Issue Docket, 1818-25, 1 vol.

Minute Books, 1809-32 (includes Circuit Superior Court of Law and Chancery, 1831-32), 3 vols.

Orders of Attendance, 1825, ca. .1 cu. ft.

Rough Docket [Process Book], 1809-28, 1 vol.; and, Process Book, 1828-1908 (includes Circuit Superior Court of Law and Chancery, 1831-51, and Circuit Court, 1852-1908), 1 vol.

Taxes on Law Process, 1817-18, 1823-24, 2 vols.

Witness Book, 1820-24, 1 vol.

Circuit Superior Court of Law and Chancery

Chancery Execution Book, 1832-1916 (includes Circuit Court, 1852-1916), 1 vol.

Chancery Executions, 1844-52, ca. .15 cu. ft.

Chancery Fee Books, 1831-51, 2 vols.

Chancery Process, see Superior Court of Law

Chancery [Rule and Issue] Docket, 1832-44, 1 vol.

Common Law Execution Books Nos. [1]-3, 1831-56 (includes Circuit Court, 1852-56), 3 vols.

Common Law Fee Books, 1831-52 (includes Circuit Court, 1852), 5 vols.

Common Law Issue Docket, 1831-54 (includes Circuit Court, 1852-54), 1 vol.

Common Law Process Book, 1831-47, 1 vol.

Copies of Judgments of Court of Appeals, 1837-69 (includes Circuit Court, 1852-69), ca. 25 items

Executions, 1832-52, ca. .85 cu. ft.

Judgment, Rule and Issue Dockets, 1831-54 (includes Circuit Court, 1852-54), 2 vols.

Memorandum Books Nos. 3-[4], 1843-56 (includes Circuit Court, 1852-56), 2 vols.

Minutes, 1832-36, 1851-86 (includes Circuit Court, 1852-86), 2 vols. See also Superior Court of Law.

Orders, 1833-67 (includes Circuit Court, 1852-67), ca. .1 cu. ft.

Process Book, 1837-39 (also Circuit Court, 1860-66, and County Court, 1875-83), 1 vol. See also Superior Court of Law.

[Rough] Common Law Rules, 1842-43, 1 vol.

Schedules of Insolvent Debtors' Estates in Superior Court No. 1, 1833-50, ca. .1 cu. ft.

Taxes upon Law Process, 1843-44, 1 vol.

Witness Books, 1831-69 (includes Circuit Court, 1852-69), 2 vols.

Circuit Court

Chancery Execution Book, see Circuit Superior Court of Law and Chancery

Chancery Executions, 1853-61, 1866-72, ca. .2 cu. ft.

Chancery Fee Books, 1852-57, 1867-1906, 5 vols.

Chancery Fees, 1875-1911, ca. .1 cu. ft.

Chancery Issue Dockets, 1856-1904, 5 vols.

Chancery Memorandum Book, 1876-1909, 1 vol.

Chancery Process Book, see Superior Court of Law

Chancery Rule Docket, 1891, 1 vol.

[Clerk's] Tax Book, 1898-1908, 1 vol.

Common Law Execution Book, 1868-1929, 1 vol. See also Circuit Superior Court of Law and Chancery.

Common Law Fee Books, 1857-61, 1858-67, 1869-75, 3 vols. See also Circuit Superior Court of Law and Chancery.

Common Law Issue Docket, 1883-1913, 1 vol. See also Circuit Superior Court of Law and Chancery.

[Common Law] References on Rules, 1893-1907, ca. 50 items

Copies of Judgments, see Circuit Superior Court of Law and Chancery

Execution Books, 1856-69, 1867-1902, 2 vols.

Executions, 1853-72, 1.4 cu. ft.

Executions on Warrants No. 3, 1854-1916, 1 vol.; and, 1861-1923, 1 vol.

Fee Books, 1853-56, 1884-1901, 1897-1919, 3 vols.

Judgment, Rule, and Issue Dockets, see Circuit Superior Court of Law and Chancery

Law Fee Book, 1861-68, 1 vol.

Law Memorandum Book, 1875-1909, 1 vol.

List of Fees and Taxes Collected, 1878-89, 1 vol.

Memorandum Books, 1856-75, 1899-1917, 3 vols. See also Circuit Superior Court of Law and Chancery.

Minutes, see Circuit Superior Court of Law and Chancery

Orders, see Circuit Superior Court of Law and Chancery

Process Book, see Superior Court of Law and Circuit Superior Court of Law and Chancery

Unidentified Suit, Exhibit A, Ledger, 1865-1905, 1 vol.

Witness Book, 1869-1943, 1 vol. See also Circuit Superior Court of Law and Chancery.

County and Superior Courts

Common Law Process Book No. 1, 1836-1941, 1 vol.

Court Papers, 1793-1935, ca. .2 cu. ft.

Judgments, Executions, and Estate Papers, 1841-1935, .75 cu. ft. (including fragments)

Memorandum Book, 1899-1927, 1 vol.

Miscellaneous Orders (copies), 1801-35, 1880, 30 items

Office Judgments [Ended Causes], 1786 [1785]-1914, ca. 10.5 cu. ft.

Petitions for Supersedeas Writs of Error, 1861-70, 11 items; and, Petitions for Writs of Habeas Corpus, 1864-65, ca. 25 items

Promiscuous Papers (including Bonds and Deeds of Trust), 1786-1821, 1863-1908, ca. .3 cu. ft.

Receipts for Taxes on Deeds and Suits Dealing with Land, 1894-1909, ca. 100 items

Summons, 1783-1864, ca. 75 items

William Sclater, Clerk, Correspondence, etc., 1870-1919, .35 cu. ft.; and, Receipts to William Sclater, 1880-82, ca. 50 items

Unspecified Court

Index to Chancery Rule Docket, n.d., 1 vol.

Election Records

Certificates of Election, 1781, 2 items

Election Returns, 1859, 1863-65, ca. .2 cu. ft.

Poll Books, 1861-66, ca. 1 cu. ft.

Polls for State Convention, 1861, ca. .1 cu. ft.

Polls Taken on Proposition to Subscribe to the Chesapeake & Ohio Rail Road Co., 1867, 10 items

See also Miscellaneous Records

Fiduciary Records

Administrators' Bonds, 1777-1838, .35 cu. ft.

Estate Papers, see Courts Records, County and Superior Courts

Guardians' Bonds, 1780-1853, ca. .35 cu. ft.

Petitions of Fiduciaries for Leave to Invest Funds in their Hands, 1867, 13 items

Schedules of Estates, 1809-41, ca. .1 cu. ft.

Trustees' Accounts, 1871, ca. .1 cu. ft.

Free Negro and Slave Records

Appraisement of Negroes Drafted to Work on Fortifications, 1865, 4 items

Certificates of Emancipation, 1789-1802, 4 items

Justice of the Peace Records

Commissioners' Accounts against the Commonwealth, 1787-1818, 19 items

Executions Returned by Constables, 1833-62, 1866-72, .7 cu. ft.

Indemnifying Bonds Returned by Constables, see Bonds/Commissions/Oaths

Justices of the Peace Appointments, 1853-65, 1868, ca. 50 items

Justices' Reports, Bonds to Keep the Peace, etc., 1877-96, .35 cu. ft.

Justices' Warrants, 1895-1912, ca. .1 cu. ft.

Warrants and Recognizances in Commonwealth Cases, 1894-1910, ca. .25 cu. ft.

Land Records

Deed Book No. 1, 1777-83, 1 vol. (copy)

Deeds of Trust, see Court Records, County and Superior Courts

Processioners' Returns, 1796-1828, ca. .15 cu. ft.

Marriage Records and Vital Statistics

Certificates of Marriage, 1781-1849, 1 vol. (copy)

Military and Pension Records

Lists of Soldiers' Families [and receipts for money to same], 1863, ca. 40 items

Military Exemption Board Proceedings, 1862, ca. .1 cu. ft.

Pension Applications Disallowed, 1902-10, 28 items

Reports of Committees [to furnish families of volunteer soldiers], 1860-65, ca. .2 cu. ft.

Road and Bridge Records

Copies of Orders Appointing Surveyors of Roads, etc., 1797-1832, ca. 50 items

Index to Road Warrants, see Township Records

Lists of Surveyors of Roads, 1786-1827, 21 items

Petitions for Roads and Mills, 1779-1820, 1883-84, ca. .1 cu. ft.

School Records
>   Accounts and Reports of School Board Bonds, 1819-61, ca. .2 cu. ft.

Tax and Fiscal Records
>   Claims Against the County, 1778-1801, ca. 50 items
>   Claims for Jury Service, 1859-60, ca. 50 items
>   County Warrants Ready for Delivery, 1886-1903, ca. 75 items
>   Delinquent Land Books, 1884-89, 1897-1903, 2 vols.
>   Delinquent Land Sales, 1884-1930, 1 vol.
>   Delinquent Lands and Insolvent Lists, 1885, 1890-1921, ca. .2 cu. ft.; and, Lists of Delinquent and Insolvent [land and personal property], 1789-1837, ca. 1865-1903, ca. 2.25 cu. ft.
>   List of Allowances against the Commonwealth, 1893-1929, 1 vol.
>   List of Vouchers Received, 1891, 1 vol.
>   Ordinary License Receipts, 1816-47, ca. .1 cu. ft.; and, Receipts to Ordinary Keepers, 1827-30, ca. 50 items
>   Personal Property Tax Lists, 1771-1817, .35 cu. ft.; and, Lists of Taxable Property in Second District, 1793, ca. 100 items
>   Receipts from the State Auditor, 1853-57, 1875-93, ca. .2 cu. ft.
>   Sale of Land for Taxes, 1833-68, ca. .2 cu. ft.
>   Tax Collection Returns, 1787-88, ca. 75 items
>   [Township and] Tax Ledger, Palmyra District, 1871-1919, 1 vol.
>   Vouchers for Payments made as Agent of Fluvanna County, 1863-65, ca. 100 items
>   Vouchers to Taxable Property, 1783-85, 1787, 1789-91, 1794, 1796-97, 1799, 1801, ca. .5 cu. ft.

Town Records
>   Town of Columbia Due Book, 1879-90, 1 vol.; and, Petty Ledger, 1891-96, 1 vol.

Township Records
>   Cunningham Township Record [Minutes], 1871-74, (also Index to Road Warrants, 1893-1930), 1 vol.
>   Fork Union Township Receipts, 1871-75, 1 vol.
>   Palmyra Township Receipts, 1871-75, 1 vol.
>   Palmyra Township Warrant Book, 1871-74 (also Clerk's Form Book), 1 vol.
>   See also Tax and Fiscal Records

Wills
>   Will Book No. 1, 1777-1808, 1 vol. (copy)

Miscellaneous Records
>   Estray Certificates, 1786-1901, ca. .3 cu. ft.
>   Insanity Papers, 1805, 1838, 2 items
>   Letter concerning Salt, 1777, 1 item; and, Reports of Agents for Distribution of Salt, 1861-64, ca. 25 items
>   Lists of Hawkers, and Peddlers, 1824-38, 11 items
>   Miscellaneous Papers (including correspondence of John Forbes, attorney, and election records), ca. 1785-1940, n.d., ca. .45 cu. ft.
>   Powers of Attorney, 1870, 1896-1911, ca. 50 items
>   Reports of Superintendents of the Poor, ca. 1870-1900, ca. .35 cu. ft.
>   Requisitions to enter Boats [on the James River], 1811-33, ca. 50 items
>   Unidentified [Clerk's personal?] Account Book, 1851-63, 1 vol.; and, Unidentified Account [or Fee?] Book, 1867-98, 1 vol. (fragment)
>   Unidentified Record Books, 1831-34, n.d., 2 vols.

Commissioner of Revenue
>   License Reports, 1881-83, 1893-98, .35 cu. ft.; and, License Returns and Reports, 1867-72, 1880-81, 1885-97, .35 cu. ft.
>   Personal Property Interrogatories, 1890 1896-97 ca. .15 cu. ft.
>   Revenue Reports under Moffett Liquor Law, 1878-80, ca. .1 cu. ft.
>   See also Tax and Fiscal Records

Sheriff
Fee Bills Returned by Sheriff [titles vary], 1834-87, .35 cu. ft.
Sheriff R. S. Campbell's Papers, 1888-1903, ca. 50 items

Treasurer
Treasurer's Orders and Warrants, 1887-1907, 1 vol.
Warrants and Vouchers Filed with Settlement Had of Board of Supervisors, 1888, ca. 150 items
See also Tax and Fiscal Records

Microfilm Records

Circuit Court Clerk
Court Records
County Court
Order Books, 1777-1867, 8 reels
Fiduciary Records
Guardians' Accounts, 1794-1852, 1 reel (part)
Land Records
Deed Books Nos. 1-19, 1777-1867, 9 reels
General Index to Deeds Nos. 1-2, 1777-1898, 1 reel
Marriage Records and Vital Statistics
Certificates of Marriages, 1781-1849, 1 reel (part)
Marriage Bonds, 1777-1804, 1 reel
Marriage Register, 1853-1923, 1 reel (part)
Register of Births (and Index), 1853-54, 1 reel (part)
Wills
Will Books Nos. 1-9, 1777-1865, 4 reels
Circuit [Superior] Court Will Book, 1831-67, 1 reel (part)
General Index to Wills, 1777-1849, 1 reel

FRANKLIN COUNTY

Formed in 1785 from Bedford and Henry counties.

Original Records

Circuit Court Clerk
Board of Supervisors Records
Receipts and Reports, 1879-1919, 1 cu. ft.
Bonds/Commissions/Oaths
Bonds and Commissions, see Court Records, County Court
Miscellaneous Bonds (including marriage bonds), 1786-1850, 7 items (including fragment)
Officials' [and Fiduciary] Bonds, 1894-1929, 1 cu. ft.
Business Records/Corporations/Partnerships
Franklin Bank Papers, Rocky Mount Loans and Trust, Receivers, 1898-1902, ca. .25 cu. ft.

Court Records
    County Court
        Court Papers (including marriage licenses), 1785-ca. 1860, 1.35 cu. ft.
        Determined Papers, 1841, 1865-1900, 25.2 cu ft.
        Fee Books, 1789, 1791, 1794, 1806, 4 vols.
        Fine Reports, 1878-92, ca. .25 cu. ft.
        Judgments, etc., 1786, ca. 50 items
        Memorandum Books, 1810-13, 1821-22, 2 vols.
        Notices and Miscellaneous Papers (including estate settlements), 1812, 1894-99, ca. .1 cu. ft.
        Order Book No. 1, 1786-89, 1 vol. (copy)
        Records [bonds and commissions, surveys, deeds, court papers, etc.], ca. 1770-1840, n.d., 1 cu. ft.
        Suit Papers, 1786-1880, 5.85 cu. ft.
        Summons, 1800, 1805-06, 1811-12, 10 items
    Circuit Court
        Common Law Miscellaneous Indictments, 1885-1927, ca. .25 cu. ft.
        Common Law Papers, 1900, ca. 50 items
        Summons and Executions, 1903-10, .35 cu. ft.
    County and Superior Courts
        Answers [to bills of complaint], 1805-06, 1811, 1815, 1817, 7 items
        Bills of Complaint, 1805-06, 1810, 1836, n.d., 5 items
        Chancery Papers (including lists of insolvents and reports of the Overseers of the Poor), 1822-1904, 119.5 cu. ft.
        Civil, Commonwealth, and Criminal Warrants, 1902-18, 1 cu. ft.
        County Receipts and [Clerk's] Reports, 1879-1941, 1 cu. ft.
        Determined Papers, 1789-1907, 46.2 cu. ft.
    Unspecified Court
        Grand Jury Presentments, 1802, 1804, 1812, 3 items
Fiduciary Records
    Administrators' Accounts, 1898-1903, ca. .25 cu. ft.
    Correspondence [re: settlement of estates, etc.], 1843, 1847, 1849-50, 1875, n.d., 7 items
    Fiduciary Bonds, see Bonds/Commissions/Oaths
    Guardians' Accounts, 1803-1929, 2.7 cu. ft.
    Inventories, 1802-99, 2 cu. ft.
    Miscellaneous Partitions [divisions of estates], 1807-97, .45 cu. ft.
    See also Court Records, County Court
Justice of the Peace Records
    Affidavits before Justices, 1788, 1801, 1805, 1812, n.d., 42 items
Land Records
    Deeds, 1786-1905, ca. 18 cu. ft. See also Court Records, County Court.
    Lists of Land Processioned, 1800, 1803-04, 4 items
    Surveys, see Court Records, County Court Records
    Warranty Deeds, 1886-87, 2 items
Marriage Records and Vital Statistics
    Marriage Bonds and Consents [and licenses], 1786-1905, 15.8 cu. ft.
    Marriage Licenses and Ministers' Returns, 1857, 1859, 1865, ca. .2 cu. ft.; and, Ministers' Returns, 1786-1868, .45 cu. ft.
    See also Bonds/Commissions/Oaths; and, Court Records, County Court
Road and Bridge Records
    See Miscellaneous Records
Tax and Fiscal Records
    Land Redeemed [before sale for delinquent taxes], 1889-91, ca. .1 cu. ft.
    Lists of Delinquents and Insolvents, 1790-1813, 32 items

Lists of Insolvents, see Court Records, County and Superior Courts
Lists of Taxable Land, 1794, 1796, 1844, 4 items
See also Miscellaneous Records

Town Records

Town of Rocky Mount Minutes and Ordinances, 1873-82, 1 vol.

Miscellaneous Records

Miscellaneous Papers (including tax tickets, fee bills, road reports, etc.; some refer to Augusta County), ca. 1770-1935, n.d., ca. .75 cu. ft.
Obligation, William Standley to Rhoda White, 1804, 1 item
Overseers of the Poor Reports, see Court Records, County and Superior Courts
Powers of Attorney, 1829, 1843, 1903-11, ca. .25 cu. ft.
Promissory Notes, 1786, 1801, 1803, 1854, 5 items

Microfilm Records

Circuit Court Clerk

Court Records

County Court

Order Books, 1786-1828, 1830-65, 7 reels

District Court

Order Books Nos. 1-5, 1789-1809, 2 reels

Circuit Superior Court of Law and Chancery

Order Books A-B, 1831-65 (includes Circuit Court, 1852-65), 1 reel

Circuit Court

Order Books, see Circuit Superior Court of Law and Chancery

County and Superior Courts

Chancery Papers, 1834-1949, 309 reels
Determined Papers, 1789-1937, 243 reels

Fiduciary Records

Guardians' Accounts, 1833-88, 6 reels
Miscellaneous Partitions, 1834, 1 reel (part)

Land Records

Deed Books Nos. 1-27, 1786-1866, 14 reels
District Court Deed Books Nos. 1-2, 1789-1814 (includes Superior Court of Law, 1809-14), 1 reel
General Index to Deeds No. 1, Grantor-Grantee A-Z, 1786-1897, 2 reels
District Court Land Suits, 1805-18 (includes Superior Court of Law, 1809-18), 1 reel (part)
Plat Books Nos. 1-2, 1792-1811, 1809-91, 1 reel

Marriage Records and Vital Statistics

Marriage Bond Book No. 1, 1786-1853, 1 reel (part)
Marriage Bonds, 1785-1912, 51 reels
Marriage Registers Nos. 1-2, 1853-1915, 1 reel (part)
Ministers' Returns, 1786-1858, 2 reels
Register of Births, 1853-79, 1 reel (part)
Register of Deaths, 1853-71, 1 reel (part)
Index to Births, Deaths, and Marriages, 1853-98, 1 reel

Wills

Will Books Nos. 1-14, 1786-1866, 7 reels
Circuit [Superior] Court Will Book No. 2, 1804-1901, 1 reel
Wills, [c. 1785-1940], 23 reels
General Index to Wills, A-Z, 1786-1948, 1 reel

FREDERICK COUNTY

Formed in 1738 from Orange County. Its government was organized in 1743, and part of Augusta County was added later.

Original Records

Circuit Court Clerk

Board of Supervisors Records
Papers [and Proceedings], 1869-1904, 3 cu. ft.

Bonds/Commissions/Oaths
Berkeley County Court (West Virginia) Constables' Bonds, 1818-43, 1 vol.

Bonds, Qualifications, and Commissions, 1782-1904, 2 cu. ft.

County Court Bond Book, 1850-70, 1 vol.

County Court Constables' Bonds, 1816-50, 3 vols.

County Court General Bonds, 1871-94, 1 vol; and, Circuit Court General Bonds, 1869-1906, 2 vols.

County Court Ordinary Bonds, 1816-50, 2 vols.; Ordinary Keepers' Bonds, 1795-1800, 1 vol.; and, Town of Winchester, Corporation Court Ordinary Bonds, 1800-17, 1 vol.

Debt Bond, 1802, 1 item

Delivery Bonds, 1811-33, ca. .1 cu. ft.

Indentures and Apprentice Bonds, ca. 1775-1875, .45 cu. ft.

Ministers' Bonds, ca. 1850, ca. 25 items

Oaths of Confederate Soldiers [on backs of blank bonds], 1865, 1 vol.

Officials' Bonds, 1899-1906, 1 vol.

Business Records/Corporations/Partnerships
Barley & Beaty Co. Ledgers Nos. 1-5, 1861-81, 5 vols.; Ledgers, 1878-79, 1882, 2 vols.; and, Journal, 1881-82, 1 vol.

Barton & Williams General Collection Journals, 1835-55, 1844-59, 2 vols.

Barton, Williams and Fauntleroy Fee Book, 1860-62 (also P. Williams & Sons Claim Book, 1866-67), 1 vol.

Crupper and Clarke Ledgers, 1807-12, 2 vols.

[F. L.] Ledger, Luray, 1818-21, 1 vol.; and, Day Book, 1827-28, 1 vol.

Garber, Gold & Co. Ledger, 1899-1900, 1 vol.

Hollingsworth & Parkins Ledger, 1811-19, 1 vol.

J. H. Griffith and Co. Day Book, 1857-58, 1 vol.

[James E. Steele's?] Day Book, 1852-55, 1 vol.

[James L. Lane's Ledger], 1818-19, 1 vol.

James Silver's and Elijah Way's Account Book, 1810-16, 1 vol.

John H. McEndrus' Ledger, 1823-25, 1 vol.

Joseph A. Nulton's Ledger, 1874-75, 1 vol.

Joseph W. Carter's Day Book, 1826-29, 1 vol.

Morgan and Joseph Lauck's Journals C-D, 1825-28, 2 vols.

R. C. Windle's Ledgers, 1840-43, 2 vols.; and, Inventory of Goods in the Store of R. C. Windle, 1845, 1 vol.

Richard S. Griffith Journal, 1847-51, 1 vol.

Subscription Book, 1850-52, 1 vol.

The Shenandoah Valley Hedge Co. Stock Certificate Book, 1886, 1 vol.

[Thomas Lawson's Account Book?], 1775-1834, 1 vol.

Unidentified Cash Book, 1878-80, 1 vol.

Unidentified Coal and Ore Book, 1816-17, 1 vol.

Unidentified Flour Book, 1810, 1 vol.

Unidentified Ledger A, 1805-06, 1 vol.; Ledger B, 1879-81, 1 vol.; Ledger C, 1791-93, 1 vol; and, Unidentified Ledgers, 1802, 1812-18, 1815, 1818-25, 1824-33, 1825-28, 1828-29, 1829, 1869, 1878-89, n.d., 12 vols.

Unidentified Record Book, 1856-67, 1 vol.

[Union Mills Day Book], 1811-14, 1 vol.

W. G. Singleton's Ledger, 1844-53, 1 vol.

W. L. & Co. Day Book, 1802-03, 1 vol.

William R. Alexander's Office Book, 1875-82, 1 vol.

Winchester & Potomac Railroad Co., Fourth [Dividend] Installment, 1833, 1 vol.

See also Court Records, County Court

Census Records

Enumeration, 1840, 1 vol.

Court Records

County Court

Blotter Books, 1841-54, 1870-92, 3 vols.

Chancery Dockets, 1870-71, 2 vols.

Chancery Hearing Docket, 1844-52, 1 vol.

Chancery Rough Docket, 1856-60 (also Partnership Record, 1905), 1 vol.

Chancery Rule Books, 1824-27, 1830-72, 6 vols.

Church Papers [suits, etc., removed from other series], ca. 1750-1800, ca. 100 items

Clerks' Correspondence, ca. 1820-65, ca. .4 cu. ft.

Commonwealth Execution Book, 1821-29, 1 vol.

Depositions, 1833, 1836-37, 2 vols.

Dockets, 1825-30, 1833-81, 1839-48, 3 vols.

Ended Causes, 1743-1904, 87 cu. ft.

Execution Books, 1760-1903, 15 vols. See also Sheriff.

Executions, 1754, 1866-69, ca. .2 cu. ft.

Indexes to Executions, 1870, n.d., 2 vols.

Fee Books, 1760-64, 1767-77, 1783-86 (includes Quartermaster's Records, 1781), 1787-98, 1801-36, 1843-55, 1859-1901, 23 vols.

Index to Judgments and Cases, 1831-50, 1 vol.

Issue Dockets, 1812, 1815, 1820-21, 1824, 1827-36, 1840-58, 13 vols.

Judgment Lien Docket, 1847-89, 1 vol.

Judgment Lien Index No. 1-2, n.d., 1 vol.

Minutes, 1761-66, 1773-80, 1782-1841, 20 vols.

Order Book No. 12, 1764-65, 1 vol.; and, 1804-08, 1 vol.

Process Books, 1835-73, 3 vols.

Quarterly Court Dockets, 1860-89, 2 vols.

Register of Criminals, 1871-1906, 1 vol.

Rough Dockets, 1829-34, 1849-52, 1865-82, 5 vols.

Rule Books, 1749-52, 1786-1804, 1806-09, 1816-24, 1831-55, 13 vols.; and, Rule Books [Order Books], 1806-09, 2 vols.

Witness Attendance Books, 1818-50, 1873-82, 1895-1923 (includes Circuit Court, 1904-23), 6 vols.

District Court

Court Papers, 1790-1850 (includes Superior Court of Law, 1809-31, and Circuit Superior Court of Law and Chancery, 1831-50), ca. .2 cu. ft.

Ended [Law] Causes, 1789-1860 (includes Superior Court of Law, 1808-31; Circuit Superior Court of Law and Chancery, 1831-51; and, Circuit Court, 1852-60), 26 cu. ft. For Ended Chancery Causes, see Superior Court of Chancery.

Execution Books Nos. 2-3, 1798-1804 [1813], 2 vols.; and, 1808-30 (includes Superior Court of Law, 1809-30), 1 vol.

Fee Books, 1789-1812 (includes Superior Court of Law, 1809-12), 5 vols.
Minute Books, 1805-15 (includes Superior Court of Law, 1808-15), 2 vols.
Order Books, 1789-90 (includes Land Record Book, 1799-1809), 1 vol.; and,
    Nos. [1]-2, 1789-1807, 2 vols.
Records [Orders], 1795-1820, 1806-19 (includes Superior Court of Chancery,
    1802-20), 2 vols.
Rule Books, 1789-1816 (includes Superior Court of Law, 1808-16), 2 vols.

Superior Court of Law
Carter et al. v. Carr, transcript, 1816, 1 vol.
Court Papers, see District Court
Docket, 1820, 1 vol.
Ended [Law] Causes, see District Court
Execution Book, see District Court
Fee Books, 1813-34 (includes Circuit Superior Court of Law and Chancery,
    1831-34), 4 vols. See also District Court.
Minutes, see District Court
Order Books, 1809-14, 1817-29, 4 vols.
[Records], 1814-17, 1 vol.
Rule Books, 1812-41 (includes Circuit Superior Court of Law and Chancery,
    1831-41), 4 vols. See also District Court.
Venire Book, 1808-17, 1 vol.

Superior Court of Chancery
[Dockets], 1812-41 (includes Circuit Superior Court of Law and Chancery,
    1831-41), 4 vols.
Ended Causes, [1777]-1851 (includes High Court of Chancery, 1777-1802, and
    Circuit Superior Court of Law and Chancery, 1831-51), 50 cu. ft. For
    Ended Law Causes, see District Court.
Execution Book, 1820-30, 1 vol.
Fee Books, 1812-25, 1828-30, 6 vols.
Order Book No. 3, 1821-23, 1 vol.
Records [Orders], see District Court

Circuit Superior Court of Law and Chancery
Bankrupt Docket, 1842, 1 vol.
Chancery Court Docket, 1841-44, 1 vol.
Chancery Execution Book, 1831-73 (includes Circuit Court, 1852-73), 1 vol.
Chancery Fee Book, 1842-51, 1 vol.
Chancery Process Books Nos. [1]-2, 1832-60 (includes Circuit Court, 1852-
    60), 2 vols.
Common Law Fee Book, 1834-49, 1 vol.
Common Law Process Book, 1833-55 (includes Circuit Court, 1852-55), 1 vol.
Court Papers, see District Court
Dockets, 1837-47, 1843-72 (includes Circuit Court, 1852-72), 2 vols. See also
    Superior Court of Chancery.
Ended Causes, see Superior Court of Chancery
Ended [Law] Causes, see District Court
Execution Books [8]-9, 1831-76 (includes Circuit Court, 1852-76), 2 vols.
Fee Book, see Superior Court of Law
Index to Chancery Order Book No. 9, 1839-47, 1 vol.
Minutes, 1831-58, 1834-39 (includes Circuit Court, 1852-58), 4 vols.
Rule Books, 1834-69 (includes Circuit Court, 1852-69), 3 vols. See also
    Superior Court of Law.

Circuit Court
Chancery Dockets, 1853-1907, 3 vols.
Chancery Execution Book, 1873-1911, 1 vol. See also Circuit Superior Court
    of Law and Chancery.

Chancery Fee Book, 1858-92, 1 vol.

Chancery Process Book, <u>see</u> Circuit Superior Court of Law and Chancery

Chancery Rough Dockets, 1860-81, 1883-91, 1894-1907, 3 vols.

Chancery Rule Books, 1853-1907, 3 vols.

C[ommon] L[aw] Dockets, 1858-90, 2 vols.

Common Law Execution Book, 1876-96, 1 vol.

Common Law Fee Book, 1858-81, 1 vol.

Common Law Process, <u>see</u> Circuit Superior Court of Law and Chancery

Common Law Rough Dockets, 1883-1923, 2 vols.

Common Law Rule Book, 1886-1916, 1 vol.

Docket Books, 1875-79, 19 vols. <u>See also</u> Circuit Superior Court of Law and
    Chancery and Winchester District Court.

Dockets, 1890-1910, ca. .5 cu. ft.

Ended Causes, 1852-1905, 23 cu. ft. <u>See also</u> Superior Court of Chancery.

Ended [Law] Causes, <u>see</u> District Court

Execution Book, 1889-1922, 1 vol. <u>See also</u> Circuit Superior Court of Law
    and Chancery.

Fee Books, 1881-94, 1898-1913, 3 vols.

Law Process Books, 1872-93, 2 vols. <u>See also</u> Circuit Superior Court of Law
    and Chancery.

Minutes, <u>see</u> Circuit Superior Court of Law and Chancery

Process Books, 1869-1907, 2 vols.

Rough Docket, 1870-82, 1 vol.

Rule Book, 1869-72, 1 vol. <u>See also</u> Circuit Superior Court of Law and
    Chancery.

Witness Attendance Books, 1868-93, 3 vols. <u>See also</u> County Court.

Winchester District Court

Docket, 1852-1917 (includes Circuit Court, 1870-1917), 1 vol.

Fee Book, 1865-70, 1 vol.

Order Book A, 1852-69, 1 vol.

Warren County Execution Book, 1856-58, 1 vol.

County and Superior Courts

Cases of Historical Interest [removed from other series], ca. 1790-1875, 1
    cu. ft.

Miscellaneous Court Papers, 1836-97, 2.45 cu. ft.

Prisoners' Schedules, 1807-47, ca. 1 cu. ft.

Unspecified Court

[Chancery Rules], 1870-71, 3 pp. (fragments)

Court Papers, 1786-1855, n.d., ca. 300 items

Dockets, 1850-56, 15 pp. (fragments); and, Docket for the Judge, 1846,
    1 item

Fee Book, 1822-24, 1 vol.

Rule Book, 1818, 7 pp. (fragment)

Unidentified Index, n.d., 1 vol.

Election Records

Abstracts of Votes, Campaign Expenses, etc., ca. 1900-40, 1 cu. ft.

Delegate Book, 1897, 1 vol.

Electoral Board Minutes, 1884 (also County Board of School Commissioners'
    Minutes, 1884-87), 1 vol.

General Registration, 1902-03, 1 vol.

Lists of Registered Voters, 1895-1954 [overlapping date ranges], 4 vols.

Polls and Ballots, 1825-ca. 1900, ca. 1 cu. ft.

Fiduciary Records

Circuit Court General Receivers' Bonds, 1871-1904, 1 vol.

Circuit Court General Receivers' Reports, 1862-65, 1869-1903, 7 vols.

Circuit Court General Receivers' Reports, 1869-99, 1 cu. ft.

Circuit Court Special Commissioners' Bonds, 1868-1901, 1871-73, 3 vols.

County Court Administrators' Bonds, 1762-84, 1786-93, 1798-1862, 1866-1914 (includes Circuit Court, 1904-14), 12 vols.; District Court Administrators' Bonds, 1797-1818 (includes Superior Court of Law, 1808-18), 1 vol.; Superior Court of Law Administrators' Bonds, 1822-44 (includes Circuit Superior Court of Law and Chancery, 1831-41), 1 vol.; and, Circuit Court Administrators' Bonds, 1866-1900, 1 vol.

County Court Commissioners' Book, 1856, 1 vol.

County Court Executors' Bonds, 1771-1885 (includes Circuit Superior Court of Law and Chancery, 1831-49), 9 vols.; Circuit Court Executors' Bonds, 1872-1914, 2 vols; and, Berkeley County Court (West Virginia) Executors' Bonds, 1824-41, 1 vol.

County Court Fiduciaries, 1850-1920 (includes Circuit Court, 1904-20), 2 vols.; and, Circuit Court Fiduciaries, 1847-89, 2 vols.

County Court General Receivers' Accounts, 1871-72, 1 vol.

County Court Guardians' Bonds, 1792-1900, 7 vols.; Circuit Court Guardians' Bonds, 1847-67, 1870-1901 (includes Circuit Superior Court of Law and Chancery, 1847-51), 2 vols.

Estate of David Hollingsworth in Account with Parkins, executor, 1859, 1 vol.

Free Negro and Slave Records

Certificates, etc., ca. .4 cu. ft.

Justice of the Peace Records

Constables' Docket, 1885-91, 1 vol.; and, No. 1, 1894-1911, 1 vol.

Constables' Executions and Returns, 1870-79, ca. 50 items

Justices' Criminal Docket, 1896-1910, 1 vol.

Justices' Dockets, 1853-88, 1856-1919, 1884-1908, 1880-1908, 4 vols.

Land Records

Deed Books Nos. 11 and 85, 1765-67, 1862-65, 2 vols.; and, Nos. 1, 7-8, 10, 13, 15, 18, 20, and 31, 1743-49, 1762-65, 1769-72, 1778-80, 1783-85, 1808-09, 9 vols. (copies)

General Indexes to Deeds, 1743-1887, 4 vols.; Circuit Court General Index to Deeds, 1793-1814, 1 vol.; and, General Indexes to Deeds Nos. 2-5, 1836-1924, 4 vols.

Plats [removed from suits], 1742-ca. 1830, ca. .3 cu. ft.; and, Plats of Land Belonging to Mrs. Charles Calaham and George Lind, n.d., 3 items

Superior Court Land Record Books, 1808-25, 1814-17, 3 vols.; and, Circuit Superior Court of Law and Chancery, 1831-36, 1 vol. See also Court Records, District Court.

Circuit Court General Index to Land Records, 1812-38, 1 vol.

Unrecorded Deeds and Wills, ca. 1885-1925, .35 cu. ft.

See also Court Records, District Court

Marriage Records and Vital Statistics

Birth and Death Certificates, 1865-75, ca. .2 cu. ft.

Marriage Registers Nos. [1]-2, 1752-1907, 2 vols.; and, 1850-61, 1 vol.

Ministers' Returns, 1782-1833, n.d., .7 cu. ft.

Register of Deaths, 1872-97, 1 vol.

Registers of Births Nos. 8-9, 1853-91, 2 vols.

Military and Pension Records

List of Persons Liable to be Enrolled in the Militia, 1853, 1 item

Militia Papers, 1812, 1825, 1833, ca. 100 items

Militia Returns and Delinquent Lists, 1811-12, 1830-34, ca. .1 cu. ft.; and, Delinquent Muster Fines, 1810-12, 1829-37, ca. .2 cu. ft.

Names of Persons Receiving Pensions, 1894, 1 vol.

Quartermaster's Records, see Court Records, County Court

Revolutionary War Pensions, 1812, ca. 50 items

Road and Bridge Records

Commissioners' Reports on Roads and Surveys, 1889-94, 1 vol.

List of Overseers of the Roads, 1813-53, 1 vol.

Minutes, Board of Road Commissioners, Shawnee District, 1884-1914, 1 vol.

North Frederick Turnpike Co. [Hampshire and Morgan Turnpike Co.] Minutes, 1850-1901, 1 vol.; List of Stockholders, 1851-1901, 1 vol.; and, Certificates, 1853-59, 1 vol.

Opequan Township Road Record, 1871-75, 1 vol.

Record of Road Overseers, 1887-88, 1 vol.

Roads, Mills, and Dams, 1743-1880 [ca. 1920], 3 cu. ft.

Stonewall Road Board Record, 1903-14, 1 vol.

School Records

School Papers, 1788-1925, .45 cu. ft.

See also Election Records

Tax and Fiscal Records

Applications for Licenses, ca. 1900, ca. .1 cu. ft.

Assessments, 1800-39, .35 cu. ft.

[Bounty] Warrants (hawks, owls, etc.), 1890-93, .35 cu. ft.

Copies of Delinquent Land Taxes, 1791-1831, ca. 25 items

County Claims, 1866, ca. 100 items

John G. Miller's Tax Book, 1858, 1 vol.; and, T. Gray Brannan's Tax Book, 1884-85, 1 vol.

Lands Sold for Taxes to Others than the Commonwealth, 1886-1913, 1 vol.

Levy Claims, 1815-54, ca. .4 cu. ft.; and, Fox Scalp Levies, 1833, ca. 50 items

List of Insolvents, 1903-15, 1 vol.

Minutes, Board of Excise Commissioners, 1890-1921, 1 vol.

Register of County Bonds Sold, 1890, 1 vol.

Rent Rolls (including Town of Winchester), 1781, 3 vols. (copies)

Surveys of Land Sold for Taxes where Deeds are Made by Clerk to Purchase, 1888-98, 1 vol.

Tax Books, 1793, 1797-98, 1802, 4 vols.

Town Records

See Tax and Fiscal Records

Township Records

Back Creek Township Board Record, 1871-75, 1 vol.

Gainsboro Township Ledger, 1872-75, 1 vol.

See also Road and Bridge Records

Wills

Exemplifications and Certificates, 1843, 6 items

Will Books Nos. 1 and 9, 1749-51, 1810-16, 2 vols.; and, Nos. 1-3, 5 and 9, 1743-70, 1783-94, 1810-16, 5 vols. (copies)

[Index to Wills], 1859-76, 1 vol.

General Index to Wills No. 1, 1743-1917, 1 vol.

Wills, 1758, 1760, 2 items (copies)

See also Land Records

Miscellaneous Records

[Appointment Book], 1826-55, 1 vol.

Crop Lien Docket (and Reservation of Title), 1897-1924, 1 vol.

Estrays, 1787-1850, ca. .2 cu. ft.

Inquests on Dead Bodies, ca. 1800-1900, .35 cu. ft.

[Lunacy Book], 1876-79, 1 vol.

Lunacy Papers, ca. 1890-1910, ca. 100 items
Morgan Papers [removed from other series], ca. 1765-1825, 1 cu. ft.
Register of Estrays, 1824-1901, 1 vol.
Settlement with Overseers of the Poor, 1796, 1 item
[Science] Lecture Book, n.d., 1 vol. (Ms.)
Unidentified List of Names [newspaper subscription list?], n.d., 1 vol.

Commissioner of Revenue
License Reports, ca. 1900, ca. .1 cu. ft.
Licenses, 1813-26, 1894-ca. 1900, ca. .3 cu. ft.; and, Licenses for Grocery and Retail
   Liquor Stores for the Years 1870-72, 1895, ca. 25 items
See also Tax and Fiscal Records

Sheriff
C. B. H[ancock, Sheriff] Journal, 1859-79 (also Judgment and Execution Book,
   1875-80), 1 vol.
[Sheriff's?] Levy Account Book, 1794, 1 vol.
Sheriffs' Receipts for Licenses, 1828-29, 1848-50, ca. 100 items

Treasurer
Land Tax Book, 1870, 1 vol.
Treasurer's Tax Book, 1883, 1 vol.
See also Tax and Fiscal Records

Microfilm Records

Circuit Court Clerk
Court Records
County Court
Minutes, 1801-41, 5 reels
Order Books Nos. 1-37, 1743-1801, 1804-06, 1841-56, 20 reels
District Court
Order Books, 1789-1809, 3 reels. See also Land Records.
Superior Court of Law
Order Books, 1809-27, 1814-29, 4 reels
Superior Court of Chancery
Order Books Nos. 1-6, 1812-31, 3 reels
Records, 1784-1825, 2 reels
Circuit Superior Court of Law and Chancery
Chancery Order Books Nos. 7-10, 1831-58 (includes Circuit Court, 1852-58),
   2 reels
Order Books, 1831-52, 2 reels
Circuit Court
Chancery Order Books, see Circuit Superior Court of Law and Chancery
Fiduciary Records
Guardians' Bonds, 1792-1865, 1 reel
Land Records
Deed Books Nos. 1-86, 1743-1867, 44 reels
Superior Court Deed Books Nos. 2-7 [No. 1 is missing], 1793-1826, 3 reels
General Index to Deeds No. 1, A-Z, 1743-1839, 1 reel; and, No. 2, 1839-76, 1 reel
Land Book [Land Causes] No. 1, 1758-1832, 1 reel
Land Record Books, 1799-1809, 1793-1817, 1808-25, 1814-20 (also District Court
   Land Records, 1789-90), 3 reels
Surveys, 1736-58, 1782-1878, 1 reel

Marriage Records and Vital Statistics
>   Marriage Bonds, 1773-98, 1 reel (part); and, Marriage Bonds Nos. 5-8 and 10-20, 1788-1850, 3 reels
>   Marriage Registers Nos. 1-2, 1782-1907, 1 reel
>   Register of Births, 1853-70, 1 reel (part)
>   Register of Deaths, 1853-70, 1 reel (part)

Military and Pension Records
>   Militia Records, 1796-1821, 1 reel (part)
>   Muster Roll, 1861-65, 1 reel (part)

Wills
>   Will Book Nos. 1-27, 1743-1865, 14 reels
>   Superior Court Will Books Nos. 1-4, 1790-1859, 1 reel
>   General Index to Wills, 1743-1917, 1 reel

GILES COUNTY

Formed in 1806 from Montgomery, Monroe (West Virginia), and Tazewell counties. Parts of Wythe, Monroe, Mercer (West Virginia), Craig, and Tazewell were added later.

Original Records

Circuit Court Clerk

Board of Supervisors Records
>   Minutes [labeled Minutes, County Court], 1903-12, 1 vol.
>   Papers (also County Claims and County and Superior Court Papers), 1814-1948, ca. 6.9 cu. ft.
>   See also Court Records, Circuit Court

Bonds/Commissions/Oaths
>   Appointment of William Adair, Special Commissioner for Public Roads, 1870, 2 items. See also Road and Bridge Records.
>   Apprentice Indentures, 1807-76, ca. 150 items
>   Bonds, ca. 1805-95, ca. 2 cu. ft.
>   Forthcoming Bonds and Receipts, 1813-16, 1869-74, ca. 50 items
>   Liquor License Bonds, 1883-84, 1889-94, ca. 50 items
>   Officials' Bonds [Board of Supervisors], 1885-1900, 1 vol.
>   Officials' Certificates and Oaths, 1807-83, ca. .2 cu. ft.
>   Stay Bonds, 1861, 20 items

Business Records/Corporations/Partnerships
>   Brotherton & Hale Ledger, 1867-70, 1 vol.
>   B. S. L. Ledger No. 1, 1903-05, 1 vol.; and, Treasurer's Cash Book No. 1, 1903-05, 1 vol.
>   C. & H. Ledger, 1848, 1 vol.; and, Ledger A, 1848-54, 1 vol.
>   Christian Snidow, Merchant, Account Book, 1829-60, 1 vol.
>   C[unningham], H[oge], and V[ass] Ledger, 1851-53, 1 vol.; and, Day Book B, 1852, 1 vol.
>   C. V. & B. Ledger A, 1853-55 (also reports to the Treasurer of the Confederate States, 1861-64), 1 vol.
>   Eggleston Springs Co. Record Book, 1901-02, 1 vol.

F. E. Dunklee and Co. Hotel and Livery Ledger, 1893-94, 1 vol.

F. N. Priddy & Co. Day Book, 1882-83, 1 vol.

G. D. French's Mill Book, 1861-65, 1 vol.; and, [Guy French's?] Ledger, 1850-62, 1 vol.

G[uy] D. F[rench] & S[ons], Merchants, Account Book, 1859-62, 1 vol.

H. Caperton and Company Claims and Receipts, 1831-32, ca. .1 cu. ft.

Henry W. Broderick, Tobacco Account, Mercer Co., 1853, 1 item

Intermont Mining, Manufacture, and Development Co. Journal, 1891-92, 1 vol.

J. & C. M. A[nderson] Ledgers A-[B], 1860-69, 2 vols.

John Anderson & Co. Correspondence, 1866-69, ca. .1 cu. ft.

John Anderson's Day Books, 1859, 1868-75, 2 vols.; and, [John Anderson's?] Merchant's Journal, Pearisburg, 1859-61, 1 vol.

John S. Wilson & Co. Accounts, 1834-41, 11 items

L. Woolwine's Journal, Giles C. H., 1870, 1 vol.

Old Dominion Bank Book Keeper's Check Book A, 1857-60, 1 vol.; Discount Ledger A, 1857-60, 1 vol.; Ledger A, 1857-65, 1 vol.; Scratch Ledger, 1860-65, 1 vol.; and, Statement Books A-[B], 1857-65, 2 vols.

[Old Dominion Bank?] Letter Books, [1859]-62, 2 vols.

Pack and Caperton Co. Papers, 1828-37, ca. .6 cu. ft.

Pack and Mahood Co. Papers, 1837, ca. 25 items

Porterfield Huppman & Co. Ledger, Mountain Lake, 1896, 1 vol.; and, [Porterfield Huppman & Co.] Hotel and Livery Ledger, 1892-95, 1 vol.

P. S. B. Ledger, 1855-58, 1 vol.

R. M. S[tafford] & C[o.] Ledger, 1861-74, 1 vol.

Thomas and Robert Brotherton's Day Book Ledgers, 1857-61, 1858, 2 vols.

T. W. Brotherton, List of Claims, 1870, 1 vol.

Unidentified Account Book, 1859-69, 1 vol.; and, Account Books L-M, 1865-71, 2 vols.

Unidentified [Attorney's] Form Book, n.d., 1 vol.

Unidentified Journals, 1839-60, 1869, 2 vols.

Unidentified Ledgers, 1861-65, 1866-67, 1866-71, 1886, 1887, 1890-91, n.d., 8 vols.

Unidentified [Merchant's] Accounts, 1863-64, 3 items

Unidentified Receipt Books, 1880-82, 2 items

Unidentified Record Books, 1853, 1870, 2 items

Unidentified Ticklers, 1860-61, 2 vols.

William F. Martin's Day Book, Princeton, Mercer Co., 1853-63, 1 vol.

Court Records

County Court

Chancery Docket, 1822-42, 1 vol.; and, Chancery Docket [labeled Chancery Law], 1871-73, 1 vol.

Chancery Rule Docket, 1871-73, 1 vol. See also Common Law Rule Docket.

Clerk's Memorandum Book, 1869-74, 1 vol.

Clerk's Register of Court Papers [Rough Minutes?] (also Memorandums of the Clerk), 1871-92, 1 vol.

Common Law Rule Docket, 1865-73 (also Chancery Rule Docket, 1866-71), 1 vol.

Commonwealth v. Johnson, transcript, 1898, 1 item

D. A. French, Clerk of Court, correspondence, 1822, 1874-89, ca. .25 cu. ft.

Execution Books, 1818-24, 1827-47, 7 vols.

Farley v. Conley, bond, 1824, 1 item

Fee Books, 1806-08, 1816-31, 1847-50, 1858-81, 1887-93, 8 vols.

Alphabet [Index] for the County Court Fee, 1832, 1 vol.

Issue Docket and Office Judgments, 1806-29, 1 vol.; and, Issue Dockets, 1836-53, 1865-71, 2 vols.

Kirk et al. v. Burton, suit papers, 1813-19, 11 items

Memorandum Books, 1831-34, 1846-53, 2 vols.; and, Memorandum Book [labeled Scott Co. Record of Administration No. 1, 1854], 1858-69, 1 vol.

Minute Book, 1822-30, 1 vol.

Orders, 1822-31, 12 items

Process Books, 1836-47, 1868-1900, 2 vols.

Recognizance, 1845, 1 item

Rule Dockets, 1806-36, 2 vols.

Schedules [of Insolvent Debtors] and County Court Papers, 1822-1906 (includes Circuit Court, 1904-06), ca. .15 cu. ft.; and, County Court Schedules, 1832-59, ca. .75 cu. ft.

Summons, ca. 1830-65, 10 items

Witness Attendance, 1836-56, 1 vol.

Superior Court of Law

Fee Book, 1823-34 (includes Circuit Superior Court of Law and Chancery, 1831-34), 1 vol.

Issue Docket, 1825-31, 1 vol.

Memorandum Book, 1825-36 (includes Circuit Superior Court of Law and Chancery, 1831-36), 1 vol.

Minute Book, 1820-33 (includes Circuit Superior Court of Law and Chancery, 1831-33), 1 vol.

Circuit Superior Court of Law and Chancery

Common Law Fee Book, 1835-45, 1 vol.

Common Law Memorandum Book, 1836-47 (also [Circuit Court] Rule Docket, 1866), 1 vol.

Execution Book [labeled Record Book], 1834-46, 1 vol.

Fee Book, 1846-51, 1 vol. See also Superior Court of Law.

Memorandum Book, see Superior Court of Law

Minutes, see Superior Court of Law

Suit Papers, 1843-90 (includes Circuit Court, 1852-90), ca. 1.2 cu. ft.

Circuit Court

Causes Referred to the Commissioner [in Chancery], 1869-96, 1 vol.

Chancery [and Common Law] Process Book, 1860-82, 1 vol.

Chancery Memorandum Book, 1858-81, 1 vol.

Commissioner's Report, F. E. Mitchell and wife v. Samuel Wohlford's exrs. et al., and Gordon Wohlford v. T. E. Mitchell et al., 1856-83, 1 vol.

Common Law Memorandum Book [Record], 1885-1910, 1 vol.

Court Papers, see County Court

Fee Book, 1852-67, 1 vol.

F. E. Snidow, Clerk of the Circuit Court and Board of Supervisors, correspondence and papers, 1900-11, ca. .1 cu. ft.

Memorandum Book, 1857-72, 1 vol.

Process Book, 1882-1901, 1 vol.

Rule Docket, see Circuit Superior Court of Law and Chancery

Suit Papers, see Circuit Superior Court of Law and Chancery

Witness Attendance Book, 1874-1904, 1 vol.

County and Superior Courts

Commonwealth Warrants, 1809-1939, ca. .8 cu. ft.

Court Papers, 1803-1948, ca. 8.85 cu. ft. See also Board of Supervisors Records.

Executions, 1806-1906, ca. 9.25 cu. ft.

Judgments, 1806-72, 23.85 cu. ft.; and, Judgments Docketed, 1852-76, 21 items

Jury Lists, 1853-1904, ca. .25 cu. ft.; and, List of Receipts for Jury Tickets, 1869, 1 item

Minutes, 1830-31, 1 item

Unspecified Court

Index to Fee Book, n.d., 1 vol.

Index to Judgment Lien Docket No. 3, 1887, 1 vol.

Superior Court Alphabet to Execution Book, n.d., 1 vol.

Election Records

Abstracts of Votes, 1870-93, ca. .3 cu. ft.

Ballots, 1850-1904, .45 cu. ft.

[List of Registered Voters], 1895, 1 vol.

Poll Books, ca. 1830-1895, 3.15 cu. ft.

See also Tax and Fiscal Records; and, Miscellaneous Records

Fiduciary Records

Administrators' Bonds, 1806, 1876, 2 items

County Court Register of Fiduciaries No. 1, 1865-70, 1 vol.

Estate Vouchers, 1815-81, 3.15 cu. ft.

Guardians' Accounts, ca. 1820-85, ca. .5 cu. ft.

James Patton Estate Papers, Augusta County, 1844, 5 items

Receipts, Estate of John Reed and Lewis Wilson, 1832-43, ca. 50 items

Reports of Dower, 1832-74, 20 items

Reports of Sales, 1843-59, 13 items

Free Negro and Slave Records

Lists of Free Negroes and Mulattoes, 1816-64, 11 items

Justice of the Peace Records

Attachments, 1877-80, 4 items

B. P. Watts, Constable, correspondence, 1868-95, ca. 100 items

Justice's Judgment and Execution Book, 1877-79, 1 vol.

Justices' Judgments, 1877-96, ca. .15 cu. ft.

Magistrates' Executions, 1836, 1868, .45 cu. ft.

Land Records

Applications for Inclusive Surveys, 1858-68, ca. 100 items

County and Township Boundary Lines [plats, reports, etc.], 1828-70, 13 items

Deeds (Partly Proven), 1810-44, ca. .2 cu. ft.

General Index to Deeds, 1806-55, 1 vol. (Ts.)

Land grant (and related papers) of Charles Neill, 1811, 4 items

Lists of Surveys, 1840-45, 4 pp.

Plats, 1813, 1903-08, n.d., ca. .1 cu. ft.

Surveyors' Level Books, n.d., 12 vols.

Unidentified Surveyor's Notes, n.d. [20th century?], 18 pp.

Marriage Records and Vital Statistics

Marriage Consents, Certificates, and Licenses, 1849-1911, ca. .3 cu. ft.

Register of Births, 1882, 1 item

Register of Births, 1st District, 1856, 1 vol.

Registers of Births and Deaths, 1859-61, 1863, 1873-74, ca. .2 cu. ft.

Military and Pension Records

Civil War Papers, see Montgomery County Military and Pension Records

Lists of Soldiers' Families in Districts 1-5, 1864-65, 5 items

Military Records [militia lists, fines, etc.], 1831-70, ca. .25 cu. ft.

Pension Applications, 1831-38, ca. 100 items

Record, State Pensioners [Confederate veterans], 1888-1903, 1 vol.

Road and Bridge Records

Freight Bills and Bills of Lading, 1892-1925, ca. .4 cu. ft.

Norfolk and Western [Railroad] Plats, 1900-10, ca. .1 cu. ft

Orders, 1831-43, ca. 25 items

Road Book, Pearisburg Precinct, 1885-96, 1 vol.

Road Commissioner's Book No. 1, 1894-1904, 1 vol.

Road Papers [appointments, orders, receipts, etc.], 1806-1940, ca. 2.15 cu. ft.

[Surveyor's] Road Book, 1849-54, 1 vol.

Walker's Creek and Holton Turnpike Co. Minute Book, 1852-61, 1 vol.

Writs of Ad Quod Damnum and related papers, 1807-53, ca. 200 items

School Records

Articles of Agreement [teachers' contracts], 1887-94, ca. .1 cu. ft.

Daily Attendance Records, 1875-95, ca. .35 cu. ft.

Pearisburg Academy Minutes, 1839-54, 1 vol.

Reports of School Commissioner, 1818-48, ca. 200 items

School Claims, ca. 1875-1900, ca. .35 cu. ft.

School Records (claims, reports, etc.), 1869-1920, ca. .2 cu. ft.

Tax and Fiscal Records

Auditors' Receipts and Financial Reports, 1854-91, ca. 125 items

County Claims, ca. 1815-60, n.d., ca. .45 cu. ft. See also Board of Supervisors Records.

Delinquent Capitation and Personal Property Taxes, ca. 1830-1900, ca. .55 cu. ft.

Delinquent Land Taxes, 1831-45, 1859-78, ca. .4 cu. ft.

Delinquent Returns, 1871, 2 items

Delinquent Tax Lists, Claims, and Election Returns, 1830-70, ca. .1 cu. ft.; Delinquent Tax Lists [Tithables], 1807-45, ca. .2 cu. ft.; and, Delinquent Tax Tickets and Lists, ca. 1805-1879, ca. .45 cu. ft.

Improper Assessment of Land, 1871-75, ca. .1 cu. ft.

List of Licenses Issued, 1871-72, 1 item

Lists of Fines Imposed and Business Reports, 1875-99, ca. .2 cu. ft.

Memorandum of Expense for Waggon [sic], 1836, 1 item

Personal Property Book, Newport District, 1876, 1 vol.

Tax Collection Ledger, 1827, 1 vol.

Township Records

Newport Township Board Minutes, 1871-75, 1 vol.; and, Ledger, 1871-75, 1 vol.

Pearisburg Township Warrant Book, No. 1, 1871-75, 1 vol.

See also Land Records

Miscellaneous Records

Charles J. Stafford Family Papers, 1869-1950, n.d., ca. 1 cu. ft.

Contracts, 1868, 5 items

Counterfeit Bank Note and related paper, 1828, 1831, 2 items

Inquests, 1814-79, 6 items

Martin Williams' personal accounts, etc., University of Virginia, 1880-85, 1 vol.

Miscellaneous Papers (including Board of Supervisors papers, election records, suit papers, etc.), ca. 1810-1940, ca. .1 cu. ft.

Overseer of the Poor, see County Officials' Records

Personal Correspondence, ca. 1785-1890, ca. .35 cu. ft.

Promissory Notes, 1806, 1833, 3 items

P. W. Strother Papers, 1871-74, ca. 25 items

Receipts [personal], 1837, 1879-92, 14 items

Sheep Accounts, 1853-1913, ca. 50 items

Unidentified Indexes, n.d., 2 vols.

Unidentified Record Books, 1853, 1870, 2 items

Commissioner of Revenue

Commissioners' Books, Land and Personal Property Taxes, 1806-72, ca. .45 cu. ft.

List of Improper Assessment of Land and Insolvent Capitation and Property, 1899, 1 item

Lists of All Persons Assessed with a License Tax, 1860-85, ca. .45 cu. ft.

Lists of Liquor Licenses, 1878-89, ca. .35 cu. ft.
Lists of Persons Applying for Business Licenses, Insolvent Capitations, and Personal Property, etc., 1885-1903, ca. .2 cu. ft.
State Personal Property Interrogatories, 1900-04, 13 items
<u>See also</u> Tax and Fiscal Records; and, Treasurer

Sheriff

Settlements with the Sheriff or Overseer of the Poor, 1807-56, ca. .1 cu. ft.
Sheriff's Papers (receipts, notes, and warrants), 1833-60, ca. .1 cu.ft
Sheriff's Qualification, 1843, 1 item
Tax Tickets, 1870, ca. 100 items

Treasurer

C. W. Walker, Treasurer, correspondence, 1871, 3 items
General Account Vouchers, 1882, 4 items
Tax Reports, 1883-1923, ca. .1 cu. ft.
[Treasurer's?] Ledger, 1891, 1 vol.
Treasurer's Report Books, Pembroke, Newport, and Walker's Creek districts, 1899-1907, 3 vols.
[Treasurer?] W. J. Woods' Reports, 1897-1900, ca. .1 cu. ft.
<u>See also</u> Tax and Fiscal Records

Microfilm Records

Circuit Court Clerk
Bonds/Commissions/Oaths
[Officials'] Bonds, 1833-65, 1 reel. <u>See also</u> Wills.
Court Records
County Court
Order Books, 1806-68, 5 reels
Circuit Superior Court of Law and Chancery
Chancery Order Books, 1831-52 (includes Circuit Court, 1852), 1 reel (part)
Circuit Court
Chancery Order Books, 1855-73 [1872], 1 reel (part). <u>See also</u> Circuit Superior Court of Law and Chancery.
Land Records
Deed Books A-L [there is no Book J], 1806-70, 5 reels
General Index to Deeds, etc., No. 1, 1806-1923, 1 reel
Surveys, 1807-45, 1 reel (part); and, Surveyors' Record, 1846-1926, 1 reel (part)
Marriage Records and Vital Statistics
Marriage Bonds, 1806-53, 5 reels
Register of Births, 1855-96, 1 reel (part)
Register of Deaths, 1855-96, 1 reel (part)
Register of Marriages, 1871-1913, 1 reel (part)
Index to Register of Births, Marriages, and Deaths, 1806-96, 1 reel
Wills
Will Books, A-B and 3-4, 1806-73, 2 reels
Circuit Court Will Book, 1856-1902, 1 reel
General Index to Wills, 1806-1953, 1 reel

GLOUCESTER COUNTY

Formed in 1651 from York County.

Original Records

Circuit Court Clerk
Board of Supervisors Records
Papers, 1870-1904, 1.5 cu. ft.
Registry of County Bonds, 1897-98, 1 vol.
Warrant Books, 1871-72, 1871-75, 2 vols.
Bonds/Commissions/Oaths
Circuit Court Bond Book, 1877-87, 1 vol.
Circuit Court Old Attachment Bonds [and related papers], 1875-77, 18 items
County and Circuit Court Bond Books, 1872-77, 1892-1901, 2 vols.; and, County and Circuit Court Bond Book No. 2, 1901-09, 1 vol.
See also Fiduciary Records; and, Land Records
Business Records/Corporations/Partnerships
Charters Granted by the Circuit Court Judge, 1888-1923, 1 vol.
H. V. Hogge's Memorandum Book, 1903, 1 vol.
P. H. Adams [railroad agent?] Letter Book, 1887, 1 vol.
Rock Landing and Weldon Account Book, 1820-34, 1 vol.
Tidewater Telephone Co. Collection Day Book, 1888-91, 1 vol.
Unidentified Account Book, 1869-71, 1 vol.
Unidentified Attorney's Receipt Book, 1872-91, 1 vol.
Unidentified Cash Book, 1860-68, 1 vol.
Unidentified Day Books, 1861-62, 1883-1906, 2 vols.
Unidentified Expense Book, 1834-69, 1 vol.
Unidentified Ledgers Nos. 1-2, 1896-1934, 2 vols.
W[yndham] K[emp]'s Ledger, 1854-60, 1 vol.; and, Cash Book, 1856-59, 1 vol.
Court Records
County Court
Bradford v. German, suit papers, 1888-89, 3 items
Clerk John R. Carey's Memorandum Books, 1847-52, 1860, 2 vols.; and, John R. Carey, Clerk of Court, Ledger and Memorandum Book, 1848-64, 1 vol.
County Court and Sheriffs' Miscellaneous Notices, 1869-78, ca. 50 items
Court Papers, 1862-1902, 15 cu. ft.
Dockets, 1837-51, 1866-94, 1896-1904, 6 vols.; and, Docket for the Judge, 1892-96, 1 vol.
Executions, 1831-41, 1866-1902 (includes Justice of the Peace Court, 1901-16), 1874-1900, 3 vols.
Fee Books, 1868-80, 2 vols.
Judgments, 1865-1903, 8 cu. ft.
Memorandum Book, 1853-69, 1 vol.
Old Court Papers, 1888-91, ca. .1 cu. ft.
Process Book, 1842-59, 1 vol.
Register of Convicts, 1871-85, 1 vol.; and, Register of Persons Convicted of Felony, 1894-1942 (includes Circuit Court, 1904-42), 1 vol.
Richardson v. Corbell, suit papers, 1886, ca. 25 items
Rough Fee Book, of Clerk's Office (also Clerk's Memorandum Book), 1839-76, 1 vol.
Rules, 1866-72, 1 vol.
Special Orders of the Circuit Court Judge, 1852-91, ca. 50 items
Witness Attendance Books, 1866-87, 1891-[1904], 3 vols.
Writ of Attachment, 1827, 1 item

Circuit Superior Court of Law and Chancery
Chancery Rule Book, 1850-80 (includes Circuit Court, 1852-80), 1 vol.
Rule Books, 1831-49, 1846-51, 2 vols.

Circuit Court
Attorney's Memorandum Book, 1888-91, 1 vol.
Burke v. Cox admr., suit papers, 1868-70, ca. 25 items
Chancery Dockets, 1874-76, 1886-96, 2 vols.
Chancery Execution Book, 1868-1948, 1 vol.
Chancery Rule Books, 1870-1917, 3 vols. See also Circuit Superior Court of Law and Chancery.
Circuit Court Papers Belonging to Chancery, 1871-79, 13 items
Clerk's Fine Receipt Book, 1900, 1 vol.
Common Law Rule Books, 1873-1920, 2 vols.
Dockets, 1853-73, 1877-85, 1887-1904, 27 vols.; and, Docket for the Judge, 1893-95, 1 vol.
Execution Books, 1853-91, 2 vols.; and, No. 2, 1892-1926, 1 vol.
Fee Books, 1889-1906, 2 vols.; and, Nos. 1-2, 1888-96, 2 vols.
Hughes v. Rowe, bill, 1881, 1 item
Issue Docket, 1897-1905, 1 vol.
Memorandum [Minute] Book, 1867-76, 1 vol.; Memorandum Book, 1891-97, 1 vol; and, No. 1, 1896-1912, 1 vol.
Miscellaneous Papers (subpoenas, presentments, etc.), ca. 1890-1915, ca. .3 cu. ft.
Moneys Deposited by Order of the Court, 1898-1940, 1 vol.
Old Chancery Subpoenas Returned, 1871-78, ca. 40 items
Page, Trustee v. Dobson's admrs., suit papers, 1875, ca. 50 items
Process Books, 1862-78, 1865-68, 2 vols.; and, [Nos. 2-4], 1865-1911, 3 vols.
Receipt Book [Chancery Papers Received by the Clerk], 1891-1903, 1 vol.
Register of Persons Convicted of Felony, see County Court
Rules, 1857-63, 1866-73, 2 vols.
Witness Attendance Book, 1866-83, 1 vol.; and, Witness and Jury Book, 1877-79, 1 vol.

County and Superior Courts
Case Papers, 1845-92, ca. .15 cu. ft.
Clerks' Correspondence and Court Papers, ca. 1885-1940, ca. .75 cu. ft.
[Clerk's] Tax Books, 1898-1904, 1898-1914, 2 vols.
Executions, 1859-1906, ca. 1 cu. ft.; and, Commonwealth Executions, 1896-1907, ca. .1 cu. ft.
Fee Books, 1860-69, 4 vols.
General Index to Judgments No. 1, 1866-1933, 1 vol.
Memorandum Book, 1870-88, 1 vol.
Miscellaneous Court Decrees (also lunacy papers, etc.), 1879-1904, ca. .5 cu. ft.
Tabb v. Furguson, suit papers, 1867-82, ca. 50 items
Witness Attendance Book [also Jury Books; titles vary], 1853-75, 1874-1903, 5 vols.

Virginia Supreme Court of Appeals
Marshall v. Keen et al., transcript, 1867, 1 vol.

Court of Common Pleas, Baltimore, Maryland
Wood and Scull v. Labb, proceedings, 1875-77, 1 item

Unspecified Court
Fee Books, 1861-63, 1865-81, 1893-1901, 4 vols.
Form Book, n.d., 1 vol.

Election Records
Lists of Registered Voters, 1898-1971, n.d. [overlapping date ranges], 219 vols.

Fiduciary Records

Circuit Court Commissioners' Bond Book No. 1, 1892-1928, 1 vol.
Circuit Court Commissioners' Bonds (also Receivers', Injunction, and Supersedeas Bonds), 1888-91, ca. 100 items
Commissioners' Accounts, 1870-86, 1 vol.
County Court [Fiduciary] Bonds, 1862-77, 2 vols.
County Court Guardians' Accounts M, 1862-90, 1 vol.
County Court Inventories, Appraisements, and Administrators' Accounts Nos. 1-2, 1862-83, 2 vols.; County Court Inventory, Administration, etc., Vol. C, 1885-94, and No. 2, 1894-1902, 2 vols.; and, County and Circuit Court Inventory, Administration Accounts, etc., No. 3, 1902-12, 1 vol.
General Index to Fiduciary Accounts, etc., 1866-97, 1 vol.
Inventory of the Stock of Goods Belonging to the Estate of A. W. Tabb, 1888, 1 vol.
John R. Carey's Estate, Executor's Account Book, 1868-69, 1 vol.
Record of Fiduciaries, 1864-85, 1 vol.

Justice of the Peace Records

Justices' Judgment and Execution Books, 1870-89, 1892-95, 1899-1912, 4 vols.
See also Court Records, County Court.
Justices' Reports, see Tax and Fiscal Records
Justices' Warrants Returned, 1879-83 (A-D) and 1886-87 (S-Y), ca. .2 cu. ft.

Land Records

Daily Index of Receipt of Deeds for Recordation, 1902-06, 1 vol.
List of Deeds Entered to Records, 1887-88, 1 item
Oyster Plats, Transfers, and Bonds, 1892-1906, ca. .25 cu. ft.
Plats of Robert Kemp's Land and of Mrs. Robert Kemp's Portion, 1903, 2 items
Processioners' Book, 1866-83, 1 vol.
Surveyors' Book A, 1733-1810, 1 vol. (copy); and, No. 1, 1817-52, 1 vol. (copy)
Unrecorded Deeds, 1885-1922, ca. .15 cu. ft.

Marriage Records and Vital Statistics

Register of Births and Deaths, 1865-90, 1 cu. ft.
[Card] Index to Births, 1867-79, ca. .25 cu. ft.

Military and Pension Records

[Confederate] Pension Applications, 1900-03, ca. .1 cu. ft.
Page-Puller Camp of Confederate Veterans, Minutes, 1893-1925, 1 vol.

Road Records

Road Book, 1886 and 1890-93, 1 vol.
Road Cases, 1890-98, ca. .25 cu. ft.

School Records

Charity School Accounts with E. B. S. Carey, 1847-76, 1 vol.; Account Book, 1876-84, 1 vol.; Minute Book, 1840-65, 1 vol.; and, Record of Debts Due and Disbursements, 1828-54, 1 vol.
Charity School Papers, 1820-1923, n.d., 1.35 cu. ft.
Public School Register, 1886-91, 1 vol.

Tax and Fiscal Records

Applications for Purchases of Delinquent Land, 1898-1946, 1 vol.
County and District Ledger, 1896-1910, 1 vol.
Delinquent Land, 1876-1926, 1 vol.
Delinquent Tax Bills, 1903, ca. .2 cu. ft.
Delinquent Tax Receipts, 1898-1901, ca. .1 cu. ft.
Insolvent and Delinquent Taxes and Land Sales, 1882-84, 1892-96, ca. .45 cu. ft.
Insolvent Capitation and Property Tax Receipts, 1894-1901, ca. .2 cu. ft.; and, Insolvent Tax Receipts, 1899, ca. 150 items.
Land Purchased by the Commonwealth, 1876-1926, 1 vol.

L. F. Miller's Tax Book, 1867-68, 1 vol.
List of Delinquent Land Sales and Taxes, 1884, 1 item
Oyster Inspectors' Reports [titles vary], 1882, 1888-89 (includes Justices'
    Reports), 1894-1908, ca. .25 cu. ft.
Reassessment Books, 1875-90, 2 vols.
Record of Insolvent Capitation and Property Tax, 1885-86, 1 vol.
Record of Lands Sold for Taxes, 1893-1919, 1 vol.
Tax Accounts, 1770-71, 1 vol.

Township Records
Records of Abingdon Township, 1871-74, 1 vol.
Records of Petsworth Township, 1871-73, 1 vol.

Miscellaneous Records
County and Circuit Court Mechanics' Liens, 1873-86, 1889-1922, 2 vols.
County Court Records of Contracts No. 1, 1891-99, 1 vol.
Record of Persons Adjudged Insane, 1901-36, 1 vol. See also Court Records,
    County and Superior Courts.
Reservation of Title to Personalty, 1900-20, 1 vol.

Sheriff
James C. Baytop's Sheriff's Book, 1867-68, 1 vol.
J. Christopher Baytop's Tax Book, 1867-68, 1 vol.
Sheriff's Notices, see Court Records, County Court

Treasurer
Cancelled Treasurer's Vouchers (and Delinquent Tax Receipts), 1897-1901, ca. .35
    cu. ft.; and, Vouchers, 1902-03, ca. .2 cu. ft.
See also Tax and Fiscal Records

Microfilm Records

Circuit Court Clerk
Court Records
County Court
Minute Books, 1820-25, 1833-42, 4 reels; and, Minute Book No. 1, 1858-67,
    1 reel
Land Records
Surveyors' Book A, 1733-1810, 1 reel (part); and, No. 1, 1817-52, 1 reel (part)
Tax and Fiscal Records
Tax Accounts, 1770-71, 1 reel

GOOCHLAND COUNTY

Formed in 1727 from Henrico County.

Original Records

Circuit Court Clerk

Board of Supervisors Records

Minutes, 1870-1907, 3 vols.; and, Minutes, Roads, 1889-1900, 1 vol.

Papers (including Road Papers), ca. 1885-1930, n.d., 6 items

Proceedings, 1876-1905, 4.95 cu. ft.; and, Miscellaneous Proceedings, n.d., .45 cu. ft.

Records (including Superintendent of the Poor Records), ca. 1870-95, .9 cu. ft.

Stubs for Warrants Issued, 1880-82, 1 vol.

Bonds/Commissions/Oaths

Bail Bonds, 1732-1843, 14 items

Bonds and Officials' Commissions, ca. 1800-50, ca. .35 cu. ft.

Commission of the Peace for Goochland County, 1730, 1 item

Commissions of Justices of Oyer and Terminer, 1763, 1768-69, 4 items

[County Court] Bonds, 1868-88, 1 vol.

Debt Bonds and Promissory Notes, ca. 1735-1840, ca. 75 items

Indemnifying Bonds, 1723, 1827-28, 4 items

Injunction Bonds, ca. 1795-1870, 29 items

Liquor License Bond, 1889, 1 item

[List of] Ordinary and Marriage Licenses [Bonds] Granted, 1779-80, 1 item

Lists of Those Who have taken the Oath of Allegiance, 1778, 4 items

[Militia] Bonds, n.d. [ca. 1860], 1 vol.

Officials' Bonds, 1788, 1820, 1828, 1846, 1887, n.d., 6 items

Ordinary and Liquor License Bonds, 1735-74, 1891, n.d., 18 items. See also Fiduciary Records.

Property Bonds, 1788-98, 9 items

Record [of Bonds], 1805-17, 1 vol.

Replevy Bonds, 1786-1828, n.d., 41 items

Stay and Appeal Bonds, 1790-1818, 15 items

See also Court Records, County and Superior Courts

Business Records/Corporations/Partnerships

B. O. Wiley's Ledger, 1836-45 and 1877-82, 1 vol.

Charter Book, 1875-1954, 1 vol.

Crutchfield and Nicholas Account Book, Cedar Point, 1848-64, 1 vol. See also William Crutchfield.

E. V. B. Account Book No. 2, 1869-70, 1 vol.

Grove James & Co. Journal, 1847-48, 1 vol.

Manakin Iron Works Account Book, 1845-51, 1 vol.; Day Book, 1849, 1 vol.; and, Ledgers, 1847-50, 2 vols.

[Mutual Assurance Society] Agency and Seal, 1822, 1 item

Unidentified Account Books, 1835-36, 1860, 2 items (fragments)

William Crutchfield Account Book, Rocketts, 1855-58, 1 vol.; Day Books, Rocketts and Cedar Point, 1850-55, 1851-59, 1853-55, 1866-70, 8 vols.; Freight Book, 1861 (also Blacksmith Shop Book, 1862-65), 1 vol.; Journal, Rocketts, 1851-57, 1 vol.; Ledger A, 1865-66, 1 vol.; and, Storage Book, 1857-67, 1 vol.

William Crutchfield Papers (business correspondence), 1866-70, n.d., 24 items

Woodson, Perkins & Co. Daybook, 1843-50, 1 vol.

Census Records

Enumerations, 1870, 1880, 5 items

Court Records
    County Court
        Attachments, 1742–43, ca. 1785–1825, 13 items
        Certificates, 1789, 1812, 1862, 3 items
        Chancery Rule Docket, 1812–23, 1 vol.
        <u>Commonwealth</u> v. <u>McLaren,</u> suit papers, 1800, 6 items
        Court Papers, 1734–1820, ca. 2.75 cu. ft.
        Docket Books, 1728–32, 1761–62, 1764–65, 1769, 1773–78, 1784, 1787, 1790, 1793–94, 1802–05, 1828–72, 12 vols.
        Escape Warrants, 1800–01, 1817, 3 items
        Execution Books, [1775–80?], 1786–1810, 1813–1903, 11 vols.; and, 1787–88, 1 item (fragment)
        Executions, 1792, 1 p.
        Fee Books, 1728–34, 1736–38, 1740–50, 1752–57, 1759–61, 1763–69, 1771, 1773–76, 1779–97, 1785–97, 1800–21, 1810–46, 1857–67, 72 vols.
        Issue Docket, Petitions, and Office Judgments [titles vary], 1788–93, 1796–1802, 5 vols.
        List of County Records in the Clerk's Office, 1769, 1 item
        Memorandum Books, 1750, 1753–55, 1785–89, 1798–1801, 1805–07, 1819–22, 1826–37, 1854–55, 16 vols.
        Minutes [Orders], 1728–31, 1734–39, 1749–50, 1753, 1759, 1762–65, 1768–80, 1782–85, 1788–99, 1803–11, n.d., 30 vols.
        Mittimus, 1738, 1 item
        Notices and Orders, 1737, 1791–1898, n.d., 44 items
        Office Judgment Books, 1787–1817, 3 vols.
        Order Books, 1862–71, 1902–04, 2 vols.; and, Nos. 1–6, 8, 10–13, 17, and 31, 1728–49, 1757–79, 1787–89, 1825–30, 14 vols. (copies)
        Index to Order Book No. 18, 1788–91, 1 vol.
        Orders, ca. 1805–25, 6 items
        Petitions [on debts], 1729, ca. 1735–1800, n.d., 36 items
        Pleas at Quarterly Sessions, 1811, 1 item
        Process Book, 1835–67, 1 vol.
        Reference Dockets, 1737, 1741–45, 1750, 1762, 1772–73, 1778–79, 9 vols.
        References and Actions to Court, 1781–84, 1 vol.
        [Rough Minutes?], 1872, 1 item
        Rule Dockets, 1789–1804, 1824–47, 5 vols.
        [Subpoena Docket?], 1797–1801, 1 vol.
        Suit Papers, ca. 1730–1815, 1875, ca. 150 items; and, Patrick Henry suit papers [removed from other series?], 1760–80, .25 cu. ft.
        Witness Attendance Books, 1870–1902, 2 vols.
        Witnesses Summoned and Action to the Courts of 1759–61, 1 vol.
        Writs and Pleas, 1728, ca. 1735–1825, n.d., 32 items
    Superior Court of Law
        Fee Book, 1822–31, 1 vol.
        Minutes, 1816–36 (includes Circuit Superior Court of Law and Chancery, 1831–36), 1 vol.
        Rule Docket Book, 1809–31, 1 vol.
        Witness Attendance Book, 1822–69 (includes Circuit Superior Court of Law and Chancery, 1831–51, and Circuit Court, 1852–69), 1 vol.
    Circuit Superior Court of Law and Chancery
        Chancery Docket Book, 1832–70 (includes Circuit Court, 1852–70), 1 vol.
        Chancery Process Book No. 1, 1831–67 (includes Circuit Court, 1852–67), 1 vol.
        Common Law Docket Book, 1832–59 (includes Circuit Court, 1852–59), 1 vol.

Common Law Rule Docket No. 1, 1831-57 (includes Circuit Court, 1852-57), 1 vol.

Docket Book, 1835, 1 vol.

Execution Book, 1846-82 (includes Circuit Court, 1852-82), 1 vol.

Executions taken from Circuit Superior Court Suit Papers, 1849, ca. 200 items

Fee Books, 1831-46, 2 vols.

Minutes, see Superior Court of Law

Orders, 1832-59 (includes Circuit Court, 1852-59), 1 vol.

Proceedings, 1835-52 (includes Circuit Court, 1852), 1.8 cu. ft.

Witness Attendance, see Superior Court of Law

Circuit Court

Chancery Docket, 1897-1906, 1 vol. See also Circuit Superior Court of Law and Chancery.

Chancery Process, see Circuit Superior Court of Law and Chancery

Chancery Rules, 1877-1904, 1 vol.

Common Law and Chancery Docket, 1880, 1 item

Common Law Docket, 1898-1927, 1 vol. See also Circuit Superior Court of Law and Chancery.

Common Law Rules, see Circuit Superior Court of Law and Chancery

Executions, 1883-1918, 1 vol. See also Circuit Superior Court of Law and Chancery.

Fee Book, 1857-68, 1 vol.

Orders, see Circuit Superior Court of Law and Chancery

Proceedings [Judgments, etc.], 1852-1904, 15.3 cu. ft.; and, Miscellaneous, n.d., .45 cu. ft. See also Circuit Superior Court of Law and Chancery.

Register of Court Costs, 1899-1910, 1 vol.

Rule Book,1858-1920, 1 vol.

Summons, 1875, ca. 75 items

Witness [Attendance] Book, 1851, 1854, 1 vol. (part). See also Superior Court of Law.

County and Superior Courts

Chancery Papers, ca. 1795-1905, .35 cu. ft.

[Clerks'] Correspondence, 1784-1941, n.d., ca. .35 cu. ft. (including fragments). See also Court Records, County and Superior Courts.

Clerk's Office Notes for the Trial of Warrants [Judgment Book], 1852-62, 1 vol.

Cocke v. Cocke, 1799, and Robertson et ux v. Cocke's admr., 1831, bills in Chancery, 2 items

Court Papers (bonds, suit papers, etc.), 1727-1900, ca. 4 cu. ft. (including fragments); and, Old [Court] Papers (including bonds, deeds, wills, election records, marriage bonds, and fiduciary records), 1728-ca. 1950, 17.55 cu. ft.

Declarations, Narrations, and Bills, ca. 1730-1870, n.d., 40 items

Depositions and Affidavits, 1790-[1856?], 9 items

Executions, 1727-1869, n.d., ca. 1.45 cu. ft.

Fee [Account] Books, [1799] 1801-46, 1818-27, 2 vols.

Judgment Liens, 1843-1917, 2 vols.

Judgments and Indictments, 1727-1821, n.d., 17 items

Memorandum Book, 1848-59, 1 vol.

Memorandums, 1730-31, 1789-1873, n.d., 22 items

Miscellaneous Court Papers [unarranged series containing suit papers, bonds, tax lists, fiduciary records, and other proceedings of the court; also, Amelia County Court Proceedings, 1747, ca. .1 cu. ft.], 1728-ca. 1870, 48.35 cu. ft.

Miscellaneous Law Papers, ca. 1840-1940, 2.7 cu. ft. See also Old [Court] Papers.

Subpoena Book, 1837-59, 1 vol.

Subpoenas and Petitions, 1729-1875, 1900, ca. 200 items

Suit Papers, 1728-1907 (also Surveyor of the Roads Papers, 1875-79, and Clerk's Correspondence, various dates), 3.85 cu. ft. See also Court Papers and Miscellaneous Court Papers.

Warrant Judgments, ca. 1860-1940, 1.35 cu. ft.

Unspecified Court

Index [to suits], n.d., 1 vol.

Election Records

Declarations of Candidacy [and other election records], 1873, 1893, 1895, 4 items

Election Returns and Abstracts of Votes, ca. 1805-90, ca. .65 cu. ft.

Poll Books, 1827, ca. 1870-1900, ca. 2.25 cu. ft.

Polling Records, 1765, 1799, 1818, 1861, 1876, 6 items

Polls, etc. 1809, 1826, 1862-63, n.d., ca. 50 items

Poll Tax and Election Records, ca. 1850-60, ca. .6 cu. ft.

[Roll of Registered Voters], 1902-03, 1 vol.

See also Court Records, County and Superior Courts

Fiduciary Records

Circuit Court [Special Commissioners'] Bonds, 1901-04, 1 vol.

County and Circuit Court Fiduciary Bonds, 1900-11, 1 vol.

Estate Papers, 1729-1805, 23 items

Executors', Administrators' and Guardians' Bonds, 1850-60, 1 vol.

Executors' Bonds, 1810-91, 1.35 cu. ft. See also Court Records, County and Superior Courts.

[Fiduciary Accounts?], 1794-1872, 1 vol.

Fiduciary Bonds and Ordinary Licenses, 1732, 1739-40, 1763, 1765, ca. 1785-1820, .45 cu. ft.

[Fiduciary Records], ca. 1850-1915, ca. .55 cu. ft.

List of Fiduciaries, 1866-72, 1 vol.

Reports and Accounts, ca. 1830-65, .45 cu. ft.

Schedule of Jesse Witt's Estate, 1827, 1 item

Widow's Dower, 1828, 1 item

See also Court Records, County and Superior Courts

Free Negro and Slave Records

Lists of Free Negroes, 1861, 1867, n.d., 3 items; and, Lists of Mulattoes and Free Negroes, 1803-12, 9 items

[Lists of] Slaves and Free Negroes, 1764, 1768, 1770, 1817, 15 items (including fragments)

Register of Free Negroes, 1804-64, 1 vol.

Justice of the Peace Records

Justices' Civil Judgments and Executions, 1899-1924, 1 vol.

Justices' [Criminal] Judgments, 1900-05, 1 vol.

Justices' Judgment and Execution Book, 1901-07, 1 vol.

Justice's Warrant, 1893, 1 item

Land Records

County Surveyor's Resignation, 1813, 1 item

Deed Books (including wills) Nos. [1]-14, 1728-88, 14 vols. (copies); and, Nos. 15-17 and 19, 1788-1800, 1804-07, 4 vols. (copies)

Deeds and Related Papers, 1765-ca. 1905, n.d., 20 items; and, Recorded Deeds and Wills, 1728-1911, 21.15 cu. ft.

[Index to Deeds?], n.d., 1 vol.

General Index to Deeds [and wills], Books 1-45, L-W, n.d., 1 vol.
General Index to Papers [deeds] in Ended Chancery Causes, B-D, n.d., 1 vol.
List of transfers, 1790, 1 item
Lists of Surveys returned by William Mayo and Peter Jefferson, 1734-35, 1745, 1748, 4 items; and, List of Surveys returned by Peter Jefferson, 1745, 1 item (copy)
Order of the General Court regarding the Goochland-Hanover boundary, 1733, 1 item (copy)
Processioner's Record, 1824, 1 item
Processioners' Returns, 1795-1820, 1 vol. (2 copies)
Processioners' Returns, ca. 1820-40, ca. .2 cu. ft.
Processioning Book, 1827-46, 1 vol.
Unidentified Indexes [to deeds?], n.d., 2 items
See also Court Records, County and Superior Courts

Marriage Records and Vital Statistics

Marriage Bond, 1770, 1 item; and, 1740, 1 item (copy)
Marriage Records, ca. 1750-1900, n.d., ca. .15 cu. ft.
Marriage Register, 1730-1853 (compilation), 1 vol. (Ts. and copy)
Index to Marriage Register, 1730-1853 (compilation), 1 vol. (Ts. and copy)
Ministers' Returns, 1788-93, ca. 1850, ca. .2 cu. ft.
Ministers' Returns, 1794-1853, 1 vol. (copy)
Register of Births, Lickinghole Township, 1871, 1 item; and, Register of Births, 1874, 1 item
Registers of Deaths and Births, 1857-58, 9 pp.
Registers of Marriages and Births, ca. 1860, 2 pp.
[Card Index to Births, ca. 1855-95], ca. .25 cu. ft.
See also Court Records, County and Superior Courts

Military and Pension Records

Applications for Exemption from the Confederate Service, 1862, ca. 75 items
Civil War and Military Government Records, 1869, n.d., 4 items
Losses Sustained by the Depredations of the British, 1781, 12 items
[Militia] Courts of Enquiry Minutes, 1861, 1 item
Militia List, 1788, 1 item
Other Military Records, 1782, 1787, 1836, n.d., 4 items
Pension Board Record, 1900-02, 1 vol.
Public Service Claims, Court Booklet (copy), 1782, 1 vol.

Road and Bridge Records

Petition [for ferry across the James River], n.d., 1 item
Petitions for Mills and Roads, and Summons to Overseers of the Roads, 1775-76, 1778, 1787-88, 1791, 7 items
Surveyor of the Roads Papers, see Court Records, County and Superior Courts
Surveyor of the Roads Record Book, 1820-68, 1 vol.
See also Board of Supervisors Records

Tax and Fiscal Records

Claims against the County, 1747-1894, n.d., 77 items
Land Tax Book, 1832, 1 vol.
Levy Papers, 1806-39, ca. .1 cu. ft.
List of Licenses Issued, 1864, 1 item
Lists of Taxable Property, 5th District, 1783, 4 pp.
Lists of Tithables, 1735-ca. 1785, n.d., ca. .75 cu. ft.; and, Tithables and Property Taxes, 1756-82, and Personal Property Tax Lists, 1783-1814, .25 cu. ft.
Mt. Upton, New York, Butternut's Tax Assessment, 1824, 1 vol.
Tithables, 1735-86 and 1746-48, 1768, 1775, 1777, 2 vols. (copies)
Unidentified List of Names [tax List?], n.d., 1 item
See also Court Records, County and Superior Court

Township Records

Lickinghole Township Journal of Proceedings, 1871-74, 1 vol.
See also Marriage Records and Vital Statistics

Wills

Wills, 1767, 1815, 1856, 3 items
Index to Wills, see Land Records
See also County Court Records, County and Superior Courts; and, Land Records

Miscellaneous Records

[Baltimore, Maryland?] City Hospital Report, 1799, 1 vol.
Bounty Warrants, 1733-41, 10 items
Certificate of Protection [bankruptcy], 1866, 1 item
Conditional Sales, 1895-96, 5 items
Estray Notices, 1777-1815, 8 items; and, ca. 1855-60, ca. 50 items
Gilmer Family Tree, 1902, 2 pp.; and, Genealogical Data, n.d., 5 items
Josiah Payne's Account Book, 1760-72, 1 vol.
Mechanics' and Miscellaneous Liens, 1872-1921, 1 vol.
Peachy R. Grattan Letters, 1827-35, 12 items
Personal Accounts [removed from suits], 1729-1886, n.d., 53 items
Personal Letters (James B. Ferguson, Thomas Miller, and others), 1797-1823, ca. 50 items
[Peter and Thomas] Jefferson Papers, 1734-49, 1773-89, ca. 50 items
Petition for a Festival, 1868, 1 item
Receipt for Payment for Subscription to the Virginia Gazette, 1774, 1 item
Receipts, ca. 1775-1920, 48 items
Stray Book, 1791-1803, 1 vol.
Superintendent of the Poor, see Board of Supervisors Records
Wyatt Freeman Papers, ca. 1820, 34 items

Commissioner of Revenue

Land Tax Book, Upper District, 1807, 1 item
[Personal Property] Tax Interrogatories and other tax records, ca. 1800-99, n.d., 27 items
See also Tax and Fiscal Records

Sheriff

Sheriffs' Return [Execution] Books, 1797-1802, 1806-07, 2 vols.
Thomas Miller, Sheriff, Account Book, 1799, 1 vol.
Thomas Miller, Sheriff, Papers, 1787-1815, ca. .2 cu. ft.

Treasurer

Delinquent Land, Property, and Capitation Taxes, 1875, 1 vol.
[Treasurer's] Ledger B, 1892-1927, 1 vol.
See also Tax and Fiscal Records

Microfilm Records

Circuit Court Clerk
  Court Records
    County Court

Complete Records [Sheriffs' Debtor Books, Bonds, etc.], 1805-17, 1 reel (part)
Minutes, 1779-82, 1803-07, 1811-18, 3 reels (parts)
Order Books Nos. 1-32, 1728-1836, 15 reels
Record Books [Orders; titles vary], 1836-71, 2 reels

Fiduciary Records
Guardians' Accounts, 1794-1822, 1 reel (part)
Land Records
Deeds, etc., No. 1 (includes wills), 1728-34, 1 reel (part)
Deed Books Nos. 2-40 (including wills), 1734-1868, 18 reels
General Index to Deeds, Wills, etc., 1728-1839, Grantors-Grantees A-Z, 2 reels
Processioners' Returns, 1795-1820, 1 reel (part)
Marriage Records and Vital Statistics
Marriage Bonds, 1730-1850, 2 reels
Marriage Register, 1730-1853 (Ms. compilation), 1 reel (part); and, Register of Marriages, 1852-1901, 1 reel (part)
Index to Marriage Register, 1730-1853 (Ms. compilation), 1 reel (part); Index to Register of Births, Deaths, and Marriages, 1852-1901 [D-Z only], 1 reel (part); and, Index to Births, 1853-77, 1 reel (part)
Military and Pension Records
Muster Roll, List of Confederate Soldiers in the War in Defense of Virginia, 1861-65, 1 reel (part)
Wills
See Land Records

GRAYSON COUNTY

Formed in 1792 from Wythe County; part of Patrick County was added later.

Original Records

Circuit Court Clerk
Bonds/Commissions/Oaths
Circuit Court Oath of Office Anti-Duelling Oath Book, 1899-1912, 1 vol.
County Court Bond Books Nos. 3-4, 1889-1903, 2 vols.; and, County Court Bond Book No. 4, 1900-05 (includes Circuit Court, 1904-05), 1 vol.
Officials' Bonds [Records], 1871-89, 1 vol.
Business Records/Corporations/Partnerships
Certificates of Incorporation, 1897-1916, 1 vol.
J. W. Wiley & Co. Account Book, 1874-75, 1 vol.
Unidentified Day Book No. 1, 1834-35 (also Memorandum Book for Account of Claims paid for 1828), 1 vol.
See also Road and Bridge Records
Court Records
County Court
[Clerk's] Tax Book, 1898-1905, 1 vol.
Common Law Process Book, 1854-88, 1 vol.
Execution Book, 1869-83, 1 vol.
Judgment Docket, 1842-71, 1 vol.
Judgment Lien Docket, 1895-[1928] (includes Circuit Court, 1904-28), 1 vol.
Order Book, 1793-94, 1 vol. (copy)
Superior Court of Law
Common Law Fee Book, 1809-33 (includes Circuit Superior Court of Law and Chancery, 1831-33), 1 vol.

Circuit Superior Court of Law and Chancery

Chancery Executions No. 1, 1834-1907 (includes Circuit Court, 1852-1907), 1 vol.

Common Law Fee Book, 1833-47 (also Witness Book, 1831), 1 vol. See also Superior Court of Law.

Common Law Process Book No. 1, 1832-75 (includes Circuit Court, 1852-75), 1 vol.

Common Law Rule Book No. 1, 1832-1908 (includes Circuit Court, 1852-1908), 1 vol.

Witness Attendance Book, 1832-54 (includes Circuit Court, 1852-54), 1 vol. See also Common Law Fee Book.

Circuit Court

Chancery Docket, 1880-1901, 1 vol.

Chancery Executions, see Circuit Superior Court of Law and Chancery

Chancery Issue Docket, 1903-23, 1 vol.

Chancery Rule Book No. 2, 1888-1923, 1 vol.

[Common Law] Order Book, 1864-67, 1 vol.

Common Law Process Book, 1876-1918, 1 vol. See also Circuit Superior Court of Law and Chancery.

Common Law Rules, see Circuit Superior Court of Law and Chancery

Execution Books, 1860-1919, 2 vols.

Judgment Lien Docket, see County Court

Witness Attendance Book, see Circuit Superior Court of Law and Chancery

County and Superior Courts

Judgments, 1797-1904, 30.45 cu. ft.

Election Records

Voter Registration Book, n.d. [ca. 1880], 1 vol.

Fiduciary Records

County Court Executors' and Administrators' Bonds, 1887-1905, 1 vol.

Land Causes, 1842-92, 1 vol.

Justice of the Peace Records

Judgments, A-Z, 1898-1918, .35 cu. ft.

Justices' Judgments Returned to County and Circuit Courts, 1879-1901, 1 vol.

Land Records

General Index to Deeds, Grantor-Grantee, n.d., 29 pp. (part)

Marriage Records and Vital Statistics

Marriage Bonds and Ministers' Returns Nos. 1-7, 1793-52, 7 vols. (copies)

Road and Bridge Records

Road Book, [1902-03?] (also Partnership Book, 1906-28), 1 vol.

Tax and Fiscal Records

Claims Paid, see Business Records/Corporation/Partnerships

Delinquent Land, 1886, 1 vol.; and, Delinquent Lands [titles vary], 1884-89, 1892-98, 1895-1913, 3 vols.

Land and Personal Property Tax Lists (also Land Assessments and Delinquent Land), ca. 1845-1935, ca. .25 cu. ft. (fragments)

Land Assessment Book, n.d. [1858?], 1 vol.

Land Books, ca. 1850, 1853-1904, 178 vols.

Personal Property Books, 1872, 1874, 1877, 1879, 9 vols.

Reassessments of Land, 1875-1900, 9 vols.

Miscellaneous Records

Contracts for Personal Property, 1890-1916, 1 vol.

Treasurer

Treasurer's [Road] Warrants, 1899-1927, 3 vols.

Microfilm Records

Circuit Court Clerk
  Court Records
    County Court
      Order Books, 1793-94, 1806-65, 4 reels
    Circuit Superior Court of Law and Chancery
      Chancery Order Book No. 1, 1832-69, (includes Circuit Court, 1852-69), 1 reel
    Circuit Court
      Chancery Orders, see Circuit Superior Court of Law and Chancery
  Land Records
    Deed Books Nos. 1-12, 1793-1868, 6 reels
    General Index to Deeds, Grantor-Grantee A-Z, 1793-1914, 2 reels
    Plat Books A and Nos. 1-4, 1739-1933, 1 reel
  Marriage Records and Vital Statistics
    Marriage Registers Nos. 1-2, 1793-1906, 1 reel (part)
    General Index to Marriages, A-Z, 1793-1953, 1 reel (part)
    Register of Births, 1853-70, 1 reel (part)
    Register of Deaths, 1853-70, 1 reel (part)
  Wills
    Will Books Nos. 1-4 [B], 1796-1869, 2 reels
    Circuit [Superior] Court Will Book No. [4] A, 1848-99, 1 reel
    General Index to Wills No. 1, 1796-1953, 1 reel

GREENE COUNTY

Formed in 1838 from Orange County.

Original Records

Circuit Court Clerk
  Board of Supervisors Records
    Claims Allowed by County Supervisors, 1871-1905, ca. 1.8 cu. ft.
  Bonds/Commissions/Oaths
    Bonds for Tavern Licenses, 1838-47, ca. 50 items
    Distillers' Bonds [Liquor License Bonds], 1903-11, 30 items
    Electoral Board Oaths, 1898-1902, 9 items
    Forfeited Bonds, 1860, ca. 50 items
    Oaths of Registration Transfers, ca. 1875, ca. 25 items
    Orphans Bound Out [Apprenticeship Bonds], 1875-78, ca. 150 items
    Refunding Bonds, 1842-60, ca. 75 items; and, Refunding Bonds of William Collins' Heirs, ca. 1865, 39 items
    Reports of Indentures of Apprentices, ca. 1855-60, ca. 50 items
    Retail Liquor License [Bonds], 1883-1906, ca. 100 items
  Business Records/Corporations/Partnerships
    Certificates of Officers, Greene County and Swift Run Telephone Co., n.d., 7 items

Court Records
    County Court

Accounts Allowed by County Court, 1874-76, 1879, 1881, 1890-98, ca. .4 cu. ft.

Civil Cases, 1871-72, 1878, n.d., ca. .3 cu. ft.

Civil Cases Disposed of by County Court, ca. 1890-1904, ca. .25 cu. ft.

Civil [Law] Cases, 1841-87, ca. .25 cu. ft.

Claims of Debt in County Court, ca. 1860-75, ca. .1 cu. ft.

Commonwealth Cases and Papers, ca. 1840-85 (also Lunacy, etc., 1885), ca. .55 cu. ft.

County Court Papers, 1874-87 (also Accounts against the Commonwealth, and Estrays, 1874-80), ca. .25 cu. ft.

Judgments, Executions, and Summons [titles vary], 1846-72, ca. .8 cu. ft.; Judgments on Notes, 1843-51, ca. 50 items; and, Judgments, Civil Cases, 1887-89, ca. 100 items. See also Lost Records.

Lost Records (executions, writs, orders, surveyors of roads, subpoenas, petitions, etc.), 1838-65, .35 cu. ft.; and, Mutilated [damaged] Papers, 1838-ca. 1845, ca. .1 cu. ft.

Office Judgments, 1859-72, ca. .2 cu. ft.

Orders, etc. [road and fiduciary], ca. 1845-55, ca. 50 items

Out-of-County Judgments, 1860-67, ca. 50 items.

Receipts of Clerks' Costs in Suits, etc., 1838-61, ca. .1 cu. ft.

Suits Brought by James T. Ship for Northern Merchants, 1838-44, ca. 50 items

    Circuit Superior Court of Law and Chancery

Returns of Circuit Court, 1847-49, ca. .1 cu. ft.

    Circuit Court

Daugherty v. Daugherty, Suit Papers, etc., 1882-97, ca. .1 cu. ft.

    County and Superior Courts

Arbitrations, 1852-57, ca. 75 items

Chancery Orders Ended, Files 1-85, 1838-ca. 1940, 30.8 cu. ft.

Criminal Case Files 1-8, 1876-92, and 1893-1909, 1.4 cu. ft.; and, Commonwealth Cases, 1873-1941, n.d., 1.1 cu. ft.

Ended Judgments, Files 1-18, 1838-1905, 6.3 cu. ft.

[Executions] Returnable, 1868-75, 1877-1907, ca. .6 cu. ft.

Old Papers, ca. 1860-1930, 18 items

Warrants, Bonds, and Summons [titles vary], 1842-92, n.d., ca. 1.4 cu. ft.

See also Fiduciary Records

Election Records

Contested Elections, 1842-45, 1864-71, ca. .15 cu. ft.

Electoral Board Commissions, 1884, 1894-95, 25 items

Lists of Voters, 1838-48, ca. .1 cu. ft.

Fiduciary Records

Administrators' Bonds, 1838-66, .35 cu. ft.

Appraisements, 1839-41, Appraisements and Sales, 1844-54 (also Summons), and Accounts of Sales and Sale Bills, 1900, ca. .65 cu. ft.; and, Inventories and Sales, 1841-75, 1877-1916, ca. .8 cu. ft.

[Fiduciary Accounts], I. B. Davis, John W. Crow, and others, ca. 1850-1905, ca. .75 cu. ft.

Settlements of Accounts Nos. 1-16, 1841-1910, ca. 1.25 cu. ft.

Summons and Appraisements, 1854-70, ca. 100 items

Vouchers of Eddins and Page, Receivers, 1903, ca. .1 cu. ft.

William Collins' Heirs, see Bonds/Commissions/Oaths

See also Court Records, County Court

Justice of the Peace Records

Civil Cases, Justices Court, 1884-88, ca. 100 items
Constables' Returns, 1839-51, 1857-67, ca. .25 cu. ft.
Judgments, Justice Court, 1897-1903, ca. .1 cu. ft.
Justices' Returns, Civil Cases, 1889-97, 1902-23, .35 cu. ft.; and, Criminal Cases, 1880-1909, 1.05 cu. ft.
Orders Summoning Magistrates, 1842-55, 37 items

Land Records

Agreements, Land Sales, 1841-53, ca. 50 items
Deeds, 1834-1905, ca. 3.5 cu. ft.
Land Patents, Plats, etc., 1838-41, ca. 50 items
[List of] Land Grants, 1884-88, 1 item
Unrecorded Deeds, 1863-71, ca. 50 items; and, Unrecorded Deeds and Old Deeds Recorded and Deed Book Lost, 1838-41, ca. .1 cu. ft.

Marriage Records and Vital Statistics

Birth and Death Records, 1890-95, ca. .1 cu. ft.
Birth [Records], 1870-96, .45 cu. ft.
Death [Records], 1870-82, 1884-89, ca. .25 cu. ft.
Marriage Certificates, Files 1-35, 1838-1904, 3.85 cu. ft.

Military and Pension Records

Affidavits for Cost, Military Law, [1869], 42 items
Applications of Wounded [Civil War] Soldiers for Commutation, 1884-87, 36 items
Pension Papers, Revolutionary War, 1831-44, 17 items

Road and Bridge Records

Judgments, Road Claims, 1870-72, ca. .1 cu. ft.
Road Cases, 1850-97, ca. .45 cu. ft.
Road Petitions, 1841-49, 1874, 1901-02, ca. .15 cu. ft.
See also Court Records, County Court

School Records

Reports of School Superintendent, 1840-60, ca. .1 cu. ft.

Tax and Fiscal Records

Commonwealth Claims, 1873-83, 1886-88, ca. .15 cu. ft. See also Court Records, County Court.
County Claims, 1848-60, ca. .3 cu. ft.
Delinquent and Erroneous Taxes, 1859-66, 1872-89, 1907, ca. .15 cu. ft.
Delinquent Lands and Sale Bills, 1838-49, 1860-63, ca. .1 cu. ft.
Homestead Claims, ca. 1870-75, ca. .1 cu. ft.
Tavern and Mer[chant] Licenses, 1843-47, 19 items

Township Records

Stanardsville Township Board Papers, Road, etc., ca. 1870-75, ca. 150 items

Wills

Wills, 1839-1911, 1 cu. ft.
Wills Left in Possession of Z. K. Page [Clerk], 1897-1909, 5 items

Miscellaneous Records

Commissions of Lunacy, Commitments, Insane, etc., 1888-99, 1901-11, ca. .1 cu. ft.
Coroners' Inquests, 1863, 1874-94, ca. .25 cu. ft.
Estray Notices, 1839-64, ca. .1 cu. ft. See also Court Records, County Court.
Pardons, 1885-98, 5 items
Petitions for Hog [stock] Law, All Districts, 1901-08, ca. 50 items
Powers of Attorney from Other States, 1842-60, ca. 50 items
Private Papers of H. T. Bray, 1898-1900, 44 items
Report of the Superintendent of the Poor, 1871-95, .35 cu. ft.

Commissioner of Revenue

Moffett Liquor Law Licenses, 1877-79, ca. .1 cu. ft
See also Tax and Fiscal Records

Sheriff

Insolvent Capitations, Tax Returns, and Summons, by I. D. Blakey, Sheriff, 1853-58,
    1887, 1900, ca. .15 cu. ft.
Sheriffs' Returns, 1841-60, and Deputy Sheriffs' Returns, 1841-58, ca. .75 cu. ft.

Treasurer

Treasurer's Reports, 1880-81, 1896, ca. .15 cu. ft.
See also Tax and Fiscal Records

Microfilm Records

Circuit Court Clerk
Court Records
County Court

Minute Books [Orders] Nos. 3-5 [Nos. 1-2 are missing], 1842-64, 2 reels
General Index to Court Orders, 1838-70, 1 reel
Record Book, 1841-81, 1 reel

Land Records

Deed Books Nos. 2-5 [No. 1 is missing], 1841-73, 2 reels
General Index to Deeds No. 1, 1838-1912, 1 reel

Marriage Records and Vital Statistics

Marriage Register No. 1, 1838-1944, 1 reel (part)
General Index to Marriage Register, 1838-1944, 1 reel (part)
Register of Births, 1853-93, 1 reel (part)
Register of Deaths, 1853-1917, 1 reel (part)

Military and Pension Records

[Confederate] Pension Record, 1900-40, 1 reel (part)

Wills

Will Books Nos. 1-2, 1838-1925, 1 reel (part)
[Superior] Court Will Book No. 1-A, 1842-91, 1 reel (part)
General Index to Wills No. 1, 1838-1949, 1 reel

GREENSVILLE COUNTY

Formed in 1780 from Brunswick County.
Parts of Brunswick and Sussex
counties were added later.

Original Records

Circuit Court Clerk
Marriage Records and Vital Statistics
Marriage Bonds, 1781-1853, n.d., ca. 1.65 cu. ft.
Marriage Certificates and Consents, 1854-59, ca. 75 items
Marriage Records, 1787-1851 (also Certificates of Strays, 1781-1831), 1 vol.
Marriage Register, 1781-1853 (Ms. compilation), 1 vol. (original and copy); and, 1851-61, 1 vol.
Index to Marriage Register, 1781-1853, 1 vol. (Ts. and copy)
Ministers' Returns, 1781-1853, ca. .1 cu. ft.
Ministers' Returns of Marriages, 1850-61, 1 vol.
Miscellaneous Records
Certificates of Strays, see Marriage Records

Microfilm Records

Circuit Court Clerk
Court Records
County Court
Minutes, 1816-22, 1840-52, 1 reel (part); and, No. 12, 1852-66, 1 reel (part)
Order Books Nos. 1-11, 1781-1856, 6 reels
Fiduciary Records
Guardians' Books, 1801-20, 1847-77, 1 reel
Land Records
Deed Books Nos. 1-10, 1781-1874, 5 reels
General Index to Deeds, 1781-1878, 1 reel
Processioners' Returns, 1796-1832, 1848-57, 1 reel
Marriage Records and Vital Statistics
Marriage License Books Nos. 1-8, 1861-1901, 4 reels
General Index to Marriage Certificates [Licenses] No. 1, 1861-1930, 1 reel
Marriage Register, 1781-1853 (compilation), 1 reel (part)
Index to Marriage Register, 1781-1853 (compilation), 1 reel (part)
Register of Births, 1853-60, 1 reel (part)
Register of Deaths, 1853-60, 1 reel (part)
Wills
Will Books Nos. 1-8, 1781-1864, 3 reels
General Index to Wills [except Common Law Wills], 1781-1904, 1 reel
Common Law Will Book, 1824-76, 1 reel (part)

HALIFAX COUNTY

Formed in 1752 from Lunenburg County.

Original Records

Circuit Court Clerk
Court Records
County Court
Court Papers, 1773, 1780-81, n.d., 11 items
Minutes, 1827-28, 8 pp. (fragment, original and copy)
Pleas [Orders] No. 1, 1752-55, 1 vol. (copy)
Land Records
Deed Books Nos. 8 and 44, 1770-72, 1837-38, 2 vols. (copies)
Surveys No. 1, 1746-1901, 1 vol. (copy)
School Records
Public School Register, High Hill School, Red Bank District, 1897-1904, 1 vol.
Tax and Fiscal Records
Lists of Tithables, 1755, 1770, 1774, 1780, n.d., 7 items (copies)
Wills
Will Books Nos. 0, 1 and 3, 1753-82, 1792-97, 3 vols. (copies)

Sheriff
List of Insolvents, 1838, 1 item
[Sheriff] Mathew Bates, Account Book, 1783-87, 14 pp. (copies)
Sheriffs' Papers, 1842-79, ca. 1.1 cu. ft.
Tax Lists, 1840, 1842, 2 items

Microfilm Records

Circuit Court Clerk
Census Records
Special Schedules, 1860, 1 reel
Court Records
County Court
Minutes Nos. 1-20, 1821-66, 6 reels
Pleas [Orders] Nos. 1-32 and 34-37, 1752-1816, 1818-21, 15 reels; and, Order
Book, 1858-66, 1 reel (part)
General Index to Order Books, Plaintiffs-Defendants, 1752-1900, 14 reels
Land Records
Deed Books Nos. 1-60, 1752-1867, 29 reels
Superior Court Deeds, see Wills
General Index to Deeds, Grantor-Grantee A-Z, 1752-1928, 6 reels
Surveys No. 1, 1751-1901, 1 reel
Marriage Records and Vital Statistics
General Index to Marriages, Males-Females A-Z, 1753-1949, 8 reels
Registers of Births, 1853-71, 1 reel (part)
General Index to Birth Records, 1853-71, 1 reel (part)
Registers of Deaths, 1853-71, 1 reel (part)
Registers of Marriages Nos. 1-3 1/2, 1782-1905, 1 reel (part); and, Marriage Bond
Register No. 1, 1753-1889 (also Ministers' Returns to 1912), 1 reel (part)

Wills

Will Books Nos. 0-3 and 6-28 [there are no Nos. 4-5], 1753-1865, 13 reels

Superior Court Will Book No. A-1, 1833-57 (includes Deeds, 1809-22), 1 reel (part)

General Index to Wills, Fiduciaries, etc., A-Z, 1752-1949, 2 reels; and, General Index to Devisees and Heirs, 1752-1949, A-Z, 3 reels

HANOVER COUNTY

Formed in 1720 from New Kent County.

Original Records

Circuit Court Clerk
  Board of Supervisors Records
    Papers, 1870-75, 1903, ca. .15 cu. ft.
  Court Records
    County Court
      Court Records [Deeds, Wills, etc.], 1733-35, 1783-92, 3 vols. (2 copies of each)
      See also New Kent County Court Records, Unspecified Court
    Superior Court of Chancery
      Dickenson v. Clark, suit papers, 1810-26, 87 pp. (copies)
    Superior Court of Law
      Writ, 1824, 1 item
    Circuit Superior Court of Law and Chancery
      Atkinson v. Allen, 1832, and Nicholas v. Foster, 1835, suit papers, ca. 100 items
      Witness Book, 1838-56 (includes Circuit Court, 1852-56), 1 vol.
    Circuit Court
      Witness Book. See also Circuit Superior Court of Law and Chancery.
    County and Superior Courts
      Court Papers (including fiduciary and suit papers), ca. 1805-70, 12.6 cu. ft.
      Executions, ca. 1810-70, 1.8 cu. ft.
  Election Records
    Election Tickets [ballots], 1870, ca. .1 cu. ft.
  Fiduciary Records
    Guardians' Bonds [removed from Court Papers], 1836-60, 7 items
    See also Court Records, County and Superior Courts
  Justice of the Peace Records
    [Justice of the Peace Docket], 1837-41, 1 vol.
  Land Records
    Deeds, 1735 and 1749, and Deeds [removed from Court Papers], 1744-1855, 25 items. See also Court Records, County Court.
  Military and Pension Records
    Affidavit of Revolutionary War Service [removed from Court Papers], 1835, 1 item
  Tax and Fiscal Records
    Henry Township Tax Bills [removed from Court Papers], 1872-73, ca. .1 cu. ft.
    [William T. H. Pollard's Tax] Book, 1843, 1 vol.

Wills
> Will Book, 1831-50, 1 vol. (2 copies)
> Wills and Inventories [removed from Court Papers], 1792-1858, 10 items. <u>See</u>
> <u>also</u> Court Records, County Court; and, Montgomery County Wills.

Miscellaneous Records
> Patrick Henry Letter, 1771, 1 item (original and copy)
> Power of Attorney [removed from Court Papers], 1817, 1 item

Microfilm Records

Circuit Court Clerk
> **Court Records**
>> **County Court**
>>> Court Records, 1733-35, 1783-92, 1 reel

> **Marriage Records and Vital Statistics**
>> Marriage Register No. 1, 1863-97, 1 reel (part)
>> Register of Births, 1853-79, 1 reel (part)
>> Register of Deaths, 1853-71, 1 reel (part)

> **Wills**
>> Old Wills, 1785-93, 1 reel (part)
>> Will Book No. 1, 1862-68, 1 reel (part)
>> [Circuit Court] Will Book, 1852-65, 1 reel (part); and, Will Book No. 1, 1862-95,
>> 1 reel (part)

Sheriff
> Deputy Sheriff Richard Littlepage's Notebook [on suits, judgments, etc.], 1784-86,
> 1 reel (Misc. Reel 563, part)

HENRICO COUNTY

Original shire established in 1634.

Original Records

Circuit Court Clerk
> **Board of Supervisors Records**
>> Accounts Allowed, 1903, ca. 50 items
>> Agreements, Contracts and Bonds, 1889-1913, .35 cu. ft.
>> Minutes, 1892, 1 item
>> Order [Minutes] Books Nos. 1-3, 1870-1905, 3 vols.
>> Index to Orders No. 6, n.d., 1 vol.
>> Paid Warrants, 1897, 1900, ca. .2 cu. ft.
>> Papers (including Circuit Court Papers, ca. 1870-1930), ca. 4.5 cu. ft.
>> Supervisors' Roads Established, 1900-34, .35 cu. ft.
>> Vouchers, 1877, 1896, ca. .15 cu. ft.
>> Warrants Drawn on the County Treasurer [Nos. 1-3; titles vary], 1875-1904,
>> 3 vols.

> **Bonds/Commissions/Oaths**
>> Appeal Bonds, A-Z, ca. 1790-1840, ca. .3 cu. ft.

Appointment, 1696, 1 p. (copy)

Attachment Bonds, ca. 1810-35, ca. .1 cu. ft.; and, Suspension, Attachment, and Forthcoming Bonds not Acted Upon, 1851-60, 12 items

Bonds and Oaths of County Officers, 1870-ca. 1890, .7 cu. ft.; and, Officials' Oaths, 1899-1902, ca. .1 cu. ft.

Circuit Court Bonds No. 2, 1884-1911, ca. .5 cu. ft.

Circuit Court Record of Bonds, 1875-1904, 1 vol.

County Court Bonds, 1850-67, 1871-75, 7 vols.

County Court Official Bonds Nos. 1-[3], 1874-1904, 3 vols.

County Court Record of Bonds Nos. 1-5, 1850-1870, 5 vols.; and, No. 6, 1866-70, 1 vol. (fragment)

County Court Records of Bonds Approved by the Court No. 1, 1875-86, 1 vol.

County Court Records of Bonds taken in the Clerk's Office No. 1, 1875-1903, 1 vol.

County Court Record of Official Bonds Nos. 1-[3], 1874-1904, 3 vols.

Declaration Bonds, 1808, 1822, 11 items

Injunction Bonds, A-Y, 1785-1846, .7 cu. ft.

Inspector's Bonds, 1782-95, ca. 75 items

Land Surveyors' Notice of Appointments, 1819-70, .35 cu. ft.

Liquor License Bonds, 1893-1904, .35 cu. ft.

Miscellaneous County Court Bonds (including fiduciary bonds), 1837-75, .35 cu. ft.

Ordinary Bonds, ca. 1785-1840, .35 cu. ft.; and, Ordinary License, 1860, 1 item

Prison Bound Bonds, 1800-28, ca. 75 items

Replevy Bonds, 1787-88, 19 items; Replevy and Stay Bonds, ca. 1790-1815, ca. .4 cu. ft.; and, [Replevy and Constables' Bonds and Executions], 1788-89, 1814-15, ca. .1 cu. ft.

Sheriffs' Bonds, 1782-93, ca. 25 items

See also Court Records, Unspecified Court

Business Records/Corporations/Partnerships

Record of Charters, 1887-1925, 1 vol.

William Halyard's [Store] Ledger C, 1799-1804, 1 vol.

See also Court Records, Circuit Court

Census Records

Assessor's Book [for the Western District], 1850, 1 vol.

Court Records

County Court

Abatements and Dismissals, 1787-88, 1806-59, 4.5 cu. ft.; and, Abatements, Dismissals, Discontinued, 1801, ca. 50 items

Bills of Injunction, 1801, 4 items

Cases Ended Nos. 1-2, 1903, .7 cu. ft.

Chancery Docket, 1872-[73], 1 vol.

Chancery Order Book, 1871-73, 1 vol.

Chancery Rule Docket, 1853-73, 1 vol.

Clerk's Receipts on Lands [Redeemed], 1899-1901, .35 cu. ft.

Closed Chancery, 1819-22, ca. 25 items

Confessed Judgments, 1855-73, 3.15 cu. ft.

Copies of Decrees in Chancery, 1858, 1861-62, 3 items

Correspondence to the County [Court], 1859, 1861, 2 items

Court Record [Minutes?], 1687, 4 pp.

Docket Books, 1797-1802, 1849-61, 2 vols.

Ended Chancery Causes, 1800-1904, 9.45 cu. ft.

Index to Ended Chancery Causes, 1800-73, 1 vol.

Ended Common Law Cases, 1820-1904, 35.6 cu. ft.

Executions, 1784-1898, 13.7 cu. ft.; and, Executions Dismissed or Unsatisfied, 1791, 26 items.

Executions [and Executions on Warrants; titles vary], 1782-1904, 26 vols.

Extracts of Judgments, 1856, 1861, 2 items

Fee Books, [1784], 1798, 1808-15, 1818, 1820-21, 1858-67, 1885-1904, 10 vols.

[Issue Docket], 1809, 1 vol. (part)

Judgments, 1783, 1788-89, 1793-1800, 1803-47, 8.55 cu. ft.; Judgments and Ended Causes, 1781-1829, 37 cu. ft.; and, Judgments at Rules, 1888, ca. 40 items

Memorandums for Subpoenas, 1862, 2 items

Minute Books, 1682-1701, 1 vol. (Ts.); 1719-24, 1784-1904, 62 vols.; and, 1752-55, 1 vol. (original and copy)

Minutes, 1819, 12 pp. (fragment)

Miscellaneous Court Records [wills, deeds, etc.], 1650-1807, 7 vols.

Notices, 1787-88, 1808, 6 items

Office Judgments, ca. 1785-1854, ca. 2.35 cu. ft.

Old Attachments and Distress Warrants, 1855-90, .35 cu. ft.

Old Continued Motions, 1817-40, .35 cu. ft.

Old Grand Jury Presentments, 1859-75, .35 cu. ft.

Old Miscellaneous Papers [including copies of deeds, wills, etc.], ca. 1835-70, .35 cu. ft.

Order Books [including wills], 1678-[1701], 1707-14, 1719-24, 1755-69, 8 vols. (originals and copies); 1737-46, 1823, 2 vols.; and, Nos. 1-19, 1781-1816, 19 vols.

Index to Order Book No. 21, n.d., 1 vol.

Orphans Court, 1697-1739, 1 vol. (original and copies). See also Minute Books.

Petitions, 1788, 5 items

Proceedings of Commissioners Respecting Records Destroyed by the British, 1774-82, 1 vol. (original, Ts., and copy)

Process Books, 1847-1902 [1870-1902 volume includes Applications to Purchase Land, 1898-1902], 2 vols.

Recognizances, 1788, 6 items

Rough Rule Dockets, 1799-1802, 1856-66, 2 vols.

Rule Dockets, 1786-90, 1856-66, 1858-72, 3 vols.

Subpoenas, 1872-86, 1902, 1.05 cu. ft.

Suits Dismissed, 1801, 1808, ca. 100 items

[Unidentified] Transcripts, 1848, 1860, 3 items

Warrants Returned and Entered, 1781, 1784, 1790-92, ca. 1805-45, 3.6 cu. ft.

Witness Attendance No. 5, 1881-90, 1 vol.

See also Wills

Superior Court of Chancery

Chancery Papers, 1850-1933 (includes Circuit Court, 1852-1933), ca. 2 cu. ft.

Court Order, 1808, 1 item

Discontinued Court Order, 1808, 1 item

Circuit Court

Attachments and Common Law Suits, see Tax and Fiscal Records

Atwater v. Gaines, order, 1875, 1 item

Chancery Dockets Nos. 2-3, 1876-96, 1883-94, 2 vols.

Chancery Execution Book No. 1, 1866-1916, 1 vol.; and, [No. 1-A, Houchens v. The Virginia Mutual Protection Assn. et al.], 1885, 1 vol.

Chancery Fee Books Nos. 1-3, 1866-89, 1886-1919, 1897-1906, 3 vols.

Chancery Order Books Nos. [1]-16, 1865-1900, 16 vols.

Chancery Cause File Ended [dismissed at rules] No. 1, 1883-1907, .35 cu. ft.; and Closed Chancery, 1868-81, ca. .2 cu. ft. See also Superior Court of Chancery.

Chancery Process Book No. 1, 1866-1944, 1 vol.

Chancery Rules, 1865-94, 1 vol.

Chancery Rules Pending, 1894, .35 cu. ft.

Chancery Suit Certificates of Deposit and Declarations of Corporations, 1903-36, .35 cu. ft.

Clerk's Dockets [Commonwealth Prosecutions], 1861-91, 2 vols.

Common Law Ended Papers, 1865-68, .35 cu. ft.; and, Common Law Ended Cases, ca. 1870-1900, 5.25 cu. ft. See also Tax and Fiscal Records.

Common Law Execution Book No. 1, 1865-1907, 1 vol.

Common Law Fee Books Nos. 1-2, 1865-1945, 2 vols.

Common Law Order Books Nos. 1-8, 1865-1904, 8 vols.

Index to Judgments, Common Law Order Books Nos. 1-7, 1867-1900, 1 vol.

Common Law Process Book No. 1, 1866-1944, 1 vol.

Common Law Rules No. 1, 1865-1904, 1 vol.

Ended Cases, 1883, 1888-89, .35 cu. ft.

Ended Chancery Causes, 1865-ca. 1935, 102.2 cu. ft.

Index to Ended Chancery Causes, 1865-1908, 1 vol.

Executions, 1870-84, .6 cu. ft.; and, No. 2, [1895]-1914, .35 cu. ft.

Extracts of Judgments, 1868, ca. .2 cu. ft.

Fee Journal, 1894-1910, 1 vol.

Fisher et al. v. R. C. & P. Railroad Co., bonds, 1893, .35 cu. ft.

Grant v. Maury, suit papers, 1902, 1.35 cu. ft.

Houchens et al. v. The Virginia Mutual Protection Assn., suit papers, 1885 (also Appointment of Church Trustees, 1900), .35 cu. ft. See also Chancery Execution Books.

Huntington v. Chesapeake & Ohio Railroad Co., exhibits and depositions, 1887, ca. 1.5 cu. ft.

Huntington v. Chesapeake & Ohio Railroad Co., Index to Suit Papers, 1887-89, 1 vol.

Issue Docket, 1866-94, 1 vol.

Kastelberge v. Kastelberge's exr. et al., exhibits, 1895-96, 4 vols.

List of Chancery Cases Stricken from the Docket and Papers not in the Office No. 1, 1896-1930, 1 vol.

Office Judgments, 1874, .35 cu. ft.; and, Office Judgments Confirmed, 1865-[74], and Common Law Cases Dismissed, 1867-98, ca. .2 cu. ft.

Old Miscellaneous Papers, 1896-99, .25 cu. ft.

Rough [Rule] Docket, 1865-68, 1 vol.

Subpoenas, 1868-1905, .7 cu. ft.; and, Miscellaneous Subpoenas, 1866-ca. 1890, .35 cu. ft.

Suit Papers, 1888-99, ca. .5 cu. ft.; and, Suit Papers and Miscellaneous Fiduciary Papers, ca. 1885-1900, .7 cu. ft.

Unidentified Transcripts, 1897-99, 1903, 4 vols.

Van Lear v. Powers et al., Account Books, Richmond Chemical Works, 1875-78 (and Statement, 1882), 3 vols.

See also Board of Supervisors Records

County and Superior Courts

Clerk's Correspondence, ca. 1885-1900, ca. 1.25 cu. ft.; and, Clerks' Notes and Correspondence, 1822-1953, ca. 50 items. See also Sheriff.

Judgment Dockets Nos. 1-5, 1844-1919, 5 vols.

Index to Judgment Dockets No. 1, 1871-1900, 1 vol.; and, Index to Judgment Docket No. 2, 1900-16, and to Judgment Lien Docket, 1917-27, 1 vol.

Judgments Docketed to Constitute a Lien on Real Estate, 1867, 1874-95, .9 cu. ft.

Record of Convicts, 1870-1944, 1 vol.

Circuit Court, Baltimore, Maryland

Rash v. National Express and Transportation Co., transcript, 1884, 1 vol.

Unspecified Court

[Attorney's Memoranda for Suits], 1878-81, ca. .2 cu. ft.

Fee Book, 1888-94, 1 vol.

Index to Criminal Docket, State, No. 1, n.d., 1 vol.

James H. Barton suit exhibits (Building Book No. 2, 1889-91; Day Book, 1894; Journal, 1891-95; Ledgers, 1890-93; and, Bills Receivable and Payable, 1892-97), 7 vols.

Miscellaneous [Court] Papers (including bonds, indentures, and Commissioners of the Roads papers), 1848-78, ca. .2 cu. ft.

Unidentified Index [to Orders], n.d., 1 vol.; and, Unidentified Index [to suits], n.d., 1 vol.

Election Records

Abstracts of Elections, 1854-90, .35 cu. ft.

Candidates for Office, 1897-1936, .35 cu. ft.

Contingent and Election Expenses, 1891, 1896-97, ca. .25 cu. ft.

Election Notices of Candidates, 1903-33, .35 cu. ft.

Poll Books, Town of Barton Heights, 1896-1904, ca. .2 cu. ft.

Record of Voters, 1902-04, 1 vol.

Rolls of Registered Voters, 1885-1943 [overlapping date ranges], 44 vols.

Rolls of Registered Voters, 1902-03, ca. .5 cu. ft.

Voter Registration Cards, 1902-04, [ca. .25 cu. ft.]

Voting List, for Constables, 1855, 1 item

Fiduciary Records

Administrators' Bonds, M-Y, ca. 1780-1800, ca. .2 cu. ft.

Circuit Court Fiduciary Bonds Nos. [1]-4, 1865-1906, 4 vols.

Circuit Court Record of Special Commissioners' Bonds No. 4, 1901-11, 1 vol.

Circuit Court Special Commissioners' Bonds No. 4, 1901-06, 1901-11, 2 vols. [both labeled No. 4]

County Court Administrators' Bonds, 1804-32, 1840-50, 7 vols. (including fragments)

County Court Executors' and Administrators' Bonds to Sell Real Estate, 1826-50, 2 vols.

County Court Executors' Bonds, 1804-50, 6 vols. (including fragments)

County Court Fiduciary Bonds Nos. 8-12, 1875-1904, 5 vols. See also Bonds/Commissions/Oaths.

County Court Guardians' Bonds, 1804-23, 1828-50, 7 vols. (including fragments)

County Court Record of Fiduciary Bonds Nos. 8-12, 1875-1904, 5 vols.

Estate Papers of Cornelius Gill, 1886, ca. 100 items

Executors' Accounts, 1891, 6 items

Executors' Bonds, A-P, ca. 1780-1805, ca. .15 cu. ft.

[Guardians' Accounts and estate papers], 1898-1912, ca. .35 cu. ft.; and Guardians' Accounts, 1783-1868, 1.8 cu. ft.

Guardians' Accounts Nos. [1]-8, 1834-1903, 8 vols.; and, 1866-74, 1 vol.

Guardians' Bonds, A-W, ca. 1780-1815, ca. .2 cu. ft.

Lewis Ginter Estate Settlement No. 1, 1901-07, .45 cu. ft. See also Wills.

Record of Fiduciary Bonds Nos. [1]-6, 1870-1911, 6 vols.

Record of Special Commissioners' Bonds Nos. 1-3, 1884-1901, 3 vols.

Special Commissioners' Bonds Nos. 1-3, 1884-1901, 3 vols.

Trustees' Accounts [of Sales] Nos. 1-2, 1878-97, 2 vols.

Trustee's Accounts of Sales Recorded Nos. 1-2, 1879-1929, .7 cu. ft.

Unidentified Index [to fiduciary accounts?], n.d., 1 vol.

See also Bonds/Commissions/Oaths; Court Records, Circuit Court; and, Wills

Free Negro and Slave Records

Appointment of Slave Patrol, 1861, 1 item

Emancipations, see Court Records, County Court

[Free Negro] Registers, 1825-57, ca. 50 items

Registers of Free Negroes and Mulattoes, 1831-65, 4 vols.

Justice of the Peace Records

Certification of Judgment, 1858, 1 item

Civil Warrants, Judgments, and Executions, 1889-1912, .7 cu ft.

Commonwealth Warrants Returned, 1872, ca. .1 cu. ft.

Constables' Executions, see Bonds/Commissions/Oaths

Criminal Cases Disposed of by Justices Nos. 2-3, 1888-1904, 2 vols.

Criminal Warrants presented by Justices with their Accounts, not called for, 1895-1901, .35 cu. ft.

Distress Warrants Returned No. 1, 1860-62, 1899-1918, .35 cu. ft.

Executions, 1881-83, ca. .1 cu. ft.; and, Unsatisfied Executions. 1840, 12 items

Executions in Judgments of Justices No. 6, 1890-1938, 1 vol.

Executions Returned by Constables, 1860-88, 1 vol.

Fine Report B, n.d., 4 items

Judgments Docketed, 1899-[1914], .35 cu. ft.

[Justices'] Executions and Warrants Returned, 1812-80, 2.1 cu. ft.

Justices' Judgment and Execution Books, 1897-1904, 1903-08, 2 vols.

Justices' Judgment No. 2, 1888-1926, 1 vol.

Pleas, 1826-29, 1 vol.

Recognizances, Warrants, and Summons, 1866-1912, .35 cu. ft.; and, Recognizances taken out of Court, 1889, ca. .25 cu. ft.

Record of Criminal Cases Disposed by Justices No. 1, 1878-87, 1 vol.

Reports, 1876-98, 1902, 1908-1909, 2.3 cu. ft.

Warrants, 1884-90, ca. 1.5 cu. ft.

Land Records

Applications on which Deeds have been Executed, A-Z, [1899-1930], 1.4 cu. ft.

Deeds, Wills, etc. [titles vary], 1677-92, 1688-1704, 1706-18, 1725-37, 1744-67, 10 vols. (originals and copies)

Deeds, 1767-74, 1 vol. (original and copy); and, Deed Books Nos. 1-169B, 1781-1904, 116 vols. See also Ledger.

Deeds [and copies of Deeds], 1808-60, 9 items

Deeds found in Taylor's desk, 1871-75, 14 items

Deeds not ready for Record No. 1, 1875-81, ca. 100 items; Deeds and Wills Partly Proved, 1782-[ca. 1835], 1.35 cu. ft.; and, Unrecorded [?] Deeds and Wills, ca. 1840, .35 cu. ft.

Deeds Recorded, 1781-1899, 23.8 cu. ft.

General Index to Deeds, 1781-1838, 1 vol.; Liber Indexes [to Deeds] by Grantor, 1781-1860, and by Grantee, 1781-1857, 2 vols.; General Index to Deeds, A-Z, 1781-1876, 2 vols.; Grantor Index to Deeds No. 1, A-H, 1781-1876, 1 vol. (Ts.); and, Grantor Index to Deeds No. 2, A-R, 1876-1907, 3 vols.

Escheator's Inquests, 1797-1808, 7 items

Land Surveyors' Reports, 1876-79, .35 cu. ft.

Ledger [temporary Deed Book], 1861-62], 1 vol.

Index to Deeds [temporary book used during the Civil War], 1860-66, 1 vol.

Maps and Plats, 1817-1904, n.d., ca. 125 items; Plats of the Prison Bounds, 1799, 1821, 2 items (copies); and, Plot, etc., of the Upper End of the County, 1884, 1 item (fragments)

Plat Book Map No. 2, n.d., 1 item

Plat Books Nos. 1-8, 1815-1908, 8 vols.

Plats of Richmond, 1901, 1 vol.

Indexes to Plots, n.d., 2 vols.

Processioners' Returns Nos. 1-2, 1775-1839, 2 vols.

Processioners' Returns Nos. 1-2, 1820-35, .7 cu. ft.; and, Processioners' Returns, 1824, 1826, ca. .2 cu. ft.

Record of Caveats [Entry Book], 1833-1914, 1 vol.

Record of Deeds not fully Proved, 1869, 1 vol.

Release Deeds Nos. 1-16, 1884-1904, 16 vols.

Grantee Index to Release Deeds No. 1, 1884-1925, 1 vol.

Surveyors' Papers (warrants and entries), 1895-1926, ca. .25 cu. ft.

See also Court Records, County Court; and, Wills

Marriage Records and Vital Statistics

Marriage Bonds Nos. 1-7, A-Y, 1781-99, 7 vols.; Marriage Bonds, A-Y, 1800-30, 12 vols.; Marriage Bonds, A-Z, 1831-50, 1.8 cu. ft.; and, Marriage Bonds and Consents, 1794, 1797-1800, 16 items

Index to Marriage Bonds, 1781-1831, 1 vol.

Marriage Certificates, Consents, and Ministers' Returns, 1781-1812, 1832-99, 10.15 cu. ft.

Marriage Licenses, 1862-99, 9.9 cu. ft.

Records at Large [Ministers' Certificates], 1815-53, 1 vol.

Register of Licenses for Marriages, 1850-62, 1 vol.; and, Register of Marriages No. 2, 1853-97, 1 vol.

Index to Marriage Register, n.d., 1 vol.

Registers of Births, 1889-92, ca. .25 cu. ft.

Registers of Births and Deaths, 1853-61, 2 vols.

Military and Pension Records

Militia Rolls, 1854-57, 5 items

[Pension Board Record of Civil War Service], 1898-99, 1 vol.

Road and Bridge Records

Application for a Road, 1859, 1 item; and, Road Applications not finally disposed of prior to 1904, [1856-97], .7 cu. ft.

Applications to Establish Roads, 1880-1923, 1 vol.

List of [Road] Hands, 1788, 1 item

Records [Minutes] of New Mechanicsville Turnpike Co., 1870-85, 1 vol.

Road Books, 1853-68, 2 vols.

Road Reports, 1875-80, 1884-91, 14 pp.

Road Vouchers, 1891-92, 1895, ca. .15 cu. ft.

Roads Established, 1895-1903, .35 cu. ft.

Turnpike [Reports] No. 1, 1880-1907, 1 vol.

See also Court Records, Unspecified Court

Tax and Fiscal Records

Accounts against the Commonwealth, 1855-58, and Clerk's correspondence about Claims, 1858, 3 items

Accounts Claimed against the County, 1788, 1862, 3 items

Accounts of County Alms House, 1890-1902, 13 items

Applications to Purchase Delinquent Land, 1899-1901 (also attachments and common law suits returnable to court and no action taken, 1895-1931), .35 cu. ft. See also Court Records, County Court

Applications to Purchase Delinquent Lands No. 2, 1900-04, 1 vol.

Assessor's Book, 1803-13, 1 vol.

Commonwealth Receipts [for purchase of land], 1889-90, ca. .1 cu. ft.

County Levy Reports and Vouchers, 1867, 1869, ca. 200 items

Delinquent Capitation and Property Taxes, 1863, 1866-76, 1878-79, 1884, 1889, ca. 1 cu. ft.

Delinquent Land, 1882-83, .25 cu. ft.

Delinquent Land Books [titles vary], ca. 1875-99, 10 vols.

Delinquent Lands Offered for Sale, 1876-83, 2 vols.

Delinquent Real Estate Redeemed No. 1, 1866-85, 1 vol.

Improper Assessments of Land, 1850, 1880, 3 pp.

Index to Lands Purchased by Parties other than the Commonwealth No. 1, 1876-85, 1 vol.; and, Index to Delinquent Lands Sold to Individuals No. 1, 1886-1911, 1 vol.

Insolvent Capitation and Property, 1891, 1901-02, 4 vols.

Insolvent License Returns, 1874-81, 22 items

[Land] Applications Settled No. 1, 1898-1900, .35 cu. ft.; and, Land Applications Settled, 1898-1909, 1.05 cu. ft.

Land Tax Books, 1813-44, ca. .5 cu. ft. (including fragments)

List of Delinquent Lands Sold No. 1, 1888-92, 1 vol.

List of Lands Sold for Taxes, 1850-58 (also Reports and Surveys, 1851-96), .35 cu. ft.; and, Reports and Surveys of Land Sold for Taxes Nos. [1]-2, 1881-1928, .7 cu. ft.

Lists of Delinquent Lands, 1845-49, 1855-63, 1865-71, ca. .4 cu. ft.; and, Lists of Delinquent Real Estate, 1873-76, 1884-86, ca. .15 cu. ft.

Lists of Delinquent Real Estate Nos. 6-11, 1892-97, 6 vols.

Lists of Disbursements on Accounts of Jurors, and Orders for Payment of Jurors, 1894-95, ca. .2 cu. ft.

Lists of Poll Tax and County Levy Returned, 1866-67, 5 items

Lists of Real Estate Delinquent for Non-payment of State Taxes, 1873-76, 1884-86, ca. .15 cu. ft.

Lists of Real Estate Returned Delinquent for the Non-payment of Taxes and Levies Nos. 1 and 3-5, 1865-74, 1882-91, 4 vols.

Names of Persons Charged with Taxes, [1786], 1 item

Orders of Publications on Tax Applications No. 1, 1898-1912, 1 vol.

Personal Property Tax Books, 1889, 1892, 1894, 1897-99, 1901, 10 vols.; and, 1852, 1 vol. (part)

Reassessments, 1870-1900, 6 vols.

Record of all Taxes and other Money Belonging to the Commonwealth, . . . 1898-1905, 1 vol.

Record of Lands Purchased by the Commonwealth Nos. 1-2, 2A, and 3 [titles vary], 1876-93, 4 vols.; Record of Lands Purchased by the Commonwealth, Fairfield and Tuckahoe Districts, 1876-1904, 2 vols.; List of Real Estate Purchased by the Commonwealth, 1891-1901, 2 vols.; and, Delinquent Lands Sold to the Commonwealth, 1902-11, 1 vol.

Index to Lands Purchased by the Commonwealth No. 1, 1876-85, 1 vol.

Return of Tax Collector for 1788, 1 item

Returns of Insolvents and Persons Removed from the County, 1786, 7 items

Sales to Individuals and Com[missioner of Revenue] and Redemptions Before Sale [titles vary], 1898-1907, 2 vols.

Schedules, 1788, 3 items

Statements of Delinquent Land Purchased by Commonwealth, 1897, 4 items

Statements of Delinquent Land Taxes Marked Paid [titles vary], 1899-1903, 1.15 cu. ft.

Surveys of Land Sold for Delinquent Taxes No. 2, 1852-94, 1 vol.

[Tax] Assessor's Book, 1803-13, 1 vol.

Tax Books, Fairfield and Northside districts, 1898-1906, 1902, 3 vols.

Tax Collections, Fairfield District, 1884, 1 vol.; Receipt Book, 1884-86, 1 vol.; and, Receipts, 1886, 1 vol.

Tax Records [assessments, land, property, and insolvents], 1891-1936, ca. .5 cu. ft. (fragments)

Tax Returns, 1787, 11 items

Vouchers for Supplies to be charged to Overseers of the Poor, 1892, ca. .1 cu. ft.

Vouchers to sustain account of collector of County Levy for 1853 and 1854, ca. 200 items

Township Records

Brookland Township Record [Minutes], 1870-75, 1 vol.

Wills

Wills, 1781-87, 1 vol. (original and copy); and, Will Books Nos. 3-5, 1802-22, 3 vols. (copies)

Wills, 1781-1900, 10.35 cu. ft.; and, Wills [and copies of wills], 1834-52, 5 items

Wills, inventories, etc., 1897-1902, .7 cu. ft.; and, Circuit Court Wills, inventories, etc. [titles vary], 1865-73, 1879-1913 (includes Lewis Ginter Estate Settlements No. 2), 1.05 cu. ft. See also Fiduciary Records.

Wills not Probated, 1819-99, 8 items

Index to Colonial Records [wills, deeds, etc.], 1677-1739, 1 vol. (original and copies)

See also Court Records, County Court; and, Land Records

Miscellaneous Records

Affidavits, 1788-90, 3 items

Appointment of Church Trustees, see Court Records, Circuit Court

Commissions of Lunacy, [1900-15], .35 cu. ft.

Crop Lien Docket, 1892-1965, 1 vol.

Coroners' Inquests, [ca. 1800]-1850, 1885-1903, ca. 1 cu. ft.

Deposition for Lunacy Hearing, 1860, 1 item

Estray Notices, ca. 1780-1880, ca. 1.2 cu. ft.

Estrays Nos. 1-2, 1806-55, 2 vols.

[Insurance companies'] Powers of Attorney, 1895-1914, .35 cu. ft.

Lists of [Tobacco] Transfers, 1788, 2 items

Mechanics' Lien Books Nos. 1-2, 1871-1910, 2 vols.

Mechanics' Liens Nos. [1]-2, 1889-1917, .7 cu. ft.

Moore Street Missionary Baptist Church Minute Book, 1875-81, 1 vol.; and, Minister's Aid Society Ledger, 1881, 1 vol.

Naturalization and Other Proceedings, rough notes, 1860, 3 pp.

Notary Public Reports, 1878-79, 15 items

Overseer of the Poor Minutes, 1869-91, 1 vol.

Overseer of the Poor Reports, 1787, 13 items

Photograph of Forest Lake, Glen Allen, n.d. [ca. 1900?], 1 item

Records of Conditional Sales of Personal Property Nos. 1-6, 1890-19[04], 6 vols.

Indexes to Personal Property Contracts Nos. 2-3, 1894-[1902], 2 vols.

Register of Physicians' Certificates No. 1, 1894-1917, 1 vol.

Reports of the Superintendent of the Poor, 1871-78, 1903, ca. .25 cu. ft.

Specifications of Vault and Clerk's Office, n.d., 2 items

Stanard's Notes [on records], 1679-1771, 1 vol. (Ts.)

Superintendent of the Poor Bills, 1887-90, ca. .3 cu. ft.; Annual Reports, 1887-88, 3 items; and, [Grocery Chits], 1889-90, ca. 200 items

Commissioner of Revenue

Land Books, 1819-32, 1835-62, 1867-69, 1877-1904, 63 vols.

License Reports, 1870, ca. .2 cu. ft.

Lists of Persons Assessed with License Taxes, 1878-88, ca. .35 cu. ft.

See also Tax and Fiscal Records

Sheriff

[Sheriffs' and] Treasurers' Reports and Settlements, 1869-94, 1897-1900, 1916, 3.15 cu. ft.

[Sheriff's Appointment?], 1861, 1 item

[Sheriff's Fee Book?], 1819, 1 vol.

Vouchers . . . not allowed in settlement with the county, 1867, ca. 100 items

Treasurer

Cancelled checks and Lists of Vouchers Issued by the Treasurer, 1892, ca. .25 cu. ft.

Index to Report of Levies, 1873-90, 1 vol.

Personal Property Tax Bills [by district], 1890, ca. .5 cu. ft.

Real Estate Tax Bills [by district], 1890, 1903-04, ca. .5 cu. ft.

Treasurer's Bimonthly Statements No. 1, 1895-98, .35 cu. ft.; and, Settlements, 1899-1902, 2 items

Warrants, 1896-97, .35 cu. ft.; Paid Warrants, 1900, ca. .1 cu. ft.; and, Warrants Drawn on the Board of Supervisors, 1888-89, 1895-97, 1903-04, .45 cu. ft.

See also Board of Supervisors Records; Tax and Fiscal Records; and, Sheriff

Microfilm Records

Circuit Court Clerk

Court Records

County Court

Miscellaneous Court Records [deeds, wills, etc.] Vols. 1-7, 1650-1807, 3 reels. See also Land Records.

Index to Colonial Records, 1677-1739, 1 reel

Orders [Minutes], 1694-1701, 1707-14, 1719-24, 1737-46, 1752-69, 4 reels; Order Books Nos. 1-19, 1781-1816, 9 reels; Minute Books Nos. 20 and 22, 1816-19, 1821-23, 1 reel; and, 1823-67, 10 reels. See also Court Records, County Court.

Fiduciary Records

Guardians' Accounts, 1813-66, 2 reels

Orphans' Court [Record Book No. 4], 1677-1739, 1 reel

Land Records

Records [deeds, wills, etc.; titles vary], 1677-1704, 1706-18, 1725-37, 1744-82, 7 reels. See also Court Records, County Court.

Deed Books Nos. 1-81, 1781-1866, 39 reels

Index to Deeds No. 1, Grantor-Grantee A-Z, 1781-1876, 2 reels

Processioners' Returns Nos. 1-2, 1795-1839, 1 reel (part)

Marriage Records and Vital Statistics

Marriage Bonds, 1781-1850, 18 reels; and, Marriage Bonds, A-Z, 1782-99, 1 reel

Index to Marriage Bonds, 1781-1831, 1 reel (part)

Records at Large [Marriages], 1815-53, 1 reel (part); and, Register of Marriages, 1853-97, 1 reel (part)

Register of Births, 1853-70, 1 reel (part)

Register of Deaths, 1853-70, 1 reel (part)

Tax and Fiscal Records

Assessor's Book, 1803-13, 1 reel (part)

Wills

Will Books Nos. 1-18, 1781-1869, 11 reels. See also Court Records, County Court; and, Land Records.

General Index to Wills No. 1, 1781-1904, 1 reel

HENRY COUNTY

Formed in 1776 from Pittsylvania County.

Original Records

Circuit Court Clerk
Board of Supervisors Records
Minutes, 1892-94, 1 vol.
Bonds/Commissions/Oaths
[Appointment of] Patrols, 1858-64, 8 pp. (copies)
Appointments, 1837-46, ca. .1 cu. ft.
[Bail and Attachment] Bonds, 1900-05, ca. .1 cu. ft.
Bonds, 1807-60, .45 cu. ft.
County Court Officials' Bonds, 1877-82, 1 vol.
County Court Record of Forfeited Forthcoming Bonds, 1867-1903, 1 vol.; and, Circuit Court Forfeited Forthcoming Bonds, 1868-99, 2 vols.
Delivery Bonds see Court Records, Circuit Court
Forthcoming Bonds, ca. 1825-50, ca. 25 items
Indentures, 1787-ca. 1860, ca. .3 cu. ft.
Justices' Commissions, 1846-68, ca. 200 items
Liquor License Bonds, 1878-1905, 1.4 cu. ft.
Officials' Bonds (also fiduciary, etc.), ca. 1860-1905, 4.1 cu. ft.; and, Officials' Oaths, ca. 1870-1904, ca. .45 cu. ft.
[Orders for] Ministers' Bonds, 1859-1903, ca. 30 items (copies)
Ordinary [and other] Bonds, 1777-ca. 1845, ca. 200 items; Ordinary Bonds, 1797, 2 items (copies); and, [Oaths of] Inn and Ordinary [Keepers], 1858-81, ca. 75 items (copies)
Replevin and Delivery Bonds, 1783-ca. 1825, 1.2 cu. ft.
Stay Bonds, 1868, ca. 60 items
Business Records/Corporations/Partnerships
County Court Record of Limited Partnerships, 1897-1902, 1 vol.
Farmer's Bank Trustees' Vouchers, 1892-93, .25 cu. ft.
Norfolk & Great Western Railroad Bonds, 1869, ca. 40 items
Unidentified Day Book, 1842-49, 1 vol.
Unidentified [merchants'] Ledgers, 1848, 1852, 1855, 1868-73, 1882-83, 1892-93, 1897-98, 8 vols.
Census Records
Enumerations, 1850, 1860, n.d., 3 vols.
Enumeration Sheets, 1870, 1880, ca. .35 cu. ft.
See also School Records
Court Records
County Court
Affidavits, 1868-70, ca. 50 items
Appeals, 1798-1861, ca. 25 items
Attachments (also warrants, judgments, etc.), 1861-90, ca. .15 cu. ft.
Bar Dockets, 1842-49, 1867-77, 3 vols.
Chancery Rule Docket, 1860-63, 1 vol.
Clerk's Dockets, 1823-39, 1867-77, 3 vols.
Clerk's [Taxes and Fines], 1881-86, 8 items
Commonwealth v. Hopper et al., suit papers, 1849, ca. 25 items
County Warrants, 1875, ca. .2 cu. ft.
Determined Papers, 1783, 1786-1802, 1805-33, 1835-1904, 58 cu. ft.

Docket, 1859, 1 item

Docket Books, 1774-84, 1820-1903, 25 vols.

Execution Books, 1778-1810, 1808-68, 1879-1904, 7 vols.

Indexes to Execution Books Nos. 4-5, n.d., 2 vols.

Executions and Executions Returned, 1778-ca. 1875, 9.35 cu. ft.

Fee Books, 1777-1904, 83 vols.

[Grand Jury] Presentments, 1834-70, ca. .2 cu. ft.

Issue and Rule Dockets [titles vary], 1802-10, 3 vols.

Jones v. Chesher, ejectment papers, 1859, ca. 50 items

Judge's Docket, 1885-1903, 1 vol.

Judgments, 1840-43, 1856, 1860-63, 1866-69, 1873-77, ca. 1.6 cu. ft.

[Lawyer's] Docket Book, 1885-1903, 1 vol.

Lien Dockets Nos. [1]-4, 1846-1911 (includes Circuit Court, 1904-11), 4 vols.

Memorandum Books (also Minutes), 1852-75, 1877-79, 1877-82, 1892-1905 [1904], 11 vols.

Motions and Attachments Abated, 1865, ca. .1 cu. ft.

Order Books Nos. 1-7, 1777-1804, 7 vols. (copies)

Pedigo v. Reynolds' admr., vouchers, 1850-73, .45 cu. ft.

Petition and Attachment Docket, 1800-08, 1 vol.

Powers v. Dillon [English suit], depositions, 1803, 2 items

Process Books, 1868-1904, 2 vols.

[References and New Causes], 1802-05, 1811-20, 2 vols.

Rule Dockets, 1786-1808, 1850-73, 8 vols.

Witness Attendance Books, 1825-1904, 6 vols.

See also County and Superior Courts

District Court

Memorandum Books, 1785-95, 1803-25 (includes Superior Court of Law, 1808-25), 5 vols.

Superior Court of Law

Docket Book, 1812-31 (also Circuit Court Memorandum Book, 1864-67), 1 vol.

Memorandum Book, see District Court

Superior Court [Papers], 1811-30, ca. .3 cu. ft.

Circuit Superior Court of Law and Chancery

Chancery Docket No. 1, 1831-40, 1 vol.

Chancery Fees No. 1, 1841-50, 1 vol.

Chancery Rule Docket, 1832-78 (includes Circuit Court, 1852-78), 1 vol.

Common Law Docket No. 1, 1831-61 (includes Circuit Court, 1852-61), 1 vol.

Common Law Executions No. 1, 1831-65 (includes Circuit Court, 1852-65), 1 vol.

Index to Common Law Executions, n.d. [1831-65?], 1 vol.

Common Law Fees No. 1, 1831-41, 1 vol.

Common Law Process No. 1, 1831-68 (includes Circuit Court, 1852-68), 1 vol.

Determined Cases, 1837-53, ca. 150 items

Dismissed at Rules, 1832, 1848, 3 items

Executions, ca. 1810-50, 1.4 cu. ft.

Fee Book, 1850-58 (includes Circuit Court, 1852-58), 1 vol.

Law and Chancery Papers, 1835-51, 3.15 cu. ft.

Memorandum Book, 1845-53, 1 vol. See also Superior Court of Law.

Summons and Warrants, 1843-69, ca. 300 items

Witness Attendance Book, 1833-54 (includes Circuit Court, 1852-54), 1 vol.

Circuit Court

Abstracts of Judgment, ca. 1875-1912, 1.75 cu. ft.

Bar Dockets, 1869-86, 1888, 5 vols.

Cases not Docketed, 1870, ca. 25 items

Chancery Minute Book, 1879-88, 1 vol.

Chancery Rule Docket No. 2, 1878-1903, 1 vol. See also Circuit Superior Court of Law and Chancery.

Clerk's Dockets, 1872-84, 1887-88, 4 vols.

Common Law Determined Papers, 1902-04, 1 cu. ft.

Common Law Docket, see Circuit Superior Court of Law and Chancery

Common Law Executions, see Circuit Superior Court of Law and Chancery

Common Law Memorandum Books, 1869-78, 1871-84, 2 vols.

Common Law Process, see Circuit Superior Court of Law and Chancery

Common Law Rule Docket No. 2, 1872-1921, 1 vol.

Commonwealth v. Adams, suit papers, ca. 1900, ca. 50 items.

Creed Docket, 1872-76, 1 vol.

Determined Cases, 1860-84, 1894-95, ca. .25 cu. ft.

Dismissed at Rules, 1855-71, 11 items

Docket Books, 1860-71, 1877-86, 1888-1915, 13 vols.

Fee Books, 1859-1900, 14 vols. See also Circuit Superior Court of Law and Chancery.

Joseph Miles Railroad Case, bill and deposition, 1895, 5 items

Judge's Dockets, 1858-59, 1882-88, 3 vols.

Judgments, 1859, ca. .3 cu. ft.; and, Judgments and Executions [also Delivery Bonds], 1861-70, ca. 75 items

Law and Chancery Papers, 1852-77, 8.75 cu. ft.

Lien Dockets, see County Court

Memorandum Books, 1854-64, 1873-1911, 11 vols. See also Superior Court of Law.

Miscellaneous Papers, 1872-1940, ca. 200 items; and, Papers (including highway papers), ca. 1875-1900, ca. 75 items

Moneys Deposited by Order of Court, 1901-22, 1 vol.

Process Books, 1876-1922, 2 vols.

Receipts for Court Papers, 1871-76, 1899-1918, 2 vols.

Register of Persons Convicted of Felony, 1883-1914, 1 vol.

Subpoenas, Judgments, etc. [labeled D-Bonds], 1855, 1883, ca. .2 cu. ft.

Summons and Warrants, see Circuit Superior Court of Law and Chancery

Witness Attendance Books, 1854-78, 1880-1908, 4 vols. See also Circuit Superior Court of Law and Chancery.

County and Superior Courts

[Clerk's Ledger], 1873, 1 vol.

Law and Chancery Papers, 1835-77, 11.9 cu. ft.

Miscellaneous Papers [also called Promiscuous Papers], ca. 1800-65, ca. .3 cu. ft.

Superior Court [Papers], 1784-1830 (includes County Court, 1784-88), ca. .5 cu. ft.

Warrants and Subpoenas, 1798-1895, .35 cu. ft.

Unspecified Court

Court Papers [unarranged, original order lost], 1814-1964, 1970, 4.25 cu. ft.

Fine Reports, 1884-86, ca. 25 items

Miscellaneous Court Papers, 1797-1904, ca. 225 items; and, Papers [suit papers, tax records, etc.], ca. 1820-1905, 1.5 cu. ft.

Persons Convicted of a Felony, 1885-91, ca. 150 items

Register for Cases Taken out of Office, 1893-98, 1 vol.

Election Records

    List of Certificates of Registration Issued, 1903-09 (and [personal property?] Contracts, 1892-94), 1 vol.

    Lists of Registered Voters, 1902-04, ca. 25 items

    Polls [titles vary], ca. 1850-1904, ca. 1 cu. ft.

    Registers [Records], 1887, 1902, ca. .15 cu. ft.

    Rolls of Registered Voters, [18]90-1928 [overlapping date ranges], 49 vols.

    See also Justice of the Peace Records

Fiduciary Records

    Accounts Current, 1777-1899, ca. 4.5 cu. ft.; and, Miscellaneous Records [fiduciary accounts], 1854-94, .45 cu. ft.

    County Court Fiduciary List, 1853-69, 1 vol.

    Estate Papers, 1853-99, ca. 50 items

    Executors' and Administrators' Bonds, 1831-59, .45 cu. ft.

    Inventory of John Rowland's Estate, 1870, 2 items

    Vouchers, ca. 1830-70, ca. 250 items

Free Negro and Slave Records

    Conscription of Free Negroes, 1863-64, ca. 25 items (copies); and, of Slaves, 1862-65, ca. 25 items (copies)

    Lists of Free Negroes, ca. 1850-60, ca. 50 items; and, 1867-1900, 14 items (copies)

    [Lists of] Slaves, 1858-66 [1865], ca. 30 items (copies)

    Miscellaneous Slave [papers], 1838, 1855, 2 items

Justice of the Peace Records

    Attachments, etc., ca. 1835-95, ca. .4 cu. ft.

    Commonwealth Sundry, 1779-1902, ca. .25 cu. ft.

    Commonwealth Warrants, 1884-87, ca. .2 cu. ft.

    Constables' and Justices' Warrants, Summons, and Accounts, 1854-59, ca. .15 cu. ft.

    Constables' Executions, 1811-1904, ca. 5.6 cu. ft.; Executions Returned Satisfied, 1853, 1855-72, ca. 1 cu. ft.; and, Returns, 1827-51, 1876-77, 1882-1925, ca. 2 cu. ft.

    Fines Imposed, 1874-76, 1893, ca. 125 items

    Index to Constables' Return Books Nos. 3 and 5, n.d., 2 vols.

    Judgments of Justices for Fines, 1874-88 (also Board of Registration letter book, 1867), 1 vol.

    Justices' Criminal Record No. 2, 1888-1912, 1 vol.

    Justices' Judgment and Execution Books, 1851-78, 1891-96, 1898-1905, 3 vols.

    [List of] Magistrates, 1797, 1 item

    Reports, 1889-91, ca. .1 cu. ft.

    Warrants and Recognizances, 1835-1900, ca. .75 cu. ft.; Warrants, 1856-69, 1885-1903, ca. .75 cu. ft.; Distress Warrants to 1887, 1893, 1895, ca. .15 cu. ft.; Miscellaneous Warrants, 1893-95, 1902, ca. 140 items; and, Miscellaneous Warrants and Witness Claims, 1878-1902, ca. 75 items

Land Records

    Deed Book No. 1, 1777-79, 1 vol. (copy)

    Deeds, 1777-1910, 8.35 cu. ft.

    Daily Index to Deeds No. 4, n.d., 1 vol.

    Indexes to Deed Books Nos. 5-6, 18, 22, 26-31, n.d., 12 vols.

    General Index to Deeds, n.d., 1 vol.

    Hairston Grant[s] Concerning Land, [1780-1848], ca. .1 cu. ft.; and, Chancery suit, ca. 1875-1905, ca. 30 items

    Maps and Surveys, 1719-1904, ca. .1 cu. ft.

    Processioners' Orders and Reports, 1807-13, ca. 50 items

    Unrecorded Deeds, 1784-1910, .75 cu. ft.

Marriage Records and Vital Statistics

Marriage Bonds, 1857-58, ca. 30 items; and, Marriage Bond and Consent, 1833, 2 pp. (copies)

Marriage Licenses, 1858, 1863, 1896, 1902, ca. 25 items

Marriage Register, 1778-1846, 1 vol. (Ts. and copy)

Index to Marriage Register, 1778-1846, 1 vol. (Ts.); and, Card Index to Marriage Register, [1778-1846], ca. .35 cu. ft.

Registers of Births and Deaths, ca. 1855-95, ca. 1.5 cu. ft.

Military and Pension Records

Appointments by the Military Authority, 1868-69, ca. 25 items

Civil War Soldiers, 1861-65, 13 items (copies)

Henry Guard, Co. H, 24th Virginia Regt. [Minutes and History], 1861-63, compiled 1899, 1 vol. (copy)

[Lists of] Veterans, 1819, 1853, 1896, 3 items

Military Orders, 1866-70, ca. 25 items; and, 1866, 1 item (copy)

Militia Lists, 1850, 9 items

Miscellaneous Civil War [items], 1863, ca. 25 items

Muster Fines, 1861, 10 items

[Orders to distribute] Salt, 1862-64, 9 items (copies)

Pension Applications Disallowed, 1902-34, .25 cu. ft.

Pension Board Minutes, 1900-09, 1 vol.

Provisions for Soldiers' Families [titles vary], 1858, 1861-70, .45 cu. ft.; and, 1861-65, 32 items (copies)

[Record of] Indigent Soldiers' Families, 1863-65, 1 vol.

Supplies for Confederate Soldiers, 1861, ca. 25 items

See also Free Negroes and Slave Papers; Justice of the Peace Records; and, Tax and Fiscal Records

Road and Bridge Records

Railroads [papers], 1859, 10 items

Road Book, 1875-92, 1 vol.

Road Papers, 1777-1896, ca. .25 cu. ft.

Surveyors of the Roads [appointments and reports], ca. 1805-75, .35 cu. ft.

Turnpike Papers, 1858-93, 25 items (copies)

School Records

Free School Registers for Districts 4-5, 12, 15, 20, and 23, 1847-53, 6 vols.

Records of School Trustees, 1894-1921, 1 vol.

[School Board Minutes], 1886-1910, 1 vol.

School Commissioners' Reports, 1837-74, ca. 150 items

School Officials [appointments] and Papers, 1858-95, 21 items (copies)

Teachers' Register, 1847, 1 vol.

Tax and Fiscal Records

[County] Accounts Allowed [titles vary], ca. 1805-1910, ca. 2.5 cu. ft.

County Levies, 1863-64, 4 items

Delinquent Land, 1784-1811, ca. 25 items; and, Delinquent Taxes and Improper Assessments [titles vary], 1873-80, 1884-90, 1892-1904, 2.15 cu. ft. See also Insolvent Lists.

Hawkers, Peddlers, and Merchants [Licenses], 1858-81, 6 items (copies)

Insolvent Lists [titles vary] (also militia fines, etc.), 1786-1810, 1850-92, ca. 2.2 cu. ft.

Jury Claims, 1869-82, ca. .5 cu. ft.

Land Books, ca. 1830-75, ca. 1.25 cu. ft. (including fragments)

Lawyers [Licenses], 1858-1902, ca. 30 items (copies)

[Licenses for] Bowling Saloons or Alleys, 1858-78, 7 items (copies)

Lists of Tax Tickets, Ridgeway, 1871-74, 1 vol.

Personal Property Books, ca. 1850-75, 1.25 cu. ft.
Reports to the Auditor, ca. 1875-95, .25 cu. ft.
Sale of Delinquent Lands, 1898-1902, 16 items
Tax List, 1779, 16 pp. (copies)
Tax Records, ca. 1780-1855, 2.7 cu. ft.
Tax Tickets, ca. 1870-1905, 1.25 cu. ft.
Tithables, 1769, 1 vol. (printed)
See also Court Records, County and Superior Courts

Township Records

Horse Pasture Township Board Order Book, 1871-75, 1 vol.
Record of Ridgeway Township Board, see Miscellaneous Records
See also Tax and Fiscal Records; Miscellaneous Records; and, Treasurer

Wills

Will Book No. 1, 1777-79, 1 vol. (copy)
Wills, Inventories, etc., 1777-ca. 1900, ca. 6.7 cu. ft.
Indexes to Will Books Nos. 9 and 13, n.d., 2 vols.
General Index to Wills No. 1, n.d., 2 vols. (copies)

Miscellaneous Records

Advertisements for Strays, 1779-80, .35 cu. ft.; and, Estrays, 1861-92, 10 items
Church Records [minutes, petitions, etc.], 1893, 1901, ca. 25 items
Coroners' Inquests, 1840-1900, .45 cu. ft.
Courthouse [supplies, repairs, etc.], 1858-1902, ca. 30 items (originals and copies); Clerk's Office [records], 1858-1902, 3 items (copies); and, Bond, specifications, etc., for building courthouse and jail, 1780, 1793, 1803, 3 items (copies)
Crop Lien Docket, 1894-1903, 1 vol.
Crop Liens to 1905 [ca. 1890-1905], .35 cu. ft.
Estray Book, 1892-1916, 1 vol.
Genealogical notes and county history, 1829-96, ca. .25 cu. ft.
Gravely Family Papers, 1855-63, ca. 25 items
Jail [Records], 1806-67, ca. 10 items; and, 1861-98, 17 items (copies)
Jonathan H. Matthews' Day Book, 1872-74, 1 vol.
Lunacy Papers [interrogatories, etc.; titles vary], ca. 1800-1900, ca. .5 cu. ft.
Lyon [Sundry] Papers, 1785-97, ca. 25 items
Mills [records of], 1800-64, ca. 25 items; and, permits, 1858-1903, 33 items (copies)
Miscellaneous Papers, 1823-1918, ca. .8 cu. ft.
New Citizens [Naturalizations], 1858-97, 5 items (copies)
Newspapers [legal notices], 1796-1811, 8 items
Notary Public Reports, 1883-85, ca. 25 items
Overseers of the Poor [titles vary] Reports, 1851-62, 1870, 1873-74, 1876, 1892-98, .8 cu. ft.; and, Settlements, 1879, 1887-1904, ca. 1.75 cu. ft.
[Personal?] Accounts, receipts, and correspondence [labeled Letterheads], ca. 1875-1900, ca. 50 items
Record of Physicians, 1886-92 (also Record of Ridgeway Township Board, 1871-75), 1 vol.
Unidentified Indexes, n.d., 2 vols.
[Unidentified number books], 1893-95, n.d., 4 vols.
Vouchers [for claims allowed], ca. 1860-1915, ca. .6 cu. ft.; and, Vouchers, courthouse repair, 1898-1900, ca. 25 items

Commissioner of Revenue

Abstracts from Books and Reports of the Commissioner of Revenue, 1884, 1886, n.d., 6 items

[Accounts paid for listing] Births and Deaths, 1859-71, 6 items (copies)

Liquor License List Returns, ca. 1835-1904, .8 cu. ft.; and, Whiskey Distillery Licenses, 1875-1903, 16 items (copies)

Lists of Licenses Returned, 1869-70, 8 items

Moffett Register Reports, 1878-80, .45 cu. ft.

See also Tax and Fiscal Records

Sheriff

Account of A. T. Jones, Deputy Sheriff, 1889, 1 vol.

Alphabetical Lists of Taxes [titles vary], 1779-80, 2 vols.

Sheriff's Cash Book, 1854-61, 1 vol.

Sheriff's Execution Books, 1843-46, 1850-54, 2 vol.

Treasurer

Samuel Smith, Treasurer, in account with Ridgeway Township, 1871, 1 vol.

[Treasurers' Ledgers], 1892-93, 1899, 2 vols.

Treasurer's Receipts for Accounts, 1894-95, 1 vol.

Treasurers' Reports, Vouchers, and Settlements, ca. 1870-1905, 5.75 cu. ft.

Treasurer's School Book, 1903-09, 1 vol.

See also Tax and Fiscal Records

Microfilm Records

Circuit Court Clerk

Court Records

County Court

Index to Criminal Orders, Defendants A-Z, 1777-1904, 1 reel

Order Books Nos. 1-10, 1777-1820, 2 reels; and, Minute Books Nos. 1-7, 1820-67, 2 reels

General Index to [Orders and Minutes], Ended Law and Chancery, Plaintiffs A-Z, 1777-1904, 4 reels

Circuit Superior Court of Law and Chancery

Chancery Order Book No. 1, 1831-67 (includes Circuit Court, 1852-67), 1 reel

Circuit Court

Chancery Orders, see Circuit Superior Court of Law and Chancery

Land Records

Deed Books Nos. 1-16, 1777-1867, 7 reels

General Index to Deeds, Grantors-Grantees A-Z, 1777-1949, 7 reels

Surveyors' Book No. 1, 1778-1877, 1 reel

Marriage Records and Vital Statistics

Marriage Bond Book No. 1, 1778-1859, 1 reel (part)

Marriage Register, 1778-1849, 1 reel (part); and, Registers of Marriages Nos. 1-2, 1853-1913, 1 reel (part)

General Index to Marriages, Males-Females A-Z, 1853-1949, 3 reels

Register of Births, 1853-71, 1 reel (part)

Register of Deaths, 1853-71, 1 reel (part)

Index to Births, Marriages, and Deaths, 1853-71, 1 reel (part)

Wills

Will Books Nos. 1-7, 1777-1867, 3 reels

General Index to Wills, Devisors-Devisees A-Z, 1777-1949, 2 reels

HIGHLAND COUNTY

Formed in 1847 from Pendleton (West Virginia) and Bath counties.

Original Records

Circuit Court Clerk
Board of Supervisors Records
Claims Audited and Allowed, 1870-90, ca. .85 cu. ft.
County Business Records Nos. 1-2, 1870-87, 1871-99, 2 vols.
Minutes [also labeled S. & P. Road, contains road records], 1884-94, 1 vol. See also Road and Bridge Records.
Record [Minutes], 1899-1910, 1 vol.
Witness Book, 1892-1917, 1 vol.
See also Miscellaneous Records
Bonds/Commissions/Oaths
County Court Bonds, 1855-89, 2 vols.
County Court Bonds Recorded Nos. 5-6, 1855-87, 2 vols.
County Court Officers Bonds Recorded, 1872-99, 2 vols.
Officers Bonds, 1872-1903, 2 vols.
School Trustees' Oaths, 1900-05, 20 items
Business Records/Corporations/Partnerships
Unidentified [merchant's] Ledgers A-B, 1891-93, 2 vols.
Court Records
County Court
Chancery Rule Docket, 1871-73, 1 vol.
Ended Causes, 1852-67, ca. 1 cu. ft.
Execution Books Nos. 1-3, 1847-1917 (includes Circuit Court, 1904-17), 3 vols.
Index to Execution Book No. 3, n.d., 1 vol.
Executions, 1889-95, 1900-07 (includes Circuit Court, 1904-07), ca. .2 cu. ft.
Executions Returned, 1859-61, 1866-79, ca. .5 cu. ft.
Fee Books [Ledgers], 1870-79, 1876-1904, 4 vols.
Issue Docket, 1847-80, 1 vol.
Order Books Nos. 4-6, 1877-1903, 3 vols.
Papers [receipts], 1837-63, 21 items
Process Book, 1870-1903, 1 vol.
Witness Attendance, 1874-1902, 1 vol.
Circuit Superior Court of Law and Chancery
Chancery Rule Docket, 1847-1903, 1 vol.
Execution Book [No. 1], 1847-61 (includes Circuit Court, 1852-61), 1 vol.
Minute Book, 1848-82 (includes Circuit Court, 1852-82), 1 vol.
Witness Attendance Book, 1848-1903 (includes Circuit Court, 1852-1903), 1 vol.
Circuit Court
Chancery Fee Books, 1874-92, 1881-1907, 2 vols.
Chancery Memorandum Book, 1888-1908, 1 vol.
Chancery Rule Docket, see Circuit Superior Court of Law and Chancery
Clerk's Reports to Auditor of Public Accounts, 1892-1908, ca. .1 cu. ft.
Common Law Execution Book No. 2, 1859-80, 1 vol. See also Circuit Superior Court of Law and Chancery.
Common Law Process Book No. 2, 1870-1919, 1 vol.

Execution Books, see County Court and Circuit Superior Court of Law and Chancery

Fee Book, 1889-1916, 1 vol.

Law and Chancery Dockets Nos. [1]-2, 1876-1905, 1875-1916, 2 vols.

Law Executions, 1869-70, 1875-80, 1902-07, ca. .35 cu. ft.

Memorandum Book, 1870-1908, 1 vol.

Memorandum of Decrees Entered, 1877-1924, 1 vol.

Minute Book, see Circuit Superior Court of Law and Chancery

Reports of Business in Highland County Circuit Court, 1896-1906, ca. 50 items

Witness Attendance, see Circuit Superior Court of Law and Chancery

County and Superior Courts

Chancery Executions, 1855-87, ca. .1 cu. ft.

Clerk's Correspondence and Receipts, A-Z, 1896-1924, ca. .2 cu. ft.

Fee Book, 1886-1916, 1 vol.

Register of Convicts, 1879-1926, 1 vol.

Election Records

Election Records [abstracts of votes, electoral board papers, etc.], 1873-1907, ca. .1 cu. ft.

[Lists of Registered Voters], 1902-11, 1 vol.

Notices of Candidacy, 1895-99, ca. 75 items

Fiduciary Records

Accounts of Fiduciaries, 1868-1916, 1 vol.

Adm[inistrato]rs Bonds No. 2, 1847-55, 1 vol.

Appraisements and Sale Bills, 1863-80, ca. .3 cu. ft.

Circuit Court Fiduciary Bond Book, 1888-1900, 1 vol.

Circuit Court Fiduciary Bonds Recorded No. 7, 1887-1901, 1 vol.

Ex[excut]ors Bonds No. 1, Personal Estate, 1847-53, 1 vol.

Ex[excut]ors Bonds No. 4, Real Estate, 1853, 1 vol.

Guardians' Bonds No. 3, 1848-54, 1 vol.

Record of Administrators' Bonds, 1852-70, 1 vol.

Sale Bills, 1884, and List of Property in the Hands of a Receiver, 1870, 3 items

Settlements of Estates, 1872, ca. .1 cu. ft.

Justice of the Peace Records

[Constables] Executions Satisfied, 1879-1904, ca. .35 cu. ft.

Judgment and Execution Books, 1891-1923, 1902-09, 2 vols.

Land Records

Miscellaneous Deeds and Related Papers, 1893-1929, ca. .1 cu. ft.

General Indexes to Deeds, 1847-1939, 3 vols.

Marriage Records and Vital Statistics

Marriage Records, 1847-53, 1 item (Ts.)

Road and Bridge Records

County Roads, Stonewall District, 1885-1913, 1 vol.

Road Commissioners' Report and Claims Allowed, 1885-98, ca. .1 cu. ft.

Road Reports [by districts], 1873-1916, .35 cu. ft.

S[taunton] & P[arkersburg] Road Claims, 1884-1903, ca. .2 cu. ft.; Road Funds, 1902-05, ca. .1 cu. ft.; and, Road Settlements, 1885-1906, .35 cu. ft.

S[taunton] & P[arkersburg] Road Records No. 2, 1884-1914, 1 vol. See also Board of Supervisors Records.

See also Miscellaneous Records; and, Treasurer

Tax and Fiscal Records

Tax Ticket, 1873, 1 item

Wills

Will of Valentine Bird (copy), 1828, 1 item

Miscellaneous Records
Certificate, 1901, 1 item
Conditional Sales Memorandum, 1870-1929, 1 vol.
Contracts and Agreements Filed, 1858-ca. 1905, ca. .1 cu. ft.
Coroners' Inquests, 1864-1900, 16 items
Estray Book, 1847-1931, 1 vol.
Insanity Commissioners' Reports, 1902-04, ca. 50 items
Mechanics' Liens, 1875-1929, 1 vol.
Overseers of the Poor Records, 1857-61, 1 vol.
Physicians' Register, 1885-1937 (also List of Road Workers, 1871-75, and Minutes
    of the Board of Supervisors, 1884), 1 vol.

Treasurer
Treasurers' Road Settlements, 1885-1904, ca. .15 cu. ft.
Treasurers' Settlements, 1879-1904, 1.75 cu. ft.

Microfilm Records

Circuit Court Clerk
  Court Records
    County Court
      Order Books Nos. 1-2, 1847-70, 1 reel
    Circuit Superior Court of Law and Chancery
      Chancery Order Book No. 1, 1848-73 (includes Circuit Court, 1852-73), 1 reel
    Circuit Court
      Chancery Orders, see Circuit Superior Court of Law and Chancery
  Fiduciary Records
    Inventories and Appraisements [also wills] Nos. 1-2, 1847-84, 1 reel
  Land Records
    Deed Books Nos. 1-3, 1847-70, 2 reels
    General Index to Deeds No. 1, 1847-1902, 1 reel
  Marriage Records and Vital Statistics
    Register of Births, 1853-78, 1 reel (part)
    Register of Deaths, 1853-78, 1 reel (part)
    Register of Marriages, 1853-1951, 1 reel (part)
  Wills
    Will Book No. 2, 1859-1924, 1 reel
    See also Fiduciary Records

ISLE OF WIGHT COUNTY

Original shire established in 1634.

Original Records

Circuit Court Clerk
Board of Supervisors Records
Records [Minutes; titles vary] Nos. 1-3, 1870-1909, 3 vols.
Bonds/Commissions/Oaths
Bonds, 1769, 1800-01, 1805, 1829, 1842, ca. .2 cu. ft.
Commissioners' Bonds (also Notary Public and Injunction Bonds, and Powers of Attorney), 1875-1904, ca. .5 cu. ft.
Court Records
County Court
Court Papers (and plats), 1828, 1838, ca. 1840-[1904], 13 cu. ft. See also Judgments.
Executions, 1769-1849, ca. 25 items
Form Book, 1771-80, 1 vol.
Judgments (also plats and court papers), ca. 1770-1850, 43.65 cu. ft.
Miscellany [court records, tax commissioner's minutes, etc.], 1775-1852, 1 vol. (copy)
Order Book, 1780-83, 1 vol.; and, Order Books [titles vary], 1746-69, 1772-83, 1795-1801, 1806-09, 11 vols. (copies). See also Land Records.
Process [Rule] Book, 1866-70 (also Minutes, 1865), 1 vol.
Rule Book, 1790-94, 1 vol.
Suit Papers, ca. 1765-85, n.d., 11 items (and fragments)
Summons, 1768-1805, 9 items (and fragments)
County and Superior Courts
Chancery Papers, ca. 1800-85, 2.4 cu. ft.
Executions, ca. 1785-1915, 5 cu. ft.
Unspecified Court
Index [to docket?], n.d., 1 vol.
Election Records
Contested Election, 1887, ca. .4 cu. ft.
Fiduciary Records
Administrators' Bonds, ca. 1775-1905, ca. 2.3 cu. ft.
Estate Papers, 1754, 1769, 1772, 6 items
Guardians' Book, 1782-89, 1 vol. (copy)
Land Records
Deed Books [titles vary], 1-2, 5-11, and 13-16, 1688-1715, 1736-65, 1772-93, 13 vols. (copies); and, Deeds and Wills, 1715-26, 1 vol. (copy)
Plats, see Court Records, County Court
Recorded Deeds, ca. 1740-1855, 2.5 cu. ft.
Unrecorded Deeds, ca. 1765-1800, ca. .2 cu. ft.
Marriage Records and Vital Statistics
Marriage Bonds, 1782-1850, ca. 2.5 cu. ft.; and, incomplete bond, 1783, 1 item
Marriage Register (compilation), 1772-1853, 1 vol. (copy); and, 1850-62, 1 vol.
Marriage Registers, 1871, 6 pp.
Ministers' Returns, ca. 1810-60, ca. .2 cu. ft.
[Register of Minister's Return] Certificates, 1828-50, 1 vol.

Tax and Fiscal Records
> Abstract of Property Book, 1788, 3 pp.
> List of Insolvent Debtors, 1778, 1 item
> See also Court Records, County Court

Wills
> Wills, etc. [tiles vary] Nos. 3 and 5-8, 1726-34, 1745-79, 5 vols. (copies)
> See also Land Records

Miscellaneous Records
> County Claims, 1787, 1863, 3 items
> Powers of Attorney, see Bonds/Commissions/Oaths

Microfilm Records

Circuit Court Clerk
Court Records
County Court
> Judgment Papers, 1799-1807, 21 reels. See also Land Records.
> Orders, 1746-52, 1759-69, 1772-83, 1795-1866, 9 reels. See also Land Records.

Fiduciary Records
> Accounts, see Wills
> Estate Paper, see Land Records
> Guardians' Accounts, 1767-1861, 4 reels. See also Land Records.

Land Records
> Deeds, Wills, and Guardians' Accounts Book A [Great Book 1], 1636-1767, 1 reel; and, Deeds and Wills [Great Book 2], 1715-26, 1 reel. See also Wills.
> Deed Books Nos. 1-40, 1688-1715, 1729-1866, 18 reels
> General Indexes to Deeds Vols. 1-2, 1688-1890, 1 reel
> Indentures, 1839-97, 1841 and 1845, 1 reel
> Recorded Deeds, 1741-1854, 5 reels
> Unrecorded Deeds, 1765-1814 (also Recorded Wills, 1780-82; Estate Paper, 1787; and, County Court Judgments, 1816), 1 reel

Marriage Records and Vital Statistics
> Marriage Bonds, 1772-1850 (also Ministers' Returns, 1810-59), 12 reels
> Marriage Register and Index, 1771-1853 (compilation), 1 reel; and, Marriage Register A, 1854-1900, 1 reel (part)
> Register of Births, 1853-76, 1 reel (part)
> Register of Deaths, 1853-74, 1 reel (part)
> Index to Births, Deaths, and Marriages, 1853-1900, 1 reel

Wills
> Record of Wills, Deeds, etc., Vols. 1-2, 1661-1719, 2 reels. See also Land Records.
> Will Books [titles vary] Nos. 3-28, 1726-1866, 11 reels
> Common Law Will Books, 1833-1902, 1 reel (part)
> Recorded Wills, see Land Records

Miscellaneous Records
> Historical Sketch of the Origin and Progress of Newport Parish, 1606-1826, by Dr. John R. Purdie, 1 reel (part)
> Record of the Vestry Meetings of Christ Church, Newport Parish, 1836-94, 1 reel (part)

JAMES CITY COUNTY

**Original shire established in 1634.
Parts of New Kent and York counties were added later.
See also City of Williamsburg, many of whose records
were recorded with those of James City County.**

Original Records

Circuit Court Clerk
  Board of Supervisors Records
    Minutes Nos. [1]-2, 1887-1908, 2 vols.
  Court Records
    County and Circuit Courts
      Clerk's Guide to Sample Forms for Certain Court Records, n.d., 5 pp. (copies)
      Minutes, 1871-82, 2 vols.
    Circuit Court, James City County and Williamsburg
      Chancery Execution Book, 1868-1916, 1 vol.
      Chancery Minutes, 1871-73, 1 vol.
      [Chancery] Order Books Nos. 6-8, 1889-1903, 3 vols.
      Chancery Rules, 1872-1911, 1 vol.
      [Common] Law Order Books Nos. [1]-4, 1865-1909, 4 vols.
      Common Law Rules, 1866-1911, 1 vol.
      Execution Book, 1866-1916, 1 vol.
      Judgment Docket, 1865-1903, 1 vol.
      Law Execution Book, 1866-1916, 1 vol.
      Law Order Book No. 5, 1885, 1 vol.
      Minutes, 1866-82, 1 vol.
      Order Book, 1879-85, 1 vol.
  Election Records
    Rolls of Registered Voters, 1900-65 [overlapping date ranges], 16 vols.
  Fiduciary Records
    James City County and Williamsburg Fiduciary Bond Book, 1865-1908, 1 vol.
  Land Records
    James City County and Williamsburg Plat Books Nos. 1-2, 1891-1918, 2 vols.
    Processioners' Books, 1890-91, 1903-04, 8 vols.
  Marriage Records and Vital Statistics
    Birth Register, 1866-84, 1 vol.
    Death Register, 1864-84, 1 vol.
  School Records
    School Commissioners' Records, 1819-61, 1 vol. (copy)
  Tax and Fiscal Records
    Tax Book, 1768-69, 1 vol. (copy)
    Tax Book, 1768-69, ca. .1 cu. ft. (unbound copies)
  Miscellaneous Records
    James City County and Williamsburg Contracts for Personal Property, 1900-18, 1 vol.

Microfilm Records

Circuit Court Clerk
    Board of Supervisors Records
        Minutes Nos. [1]-2, 1887-1908, 1 reel (part)
    Land Records
        Deed Books Nos. 1-2, 1854-61, 1865-74, 1 reel
    Tax and Fiscal Records
        James City County-Williamsburg Tax Book, 1768-69, 1 reel

KING AND QUEEN COUNTY

Formed in 1691 from New Kent County.

Original Records

Circuit Court Clerk
    Court Records
        County Court
            Longest v. Williams, complaint, 1867, 1 item
            See also Tax and Fiscal Records
    Land Records
        Court Records [deeds and related papers], 1763-1868, n.d., ca. .1 cu. ft. (copies)
        Deed, 1719, 1 item (original and copy); Deeds, 1840, 1858, 3 items (copies); and,
            Deed, 1850, 1 item
        Plat, n.d., 1 item (copy)
        Plat Book, 1823-78, 1 vol. (copy)
    Road Records
        Road Surveyor's Record Book, 1851-70, 1 vol.
    Tax and Fiscal Records
        Tax Accounts, Executions, etc., 1779, 1786-87, 1 vol. (copy)
        Tax Assessor's Book, 1841-42, 1 vol.
        See also Sheriff

Sheriff
    Sheriff's Tax Book, 1821, 1 vol.

Microfilm Records

Circuit Court Clerk
    Court Records
        County Court
            Minute Book, 1858-66, 1 reel
        Circuit Superior Court of Law and Chancery
            Chancery Order Book, 1831-58 (includes Circuit Court, 1852-58), 1 reel
            Records, 1831-51, 1 reel

Circuit Court
> Chancery Order Book, 1859-[74], 1 reel. <u>See also</u> Circuit Superior Court of
> Law and Chancery.
> Order Book [1854-67], 1 reel

Wills
> Will Book, [1864-93], 1 reel

KING GEORGE COUNTY

**Formed in 1720 from Richmond County. Part of
Westmoreland County was added later.**

Original Records

Circuit Court Clerk
Court Records
County Court
> Orders and Judgments [titles vary], 1721-90, 4 vols. (copies)

Fiduciary Records
> Fiduciary Accounts No. 3 (Bonds, 1739-65, and Orphans' Accounts, 1740-61),
> 1 vol. (copy); and, Fiduciary Accounts, 1794-1807, 1 vol. (copy)
> Inventories [Book 1], 1721-44, 1 vol. (copy). <u>See also</u> Land Records.
> Orphans' Accounts, 1740-61, 1 vol.

Land Records
> Deed Books Nos. 1-6, 1721-84, 7 vols. (copies)

Marriage Records and Vital Statistics
> [Index to] Marriages, 1786-1850 (Ts.), 1 vol. (copy)
> Marriage Bond, 1802, 1 item (copy)

Military and Pension Records
> [Militia] Court of Inquiry Order Book, 1789-1812, 1 vol.

Tax and Fiscal Records
> Rentals, 1769-70, 1773, 28 pp. (copies)

Wills
> Will Books Nos. 1-3, [1752]-1846, 3 vols. (copies)

Microfilm Records

Circuit Court Clerk
Bonds/Commissions/Oaths
> Bonds, 1765-1874, 2 reels. <u>See also</u> Land Records.

Court Records
County Court
> Order Books, 1721-1812, 5 reels; and, Order Books [Minutes] Nos. 5A-13,
> 14B, and 16-17, 1790-1869, 9 reels

Circuit Superior Court of Law and Chancery
> Order Books, 1831-70 (includes Circuit Court, 1852-70), 1 reel (part)

Circuit Court
> Order Books, <u>see</u> Circuit Superior Court of Law and Chancery

Fiduciary Records

Fiduciary Accounts [bonds and inventories, etc.; titles vary] Books Nos. 3-12, 1740-1872, 5 reels

General Index to Fiduciary Accounts No. 1, 1721-1921, 1 reel

Inventories [Book 1], 1721-44, 1 reel (part). See also Land Records.

Orphans' Accounts, 1740-61, 1 reel (part)

Land Records

Deed Books Nos. 1-19, 1721-1868 (also Bonds, 1723-38, and Inventories, 1745-65), 11 reels

General Indexes to Deeds Nos. 1-2, 1721-1892, 1 reel; and, [Embrey's] General Index [to deeds, wills, etc.], 1721-1924, 6 reels

Land Causes, 1792-1813, 1831-33, 1 reel

Marriage Records and Vital Statistics

[Index to] Marriages, 1786-1850 (Ts.), 1 reel

Record of Births, 1871-1917, 1 reel (part)

Register of Marriages No. 1, 1856-1930, 1 reel (part)

Military and Pension Records

[Militia] Court of Inquiry Order Book, 1789-1812, 1 reel (part)

Militia Record [Regimental Court], 1824-60, 1 reel

Wills

Will Books Nos. 1-4, [1752]-1901, 2 reels

General Index to Wills, A-Z, 1752-1948, 1 reel. See also Land Records.

KING WILLIAM COUNTY

Formed in 1701 from King and Queen County.

Original Records

Circuit Court Clerk
  County Records
    County Court
      Record Books [deeds, wills, etc.] Nos. 1-19, 1701-1884, 19 vols. (copies)

      Index to Photostat Copies of Old Records of K[ing] W[illia]m Co[unty] No. 1, 1701-1885, 1 vol. (copy)

  Land Records
    Plat of Town Lots [West Point?], see New Kent County Land Records

    See also Court Records, County Court

  Military and Pension Records
    Compiled Service Records of King William County Confederate Soldiers, [1861-65], .45 cu. ft.

  Wills
    Will of William McGeorge, 1825, 1 item

    See also Court Records, County Court

  Miscellaneous Records
    Benjamin C. Spiller's Account Book, 1783-84, 1 vol.

Sheriff

[Sheriff] Thomas Moore's Account Book, 1819, 1 vol.

Microfilm Records

Circuit Court Clerk
Court Records
County Court

Records [including deeds, wills, etc.] Nos. 1-19, 1701-1884, 16 reels
General Index to Records, 1701-1885, 1 reel

LANCASTER COUNTY

**Formed in 1651 from Northumberland
and York counties.**

Original Records

Circuit Court Clerk
Bonds/Commissions/Oaths

Apprentice Bonds and Records, 1722-97, 12 items
Bonds (ordinary, officials', etc.), 1721-99, ca. .25 cu. ft.
County Court Bonds, 1791-1885, 2.7 cu. ft.
[Debt] Bonds and Promissory Notes, 1722-99, ca. 100 items
Militia Commissions, etc. 1787-93, 8 items
Minister's Bond, 1810, 1 item
Oaths of Allegiance, 1777-78, 4 items
Ordinary Bonds, 1831, 2 items
See also Fiduciary Records

Business Records/Corporations/Partnerships

[Benjamin Waddey's] Merchant's Account Book, 1809-15, 1 vol.; and, Journal, 1834-36, 1 vol.
[Jonathan S. Chowning's] Day Book, Merry Point, 1855-58, 1 vol.; and, Journal, 1855-59, 1 vol.
Schedule of Debts Claimed of the United States by McCall Dennistoun and Co., 1783, 1 item
Thomas West's Tavern Ledgers, 1809, 1813-15, 2 vols.
Unidentified Account Books, 1796-97, 1813-17, 2 vols.
Unidentified Journal, [1832] 1833-34, 1 vol.
Unidentified Ledgers, 1799-1801, 1804-09, 1838-41, 4 vols.
W[arner] E[ubank]'s Ledger, 1845-49, 1 vol. See also Sheriff.

Court Records
County Court

Appeals and Land Causes No. 39, 1795-1823, 1 vol. (original and copy)
Attachments, 1782-95, 7 items
Chancery Papers, 1800-57, ca. 1.8 cu. ft.
Court Papers, 1770-1899, 18 cu. ft.
Criminal Suit Papers, 1772-1807, ca. .1 cu. ft.
Docket Book, 1801-04, 1 vol.
Execution Books, 1786-99 (includes estrays), 1801-05, 1828-56, 3 vols. See also Plea Book.
Executions, 1783-99, 8.1 cu. ft.
Fee Books, 1772, 1813-16, 1835-37, 1841, 4 vols.

General Index [to records of the County Court, 1652-1881] 1 vol. (original and copy)

Henry Towles, Clerk of the County Court, Ledger, 1796-98, 1 vol.

Issue Dockets [titles vary], 1823-32, 1844-66 and 1848-68, 2 vols.

Judgments, 1702-1876, 20.7 cu. ft.

Minute Book No. 2, 1801-04, 1 vol.

Miscellaneous Court Records, 1725-95, n.d., ca. 50 items (and fragments)

Orders, etc. [including wills and deeds; titles vary], 1655-66, 1 vol.; Nos. 1, 3-8, 10-11, and 14-18, 1666-80, 1686-1743, 1752-64, 1767-89, 14 vols. (originals and copies); No. 2, 1680-86, 1 vol. (copy); and No. 9, 1743-52, 1 vol. Orders Nos. 12-13 are bound with Deeds, etc., Nos. 17-18; Orders No. 14 includes Marriages, 1794-1852, and No. 16 includes Criminal Cases, 1770-78. See also Land Records; and, Wills.

Index to Order Book No. 8, 1729-43, 1 vol. (copy)

Plea Book, 1752-96, and Execution Book, 1791-96, 1 vol.

Rule Book, 1801-03, 1 vol.

Suits involving Negroes, 1791-92, n.d., 14 items

Superior Court of Law

Judgments, 1809-49 (includes Circuit Superior Court of Law and Chancery, 1831-49), 3.6 cu. ft.

[Writs of] Execution, 1817-35 (includes Circuit Superior Court of Law and Chancery, 1831-35), .25 cu. ft.

Circuit Superior Court of Law and Chancery

Chancery Papers, 1832-51, 2.7 cu. ft.

Court Papers, 1849-50, ca. .1 cu. ft.

Executions, see Superior Court of Law

Judgments, see Superior Court of Law

Circuit Court

Chancery Papers, 1852-99, ca. 3.25 cu. ft.

Court Papers, 1858-89, ca. .35 cu. ft.

Executions, 1854-68, ca. .2 cu. ft.

Judgments, 1853-85, 2.7 cu. ft.

County and Superior Courts

Court Papers, 1789-1905, n.d., ca. 3.15 cu. ft.

Executions, 1726-1831, .45 cu. ft.

Subpoenas, 1843-48, ca. .1 cu. ft.

Suit Papers, 1787-1827, n.d., ca. 100 items

Election Records

Polls, ca. 1750-90, 1798-1887, ca. 1 cu. ft.

Fiduciary Records

Administrators' and Executors' Bonds, 1725-79 (and various other bonds, 1780-99), ca. .7 cu. ft.

Estate Appraisements and Accounts, 1850-54, 1 vol.

Estate Papers (inventories, etc.), 1651-1797, n.d., 43 items; Divisions and Settlements of Estates, and Widows' Dower, 1749-78, 13 items; and, Col. Burgess Smith's estate papers, 1768-79, 26 items

Guardians' Bonds and Records, 1720-99, 1818-19, n.d., ca. .45 cu. ft.

Inventory of the estate of Teague Carroll, 1666, of Hugh Brent, 1716, and of Christopher Hodgkinson, 1777, 3 items; and, Inventories, 1650-1799, 2.7 cu. ft.

Orphans' Account Books, 1839-63, 1842-48, 1856-70, 4 vols.

See also Bonds/Commissions/Oaths

Free Negro and Slave Records

Emancipation Bills, 1790, 4 items
Patrollers' Accounts, 1788-98, n.d., 13 items
Register of Free Negroes, 1803-60, 1 vol.
See also Court Records, County Court; Land Records; and, Tax and Fiscal Records

Justice of the Peace Records

[Justices' Reports of] Criminal Cases, 1807-95, 1898, .45 cu. ft.

Land Records

Deeds, 1661-1801, 1818, .9 cu. ft.; and, County Court Deeds, 1791-1899, 2.7 cu. ft.
Deeds, etc. [also wills and orders; titles vary] No. 1, 1652-57, 1 vol. (copy); Nos. 2, 4, 6-7, 9, 11-19, and 21, 1654-1702, 1666-1782, 15 vols. (originals and copies); and, 1699-1800 (also Wills, 1661-1787), 1 vol. See also Court Records, County Court; and, Wills.
Index to Deeds and Wills, 1653-1800, 1 vol. (copy)
Ejectments, 1751-52, n.d., 5 items
Land and Property Records (including deeds, bills of sale for slaves, etc.), 1665-1798, ca. 75 items
Land Causes, see Court Records, County Court
[Land] Papers (including plats), 1711, 1726, 1743, 1785, 1787, 1798, 6 items (copies)
Processioners' Returns, 1820, 18 pp. (copies)
Surveys and Boundary Agreements, 1711-99, 14 items

Marriage Records and Vital Statistics

Marriage Bonds and Records, 1679, 1701-1848, ca. 1.5 cu. ft.
Marriage Bonds Nos. 1-5, 1701, 1715-1848, 5 vols. (copies)
Marriage Certificates, 1854-64, .45 cu. ft.
Marriage Contracts, 1765, 1770, 1786, 3 items (copies)
Marriage Licenses and Consents, 1852-1915, ca. 2.5 cu. ft.
Marriage Register, 1715-1852, 1 vol. (Ts. and copy)
Index to Marriage Register, 1715-1852, 1 vol. (Ts. and copy)
Ministers' Returns, 1782-1849, 1 vol. (copy)
Ministers' Returns, 1782-1849, ca. 75 items.
Register of Deaths, 1853-70, 1 vol.
Registers of Births, 1854-95, .45 cu. ft.
Registers of Births and Deaths, ca. 1855-95, .25 cu. ft.
Registers of Deaths, 1870-85, .45 cu. ft.
See also Court Records, County Court

Organization Records

Sons of Temperance, 152nd Division, Record Book, 1848-52, 1 vol. [pp. 1-4 missing]

Road and Bridge Records

Road Records, 1746-99, n.d., ca. 50 items

Tax and Fiscal Records

Delinquent Land, 1872-92, 11 items
G. Carter's List of Negroes Exempted from Tax, 1787, 1 item
Land Taxes, 1782-97, ca. .1 cu. ft.
Lists of Tithables and Tax Records, 1734-98, 13 items
Personal Property Taxes, 1782-89, ca. .15 cu. ft.
Rentals (Rent Rolls), 1773, 2 vols. (copies); Rent Rolls for Christ Church Parish, 1721, 1748, 1750, 7 pp. (copies); and, Rental for White Chapel Parish, 1750, 2 pp. (copies)

Tithables, 1745-46, 1775-81, n.d., 1 vol. (copy)

Tithables, ca. 1745-1800, ca. .15 cu. ft.; and, 1784-85, 1795-99, ca. .1 cu. ft. (copies)

Wills

Will and inventory of Tobias Hunter, 1668-69, 1 item; Will (and copy) and letter of administration on the estate of William King, 1716, 3 items; and, Will and letter of administration on the estate of Walter Armes [Arends?], 1718, 1 item

Wills, 1700-1819, .9 cu. ft.; and, County Court Wills, 1750-1836, .45 cu. ft.

Wills and administrations, [1726]-97, 9 items

Wills, etc. [includes deeds], 1653-99, 1 vol.; No. 10, 1709-27, 1 vol. (copy); and, Nos. 5, 8, 20, and 22, 1674-1709, 1770-95, 4 vols. (originals and copies). See also Land Records.

See also Court Records, County Court

Miscellaneous Records

Accounts and Claims (including personal accounts), 1745-98, ca. 75 items

Ewing Goode genealogical data, n.d., 1 item

Lectures on the Powers of Congress, n.d., 1 vol. (Ms.)

Mill Records, 1760-97, n.d., 41 items

Powers of Attorney, 1722-99, 22 items

Reports of Overseers of the Poor, 1789, 1792, 4 items

Tobacco [Inspectors'] Records, 1757-91, 26 items

Sheriff

Eubank Sheriff Book [Account Book], 1852, 1 vol.

Microfilm Records

Circuit Court Clerk

Bonds/Commissions/Oaths

Bonds, 1719-49, 1 reel (part); and, County Court Bonds, 1791-1885, 6 reels

Criminal Trial Bonds, 1772-1807, 1 reel (part)

Miscellaneous Bonds, 1721, 1740-90, 1 reel (part)

Ordinary Bonds, 1790-99, 1 reel (part)

Court Records

County Court

Appeals and Land Causes [titles vary], 1795-1885, 2 reels

Chancery Papers, 1800-99, 7 reels

Court Papers, 1653-1899, 49 reels

Criminal Papers, 1807-98, 1 reel

Executions, 1726-1899, 24 reels

General Index to Records, 1652-1881, 1 reel

Judgments, 1702-1876, 89 reels

Orders, etc. [titles vary] Nos. 1-7, 9-11, and 14-18, 1655-1729, 1743-64, 1767-89 (also Ministers' Returns, 1794-1852), 8 reels; and, Order Books [nonconsecutively numbered], 1789-1866, 12 reels

Subpoenas, 1843-48, 1 reel (part)

Superior Court of Law

Executions, 1817-35 (includes Circuit Superior Court of Law and Chancery, 1831-35), 1 reel (part)

Judgments, 1809-48 (includes Circuit Superior Court of Law and Chancery, 1831-48), 13 reels

Circuit Superior Court of Law and Chancery

Chancery Order Book No. 1, 1831-60 (includes Circuit Court, 1852-60), 1 reel
Chancery Papers, 1832-51, 7 reels
Court Papers, 1849-50, 1 reel (part)
Executions, see Superior Court of Law
Judgments, see Superior Court of Law

Circuit Court

Chancery Order Book, see Circuit Superior Court of Law and Chancery
Chancery Papers, 1852-97, 10 reels
Court Papers, 1858-89, 1 reel (part)
Executions, 1854-68, 2 reels (part)
Judgments, 1853-80, 10 reels

County and Superior Courts

Court Papers, 1789-1920, n.d., 13 reels

Election Records

Polls, 1752-99, 4 reels

Fiduciary Records

[Administrators' and Executors'] Bonds, 1750-99, 1 reel; and, Administrators' Bonds, 1790-99, 1 reel (part)
Estate Books [nonconsecutively numbered], 1796-1850, 1854-63, 8 reels
General Index to Fiduciary Accounts, etc., No. 1, 1750-1912, 1 reel
Guardians' Bonds, 1720-99, 1818-19, 2 reels (parts)
Inventories, 1650-1799, 11 reels
Orphans' Accounts, 1824-42, 2 reels

Land Records

Deeds, 1660-1899, 7 reels; and, County Court Deeds, 1791-1836, 3 reels
Deeds, etc. [nonconsecutively numbered], 1652-1770, 6 reels; and, Deed Books [nonconsecutively numbered], 1770-1866, 9 reels
General Index to Deeds No. 1, 1750-1900, 1 reel
See also Court Records, County Court

Marriage Records and Vital Statistics

Marriage Certificates, 1854-65, 1 reel (part)
Marriage Licenses, 1852-1915, 4 reels
Marriage Register, 1715-1852 (Ms. compilation), 1 reel (part); and, Register of Marriages, 1848-62, 1 reel (part)
Index to Marriage Register, 1715-1852 (Ms. compilation), 1 reel (part)
Marriage Record, 1854-1901, 1 reel (part)
Registers of Births, 1853-95, 2 reels (parts)
Registers of Deaths, 1853-85, 2 reels (parts)
See also Court Records, County Court

Tax and Fiscal Records

Delinquent Lands, 1791-1892, 1 reel (part)
Land Taxes, 1782-97, 1 reel (part)
Personal Property Taxes, 1782-97, 1 reel (part)
Tithables, 1745-99, 1 reel (part)

Wills

Wills, 1700-90, 1795-1819, 4 reels; and, County Court Wills, 1750-1836, 1 reel
Wills, etc. [nonconsecutively numbered], 1674-1727, 1770-1925, 5 reels. See also Land Records, Deeds, etc.
General Index to Wills No. 1, 1669-1950, 1 reel
See also Land Records

LEE COUNTY

**Formed in 1792 from Russell County.
Part of Scott County was added later.**

Original Records

Circuit Court Clerk
Board of Supervisors Records
County Claims and Supervisors' Warrants, 1876-80, .35 cu. ft.; and, Old Claims (Supervisors' Warrants and Vouchers), 1861-84, .35 cu. ft
Ledger [Minutes of Road Board and Board of Supervisors], 1898-1909, 1 vol.
Warrants Paid, 1898-1903, .35 cu. ft.; and, Warrants, 1903-05, ca. .35 cu. ft. See also Miscellaneous Records.
Business Records/Corporations/Partnerships
[Castelton Wade's?] Account Book, 1883-93, 1 vol.
Court Records
County Court
Arrest Warrants, 1867-96, ca. .25 cu. ft.
[Clerk's] Tax Book, 1898-1910 (includes Circuit Court, 1904-10), 1 vol.
Execution Books, 1831-1917 (includes Circuit Court, 1904-17), 6 vols.; and, 1834-40, 1857-59, 1868-92, 1894-1904, 4 vols. Some of these volumes may be from the Circuit Court.
Fee Books, 1830-53, 1832-89, 1838-47, 1842-48, 1893-1904, 6 vols. Some of these volumes may be from the Circuit Court.
Issue Dockets, 1838-1900, 4 vols.
Memorandum Book, 1877-93, 1 vol.
Minute Books, 1888-90, 1896-98 [labeled S. E. Ledger], 2 vols.
Process Books, 1836-43, 1898-[1904], 2 vols.
Witness Attendance Books, 1867-1909 (includes Circuit Court, 1904-09), 3 vols.
Circuit Superior Court of Law and Chancery
Chancery Court Reference Docket, 1832-33, 1 vol.
Chancery Process Book No. 1, 1832-93 (includes Circuit Court, 1852-93), 1 vol.
Chancery Rules No. 1, 1834-40, 1 vol.; and, Chancery Rules, 1840-77 and Fees, 1858 (includes Circuit Court, 1852-77), 1 vol.
Common Law Court Issue Docket No. 1, 1831-34, 1 vol.
Common Law Executions, 1848-82 (includes Circuit Court, 1852-82), 1 vol.
Common Law Process No. 1, 1834-53 (includes Circuit Court, 1852-53), 1 vol.
Common Law Rules No. 1, 1832-96 (includes Circuit Court, 1852-96), 1 vol.
Execution Book, 1833-87 (includes Circuit Court, 1852-87), 1 vol.
Fee Book, 1845-58 (includes Circuit Court, 1852-58), 1 vol.
Issue Docket for the Bar, 1838-58 (includes Circuit Court, 1852-58), 1 vol.
Witness Attendance Book, 1831-45, 1 vol.
Circuit Court
[Bar] Issue Dockets [titles vary], 1858-67 (also memorandum of papers taken out of clerk's office by attorneys, 1852-54), 1 vol.; and, 1858-82, 1874-1904, 1891-98, 1895-1905, 6 vols. See also Circuit Superior Court of Law and Chancery.
Chancery Execution Book, 1887-1906, 1 vol.
Chancery Process, see Circuit Superior Court of Law and Chancery

Chancery Rule Docket No. 2, 1896-1912, 1 vol. See also Circuit Superior Court of Law and Chancery.

[Clerk's] Tax Book, 1898-1904, 1 vol. See also County Court.

Common Law Execution Nos. 4-6, 1892-1906, 3 vols. See also Circuit Superior Court of Law and Chancery.

Common Law Process Books, 1878-1913, 1886-95, 2 vols. See also Circuit Superior Court of Law and Chancery.

Common Law Rule Docket No. 2, 1896-1923, 1 vol. See also Circuit Superior Court of Law and Chancery.

Execution Books, see County Court and Circuit Superior Court of Law and Chancery

Fee Book [labeled Road Book], 1858-59 and 1867-93, 1 vol.; and, 1859-82, 1893-97, 2 vols. See also Circuit Superior Court of Law and Chancery.

Memorandum [Process?] Book, 1899-1904, 1 vol.; and, Memorandum Book, 1899-1906, 1 vol.

[Minute Book], 1873-82, 1 vol.

Process Book No. 2, 1853-78, 1 vol.

Slemp v. Pardee et al., transcripts, 1903, ca. .45 cu. ft.

Witness Attendance Book, 1874-1909, 1 vol. See also County Court.

County and Superior Courts

Old Judgments, 1885-1912, .35 cu. ft.

Unspecified Court

Index [to suits?], n.d., 1 vol.

Fiduciary Records

Settlements of Fiduciaries (Recorded), 1860-1902, 9.8 cu. ft.; and, Fiduciary Settlements, 1868-1934, 1.4 cu. ft.

Justice of the Peace Records

Cases Disposed of by Justices No. 7, 1889-1906, 1 vol.

Justices' Judgment and Execution Docket, 1897-99, 1 vol.

Justices' Judgments, 1887-1906, 1 vol.

[Justices'] Reports of Criminal Cases, 1898-1909, .7 cu. ft.

Justices' Summons, 1848-79, .35 cu. ft.

Justices' Warrants, ca. 1880-1905, .35 cu. ft. See also Court Records, County Court.

See also Miscellaneous Records

Land Records

Deeds Recorded, 1872-1911, 2.1 cu. ft.

Index to Deed Books 1-17, 1793-1876, 1 vol. (Ts.)

Index to Deeds No. 1, 1803-30, 1 vol. (Ts.)

Transfer of Real Estate [No. 1], 1892-1921, 1 vol.

Road and Bridge Records

Road Board Reports, 1886-96, .35 cu. ft.

Road Warrants, 1896-1911, .7 cu. ft.; and, Road Warrants Paid, 1900-06, .35 cu. ft. See also Miscellaneous Records.

Yokum Road Fund Warrants, 1901-04, ca. .15 cu. ft.

See also Board of Supervisors Records; and, Treasurer

Tax and Fiscal Records

Lands Sold for Taxes to Others than the Commonwealth, 1886-1934, 1 vol.

List of Delinquent Real Estate, 1895-1900, 1 vol.

List of Real Estate Sold for Non-payment of Taxes and Purchased by the Commonwealth, 1886-1931, 1 vol.

Record of Delinquent Lands, 1884-89, 1 vol.

Record of Improper Assessments, 1886-1916, 1 vol.

Record of Insolvent Capitation and Property Tax, 1887-1907, 1 vol.

Warrant Stubs, 1901-06, ca. .3 cu. ft.

See also Miscellaneous Records

Wills

Miscellaneous Wills, 1794-1832 [approximate date range of Will Book No. 1 which is missing], 1 vol. (copy)

Wills (Recorded), 1836-1913, .7 cu. ft.

Miscellaneous Records

Miscellaneous Papers [unarranged Justices' reports, claims and warrants, etc.], ca. 1880-1925, ca. 13.3 cu. ft.

Promissory Notes, 1839-53, ca. .1 cu. ft.

Reports of Superintendents of the Poor (also Liquor License Returns), 1883-89, .35 cu. ft.

Treasurer

Day Book [Treasurer's Highway Account Book], 1896-1936, 1 vol.

Treasurer's Settlements, 1876-78, 1885, ca. .45 cu. ft.

Treasurer's Settlements No. 3, 1900-03, 1 vol.

See also Tax and Fiscal Records

Microfilm Records

Circuit Court Clerk

Court Records

County Court

Order Books Nos. 1-9, 1808-67, 4 reels

Superior Court of Law

Order Books A-B, 1809-31, 1 reel (part)

Circuit Superior Court of Law and Chancery

Order Book No. 1, 1832-68 (includes Circuit Court, 1852-68), 1 reel (part)

Circuit Court

Order Book, see Circuit Superior Court of Law and Chancery

Land Records

Deed Books Nos. 1-15, 1793-1869, 7 reels

General Indexes to Deeds Nos. 1-2, 1793-1886, 1 reel

Surveyors' Records Nos. 1-4, 1794-1815, 1820-1944, 2 reels

Marriage Records and Vital Statistics

Marriage Record Nos. 1-2, 1830-36, 1850-1916, 1 reel

Register of Births, 1853-77, 1 reel (part)

Register of Deaths, 1853-77, 1 reel (part)

Wills

Miscellaneous Wills, 1794-1832, 1 reel

Will Books Nos. 2-3, [No. 1 is missing], 1833-88, 2 reels

Superior Court Will Book, 1846-1901, 1 reel

General Index to Wills, 1793-1944, 1 reel

Miscellaneous Records

Record of Overseers of the Poor, 1838-70, 1 reel

LOUDOUN COUNTY

Formed in 1757 from Fairfax County.

Original Records

Circuit Court Clerk
Bonds/Commissions/Oaths
>Commission of Oyer and Terminer, 1771, 1 item
>Index to Ordination Bonds, see Marriage Records and Vital Statistics
>Index to Ordination Bonds, etc., [1785-1852], 5 pp. (Ts.)

Court Records
County Court
>Court Papers, 1760-68, 3 items
>Letter, Samuel Shepard to Charles Binns, Clerk of Court, 1803, 1 item
>Order Books A and G, 1757-62, 1776-83, 2 vols. (copies)

Circuit Court
>Memorandum of Court Records . . . Loudoun County, 1757-1904 [compiled
>ca. 1930], 5 pp. (copies)

Land Records
>Deed Books A-B, D, F-G, I, L-O, T-U, and X, 1757-61, 1763-65, 1767-73, 1775-
>85, 1791-93, 1796-97, 13 vols. (copies)

Marriage Records and Vital Statistics
>Marriage Bonds and Ministers' Returns, 1785-1856, n. d. [broken series] .25 cu.
>ft.
>Marriage Bonds, 1786-99 (also Ordination Bonds, 1785-1852), 1 vol. (copy)
>Index to Marriage Bonds, [1786-99], 1 vol. (Ts. and 2 copies)
>Marriage License, 1843, 1 item

Military and Pension Records
>Militia Records [appointments, fines, muster rolls, etc.], 1812-32, 30 items
>Order to Raise Militia, 1796, 1 item

Tax and Fiscal Records
>Land Taxes, 1781-1842, .5 cu. ft.
>Personal Property Taxes, 1782-98, 1801-33, n. d., 1 cu. ft.
>Rentals, 1769, 1771-72, 34 pp. (copies). See also Fairfax County Tax and Fiscal
>Records.
>Tithables, 1758-86, 3 vols. (copies)

Wills
>Will Books A-C, H, and S, 1757-81, 1783-88, 1806-09, 1829-30, 5 vols. (copies)

Microfilm Records

Circuit Court Clerk
Court Records
County Court
>Order Books A-Z, 1757-1807, and Nos. 1-5, 1807-12, 11 reels
>Minute Books, 1812-66, 10 reels

Circuit Superior Court of Law and Chancery
>Chancery Order Books A-C, 1831-53 (includes Circuit Court, 1852-53),
>2 reels

Circuit Court
>Chancery Order Books D-E, 1854-66, 1 reel. See also Circuit Superior Court
>of Law and Chancery.

Election Records
>Poll Book, 1801-21, 1 reel (part)

Fiduciary Records
Guardians' Accounts A and C-E, 1759-1823, 1838-70, 2 reels
Land Records
Deed Books A-Z and 2A-5U (also inventories and accounts), 1757-1865, 48 reels
Superior Court Deed Book A, 1809-44, 1 reel (part)
General Index to Deeds, 1757-1878, 3 reels
Land Causes, 1757-73, 1 reel part
Land Records, 1809-45, 1 reel (part)
Miscellaneous Deeds, 1774, 1791, [2 items], 1 reel (part)
Marriage Records and Vital Statistics
Marriage Bonds, etc., 1779-1850, 1 reel (part)
Marriage Records, 1760-1880 (Ts.), 1 reel; 1760-92, 1 reel (part); and, Marriage
Records [Ministers' Returns], 1793 [1794]-1866, 1 reel; and, Marriage
Records Nos. 1-4, 1852-1914, 1 reel
Registers of Births Nos. 1-2, 1853-59, 1864-66, 1 reel (part)
Registers of Deaths, 1853-66, 1 reel (part)
Military and Pension Records
Militia Records, 1793-1809, 1805-27, 1 reel (part)
Minute Book [Revolutionary War Records], 1780-83, 1 reel (part)
Roster of Confederate Soldiers, 1861-65, 1 reel (part)
Tax and Fiscal Records
Tithables, 1758-99, 1 reel
Wills
Will Books A-2Q (including inventories, etc.), 1757-1866 12 reels
Index to Wills, 1757-1871, 1 reel (part)
General Index to Wills Vol. 1, 1757-1949, 1 reel (part)
[Superior Court] Will Books A-B, 1810-88, 1 reel (part)
Index to [Superior Court] Will Books, 1816-1904, 1 reel (part)

LOUISA COUNTY

Formed in 1742 from Hanover County.

Original Records

Circuit Court Clerk
Bonds/Commissions/Oaths
Minister's Bond, 1815, 1 item
Business Records/Corporations/Partnerships
[Chiles & Levy?] Ledger, 1882, 1 vol.
Louisa Milling & Mfg. Co. Account Book, 1875, 1 vol.; and, Ledgers C-D, 1872-
77, 2 vols.
Negro Book [unidentified account book], 1847-53, 1 vol.
Philip T. Hunt's Account Book, 1860-61, 1 vol.; [Day Book], 1854-58, 1 vol.; and,
Ledger A, 1854-56, 1 vol.
[R. E. Perkins & Bros.?] Invoice Book, 1885-86, 1 vol.
Shepherd Hunter and Company Day Book, 1835-37, 1 vol.; and, Journal, 1835-38,
1 vol.
Unidentified Account Books, 1784-85, 1841, 1850, 3 vols.
Unidentified Ledger, 1849, 1 vol.

Court Records
    County Court

        Blotter, 1817, 1 vol.

        Chancery Rules, 1801-21, 8 vols.

        Common Law Rules, 1806-14, 3 vols.

        Court Papers [appointments, etc.], ca. 1790-1865, 15 pp. (copies)

        Dockets, 1761-65, 1782-83, 1787-90, 1795-1800, 1812-14, 1831-50, 8 vols. See also Issue Dockets.

        Execution Book, 1767-69, 1 vol.

        Fee Books, 1769, 1771-73, 1780-86, 1788-91, 1793, 1795, 1797-1800, 1802-05, 1808, 1810-21, 1824-26, 1828, 1831-32, 1835-36, 1838-40, 1842-43, 1848, 1851-52, 56 vols. See also Fiduciary Records.

        Issue Dockets, 1773-79, 1783-86, 1789-1803, 1806-09, 1811-21, 1850-60, 12 vols. See also Dockets.

        Juror Attendance, 1808-18, 1853-71, 2 vols.

        Memorandum Books, 1768-73, 1776-78, 1782-88, 1790-1814, 1816-18, 1820-42, 1844-49, 40 vols.

        Minute Books, 1771-73, 1790-91, 2 vols.; and, 1788-90, 1 vol. (copy)

        Minutes, 1770, 1 p. (and fragment)

        Order Books, 1742-48, 1760-82, 3 vols. (copies)

        Orders [Minutes], 1773, 1 vol. (copy)

        Process Books, 1843-70, 2 vols.

        Rough Rule Dockets, 1814-24, 2 vols.

        Rule Dockets, 1786, 1795-99, 4 vols.

    Superior Court of Law

        Fee Book, 1809-25, 1 vol.

        Memorandum Books, 1818-30, 2 vols.

    Circuit Superior Court of Law and Chancery

        Memorandum Book, 1831-44, 1 vol.

    Circuit Court

        Juror Attendance, 1853-70, 2 vols.

        Law and Chancery Dockets, 1867-68, 4 items

        Witness Fees, 1852-53, 1 vol.

    County and Superior Courts

        Miscellaneous Records [summons, bonds, etc.], 1782-1859, ca. 50 items

        Receipt Book, 1809-11, 1 vol.

        Tax Books, 1807-41, 6 vols.

Election Records

    Poll Book, 1901, 1 vol.

Fiduciary Records

    Estate Book, William Trice, 1812, 1 item

    Estate [Papers], P. A. Anderson, ca. 1820-35, ca. 25 items

    Guardians' Bonds and Accounts, 1767-1819, 1 vol. (copy)

    Inventory Book, 1743-66 (also Fees, 1791-97), 1 vol. (copy)

Free Negro and Slave Records

    Free Negroes Registered, 1809, 2 items

    See also Business Records/Corporations/Partnerships

Land Records

    Deed Books A-D 1/2 [titles vary], 1742-74, 6 vols. (copies)

    Processioners' Returns, 1812-24, ca. .1 cu. ft. (1 vol., unbound); and, 1817-18, .25 cu. ft.

Marriage Records and Vital Statistics

    A List of Marriage Bonds and Licenses, 1767-1800, 1 item (Ts.)

    List of Returns, ca. 1785-1850, 40 pp. (Ts.)

    Marriage Consents, n.d., 2 items

Marriage Licenses [and consents], 1860-67, 1876-77, .2 cu. ft.
Marriage [Ministers'] Returns, 1781-1853, 1 vol.
Marriage Records [bonds and consents], 1766-1849, ca. 5 cu. ft.
Marriage Register, 1766-1861 (compilation), 1 vol. (Ts. and copy); and, Register of Licenses for Marriage, 1850-61, 1 vol.
Index to Marriage Register, 1763-1861, 2 vols. (Ts. and copy)
Ministers' Returns, 1780-1853, ca. .2 cu. ft.

Organization Records
Grand Royal Arch Chapter of Virginia, Dove Chapter No. 44, Treasurer's Book, 1855-71, 1 vol.

Tax and Fiscal Records
Delinquent Land Taxes, 1895-96, 29 pp.
Insolvent Lands, 1782-84, 3 items
Land Book, 1797, 1 vol.
Personal Property Book, 1804, 1 item
Taxable Property, 1782-86, n.d., ca. .25 cu. ft.
Tithables, 1767-84, 1 vol. (copy)
Tithables, 1767-84, .5 cu. ft.

Wills
Will Books Nos. 1-2, 1746-61, 1767-83, 2 vols. (copies)
Will of David Arnett, 1737, 2 pp. (copies)
Wills not Fully Proven, 1757-1902, 1 vol. (copy)

Miscellaneous Records
Unidentified Indexes, n.d., 2 vols.

Sheriff
[Sheriffs' Tax Collection Books], 1799, 1833, 2 vol.

Microfilm Records

Circuit Court Clerk
Court Records
County Court
Minutes, 1794-95, 1800-08, 1810-60, 8 reels
Order Books, 1742-48, 1760-82, 1790-1810, 6 reels (parts)

Fiduciary Records
Guardians Bonds and Accounts, 1767-1819, 1 reel (part)
Inventory Book, 1743-90, 1 reel

Land Records
Deed Books A-FF (including Wills, etc.), 1742-1865, 17 reels
General Indexes to Deeds Nos. 1-2, Grantors-Grantees, 1742-1872, 2 reels
Survey[or]s Book, 1805-70, 1 reel (part)

Marriage Records and Vital Statistics
Marriage Bonds (also consents and certificates), 1766-1877, 20 reels
Marriage Register, 1766-1861 (Ms. compilation), 1 reel; and, Marriage Register No. 3, 1865-1941, 1 reel (part)
Index to Marriage Register, 1766-1861 (Ms. compilation), 1 reel; and, Index to Marriage Register No. 3, 1865-1941, 1 reel (part)
Ministers' Returns, 1780-1849, 3 reels
Register of Births, 1864-71, 1 reel
Register of Deaths, 1864-70, 1 reel (part)

Military and Pension Records
Court of Militia [Enquiry], 1814, 1 reel (part)
Muster Roll, 1861-65, 1 reel (part)

Wills
    Will Books Nos. 1-16, 1745-1865, 7 reels
    [Superior] Court Wills, 1810-1901, 1 reel
    General Index to Wills No. 1, 1742-1947, 1 reel
    See also Land Records

Sheriff
    [Sheriffs' Debtors Books], 1785-1812, 1 reel

LOWER NORFOLK COUNTY

See Norfolk County.

LUNENBURG COUNTY

Formed in 1745 from Brunswick County.

Original Records

Circuit Court Clerk
  Board of Supervisors Records
    Papers [titles vary], 1867-1909 (also County Court Papers), ca. 2.85 cu. ft.
  Bonds/Commissions/Oaths
    Commissions of Oyer and Terminer, 1753-64, 10 items
    [Delivery, Ferry, and Replevy] Bonds, 1752-67, 12 items
    District School Trustees' Official Oaths, 1894-1904, ca. 50 items
    Indentures, 1830-50, ca. 50 items
    Militia Appointment, 1775, 1 item
    Oaths to the Government and Test, 1764-70, 1 item
    Officials' Bonds, 1753-61, 1776-81, ca. 150 items; and, Officials' Oaths, 1887-1905, ca. .4 cu. ft.
    Ordinary Bonds, 1748-57, 1760-61, ca. 150 items
    Registration Oaths, 1870, n.d., ca. 100 items
    See also Election Records; and, Road and Bridge Records
  Business Records/Corporations/Partnerships
    Miles Jordan and Co., bills, receipts, and orders, 1809-19, n.d., ca. .75 cu. ft.
    South Side Railroad Co., freight receipts, 1863, 9 items
  Court Records
    County Court
      Chancery Rules, 1805-16, 2 vols.
      Clerk John Yates' Papers [correspondence, tax records, etc.], 1852-53, 1889-1905, ca. 1 cu. ft.
      [Clerk's Notebooks?], 1893-1900, 5 items
      County Court Appeals, Mill and Road Papers Removed from the Docket, 1873, ca. .1 cu. ft.
      Court Papers [and Justices' Judgments; titles vary], 1849-1905, ca. 9.6 cu. ft. See also Board of Supervisors Records.

Docket, 1746-49, 9 pp.
Execution Books, 1765-67, 1791-96, 2 vols.
Executions, 1748-1872, ca. 7.5 cu. ft.
Fee Books, 1751, 1778, 2 vols.
Issues, 1831, 3 items
Judgments [Causes Determined; titles vary], ca. 1745-1825, 1827, 1831, n.d., ca. 29.4 cu. ft.
[Jury Tickets], 1873-78, 1890-91, ca. 75 items
Memorandum Books, 1806-12, 1816-21, 4 vols.
Memorandums, 1749, 8 pp.; and, 1803, 3 items
Minutes, 1747-48, 1753, 1764-67, 1804-05, 4 vols.
Orders, 1752-53, 1760, 1762, 1784, 1840, 6 items
Orders and Judgments [titles vary], 1753-54, 1758, 1763, 1824-28, 5 vols.; and, Order Books Nos. 7-8, 1761-62, 2 vols. (copies)
Index to Order Book, n.d., 1 vol.
Presentments of the Grand Jury, 1871-79, 25 items
Rough Order Books, 1752-53, 1758-59, 1762, 3 vols.
Rule Dockets [titles vary], 1803, 1807-18, 5 vols.
Subpoenas, 1747-1892, ca. 100 items

Superior Court of Chancery
Summons, 1820, 1 item

Superior Court of Law
Memorandum Books, 1818-29, 2 vols.

Circuit Superior Court of Law and Chancery
Chancery Rules, 1847-74 (includes Circuit Court, 1852-74), ca. 25 items
Subpoena [Mecklenburg County Circuit Court], 1832, 1 item

Circuit Court
Chancery Rules, see Circuit Superior Court of Law and Chancery
Jury Tickets, 1890, n.d., 4 items
Law Decisions, 1868, ca. 50 items
Presentments of the Grand Jury, 1852, 1867-70, 1895, 51 items
Subpoenas, 1860-81, 1885-86, 1893, ca. .1 cu. ft.

Election Records
Abstracts of Votes, 1872-1910, ca. .2 cu. ft.
Ballots, 1870-94, n.d., ca. 3.6 cu. ft.
Notices of Candidacy and Statements and Oaths Under Pure Election Law, 1895-1905, ca. 25 items
Polls, 1792, 1813, 1819-22, 1825-26, 1828-30, 1833-66, ca. 1.6 cu. ft.
Poll Taxes Paid, A-Z, 1903-10, ca. .1 cu. ft.

Fiduciary Records
Accounts Current, 1750-54, ca. 50 items. See also Wills.
Administrators' Bonds, 1748-54, 1856-62, ca. 200 items
Executors' Bonds, 1760-61, 1837-46, 1851-59, ca. .2 cu. ft.
Guardians' Accounts, 1753-59, 78 items
Guardians' Bonds, 1750-62, 40 items
Vouchers, L. L. Burnett's Estate, 1849-63, ca. .35 cu. ft.
See also Wills

Free Negro and Slave Records
Lists of Free Negroes and Mulattoes, 1802-03, 13 pp.
See also Miscellaneous Records

Justice of the Peace Records
Appointments of Justices, 1853-61, 13 items
Commonwealth Recognizances to Keep the Peace, 1877-93, ca. 100 items
Justices' Judgments, see Court Records, County Court

Reports of Fines, 1889-1904, ca. .35 cu. ft.

Satisfied Executions Returned by Constables, 1842-75, ca. .5 cu. ft.

Sundry Judgments and Returns by Constables to which they or Plaintiffs are Entitled, 1858-68, ca. 50 items

Land Records

Deed Book No. 3, 1752-54, 1 vol. (2 copies)

Deeds, 1743-1822, 1824-39, ca. 2.5 cu. ft.

[Deeds and Wills], 1749-1890, ca. .35 cu. ft.

Deeds of Trust, 1759-1823, ca. 100 items

Lists of Transfers, 1870-1905, ca. .35 cu. ft.

Processioners' Returns, 1803-04, 1808, 1812, 1814, 1816, 1820, 1824, 1828, 1840, 1844, 1856, ca. .5 cu. ft.

Marriage Records and Vital Statistics

Marriage Consents and Certificates, 1850-79, 1885, ca. .5 cu. ft.

Register of Colored Births, 1871, 1 item

Registers of Births, 1865-72, 1875-77, 1879, 1888, 1892-93, 1895, ca. .25 cu. ft.

Registers of Deaths, 1865, 1867, 1875-76, 1878, 1880, 1882, 1884-88, 1890, 1892-93, ca. .25 cu. ft.

Road and Bridge Records

[Road Reports, Petitions, and Bonds], 1751-1861, 1882, ca. .15 cu. ft.

Road Surveyors Appointed, 1862-69, 1875, ca. 100 items

School Records

School Papers [bonds and reports], 1836-60, ca. .1 cu. ft.

Teacher Certificate, 1893, 1 item

Tax and Fiscal Records

Duplicate Tax Accounts, 1866-74, ca. 25 items

Fifteen-cent bank note printed by Lunenburg County, 1862, 1 item

Land Assessment, 1856, 1 item

Land Tax, 1846, 1 item

Personal Property Books, ca. 1785-1850, 56 vols.

Personal Property Tax Interrogatories, 1888-95, ca. .25 cu. ft.

Record of All the Real Estate Returned Delinquent for Non-payment for 1865-71, 1873, 4 items

Tax Tickets, 1865, 1878, 1880, 1894, ca. 250 items

Tithables, 1782, 1785, 1787, 1810, 1865, 1880, 1894, ca. .1 cu. ft.; and, 1748-52, 29 items (copies). See also Personal Property Taxes.

Vouchers for the County Levy, 1757-58, 1771, ca. 100 items

Wills

Will and Estate Papers of James Cocke, 1753-61, ca. .1 cu. ft

Wills, 1748-61, ca. 50 items

[Wills, Inventories, Appraisements, and Accounts], 1747-62, 1810, 1890-91, ca. .4 cu. ft.

See also Land Records

Miscellaneous Records

Annual Reports of the Superintendent of the Poor, 1851-1904, ca. .3 cu. ft.

Book of Don Alphonso, Season Commencing March 1802, 1 item (blank, Ms. caption)

Claims Allowed, 1867-78, ca. .5 cu. ft.

Commitment Proceedings, 1903, 4 items

Contracts, 1865-66, ca. .15 cu. ft.

Crop and Vendors Liens, A-Z, 1892-1911, ca. .1 cu. ft.

Entries of Estrays, 1773-97, 1 vol.

Estrays, 1774-78, ca. .1 cu. ft.

John C. Epes' Account Book (including List of Negroes), 1844, 1 vol.; and, letter, 1847, 1 item.
[List of Wolf Scalps], 1748, 1 item
Unidentified Index, n.d., 1 item

Microfilm Records

Circuit Court Clerk
  Court Papers
    County Court
      Minute Books, 1817-19, 1822-32, 1842-66, 3 reels
      Order Books Nos. 1-31, 1746-1865, 13 reels
  Fiduciary Records
    Guardians' Accounts, 1791-1810, 1828-51, 1 reel
  Free Negro and Slave Records
    See Wills
  Land Records
    Deed Books Nos. 1-37, 1746-1869, 15 reels
    Superior Court Deed and Will Book, 1811-88, 1 reel
    Index to Deeds, Grantors-Grantees A-Z, 1746-1900, 2 reels
    Processioners' Returns, 1808-16, 1820-28, 1848-70, 1 reel
  Marriage Records and Vital Statistics
    General Index to Marriages, 1746-1929, 1 reel (part)
    Index to Marriage Bonds, 1746-1850, 1 reel (part)
    Marriage Register, 1853-1929, 1 reel (part)
    Register of Births, 1853-89, 1 reel (part)
    Register of Deaths, 1853-70, 1 reel (part)
    Register of Marriage Licenses No. 1, 1850-72, 1 reel (part)
  Wills
    Will Books Nos. 1-14, 1746-1916, 5 reels
    General Index to Wills, Estates, etc., 1746-1949, 1 reel (part)
    Index to Devisees and Heirs, 1746-1949, 1 reel (part)
    See also Land Records

MADISON COUNTY

Formed in 1792 from Culpeper County.

Original Records

Circuit Court Clerk
  Board of Supervisors Records
    Index to Supervisors Order Book, n.d., 1 vol.
  Bonds/Commissions/Oaths
    Bonds, ca. 1800-75, ca. .3 cu. ft.
    Officials' Bonds, ca. 1825-80, ca. .45 cu. ft. See also Fiduciary Records.
    Registration Oaths, Act of 1867, ca. 100 items
  Business Records/Corporations/Partnerships
    Gwin & McClung Receipt Book, 1849-58, 1 vol.
    Sale Book of the Goods of L. & H. Barnes and Co., 1835, 1 vol. See also Fiduciary Records.

Census Records
    Enumeration, 1880, ca. .1 cu. ft.
Court Records
    County Court
        Court Claims, 1810-39, ca. .15 cu. ft.
        Executions, ca. 1810-80, ca. 1.25 cu. ft.
        Fee Books, 1793, 1795, 1801-05, 7 vols.
        Memorandum Book, 1866-1919 (includes Circuit Court, 1904-19), 1 vol.
        Office Judgments, ca. 1795-1845, ca. 2.35 cu. ft.
    Circuit Court
        Chancery Papers, 1873, ca. .45 cu. ft.
        Fee Book, 1893-1912, 1 vol.
        [Issue] Dockets, 1868-72, 3 vols.
        [Judgment and Execution Book], 1852-59, 1 vol.
        Law and Chancery Docket, 1869-79, 1 vol.
        Memorandum Book, see County Court
        Thomas et al. v. Thomas, Trustee et al., transcript, 1882, 1 vol.
        Witness Attendance Books, 1858-1919, 2 vols.
    County and Superior Courts
        Court Papers, 1795-1892, n.d., ca. 1.9 cu. ft. (including fragments)
    Unspecified Court
        [Clerk's?] Account Book, 1881-89, 1 vol.
        Indexes [to order book and to suits?], n.d., 2 vols.
Election Records
    List of Registered Voters, 1861-96, 1 vol.
    Voters Registered without Challenge, 1869, 1 vol.
Fiduciary Records
    Account of James M. Glassell with Henry Barnes his agent, 1830, 1 item
    Appraisement and Sale Books [estates of Aylor, Banks, Carpenter, Cave, Collins
        and Yager, Daniel, Hood, Kean, Shirley, Tatum, and Weaver], 1853, 1885-
        1902, 12 vols.
    Bonds of Fiduciaries, Officers, etc., ca. 1820-50, ca. .45 cu. ft.
    Estate Papers of Ann Brookings, 1834-45, and of Thomas Shirley, 1838-44 (see
        also Appraisement and Sale Books), ca. 50 items
    Fiduciary Bonds, ca. 1850-70, ca. .25 cu. ft.
    Guardians' Accounts, 1819-83, 19 items
    Henry Barnes' Vouchers, 1827-48, ca. .2 cu. ft. See also Business Records/
        Corporations/Partnerships.
    Register of Fiduciaries, 1887-1907, 1 vol.
    Index to Fiduciary Book No. 1, n.d., 1 vol.; and, Index [to fiduciaries?], n.d.,
        1 vol.
    Settlement of Lewis Harrison, 1850-65, 1 vol.
Justice of the Peace Records
    Constables' Returns, 1807-34, 1838-52, 1859-61, 1877, .35 cu. ft.
Land Records
    Deeds, ca. 1795-1850, ca. 2.3 cu. ft.
    Deeds of Trust, 1850-53, ca. 50 items
    General Index to Deeds No. 1, Grantors A-K, 1793-1914, 1 vol.
    Map of Casey and Reddish Land now owned by Tanner et al., 1899, 1 item
    Unidentified map showing the Rapid Ann [sic] River, n.d., 1 item
Marriage Records and Vital Statistics
    Consents, 1866, 1874-78, ca. 150 items
    Marriage Bonds [and consents], 1793-1850, 3 cu. ft.
    Marriage Licenses [and consents], 1855-86, 2 cu. ft.

Ministers' Returns, 1793-1854, ca. .5 cu. ft.
Register of Births, 1853-71, 1 vol.
Register of Births, 1853, 1 item
Registers of Births and Deaths, 1883-84, 13 pp.
Index to Registers of Births, Deaths, and Marriages, 1853-71, 1 vol.
Military and Pension Records
Military Exemptions, 1862, ca. 100 items
Road and Bridge Records
Road Book, 1866-97, 1 vol.
Road Claims, 1826-27, 1830, 1842, 1876, ca. .15 cu. ft.
Tax and Fiscal Records
County Claims, ca. 1815-70, 1 cu. ft.
List of All Persons Assessed with a License Tax, 1882, 1 item
Personal Property Book, 1821, 1 vol.
Miscellaneous Records
Estray Warrants, 1800-25, ca. .2 cu. ft.
Stray Book, 1793-1810, 1 vol.
Unidentified Account Book, 1861-66, 1 vol.; and, Account Book, Madison C. H., 1877-78, 1 vol.
Unidentified Day Book, 1863-65, 1 vol.
Unidentified Note/Receipt Book, 1858-60, 1 vol.

Treasurer
Receipt Book of G. H. Taylor, Treasurer, 1893, 1 vol.
Treasurer's Reports, 1871-74, 7 pp.
[Treasurers'] Warrant and Order Book A, 1871-1907, 1 vol.

Microfilm Records

Circuit Court Clerk
Court Records
County Court
Order Books Nos. 1-12, 1793-1863, 4 reels
Land Records
Deed Books Nos. 1-24, 1793-1871, 11 reels
General Index to Deeds, Grantors-Grantees A-Z, 1793-1949, 4 reels
Land Warrants [Entry Book], 1805-88, 1 reel (part)
Processioners' Returns, 1796-1800, 1 reel (part)
Surveys Nos. 1-2, 1792-1803, 1805-88, 1 reel (part)
Marriage Records and Vital Statistics
Marriage Register No. 1, 1793-1905, 1 reel (part)
Indexes to Marriages, Males-Females A-Z, 1793-1949, 1 reel (part)
Military and Pension Records
Muster Rolls, 1812, 1861-65, 1 reel (part)
Wills
Will Books Nos. 1-12, 1793-1866, 6 reels
General Index to Wills, 1793-1905, 1 reel (part)
[Superior] Court Will Book No. 1, 1820-66, 1 reel (part)
General Index to [Superior Court] Wills, 1820-1943, 1 reel (part)
Miscellaneous Records
Hebron Lutheran Church Records, 1754-1866, 1 reel (part)

MATHEWS COUNTY

Formed in 1790 from Gloucester County.

Original Records

Circuit Court Clerk
Court Records
County Court
Fee Book, 1795, 1 vol. (copy)
Land Records
Plat Books, 1817-68, 2 vols. (copies)
Indexes to Plat Books, 1817-1921, 1855-68, 3 items (copies)
Marriage Records and Vital Statistics
Marriage Licenses, 1827-35, 1839-50, 1 vol. (copy)
Register of Marriages, 1857, 1 item (Ms. copy)

Microfilm Records

Circuit Court Clerk
Business Records/Corporations/Partnerships
James S. Shipley [Merchant] Account Books, 1855-58, 1865, 1868-71, 1 reel (part); and, Day Book, 1855-61, [1865]-68, 1 reel (part)
John G. Forrest's Day Book, 1852-60, 1 reel (part)
Unidentified Tavern Journal, 1842-43, 1 reel (part)
Court Records
County Court
Chancery Docket Book, 1805-35, 1 reel (part)
Fee Books, 1795, 1799, 1823, 1825, 1827, 1829, 1833-35, 1837-42, 1844-45, 1849, 1853, 1855, 1857-58, 2 reels
Process Book, 1831-61, 1 reel (part)
Rule Dockets, 1796-1853, 1 reel (part)
Superior Court of Law
Law Execution Book, 1809-31, 1 reel (part)
Plea Book, 1814-30, 1 reel (part)
Rule Docket, 1809-30, 1 reel (part)
Circuit Superior Court of Law and Chancery
Execution Book, 1842-66 (includes Circuit Court, 1852-66), 1 reel (part)
Fee Books, 1832-34, 1836-39, 1843, 1845-48, 1 reel (part)
Minute Books, 1831-62 (includes Circuit Court, 1852-66), 1 reel (part)
Process Book, 1831-40, 1 reel (part)
Rule Dockets, 1831-58 (includes Circuit Court, 1852-58), 1 reel (part)
Writ Docket Book, 1840-43, 1 reel (part)
Circuit Court
Execution Books, see Circuit Superior Court of Law and Chancery
Fee Books, 1852-56, 1859, 1861, 1868-70, 2 reels (parts)
Minute Books, see Circuit Superior Court of Law and Chancery
Rule Dockets, see Circuit Superior Court of Law and Chancery
Subpoena Docket Book, 1854-63, 1 reel (part)
Suit Dockets, 1865-68, 1 reel (part)

Fiduciary Records
    Executors' Bond Book, 1795-1825, 1 reel (part)
    Guardians' Bond Book, 1806-22, 1 reel (part)
Land Records
    Plat Books, 1817-1921, 1855-1911, 2 reels

Sheriff
    Baldwin Foster's [Sheriff's?] Account Book, 1849-50, 1868-[70], 1 reel (part)
    Sheriff's Fee Book, 1840-41, 1 reel (part)

MECKLENBURG COUNTY

Formed in 1764 from Lunenburg County.

Original Records

Circuit Court Clerk
Board of Supervisors Records
    County Warrants and State Claims Allowed by the Board, 1871-82, ca. 50 items
Bonds/Commissions/Oaths
    Appointments of Registrars and Judges of Elections, 1897, ca. 50 items
    Appointments of Processioners, 1823-24, ca. 50 items
    [Apprentice] Indentures, 1794-1837, ca. .1 cu. ft.
    Attachment Bonds, 1787-88, 1800-09, ca. 50 items. See also Circuit Court
        Injunction Bonds.
    Bail Bonds and Recognizances by Justices, 1875-84, ca. 100 items
    Bonds of Clerks [of Court], 1818-65, 20 items
    Bonds of Commissioners of Revenue, 1810-32, ca. 25 cu. ft.
    Certificates and Oaths, 1867, 1870-72, 1902, ca. 50 items
    Circuit Court Injunction Bonds [also attachments, appeal bonds, etc.], 1885-
        1906, ca. 50 items
    Circuit Court Oaths, Officer Qualifications, etc., 1870-1904, ca. .1 cu. ft.
    Circuit Court Refunding Bonds, ca. 1880-1900, 36 items
    Constables' Bonds, 1805-19, ca. 50 items
    Delivery Bonds, 1815-20, ca. .1 cu. ft.
    Judgment Bonds, 1808-15, ca. 50 items
    Liquor License Bonds, 1898-1900, 19 items
    Miscellaneous Bonds, [Bonds of Assessors], 1900, 6 items
    Oaths of Judges and Registrars of Elections, 1884, ca. 25 items
    Officials' Bonds, 1793-1819, 1870-1905, ca. .45 cu. ft. See also Fiduciary
        Records; and, Land Records.
    Ordinary Bonds, 1799, 1802, 1823, 1825, 7 items
    Replevy Bonds, 1786-87, n.d., 5 items
    Supersedeas Bonds, etc., 1832-1907, ca. .1 cu. ft.
    Whiskey Bonds, 1877-99, ca. .25 cu. ft.
    See also Business Records/Corporations/Partnerships; Court Records, County and
        Superior Courts; Military and Pension Records; and, Road and Bridge
        Records

Business Records/Corporations/Partnerships

Charter Book No. 1, 1867-1902 (also Register of Bonds Issued to the County Court for War Purposes, 1861-65), 1 vol.; and, Charter Book I, 1902-18, 1 vol.

Geoghegan Tarwater & Co., [Clarksville?], Account Book, 1852-56, 1 vol.

Land and Toone Ledger, 1874-87, 1 vol.

Samuel J. Watson's [doctor's] Account Book, 1848-54, 1 vol.

Samuel S. Davis' Account Book, 1810-14, 1 vol.

Court Records

County Court

Chancery Papers, 1823, 1837, 1852, 1858, 1872, ca. 2.3 cu. ft. See also County and Superior Courts.

Commonwealth Papers of John Ervin and Others, 1880-92, ca. 100 items

Commonwealth v. Mollett, suit papers, 1792, 2 pp.

Court Papers, 1854-1904, 12 cu. ft.

Day Book (also register of serial numbers of paper money issued by the County Court), 1862-63, 1 vol.

Decrees, 1870-73, ca. .1 cu. ft.

Dismissions at Rules, Abatements, and Judgments Confessed in Office, 1835, 4 items; and, Dismissions at Rules, 1866-72, ca. 50 items

Executions, 1850-52, 1854-56, 1858-1904, ca. .7 cu. ft.

Fee Book, 1768, 1 vol.

Hardy v. Endly et al., road suit papers, 1884-85, ca. 25 items

Hutcheson and Hutcheson v. Richardson, deposition, 1870, 36 pp.

Lists of Fees, [ca. 1895], 3 items

Order Book No. 1, 1765-68, 1 vol. (copy)

Orders to be delivered, 1828-39, ca. .1 cu. ft.

Index to Old Orders, etc., of Interest, 1793, 1 vol.

Petitions, Reports, etc. [titles vary], 1799-1817, 1835, ca. 150 items

Presentments, 1810-35, 1878-84, ca. .15 cu. ft.

Quarterly Court Rules, 1796-1802, 1 vol.

Recognizances, 1864-78, ca. .1 cu. ft.

Subpoenas, ca. 1870-1900, ca. .6 cu. ft.

Suit Papers, 1863-93, ca. .25 cu. ft.

Summonses, 1787, 2 items

General Court

Execution, 1789, 1 item

Superior Court of Law

Order Book No. 2, see Land Records

Rule Book No. 1, 1809-31, 1 vol.

Circuit Superior Court of Law and Chancery

Chancery Dockets, 1828, 1851, 2 items

Chancery Executions, 1833-46, ca. .1 cu. ft.

Chancery Forms, 1833, ca. 50 items

Clark v. Clark, vouchers, 1835, ca. 75 items

Common Law Dockets, 1851, 1 item

Common Law Orders Nos. 1-2 and 4, 1831-42, 1844-53 (includes Circuit Court, 1852-53), 3 vols.

Decrees, ca. 1845-1900 (includes Circuit Court, 1852-1900), ca. .25 cu. ft.

Executions, 1846-50, ca. .35 cu. ft.

Subpoena, see Lunenburg County Court Records

Witness Attendance Claims, 1833-45, ca. .1 cu. ft.

Circuit Court

Chancery Dockets, 1854-55, 1858-69, 1871-79, 1881-95, 66 items

Chancery Orders No. 6, 1879-83, 1 vol.

Chancery Papers, 1873, ca. 100 items

Common Law Dockets, 1852-65, 1868-97, 72 items

Common Law Orders Nos. 5-9, 1853-1906, 6 vols. See also Circuit Superior Court of Law and Chancery.

Common Law Papers, 1892-96, 1912, ca. .15 cu. ft.

Court Papers, 1874, 1889-1902, ca. .2 cu. ft.

Decrees, see Circuit Superior Court of Law and Chancery

Dismissions in Chancery, 1885-88, ca. 25 items

Executions, 1851-61, 1866-79, 1881-1903, 1.75 cu. ft.

Executions to lie in Office, A-D, H-J, and P-Z, 1862-80, ca. .2 cu ft.

[Fiduciary] Accounts Notified from Circuit Court, 1886-87, ca. .1 cu. ft.

Judgments Satisfied, [ca. 1900], ca. .25 cu. ft.

Lists of Fees, 1897-98, n.d., 22 pp.

Money Deposited by Order of Court, 1891-1940, 1 vol.

Papers Removed from Court Papers in 1924, [ca. 1900], ca. .25 cu. ft.

Subpoenas in Chancery, Subpoenas for Witnesses, etc., ca. 1875-1900, ca. .5 cu. ft.

Witness Dockets, 1868-95, 1897, 56 items

County and Superior Courts

Chancery Causes Nos. 1-240, [1764-ca. 1905], 69 cu. ft.

Court Papers [including appointments and oaths, military exemptions, etc.], 1792-1907, ca. .6 cu. ft.

Fees [titles vary], 1819-75, ca. .5 cu ft.

Judgments [and related papers], 1782-1905, ca. 60.3 cu. ft.

Miscellaneous Papers, ca. 1760-1905, ca. 1.2 cu. ft.

Reports of Clerks of Courts, 1886-99, ca. .15 cu. ft.

Suit Papers, 1808-93, ca. .4 cu. ft.

[Writings] Not Admitted to Record, 1788-1904, ca. .1 cu. ft.

Unspecified Court

Unidentified [Chancery?] Index, n.d., 1 item

Election Records

[Abstracts of Votes], 1870, 1883, n.d., 16 items; and, Abstracts for Railroad Subscription District Officers and other papers, 1883, 2 items

Lists of Candidates, 1895, 10 items

Lists of Names Improperly on Registration Books, 1882-83, 8 items

Petition to Change Voting Precinct to LaCrosse, n.d., 1 item

Poll Books, 1834, 8 items

Registered Voters, 1911 [1902-64], 1 vol.

Rolls of Colored Voters Registered at Pearson's Store and Baskerville Precincts, 1892-1900, 2 vols.

Rolls of Registered Voters, 1902, 13 pp.

See also Bonds/Commissions/Oaths

Fiduciary Records

Administrators' and Executors' Bonds, 1765-1860, 1865-71, ca. 1.1 cu. ft.

Assignment of Bankrupt's Effects, 1874, 1 item

Bonds of Fiduciaries [and other bonds, including Officials' Bonds], 1861-64, 1872-1905, .6 cu. ft. See also Land Records.

Bonds of Special Commissioners, 1885-1905, .35 cu. ft.; and, Copies of Bonds of Special Commissioners, 1890-98, ca. .1 cu. ft.

Circuit Court Accounts of Executors, Administrators, Guardians, Trustees, etc., 1832-1901, ca. .1 cu. ft.

Circuit Court Executors', Administrators', and Guardians, Bonds, 1841-42, ca. 50 items

Estate Papers and Vouchers, 1796-1874, ca. .75 cu. ft.

Guardians' Accounts, 1766-93, 1 vol.

Guardians' Accounts, 1781-1873, 1876, ca. 2.35 cu. ft. See also Inventories, Appraisements, etc.

Guardians' Bonds, 1765-1831, 1861-71, .75 cu. ft.

Guardians' Books, 1800-35, 3 vols.; and, Nos. 3-5, 1835 [1822]-79, 3 vols.

Inventories, Appraisements, Accounts of Sale [including guardians' accounts], 1783-1904, 8 cu. ft.; and, Inventory and Accounts of John Bennett Goode, 1800-33, .45 cu. ft.

Free Negro and Slave Records

Lists of Slaves [and correspondence], 1863-64, n.d., ca. .1 cu. ft.

Registers of Free Negroes, 1827, 1831, 1838-39, 1842, 5 items

Justice of the Peace Records

Attachments, Appeals, and Removed Warrants, 1885-94, ca. 100 items

Civil Warrants [and Executions], 1870-1904, ca. 2.45 cu. ft.

[Commonwealth Court Suits], 1837, 1842, 1846-56, ca. .15 cu. ft.

Constables' Returns, ca. 1820-75, ca. .6 cu. ft.

Criminal Warrants [titles vary], 1855, 1860-89, ca. .55 cu. ft.; and, Commonwealth Warrants, 1890-1905, 1 cu. ft.

Judgments and Executions, 1900-01, 2 pp.

List of Judgments Obtained by Thomas F. Goode, 1858-68, 1 vol.

Magistrates' Reports, see Miscellaneous Records

Miscellaneous Papers, 1888-1900, ca. .2 cu. ft.

Papers Returned . . . by D. Ostin, Constable, 1857-58, 9 items

Reports of Fines [Lists of Criminal Case Disposed], 1888-90, ca. .1 cu. ft.

See also Bonds/Commissions/Oaths

Land Records

Condemnation of Land for Atlantic and Danville Railway Co., 1889, ca. 25 items

Deed Books Nos. 2 and 4, 1768-71, 1773-76, 2 vols. (copies)

Deeds, 1765-1905, 12.8 cu. ft.; and, Copies of Deeds and Wills, A-Z, 1824-66, 36 items. See also Court Records, County and Superior Courts.

Deeds and Bonds (including officials' bonds), 1858-69, 1872, ca. .75 cu. ft.

Deeds Partly Proved, A-D, ca. 1790-1830, ca. .2 cu. ft.

Old Land Grants, etc. [deeds, plats, and surveyors' notes], ca. 1765-1850, ca. .2 cu. ft.

Processioners' Reports, 1845-72, 1 vol.

[Processioners' Returns], 1808, 1858, ca. 100 items

Release Deeds No. 1, 1884-1916, 1 vol.

Rough Index to Deed Book No. 52, 1892-94, 12 pp.

Superior Court Deed Book No. 1, 1810-13 (also Order Book No. 2, 1821-24 [and unidentified volume No. 4, 1929-31?]), 1 vol.

Marriage Records and Vital Statistics

Marriage Bonds and Consents, 1770-1850, ca. 4 cu. ft.

Marriage Certificates and Consents, 1850-61, .9 cu. ft.; Certificates [of age], 1836, 2 items; and, Consents, 1890-91, 2 items

Marriage Licenses, 1862-1905, ca. 9.8 cu. ft.

Marriages and Returns of Ministers, 1785-1854, 1 vol.

Returns of Ministers prior to 1854, compiled by N. G. Hutcheson, Clerk of the Circuit Court, 1939, 1 vol.

Index to Marriages and Ministers' Returns, 1785-1854, 1 vol.

Registers of Births and Deaths, 1856-64, 1866-67, 1869-[96], ca. 1.5 cu. ft.

Military and Pension Records

County Court Rosters of Ex-Confederate Soldiers and Sailors, 1899, 3 items

Lists of Goods Furnished to Soldiers and Their Families, 1863-64, 14 items

Petitions, Claims [Military] Exemptions, 1862-63, n.d., ca. 25 items. See also Court Records, County and Superior Courts.

Reports of Indigent Families in the 20th and 98th Regiments, and Bond, 1864, n.d., 3 items.

Road and Bridge Records

County Court Notices of Surveyors of Roads, 1874-77, .35 cu. ft.
County Court [Road and Bridge Papers], 1827, 1874-1902, ca. .1 cu. ft.
Map of Tuckersmill and Keysville Roads, n.d., 1 item
Old Road Papers, 1857-74, ca. .1 cu. ft.
Reports of Commissioners of Roads, 1876-88, ca. .1 cu. ft.
Road Orders Returned, 1828-53, ca. .1 cu. ft.
Road Papers [including bonds, reports, and petitions], 1887-92, ca. 50 items

Tax and Fiscal Records

Abstracts of Property, Land, and License Taxes, 1886-89, 1891, 1896, 8 items
[County Claims], 1852-60, ca. 50 items
Delinquent Land Taxes, 1833, 1865-74, ca. 50 items
Insolvent Capitation and Property, 1872-79, 15 items
Insolvent Fees, 1845-57, ca. 350 items
Insolvent License Taxes, 1873, 1875, 1877, 5 items
J. H. Drumright's [Tax?] Account Book, 1875, 1 vol.
Land Books, 1780-98, 1790-1810, 1813-97, 1900, 24 vols.
Lists of All Persons Assessed with a Tax of Two and One-half or Five Per
     Centum, 1872-76, 16 items
[Personal Property Book], 1884 and 1886, 1 vol.; and, 1787, 1789-92, 1794, 1796-
     97, 1799-1807, 1812, 1814, 1816, 1818-19, 1821-24, 1826, 1832, n.d., 50 items
Register of Bonds Issued, see Business Records/Corporation/Partnerships
Register of Serial Numbers of Papers Money, see Court Records, County Court
Supplementary [Tax] Lists, 1877-78, 3 items
Tax Receipt Stubs, 1880, 1 vol.
Tax Tickets, 1860, 1872, ca. .1 cu. ft.

Wills

Copies of Wills, see Land Records
Will Books Nos. 1-3, 1765-98, 3 vols. (copies)
Superior Court [of Law] Will Book No. 1, 1810-22, 1 vol.
Circuit Court Will Books Nos. 1-2, 1831-1904, 2 vols.
Wills, 1764-1904, 2.7 cu. ft.
Wills Probated in Circuit Court, 1837-1901, ca. 25 items

Miscellaneous Records

Annual Reports of Superintendent of the Poor, 1883-86, ca. 100 items
Blueprint [of cannon monument at courthouse], n.d., 1 item
Certificates of Physicians Recorded, 1892-93, 1 vol.
Estrays, 1810-20, ca. .1 cu. ft.
Inquisitions, etc. [petitions, lists of tithables, and magistrates' reports], 1798-
     1882, ca. .2 cu. ft.
Mechanics' Liens to 1892, ca. 25 items
Poor House Papers, 1877, ca. 50 items
Records of the Vestry of St. James P. E. Church, Boydton, 1876-1907, 1 vol.
Vouchers of Superintendent of the Poor, 1885, 1889, ca. 150 items

Commissioner of Revenue

Application for a Liquor License, 1900, 1 item
License Interrogatories, 1875, 10 items
Licenses Granted, 1867, 15 items
Licenses to Retail Liquor Dealers, 1890-91, 2 items
Lists of All Persons Assessed with a License Tax, ca. 1870-95, ca. .2 cu. ft.
Lists of Tithables, ca. 1790-1815, ca. .1 cu. ft. See also Miscellaneous Records.
Merchants' License Reports and Interrogatories, 1901-02, 46 items
Moffett Liquor Law [Returns], 1878-88, 1890, 1892, 1895, ca. .2 cu. ft.

Ordinary and Retail Licenses, 1816-18, ca. 25 items
Tax Reports of Bank Stocks, 1889-92, 1894, 6 items
See also Tax and Fiscal Records

Sheriff
Sheriff's Receipts for County Claims, 1842-51, ca. 50 items

Treasurer
Report of Taxes Collected on Delinquent Lands and Paid to Treasurer, 1888, 1 item
Treasurer's Reports [titles vary], 1880-94, ca. .15 cu. ft.
See also Tax and Fiscal Records

Microfilm Records

Circuit Court Clerk
Court Records
County Court
Order Books Nos. 1-29, 1A-3A and 5A-6A, 1765-1843, 1849-58, 13 reels
Fiduciary Records
Fiduciary Book, 1765-1850, 1 reel (part)
Guardians' Accounts, 1766-93, 1802-65 2 reels (part)
Guardians' Bond Book, 1765-1850, 1 reel (part)
Free Negro and Slave Records
Registers of Free Negroes Nos. 1-2, 1809-65, 1 reel
Land Records
Deed Books Nos. 1-37, 1765-1870, 18 reels
General Index to Deeds, Grantors-Grantees A-Z, 1765-1933, 4 reels
Marriage Records and Vital Statistics
Marriage Bonds, 1765-1810 (Ts.), 1 reel (part)
Marriage Bonds and Consents, 1770-1847, 20 reels; and, Marriage Licenses, Consents, etc., 1848-1912, 33 reels
Marriage Certificates, Consents, etc., 1782-1909, 10 reels
Marriage Register No. 1, 1864-1929, 1 reel (part)
Marriage Returns of Ministers, 1785-1854, 1 reel (part)
General Index to Marriages, Males-Females A-Z, 1854-1929, 1 reel
Wills
Will Books Nos. 1-21, 1765-1866, 9 reels
Superior Court [of Law] Will Book No. 1, 1810-22, 1 reel (part)
Circuit Court Will Book No. 1, 1831-92, 1 reel (part)
General Index to Wills and Lists of Heirs, Decedents A-Z, 1765-1948, 1 reel

MIDDLESEX COUNTY

Formed in 1669 from Lancaster County.

Original Records

Circuit Court Clerk
Bonds/Commissions/Oaths
Apprentice Bond, 1775, 1 item
Bonds, 1724-1806, ca. 25 items
Court Records
County Court
Chancery Suits, 1754-1820, 1.35 cu. ft.
Court Papers, 1754-1802, 1818, 8.55 cu. ft.
Execution and Order, 1824, 2 items
Grand Jury Presentments, ca. 1750-1800, n.d., ca. 50 items
Miscellaneous Court Papers, 1747-1855, n.d., ca. 200 items (including fragments)
Order Books, 1673-80 (includes deeds and wills), 1680-94, 1732-37, 1740-44 and 1782-83 (one volume, including deeds), 1745-67 (includes wills, inventories, slaves, and horses), 1769-84 (includes deeds and executions), and 1764-86, 10 vols. (originals and copies); Order Books Nos. 4-[6], 1705-1826, 3 vols. (originals and copies); Order Book No. 3, 1694-1705, 1 vol. (two copies); and, Order Book, 1767-69, 1 vol. (copy)
[Card] Index to Orders, 1721-26, ca. .1 cu. ft.
Fiduciary Records
Estate Papers, 1742-1800, 1842, ca. 25 items
Orphans Book, 1760-1820 (also Marriage Returns, 1785-1826), 1 vol. (copy)
Summons for Guardian, 1760, 1 item
See also Court Records, County Court
Free Negro and Slave Records
Slave Records [receipts, criminal papers, etc.], 1764-1800, 13 items
See also Court Records, County Court
Land Records
Deeds, etc., 1687-1750, and Miscellaneous Records, 1752-1831 (compiled from loose papers), 1 vol. (copy); Deed Books Nos. 2-[4], 1679/80-1720, 3 vols. (originals and copies); Deed Books, 1740-85, 3 vols. (originals and copies); and, Deed Book No. 11, 1791-99, 1 vol. (copy). See also Court Records, County Court.
Deeds, 1751-1820, 1827, 1831, .9 cu. ft.
Surveys, 1735-1807, 1 vol. (original and copy)
Marriage Records and Vital Statistics
Marriage Bonds, 1740-1852, ca. 1.7 cu. ft.
Marriage Contract, 1789, 1 item
Marriage Register, 1740-1854 (Ms. compilation), 1 vol. (original and copy)
Index to Marriage Register, 1740-1854, 1 vol. (Ts. and copy)
Ministers' Returns, 1785-1811, 1813, 1823-54, ca. 50 items
See also Fiduciary Records
Military and Pension Records
Inventories of Stores, etc. [militia records found in the back of Christ Church Parish Register], 1678/9-82, 1 vol. (copy)

Tax and Fiscal Records

    Claims against the County, 1794-98, 18 items

    County Levy, 1796, 1 item

    Lists of Insolvents, 1794, 1796, 1798, 3 items

    Tithables, 1769, 2 items

Wills

    Wills, etc., 1675-1798 (compiled from loose papers), 1 vol. (copy); and, Will Books
        [A]-H, 1698-1734, 1740-93, 1795-98, 8 vols. (originals and copies)

    Wills, 1749-1813, 28 items

    See also Court Records, County Court

Miscellaneous Records

    Mill Petitions, 1763, 1777, n.d., 3 items

    Personal Account, 1845 , 1 item

    Tobacco [Inspector's] List, 1798, 1 item

Microfilm Records

Circuit Court Clerk

Business Records/Corporations/Partnerships

    Elliott P. Jones' Day Book, Wilton Plantation, 1856-58, Lumber Mill Day Book,
        1858-61, and Lumber Mill Register, 1858-61, 1 reel (part)

    Jones and Wake, Merchants, Account Books, 1859-62, 1 reel (part)

    Thomas Henry Dunn, M. D., Middlesex County, Account Book, 1852-53, and
        Mathews County Account Book, 1855, 1857, 1 reel (part)

Court Records

County Court

    Execution Books, 1799-1802, 1820-24, 1 reel (part). See also Order Books.

    Fee Book, 1832-47, 1 reel (part)

    Form Book, 1807, 1 reel (part)

    Minute Book, 1823-27, 1 reel (part)

    Order Book [No. 1], 1673-80 (includes wills and deeds), 1 reel (part); Order
        Books Nos. 2-6, 1680-1726, 3 reels; Orders, 1732-37, 1740-44 and 1782-
        83 (includes Deeds, 1736-39), 1 reel; Orders, 1758-67 (includes Wills,
        1794-95), 1 reel (part); Orders, 1745-58, 1767-82, 1784-97, 1799-1804
        (includes Executions, 1769-72), 1807, 1811-15, 1821, 1829-65, 10 reels;
        and, Orders, 1783-84 (includes Deeds, 1785-91), 1 reel (part)

    Rule Book, 1799-1817, 1 reel (part)

Superior Court of Law

    Order Book, 1813-25, 1 reel (part)

Circuit Superior Court of Law and Chancery

    Chancery Order Books, 1831-52 (includes Circuit Court, 1852), 1 reel (part)

    Common Law Execution Book, 1831-45, 1 reel (part)

    Common Law Order Books, 1831-57 (includes Circuit Court, 1852-57), 2 reels

Circuit Court

    Chancery Order Book, see Circuit Superior Court of Law and Chancery

    Common Law Order Books, see Circuit Superior Court of Law and Chancery

Fiduciary Records

    Administrators' Bond Books, 1767-1810, 1821-35, 1 reel

    Guardians [Account] Books Nos. [1]-3, 1820-31, 1825-57, 1 reel (part)

    Guardians' Bonds, 1767-1850, 1 reel

    Healy estate, administrator's and guardian's [accounts], 1837-55, 1 reel (part)

    Orphans Book, 1760-1820 (also Marriage Returns, 1785-1826), 1 reel

Land Records

Deeds, etc. (also miscellaneous records) Nos. [1]-3, 1687-1750, 1679-1720, 2 reels; Deed Books, 1740-85, 2 reels; and, Deed Books Nos. 11-22, 1791-1865, 12 reels. See also Court Records, County Court.

General Indexes to Deeds Vols. A and 1, 1675-1897, 1 reel

Processioners' Returns, 1826-38, 1 reel

Surveys, 1735-1807, 1832-35, 1837-47, 2 reels

Marriage Records and Vital Statistics

Marriage Bonds, 1740-1852, 10 reels

Marriage Register, 1740-1854 (compilation), 1 reel (part); Marriage Register, 1853-76, 1 reel (part); and, Nos. 1-3, 1861-1904, 1 reel (part)

Index to Marriage Register, 1740-1854 (compilation), 1 reel (part)

Marriage Returns, see Fiduciary Records

General Index to Marriages, 1854-1934, 1 reel (part)

Register of Births, 1853-96, 1 reel (part)

Register of Deaths, 1853-96, 1 reel (part)

Miscellaneous Records of Marriages and Deaths [and Births], 1663-1763, 1 reel (part)

Index to Register of Births, Marriages, and Deaths, 1853-96, 1 reel (part)

Military and Pension Records

Muster Rolls, 1861-65, 1 reel (part)

School Records

School Commissioners' Minute Book, 1818-29, 1 reel (part)

Wills

Wills, etc., 1675-1798, 1 reel; Will Books [A]-G, 1698-1734, 1740-93, 3 reels; Wills, 1795-98, 1 reel (part); and, Will Books Nos. 2-9, 1799-1869, 8 reels. See also Court Records, County Court.

Superior Court [of Law] Will Book, 1819-44, 1 reel

[Circuit Superior Court of Law and Chancery] Common Law Will Book No. [1], 1844-90, 1 reel (part)

General Index to Wills No. 1, 1675-1950, 1 reel; and, General Indexes to Decedents, Devisees and Heirs Nos. 1-2, 1675-1935, 1 reel

Miscellaneous Records

Guthrie Family Records, [1686-1946], 1 reel (part)

Sheriff

Sheriff's Book, 1829, 1 reel

MONTGOMERY COUNTY

Formed in 1776 from Fincastle County.
Parts of Botetourt and Pulaski counties
were added later. Some Fincastle County
records, 1772–76, are filed with those
of Montgomery County.

Original Records

Circuit Court Clerk
Bonds/Commissions/Oaths
Bond of Non-Signers of the Oath of Allegiance, 1779, 1 item. <u>See also</u> Miscellaneous Records.
Bonds and Promissory Notes [including notes prior to 1772 from Augusta and Frederick counties, possibly related to the estate of James Patton], 1751–1808, 14 items
Fincastle County Bond, 1774, 1 item (copy)
Militia Officers [commissions, etc.], 1787–1817, ca. 50 items
Oaths of Allegiance, 1774–75, 1777–79 (also Bond of Non-Signers of the Oath), 14 pp. (copies); and, 1777–79, 9 items
Business Records/Corporations/Partnerships
<u>See</u> Marriage Records and Vital Statistics
Court Records
County Court, Fincastle County
Minutes, 1773–77, 1 vol. (Ts.)
Summonses, 1774–75, 2 items (copies)
County Court
Advertisements, 1773, 1786, 1803, 3 items
Fee Alphabet [index to fee book], 1823, 1 item
Grand Jury Presentments, 1779, 1786, 1827, n.d., 5 items
Memorandums, [1772–76], 12 items
Minutes [and docket], 1779, 2 items
Order Books Nos. 1–3, 1773–82, 3 vols. (copies). <u>See also</u> Marriage Records and Vital Statistics.
Records and Notes, 1776–1900 (compilation), 1 vol. (Ts. and copy)
Suit Papers [including papers from Augusta County; <u>see also</u> Bonds/Commissions/Oaths], 1753–1802, ca. 50 items
Summons, 1783, 1 item (copy)
Writ Docket, 1867–73, 1 vol.
County and Superior Courts
Miscellaneous Court Records, [1772]–1834, 44 items
Election Records
Presidential Poll, 1844, 1 item
Land Records
[Commissioners'] Accounts of Certificates/Warrants [issued to County Surveyor], 1781–98, 1 vol.
Deed Book A, 1773–89, 1 vol. (copy)
Deeds and Related Papers [including items from Augusta County; <u>see also</u> Bonds/Commissions/Oaths], 1753–1805, n.d., 14 items
Deeds and Wills B, 1773–97, 1 vol. (copy)
Entry Books A–E, 1773–77, 1780–1883, 5 vols. (copies)

Land Records, 1767-94, n.d., 26 items

Patents and Grants [including items from Augusta County dated prior to 1772], 1750-1859, 23 items

Record of Plotts [sic] A, 1773-82, 1 vol. (copy)

Marriage Records and Vital Statistics

Fincastle County Marriage Bonds [and consents], 1773-75, 8 items; and, 1773-75, 3 items (copies)

List of Marriage Licenses Issued, 1850-61 (also Crush & Wade Expense Accounts, 1863-65), 1 vol.

Marriage Bonds and Records, 1777-1865, ca. 3.35 cu. ft.

Marriage Records and [ministers'] Ordinations, 1782-1835, 1838, n.d., 25 items; and, Pulaski County Marriage Records, 1844-57, 8 items

Marriage Register, 1777-1853, 1 vol. (original and copy)

Index to Marriage Register, 1777-1853, 1 vol. (Ts. and copy)

Ministers' Returns, 1841-53 (also County Court Order Book, [1866]), 1 vol.

Ministers' Returns, 1780-1853, ca. .25 cu. ft.

Records of Marriage Certificates, [1818] 1820-41, 1 vol.

Military and Pension Records

Civil War Papers (orders, etc., including conscript reports from Giles, Craig, Floyd, Botetourt, Roanoke, and Pulaski counties, and from Mercer, Greenbrier, and Monroe counties, West Virginia), 1861-65, ca. 100 items

Courts Martial [proceedings], 1776, 1781-83, 13 items. See also Fincastle and Montgomery County Revolutionary War Records.

Fincastle and Montgomery County Revolutionary War Records, 1775-83, 1 vol. (copy)

Militia Claims [and related papers], 1775-98, 1811, n.d., 24 items

Militia Fines, 1787, ca. 300 items

Militia Lists, 1781-84, 1787, n.d., 43 items; and, 1781-83, n.d., 39 pp. (copies). See also Fincastle and Montgomery County Revolutionary War Records.

Papers Belonging to the J. F. Preston Camp #33, 1895-1900, 11 items

Revolutionary War Claims and Bounty Land Papers, 1777-80, 1834-43, n.d., ca. 50 items

See also Bonds/Commissions/Oaths

Road and Bridge Records

Road Petitions [and related records], 1794-1862, n.d., 15 items

Tax and Fiscal Records

[List of] Insolvents, 1799, 1 item

List of Taxable Property, [1781], 25 pp. (copies)

Lists of Delinquent Taxes, 1773, 1783, 1787-88, 1797-99, 1818, n.d., 28 items

Lists of Taxes Collected, 1787-89, 9 items

[Taxes not collected because of] Removals from the County, 1787, 3 items

Tithables, 1779, 1783-84, 2 items (copies); and, 1782-84, 1796-99, 11 items

Wills

Will Book No. 1, 1797-1809, 1 vol. (copy)

Will of William Winston, Hanover County, 1772, and of Charles Sinclair, Orange County, North Carolina, n.d., 2 items

See also Land Records

Miscellaneous Records

An Act to amend an act entitled "an act suspending in part the operation of the act concerning escheat and forfeiture from British subjects," 1782, 1 item (Ms.)

Circular Letters from governors, 1788-1809, 6 items

Committee of Safety Journal, 1775-76, 1 vol.; and, Minutes, 1775-76, 1 vol.

Contract, etc., for Courthouse and Jail, 1788-1863, 6 items

Correspondence and Papers of William Ingles, William Preston, William Christian, Andrew Lewis, and others, 1774-1824, 41 items

Impressed Property Records [public service claims], 1774-83, n.d., 24 items. See also Fincastle and Montgomery County Revolutionary War Records.

Letter from Arthur Campbell, 1776, 1 item

Papers related to Tories, 1779-89, n.d., 14 items

Personal Accounts [including items from Augusta County; see also Bonds/ Commissions/Oaths], 1752-94, ca. 25 items

Microfilm Records

Circuit Court Clerk
Court Records
County Court

Order Books Nos. 1-2, 1773-88, and Nos. 3-32, 1778-80 and 1788-1855, 9 reels; and, Order Book, 1859-67 [1868], 1 reel (part)

General Index to County Court Order Books, A-Z, 1773-1855, 1 reel

Circuit Superior Court of Law and Chancery

Chancery Order Book No. 1, 1831-66 (includes Circuit Court, 1852-66), 1 reel

Circuit Court

Chancery Orders, see Circuit Superior Court of Law and Chancery

Land Records

Deed Book A, 1773-89, 1 reel (part); Deeds and Wills B, 1773-97, 1 reel (part); and, Deed Books C-R, 1797-1868, 8 reels

General Index to Deeds, Grantors-Grantees A-Z, 1773-1933, 4 reels

Record of Plotts [sic] A, 1773-82 (also index to warrants to colonial soldiers of Fincastle, 1773-80), 1 reel (part); and, Records of Plotts [sic] B-F, 1782-1890, 3 reels

General Index to Plotts [sic], 1773-1890, 1 reel

Marriage Records and Vital Statistics

Marriage Bonds, 1778-1865, 13 reels; Fincastle County Marriage Bonds, 1773-75, 1 reel; and, Pulaski County Marriage Bonds, 1844-57, 1 reel

Marriage Certificates, 1813-41, 1 reel

Marriage Records, 1785-1803, 1850-61, 1 reel

Marriage Register, 1777-1853 (compilation), 1 reel (part); and, Marriage Register No. 1, 1854-1902, 1 reel

Index to Marriage Register, 1777-1853 (compilation), 1 reel (part)

Ministers' Returns, 1780-1853, 2 reels

Register of Births, 1853-68, 1 reel (part)

Register of Deaths, 1853-68, 1 reel (part)

Military and Pension Records

Soldiers' [service] Records, 1818-39, 1 reel

See also Land Records

Wills

Will Books Nos. 1-10, 1797-1874, 4 reels. See also Land Records.

Superior Court Will Book No. 1, 1821-89, 1 reel

General Index to Wills, A-Z, 1773-1952, 1 reel

NANSEMOND COUNTY

**Established in 1637 as Upper Norfolk,
the name Nansemond was adopted in 1646.
The county became the independent city of
Nansemond in 1972, and merged with the
City of Suffolk in 1974. The entire
area is now known as Suffolk.**

For listing of records, see A Preliminary Guide to Pre-1904 Municipal Records, City of
   Suffolk entry.

NELSON COUNTY

Formed in 1807 from Amherst County.

Original Records

Circuit Court Clerk
   Bonds/Commissions/Oaths
      Bonds Taken in Court, 1867-93, 2 vols.; and, Official Bonds Taken in Court, 1893-
         1911, 2 vols.
      Circuit Court Bond Books, 1891-1919, 2 vols.
      County Court Bonds, 1852-67, 3 vols.
   Business Records/Corporations/Partnerships
      Invoice Book (An Inventory of Goods on Hand in Store of Lofftus and Jones),
         1839, 1 vol.
   Court Records
      County Court
         Chancery Rule Book, 1853-72, 1 vol.
         [Clerk's] Tax Book, 1898-1915 (includes Circuit Court, 1904-15), 1 vol.
         Complete Collection of Forms of the best kind for the use of Clerks, by
            Spottwood Garland, 1798 (also A List of Marriage Licenses issued by
            Clerk's Office, 1814-19), 1 vol.
         Execution Books A-E, G-H, J-K and M-N, 1808-22, 1824-42, 1850-93, 11 vols.
         Fee Books, 1808-34, 1836-72, 1880-89, 1893-1904, 66 vols.
         Law Issue Docket, 1827-29, 1 vol.
         Law Rules 1852, [1853-72], 1 vol.
         Memorandum Book, 1870-86, 1 vol.
         Memorandum Docket and Estray Book and Title to Property Retained, 1890-
            1900 (also [Records of Insane Persons], 1901-03), 1 vol.
         Quarterly Session Minutes, 1876-1900, 1 vol.
         Warrant Book, 1884-89, 1 vol.
      Superior Court of Law
         Fee Books, 1816, 1819-30, 4 vols.
      Circuit Superior Court of Law and Chancery
         Chancery Fee Books, 1831-53 (includes Circuit Court, 1852-53), 4 vols.
         Fee Book, 1831-35, 1 vol.
         Law Fee Books, 1835-39, 1843-51, 4 vols.
         Process Book, 1843-58 (includes Circuit Court, 1852-58), 1 vol.
         Sleeping Docket, 1847-72 (includes Circuit Court, 1852-72), 1 vol.
         Writ of Summons, 1836, 1 item

Circuit Court

 Chancery Dockets, 1874-1909, 2 vols.

 Chancery Fee Books, 1854-90, 1892-1900, 11 vols. See also Circuit Superior
  Court of Law and Chancery.

 Chancery Memorandum Books, 1861-1915, 3 vols.

 Chancery Minutes, 1860-62, 1866-99, 1 vol.

 Chancery Rule Docket, 1887-1910, 1 vol.

 [Clerk's] Tax Book, 1899-1903, 1 vol. See also County Court.

 Common Law Docket, 1887-1922, 1 vol.

 [Common Law] Docket for the Clerk, 1868-90, 1 vol.

 Common Law Fees, 1852-55, 1857-68, 1879-94, 1896-1905, 8 vols.; and,
  Ledger [Law Fees], 1892-94, 1 vol.

 Common Law Memorandum, 1871-79, 1887-1921, 2 vols.

 Common Law Minutes, 1866-89, 1 vol.

 Docket, 1891-1903, 1905, 1907, 1 vol.

 Docket for Fines and Costs, 1878-1928, 1 vol.

 Fee Books, 1870-78, 1902-40, 2 vols.

 Issue Docket, 1857-73, 1 vol.

 [Jury Fees], 1895-1926, 1 vol.

 Jury List, 1859-77, 1 vol.

 Law Fee Books, 1873-80, 2 vols.

 Ledger [Clerk's Writ Tax], 1894-1911, 1 vol.

 Minute Book, 1900-19, 1 vol.

 Process Book, 1858-93, 1 vol. See also Circuit Superior Court of Law and
  Chancery.

 Receipt Book for Chancery Causes, 1874-83, 1 vol.

 Sleeping Docket, see Circuit Superior Court of Law and Chancery

 Witness Attendance Books, 1851-1903, 1902-21, 2 vols.

County and Superior Courts

 [Clerk's Ticket Register], 1872-1903, 1 vol. [labeled Nevada, Oregon,
  Washington, Idaho]

 [Descriptive List of Persons Convicted of Felony and other Infamous
  Offenses in the County], 1870-1919, 1 vol.

 Memorandum Book, 1886-1907, 1 vol.

Unspecified Court

 [Index to Court Cases], n.d., 1 vol.

Election Records

List of White Voters Registered at New Market Precinct, 1897, 1 vol.

Record [Minutes of Electoral Board], 1884-1961, 1 vol.

Roll of Registered Voters, 1902-03, 1 vol.

Fiduciary Records

Circuit Court Record of Fiduciary, 1850-1906, 1 vol.

County Court Record of Fiduciary, 1850-1904, 1 vol.

Fiduciary Bonds, see Bonds/Commissions/Oaths

Index [to Fiduciaries], n.d., 1 vol.

[Receivers'] Bond Book, 1873-91, 1 vol.

Register of Fiduciaries, 1870-1901, 1 vol.

Settlement of Accounts of Amey Warwick, 1844, 14 items

Justice of the Peace Records

Justices' FiFa [Execution] Books, 1829-41 [1828-37], 1860-74, 1877-91, 1886-
 1937, 4 vols.

Land Records

Daily Index of Receipts of Deeds for Recordation, 1902-05, 1919, 1 vol.

General Indexes to Deeds, 1808-1909, 3 vols.; General Indexes to Deeds, Grantors-Grantees, 1808-1915, 4 vols.; General Index to Deeds, 1809-67, 1 vol. (original and Ts.); General Index to Deed Books, 1867-78, 1 vol.; and, Indexes [to Deeds], 1877-1915, 2 vols.

Marriage Records and Vital Statistics

Marriage Register, 1808-78 (compilation), 1 vol. (copy)

Index to Marriage Register, 1808-78, 1 vol. (Ts.)

See also Court Records, County Court

Millitary and Pension Records

Pension Roll of Nelson County Pensions under Act of 1900 continued under Act of 1902, 1902-07, 1 vol.

Road and Bridge Records

Road Books, 1848-75, 1892-93, 2 vols.; and, [Road Book], 1878-91 and 1894-99 (also Delinquent Land Taxes Received by W. J. Kidd, Clerk, 1898-99), 1 vol. [labeled Mass.]

School Records

Annual Report, 1872, 1 item

Articles of Agreement [Contracts], 1871, 1873-75, n.d., 7 items

Monthly and Term Reports, 1871-74, 1876, n.d., 87 items

Tax and Fiscal Records

Aggregate Expenditures 189[?], 1891-1910, 1 vol.

Delinquent Lands Redeemed, 1899-1930, 1 vol.

Delinquent Real Estate, 1883-89, 1 vol. See also Road and Bridge Records.

Lands Sold for Taxes and Purchased by the Commonwealth [Vol.] A, 1876-1923, 1 vol.

Personal Property Book, 1878, 1 vol.

Miscellaneous Records

Crop Lien Docket, 1890-1965, 1 vol.

Estray Book, see Court Records, County Court

Messages Received and Sent, Toll Station at Jonesboro, 1901-10, 1 vol.

[Records of Insane Persons], see Court Records, County Court

Title to Property Retained, see Court Records, County Court

Sheriff

[Sheriff's Levy Book], 1833-34, 1 vol.

Microfilm Records

Circuit Court Clerk
Court Records
County Court

Order Books, 1808-11, 1813-17, 1820-68, 4 reels

Land Records

Deed Books Nos. 1-16, 1808-67, 8 reels

Superior Court Deeds, etc., Book A [includes wills] 1811-31, 1 reel (part)

General Index to Deeds, Grantor-Grantee A-Z, 1808-1915, 2 reels

See also Wills

Marriage Records and Vital Statistics

Marriage Register, 1808-78 (compilation), 1 reel (part); and, Marriage Register, 1854-1926, 1 reel (part)

General Index to Marriages No. 1, 1854-1922, 1 reel (part)

Register of Births, 1853-72, 1 reel (part)
Register of Deaths, 1853-72, 1 reel (part)
Index to Registers of Births, Marriages, and Deaths, 1853-72, 1 reel (part)
Wills
Will Books A-M, 1808-67 (there is no Book I; Book L includes Circuit Court Trustee Accounts, 1856-63, and Book M includes Deeds, 1816-47), 5 reels
General Index to Wills, etc., 1808-1927, 1 reel
See also Land Records

NEW KENT COUNTY

Formed in 1654 from York County.

Original Records

Circuit Court Clerk
Board of Supervisors Records
Officers' Accounts, 1871-80, 12 items
Papers, 1872-1906, ca. 1.25 cu. ft.
Bonds/Commissions/Oaths
Appointments and Commissions, ca. 1860-1900, n.d., ca. 25 items
Appointments of Commissioners of Election, 1864, 1 item
Bond to sell a slave, 1858, 1 item
Bonds to negotiate loans, 1861, 2 items
Electoral Board Oaths, 1884-98, 25 items
Examination of Officials' Bonds, 1881-1904, ca. 25 items
Forthcoming Bonds, 1820-21, ca. 1875-80, ca. 25 items
Fyke and Weir Fishing Oath, 1882, 1 item
Injunction and Suspending Bonds, 1892-99, 9 items
Liquor License Bonds [and petition against], ca. 1880-1900, ca. .25 cu. ft.
[List of] Bonds issued and dated May 14, 1861, 2 pp.
Merchants' License [Bonds], 1859, 6 items
Militia Officer's Bonds, 1861, 2 items
Ministers' Bonds, 1867-1900, 8 items
[Oath for] License to practice law, 1894, 1 item
Officials' Bonds and Oaths, ca. 1865-1905, n.d., ca. .5 cu. ft.
Ordinary Bonds, 1859-60, 2 items
Oystermen's Bonds, 1866-80, 10 items
Petitions and Miscellaneous Papers [concerning bonds], ca. 1870-1900, n.d., 22 items
Retail and Bar License Bonds, 1877-92, ca. 125 items
Superior Court Delivery Bonds, 1820-21, 16 items
Business Records/Corporations/Partnerships
Agreements, etc. [including bankruptcy], 1859-90, 7 items; and, Taliaferro and Vaiden, agreement to run a sawmill, 1858, 27 items
Northern Neck Mutual Fire Assn. [and other] insurance policies, 1880-87, 9 items
Census Records
Enumeration, 1880, 1 vol.
Enumeration Sheets, 1870, 3 pp.

Court Records
  County Court
    Miscellaneous Papers, E. M. Crump, Clerk, 1879-80, 3 items; and, Julian N.
      Harris, Clerk, 1892, n.d., ca. 25 items
    Qualification and Vacation Orders, ca. 1870-1900, n.d., ca. 25 items
    Witnesses, 1858-84, 1893-98, 15 items
  Circuit Superior Court of Law and Chancery
    Fees, 1839-48, 6 items
  Circuit Court
    Memorandums, 1879-86, ca. 50 items
    Report of the Clerk of Court, n.d., 1 item
    Reports of Business in Circuit Court, 1872-99, 21 items
  County and Superior Courts
    Attorney's Memorandums [and correspondence regarding suits], 1849-1904,
      ca. 50 items
    [Commonwealth Cases], A-Z, ca. 1865-1905, ca. 6 cu. ft.
    Grand Jury Drawn, 1827, 1858-59, 1870-1904, n.d., ca. .35 cu. ft.; and,
      Presentments, 1820-59, 8 items
    Jury Dockets, Venire Facias, 1827, 1850-1904, n.d., ca. .5 cu. ft.
    [Law and Chancery Suits], A-Z, 1820-1904, ca. 12 cu. ft.
    Orders, Correspondence, etc. [re: dockets and terms of court], 1872-1900,
      n.d., 18 items
    Summonses, 1859, 1870-1904, ca. 50 items
    Warrants, Judgments, and Executions [titles vary], 1812-1904, ca. 3 cu. ft.
  Unspecified Court
    Examination and Reports on Condition of the Clerk's Office and Books, etc.,
      1858-91, ca. 25 items
    Jury instructions [unidentified suits], n.d., 15 items
    List of Fees due Philip B. Winston, Hanover County Clerk [and miscellaneous
      fees], 1838, 3 items
Election Records
  Abstracts of Votes, 1870-1901, ca. 75 items
  Certificates of Election, 1851-63, 1870-1900, ca. .1 cu. ft.
  Election Expenses, 1903, 4 items; and, Declaration of Expenses of Manley H.
    Barnes, 1903, 4 items
  Election Records, 1866, 6 items; and, Miscellaneous Papers (including accounts),
    1859, 1871-1903, 23 items
  Judges of Elections Papers, 1872 [1873], 1883-84, 3 items
  [List of] District Officers, 1891, 1 item
  List of Persons who Paid Capitation Tax, 1901-03, 1 item
  List of Voters, 1866, 13 pp.
  List of White Voters, 1871-73, and Colored Voters, 1870-73, Cumberland
    Precinct, 2 vols.
  Notices of Candidacy, 1895, 1903, 3 items
  Petitions and Notices, 1870-89, 11 items
Fiduciary Records
  Carrie O. Hoard's Papers and Receipts, 1876-81, ca. 25 items
  Divisions of estates (including slaves), 1846, 1863, n.d., 6 items
  Fiduciary Bonds, 1851-53, ca. 50 items
  Fiduciary Records [guardians' accounts, wills, accounts, etc.], 1827-1904, n.d.,
    ca. 3.4 cu. ft.
  Guardians' Bonds, 1851-53, 19 items
  Miscellaneous Papers, 1853-1904, n.d., 10 items
  Receivers' Bonds, 1894, 2 items

Siefred Orphans [apprenticeship paper], 1871, 1 item
Special Commissioners' Bonds, 1888-1904, ca. 50 items
[Trusteeship Records], ca. 1830, 1868-1902, ca. .45 cu. ft.

Free Negro and Slave Records
Bureau of Refugees, Freedmen and Abandoned Land, letters, 1866, 2 items
Lists of Free Negroes, 1855, 1866, 2 items
See also Bonds/Commissions/Oaths; and, Fiduciary Records

Justice of the Peace Records
Justice of the Peace Reports, 1890, 1892-1903, .45 cu. ft.
Justices' Attendance in County Court, ca. 1855-70, ca. 25 items
Warrants Returned, 1881-92, 1895, 1898-99, .45 cu. ft.; and, Warrants Returned
    Unsatisfied, 1866-79, .45 cu. ft.

Land Records
Deeds, 1697-1827, 1 vol. (copies)
Deeds, 1817-1903, 16 items; and, Deeds for Delinquent Land, 1870, 1888, 3 items
Land Grants, 1674, 1679, 2 items
List of Transfers of Real Estate, 1866, 1 item
Lists of [Deeds and] All Writings Admitted to Record, 1890-1904, ca. .1 cu. ft.
Miscellaneous Papers, 1880-1904, 10 items
Plats and Surveys, 1888-1900, 8 items; and, Plat of Town Lots [West Point?],
    n.d., 1 item
Processioning Books, 1867, 1880-81, 2 vols. (copies)
Processioning Reports, 1867-70, 1880-81, ca. .25 cu. ft.
Rough [notes] of Apportionment of the County in Processioning Precincts, 1866,
    6 pp.
[Surveyor's Book], 1881, ca. .1 cu. ft. (unbound)

Marriage Records and Vital Statistics
Affidavit of Jim Lee's birth date, 1878, 1 item
Certification of Register of Births, 1866, 1 item
Lists [Registers] of Births, 1870-96, ca. .75 cu. ft.
Lists [Registers] of Deaths, 1870-96, ca. .45 cu. ft.
Marriage Certificates, 1850-68, ca. 125 items
Marriage Licenses, 1862-77, 1902, 8 items
Petition to Establish a Marriage Contract, 1866, 1 item

Military and Pension Records
Applications for Commutation, etc., [ca. 1885], 11 items
List of Pensioners, Act of 1900, 1903, 2 pp.
Military Orders after the [Civil] War, 1868-70, ca. 50 items
Militia Order, 1858, 1 item
Reports, Commissioners for the Benefit of the Barhamville Grays, etc., and
    Committee Expenditures for Volunteers, 1861, ca. 58 items

Road and Bridge Records
Blueprints for proposed bridges, n.d., 3 items
Bridge Papers, 1858-ca. 1905, n.d., ca. .45 cu. ft.
Chesapeake & Ohio Railroad Co. condemnation notice, 1881, 1 item
Records of Overseers and Supervisors, 1866-1901, n.d., ca. 75 items
Road Accounts, ca. 1870-1905, ca. 1 cu. ft.
Road Papers, 1881-98, ca. .2 cu. ft.; and, Miscellaneous Road Papers, 1873-1900,
    n.d., ca. 50 items
[Road Petitions], 1858-1902, n.d., ca. .2 cu. ft.

School Records
Census, 1875, 1 vol.
Condemnation of Land for Schools, 1872-1906, n.d., 22 items
Papers [including annual reports], 1874-82, 19 items
Superintendent's Papers, 1872, 1886, 1894, 1897, 4 items
Weir's Creek School District Papers, 1872, 6 items

Tax and Fiscal Records

Accounts against the Commonwealth, ca. 1820-1900, ca. .45 cu. ft.

Accounts against the County, 1850-ca. 1900, n.d., ca. .5 cu. ft.

Alms House Accounts, 1884-1902, 4 items

Applications for Liquor Licenses, 1904 [also petition, 1886], 14 items

Applications to Purchase Delinquent Land, ca. 1870-1900, ca. .2 cu. ft.

Delinquent Land and Property Taxes, 1862, 1865-67, 6 items

Delinquent Land and Town Lots, ca. 1870-1900, n.d., ca. 1.5 cu. ft.

Delinquent Land Sold for Taxes, 1891-1903, 9 pp.; and, Delinquent Lands Redeemed and Sold, 1891, 1895, 13 items; and, Delinquent Lands Redeemed before being Sold, ca. 1885-1900, n.d., ca. .25 cu. ft.

Delinquent Taxes other than Land, 1866, 1 item

Erroneous Assessments, 1868-ca. 1905, ca. 75 items; and, Improper Assessments, ca. 1870-1900, 1903, 33 pp.

Homestead Petitions, 1874-83, 9 items

Land Books (also Reassessments and Supplements), 1863, 1865-66, 1870, 1875, 1880, 1882, 1884, 1886, 1889-91, 1899-1902, 13 vols.

Land Tax Supplement Sheet, 1876-83, 1 p.

Oyster Licenses and Reports, 1876-99, ca. .15 cu. ft.

Personal Property Books (and Supplements), 1863, 1865, 1866-85, 1887-88, 1890, 1892-1904, 53 vols.

Personal Property, Capitations, and Insolvents, 1867-1907, ca. 1 cu. ft.

Reassessments, 1885, 2 pp.

Recapitulation of Assessments, 1902, 1 p.

Reports of Bonds, Money, Taxes, etc. [titles vary], 1883, 1885-ca. 1905, ca. .6 cu. ft.

Tax Collectors, Assessors, etc., Papers, 1873-84, n.d., 6 items; and, Miscellaneous Papers, 1869-ca. 1905, n.d., ca. 25 items (including fragments)

Tax Petitions and Orders, 1871-1900, n.d., ca. 75 items

Values of Tracts of Land, 1866, 1869-1880, 1885-86, ca. .25 cu. ft.

Township Records

Division of the County into Townships, 1870, 2 items

St. Peter's Township Receipt Book, 1871, 1 vol.

Miscellaneous Records

Appointments of Church Trustees, etc., 1868-99, n.d., 12 items

Coroner's Inquests, 1866-1904, ca. .2 cu. ft.

Examination and Reports of Condition of the Jail, 1820-93, n.d., ca. 25 items

Fence Law Petitions, 1866, 1869, 12 items

[Lunacy Papers], A-Z, 1866-1904, n.d., ca. .45 cu. ft.

Mechanics Lien, 1903, 1 item

Memorials and Resolutions, n.d., 4 items

Miscellaneous Records, n.d., ca. 25 items (including fragments)

Naturalization Report, 1848, 1 item

Overseers of the Poor Orders and Accounts, 1866-69, 1873, 1890-1904, ca. .25 cu. ft.

Personal Accounts, notes, etc., 1825, 1859-1904, ca. 25 items

Plat of the Courthouse and Prison rules, 1829, and construction and repairs, 1860-ca. 1905, n.d., ca. 50 items

Powers of Attorney, 1875, 1879-1901, ca. 50 items

Reports of Superintendents of the Poor, 1866-80, ca. 1900, 17 items

Sale of Poor House Land and [Railroad] Ties, 1892, 7 items

Vaccination Reports, 1895, 1899, 2 items

Commissioner of Revenue
Liquor Law [Returns of Wholesale and Retail Sales and Purchases], 1883, 1 p.
Lists of All Persons Assessed with a License Tax, 1869, 1880, 2 items
See also Tax and Fiscal Records

Sheriff
Resignation of Sheriff James Pollard, 1865, and [other] resignations, 1871-[97], ca. 25 items

Treasurer
Treasurer's Bimonthly Reports, 1888-99, ca. .1 cu. ft.
Treasurer's Settlements, 1886-1904, ca. 1.8 cu. ft.
See also Tax and Fiscal Records

NEW NORFOLK COUNTY

Formed in 1636 from Elizabeth City County.
It was divided into Upper and Lower
Norfolk counties in 1637 and became
extinct. See Nansemond and
Norfolk counties.

NORFOLK COUNTY

Formed in 1691 from Lower Norfolk County.
Norfolk County became extinct in 1963,
when it was consolidated with the
City of South Norfolk to form
the City of Chesapeake.

For listing of records, see A Preliminary Guide to Pre-1904 Municipal Records, City of Chesapeake entry.

NORTHAMPTON COUNTY

**Original shire established in 1634,
and first called Accawmac[k].
The name was changed in 1643.
See also Accomack County.**

Original Records

Circuit Court Clerk
Court Records
County Court
Abstract of Judgment, 1901, 1 item
Accawmack Orders, Deeds, etc., No. 1, 1632-40 (original and Ts.), 2 vols.
(copies); and Accawmack Orders, Deeds, and Wills No. 2, 1640-45 (Ts.),
1 vol., and original and Ts., 2 vols. (copies)
Executions, 1851, 1879-85, 1893-97, ca. .2 cu. ft.
Minute Books, 1754-83, 5 vols. (copies)
Order Books Nos. 6-[7], 10-12, and 15-18, 1655-64, 1674-89, 1710-29, 9 vols.
(copies)
Circuit Court
Executions [titles vary], 1876-ca. .5 cu. ft.; and, Executions, etc., Returned,
1877, ca. 50 items
Land Records
Deeds, Wills, etc., 1657-66, 1668-80, 1711-25, 4 vols. (copies); Deeds, etc. [titles
vary], Nos. 3-5, 7-8, and 11-12, 1645-68, 1680-1707, 6 vols. (copies); and,
Deeds Nos. 19 and 21, 1750-63, 1771-85, 2 vols. (copies)
Land Causes, 1731-54, 1 vol. (copy)
Surveyors' Records Nos. 1-2, 1784-1833, 2 vols. (copies)
See also Land Records; and, Wills
Marriage Records and Vital Statistics
Marriage Register, 1706-1853 (compilation), 1 vol.
Tax and Fiscal Records
Tithable List, 1670, 1 item (copy); and, Tithables, 1662-64, 1675-77, 15 pp.
(copies)
Wills
Wills and Deeds, 1657-66 (Ts.), 1 vol. (copy); Wills and Inventories [titles vary]
Nos. 18, 20-21, and 25, 1733-40, 1750-60, 1772-77, 4 vols. (copies); [Wills]
Orders No. 9, 1664-74, 1 vol. (copy); and, Wills No. 19, 1708-17, 1 vol. (copy)
See also Court Records, County Court; and, Land Records.

Microfilm Records

Circuit Court Clerk
Court Records
County Court
Minute Books, 1754-83, 1 reel
Order Books [titles vary] Nos. 1-2, 6-[8], 15-24, and 30-44, 1632-45, 1655-
64, 1710-58, 1783-1865, 18 reels
[Superior Court Pleas] Complete Records, 1819-28, 1843-83, 1 reel (part)
See also Land Records.

Fiduciary Records

Orphans' Accounts Nos. 1-4, 1731-1850, 1 reel

See also Wills.

Land Records

Deeds, Wills, etc., Nos. 3-5, 7-8, and 11-12, 1645-[56], [1654]-68, 1680-1707, 3 reels (parts); Deeds, Wills, etc., 1657-66, 1668-80, 1718-25, 3 reels (parts); and, Deeds, etc., Nos. 18-36, 1733-1867, 17 reels

Indexes to Deeds, Grantors-Grantees A-Z, 1632-1917, 3 reels

Land Causes, 1754-71, 1815-67, 1 reel (part); and, Common Law Land Causes, 1835, 1 reel (part)

Processioners' Returns, 1795-1828, 1831-87, 1 reel (part)

Surveyors Records Nos. 1-2, 1784-1833, 1 reel (part)

See also Court Records, County Court; and, Wills.

Marriage Records and Vital Statistics

Marriage Register [No. 1], 1706-1853 (Stratton Nottingham compilation), 1 reel; and, Nos. 2-3, 1853-1922, 1 reel (part)

General Index to Marriage Registers, 1853-1922, 1 reel (part)

Register of Births, 1853-70, 1 reel (part)

Register of Deaths, 1853-70, 1 reel (part)

Tax and Fiscal Records

Tithables, 1662-64, 1675-77, 1 reel (part)

Wills

[Wills] Order Books [titles vary] Nos. 9-14, 1664-1710, 2 reels; Wills No. 19, 1708-17, 1 reel; Wills, etc., 1711-18, 1 reel (part); Wills, etc., Nos. 15 and 26, 1717-33, 1 reel (part); and, Wills and Inventories [titles vary] Nos. 18-39, 1733-1897, 13 reels

Superior Court Will Book No. 33A, 1811-30, 1 reel (part); and, Wills and Inventories No. 38A, 1831-1901, 1 reel (part)

General Indexes to Wills, 1632-1950, 1 reel

See also Court Records, County Court; and, Land Records.

Miscellaneous Records

Hungars Parish Record, 1758-82, 1 reel (part)

NORTHUMBERLAND COUNTY

Formed ca. 1645 from the district of Chickacoan, the area between the Potomac and Rappahannock rivers.

Original Records

Circuit Court Clerk

Court Records

County Court

Minutes, 1718-20, 1793-1807, 5 vols. (copies)

Order Books, 1652-1770, 1773-83, 17 vols. (copies)

Land Records

Deeds and Orders, 1650-52, 1 vol. (2 copies).

Record Books [deeds, wills, and fiduciary accounts], 1652-72, 1706-29, 1738-87, 23 vols. (copies)

Marriage Records and Vital Statistics
> Marriage License, 1842, 1 item

Wills
> District Court Wills, 1789-1825, 28 pp. (copies)

Microfilm Records

Circuit Court Clerk
Court Records
County Court
> Fee Books, 1718-24, 1727-37, 1740-49, 1785 (includes Marriage Licenses),
> 1 reel
> Order Books, 1652-1871, 21 reels. See also Land Records.

District Court
> Order Books, 1789-1811 (includes Superior Court of Law, 1808-11), 2 reels

Superior Court of Law
> Order Books, 1812-30, 1 reel (part). See also District Court.

Circuit Superior Court of Law and Chancery
> Chancery Order Books, 1831-71 (includes Circuit Court, 1852-71), 1 reel
> (part)
> Common Law Order Book No. 1, 1831-54 (includes Circuit Court, 1852-54),
> 1 reel (part)

Circuit Court
> Chancery Orders, see Circuit Superior Court of Law and Chancery
> Common Law Orders, see Circuit Superior Court of Law and Chancery

Fiduciary Records
> Estate Books A-E, 1847-67, 2 reels. See also Land Records.
> Guardianship Accounts, 1824-43, 2 reels; and, Nos. 1[A]-4, 1843-65, 2 reels
> General Index to Fiduciary Acocunts, etc., 1749-1950, 1 reel

Land Records
> Deeds and Orders [Record Books] 1650-52, 1 reel; Record Books (including wills),
> 1652-72, 1706-29, 1738-49, 4 reels; Record Books Nos. 1-34, 1749-1846,
> 28 reels; Record Book [Deeds] A, 1847-52; and, Deed Books B-C, 1847-66,
> 1 reel
> District Court Orders, Deeds, etc. [Record Book], 1789-1825 [1849], 1 reel
> General Index to Deeds No. 1, 1749-1892, 1 reel
> Land Causes Nos. [1]-2, 1846-73, 1 reel
> Processioners' Reports, 1795-1839, 1 reel

Marriage Records and Vital Statistics
> Birth Register, 1853-96, 1 reel (part)
> Death Register, 1853-96, 1 reel (part)
> Marriage Licenses, see Court Records, County Court
> Marriage Records, 1735-1853, 1 reel (part)
> Marriage Register, White, 1854-1917, 1 reel (part)
> St. Stephen's Parish Record of Births and Deaths, 1650 [1661]-1810, 1 reel

Wills
> Will Book A, 1847-72, 1 reel. See also Land Records.
> General Index to Wills No. 1, 1749-1950, 1 reel

NOTTOWAY COUNTY

Formed in 1788 from Amelia County.

Original Records

Circuit Court Clerk
Court Records
County Court
Bills of Complaint, 1789, 2 items
Minute Book, 1860-64, 1 vol.
Order Books Nos. 1-2, 1793-1801, 2 vols. (copies)
Wills
Will Books Nos. 1-2, 1789-1809, 2 vols. (copies)
Will [removed from Will Book No. 9], 1850, 1 p.

Microfilm Records

Circuit Court Clerk
Court Records
County Court
Minute Books Nos. 1-3, 1840-64, 2 reels
Order Books Nos. 1-11 and 13-14, 1793-1812, 1814-20, 1823-54, 6 reels
Index to Court Order Books, 1793-1854, 1 reel
Land Records
Deed Books Nos. 1-4, 7-8, and 10, 1789-1816, 1824-29, 1836-42, 3 reels
Marriage Records and Vital Statistics
Register of Marriages, 1865-97, 1 reel (part)
The Reverend John Cameron's Marriage Register, Bristol, Cumberland, and Nottoway parishes, 1784-1815, 1 reel (part)
Wills
Will Book Nos. 1-8, 1789-1845, 4 reels

[OLD] RAPPAHANNOCK COUNTY
Formed in 1656 from Lancaster County.
Became extinct in 1692 when it was
divided into Essex and Richmond
counties. See Essex County entry.

ORANGE COUNTY

Formed in 1734 from Spotsylvania County.

Original Records

Circuit Court Clerk
Court Records
County Court
Minute Book No. 2, 1774-89, 1 vol. (copy)
Order Books Nos. 1-2, 4, [4A], and 5, 1734-41, 1743-54, 5 vols. (copies)
Land Records
Deed Books Nos. 3, 5, 7, 9-12, and 14, 1738-44, 1741-59, 1765-68, 8 vols. (copies)
Deeds, etc., 1713-26, 1 vol. (copy)
Marriage Records and Vital Statistics
Marriage [and other] Licenses Listed in Fee Books, 1752-70, 7 pp. (copies)
Marriage Bonds and Ministers' Returns Nos. 1-16, 1775-1854, 16 vols. (copies)
Index to Marriage Bonds and Ministers' Returns, 1775-1854, 1 vol. (Ts. and copy)
Marriage Register No. 1, 1757-1867, 1 vol. (original and copy)
Military and Pension Records
Militia [or tax?] List, n.d., 1 item
Tax and Fiscal Records
Lists of Tithables, 1736-39, 1782, n.d., 16 items (copies); and, 1736-37, 1739, 1749, 1752-55 (Ts), 27 pp. (copies)
Tax Book, 1843-44, 1 vol.
Wills
Will Books Nos. 1-3 and 5, 1735-1801, 1814-21, 4 vols. (copies)
Miscellaneous Records
Miscellaneous Papers [including writs, petitions, claims, surveys, tax records, and suit papers], ca. 1735-80, 1851-53, n.d., 107 items (copies)

Microfilm Records

Circuit Court Clerk
Bonds/Commissions/Oaths
Bonds, 1735-1805, 1 reel (part)
Oaths of Office, 1879-1903, 1 reel (part)
Ordinary Licenses [Bonds], 1738-1809, 1 reel (part)
Court Records
County Court
Criminal Warrants, 1867-90, 2 reels
Judgments, 1735-1903, 258 reels
Minute Books Nos. 1-4, 1764-1806, 2 reels; and, Minutes, 1825-52, 1856-67, 4 reels
Order Books Nos. 1-8, 1734-77, 4 reels; and, Order Books [Minutes], 1801-11, 1816-24, 1852-56, 4 reels
General Indexes to Orders and Minutes Nos. 1-3, 1734-1806, 2 reels
See also Land Records.
Superior Court of Law
Judgments, 1819-31, 20 reels
Minutes, 1809-31, 1 reel (part)

Circuit Superior Court of Law and Chancery
Judgments, 1832-51, 42 reels
Minutes, 1831-39, 1841-85 (includes Circuit Court, 1852-85), 1 reel (part)
Circuit Court
Final Chancery Decrees Vols. 1-40 and 52, 1868-96, 38 reels
Judgments, 1852-99, 1901-16, 86 reels
Minutes, see Circuit Superior Court of Law and Chancery
Orange Humane Society suits, 1883-85, 2 reels
County and Superior Courts
Miscellaneous Papers (including estate vouchers and suit papers), 1724-ca.
1900, 2 reels (and 4 reels, parts)
Fiduciary Records
Executors and Administrators Bonds Vol. 88, 1827-47, 2 reels
Guardians' Accounts, 1827-52, 1 reel (part)
See also Court Records, County and Superior Court
Free Negro and Slave Records
Free Negro [registrations], ca. 1850-60, 1 reel (part)
Land Records
Deed Books Nos. 1-45 (including court records, marriage records, and vital
statistics), 1734-1865, 20 reels
Deeds Partly Proven, 1737-1878 (also Deeds and Miscellaneous Papers after
1800; and Deeds, 1800-50), 3 reels
General Indexes to Deeds Nos. 1-3, 1734-1892, 2 reels; and, General Indexes to
Deeds Vols. 1-8, 1734-1944, 5 reels
Lands Processioned, 1795-1804, 1 reel (part)
Plats, 1839-92, 1 reel (part)
Marriage Records and Vital Statistics
Birth Records, 1866-95 (Ts), 1 reel (part)
Marriage Bonds, 1775-1853, 9 reels
Marriage Licenses, 1854-1911, 12 reels
Marriage Registers Nos. 1-3, 1757-67, 1854-1938, 2 reels; and, 1784-1873, 1 reel
(part)
Index to Marriage Registers [Nos. 2-3], Males-Females, 1854-1938, 1 reel (part)
See also Land Records.
Organization Records
Gordonsville Building Association Papers, 1880, 1 reel (part)
Orange Union Agricultural Society Papers, 1847, 1 reel (part)
Road and Bridge Records
Railroad Papers, 1845-57, 1 reel (part)
[Road Papers], 1735-1851, 1 reel (part)
Tax and Fiscal Records
Tithables, 1736-82, 1 reel (part)
Wills
Will Books Nos. 1-12, 1735-1864, 6 reels; Nos. 1-15, 1735-1906, 8 reels; and,
Original Wills Vols. 1-21, 1735-1904, 33 reels
Index to Wills No. 1, 1734-1947, 1 reel
Miscellaneous Records
Inquisitions, 1735-39, 1 reel (part)
Old Lunacy Papers, ca. 1900, 1 reel (part)
Petitions, 1735-1863, 1 reel (part)
Public Buildings, Papers and Plans, 1765-1894, 1 reel (part)

PAGE COUNTY

Formed in 1831 from Rockingham and Shenandoah counties.

As of 1 July 1985 there were no original records from Page County in the Virginia State Library.

Microfilm Records

Circuit Court Clerk
  Court Records
    County Court
        Minute Books Nos. 1-6, 1831-68, 3 reels
        Index to Minute Books No. 1, 1831-1904, 1 reel (part)
    Circuit Superior Court of Law and Chancery
        Chancery Order Book No. 1, 1831-59 (includes Circuit Court, 1852-59), 1 reel (part)
        Common Law Order Book No. 1, 1831-59 (includes Circuit Court, 1852-59), 1 reel (part)
  Fiduciary Records
        Administrators' Bonds No. 1, 1850-65, 1 reel (part)
        Executors Bonds' No. 1, 1850-86, 1 reel (part)
        Guardians Bonds' Nos. 1-2, 1850-70, 1 reel (part)
  Land Records
        Complete Record [Chancery Land Causes] No. 1, 1843-56, 1 reel (part)
        County Surveyors' Book No. 1, 1831-1928, 1 reel (part)
        Deed Books A-H and J-M, 1831-67, 6 reels
        General Index to Deeds, Grantors-Grantees A-Z, 1831-52, 7 reels
  Marriage Records and Vital Statistics
        Register of Births, 1865-72, 1 reel (part)
        Register of Deaths, 1864-72, 1 reel (part)
        Registers of Marriages Nos. 1-2, 1831-1906, 1 reel (part)
  Wills
        Will Books A-H and J, 1831-66, 3 reels
        General Index to Wills, A-Z, 1831-1944, 1 reel

PATRICK COUNTY

Formed in 1790 from Henry County.

Original Records

Circuit Court Clerk
  Marriage Records and Vital Statistics
        Marriage Register, 1791-1953 (compilation), 1 vol. (original and copy)
        Index to Marriage Register, 1791-1853, 1 vol. (Ts. and copy)
  Wills
        Will Book No. 1, 1791-1823, 1 vol. (copy)

Microfilm Records

Circuit Court Clerk
  Court Records
    County Court
      Order Book O, 1791-1800, and Nos. 1-8, 1800-64, 3 reels
    Circuit Superior Court of Law and Chancery
      Chancery Order Books Nos. 1-2, 1832-75 (includes Circuit Court, 1852-75), 1 reel
  Land Records
    Deed Books Nos. 1-17, 1791-1866, 9 reels
    General Index to Deeds, Grantors-Grantees A-Z, 1791-1949, 4 reels
  Marriage Records and Vital Statistics
    Marriage Registers Nos. 1-3, 1791-1912, 1 reel
    Register of Births, 1853-96, 1 reel (part)
    Register of Deaths, 1853-70, 1 reel (part)
    Index to Births, Marriages, and Deaths, 1853-1912, 1 reel
  Military and Pension Records
    [Civil War] Muster Rolls, 1861-65, 1 reel (part)
  Wills
    Will Books Nos. 1-6, 1791-1867, 3 reels
    General Index to Wills No. 1, 1791-1949, 1 reel

PITTSYLVANIA COUNTY

Formed in 1766 from Halifax County.

Original Records

Circuit Court Clerk
  Bonds/Commissions/Oaths
    Ordinary Bonds, S-Z, ca. 1825, ca. .1 cu. ft.
  Business Records/Corporations/Partnerships
    Anthony & Grasty Ledger A, 1839, 1 vol.
    Unidentified Ledger, 1787-1828, 1 vol.
  Court Records
    County Court
      Appeals, Attachments, and Motions, 1836-54, 1 vol.
      Docket Book [issues, rules, etc.], 1767-70, 1782, 1789-1850, 1 vol.
      Executions, 1767-1845, 6.3 cu. ft.
      Executions No. 1, 1767-91, 1 vol.
      Fee Books, 1767-86, 1795-1806, 1812, 1846-48, 13 vols.; and, Fee Book (with lists of Negroes removed from Georgia and South Carolina and reported), 1779, 1 vol.
      Issue Docket, 1772-82, 1 vol.
      Minutes, 1772-77, 1824-25, 2 vols.; and, Quarterly Session Minutes, 1806-11, 3 vols.
      Petition Docket, 1797, 1 vol.
      References and New Causes, 1770-72, 1 vol.

Fiduciary Records

Executors' and Administrators' Bonds, 1834-52, ca. .35 cu. ft.; and, Administrators' Bonds, 1810, ca. .1 cu. ft.

Guardians' Bonds, 1777-1852, ca. .25 cu. ft.

Inventory of Goods sold by Rawlins and Coleman, agents, for George Townes, trustee, 1842, 1 vol.

Justices of the Peace Records

Constables' Executions, 1854-95, 1.8 cu. ft.

Land Records

Deeds, 1767-1840, ca. 11.5 cu. ft.

List of Conveyances for Auditor of Public Accounts, 1883, 1 vol.

Processioners' Book, 1796-1812, 1 vol.

Marriage Records and Vital Statistics

Marriage Bonds, 1810, 15 items

See also Miscellaneous Records, Arithmetic Book.

Military and Pension Records

Militia Bonds, 1860-61, 1 vol. (original and copy)

Proceedings of the Board of Exemptions, 1862, 1 vol.

Tax and Fiscal Records

Miscellaneous [Tax] Lists [of insolvents, numbers of people, etc.; titles vary], 1782, 1785, 10 items

Tithables, 1767-85, ca. .65 cu. ft.

Tithables, 1767-85 (and Miscellaneous Lists, 1782, [1784], 1785), 1 vol. (copy)

Wills

General Index to Wills No. 1, 1767-1949, 1 vol. (copy)

Miscellaneous Records

Arithmetic Book [contains birth records, 1792-1826], n. d., 1 vol. (Ms.)

Estrays, 1822-26, ca. .1 cu. ft.

Microfilm Records

Circuit Court Clerk

Court Records

County Court

Court Records [Orders] Nos. 1-47, 1767-1866, 16 reels

Index to Court Orders, Plaintiff-Defendants A-Z, 1767-1904, 4 reels

Judgments, 1767-1810, 66 reels; and, Miscellaneous Judgments, ca. 1765-1800, 4 reels

Fiduciary Records

Accounts Current Nos. 1-28, 1770-1866, 11 reels. See also Wills, Superior Court Will Books.

General Index to Accounts Current, Inventories, etc., No. 1, 1767-1949, 1 reel

Land Records

Deed Books Nos. 1-61 [including wills], 1767-1866, 27 reels; and, Deeds and Wills No. 11, 1780-1820, 1 reel

Index to Deeds, Grantors-Grantees A-Z, 1767-1889, 3 reels

Old Surveys Nos. 1-2, 1746-82, 1770-1829, 1 reel (part); and, Old Surveys, 1820-63, 1 reel (part)

Processioners Returns, 1812-34, 1 reel (part)

Record Book [Land Records], 1737-70, 1 reel (part)

Marriage Records and Vital Statistics

Marriage Bonds, 1767-1859, 17 reels; and, 1767-1862, 1 reel (part)
Marriage Licenses, 1861-1912, 25 reels
Marriage Register No. 2, 1861-1900, 1 reel (part)
Index to Marriage Register No. 2, 1861-1900, 1 reel (part)
Ministers' Returns, 1770-1860, 3 reels
Register of Deaths, 1853-96, 1 reel (part)
Registers of Births, 1853-96, 1 reel (part)
Index to Births, Marriages, and Deaths, 1853-96, 1 reel (part)

Military and Pension Records

[Civil War] Muster Rolls, 1861-65, 1 reel (part)

Wills

Will Books Nos. 1-2, 1814 [1820]-80, 1 reel
Superior Court Wills, Inventories, and Accounts Current Nos. 1A-2A, 1809-65, 1 reel
General Index to Wills No. 1, 1767-1948, 1 reel
See also Land Records, Deed Books.

Miscellaneous Records

Camden Parish Vestry Book, 1767-1852, 1 reel

POWHATAN COUNTY

Formed in 1777 from Cumberland County; part of Chesterfield County was added later.

Original Records

Circuit Court Clerk

Board of Supervisors Records

Allowances, 1889, ca. 50 items
Letters and Oaths, 1873-1916, ca. .15 cu. ft.
Vouchers and Accounts, 1876-1907, 1.4 cu. ft.

Bonds/Commissions/Oaths

Appeal Bonds, 1786-95, ca. .1 cu. ft.
Apprentice Bonds, 1795-1817, ca. 50 items; and, Indentures of Apprenticeship Returned, 1818, ca. .1 cu. ft.
Bail Bonds, 1794, ca. 50 items
Bonds to Stay Executions, 1810, 1816, ca. .1 cu. ft.
Circuit Court Bonds, 1903-07, ca. .1 cu. ft.; and, Copy Circuit Court Bonds, 1887-1914, ca. .15 cu. ft.
Docket of Replevin Bonds, 1783-87, 1 vol.
Execution Bonds, 1814, ca. 25 items; and, Receipts for Sale and Execution Bonds, 1816, ca. 25 items
Indemnifying Bonds, 1822, 17 items
Injunction Bonds, 1794-1822, ca. .1 cu. ft.
Lists of Persons who took the Oath of Allegiance, 1777, 9 items
Officials' Bonds, 1777-93, 1825-46, ca. 150 items; Officials' Bonds and Oaths, 1895-1913, ca. 100 items; and, Oaths of Office, 1895-96, 10 items
Ordinary Bonds, 1777-78, ca. 25 items.

Replevy Bonds, 1783-1887, .35 cu. ft.; and, Replevy and Delivery Bonds, 1791-95, ca. .1 cu. ft.

Statements of and Receipts for Costs on taking Stay Bonds under the Execution Law, 1809-14, 1 vol.

Business Records/Corporations/Partnerships

B. S. Morrison's Day Book, 1831-34, 1 vol.

Cardozo Oldner & Co. Sales Books, 1845-46, 2 vols.

[Charles C. White's?] Account Book, 1891, 1 vol.

Fortune and Harris Day Book, 1853-55, 1 vol.

[George W. Williams'] Journal, 1845-48, 1 vol.

[James M. Whitlock's?] Day Books, 1839-42, 1841-42, 2 vols.,; and James M. Whitlock's [H. W. Whitlock & Son?] Ledger, 1835-43, 1 vol.

J[oseph] B. Davis' Journals [Ledgers] Nos. [1]-3, 1831-34, 3 vols.; and, Ledger, 1822-28, 1 vol.

J[no] M. S[tratton]'s Day Book, 1853-54, 1 vol.; and, Ledger A, 1853-54, 1 vol.

[J. S. Taylor's?] Ledger, 1846-48, 1 vol.

[M. O. Lomenco's?] Accounts of Sales, 1897, 1 vol.

M. P. Atkinson and Co. Ledger, 1829-31, 1 vol.

[O. C. Swann, Jr.'s?] Cash Receipt Book, 1849-51, 1 vol.

S. B. and F. O. Drake's Blotter, 1840-45, 1 vol.

Scott, Skipwith & Co. Day Book, 1854-55, 1 vol.; and, Scott, Skipwith & Co. [Scott, Skipwith & Cardozo] Ledger, 1854-56, 1 vol.

Unidentified Account Books, 1777-82, 1890-91, 2 items

Unidentified Day Books [Ledgers; titles vary], 1804-07, 1823-31, 1838-39, 1845-46, 1852-55, 1881-1917 (includes Index to Order Book 11), 9 vols.

William C. Scott's Journal, 1843-63, 1 vol.

William E. Davis' Day Book, 1831-32, 1 vol.

Court Records

County Court

Appeals, 1805-12, 1 vol.

Chancery Issue Docket, 1830, 1 vol.

Chancery Rule Dockets, 1806-30, 2 vols.

[Clerk's Delinquent Tax Book?; and Index to Order Book 11], [1888-1904], 1 vol.

Clerk's Ledger, 1894-98, 1 vol.

[Clerk's] Statement of Taxes, 1899, 1 vol.

Common Law Rule Dockets, 1812-17, 1819-71, 4 vols.

Commonwealth v. A. S. Mayo, Clerk, suit papers, 1886, ca. .1 cu. ft.

Commonwealth v. Bell, transcripts, 1885, 4 items

Continued Motions, 1832-44, ca. 75 items

Court Papers, 1828-1900, ca. .7 cu. ft.

Criminal Prosecutions, 1807-34, 1847-56, ca. .4 cu. ft.

Dockets [New Causes], 1778-80, 1787, 1790, 4 items

Execution Dockets Nos. 3-19, 1791-1904, 18 vols.; and, No. 11, 1 vol. (Ms. copy)

Executions, 1777-1887, 12.8 cu. ft.

Fee Books, 1786-1867, 1871-94, 25 vols.

Grand Jury Presentments, 1798-1815, ca. 100 items

Issue Dockets, 1815-26, 1836-73, 1888-1923 (includes Circuit Court, 1904-23), 6 vols.

Judgments Docketed, 1843-71, ca. .1 cu. ft.

Memorandum [Minute] Books, 1789-91, 1800-02, 1814-15, 1824-28, 1834-40, 1842-47, 1851-67, 1870-1914 (includes Circuit Court, 1904-14), 16 vols.

Memorandum Book of A. S. Mayo [Clerk's Form Book, Law Entries], 1865-84, 1 vol.

Memorandum Book of Subpoenas, 1804-07, 1 vol. See also Subpoena Dockets.

Office Judgments Nos. I-III, 1786-1817, 3 vols.

Office Judgments, 1787-1871, 5.45 cu. ft.

Process Books Nos. 1-2, 1835-82, 2 vols.

Receivers Book, 1882-1900, 1 vol.

Rough Dockets, 1814-23, 1832-71, 2 vols.

Rough Rule Docket, 1799-1804, 1 vol.

Subpoena Dockets, 1813-16, 1823-24, 1832-36, 1841-42, 1845-46, 7 vols.

Subpoenas Returned in Suits on Docket, 1866-70, ca. 75 items

Suit Papers, 1795, ca. 75 items

[Warrant] Dockets, 1820-25, 1820-27, 4 vols.

Witness Attendance Books, 1807-13, 1823-74, 1883-96 [1920-22] (includes Circuit Court, 1920-22), 7 vols.

Superior Court of Law

Executions Dockets Nos. [1]-4, 1809-31, 4 vols.

Executions, 1810-1904 (includes Circuit Superior Court of Law and Chancery, 1831-51; and Circuit Court, 1852-1904), 8.2 cu. ft.

Fee Books, 1809-33 (includes Circuit Superior Court of Law and Chancery, 1831-33), 4 vols.

Issue Docket, 1816-20, 1 vol.

Judgments Confessed in the Clerk's Office, 1822-71 (includes Circuit Superior Court of Law and Chancery, 1831-51; and Circuit Court, 1852-71), ca. .25 cu. ft.; and, Judgments, etc., 1816, ca. 100 items

Rough Dockets, 1809-38 (includes Circuit Superior Court of Law and Chancery, 1831-38), 2 vols.

Rule Docket, 1820-31, 1 vol.

Subpoena Docket, 1824-25, 1 vol.

Witness Attendance Books, 1809-16, 1828-36 (includes Circuit Superior Court of Law and Chancery, 1831-36), 2 vols.

Witness Orders, 1812-59 (includes Circuit Superior Court of Law and Chancery, 1831-51, and Circuit Court, 1852-59), .45 cu. ft.

Circuit Superior Court of Law and Chancery

Chancery Issue Docket, 1832-55 (includes Circuit Court, 1852-55), 1 vol.

Chancery Rule Docket No. 1, 1831-57 (includes Circuit Court, 1852-57), 1 vol.

Common Law Rule Docket No. 2, 1843-64 (includes Circuit Court, 1852-64), 1 vol.

Execution Dockets Nos. [1]-6, 1831-60 (includes Circuit Court, 1852-60), 6 vols.

Executions, see Superior Court of Law

Fee Books, 1834-54 (includes Circuit Court, 1852-54), 4 vols. See also Superior Court of Law.

Issue Docket, 1831-43, 1 vol.

Judgments Confessed, see Superior Court of Law

Motion Docket, 1832-42, 1 vol.

Process Books Nos. 1-3, 1831-78 (includes Circuit Court, 1852-78), 3 vols.

Rough Docket, 1838-49, 1 vol. See also Superior Court of Law.

Rule Docket, 1832-43, 1 vol. See also Superior Court of Law.

Subpoena Dockets, 1831-38, 1842-45, 1850-51, 7 vols.

Witness Attendance Book, 1836-48, 1 vol. See also Superior Court of Law.

Witness Orders, see Superior Court of Law

Circuit Court

Chancery Issue Dockets, 1855-1900, 3 vols. See also Circuit Superior Court of Law and Chancery.

Chancery Rule Dockets Nos. 2-[3], 1857-1900, 2 vols. See also Circuit Superior Court of Law and Chancery.

[Clerk's] Ledger [Tax Book], 1887-1917, 1 vol.

Common Law Issue Dockets, 1864-72, 1875-1900, 2 vols.

Common Law Rule Docket No. 3, 1864-98, 1 vol. See also Circuit Superior Court of Law and Chancery.

Cost Book No. 1, 1888-1921, 1 vol.

Court Papers [unarranged], 1886-1930, 1.4 cu. ft.

Execution Dockets Nos. 7-8, 1860-1922, 2 vols. See also Circuit Superior Court of Law and Chancery.

Executions, see Superior Court of Law

Farmville and Powhatan Railroad Co. v. Powhatan Co., depositions, 1890, 8 items

Fee Book, 1871-92, 1 vol. See also Circuit Superior Court of Law and Chancery.

Index to Order Book 11, see Business and Organization Records, Unidentified Day Books

[Inventory of books located in the Clerk's office], n. d. (includes list of warrants issued, 1937, and list of available funds in Macon District, 1913-14), 1 vol.

Issue Dockets, see County Court

Judgments Confessed, see Superior Court of Law

Memorandum Books, see County Court

Nicholls v. Rudd et als. and Conquest Tie and Lumber Co., transcript, 1899, 1 vol.; and, Papers from the Office of Commissioner Guy, 1891-93, 43 items [in book backs]

Process Books, see Circuit Superior Court of Law and Chancery

Receivers Book, 1878-97, 1 vol.

Rule Docket, 1849-71, 1 vol. (includes Superior Court, 1849-51)

Witness Attendance Book, 1890-97, 1 vol. See also County Court.

Witness Orders, see Superior Court of Law

County and Superior Courts

Card Index to Court Cases, 1807-1930, ca. .5 cu. ft.

Extracts of Judgments and Decrees [including Justices'] Entered on Lien Docket, 1881-89, ca. .1 cu. ft.

Judgment Docket No. 1, 1843-84, 1 vol.

Judgments, etc. [includes deeds and fiduciary papers], 1777-1881, 17.15 cu. ft.; and, Copy Judgments, 1820, 1825-26, ca. .2 cu. ft.

Miscellaneous Papers, 1776-1919, ca. 1 cu. ft. (including fragments); Old General and Miscellaneous Papers, 1868-97, ca. .1 cu. ft.; and, Miscellaneous Bills from County Clerk's Office, 1900-10, ca. .15 cu. ft.

Old [Executions], etc., 1871-99, ca. .15 cu. ft.

Old Papers which may be called for [including deeds, bonds, road papers, and fiduciary papers], 1854-63, ca. .1 cu. ft.

Reports of Fines and Costs, 1888-91, 11 items

Circuit Court, District of Columbia, Washington County

Chancery Causes, 1848, 2 items.

Election Records

Applications of Candidates, 1895-1901, ca. .1 cu. ft.

General Registration, 1902-03, 1 vol.

Political Papers [contested elections, etc.], 1893-96, ca. 50 items

Poll Books, 1786-1830, 1885-87, 2 vols.

Poll Returns for Electors, 1798-1804, ca. 25 items

Registration Oaths, 1867, 1889, 9 items

Rolls of Registered Voters, Colored, 1897, 1 vol.; Rolls of Registered Voters, White, ca. 1890-1900, 1 vol.; and, Rolls of Registered Voters, White and Colored, 1889, 2 vols.

Fiduciary Records

Account of the Estate of G. P. Scruggs, 1843-56, 2 items; and of Edward Scott, 1856-58, 3 items

Accounts and Reports Undecided, 1822-48, ca. .1 cu. ft.

Circuit Court Register of Fiduciaries, 1850-57, 1 vol.

Claims [and accounts], 1853-92, 2 items

Cleon A. Crawford, Jr., in account with W. C. Scott, Guardian, 1853-57, 1 item

County Court Register of Fiduciaries, 1850-93, 1 vol.

Day Book or Journal for the Estate of Robert Goode, 1809-13, 1 vol.

Executors' Bonds, 1777-96, 1809-13, ca. .1 cu. ft.; and, Executors and Administrators Bonds, 1777-95, ca. 50 items

Guardians' Bonds, 1777-84, ca. 100 items

Inventories, Appraisements, and Settlements, 1777-93, ca. .1 cu. ft.

See also Wills, Inventories, Accounts, etc.; and, Court Records, County and Superior Courts, Judgments and Old Papers.

Free Negro and Slave Records

Register of Free Negroes and Mulattoes, 1820-65, 1 vol.

See also Bonds, Apprentice Bonds.

Justices of the Peace Records

Abstracts of Judgments, 1892-1906, ca. 100 items. See also Court Records, County and Superior Courts, Extracts of Judgments.

[Constable's] Fee Book, 1823-27, 1 vol.

Criminal Warrants Disposed of by Justices, 1854-57, 1876-81, ca. 150 items

Distress Warrants, Executions, and Judgments Satisfied, 1876, 1880-81, ca. 100 items

[Judgment and Execution Book], 1807-22, 1 vol.

Judgment Lien Docket, 1885-1922, 1 vol.

Justices' [Executions] Satisfied, 1882-85, ca. 100 items; Warrants Satisfied, 1833-36, ca. 25 items; and, Executions of Justices and County Court, Satisfied, 1880-1913, ca. .25 cu. ft.

Justices' Executions not Satisfied, 1875-1914, ca. 1.1 cu. ft.

Justices' Judgments [Criminal Judgments Returned to Court], 1889-1931, 1 vol.

Justices' Judgments upon which no executions have been issued, 1887-1909, ca. .1 cu. ft.

Justices' Record [Minute] Books, 1877-94, 1887-1904, 2 vols.

Justices' Reports, 1890-1913, ca. .5 cu. ft.

Old Warrants, 1869-97, ca. .3 cu. ft.

Warrants [Executions], 1834, ca. 150 items; and, Executions on Warrants Returned, 1851-75, ca. .4 cu. ft.

Warrants Satisfied and Warrants [Unsatisfied], 1874, ca. 100 items

Land Records

Deeds, 1777-96, ca. .35 cu. ft.; and, Miscellaneous Deeds Recorded, 1866-1921, 21 items

Daily Index of Receipt of Deeds for Recordation, 1902-09, 1 vol.

General Index to Deeds, n. d., 1 vol.; Reverse Index to Deeds, 1845-88, 1 vol.; and, Direct Indexes to Deeds, 1797-1900, 1845-87, 2 vols.

Deeds and Wills Partly Proved and Continued, 1810, 1822-52, ca. .35 cu. ft.

[Lists of Conveyances], 1786, 2 items

Processioner's Returns, 1804, ca. 75 items

See also Court Records, County and Superior Courts, Judgments and Old Papers.

Marriage Records and Vital Statistics

Marriage Bonds, 1777-1868, ca. 1.6 cu. ft.

Marriage Register, 1777-1853 (compilation), 1 vol. (original and copy); and, Marriage License Register, 1850-72, 1 vol.

Index to Marriage Register, 1777-1853 (compilation), 1 vol. (Ts. and copy)

Ministers' Returns, 1820-50, 1 vol.

Ministers' Returns, 1800-54, ca. .1 cu. ft.

Registers of Births and Deaths, 1857-91, 4 items; and, Reports of Births and Deaths, 1869-78, ca. .15 cu. ft.

Organization Records

Dover Lodge #28, A. F. & A. M., vouchers, 1899-1901, ca. 50 items

Powhatan [Masonic] Lodge Minutes, 1874-81, 1 vol.

Road and Bridge Records

Commissioner of Roads Settlements, 1888, ca. 100 items

Copy Orders [Road Surveyors], 1853-67, ca. 100 items

Farmville & Powhatan Railroad Co. condemnations, 1888, ca. .15 cu. ft.

Old Road Petitions, 1872-82, 11 items; and, Old Accounts [and petitions], 1903, 15 items

Road Board Book, Huguenot District, 1885-90, 1 vol.

Road Books, 1839-65, 1879-90, 2 vols.

Road Claims, 1892, ca. 100 items

Road Warrants, 1902, ca. 150 items; and, Cancelled Warrants [including County Levy], 1901, ca. .1 cu. ft.

See also Court Records, County and Superior Courts Old Papers.

School Records

Cancelled School Warrants, 1900-04, ca. .25 cu. ft.

School Funds, 1887-1900, ca. .1 cu. ft.

Tax and Fiscal Records

Applications to purchase [delinquent] lands, 1898-1922, .35 cu. ft.

Bar Room Licenses, 1878-87, ca. 75 items

Cancelled Warrants on Account, 1903, ca. .15 cu. ft.

Capitation Taxes, 1903-05, 10 items

Delinquent Land Books, 1884-1905, 4 vols.

Delinquent Land Sales, 1883-1904, 1.4 cu. ft.; and, Delinquent Land Sales to Individuals, 1889, ca. 50 items

Delinquent Lands and Insolvent Capitation and Property Tax Tickets, 1902, ca. .1 cu. ft.

Delinquent Tax Tickets, 1872, 1875-1906, ca. 2.35 cu. ft.

Insolvent Capitation and Property, 1898-99, 7 items

Interest on Warrants, 1898, 1903, ca. 125 items

Levies, 1882, 1896-98, ca. 125 items. See also Road and Bridge Records, Road Warrants.

List of Real Estate Purchased by Individuals, 1876-83, 1 vol.

Lists of Retail Merchants Licenses issued by the Treasurer, 1892-1922, ca. .1 cu. ft.; and, Lists of Retail Merchants Licenses, 1872-73, 6 items

Old Reports of Liquor License Returns, 1891-99, 6 items

Returns of Delinquent Lands, 1876, 1884-94, 1896-99, 1901-07, ca. .5 cu. ft.

Statements and Warrants paid in, 1902, ca. 150 items

Statements of Delinquent Taxes, 1894-98, ca. .1 cu. ft.

Tax Book in Debt, 1786, 1 vol.

Taxes Collected [in Macon Township], 1871, 1 vol.

[Tax Fees Received], 1884-85, 1 vol.

Tax Receipts, 1882-86, 1888-1900, ca. 200 items

Treasurer's List of Poll Taxes Paid, 1903-04, 9 items

Treasurer's Record, 1871-72, 1 vol.

Warrants, 1879-84, ca. 100 items; Warrants paid by J. A. Tilman, 1882, ca. 200 items; and Warrants and Vouchers, Settlement with Treasurer, 1885-86, ca. 200 items

See also Court Records, Circuit Court Inventory of Books.

Wills

Will Book No. 1, 1777-95, 1 vol. (copy)

Wills, 1786-94, and Miscellaneous Wills Recorded, 1864-93, ca. 25 items

Wills, Inventories, Accounts, etc., 1793-96, ca. .1 cu. ft.

General Index to Wills, 1795-1800, 1 vol.

See also Land Records, Deeds and Wills Partly Proved.

Miscellaneous Records

Account, Warrock to Mercer, 1856, 1 item

Correspondence and Accounts, 1876-77, 1903, n. d., 4 items

Estrays, 1793-1814, ca. .15 cu. ft.

[Minute] Books of the Overseers of the Poor, 1852-58, 1860-70, 2 vols.

Overseers of the Poor Allowances, 1826-32, 1 vol.

Stray Books, 1777-86, 1820-65, 2 vols.

Unidentified Index, n.d., 1 vol.

Sheriff

Execution Book, 1807-09, 1813-22, 3 vols.

Fee Book, 1803-09, 1813-14, 1 vol.

Land Tax Book, n.d., 1 booklet

Miscellaneous Papers, 1808-27, n.d., 37 items (includes correspondence, deed of trust, militia fines, sheriff's fees)

Notes and Receipts, 1804, 1818-22, n. d., 22 items

Register of stud fee, n.d., 1 booklet

Returns, 1788, 14 items

Tax Account Book 1804-05, 1 vol. (includes muster fines, 1804; accounts for sale of foodstuffs, 1806, 1812-22); Tax Account Book, 1814-15, 1 vol.

Thomas Watkins's Fee Book, n.d., 1 vol.

Microfilm Records

Circuit Court Clerk
Court Records
County Court

Order Books Nos. 1-30, 1777-1860, 13 reels

Land Records

Deed Books Nos. 1-2, 1777-1866, 10 reels

[Superior] Court Deeds and Wills No. 0, 1809-98, 1 reel (part)

General Index to Deeds, Grantors-Grantees A-Z, [1777-1920], 2 reels; and, Supplementary General Index to Deeds Nos. 1-4, Grantors-Grantees, 1921-48, 2 reels

Marriage Records and Vital Statistics

Marriage Bonds, 1777-1845, 5 reels; and, Marriage Bonds, Consents, and Certificates, 1846-68, 2 reels

Marriage Register, 1777-1853 (compilation), 1 reel (part); and, 1853-1935, 1 reel (part)

Index to Marrige Register, 1777-1853 (compilation), 1 reel (part); and, General
    Index to Marriages, 1853-1935, 1 reel (part)
Ministers' Returns, 1780-1854, 2 reels
Register of Births, 1853-71, 1 reel (part)
Register of Deaths, 1853-71, 1 reel (part)
Index to Births, Marriages, and Deaths, 1853-71, 1 reel (part)

Military and Pension Records
Powhatan Artillery Muster Roll, 1861-65, 1 reel (part)
Records, Powhatan Cavalry Troop Co. E, 4th Regt., 1861-65, 1 reel (part)

Wills
Will Books Nos. 1-16, 1777-1868, 6 reels. See also Land Records, Deeds and
    Wills.
General Index to Wills No. 1, 1777-1947, 1 reel

PRINCE EDWARD COUNTY

Formed in 1753 from Amelia County.

Original Records

Circuit Court Clerk
Bonds/Commissions/Oaths
Appeal Bonds, ca. 1795-1820, ca. .1 cu. ft
Apprentice Indentures, A-W, ca. 1800-70, ca. .15 cu. ft.
Bond Book No. 1, 1903-10, 1 vol.
General Index to Bond Books, n. d., 1 vol.
Bonds, ca. 1795-1840, ca. 100 items. See also Court Records, County and
    Superior Courts, [Miscellaneous Records]; Military and Pension Records,
    War Material; and, Tax and Fiscal Records, Tax Tickets.
Injunction Bonds, A-Z, ca. 1800-50, ca. .2 cu. ft.; and, Injunction Bonds, ca. 1790-
    1820, ca. .15 cu. ft.
Inspections' Bonds, 1798-1847, 1 vol.
Justice of the Peace Commission, 1759, 1 item
Officials' Bonds and Oaths, 1903-20, ca. .45 cu. ft.
Records of Bonds Nos. [1]-4, 1872-1904, 4 vols.
Replevy Bonds, ca. 1795-1820, ca. .1 cu. ft.
Business Records/Corporations/Partnerships
Brightwell & Davis Journal, 1859-60, 1 vol.
[Butler & Hooper?] General Merchandise Ledger, 1874-78, 1 vol.
[J. G. Cheadle's?] Tobacco Sales Book [and personal accounts], 1821-57, 1 vol.
[Tavern Account?] Book, 1876, 1 vol.
Census Records
U. S. Census, 1880, 1 vol.
Court Records
County Court
Chancery Docket, 1805-30, 1 vol. See also Land Records, Index.
Chancery Issues, 1831-56, 1 vol.
Chancery Rules, [1807?]-49, 3 vols.
Court Papers, 1773-1861, 45 cu. ft.
Docket Book, 1784-86, 1 vol.

Executions, 1788-1904 [Law Executions No. 2, 1870-1904], 12 vols.

Executions, A-Y, ca. 1800-35, and 1837-90, ca. 7.5 cu. ft.

Fee Books A-F, 1754-59, 4 vols.; and, 1760-1898, 36 vols.

Form Book, 1760, 1 vol.

Issue Dockets, 1786-94, 1817-53, 2 vols.; and, Issue and Petition Docket, 1808-17, 1 vol.

Judgment Lien Docket No. 2, 1875-1904, 1 vol.

General Index to Judgment Lien Docket, n. d., 1 vol.

Judgments, 1807-14, 1 vol.; and, Office Judgments, 1814-46, 1839-72, 5 vols.

Law and Chancery Process, 1836-96, 1 vol.

Law Issues, 1853-1904, 1 vol.

Law Rules, 1838-70, 1 vol.; and, Rules, 1870-73, 1 vol.

Memorandum Books, 1856-60, 1867-69, n. d. (undated volume includes Circuit Court, 1888), 3 vols.

Minutes, 1754-55, 1764-68, 1771-1904, 36 vols.

General Index to Minute Books, n. d., 1 vol.

Miscellaneous Papers [including lunacy papers], 1872-81, ca. 100 items

Office Judgments, 1869-[1904], ca. 100 items. See also Judgments.

Order Books Nos. 3-4 and 6 (pt. II), 1765-81, 3 vols.; and, Nos. 1, 3-5, and 10, 1754-58, 1765-81, 1791-93, 5 vols. (copies [2 copies of Nos. 4-5 and 10])

Reference and Petition Docket, 1788-93, 1 vol.

Rule Dockets, 1796-1838, 5 vols.

Summons, 1871, ca. 150 items

Witness Attendance, 1807-83, 3 vols.

District Court

Allotment of Judges and Appointment of Clerk, 1789-92, 1 vol.

Court Papers, A-Y, 1789-99 (including [Superior Court] Miscellaneous, n. d.), 4 cu. ft; and, 1804-15 (including Superior Court of Law, 1809-15), 2 cu. ft.

Docket Books, 1789-93, 1808-[31] (includes Superior Court of Law, 1809-31), 2 vols.

Executions, 1790-1809, 2 vols.

Fee Books, 1790-1831 (includes Superior Court of Law, 1809-31), 4 vols.

Form Book, n. d., 1 vol.

Records, 1789-1841 (includes Superior Court of Law 1809-31, and Circuit Superior Court of Law, 38 items Cts.)

Rules, 1790-1831 (includes Superior Court of Law, 1809-31), 2 vols.

Witness Attendance, 1790-1831 (includes Superior Court of Law, 1809-31), 2 vols.

Superior Court of Law

Court Papers, 1816-36 (includes Circuit Superior Court of Law and Chancery, 1831-36), 2 cu. ft. See also District Court, Court Papers.

Docket, see District Court

Fee Book, see District Court

Rules, see District Court

Witness Attendance, see District Court

Circuit Superior Court of Law and Chancery

Chancery Court Chancery Fees, 1844-54 (includes Circuit Court, 1852-54), 1 vol.

Chancery Docket, 1832-58 (includes Circuit Court, 1852-58), 1 vol.

Chancery Fees, 1831-43, 1 vol.

Chancery Rules, 1832-84 (includes Circuit Court, 1852-84), 1 vol.

Common Law Docket, 1832-58 (includes Circuit Court, 1852-58), 1 vol.

Common Law Executions, 1831-43, 1 vol.; and, Executions, 1843-[58] (includes Circuit Court, 1852-58), 1 vol.

Common Law Rules, 1832-67 (includes Circuit Court, 1852-67), 1 vol.

Court Papers, B and R, 1845, n. d., 1 cu. ft; and, 1836-53 (includes Circuit Court, 1852-53), 10 cu. ft. See also Superior Court of Law.

Law Fees, 1831-64 (includes Circuit Court, 1852-64), 3 vols.

Law Process, 1831-67 (includes Circuit Court, 1852-67), 2 vols.

Minutes, 1846-70 (includes Circuit Court, 1852-70), 1 vol.

Records, see Superior Court of Law

Witness Claims, 1844-1907 (includes Circuit Court, 1852-1907), 1 vol.

Circuit Court

Chancery Dockets, 1860-74, 1870-[84], 1880-88, 1885-1904, 4 vols. See also Circuit Superior Court of Law and Chancery.

Chancery Fees, 1855-70, 2 vols. See also Circuit Superior Court of Law and Chancery.

Chancery Rules, 1884-1920, 1 vol. See also Circuit Superior Court of Law and Chancery.

[Clerk's] Tax Book, 1898-1904, 1 vol.

Court Papers, 1853-55, ca. 1.5 cu. ft. See also Circuit Superior Court of Law and Chancery.

Execution Book, 1850-58, 1 vol. See also Circuit Superior Court of Law and Chancery, Common Law Executions.

Executions, 1837-1904, ca. 3.95 cu. ft.

Fee Book, 1896-1923, 1 vol.

Hubard v. Farmville Banking and Insurance Co., suit papers, ca. 1900, .25 cu. ft.

Law Docket, 1859-74, 1 vol. See also Circuit Superior Court of Law and Chancery.

Law Executions, 1881-1902, 1 vol.; and, Execution Book No. 3, 1902-27, 1 vol.

Law Fees, 1855-56, 1867-1919, 5 vols. See also Circuit Superior Court of Law and Chancery.

Law Papers, 1856-1905, 6.4 cu. ft.

Law Process, see Circuit Superior Court of Law and Chancery

[Law] Witness Claims, 1883-1907, 1 vol. See also Circuit Superior Court of Law and Chancery.

Memorandum Books, 1855-1911, 7 vols. See also County Court.

[Minutes], 1870-1908, 1 vol. See also Circuit Superior Court of Law and Chancery.

Moneys Deposited by Order of Court, 1899, 1 vol.

Rules, 1868-84, 1 vol. See also Circuit Superior Court of Law and Chancery, Common Law Rules.

Summons, 1868-72, ca. .25 cu. ft.; and, Subpoenas, n. d. [ca. 1790-1850], ca. .6 cu. ft.

Vouchers, Attendance at Court [Witnesses M-W], 1860, and Witness Attendance A-L, 1850-54, ca. .1 cu. ft.

County and Superior Courts

Cash Books, 1873-74, 1901-09, 2 vols.

[Clerk's] Tax Book, 1898-1912, 1 vol.

Decrees, Inventories, etc., 1870-86, ca. 100 items

[Miscellaneous Records] Bonds, Notes to Clerk, Plat, etc., ca. 1870-85, ca. 50 items

Unspecified Court

Judgment Liens, 1880-89, 1 vol.

Election Records

Accounts, Judges of Elections, 1876-78, n. d., ca. 25 items

Election Records [abstracts, etc.], 1795-1884, ca. 2.35 cu. ft.
List of Voters, 1860-66, 1 vol.; and, List of White Voters, 1883, 1 vol.
Poll Books, 1870-1910, ca. 6 cu. ft.
Voter Registration, Buffalo District, 1902-03, 1 vol.

Fiduciary Records

Administrators' Bonds, A-W, [ca. 1750]-1850, ca. .5 cu. ft.
[Estate] Papers, Executor of Ab. Watson, 1821, ca. 50 items
Executors' Bonds, A-Y, [ca. 1775]-1850, ca. .5 cu. ft.
Fiduciary Bonds, etc., 1903-[13], ca. .2 cu. ft.
Guardians' Accounts, 1763-1869, 4 vols.
Guardians' Accounts, A-W, [ca. 1750]-1856, ca. .5 cu. ft.
Guardians' Bonds, A-Z, ca. 1775-1850, ca. .75 cu. ft.
Inventories, A-W, ca. 1775-1855, ca. 1.25 cu. ft. See also Court Records, County and Superior Courts, Decrees.

Free Negro and Slave Records

List of Colored Persons Living together as Man and Wife, 1866, 1 item
Lists of Free Negroes, 1801-11, 1821, 1857-60, 24 items. See also Military and Pension Records, War Material.

Justice of the Peace Records

Constables' Executions, 1842-[86?], 3 vols.
Constables' Fifa's [Executions] Satisfied, 1852-74, ca. .5 cu. ft.
Justices Court Civil and Criminal Warrants, 1872-93, and Criminal Warrants, 1894-1904, ca. 1.45 cu. ft.
Justices' [Criminal] Reports, 1888-1904, ca. .8 cu. ft.
Justices' Execution Record, 1882-1931 (and Witness Attendance Record, 1908-32), 1 vol.
Justices' Judgments Returned, 1876-86, 1 vol.
Index to Judgments Returned, [1876-86], 1 vol.
List of Justices for 1861, 1 item

Land Records

Alienations, 1787-88, 1 item
Conveyances [Deeds Recorded], 1872-85, 1892-1905, 3 vols.
Deed Books Nos. 5-6, 1772-83, 2 vols. (copies)
General Indexes to Deeds Nos. 1-2, n. d., 2 vols.
Deeds, Morton to Morton [and others], 1837, 14 items
Deeds not Recorded for want of Tax and Stamp, n. d., 5 items
District Court Deeds, 1789-1809, ca. 50 items
Index to Chancery [illegible word] Land (and County Court Chancery Docket, 1872), 1 vol.
Jacob's Official Map of Prince Edward County, 1878, 1 item; and, maps and blueprints, n. d. [20th century], ca. 1 cu. ft.
[List of Deeds], Grantor B, n. d., 1 item
Original Surveys, Farmville, ca. 1800-35, 1 vol.
Plat, see Court Records, County Court [Miscellaneous Records]
Processioners' Returns, 1796-1812, 1820-24, 1831, 1843, 4 vols.
Record of Releases No. 1, 1884-1920, 1 vol.

Marriage Records and Vital Statistics

Birth and Death Records, 1853-96, 2 cu. ft.
Marriage Licenses, 1861-70, 1 vol
Marriage Register, 1850-59, 1 vol.
Register of Births, Marriages, and Deaths, [1853-79], 1 vol.

Military and Pension Records

Orders for Provisions and Clothing, 1861-65, ca. .15 cu. ft.
Payments . . . to Committee for Supplies to Soldiers, 1861-64, ca. 100 items
War Material [including bonds, list of free Negroes, etc.], 1861-65, ca. .1 cu. ft.

Organization Records
>Citizens Committee, Organization of Campaign Club Officers, etc., 1876, ca. 50 items

Road and Bridge Records
>Claims for Work on Roads, 1880, 1 vol.
>Road and Bridge Orders, 1864-69, 14 items
>Road Papers, 1873-79, ca. .2 cu. ft.

School Records
>Superintendent of School Receipts, 1886, ca. 100 items

Tax and Fiscal Records
>Capitation Tax Tickets, 1876, ca. 200 items
>Circuit Court Delinquent Lands No. 1, 1884-89, 1 vol.
>Circuit Court Delinquent Town Lots Sold, 1887-89, 1 vol.
>Commissioners' Vouchers, Property Tax, ca. 1790-1825, ca. .2 cu. ft.
>Delinquent Land, 1867, 1869, ca. .25 cu. ft.
>Delinquent Land Sold to Individuals, 1876-1925, 1 vol.
>Delinquent [Tax] Lists, 1869, 1871, 1874-78, 1880-1903, ca. 2.75 cu. ft.
>Delinquent Tax, Petition for Relief, 1886, 1 item
>Lands Purchased by the Commonwealth No. 1, 1876-1900, 1 vol; and, 1876-1912, 1 vol.
>Land Tax, 1787-1810, ca. .5 cu. ft.; and, 1839, 1859, 2 items
>License Reports, 1884-1914, ca. .35 cu. ft.
>Liquor Licenses, 1874-75, 1884-86, ca. .25 cu. ft.
>List of Persons Taxed [with a license tax], 1874-84, ca. .1 cu. ft.
>[Merchants', etc.] Licenses, ca. 1870-75, ca. .1 cu. ft.
>Merchants' Receipts, no value, 1872, ca. 100 items
>Personal Property Assessments [Interrogatories], 1866-67, 1870, ca. .5 cu. ft.
>Personal Property [Tax], ca. 1795-1830, 1859, ca. .25 cu. ft.
>Property and Land Taxes, ca. 1800-60, 3 cu. ft.
>Rent Rolls [Heads of Household; Lists of White Persons and Buildings], 1784-85, 8 items
>Taxable Property, 1782-1810, ca. 1 cu. ft.
>Tax Tickets and Bonds, 1864-65, ca. 100 items
>Tithables, 1767, 1773-75, 1777, 1783, 23 items
>Treasurer's Accounts, 1862-63, 1871, ca. .1 cu. ft.
>Treasurer's Report [Warrants], 1880, ca. 50 items
>Vouchers, Receipts, and Warrants, ca. 1875-90, ca. .35 cu. ft.

Township Records
>Buffalo Township Board Minutes, 1870-73, 1 vol.; and, Clerk's Tickets, 1872-79, 1 vol.
>Farmville Township Record of Town Board Vol. 1, 1871-93 (includes Magisterial District records, 1875-93), 1 vol.
>Lockett Township Board Minutes, 1870-71, 1 vol.; and, Record of Town Board Vol. 1, 1871-75, 1 vol.

Wills
>Will Books Nos. [1] and 3, 1754-84, 1795-1807, 2 vols. (copies)

Miscellaneous Records
>Coroners' Inquests, ca. 1810-60, ca. 75 items
>Crop Liens Nos. 1-2, 1892-1906, 2 vols.
>Docket of Bargain, Sales, and Other Conveyances, ca. 1790-1820, 1 vol.
>Estray Books, 1784-87, 1798-1851, 3 vols.
>Mechanics Lien Docket, 1889-1909, 1 vol.
>Miscellaneous Papers, 1861-74, 1892, ca. 75 items
>Miscellaneous Small Claims Against the County, 1877, ca. 25 items
>Record of Conditional Sale of Personal Property, 1891-1912, 1 vol.
>Reports of Superintendent of the Poor, 1868, 1877, ca. 100 items

Microfilm Records

Circuit Court Clerk
  Court Records
    County Court
      Order Books Nos. 1-28, 1754-1869, 12 reels
    District Court
      Order Books, 1789-1830 (includes Superior Court of Law, 1809-30), 3 reels
      Records at Large, 1789-92, 1795-98, 1 reel
    Superior Court of Law
      Orders, see District Court
    Circuit Superior Court of Law and Chancery
      Order Books, 1831-58 (includes Circuit Court, 1852-58), 1 reel
    Circuit Court
      Orders, see Circuit Superior Court of Law and Chancery
  Fiduciary Records
    Guardians' Accounts, 1764-1869, 1 reel
  Land Records
    Deed Books Nos. 1-28, 1754-1866, 12 reels
    [Superior] Court Deeds, 1789-1816, 1 reel (part)
    General Index to Deeds, Grantors-Grantees A-Z, 1754-1916, 2 reels
  Marriage Records and Vital Statistics
    Marriage Bonds, 1754-1850, 1 reel
    Marriage [Licenses], 1850-59, 1 reel (part)
    Register of Births, 1853-96, 1 reel (part)
    Index to Births, 1853-96, and to Marriage Bonds, 1754-1850, 1 reel
    Register of Marriages No. 1, 1854-1919, 1 reel (part)
    General Index to Marriages, Male-Female A-Z, 1850-1949, 1 reel
    Register of Deaths, 1853-68, 1 reel (part)
  Military and Pension Records
    Muster Roll, 1861-65, 1 reel (part)
  Wills
    Will Books Nos. 1-12, 1754-1869, 4 reels
    District Court Will Books Nos. 1-2, 1789-1829 (includes Superior Court of Law, 1809-29), 1 reel (part)
    Circuit Superior Court Will Books, 1833-99 (includes Circuit Court, 1852-99), 1 reel (part)
    General Index to Wills A-Z, 1754-1915, 1 reel

PRINCE GEORGE COUNTY

Formed in 1702 from Charles City County.

Original Records

Circuit Court Clerk
  Court Records
    County Court
      Chancery Bill, 1743, 1 item
      Execution, 1758, 1 item

Execution Book, 1801-03 (and Process Book, 1801-04), 1 vol.
Minutes, 1737-40, 1 vol. (original and copy)
Order [Warrant] to Electors, 1776, 1 item
Orders [and Returns of Executions], 1714-20, 1 vol. (original and copy)
Writ of Attachment, 1773, 1 item

County and Circuit Courts

Court Papers [fiduciary records, deeds, wills, leaf from Record Book, etc.], 1728-1884, 25 items

Justices of the Peace Records

Thomas E. Shands' Judgment Book, 1829-33, 1 vol.

Land Records

Deeds, etc, 1713-28, 1759-60, 2 vols. (originals and copies); and, Deed Book, 1787-92, 1 vol. (original and copy)
Record of Deeds, etc., 1713-28, 1787-92 (compiled indexes), 2 vols.
Deeds, 1728, 1733, 1744, 4 items; and, Records [Deeds, Wills, etc., from Record Book], 1733, 24 pp. (originals and copies)
Plat [Osborne's?], see Amelia County, Land Records
Surveyor's Platt Book, 1711-24, 1 vol. (copy)
Surveyor's Records of Robert Bolling, 1711-21, 3 items

Military and Pension Records

Record of Proceedings of Court Martials [sic], 62nd Regt., 1793-1814, 1 vol.

Tax and Fiscal Records

List of Insolvents and Removals Returned, 1810, 5 pp.

Wills

Wills, 1753-67, 5 items
See also Land Records, Deeds, etc., and Records.

Microfilm Records

Circuit Court Clerk

Court Records

County Court

Minute Book, 1737-40, 1 reel
Orders [and Returns of Executions], 1714-20, 1 reel; and, Order Book, 1811-14, 1 reel

Fiduciary Records

Inventories and Accounts, 1835-41, 1 reel

Land Records

Deeds, etc. (including wills), 1713-28, 2 reels
Deed Books, 1759-60, 1787-92, 2 reels; and, Nos. 18, 22, and 24, 1842-46, 1851-58, 2 reels
Surveyor's Platt Book, 1711-24, 1 reel
Surveyor's Records, 1794-1879, 1 reel

Marriage Records and Vital Statistics

Register of Marriages, Births, and Deaths, 1865-1904, 1 reel (part)

Military and Pension Records

Muster Roll, 1861-65, 1 reel (part)

PRINCE WILLIAM COUNTY

Formed in 1730 from Stafford
and King George counties.

Original Records

Circuit Court Clerk
Bonds/Commissions/Oaths
Bond Book, 1753-86, 1 vol. (2 copies)
Business Records/Corporations/Partnerships
Bull Run Coal & Iron Co., Warrenton, Minutes of the Board of Directors, 1891-93, 1 vol.

C. C. Jolliffe [Jolliffe & Co.] letter, 1866, 1 item

Hynson and Co. Account Book, 1884, 1 vol.
Court Records
County Court
Carrington for Mitchell v. Pleasants, suit paper, 1866, 1 item

Court Papers, 1731-1806, n. d., 14 items

Execution, 1756, 1 item

Fee Books, 1797, 1813-16, 1819-22, 1825-26, 6 vols.

Indexes to Execution Books, 1838-41, 1850, 1854, 1858, n.d., 8 vols.

Memorandum Book (and index to suspended cases), 1871-86, 1 vol.; and, Memorandum Book, 1883-97, 1 vol.

Minute Book, 1752-53, 1 vol. (2 copies)

Order Books, 1754-57, 1766-69, 3 vols. (copies); and, 1759-61, 1 vol. (original and copy)

Writ, 1752, 1 item (original and copy)
District Court
Court of Appeals Record Book, 1797-1800, 1 vol. (copy)

Records at Large, 1798-99, 1 vol.

Record of Pleadings, 1803-04, 1 vol. (original and copy)
Circuit Court
Chancery Fee Books, 1852-80, 1898-1912, 3 vols.

Chancery Rules, 1853-75, 1 vol.

Common Law Docket, 1865-73, 1 vol.

Common Law Fee Book, 1865-68, 1 vol.

Fee Books, 1865-79, 1885-1911, 5 vols.

Memorandum Books for Suits, 1866-89, 1900-07, 5 vols.

Orders and Correspondence, see Wills, Carbon Copies

Suit Papers, 1898, ca. .1 cu. ft.

Witness Book, 1897-1910, 1 vol.
County and Superior Courts
Clerk's Letter Book, 1891-99, 1 vol.
Election Records
Lists of Registered Voters, Hoadley Precinct, 1902-04, 1 vol.
Fiduciary Records
Administrator's Bond, 1751, 1 item

Administrators' Bonds, 1753-82, 1 vol.

Estate Papers, 1884, ca. 50 items
Justices of the Peace Records
Justices' Civil Judgments and Executions, 1890-1913, 1 vol.

Land Records

County Records [Deeds, etc.], 1743-1837, n. d., .25 cu. ft. (copies)

Deeds, Liber A, 1731-32, 1 vol. (original and copy); Libers B, E, M, P, and R, 1732-35, 1740-41, 1749-52, 1761-64, 1768-71, 5 vols. (copies); and, Deed Books Nos. 38-53, 1887-1904, 16 vols.

Index to Deed Book No. 40, n. d., 1 vol.; and, Daily Index of Receipts for Recordation, 1902-03, 1 vol.

Land Causes, 1789-1811, 1805-16, 1805-43, 4 vols. (copies)

List of County Landholders, 1762, 1 item (copy); and, List of Landholders, Prince William and Fairfax, who reside elsewhere, [1743-44], 1 item (copy)

Plats from Land Causes, 1789-1843, ca. .25 cu. ft. (copies)

Redemption of Land [suit papers], 1898-1913, 1 vol.

See also Wills, Carbon Copies.

Road and Bridge Records

District Road Funds Day Book, 1891-1915, 1 vol.

School Records

Library Record, Brentsville School, 1867-69, 1 vol.

Tax and Fiscal Records

Delinquent Lists [capitation, land, and personal property], 1870-86, 1898-1902, 1.4 cu. ft.

Rentals, 1752-54, 3 items (copies); and, Rent Rolls, 1737-39, 1753-54, 1760-61, 1767, 1773, 1777, 10 items (copies)

Tax Book, 1898-1909, 1 vol.

Tithables List, 1747, 1 item

Warrant [stub] Book, 1896-98, 1 vol.

Town Records

Corporation of Brentsville Minutes, 1882-91, 1 vol.

Township Records

Dumfries Township Records, 1871-75, 1 vol.

Wills

Carbon Copies of Wills, Deeds, Orders, and Correspondence, A-Z, 1894-1922, ca. .25 cu. ft.

Will books C, and G-I, 1734-44, 1778-1809, 4 vols. (copies)

Will of James Harrill, 1756, 2 items (originals and copies)

See also Land Records, County Records [Deeds, etc.].

Miscellaneous Records

Genealogical notes of Mrs. M. M. Magow, Gainesville, 1897, ca. .2 cu. ft.

[List of participants in a field day?], n. d., 3 pp.

Receipt [promissory note?], William P. Mered[ith], n. d., 1 item (fragment)

Unidentified Indexes, 1856, n. d., 2 vols.

Unidentified Photograph, Earl A. McGarry, Shenandoah Junction, W. Va., photographer, [ca. 1890], 1 item.

Microfilm Records

Circuit Court Clerk

Bonds/Commissions/Oaths

Bond Books, 1753-86, 1815-47, 1852-73, 1 reel (part)

Court Records

County Court

Minute/Order Books, 1752-57, 1759-69, 1804-06, 1812-14, 1833-50, 1853-69, 5 reels

District Court
> Order Books, 1793-99, 1804-07, 2 reels

Superior Court of Chancery
> Ended Chancery Papers, [1802]-1935 (includes Circuit Superior Court of Law and Chancery, 1831-51, and Circuit Court, 1852-1935), 50 reels

Circuit Superior Court of Law and Chancery
> Chancery Order Book No. 1, 1837-52 (includes Circuit Court, 1852), 1 reel (part)
>
> Ended Chancery Papers, <u>see</u> Superior Court of Chancery

Circuit Court
> Chancery Order Book No. 2, 1852-70, 1 reel (part). <u>See also</u> Circuit Superior Court of Law and Chancery.
>
> Ended Chancery Papers, <u>see</u> Superior Court of Chancery

Fiduciary Records
> Administrators' Bond Book, 1782-83, 1 reel

Land Records
> Deed Books A-B, D-E, I, L-M, P-R, T-Z, and Nos. 1-4, 7-13, 16, 19-21, and 23-26, 1731-35, 1738-41, 1745-46, 1748-52, 1761-71, 1774-1813, 1818-34, 1840-41, 1845-52, 1854-69, 15 reels
>
> District Court Deed Book B, 1795-99, 1 reel (part)
>
> General Index to Deeds Vol. A, 1732-99, and Vols. 1A-2, A-Z, 1799-1887, 1 reel
>
> Land Causes, 1789-1849, 2 reels
>
> Land Record, 1835-43, 1 reel (part)
>
> Plat Book, 1789-1858, 1 reel (part)

Marriage Records and Vital Statistics
> Marriage Register No. 1, 1859-1936, 1 reel (part)
>
> General Index to Marriage Register, Male-Female, 1859-1946, 1 reel (part)
>
> Register of Births, 1864-70, 1 reel (part)
>
> Register of Deaths, 1864-70, 1 reel (part)

Tax and Fiscal Records
> Tithables, 1747, 1 reel (part)

Wills
> Will Books C and G-R, 1734-44, 1778-1872, 6 reels
>
> General Index to Wills, 1734-1951, 1 reel

PRINCESS ANNE COUNTY

**Formed in 1691 from Lower Norfolk County.
It became extinct in 1963, after its
consolidation with the city of
Virginia Beach.**

For listing of records, see <u>A Preliminary Guide to Pre-1904 Municipal Records</u>, City of Virginia Beach entry.

PULASKI COUNTY

Formed in 1838 from Montgomery
and Wythe counties.

Original Records

Circuit Court Clerk
Marriage Records and Vital Statistics
Marriage Licenses, 1844-57, 8 items (copies)
See also Montgomery County Marriage Records.
Military and Pension Records
See Montgomery County Military and Pension Records

Microfilm Records

Circuit Court Clerk
Court Records
County Court
Order Books, 1839-62, 1 reel
Circuit Superior Court of Law and Chancery
Chancery Order Book No. 1, 1839-75 (includes Circuit Court, 1852-75), 1 reel
Order Book No. 1, 1839-57 (includes Circuit Court, 1852-57), 1 reel (part)
Circuit Court
Chancery Order Book, see Circuit Superior Court of Law and Chancery
Order Book No. 2, 1857-76, 1 reel (part). See also Circuit Superior Court of Law and Chancery.
Land Records
Deed Books Nos. 1-3, 1839-67, 2 reels
General Index to Deeds, Grantors-Grantees A-Z, 1839-1909, 2 reels
Marriage Records and Vital Statistics
Marriage Records, 1839-57, 1850-1902, 1 reel
Register of Births, 1853-70, 1 reel (part)
Register of Deaths, 1853-70, 1 reel (part)
Register of Marriages, 1854-1933, 1 reel
Index to Register of Births, Marriages, and Deaths, 1853-1933, 1 reel
Wills
Will Books Nos. 1-2, 1840-71, 1 reel (part)
Circuit Court Will Book No. 1, 1848-1902, 1 reel (part)
General Index to Wills, A-Z, 1839-1909, 1 reel (part)

RAPPAHANNOCK COUNTY

Formed in 1833 from Culpeper County.

Original Records

Circuit Court Clerk
Board of Supervisors Records
See Road and Bridge Records
Bonds/Commissions/Oaths
Circuit Court Record of Forfeited Forthcoming Bonds, 1897, 1899, 1 vol.
County Court Bonds of Officers, 1875-95, 1 vol.; Bond Book No. 2 [Officials'
Bonds], 1895-1932 (includes Circuit Court, 1904-32), 1 vol.; and, Bond Books
[Officials' Bonds], 1895-1919, 1896-1920, 2 vols.
Business Records/Corporations/Partnerships
Rappahannock Home Mutual Fire Insurance Co. Ledger [of values], 1896-1924,
1 vol.
Court Records
County Court
Execution Books A-D, 1833-42, 1841-52, 1849-80, 1876-1903, 4 vols.
Fee Book, 1890-1902, 1 vol.
Circuit Superior Court of Law and Chancery
Execution Books A, 1833-52, 1835-1913 (includes Circuit Court, 1852-1913),
2 vols. [both labeled A]
Circuit Court
Chancery Memorandum Book No. 2, 1886-1936, 1 vol.
Execution Books B-C, 1852-71, 1869-1917, 2 vols. See also Circuit Superior
Court of Law and Chancery.
Law Docket, 1898-1953, 1 vol.
Memorandum Books, 1858-65, 1870-1935, 2 vols.
County and Superior Courts
Register of Descriptive Lists of Persons Convicted of Felony and Other
Offences, 1883-85, 1900, 1908, 1921, 1 vol.
Election Records
General Registration [of Voters], 1902-03, 1 vol.
Lists of Voters [by precincts], 1902-60 [overlapping date ranges], 20 vols.
Proceedings of Electoral Board, 1884-1937, 1939, 1950, 1 vol.
Fiduciary Records
Bonds of Commissioners, 1875-1905, 1 vol.
Fiduciary Record, 1870-1908, 1 vol.
Land Records
Indexes to Deeds I-II, Grantor-Grantee, ca. 1833-1936, 2 vols.; and, General
Indexes to Deeds Nos. 1-2, Grantor-Grantee, 1833-1935, 1874-1935, 2 vols.
Road and Bridge Records
Records [Proceedings of the Board of Supervisors While Sitting as Road Board],
1889-96, 1 vol.
Road Book, 1836-59, 1 vol.; and, Road Book A, 1883-1900, 1 vol.
Tax and Fiscal Records
Delinquent Lands, ca. 1890-1900, 1905, 1 vol.
Delinquent Real Estate Sold for Non-payment of Taxes, 1899-1904, 1 vol.
Miscellaneous Records
Estrays, 1833-1910, 1 vol.
Mechanics Lien Record A, 1893-99, 1 vol.

Record of Persons Adjudged Insane, 1901, 1 vol.
Reservations of Titles to Personalty, 1894-1922, 1 vol.

Microfilm Records

Circuit Court Clerk
Court Records
County Court
Minute Books A-H, 1833-66, 3 reels
General Index to Minute Books No. 1, 1833-95, 1 reel
Circuit Superior Court of Law and Chancery
Chancery Order Books A-B, 1833-71 (includes Circuit Court, 1852-71), 1 reel
Minute Book, 1833-46, 1 reel
Order Books A-B, 1833-56 (includes Circuit Court, 1852-56), 2 reels
Circuit Court
Chancery Order Books, see Circuit Superior Court of Law and Chancery
Order Books, see Circuit Superior Court of Law and Chancery
Fiduciary Records
Administrators' Bonds, 1833-50, 1 reel (part)
Executors' Bonds, 1833-50, 1 reel (part)
Guardians' Bonds, 1833-50, 1 reel (part)
Land Records
Deed Books A-L, 1833-67, 6 reels
Index to Grantors, 1833-1952, 2 reels; and, Index to Grantees, 1833-52, 1 reel
Division of Lands, 1833-47, 1 reel (part)
Land Causes, 1839-49, 1 reel (part)
Marriage Records and Vital Statistics
Register of Births, 1853-70, 1 reel (part)
Register of Marriages, 1833-1939, 2 reels
Wills
Will Books A-D, 1833-66, 2 reels
[Superior Court], Wills, 1833-78, 1 reel
General Index to Wills, 1833-1952, 1 reel

RICHMOND COUNTY

Formed in 1692 from [Old] Rappahannock County.

Circuit Court Clerk
Board of Supervisors Records
Board of Supervisors Papers, 1870-71, .1 cu. ft.
Papers for Board of Supervisors, 1879-85, 25 items
Bonds/Commissions/Oaths
Bond, Ally and Brown v. Darby and others, 1818, 1 item
Bonds, 1812-18, 1904, 34 items
Executions Stay Bonds, 1810, ca. 60 items
Justices and Sherrifs Commissions, 1782-1841, .1 cu. ft.
Oaths, 1903, 50 items
Oaths and Commissions, 1882, 15 items

Official Commissions and Accounts, 1813-26, .1 cu. ft.
Refunding Bonds, 1856-58, ca. 30 items
Recognizance Bonds, 1873-75, 21 items
Stay Bonds, 1810, .1 cu. ft.
Upshaw v. Snead Bond, 1818, 3 items
See also Fiduciary Records.

Business Records/Corporations/Partnerships

Howell & Taylor Correspondence Book, 1793-95, 1 vol. (first few pages are a memorandum book)
J. P. Cauthorn's Ledger, 1837, 1 vol.
Mangorike Wharf Co. Subscription Book (includes Board of Directors' Minutes), 1872-74, 1 vol.
Martin Sisson's Account Book, 1849-51, 1 vol.
Matthew Glenn's Day Book, 1849-51, 1 vol.
P & J Journal, 1812-14, 1 vol.
R. B. Sydnor's Account Ledger, 1849-52, 1 vol.
Rodham Davis New Ledger, 1804-07, 1 vol.
Unidentified Account Journal, 1847-52, 1 vol.
Unidentified General Account Book, 1848-49, 1 vol.
William Garner's Account Book, 1806-12, 1820, 1835, 1 vol. (includes list of births and marriages)

Court Records

County Court

Applications, capias, 1889-1901, .14 cu. ft.
Carter v. Baker, suit papers, 1770, 4 items
Chancery Abatements, 1849, 12 items
Chancery Abatements Department, 1803-30, 18 items
Commonwealth Plea Book, 1891-1904, 1 vol.
Contract of Jacob Gordy and D. A. Parlaz, 1869, 25 items
Court Docket, 1850-83, 1 vol.
Court Papers, 1764, 1771-79, 1784-1814, 1818-97, 1901-03, 7.47 cu. ft.
Criminal Records, 1710-54, 1 vol.
Declarations in Slander, etc., 1818, .1 cu. ft.
Downing v. Yerby, suit papers, 1787-89, and Yerby v. Downing, suit papers, 1789-92, 25 items
Ended Papers, 1820, 1828-29, .5 cu. ft.
Execution Book, 1797-1800, 1 vol.
Executions, 1765-67, 1802-05, 1809-18, 1820-1900, 5.45 cu. ft.
Fee Books, 1828-30, 1871-93, 3 vols.
Fees to the clerk, 1876-84, .1 cu. ft.
Glascock v. Glascock, suit papers, 1754, 10 items
Grand Jury Presentments, Declarations and Bonds, Capias, 1812-15, .14 cu. ft.
Green v. White, suit papers, 1797, 25 items
Griffen v. Tarpley, suit papers, 1762, 25 items
Hamack v. Hamack, suit papers, 1818, 9 items
Issue Docket, 1838-50, 1 vol.
Judges Docket Book, Chancery, 1871-73, 1 vol.
Judgments 1810-11, 1813-14, 1817-22, 1824, 1826-30, 1833, 1837-46, 1850, 1853, 1855-73, 3.19 cu. ft.
Jury Docket, 1897-1903, 1 vol.
List of Causes Remaining on the Chancery Docket, 1814, 1 item
Memo Book, 1821-41, 1 vol.
Miscellaneous Records, 1699-1724, 1 vol.
Monthly Reference, 1825-30, 1839-54, .21 cu. ft.

Order Books, Nos. 1-15, 21, 1692-1762, 1779-94, 16 vols.

Parsell v. Saunders, and Parsell v. Redmon, Chancery suit papers, 1819, .1 cu. ft.

Presentments of Grand Jury and Capias, 1765-67, .1 cu. ft.

Register of Warrants, 1872-88, 1 vol.

Rule Books, 1750-1860, 2 vols.

Subpoenas, F. C. Bonds, Notices, etc., 1817-19, .1 cu. ft.

See also Fiduciary Records, Division of Land, County Court Chancery Papers.

Superior Court of Law

Court Papers, 1816-31, 1.11 cu. ft.

Declarations and Capias, 1824, .1 cu. ft.

Declarations and Forthcoming Bonds, 1809-10, 1820, .14 cu. ft.

Executions, 1809-28, 1.24 cu. ft.

Fee Book, 1825-27, 1 vol.

Forthcoming Bonds and Papers, 1819, .1 cu. ft.

Grand Jury Presentments, Declarations and Bonds, 1823-24, .1 cu. ft.

Judgments, 1816, 1821-23, .21 cu. ft.

Circuit Superior Court of Law and Chancery

Chancery Court Court Docket, 1831-51, 1 vol.

Chancery Executions, 1834-41, .1 cu. ft.

Chancery Fee Book, 1833-41, 1 vol.

Court Papers, 1831-39, 1842-49, 1.37 cu. ft.

Declarations and Forthcoming Bonds, 1835-38, .1 cu. ft.

Docket Book, 1831-48, 1 vol.

Docket of Motions, 1832-42, 1 vol.

Executions, 1833-41, .6 cu. ft.

Forthcoming Bonds and Papers, 1833, .1 cu. ft.

Judges Chancery Docket, 1842-53, 1 vol.

Process Book, Law, 1831-40, 1 vol.

Rough Docket, 1831-47, 3 vols.

Circuit Court

Affidavits and Original Bills in Chancery, 1892-96, .1 cu. ft.

Chancery Papers, 1875-77, .21 cu. ft.

Clerks Correspondence, 1896-1920, 1 cu. ft.

Clopton v. Clopton, suit papers, 1894-96, 22 items

Commonwealth Cases, 1850-57, 17 items

Confessions of Judgments, 1868-97, .1 cu. ft.

Court Papers, 1850-51, 1866, 1872-85, 1893, 1895-1900, 1904, .35 cu. ft.

Docket Book, 1901-19, 1 vol.

Efford et al. v. Parsons, suit papers, 1894-98, 12 items

Execution Book, 1869, 1 vol.

Executions, 1851-90, 1895-1902, .66 cu. ft.

Grand Jury List, 1901-18, 1 item

Harwood v. Haynes, suit papers, 1873, 4 items

Issue Book, Memo Book of Suits Filed, 1876-1916, 1 vol

Judgments, 1866-67, 25 items

Mangorike Wharf Company v. Owners of Steamboat Wenonah and Matilda, suit papers, 1874, 1 item

Records, 1885-1901, .1 cu. ft.

Rough Docket, 1856-66, 1 vol.

Suits Dismissed, 1852-59, .1 cu. ft.

County and Superior Court

Court Papers, 1807-58, .2 cu. ft.

Executions, 1849, .1 cu. ft.

Reports, 1816-49, .1 cu. ft.

Rules and Abatements, 1844-49, 30 items

County and Circuit Court

Commonwealth Cases, 1903, 1 item

Confessed Judgments, 1855-73, 6 items

Court Papers, 1860-76, 1900-05, .24 cu. ft.

Executions, 1903-13, 40 items

Fee Book, 1891-1919, 1 vol.

Indictments, Warrants, Executions, 1885-95, 1900-04, .1 cu. ft.

Miscellaneous Papers, 1848-73, .1 cu. ft.

Monthly Reference, 1856-58, 50 items

Witness Attendance, 1873-1913, .1 cu. ft.

See also Tax and Fiscal Records, Land Tax Book, 1826.

Superior Courts

Court Papers, 1809-21, 1824-28, .83 cu. ft.

Executions, 1828-29, .1 cu. ft.

Judgments, 1809-11, 1821-22, 1824, 1826-28, 1830, .86 cu. ft.

Narratio [Judgments], 1809-16, .1 cu. ft.

Unidentified Court

Chancery Docket, 1853-79, 1 vol.

Court Docket, 1848-1901, 1 vol.

Execution Books, 1823-31, 1834-78, 2 vols.

Fee Books, 1809-26, 1830-36, 1844-70, 6 vols.

Judges Docket, 1831-1901, 3 vols.

Law Execution, 1831-39, 1 vol.

Process Book, Chancery, 1832-78, 1 vol.

Rough Docket of Appearances, 1814-22, 1 vol.

Witness Book, 1867-68, 1 vol.

See also Business Records.

Election Records

Abstract of Voters, 1853-55, 19 items

Abstract of Votes (titles vary), 1868-97, 1903-07, .1 cu. ft.

Ballots, n.d., 50 items

Certificates of Election, 1866-74, 30 items

Congressional Poll, 1813, .1 cu. ft.

Election Returns, 1835-36, 1848-49, 1853-57, 1866, .56 cu. ft.

Poll Books, 1895-97, 1901, 15 vols.

Poll Records, 1850-61, ca. 100 items

Polls, 1827-30, .35 cu. ft.

Polls, County Officers, 1852, 1864-65, .28 cu. ft.

Polls, Statewide and Local, 1858, ca. 100 items

Polls Taken, 1735, 5 items

Polls Taken for a Member of Congress 1821, .1 cu. ft.

Register of Voters, 1853-55, .21 cu. ft.

Fiduciary Records

Accompanying vouchers-estate of Brockenbrough, 1862, 40 items

Account Book, 1724-83, 2 vols. (also includes deeds and bonds)

Account Book #3, 1778-1821, 2 vols.

Account of Sales and inventory of personal property of John C. Mitchel, 1860, 1 vol.

Account of Settlement of Estate, 1842-45, .14 cu. ft.

Accounts, 1846-49, 1852-76, 1897, .34 cu. ft.

Accounts, Account Sales, Division of Estates, 1794-96, .1 cu. ft.

Accounts and Reports Ending, 1893, .1 cu. ft.

Accounts and Reports of Divisions, 1803-06, 1816-36, .5 cu. ft.

Accounts of Daniel Thomas with Crabb and Belfield, 1854, 8 items

Accounts of Sales, 1868-79, .14 cu. ft.

Accounts, Reports of Commissioners, and Settlements, 1870-78, .1 cu. ft.

Accounts, Reports of Divisions A-L, 1868-79, .14 cu. ft.

Accounts, Reports of Divisions, Accounts of Sales, 1838-67, 1.4 cu. ft.

Accounts, Reports of Divisions, Accounts of Settlements, 1810-14, 1860-68, .28 cu. ft.

Administration and Commissioners Accounts, 1896-1907, .1 cu. ft.

Administration Bonds, 1824-50, 1 vol.

Administrators, Executors, Guardians Accounts, 1811-20, .1 cu. ft.

Bonds of Administrators, 1896-1910; Guardians' Bonds, 1893-1902, .14 cu. ft.

Bonds of Administrators, Guardians, Executors, 1883-87, .1 cu. ft.

Bonds to Alderson, 1850, .1 cu. ft.

C. C. Carters's Estate Vouchers, 1851-52, 50 items

Copy of Proceedings of Settlement of the estate of John Tayloe, 1797, 1 item

Division of Land, County Court Chancery Papers, 1802, 1811, .14 cu. ft.

Dominic Bennehan's Estate Papers, 1832, .14 cu. ft.

Estate Affairs of L. D. Warner, 1895, 1 cu. ft.

Estate of Joseph Scates, Vouchers, 1853, 40 items

Estate Sales, 1900-1904, 10 items

Estate Vouchers, 1852-59, .21 cu. ft.

Execution Bonds, 1824-49, 1 vol.

Executors' and Administrators' Accounts, Jno. F. B. Jeffries with J. T. Jeffries, 1843-49, 25 items

Executors' Bonds, 1808-23, ca. 30 items

Fiduciary Accounts, 1849-70, .1 cu. ft.

Fiduciary Circuit Court Papers, 1859-1921, .14 cu. ft.

Fiduciary Reports, 1820-21, 1849-57, .21 cu. ft.

Inventories, 1812-17, 14 items

Inventories, Appraisements, and Accounts of Sales, 1893, .1 cu. ft.

List of Payment--Clement Estate, n. d., 1 item

M. A. Jeffries' Estate Papers, 1872, 25 items

Rains' Estate Vouchers, 1847, 40 items

Receipts of Sales to Nancy Oldham, 1829, 1 item

Reports, 1828-29, .1 cu. ft.

Reports, Accounts, etc., Admitted to Record, not recorded, 1820-34, .34 cu. ft.

Reports, Accounts of Sales, 1838-39, .14 cu. ft.

Reports, Accounts of Sales, Division of Estates, 1794-96, .1 cu. ft.

Reports and Accounts of Administrators to record, not recorded, N-R & S, 1832-34, .1 cu. ft.

Reports and Division of Estates, 1797-1865, .1 cu. ft.

Reports and Divisions, etc., 1769-1880 , 1.03 cu. ft.

Reports and Divisions of Estates, Executors, 1815-60, .28 cu. ft.

Reports Lying for Exceptions, 1815-32, 1838-49, .44 cu. ft.

Reports Lying for Exceptions over 60 days, 1839-58, .1 cu. ft.

Reports of the Settlement, (Executors', Administrators', and Guardians' Accounts and Divisions), 1817-18, 1824-28, .3 cu. ft.

Vouchers, 1808-70; .74 cu. ft.

Vouchers for Brockenbrough, 1850, 23 items

Vouchers for Capt. Wm. Webb, 1856, 1 cu. ft.

Vouchers for G. B. Burch, 1846-47, 17 items

Vouchers for John Cundiffe, 1855, 18 items

Vouchers for John Jeffries, 1852-53, 32 items

Vouchers for Pursell with Peter Rice, 1854, 25 items
Vouchers for Capt. Wm. Webb, 1856, .1 cu. ft.
Vouchers, Guardians', Administrators', Trustees', 1859-64, .1 cu. ft.
See also Wills; Miscellaneous Records, Papers of Various Kinds Deposited in the
    Clerk's Office by George Saunders.

Free Negroes and Slave Records

Free Negro Register, 1825; 1853-56, 1 item
Lists of Free Negroes and Mulattoes, 1816-27, 9 items
Sundry Petitions and Lists of Free Negroes, 1853, 22 items

Justice of the Peace Records

Attachments, Warrants, Recognizances from Justice of the Peace, 1860-89,
    .14 cu. ft.
Executions (titles vary), 1807-33, 1837-99, .71 cu. ft.
Judgments Docketed, 1865-94, .14 cu. ft.
Justice's Execution Book, 1897-1922, 1 vol.
Papers in Criminal Cases from Justices Courts, 1885-1900, .1 cu. ft.
Warrants and Judgments, 1899-1914, .14 cu. ft.

Land Records

Andrew Leckie Garland's Survey Notes, 1869-1939, .9 cu. ft.
Daily Index of Deeds for Recordation, 1902-10, 1 vol.
Deed Books Nos. 1-16, 1692-1793, 15 vols.
Deeds, 1802, 1838, 1848, 1859-60, 17 items
Deeds and Bonds Recorded, 1820-38, 4 items
Deeds and Narrations, 1818, 11 items
Deeds, Bills & Fees, 1712, 2 items
Folly Neck Land Grant, 1663-68, 2 items
List of Conveyances, 1817-38, .1 cu. ft.
List of Deeds, etc., 1888, 1 item
Map of Grove Mount, Mitchell's Estate, 1843, 1 item
Map of Kenova, West Virginia, n. d., 1 item
Map of Sabine Hall, Estate of Landon Carter, 1820, 1 item
Miscellaneous Plats, 1801-08, n. d., 18 items
Plat of Brockenbrough Land, 1795, 1 item
Plat of Daniel Sunderland, 1833, 1 item
Plat of prison bounds, 1800, 1 item
Plat of Warsaw, 1846, 1 item
Processioners Reports, 1821, 1829, 2 items
Processioners Returns, 1817, 1833, .14 cu. ft.
Rental Rolls (titles vary), 1721, 1744, 1746, 1751, 1765-66, 1768, 1770, .2 cu. ft.
Turbeville Survey, n. d., 1 item
See also Fiduciary Records; Tax and Fiscal Records.

Marriage Records and Vital Statistics

Births, 1889, 1895, 2 items
Blank Marriage Certificates, n. d., .1 cu. ft.
Cohabitation Records, 1866, 3 items
Marriage Bonds, 1902-09, .14 cu. ft.
Marriage Licenses, 1841-56, 39 items
Marriage Returns, 1815-25, 1829-37, 25 items
Register of Births and Deaths, 1853-62, 9 vols.
Register of Deaths, 1876, .1 cu. ft.
See also Tax and Fiscal Records, Land Tax Book, 1826.

Military and Pension Records
Applications for Pensions, 1900, 25 items
Blank Certificates for Pensions for Widows of Confederate Soldiers, Sailors and Marines, 1900-1902, .14 cu. ft.
Certificates for Pensions, 1900, 25 items
Pension Records, 1869, 30 items

Road and Bridge Records
Claims for Roads, 1902, 30 items
List of Roads, 1839-55, 2 items
Petitions of William D. Miskell for Public Road to Totusky Creek and Public Lands at Lessins Landing, 1853, 14 items
Plat of Road from Warsaw to Rappahannock Ferry, 1873, 11 items
Reports of Commissioners to lay off Road Districts, 1875, 15 items
Writs, etc., to Surveyors of Roads, 1861-69, .14 cu. ft.

School Records
Record of School Commissioners, (includes estrays), n. d., 1 vol.
School Receipts, 1879-80, 30 items

Tax and Fiscal Records
Accounts Certified, 1899-1903, 8 items
Accounts of Taxes to be Collected, 1876-98, 1 vol.
Audited Accounts, 1871-80, .45 cu. ft.
Circuit Court Tax Book, 1898-1905, 1 vol.
County Court Tax Books, 1898-1904, 2 vols.
County Taxable Land Lists, 1813-71, .1 cu. ft.
Fines, 1895-98, 3 items
Land Tax, 1814, 1818, 1820, 1823, 1830, 1834, 1836, 1845-47, 1853-58, 1867, 1869, 1871, n. d., 8 booklets and .1 cu. ft.
Land Tax Book, 1826, 1 vol. (includes draft indexes to Deed Book, Wills Books, County and Circuit Court Order Books and Execution Books, and Vital Statistics)
Liquor Licenses and Administrators and Commissioner's Accounts, 1883-1907, 1 cu. ft.
List of Liquor Licenses, Reports of Licenses, Oyster Licenses, Oyster Inspectors Reports, 1876-1903, .21 cu. ft.
List of Land Sold for Delinquent Taxes, 1898-99, 1 vol.
List of Persons who Paid Capitation Tax, 1903-05, .1 cu. ft.
Personal and Fee Book, 1854-55, 1 booklet
Personal Property Interrogatories, 1888, 1890, .35 cu. ft.
Personal Property Tax, 1845, .1 cu. ft.
Record of Land Tax Lists and Tangible Property, 1796-1813, 1 vol.
Tax Book, 1867-68, 1 vol.
Tax Ticket, 1879, 1 item

Township Records
Check Book, Marshall Township, 1 vol.
Minutes of Stonewall Township, 1871-75, 1 vol.
Receipts, 1872, 4 items

Wills
John Tayloe's Will, 1744, 2 items
Landon Carter's Will, 1799, 1 item
Records Recorded (includes wills and inventories) 1699, 5 items
Will Books Nos. 4-7, 9, 1717-87, 1794-1822, 5 vols.
Wills and Inventories, 1699-1717, 1796-97, 2 vols. and 1 cu. ft.
Wills Not Admitted to Record, 1773, 1819, 2 items
See also Tax and Fiscal Records, Land Tax Book, 1826.

Miscellaneous Records

Duplicate account of licenses, 1862, 1 item

James E. Kilgro v. George W. Legget, suit papers, 1887, 1 vol.

List of Warrants Issued from the Auditor's Office, 1791-95, 1 vol.

Miscellaneous Papers, 1870, 1880, 1890, 1900-34, .24 cu. ft.

Miscellaneous Records, 1699-1724, 1 vol.

Overseer of the Poor Indentures, 1846-48, .1 cu. ft.

Overseer of the Poor Minute and Account Book, 1869-70, 1 vol.

Overseer of the Poor Minute Book, 1786-1842, 1 vol.

Overseer of the Poor Papers, 1837-59, .28 cu. ft.

Oyster Plat of Captain Simson, n. d., 1 item

Oyster Reports, 1878, 1897-98, 1904, .35 cu. ft.

Papers in Lunacy and Inquests, 1868-96, 27 items

Papers of Various Kinds Deposited in the Clerk's Office by George Saunders, 1838, 5.11 cu. ft.

Papers Relating to the Catching of Oysters, Bond, etc., 1860, .1 cu. ft.

Personal letters to Mrs. Nancy Oldham, 1836, .45 cu. ft.

Persons Adjudged Insane, 1903-30, 1 vol.

Proceedings for Commitments of the Insane (titles vary) 1903-1908, .1 cu. ft.

Record of the Proceedings of the Overseer of the Poor, 1843-56, 1 vol.

Register of Oyster Inspectors, 1844, 1 item

Report of Supervisor of the Poor, 1884, .14 cu. ft.

Richmond County Licenses, 1798-1812, 44 items

Superintendant of the Poor, 1884, .14 cu. ft.

Vouchers, Roads, Township Board, 1873-74, 50 items

Treasurer

License Tax Receipt Book, 1874-78, 1 vol.

Tax Tickets, 1879, 50 items

Treasurer's Reports, 1881-93, 1 vol.

Treasurer's Statement to Board of Supervisors, 1886, .1 cu. ft.

Vouchers for Disbursement of County levy turned into the Board of Supervisors, 1904, .1 cu. ft.

Microfilm Records

Circuit Court Clerk
Court Records
County Court

Chancery Court Orders, 1815-28, 1848-49, 1856, 1 reel

Criminal Trials, 1710-54, 1 reel (part)

Execution Book, 1786-97, 1 reel (part)

Order Books Nos. 1-21, 24-31, 1692-1794, 1816-71, 16 reels

Orders, 1795, 1809-10, 1814-16, 2 reels

Rule Books, 1786-1805, 1816-41, 1850-73, 2 reels

Superior Court of Law

Orders, 1809-31, 2 reels

Circuit Superior Court of Law and Chancery

Law Order Book, 1831-1840, 1 reel (part)

Order Books, 1841-50, 1 reel

Superior and Circuit Courts
> Chancery Order Book, 1831-61, 1 reel (part)

Fiduciary Records
> Account Books Nos. 1-11, 1724-1866, 9 reels
> Guardian Bonds, 1824-50, 1 reel
> See also Wills.

Land Records
> Deed Books Nos. 1-30, 1692-1869, 20 reels
> General Index to Deeds, Nos. 1, 2, 1692-1915, 1 reel
> Processioners' Book 1796-1817, 1 reel (part)
> Processioners' Returns, 1838-46, 1 reel (part)

Marriage Records and Vital Statistics
> Marriage Bonds, 1824-50, 1 reel (part)
> Register of Births, 1853-95, 1912-14, 1 reel (part)
> Register of Deaths, 1853-95, 1912-17, 1 reel (part)
> Register of Marriages, 1853-1906, 1 reel (part)

Wills
> Will Books Nos. 4-11 (titles vary), 1717-1879, 5 reels
> Wills and Inventories, 1699-1717, 1 reel
> General Index to Wills, 1699-1950, 1 reel

Miscellaneous Records
> Miscellaneous Records, 1699-1724, 1 reel
> North Farnham Parish Record, 1672-1801, 1 reel (part)
> Overseers of the Poor Records, 1786-1856, 2 reels

ROANOKE COUNTY

**Formed in 1838 from Botetourt County.
Part of Montgomery County was added later.**

Original Records

Circuit Court Clerk
Bonds/Commissions/Oaths
> Circuit Court Bond Book #3, 1904-09, 1 vol.
> Circuit Court Official and Injunction Bonds Nos. [1]-2, 1876-1903,
> 2 vols.
> County Court Bond Book II A, 1901-04, 1 vol.
> County Court Official and Fiduciary Bonds Nos. 1-2, 1875-1901, 2 vols.
> Oaths of Office, 1895-1915, .35 cu. ft

Court Records
County Court
> Common Law Form Book, ca. 1838, 1 vol.
> Commonwealth Cases Claims Allowed, 1879-94, .45 cu. ft.
> J. L. Hannah, adm. v. Mary Woodson, suit papers, 1879, 4 vols.
> Judgment and Executions, 1843-58, .35 cu. ft.

Circuit Court
> Memorandum Book, Common Law, 1857-71, 1 vol.
> Roland v. Southern Carriage Works, Receiver, suit papers, 1893-99, .35 cu.
> ft.

County and Circuit Courts
Common Law Papers, 1888-94, 5 cu. ft.
Condemnations Nos. 1-62, 1850-1906, 1 cu. ft.
Criminal and Commonwealth Cases, 1855-1908, 3 cu. ft.
Criminal Justice Warrants, Justice Executions, 1883-1940, 2 cu. ft.
Judgments, 1839-72, 2 cu. ft.
Judgments and Executions Books, 1882-1915, 9 vols.
Miscellaneous Papers, 1850-1938, 2.45 cu. ft.
Old Abstracts and General Correspondence, ca. 1884-1907, 2 cu. ft.
Sale Bills, 1863-1910, 1 cu. ft.
Unidentified Court
Chancery Forms [Judgment Docket], 1888-94, 1 vol.
Condemnation Proceedings, 1882-1934, 1 vol.
Memorandum Book, 1838-58, 1 vol.
Election Records
Abstracts of Votes, 1860-1958, 1 cu. ft.
Fiduciary Records
Appraisement Bill of Personal Estate of John T. Mills, 1893-94, 1 vol.
Cash Book #2, John T. Mills Estate, 1893, 1 vol.
Inventories and Appraisements, 1845-1946, 2 cu. ft.
Inventories, Appraisements, and Sale Bills, 1895-1957, .35 cu. ft.
Free Negro and Slave Records
Register, 1835-65, 1 vol.
Land Records
Deeds, 1838-1905, 8 cu. ft.
Deeds for School District, 1871-86, ca. 50 items.
Maps Shown in plat book, 1889-1927, .35 cu. ft.
Releases 1-9, 1884-1925, 3 cu. ft.
Road and Bridge Records
Diagram of Road Survey on Mason's Creek, 1891, 1 item.
Miscellaneous Records
Crop Lien Docket No. 1, 1893-1962, 1 vol.
Day Book No. 2, 1890-1892, 1 vol.
[General] Index to Judgment Lien Dockets, Defendants, A-Z, 1843-1971, 5 vols.
Inquests, 1838-1916, .45 cu. ft.
Insane Register, 1900-[1936], 1 cu. ft.
Ledgers, 1893, 2 vols.
Lunacy Papers, 1887-1936, 1 cu. ft.
Receipt Book for Acts of Assembly, Jury Tickets, 1897-1942, 1 vol.
Unidentified Volume, 1852, 1885-86, 1 vol.

Microfilm Records

Circuit Court Clerk
Bonds/Commissions/Oaths
See Wills
Court Records
County Court
Order Books, A-F, 1838-68, 3 reels
Superior and Circuit Courts
Order Book 1, 1838-1866, 1 reel
Fiduciary Records.
See Wills

Land Records
    Deeds Books A-G, 1838-69, 4 reels
    General Index to Land Records [Deeds], A-Z, 1838-1923, 5 reels
    Surveyors Records Nos. 1, 2, 1840-68, 1 reel
Marriage Records and Vital Statistics
    Marriage Licenses, 1838-53, 1 reel (part)
    Register of Births, 1853-85, 1 reel (part)
    Register of Deaths, 1853-81, 1 reel (part)
    Register of Marriages 1, 1853-1919, 1 reel (part)
Wills
    Circuit Court Will Book A, 1841-1869, 1 reel (part)
    Will Book 1, 1838-1903, 1 reel (part)
    General Index to Wills 1, 1838-1953, 1 reel
    Wills, Inventories, Appraisements Nos. 1-5, 1838-1870, 3 reels
    General Index to Wills, etc., A-Z, 1838-1940, 1 reel
Miscellaneous Records
    History and Wars of Roanoke County, 1671-1945, 1 reel

ROCKBRIDGE COUNTY

**Formed in 1778 from Augusta and Botetourt
counties. An additional portion of Botetourt
County was added later.**

Circuit Court Clerk
  Bonds/Commissions/Oaths
    Delivery Bonds, 1824-1827, .14 cu. ft.
    Ordinary Bonds, 1819-1850, .14 cu. ft.
  Business Records/Corporations/Partnerships
    John and Daniel Hoffman's Account Book, 1809-13, 1 vol.
    Junction Valley Turnpike Company, receipts, 1851, 31 items; receipt book, 1851,
        1 vol.; vouchers, 1850, 1852, ca. 100 items
    Ledger for Blacksmith's Shop, 1794, 1 booklet.
    North River Navigation Company Receipts, 1856-57, 30 items
    Watkins & Jones Day and Account Book, 1877, 1 vol.
  Court Records
  County Court
    Chancery Rough Docket, 1871-73, 1 vol.
    Chancery Rule Docket, 1799-1803, 1 vol.
    Common Prosecution Papers, ca. 1845-48, ca. 100 items
    Court Dockets, 1786-99, 1837-47, 1856-58, 4 vols.
    Court Papers, 1785-1830, 1886, .14 cu. ft.
    Criminal Prosecution Papers, 1826-92, .14 cu. ft.
    Docket Book, 1779-82, 1 vol.
    Fines, 1889-90, .14 cu. ft.
    Form Book, 1808, 1 vol.
    Judgments Confessed, 1820-31, 1 vol.
    List of Jurors, 1853-58, 30 items
    Loose Papers, 1778-1848, 22 items
    Memorandum Books, 1784-1801, 1821. (Volume for 1787-93 includes a form
        book) 7 vols., and .14 cu. ft.

Minute Books, 1778-79, 1785-1811, 22 vols.
Presentments, 1850-58, 30 items
Process Book, 1835, 1 vol.
Rough Docket, 1787-90, 1 vol.
Rule Dockets, 1786-99, 1821-57, 4 vols.
Rules Docket and Office Judgments, 1786-95, 1 vol.
Schedules, 1812-17, ca. 100 items
Witness Books, 1831-77, 2 vols.

County and Circuit Courts
Juror Lists, 1853-58, 30 items
Receipts, 1867-71, 40 items

Unspecified Court
Execution Docket, 1828-39, 1 vol.
Executions, 1842-44, 1877-95, 1879-82, 3 vols.
Fee Book, 1841-42, 1 vol.
Form Booklets, n. d., 3 booklets
Issue Docket, 1815-21, 1 vol.
Memorandum, 1815-26, 1852-67, 5 vols.
Minute and Form Book, 1863-65, 1 vol.
Rough Docket, 1808-15, 1868-77, 3 vols.
Witness Books, 1807-30, 1871-76, 3 vols.

Election Records
Election Tickets, 1891, 50 items
Lists of Voters, 1863, 30 items
Polls, 1802-38, 1851-58, 1860-65, 1.45 cu. ft.
Republican tickets, 1886, ca. 50 items
Senators' Poll, 1857, 1 item

Fiduciary Records
Administrator's Bonds, 1794-1810, 1815-23, 1837-39, 3 vols.
Estate Accounts of John Letcher, 1829-30, 1 item
Executors' Bonds, 1782-93, 1799-1805, 1811-15, 1835-39, 6 vols.
Guardians' Bonds, 1784-1803, 2 vols.

Free Negro and Slave Records
Certificate of a Free Negro, 1836, 1 item
Petition Against Free Negroes Remaining in Virginia, 1855, 1 item
Register of Free Negroes, 1831-50, 1 vol.

Justice of the Peace Records
Warrants and Summons, 1826-98, .9 cu. ft.

Land Records
Bedford County Processioning Records, 1814, 3 items
Deeds, 1787, 1799, 1821, 4 items
Kentucky Land Grant, 1792, 1 item
Land Books, 1820-22, 2 vols.
List of Conveyances, 1861, n.d., 1 booklet and 1 item
List of Grants, 1800, 1 item
List of Transfers, 1816, 1 item
Processioner's Lists, 1813, 1818, 2 vols.
Processioner's Reports, 1812-22, ca. .1 cu. ft.
Processioning Books, 1812-13, 1816-17, 1820-21, 6 vols.

Marriage Records and Vital Statistics
Marriage License, 1838, 1 item

Military and Pension Records
Roll of Company K, 93rd Regiment, 1861, 1 booklet

Organization Records

Democratic Executive Committee Minutes, 1901-09, 1 vol.

Road and Bridge Records

Assignment of Labor to Roads, 1846, 1850, 1854, 1862, 4 items

Road Accounts, 1841-42, 1845-46, 1849, 1855-56, 1858-59, 1862, 1867-68, n. d., 14 booklets; 1839-40, 1842-43, 1845-50, 1852-58, 1869, n. d., 1 cu. ft.

Surveyors of Road, 1870, 20 items

School Records

Reports, Orders, and Accounts of School Commissioners, 1837, 1839-42, 1.14 cu. ft.

Tax and Fiscal Records

Accounts and Sales of Delinquent Land, 1818, 1 vol.

Delinquent and Insolvent Lists, 1792-93, 1 item

Delinquent Land Lists, 1791, 1825, 10 items

Delinquent Tax Lists, 1803-30, .14 cu. ft.

Insolvent Land Lists, 1802, 1812, 2 items

Insolvent List of 1838-39, 1 item

Insolvent Personal Property for 1807, 1807-08, 2 items

Insolvent Schedules, 1820-28, 1834-38, 1840-44, 4 vols.

James McClung's Personal Property Tax, n. d., 1 vol.

List and Vouchers for Taxes, 1850-54, 40 items

List of Attornies Taxes, 1787-89, 1 vol.

List of Collection of Revenue Tax, 1787, 1 item

Personal Property Tax Books, 1846-47, n. d., 4 vols.

Rough Personal Property Tax Books, 1780, 1794, 1806, n. d., 6 booklets

See also Miscellaneous Records.

Miscellaneous Records

Certificates of Insanity, Inquisitions, 1820-49, 50 items

Frances Jenks' Papers, 1886, ca. 100 items

J. P. Moore's Receipts, ca. 1873, .35 cu. ft.

James Campbell's Exercise Book, n. d., 1 item

James W. McClung's Papers, 1779-1896, 1.45 cu. ft.

Miscellaneous Account Book, 1828, 1 booklet

Miscellaneous Accounts, 1816-17, 1828, 1847-68, ca. 100 items

Miscellaneous Accounts and Vouchers, ca. 1850-65, ca. 100 items

Miscellaneous Papers, 1784-1884, .1 cu. ft.

Miscellaneous Papers, Accounts, and Delinquents, ca. 1840-50, ca. 100 items

Microfilm Records

Circuit Court Clerk

Court Records

County Court

Minute Books, 1825-67, 6 reels

Order Books, 1778-21, 6 reels

Superior Court of Law

See Land Records (Reel 20)

Circuit Superior Court of Law and Chancery

Order Books, 1831-51, 1 reel

Circuit Court

Order Books, 1852-67, 2 reels

Unspecified Court

Index to Decided Causes, 1778-1948, 1 reel

Land Records
    Circuit Court Deed Book 1, 1809-14, 1 reel
    Deed Books A-JJ, 1778-1868, 17 reels
    General Index to Deeds Nos. 1, 2, 1778-1887, 2 reels
    Plat Record Book 1, 1787-99, 1 reel
    See also Marriage Records and Vital Statistics.
Marriage Records and Vital Statistics
    Birth Register Nos. 1, 2, 1853-96, 1 reel
    Marriage Bonds, 1778-1838, 10 reels
    Marriage Register Nos. 1, 1-A, 2, 1778-1913, 2 reels
    General Index to Marriage and Birth Registers, 1778-1918, A-Z, 1 reel
    Record of Marriages, 1782-1866, [contains Surveys, 1779-1806], 1 reel
Military and Pension Records
    Muster Roll, 1861-65, 1 reel
Wills
    Circuit Court Will Book 1, 1809-74, 1 reel
    Will Books Nos. 1-18, 1778-1868, 10 reels
    General Index to Wills, 1778-1925, 1 reel

ROCKINGHAM COUNTY

Formed in 1778 from Augusta County.

Original Records

Circuit Court Clerk
  Bonds/Commissions/Oaths
    Oaths, 1895, 20 items
    Officials' Bonds, 1860-62, 1865-66, ca. 100 items
    Officials' Commissions, 1870, 1875, ca. 50 items
    Road Surveyors' Commissions, 1855-56, 1858, .1 cu. ft.
    Surveyors of Roads Appointments, 1842-44, 1846, 1847, 1852-53, ca. 50 items
    See also Court Records, County Court Miscellaneous Papers.
  Business Records/Corporations/Partnerships
    Account Book of John Karacofe, 1841-52, 1 vol.
  Court Records
  County Court
    Attachments, 1783, 1784, 1791, .1 cu. ft.
    Chancery Papers, 1799, 1806, 1828, 1830-39, .1 cu. ft.
    Civil Suits, 1799-1820, 1822-27, 1831-55, 1861-79, 1893-1906, .52 cu. ft.
    Commonwealth Cases, 1792, 1794-1813, 1820, 1829-35, 1851-71, 1894, .4 cu.
        ft.
    Court Papers, 1765-1901, n. d., 4.1 cu. ft.
    Docket [Book], 1852-53, 2 items
    Executions, 1809, 1819, .14 cu. ft.
    Judgments, 1785, 1792, 1797, 1809-15, 1819-20, 1872, 1.7 cu. ft.
    Office Judgments, 1815, ca. 100 items
    Subpoenas, 1855, 1858-59, 1868, .175 cu. ft.
    Suit Papers, 1772-1841, 1858, 1881, .175 cu. ft.

Superior Court of Chancery
>Chancery Paper, 1816, 1 item

Circuit Court
>Judgments, 1867-68, ca. 50 items

County and District Courts
>Suit Papers, 1785-1801, 1829, ca. 50 items

County and Superior Courts
>Court Papers, 1800-08, 1817-18, 1850-52, .175 cu. ft.

County and Circuit Courts
>Civil Suits, 1856-60, n. d., ca. .1 cu. ft.
>Court Papers, 1841-86, .21 cu. ft.
>Judgments, 1853-61, ca. .1 cu. ft.
>Summons & Judgments, 1857-69, 20 items

Circuit and Superior Courts
>Court Papers, 1846-61, ca. 50 items.

Hustings Court of Town of Harrisonburg
>Court Papers, 1868-69, ca. 50 items
>Executions, 1869, ca. .1 cu. ft.

Election Records
>Abstracts of Votes, 1872-73, 1876-80, 1887-89, 1892, 1896-1901, n. d., 72 items
>Election Returns, 1874-75, 1884-85, 1901, 11 items

Fiduciary Records
>Administrators' Bonds, 1778-1815, 1 vol.
>Administrators', Executors', Guardians' Bonds, 1864-65, 27 items
>Appointments of Guardians' Administrators', and Curators', n. d., 30 items
>Curators' Bonds, 1815, 1820, 1841-86, 20 items
>Estate Inventories and Sales, 1804, 1864-65, 1874, 7 items
>Homestead Act Inventories, 1870-73, 48 items

Free Negro and Slave Records
>Free Negro Paper, 1839, 1 item
>Proof of Freedom, 1825, 2 items

Justice of the Peace Records
>Judgments, 1867, 1868, ca. 50 items
>Summons, 1870, 17 items
>Summons and Attachments, 1866-67, ca. 50 items
>Summons and Executions, 1860, 1868-69, ca. 35 items
>Warrants, 1870-79, 1881-86, 12 items
>See also County and Circuit Courts, Judgments, Summons and Judgments; Circuit and Superior Courts, Court Papers.

Land Records
>Deed Books, 1805-07, [1809]-1817, 1823-24, 1827-32, 1838-39, 1841-49, 1852-63, 23 vols.
>Deeds, 1783, 1799-1800, 1809, 1811, 1818-21, 1830-31, 1833-35, 1837, 1839, 1866, 1868, 1882, 1897, n. d., 31 items
>Divisions of Land, 1865-66, 2 items
>List of Surveys prior to 1810, 1 item
>Plats, 1853-54, 1866, 6 items
>Surveys, n. d., 20 items

Marriage Records and Vital Statistics
>Marriage license, 1870, 1 item

Military and Pension Records
>Strength Report of Company of Militia of 1st Battalion of 116th Regiment, 1843, 1 item

Road and Bridge Records

 Certificate for individuals who worked on public roads sworn before Justice of
  the Peace, 1855, . 1 cu. ft.
 County [Road] Claims, 1822, ca. 100 items
 List of Road Claims, 1857, 1859-60, 2 vols., 1 item
 Petitions for Roads, 1850-59, 1868, 1871, 1873, 1877, 1884, 1887, n. d., .1 cu. ft.
 Road and Bridge Petitions and Reports, 1874, ca. 50 items
 Road Petitions, Reports, and Allowances, 1813-99, .67 cu. ft.
 Specification for Wrought Iron Highway Bridge, n. d., 1 item
 See also Court Records, County Court, Court Papers.

School Records

 School Commissioners' Report, 1857, 4 items

Tax and Fiscal Records

 Assessments for License Tax, 1858, 20 items
 Delinquent Lands, etc., 1875-82, 1884, 1891-92, .42 cu. ft.
 Delinquent Tax List, 1851, 1853-54, 1856, 1862-65, 1868-69, 1871, 39 items
 Improper Assessments of Land, 1872, 1 item
 Joseph Craven's and H. J. Gambill's Tithables for 1819, 1 item
 Liquor Law Licenses, 1880, 3 items
 List of Delinquent Real Estate Sold, 1895-97, 6 items
 List of Free Negroes returned delinquent, 1862, 1 item
 List of Persons assessed with License Tax, 1866, 1 item
 List of Tithables in Southwest District, 1818, 2 items
 List of Tithables in Southwest District of Harrisonburg, [1819], 1 item
 List of Tithables in the Northwest District, n. d., 1 item
 Lists of Delinquent Capitation and Property Taxes, 1866-67, 3 items
 Lists of Delinquent Personal Property Taxes, 1850-52, 5 items
 Lists of Delinquent Real Estate Taxes, 1850-52, 6 items
 Lists of Land Sold for Taxes, 1845-47, 1850-1852, 25 items
 Personal Property Tax Lists, 1789-98, 1802-05, 1807, 1810-11, 1813-14, 1816-24,
  1828, 1830, 1832-33, 1836-42, 1844-45, 81 vols.
 Sheriff's Receipts for Licenses [merchants', taverns'] Paid, 1845-57, ca.
  100 items
 Tax and Delinquent Returns, 1801, 1806, 2 items
 Tithables, 1817, 1 item.

Wills

 Wills 1784, 1870, n. d., 3 items

Miscellaneous Records

 Accounts of the Commonwealth allowed by the Court, 1826-74, ca. 50 items
 Accounts of the County Agent, 1845-51, ca. 50 items
 [Clerk's] Incoming Correspondence, 1850-52, ca. 50 items
 Estrays, 1834-40, .1 cu. ft.
 Inquisitions, 1836, 1838, 1840-42, 6 items
 Letter from Reuben Shirreffs to J. S. Messerly, 1894 [Jail plans], 1 item
 Obituary of Hugh Craig, [1879], 1 item
 Overseers of the Poor, Apprenticeship Indentures, 1848-55, 16 items
 Overseers of the Poor, Court Orders to Bind Children as Apprentices, 1848-55,
  14 items
 Powers of Attorney, 1824, 1827, 1829, 4 items
 Receipts to the County Agent, 1830-50, 33 items
 Reports of the Jailor, 1884, 1894, 3 items
 Reports of the Overseers of the Poor, 1856, 1863, 3 items

Commissioner of Revenue
    Auditor's Receipt for taxes paid, 1900, 1 item
    Interrogatories to Merchants concerning Gross Sales, 1860, 1861, 20 items
Sherriff
    Lists of claims and tickets paid by Sheriff, 1854, 1855, 3 items
Treasurer
    Statement of Receipts and Disbursements made by County Treasurer, 1890, 4 items
    Statement of Warrants paid by County Treasurer, 1890, 4 items

Microfilm Records

Circuit Court Clerk
  Court Records
    County Court
      Common Law Minutes 1, 1831-45, 1 reel (part)
      Common Law Orders 2, 1842-54, 1 reel (part)
      Judgments and Orders Nos. 1-7, 1778-84, 1786-1804, 3 reels
      Minute Books Nos. 1-31, 1778-86, 1791-1834, 1836-40, 1843-65, 12 reels
    Superior and Circuit Courts
      Chancery Court Records, 1831-1865, 1 reel
  Fiduciary Records
    Administrators' Bonds, 1778-1874, 1 reel
    Executors' Bonds, 1778-1815, 1819-54, 1 reel
    Guardians' Bonds, 1779-1864, 2 reels
  Land Records
    Deed Books 0-35, 1778-1863, 20 reels
    Deed Records, etc. Nos. 1-4, 1809-53, 1 reel
    General Index to Deeds, 1778-1863, 1 reel
    General Index to Surveys, 1761-1836, 1 reel (part)
    Land Causes, 1810-48, 1 reel
    Superior Court Deed Book, 1809-52, 1 reel
    Survey Books (0-1)-B, 1750-52, 1761-75, 1780-1876 2 reels
    Survey Entry Books A-D, 1776-1880, 1 reel
  Marriage Records and Vital Statistics
    Marriage Bonds, 1778-1816, 2 reels
    Marriage Registers, 1778-1904, 1 reel
    Index to Marriage Register, Females, 1778-1939, 1 reel
    Index to Marriage Register, Males, 1778-1939, 1 reel
    Register of Births, 1862-70, 1 reel (part)
    Register of Deaths, 1862-70, 1 reel (part)
  Military and Pension Records
    Muster Roll, 1861-65, 1 reel (part)
  Wills
    Will Book A, 1803-63, 1 reel
  Miscellaneous Records
    Minute Book, Overseers of Poor, 1782-1863, 1 reel

RUSSELL COUNTY

Formed in 1786 from Washington County.

Circuit Court Clerk
Board of Supervisors Records
Papers, 1878-1922, 9 cu. ft.
Bonds/Commissions/Oaths
Bond Books, 1887-95, 1 vol.
Bonds 1872-75, 1902-05, .1 cu. ft.
Bonds and Orders, 1882-95, 39 items
Circuit Court Bond Books, 1893-94, 2 vols.
Oaths of Office and Officials' Bonds, 1849-1919, 2 cu. ft.
Record of Forfeited Forthcoming Bonds, 1895-1925, 1 vol.
Business Records
C. Wallace & Company, Account Book, 1888-89, 1 vol.
Castlewood Grocery Company, Inc., Receipt Book, Mew, Virginia, 1914, 1 vol.
Thomas Alderson and Thomas Creigh, Articles of Partnership, 1816-22, 1 vol.
Court Records
County Court
Attachments, Indictments, Appeals, 1850-96, 2 vols.
Capias, 1871-79, 1881-86, .21 cu. ft.
Chancery Process Book No. 1, 1835-81, 1 vol.
Common Law Process Books Nos. 1-2, 1835-1904, 2 vols.
Commonwealth v. Judgment For Felony, Colbert C. Musick, suit papers, 1888, 40 items
County Court Papers, 1846-1903, 18.14 cu. ft.
Execution Books Nos. [4]-8, 1822-83, 5 vols.
Fee Books, 1822-35, 1844-99, 9 vols.
Fifas, 1870-80, 1896-1904, .28 cu. ft.
Index to Common Law Order Book No. 23, 1885, 1 vol.
Index to Executions Nos. 1-2, 1831-79, 2 vols.
Index to Judgments and Decrees No. 1, 1835-53, 1 vol.
Index to Orders No. 1, 1835-53, 1 vol.
Indictments, 1894-95, 1899-1902, .21 cu. ft.
Issue Dockets at Law, 1824-76, 2 vols.
Issue Docket in Chancery, 1824-73, 1 vol.
Issues, 1857-70, 1896-1904, 2 vols.
Memorandum Books, 1865-1902, (including Board of Exemption Minutes, 1862-1864) 7 vols.
Minutes, 1871-1896, 1903 (including list of Candidates, 1903, and Warrants, 1895-99), 6 vols.
Order Book No. 1, 1786-91, 1 vol.
Receivers Record, Froley v. Smith in Chancery, 1826, 1 vol.
Rule Dockets at Law, 1824-73, 2 vols.
Summons, 1883, 50 items
Witness Books, 1853-1916, 5 vols.
Circuit Superior Court of Law and Chancery
Index to Chancery Orders and Decrees No. 1, n.d., 1 vol.
Index to Common Law Orders &c. No. 1, 1831-38, 1844-46, 1 vol.
Circuit Court
Bar and Reference Docket, Nos. 1-4, 1880-1908, 4 vols.
Chancery Executions, 1904, 10 items
Chancery Executions Nos. 1-2, 1834-1916, 2 vols.
Chancery Fee Book No. 2, 1874-93, 1 vol.

Chancery Process Book, 1897-1921, 1 vol.
Chancery Process Book [and Receipts], 1832-97, 1 vol.
Chancery Rule Dockets, 1824-73, 1890-1922, 2 vols.
Common Law Rules Nos. 1-2, 1850-1923, 2 vols.
Court Papers, 1898-1902, .1 cu. ft.
Executions, 1868-1915, 1.45 cu. ft.
General Index to Judgments No. 2, 1884-1916, 1 vol.
Indictments and Abstract of Judgments, 1880-1900, 2 cu. ft.
Issues and Causes, 1871-82, 1 vol.
Issues at Common Law No. 3, 1850-68, 1 vol.
[Law] Execution Books Nos. 2-4, 1855-1910, 3 vols.
Index to Law Execution Book No. 4, [1896-1910], 1 vol.
Law Executions, 1904, ca. 45 items
Law Fee Books Nos. 3-5, 1850-1904, 3 vols.
Memorandum Books, 1859-1909 [the volume for 1858-75 includes Witness
    Book, 1840-53], 7 vols.
Minute Books, 1877-1907, 3 vols.
Process Book No. 2, 1895-1921, 1 vol.
Reference Docket No. 1, 1873-84, 1 vol.
Settlement of Receivers of Court, 1898, 1 vol.
Witness Attendance Book, 1898-1908, 1 vol.

County and Superior Courts
Judgment Docket No. 1, 1843-74, 1 vol.

County and Circuit Court
County Fines, 1883-84, .1 cu. ft.
Court Papers, 1872-1902, .45 cu. ft.
Judgments, 1894-1917, .42 cu. ft.
Law Executions No. 9, 1881-1912, 1 vol.
Law Motions, 1873-1906, 24 cu. ft.
Register of Persons Convicted of Felonies, 1880-1956, 1 vol.

Superior and Circuit Courts
Chancery Court Docket No. 1, 1832-72, 1 vol.
Chancery Fee Books, 1831-74, 1 vol.
Chancery Rule Book No. 1, 1831-90, 1 vol.
Common Law Process Book No. 1, 1832-72, 1 vol.
Minute Book, 1848-77, 1 vol.

Unspecified Court
Common Law Executions No. 1, 1832-55, 1 vol.
Fee Book, 1826-49, 1 vol.
Order [Index] to Fee Book, n.d., 1 vol.

Election Records
Election Records, 1884-1925, .28 cu. ft.
Election Returns, 1873-80, .1 cu. ft.
General Registration of Voters, 1902-03, 1 vol.
Returns of Local Elections, 1889, 30 items
Sheriff's Return of Qualified Voters, 1904-07, 1 vol.

Fiduciary Records
Registers of Fiduciaries, 1850-1912, 2 vols.

Justice of the Peace Records
Causes Determined, 1885, 1888-89 .14 cu. ft.
Common Causes for Justice of Peace, 1889-90, .14 cu. ft.
Commonwealth Warrants, 1892, 1894, 1900, 1902-05, .35 cu. ft.
Justice of the Peace Judgment and Execution Books, 1889-1907, 5 vols.
Justice of the Peace Warrants, 1884-99, 3 cu. ft.
Justices' Criminal Record, 1888-1906, 1 vol.
Reports of Criminal Cases, 1880-90, .1 cu. ft.

Land Records
Circuit Court General Index to Deeds Nos. 1-5, 1791-1913, 4 vols.
Deeds, 1890-1911, 3 cu. ft.
Index to Deed Books, n. d., 17 vols.
Index to Land Titles No. 1, 1787-1846, 1 vol.
Land Entry Book 19, 1768-1908, 1 vol.
Lists of Conveyances, 1882-92, .2 cu. ft.
Lists of Deeds, 1894-1902, 38 items
Plat of proposed Road from the main Mocasin Road to Cumberland Gap of Fincastle Road, n. d., 1 item
Transcripts of Deeds, 1890-1905, 1 vol.

Marriage Records and Vital Statistics
Marriage Registers, 1853-1908, 2 vols.
Register of Births and Deaths, 1895, 5 items

Military and Pension Records
Confederate Pension Applications, 1903-06, 30 items

Road and Bridge Reports
Commissioner of Roads Reports, 1867-1871, 30 items
Road Book, 1850-65, 1 vol.
Road Reports, 1853-60, 40 items
Road Reports by Surveyors, 1883, 57 items.
Road Tools Furnished Overseers, 1884, 1 vol.

Tax and Fiscal Records
County Levy Papers, 1872-1878, .21 cu. ft.
Delinquent Taxes, 1898, .1 cu. ft.
Erroneous Land Tax, 1882-99, .14 cu. ft.
Forms for Taxes Received, 1882-91, .1 cu. ft.

Wills
Wills and Lists of Heirs, 1871-1912, 3 cu. ft.

Miscellaneous Records
Claims Against the Commonwealth, 1876-78, .1 cu. ft.
Commonwealth Accounts, 1872-75, .1 cu. ft.
Deeds of Personalty Nos. 1-3, 1855-1908, 3 vols.
General Index to Judgment Lien Docket, 1870-1902, n. d., 2 vols.
Judgment Lien Dockets Nos. 2-9, 1874-1909, 4 vols.
License Returns, 1872-77, .1 cu. ft.
Licenses, 1894-1904, .14 cu. ft.
List of Licenses, 1895, 1897-98, 11 items
Miscellaneous Accounts and Papers, 1881-82, .14 cu. ft.
Miscellaneous Papers, 1875, 1881-82, 1900-04, . 21 cu. ft.
Record of Physicians' Certificates, 1892-1912, 1 vol.
Reservation of Title to Personalty Nos. [1], 1890-1919, 1 vol.
Warrants for Jurors, 1857-58, 40 items

Treasurer
Treasurers' General Ledger [with Board of Supervisors] 1871-1906, 1 vol.

Microfilm Records

Circuit Court Clerk
Court Records
County Court
Chancery Order Book, 1821-30, 1 reel (part)
Law Order Books Nos. 1-15, 1786-1867, 5 reels
General Index to County Court Law Order Books, A-Z, 1786-1904, 5 reels

Superior and Circuit Courts
Chancery Order Book 1, 1831-1872, 1 reel (part)
Land Records
County Surveyors Books Nos. 1, 2, 1786-1908, 1 reel
Deed Books Nos. 1-15, 1787-1869, 7 reels
General Index to Deeds, A-Z, 1787-1917, 2 reels
Superior Court Deed Book [Land Causes], 1809-17, 1 reel
Marriage Records and Vital Statistics
General Index to Marriage Licenses, 1853-1930, 1 reel (part)
Marriage Register 2, 1853-1908, 1 reel (part)
Register of Births, 1853-66, 1 reel (part)
Register of Deaths, 1853-66, 1 reel (part)
Wills
Will Books Nos. 2-7, 1803-1866, 2 reels
General Index to Wills and Fiduciaries, 1803-1929, 1 reel

SCOTT COUNTY

Formed in 1814 from Lee, Russell, and Washington counties.

Circuit Court Clerk
Board of Supervisors Records
Board of Supervisors Warrants, 1871, 1872, 1894, ca. 100 items
Vouchers in Settlement with Board of Supervisors, 1885, 1886, .175 cu. ft.
Bonds/Commissions/Oaths
Bonds relative to repairs on public buildings & districting the county of Scott,
1829-65, .1 cu. ft.
Bonds that Judgment has been rendered on, 1893, ca. 50 items
Commissioners' and Testimonial Bonds, 1820-62, 1866-87, .175 cu. ft.
Commonwealth Bonds, 1893-99, ca. 50 items
Commonwealth Bonds, Recognizance of Witness and Certificates of
Commitment, 1892-95, .1 cu. ft.
Constable Bonds 1815-25, 1827-42, 1844-47, 1850-70, 1872-74, 1889, .1 cu. ft.
Forthcoming Bonds, 1815-21, 1851-88, 1892-1901, .175 cu. ft.
Indemnifying Bonds, 1859-67, ca. 50 items
Liquor Bonds, 1873-93, .1 cu. ft.
Ministers' Bonds, 1887-99, ca. 60 items
Miscellaneous Bonds, 1815, 1819, 1821-26, 1828, 1830-31, 1833, 1837-53, 1856,
1858, 1860-62, 1864-69, 1876-77, 1882, 1885-93, .14 cu. ft.
Oaths, 1861-65, 1870-99, .28 cu. ft.
Oaths of Officers, 1878-87, .1 cu. ft.
Officers' Commissions, ca. 1815-52, .14 cu. ft.
Officials', Administrators', etc. Bonds, ca. 1900-06, .14 cu. ft.
Officials' Bonds, 1851-79, 1881-99, .35 cu. ft.
Officials' Oaths, 1903-05, .14 cu. ft.
Ordinary Bonds, 1828-53, ca. 100 items
Physicians' Bonds, 1887-93, 14 items
Prison Bounds Bonds, 1821-47, .1 cu. ft.
Recognizance Bonds (before Justice of the Peace) 1823-87, 1891-1903, .21 cu. ft.
Replevy Bonds, 1815-41, 18 items

School Commissioners' Bonds, 1831-55, ca. 50 items
Township Officers Bonds, 1870-73, ca. 100 items
See also Miscellaneous Records; Commissioner of Revenue

Business Records/Corporations/Partnerships

E. L. Davidson & Bros. Account Book, 1889-92, 1 vol.
E. L. Davidson & Bros. Bank and Rent Book, 1889-94, 1 vol.
E. L. Davidson & Bros. Bank Book, 1889-93, 1 vol.
E. L. Davidson & Bros. Business Order Book, 1898-99, 1 vol.
E. L. Davidson & Bros. Day Book #4, 1890, 1 vol.
J. H. Midkiff Account Book, 1898-99, 1 vol.
Unidentified Bill Book, 1890-95, 1 vol.
Unidentified Day Books, 1882-1905, 1891 [#7], 1891-92, 1893-94 [#13], 6 vols.
Unidentified Journal (Hardware Lists), 1892, 1 vol.

Court Records

County Court

Arrest Warrants, 1826, ca. 60 items
Bills of Indictment and Decrees, 1823-25, .1 cu. ft.
Capias, 1824-99 (broken series), 30 items
Causes Determined, 1816-89, 1898, 12.42 cu. ft.
Chancery Causes Determined, 1815-70 (broken series), 2.45 cu. ft.
Civil Executions, 1889-1905, .80 cu. ft.
Common Law Causes Determined, 1880-1903, .91 cu. ft.
Commonwealth Capias pro fine, 1893-1905, .42 cu. ft.
Commonwealth Causes Determined, 1868, 1881-1902, .28 cu. ft.
Commonwealth Executions, ca. 1821-81, 1887-1905, 2.17 cu. ft.
Commonwealth Executions and Capias pro fine, 1881-87, .35 cu. ft.
Commonwealth Grand Jury Subpoenas, 1893-97, .1 cu. ft.
Commonwealth Rules Discharged, 1889-93, ca. 60 items
Commonwealth v. Dean, suit papers, 1879, ca. 100 items
Commonwealth v. Wayne Powers et al., suit papers, 1884, 39 items
Commonwealth Venire Facias, 1860-1929, .1 cu. ft.
County Court I. O. U. Notes, 1856-79, ca. 60 items
Execution Book, 1815-21, 1 vol.
Executions, ca. 1818-87, 4.2 cu. ft.
Fifas, Casas, ca. 1823-45, ca. 100 items
Grand Jury Subpoenas, 1888-91, .1 cu. ft.
Indictments, 1825-78 (broken series), .32 cu. ft.
Judgments, Rules and Declarations, 1817-1903, .5 cu. ft.
[A] List of Witnesses Allowances, 1867-70, 1 vol.
Lists of Veniremen, 1893-95, ca. 40 items
Memorandum and Execution Book, 1867-70, 1 vol.
Petitions, ca. 1885-1900, ca. 100 items
Process Book, 1881-88, 1 vol.
Receipts, 1867-69, ca. 35 items
Subpoenas, 1860-99 (broken series) .5 cu. ft.
Subpoenas, Jury Lists, etc. 1881-90, .28 cu. ft.

Superior Court of Law

Causes Determined, 1815, 1817, 1819-23, 1825, 1827, 1829-31, 1.23 cu. ft.
Chancery Causes Determined, 1820, ca. 100 items

Circuit Superior Court of Law and Chancery

Causes Determined, 1831-50, 1.75 cu ft.
Chancery Causes Determined, 1832-50, 1.44 cu. ft.
Commonwealth Executions, 1845, .1 cu. ft.
Orders granting writs of prohibition to which have not been perfected by
    applicants, 1843, 7 items
Presentments of the Grand Jury, 1846, ca. 50 items

Circuit Court

Abstracts of Judgments from Circuit Court, 1886, 1893-94, .1 cu. ft
Abstracts of Law Judgments, 1891, 1899, .14 cu. ft.
Cases, Fifas, Orders Filed by William H. Morison, 1860, ca. 50 items
Causes Determined, 1851-61, 1866-81, 4.52 cu. ft.
Chancery Causes Determined, 1852-98 (broken series), 3.53 cu. ft.
Chancery Causes Dismissed at Rules, 1875-81, ca. 100 items
Chancery Executions, 1858-93, .7 cu. ft.
Chancery Fee Book #5, 1900-07, 1 vol.
Chancery Fifas, 1893-98, .14 cu. ft.
Chancery Suit Papers, ca. 1870-1941, 1.75 cu. ft.
Claims, 1856-60, ca. 40 items
Credits certified from Circuit Court, 1891, 1 item
Criminal Cases, 1890-1913, .245 cu. ft.
Decree, 1899, 1 item
Ejectment Cases Determined, 1873, 8 items
Executions, 1874-93, 1897-1905, 1.37 cu. ft.
Fifas, 1881-85, 1893-1905, .42 cu. ft.
Judgments, Executions, Writs of Possession, 1893-1920, .42 cu. ft.
Lists of Judgments, 1892-1902, 22 items
Process Book, 1887-95, 1 vol.
Record of Witnesses Attendance, 1841-66, 1 vol.
Samuel Field's Papers, 1889, ca. 40 items
Suit Papers, 1894-97, .1 cu. ft.
William C. Fugate v. U. Fugate, suit papers, 1874, .14 cu. ft.
Writs of Possession, 1881-87, 19 items

Corporation Court of Bristol

Depositions, 1901, .25 cu. ft.

Superior Court of Law and Circuit Superior Court of Law and Chancery

Causes Determined, 1829-35, 1845-58, ca. 100 items
Executions, ca. 1821-45, .56 cu. ft.

County and Superior Courts

Bills in Chancery, 1833-40, 1843-44, 1871-73, .1 cu. ft.
Subpoenas, 1825-1831, 1839-40, 1842, 1844, ca. 40 items

County and Circuit Courts

Commonwealth Causes Determined, 1892-1910, ca. 100 items
Court Orders, 1860, 1869-70, ca. 50 items
Miscellaneous Papers (including marriage bonds), 1849-1900, .41 cu. ft.

Circuit and Superior Courts

Commonwealth Executions, 1845-70, ca. 100 items
Executions, 1845-74, .455 cu. ft.

Unspecified Court

Account Book of Moneys Received and Spent in Chancery Cases, 1893-1909,
    1 vol.
Chancery Causes Determined, 1825, ca. 50 items
Chancery Causes partly burned up by fire, 1885, ca. 100 items
Execution Books, 1826-29, 1876-90, 2 vols.
Final Decrees, 1832, 1866-67, 1870-71, 26 items
Jackson v. Hayes, [Account of lumber brought and sold for 1890], 1897,
    1 vol.
Lists of Sales on Executions, ca. 1831-41, ca. 100 items
Memorandum Book, 1897-1909, 1 vol.
[Unidentified Chancery Docket Book], 1859-68, 1 vol.
W. E. Taylor Case, 1904, .42 cu. ft.

Election Records
　　Abstract of Votes, 1871-76, .1 cu. ft.
　　Ballots, 1884, 1891-92, .4 cu. ft.
　　Campaign Contribution and Expense Reports, 1903, ca. 60 items
　　Certificates of Candidates, 1899, ca. 75 items
　　Certificates of Voter Registration, 1904, ca. 75 items
　　Commissioners' Certificates of Elections, 1887, 1889, 10 items
　　Democratic Ballots, [1846], ca. 100 items
　　Lists of All Persons who paid State Poll Tax, 1903-07, 2 booklets
　　Notices of Candidacy, 1903, 23 items
　　Poll Books, 1889-93, 1898, n. d., .6 cu. ft.
　　Writs, Certificates, Elections of Overseers of Poor, 1824-48, .1 cu. ft.

Fiduciary Records
　　Accounts Filed with James Fullen Schedule at suit of Fletcher et als., 1817, .1 cu. ft.
　　Administrators' Accounts, 1899-1900, 2 items
　　Administrators' and Guardians' Bonds, 1904-33, .42 cu. ft.
　　Administrators', Executors', Curators' Bonds, 1815-40, 1845-57, 1860, 1862-66, 1881-99, .42 cu. ft. See also Bonds/Commissions/Oaths, Officials', Administrators', etc. Bonds.
　　Appraisements, 1858-69, 29 items
　　Commissioner's Report on Fiduciaries Bonds, 1887, ca. 50 items
　　Commissioner's Reports on Estates, 1893-1903, .21 cu. ft.
　　Estate Settlements, ca. 1860-1870, .175 cu. ft.
　　Fiduciary Accounts, 1860-64, 15 items
　　Fiduciary Settlements, (Do-W), [1868] 1872-1935, 5 cu. ft.
　　Guardians' Accounts, 1863-70, .1 cu. ft.
　　Guardians' Bonds, 1833-73, 1881-87, 1893-99, .2 cu. ft.
　　Papers relating to estate of John McKinney, deceased, 1833, ca. 100 items
　　Record of Personal Representatives, Wills, etc., #1, 1870-95, 1 vol.
　　Sale Bills, 1878-1915, .1 cu. ft.
　　Settlements, 1859-60, 1862, 1864, 1866-71, .14 cu. ft.
　　See also Bonds/Commissions/Oaths; Wills; Miscellaneous Records.

Justice of the Peace Records
　　Attachments, 1818-61, .14 cu. ft.
　　Bench Warrants, 1885-90, ca. 40 items
　　Civil Executions, 1893-99, ca. 50 items
　　Civil Warrants, 1869-1917, ca. 50 items
　　Civil Warrants Returned, 1899, ca. 30 items
　　Civil Warrants returned from Justice of the Peace, 1887-1917, .21 cu. ft.
　　Commonwealth Warrants returned from Justices of the Peace, 1880-1923, (broken series) .21 cu. ft.
　　Executions Granted by Magistrates, 1821-71, 1.05 cu. ft.
　　Fines imposed out of Court, 1832, ca. 50 items
　　Justice Certificates, 1893, ca. 40 items
　　Reports of Criminal Cases, 1888-89, 10 items
　　Warrants, 1893-1918, .1 cu. ft.

Land Records
　　Deeds, 1817-49, 5.85 cu. ft.
　　Land Grants and Surveys, 1888-93, 7 items
　　List of Grants from Land Office, 1893-99, 6 items
　　Miscellaneous Copies of Deeds and Petitions, 1893, ca. 50 items
　　Patents, 1796, 1798, 2 items
　　Plats, 1888, 8 items

Reports and Plats of Partitions Extracted from files, ca. 1868-90, 25 items
Reports of Surveyors and Entries of Land, ca. 1815-60, ca. 50 items
See also Miscellaneous Records.

Marriage Records and Vital Statistics

Marriage Records, 1815-1844, 1853-94, 3 vols.
Register of Births, 1890, 1892, 1894, 8 items
Register of Deaths, 1892, 1894, 4 items
See also County and Circuit Courts, Miscellaneous Papers.

Military and Pension Records

Delinquent Returns, 124th Regiment, 1820-41, .15 cu. ft.
Militia List, 1855, 1 item
Regimental Reports of military officers, 1849-50, ca. 40 items

Organization Records

Day Book, Mendota Exchange of the Farmers' Alliance, 1890-92, 1 vol.

Road and Bridge Records

DeKalb Road Warrants, 1887-90, .1 cu. ft.
Overseers of Roads and Road Reports, 1815, 1818, 1820, 1823, 1872, 1879, 1893, 20 items
Report of Commissioners Laying off County into Road Precincts, 1870, ca. 50 items
Road Accounts, 1898-1908, .14 cu. ft.
Road Boards, Capias Pro fine, 1893-99, 25 items
Road Book, 1888-95, 1 vol.
Road Commissioners' Reports, 1892-93, .1 cu. ft.
Road Fund Ledger, 1896-1900, 1 vol.
Road Levy, 1898, ca. 100 items
Road Map of Road from Pattonville to Fairview and C. & O. R. R. Maps, 4 items
Road Petitions, 1815, 1868-69, 1871, 1875, 1877, 6 items
Road Reports, 1865-1903, .45 cu. ft.
Road Reports and Petitions, 1892, 1893, ca. 100 items
Road Settlements, 1900, 1 item
Road Warrants, 1886-1903, .42 cu. ft.
Road Warrants Booked, 1886-87, .14 cu. ft.
Writs of Ad quod damnum and Inquisitions for Mills and Roads, 1818-60, ca. 100 items
See also Miscellaneous Records, Inquests and Dead Bodies, Ferry Bond, Turnpike, and Road Papers.

School Records

Arrearage Grand Staff, County, and District School Warrants, 1894-1896, 1898, 1899, .28 cu. ft.
Arrearage County and District School Fund, 1896-97, ca. 100 items
County School Warrants, 1886-88, .245 cu. ft.
Grand Staff [School] Warrants, 1886, ca. 50 items
School Commissioners' Reports, 1821-42, 1847-59, .1 cu. ft.
School Reports, 1898-99, .1 cu. ft.
School Statements, 1880-1883, 4 items
State School Settlement, 1889, ca. 100 items
Vouchers, State, County, District School Fund, 1883, ca. 40 items

Tax and Fiscal Records

Account of County Levy #1, 1891-95, 1 vol.
August Levy, 1870, 20 items
County Levy, 1860, ca. 40 items
District Pay Sheets, 1892, 1897, 9 items
Estillville District Road levy exonerated, 1886, ca. 100 items

Land [Tax] Book, 1821, 1 vol.

Land [Tax] Book, North District, 1822, 1 vol.

Receipts for Private Entertainment Tax, 1823-34, ca. 75 items

Records of all Taxes Belonging to Commonwealth of Virginia Collected, 1898-1909, 1 vol.

Statements of Various Classes of Taxation, 1891, 1893, 2 items

Tax Tickets, 1887, 1893, .1 cu. ft.

Tax Tickets Returned Not Found, 1886, ca. 50 items

Taxes Due by District and Type of Tax, 1883, 1885, 1890, .14 cu. ft.

Vouchers for settlement of County Levy, 1892-94, 1896, .42 cu. ft.

See also Fiduciary; School Records; Commissioner of Revenue; Treasurer.

Wills

Wills and Settlements of Estates, 1845-52 [1868], 2 cu. ft.

Miscellaneous Records

Accounts accompanying W. H. Fisher's Schedule at suit of Wolf et. al., 1825, 37 items

Accounts filed with John Fullen, 1820, ca. 75 items

Articles of Agreement, 1830-52, ca. 50 items

Bayard Pendleton Letters, 1904, 5 items

Bills presented to Court, 1861, ca. 40 items

Certificates of Estray, 1815-46, 1863, .1 cu. ft.

Claims allowed, 1820-38, 1841-56, 1858, 1860, 1864, 1868-70, 1880-86, .735 cu. ft.

County Claims, 1870, 1883, 1890-91, .28 cu. ft.

County Warrants and Claims in Settlement, 1887, .1 cu. ft.

Court Claims, 1871-75, ca. 60 items.

Indentures Binding Out People (Overseer of the Poor), 1827-71, .1 cu. ft.

Inquests on Dead Bodies, Ferry Bond, Turnpike and Road Papers, 1852, ca. 35 items

Interrogatories by Commissioners, ca. 1857-1869, .14 cu. ft.

Jury allowances, 1887-93, .14 cu. ft.

List of Claims Against the State Sent to the Auditor, 1899, 1 item

Lunacy Papers, 1901-02, .16 cu. ft.

Lunacy Warrants, 1889-1900, .125 cu. ft.

Miscellaneous County and Court Papers, 1858-86, .63 cu. ft.

Papers relating to sales of Delinquent and Forfeited Lands, 1840-50, ca. 35 items

Pardons granted by Governor, 1898-1906, 19 items

Poor House Warrants Booked, 1887, 6 items

Promiscuous Papers Found, 1875, .14 cu. ft.

Receipts upon which Licenses have been granted, 1838-53, ca. 100 items

Reports of Overseers of Poor, 1848, ca. 60 items

Reports of Superintendent of Poor Farm, 1872, 1920-21, ca. 35 items

Schedule of Insolvent Debtors, 1847-49, ca. 75 items

Scott County Accounts, 1866, ca. 100 items

Scott County Notes, 1848, 1851, 1853-54, 1857-62, 1867, 1869, 1871, 1873, 1877, 1879, ca. 35 items

Sundry Claims, 1859, ca. 50 items

Unidentified Accounts, 1892, .1 cu. ft.

Warrants, 1861, 1872, 1876-77, 1879, ca. 35 items

Witness and Juror Pay Warrants, 1867-87, .28 cu. ft.

Commissioner of Revenue

Erroneous Assessment of Land, 1886, 28 items

Improper Assessment of Land, 1876, 1 item

Insolvent License Report, 1877, 1 item

License Reports, 1879-84, 1893-1901, .14 cu. ft.

License Returns, 1884-85, .1 cu. ft.

Liquor License Reports [and Bonds], 1891, 41 items

Lists of Licenses, 1887, 1889, 9 items

Reports, Accounts, Certificates of Oaths of Commissioner of the Revenue, 1824-52, ca. 50 items

Schedules of Insolvent Debtors, 1820-24, 1826-48, .19 cu. ft.

State Personal Property Interrogatories, 1871-97 (broken series), 4 cu. ft.

See also Circuit Court Clerk, Tax and Fiscal Records; Treasurer.

Sheriff

Settlements with Sheriff in relation to County Funds, 1821-67, ca. 100 items

Sheriff's Reports, 1896-98, 27 items

Treasurer

Capitation and Property, County Purposes, 1872, 7 items

Claims sent to Auditor, 1893, 17 items

Delinquent and Improper Assessment of Lands, 1901-03, .2 cu. ft.

Delinquent Capitation and Property Tax Lists 1870, 1884-91, 1898-99, .6 cu. ft.

Delinquent Capitation, Land, and School Tax Lists, 1870-71, 15 items

Delinquent Land and Capitation Taxes, 1870-71, 1891, .14 cu. ft.

Delinquent Land County Purposes, 1870-72, 4 items

Delinquent Lands Lists, 1872, 1887, 1889, 1891-1900, 1904, .38 cu. ft.

Delinquent Lands sold to Commonwealth, 1885-99, 1901, .14 cu. ft.

Delinquent Returns for School Levy, 1872-73, 1878, 8 items

Delinquent Tax Tickets, 1890-1893, 1895, 1898, 1903, .45 cu. ft.

Insolvent and Delinquent Capitation and Property Lists, 1870-71, 1885-86, 1897-98, ca. 70 items

Insolvent Capitation and Property Tax Lists, 1876-77, 1882, 1895, 1898, 1900-02, .2 cu. ft.

Insolvent Capitation Lists, 1903, ca. 60 items

Register of Payments Sent to Auditor, 1893-98, 1 vol.

Report of Treasurer—Land and Surveys, 1894-96, 9 items

Reports of Superintendent of Poor and Treasurer, 1887-92, 24 items

State and County Levy Delinquents, 1884-85, ca. 50 items

State Levies Delinquent, 1875-80, .1 cu. ft.

Treasurer's Account Book, 1891-98, 1 vol.

Treasurer's Account of Arrearage and Grand Staff School Fund, 1891-1903, 3 vols.

Treasurer's Account of County and District School Fund, 1896-99, 1901-02, 2 vols.

Treasurer's Reports, 1898-99, 10 items

Treasurer's Reports of County Levy, 1899, ca. 35 items

Treasurer's Reports of Sale of Delinquent Lands, 1840-86, .2 cu. ft.

See also Commissioner of Revenue; Circuit Court Clerk, Tax and Fiscal Records.

Microfilm Records

Circuit Court Clerk
Bonds/Commissions/Oaths
Bond Records, 1832-87, 1 reel (part)
Court Records
County Court
Ledger Index to Docket Cases, 1815-70, 1 reel (part)

Minute Books Nos. 1-13, 1815-66, 5 reels

General Index to Minute Books, 1815-1902, 1 reel

Order Books Nos. 1-5, 1831-80, 2 reels

General Index to Order Books, 1831-1913, 1 reel

Superior Court of Law
Superior Court Order Book 1, 1825-31, 1 reel (part)
Circuit Superior Court of Law and Chancery
Chancery Court Order Book 1, 1831-53, 1 reel (part)
Chancery Court Records at Large, 1837-47, 1 reel (part)
Circuit Court
Chancery Court Order Books No. 2, 3, 1855-78, 1 reel (part)
Superior and Circuit Courts
General Index to Chancery Order Books, 1831-1913, 1 reel
Land Records
Deed Books Nos. 1-13, 1815-66, 5 reels
General Index to Deeds, Nos. 1-15, 1815-1960, 8 reels; Nos. 1-2 (Books 1-37), n.d,
1 reel
Entry Book, 1816-58, 1 reel (part)
Land Title Book, 1816-58, 1 reel (part)
Surveyor's Records, 1816-81, 1 reel (part)
Writings Partially Proved, 1817-24, 1 reel (part)
Marriage Records and Vital Statistics
Consents, 1845-69, 1 reel
Marriage Bonds, 1815-84, 2 reels (part)
Marriage Licenses and Consents, 1841-1900, 19 reels
Marriage Licenses Returned, 1873-74, 1 reel (part)
Marriage Registers Nos. 1-11, 1815-1963, 4 reels
General Index to Marriages, A-Z, 1815-1945, 1 reel
Ministers' Returns, 1815-60, 1 reel
Register of Births, 1853-70, 1 reel (part)
Register of Deaths, 1853-70, 1 reel (part)
Wills
Will Books Nos. 1-5, 1816-68, 2 reels
General Index to Wills, 1815-45, 1 reel (part)
General Index to Wills and Inventories, 1816-90, 1 reel (part)

SHENANDOAH COUNTY

Formed in 1772 from Frederick County.
Originally named Dunmore County, present
name adopted in 1778.

Original Records

Circuit Court Clerk
Board of Supervisors Records
Board of Supervisors' Minutes, 1884-98, 1 vol.
Bonds/Commissions/Oaths
Bond Book, 1877-90, 1 vol.
Bond Book C, 1903-22, 1 vol.
Commissioner's Bond Book B, 1890-1903, 1 vol.
Execution Bond Book N, 1851-58, 1 vol.
Official Bond Books, 1893-1915, 1 vol.
Superior Court of Law and Circuit Superior Court of Law and Chancery Bond
Book (also includes deeds), 1809-33, 1863, 1 vol.

Business Records/Corporations/Partnerships

Fravel Sash & Door Co. Invoice Copy Book, 1901-05, 1 vol.
Unidentified Ledgers, 1862-99, 1904-06, 4 vols.
Unidentified Receipt and Notebook, 1883-86, 1 vol.
Unidentified Time Book and Pay Roll, 1903-04, 1 vol.

Court Records

County Court

Common Law Rule Docket, 1871-73, 1 vol.
Docket, 1881-1904, 1 vol.
Execution Books, 1806-15, 1842-51, 1858-1924, 5 vols.
Fee Books No. 3 and unnumbered, 1871-74, 1881-93, 4 vols.
Final Process Book, 1851-58, 1 vol.
Issue Docket, 1842-58, 1 vol.
Minute Book, 1774-80, 1 vol.
Order Book, 1871-94, 1 vol.
Original Process Book, 1897-1909, 1 vol.
Process Books, 1772-74 (Dunmore Co.), 1784-86, 1871-94, 3 vols.
Record Book 6 [Chancery Order Book], 1824-34, 1 vol.
Record of Judgments Nos. 1 and 2, 1838-86, 2 vols.
Rule Book, 1841-71, 1 vol.
Witness Attendance Books, 1872-81, 1892-1901, 2 vols.

Circuit Court

Chancery Issues, 1875-90, 1 vol.
Chancery Issues Dockets, 1884-1906, 2 vols.
Chancery Issues Record, 1896-97, 1 vol.
Chancery Rule Dockets Nos. 2, 4, and unnumbered volume [1892-99], 1876-1922, 3 vols.
Common Law and Chancery Issue Docket, 1866-74, 1 vol.
Common Law Order Book C, 1856-75, 1 vol.
Execution Books, Nos. 2-5, 1874-1930, 5 vols.
Fee Books, 1875-99, 2 vols.
Final Process Books, 1851-1917, 4 vols.
Law Issues No. [1], 2, and unnumbered volume (1875-82) [Common Law Issue Dockets], 1875-1904, 3 vols.
Law Rules, 1871-97, 2 vols.
Minute Book, 1904, 1 vol.
Moneys Deposited by Order of Circuit Court, 1899-1906, 1 vol.
Original Process Book, 1890-96, 1 vol.
Witness Attendance Books, 1873-1904, 2 vols.

County and Circuit Court

Book of Preservation No. 1 [copies of notes filed with Clerk], 1898-1916, 1 vol.
Execution Book, 1885-1911, 1 vol.
Fee Book, 1894-1912, 1 vol.
Final Process Book, 1869-84, 1 vol.
Record of Warrants, 1875-94, 1 vol.
Witness Attendance Book, 1900-14, 1 vol.

Circuit and Superior Courts

Circuit and Circuit Superior Court of Law and Chancery Execution Book 1, 1831-73, 1 vol.
Circuit and Circuit Superior Court of Law and Chancery Rule Docket, 1831-62, 1 vol.
Circuit, Superior Court of Law, and Circuit Superior Court of Law and Chancery Minute Book, 1827-58, 1 vol.

Unidentified Court
>   Clerk's Form Book, n. d., 1 vol.
>   Fee Books, 1844-45, 1868-1919, 7 vols.
>   Index to Judgments, Nos. 1 & 2, 1840-86, 1 vol.
>   Register of Persons Convicted of Felony, 1872-1927, 1 vol.

Election Records
>   General Registration, 1902-03, 1 vol.
>   Lists of Registered Voters, Nos. 1-2, 1902-34, 2 vols.
>   White and Colored Voters of Strasburg, Va., Davis District, 1904-33, 1 vol.

Fiduciary Records
>   Administration Bond Books, 1869-1912, 3 vols.
>   Administrators', Guardians' & Executors' Bonds, 1879-1910, 1 vol.
>   Executors' Bond Books, 1869-1909, 1 vol.
>   Guardian Bonds, 1886-1920, 3 vols.
>   Record of Guardians, 1862-85, 1 vol.
>   Record of Guardians and Fiduciaries, 1886-1923, 1 vol.
>   Register, Memorandum of Facts Furnished by Persons Moving for Appointment of Personal Representative of a Decedent, n. d., 1 vol.

Justice of the Peace Records
>   Cases Disposed of, 1888-1915, 1 vol.
>   Executions Dockets [A], C, D, 1845-49, 1859-1920, 3 vols.
>   Judgment and Execution Books, 1886-1915, 2 vols.
>   Receipts, 1870-1920, 1 vol.

Land Records
>   Daily Index of Receipt of Deeds for Recordation, 1904-10, 1 vol.
>   Indexes to Deed Books Nos. 1 and 2, 1772-1875, 2 vols.
>   Index to Deeds of Release, No. 1, 1885-1918, 1 vol.
>   Original Deed, 1812, 1 item.

Marriage Records and Vital Statistics
>   Marriage Bonds, Licenses, Consents, 1772-1904, 20.7 cu. ft.
>   Ministers' Returns, 1772-1877, .9 cu. ft.

Military and Pension Records
>   <u>See</u> Miscellaneous Records; Ledger for Physicians, Dentist and Optometrists

Road and Bridge Records
>   Road Book, 1881-85, 1 vol.

Tax and Fiscal Records
>   Delinquent Land Books, 1890-1907, 3 vols.
>   Notes and Bills Receivable, 1904, 1 vol.
>   Records of Delinquent Lands, 1884-89, 1 vol.
>   Rentals for Dunmore County (photoprints) 1774-76, 56 items
>   Taxes Received in the County Court, 1892-99, 1 vol.

Wills
>   Circuit Court and County Court Index to Wills (transcribed), 1835-75, 1 vol.
>   Will Book C, 1789-91, 1 vol.

Miscellaneous Records
>   Appraisement of Estrays, 1881-1918, 1 vol.
>   County and Circuit Court Estray Book, 1865-1922, 1 vol.
>   County Court and Circuit Court Mechanics Lien Record, 1898-1918, 1 vol.
>   County Court Mechanics Liens, No. 1, 1872-97, 1 vol.
>   Crop Lien Docket, No. 1, 1894-1938, 1 vol.
>   General Index to Miscellaneous Lien Book, n. d., 1 vol.
>   Index, n. d., 1 vol.
>   Judgment Lien Docket No. 1, 1840-69, 1 vol.

Indexes to Judgment Lien Docket No. 1, 1840-69, 1 vol.; Nos. 2-3, A-H, M-P, U-Z, n.d., 4 vols.; No. 3, 1887-94, 1 vol.

Ledger for Physicians, Dentists and Optometrists (also includes a list of Confederate pensioners), 1886-1919, 1 vol.

Microfilm Records

Circuit Court Clerk
  Court Records
    County Court
      Minute Books, 1810-65, 5 reels
      General Index to Minute Books, 1831-82, 1 reel
      Order Books, 1772-88, 1791-1811, 5 reels
    Circuit Superior Court of Law and Chancery
      Chancery Orders, 1831-57, 1 reel (part)
  Land Records
    Deed Books A-ZZ, Nos. 1-7, 1772-1867, 29 reels
    General Index to Deeds, 1772-1884, 3 reels
    Surveyors Book, 1785-1817, 1826-1921, 1 reel
  Marriage Records and Vital Statistics
    Marriage Bonds, 1772-1860, 18 reels
    Marriage Licenses, 1860-1912, 21 reels
    Marriage Registers, 1781-1856, 1882-1915, 1 reel (part)
    Index to Marriage Register, 1882-1915, 1 reel (part)
    Minister Returns, 1772-1877, 3 reels
    Register of Births, 1853-71, 1 reel (part)
    Register of Deaths, 1853-71, 1 reel (part)
    Register of Marriages, 1854-82, 1 reel (part)
  Military and Pension Records
    Muster Roll in the War in Defense of Virginia, 1861-65, 1 reel (part)
  Wills
    Circuit Court Wills and Settlements A, 1856-92, 1 reel (part)
    Superior Court Wills and Accounts, 1809-63, 1 reel (part)
    Will Books A-Z, Nos. 1-11, 1772-1866, 17 reels
    General Index to Wills, 1772-1925, 1 reel

SMYTH COUNTY

**Formed in 1832 from Washington and Wythe counties.
As of 1 July 1985 there were no original records from
Smyth County in the Virginia State Library.**

Microfilm Records

Circuit Court Clerk
  Court Records
    County Court
      Order Books Nos. 1-12, 1832-66, 4 reels

Circuit Superior Court of Law and Chancery
Chancery Order Book 2, 1846-47, 1 reel (part)
Circuit Court
Chancery Order Book No. 3, 1857-72, 1 reel (part)
Circuit and Superior Courts
Chancery Order Book 1, 1832-56, 1 reel (part)
Land Records
Deed Books Nos. 1-8, 1832-65, 4 reels
General Index to Deeds, 1832-1929, 2 reels
Surveyors Book, 1833-90, 1 reel
Marriage Records and Vital Statistics
Marriage Registers A, No. 1, 1832-1915, 1 reel
Register of Births No. 1, 1857-85, 1 reel (part)
Register of Deaths No. 1, 1857-96, 1 reel (part)
Wills
Will Books A, 1-4, 1832-98, 2 reels
General Index to Wills, 1832-1913, 1 reel

SOUTHAMPTON COUNTY

**Formed in 1749 from Isle of Wight County.
Part of Nansemond County was added later.**

Original Records

Circuit Court Clerk
Board of Supervisors Records
Board of Supervisors' Papers, 1870-73, .25 cu. ft.
Bond/Commissions/Oaths
Appointments, 1786-1860 (broken series), 38 items
Apprentice Indentures, 1804-94, .5 cu. ft.
Bastardy Bonds, 1804, 1824, 3 items
Bonds, Correspondence, Estrays, etc., 1749-1824, 1893, .5 cu. ft.
Bonds of Coroners, Escheators, and Ministers of the Gospel, 1811-60, .1 cu. ft.
Bonds to Retail Ardent Spirits, 1878, .1 cu. ft.
Election Commissioners' Appointments and Oaths, 1839-40, 17 items
Executions [Oaths], 1870-73, .1 cu. ft.
Liquor Bonds, 1879-89, ca. .5 cu. ft.
Minister's Bond and Certificate of Ordination, 1803 and 1810, 2 items
Official Bonds, 1749-1903, .95 cu. ft.
Official Bonds and Oaths of Office, 1881-1903, .6 cu. ft.
Ordinary Bonds, 1772-73, 1807 and 1826, 7 items
Recognizance Bonds, 1861-66, 7 items
Refunding Bonds, 1833-66, ca. 35 items
Register of Free Negroes [Officials' Bond Book], 1860-62, 1 vol.
Replevy Bonds, 1773-74, .2 cu. ft.
See also Court Records, County and Circuit Courts; Election Records; Road and Bridge Records.
Census Records
Nicholas Magett's District, 1790, 1 item

Court Records
   County Court

      Bills in Chancery, 1763, 3 items
      Chancery Papers, 1750-1831, 15 cu. ft.
      Chancery Rule Dockets, 1801-39, 1870-77, 2 vols.
      Common Law Mesne Process Book, 1869-1904, 1 vol.
      Docket, 1798, 1 vol.
      Execution Books, 1800-42, 5 vols.
      Executions, 1749-1904 (broken series), 13.85 cu. ft.
      Executions and Attachments, 1806, 1822, 1850-51, 1858, 1891, 13 items
      Index to Fee Book, 1880-81, 1 vol.
      Issue Dockets, 1784-86, 1788-91, 2 vols.
      Judgments, 1750-1831, 1833, 1836, 1838, 1840-43, 1859, 57.3 cu. ft.
      Memorandum Book, 1825-36, 1 vol.
      Minute Book (Court of Oyer and Terminer, Quarterly Sessions), 1803-04, 1 vol.
      Minute Books, 1749-51, 1754-65, 1771-74, 1811-12, 1816-19, 7 booklets and 3 vols. See also Miscellaneous Records, Proceedings of the Committee of Safety.
      Order Book No. 1, 1749-54, 1 vol.
      Petitions, 1754, 1773, 1802-04, n. d., 17 items
      Pleas, 1790, 1 item
      Presentments (titles vary) 1749-1866 (broken series), .3 cu. ft.
      Process Book, 1836-69, 1 vol.
      Rule Dockets, 1784-1800, 1808-73, 8 vols.
      Summons, 1801, 1823, 1828, 1882, 1893, n. d., 34 items
      Warrants, 1866, 3 items
      Witness Books, 1807-75, 2 vols.

   Superior Court of Law

      Ejectment Suit, 1823, 1 item
      Execution Books, 1809-31, 2 vols.
      Executions, 1809-31, 1.5 cu. ft.
      Judgments, 1825, 1831, .2 cu. ft.
      Murder Trial Deposition, 1824, 1 item
      Rule Dockets, 1809-31, 2 vols.
      Rules, 1812-16, 1 vol.

   Circuit Superior Court of Law and Chancery

      Chancery Process Book No. 1, 1831-83, 1 vol.
      Chancery Rule Docket No. 1, 1831-76, 1 vol.
      Common Law Rule Docket, 1831-43, 1 vol.
      Executions, 1831-51, .65 cu. ft.
      Judgments, 1832, 1835-38, 1840-50, 2.37 cu. ft.
      Witness Book, 1839-75, 1 vol.

   Circuit Court

      Chancery Executions, 1871, .15 cu. ft.
      Common Law Mesne Process Book, 1869-96, 1 vol.
      Common Law Mesne and Final Process Book, 1897-1911, 1 vol.
      Criminal Papers, 1877, .1 cu. ft.
      Executions, 1851-54, 1857, .2 cu. ft.
      Judgments, 1851-63, 1897-1904, 1.2 cu. ft.

   County and Superior Courts

      Chancery Papers, 1831-51, 11.9 cu. ft.
      Executions, 1835, 1848, 1850, .3 cu. ft.
      Judgments, 1831-51, 14.35 cu. ft.

County and Circuit Courts

Accounts of Sale [Jury Claims], 1859-62, ca. 75 items

Chancery Papers, 1851-87, 1890-96, 1898-1904, n. d., 9.8 cu. ft.

Commonwealth Papers and Causes and Peace Bonds, 1811-1903 (broken series), 1 cu. ft.

Court Papers (includes appraisements, bonds, licenses, road petitions, election and tax papers), 1754-1904 (broken series), 7 cu. ft.

Docket, 1897-1911, 1 vol.

Executions, 1852, 1854, 1855, 1857-59, 1870-73, .75 cu. ft.

Judgment Docket, 1843-73, 1 vol.

Judgments, 1851-1904, 9.1 cu. ft.

Subpoenas, 1845-1902, .5 cu. ft.

Unspecified Court

Chancery Dockets, 1836-60, 1839-71, 2 vols.

Chancery Execution Book No. 1, 1832-1901, 1 vol.

Common Law Execution Book No. 1, 1831-43, 1 vol.

Common Law Process Book No. 1, 1832-69, 1 vol.

Common Law Rule Docket No. 2, 1843-85, 1 vol.

Deposition, n. d., 1 item

Fees due to the Clerk of High Court of Chancery, 1793, 1 item

Index to Rule Book, 1829, 1 vol.

Notes, 1873, 1876, 1878, 1895, n. d., 5 items

Recognizances, 1872-82, .10 cu. ft.

Special Bail, 1823, 1 item

Unidentified Indexes, n. d., 3 vols.

Warrant of Identity, 1824, 1 item

Election Records

Lists of Voters, 1853, 1855-59, n. d., .3 cu. ft.

Polls and Election Returns, 1777-1877 (broken series), 7.15 cu. ft.

Writs of Election, 1810, 1857-59, 1870, 8 items

See also Court Records, County and Circuit Courts.

Fiduciary Records

Accounts Current (Guardian and Estate), 1793-1855 (broken series), 1.85 cu. ft.

Administrators' Bonds, 1749-1850, 2 cu. ft.

Administrators' Bonds and Assorted Papers, 1762, 1781-83, 6 items

Administrators' Bonds and Guardians' Bonds, 1822-30, 1850-60, 1895-99, 1 cu. ft.

Allotments of Dower, 1866, 2 items

Assignment of Dower, 1810, 1 item

Circuit Court List of Fiduciaries, 1850-1904, 1 vol.

County Court List of Fiduciaries, 1850-1911 (includes Circuit Court, 1904-11), 1 vol.

Court Orders Concerning Estates, 1804-05, 7 items

Executor's Bond, 1810, 1 item

Estate Papers, 1875, 1881-89, 1903-04, 53 items

Fiduciary Bonds [Guardians' and Administrators'], 1870-95, 1899-1902, .9 cu. ft.

Guardians' Accounts, 1750-1902 (broken series), 6.8 cu. ft.

Guardians' Accounts Books No. 1 and unnumbered, 1751-72, 1810-36, 2 vols.

Guardians' Bonds, 1750-79, 1782-1839, 1.8 cu. ft.

Guardians' Bonds and Accounts, 1751, 1809, 1814, 1817, 5 items

Guardians', Administrators', Executors' Accounts, and Inventories, 1903-1911, .35 cu. ft.

Inventories, Accounts, and Sales, 1749-1824 (broken series), 2.6 cu. ft.

Inventories, Wills, and Deeds (copies), ca. 1795-1820, .15 cu. ft.

Lists of Probates, 1761-62, 2 items

Record of Commissioner of Accounts, 1879-1903, 1 vol.

Relinquishment of Guardianship, 1801, 1 item

Trustee Accounts, 1904, 2 items

See also Court Records, County and Circuit Courts, Court Papers; Wills, Wills and related papers.

Free Negroes and Slave Records

Apprentice Indentures—colored children, 1820-39, .2 cu. ft.

Lists of Free Negroes, 1801, 1803, 1822, 5 items

Registers of Free Negroes, 1789-1864, 2 vols.

Justice of the Peace Records

Executions Returned by Constables, 1816-23, 1833-49, 1851-60, .45 cu. ft.

Executions Returned by Constables, 1829-49, 1860-94, 1 vol.

List of Magistrates nominated in the Commission of the Peace from June 1777 to [1796], 1 item

See also Court Records, County Court.

Land Records

Deed Books, Nos. 2-4, 6, 7, 1753-73, 1782-93, 5 vols.

Deeds, 1749-1866, 1873-1904, 18.9 cu. ft. See also Fiduciary Records, Inventories, Accounts, and Deeds.

Deeds Partly Proved, 1759-1839, 1.35 cu. ft.

Deeds related to Jerusalem (Courtland), 1811, 1828, 1869, 13 items

Drawing of Boundary Line, 1810, 1 item

List of Conveyances, 1753, 1 item

List of Land Transfers, 1818-19, 1 item

Processioners' Reports, 1795, 1800, 1804, 1807, 1823, 1836, 1841, 1875, 1890, n. d., .45 cu. ft.

Processioners' Reports, 1836-91, 1890-1910, 2 vols.

Processioners' Returns, 1830, 1845, 1850-52, 1854, 1858, .45 cu. ft.

Marriage Records and Vital Statistics

Certificates to obtain Marriage Licenses, 1864-1869, .35 cu. ft.

Marriage Bonds and Consents, 1750-1855, n. d., ca. 4.7 cu. ft.

Marriage Index, 1813, 1 vol.

Marriage Licenses, 1863-64, 1871, .15 cu. ft.

Marriage Records, 1759-1841 (broken series), 10 items

Marriage Registers, 1750-1853, 4 vols. (2 copies)

Marriage Registers, 1863-64, 2 items

Index of Marriage Register, 1750-1853, 2 vols. (2 copies)

Ministers' Returns, 1783-1851, .25 cu. ft.

Ministers' Returns, 1817-46, 1849-53, 2 vols.

Registers of Births, 1883, 1885-86, 1888-89, 1891-96, .50 cu. ft.

Registers of Deaths, 1883, 1885-89, 1891-92, 1894-96, .65 cu. ft.

See also Court Records, County Court, Judgments.

Military Records

Certificate of Service as Guard, 1801, 1 item

Lists of Pensioners, 1797, 1804, 3 items

Militia Commissions, 1801, 1812, 1816, 1818, 1821, 5 items

Receipts for Soldiers' Families, 1863-65, 8 items

Road and Bridge Records

Allowances for Surveyors of Roads, 1858-59, 1861, 1863-68, ca. 50 items

Bridge and Road Repair and Construction Reports, 1758-1890, .1 cu. ft.

Bridge and Road Reports, 1857-65, 1875-77, 1884-90, .35 cu. ft.

Ferry Report (South Quay Ferry), 1856, 2 items

List of Hands belonging to a Road, n. d., 1 item

Overseer of the Road Papers and Appointments, 1875-94, .2 cu. ft.

Payment of Keeping a Free Ferry, 1868, 1 item

Reports of Commissions on Bridges, Roads, etc., 1874-79, ca. 50 items

Road Petitions, 1754, 1773, 1802, 1803, n. d., 17 items

Surveyors of Road Appointments, 1800-04, 1823, 14 items

See also Court Records, County Court, Judgments; County and Circuit Courts, Court Papers.

School Records

Jerusalem Military School Subscription, n. d., 1 item

School Commissioners' Reports, 1849-60, .2 cu. ft.

See also Court Records, County Court, Judgments.

Tax and Fiscal Records

Applications to Purchase Delinquent Lands, 1889-92, 1894-95, 1898, .15 cu. ft.

Delinquent for Non-Payment of Taxes on Land, Capitation and Personal Property Lists, 1867-79, 1882-89, 1891-94, 1896-98, 1901-04, ca. 1.65 cu. ft.

Improper Assessment of Land and Delinquent Taxes, 1898, ca. .1 cu. ft.

Insolvent Lists [titles vary], 1791, 1793-94, 1803, 1806, 1809, 9 items

Licenses and payment receipts, 1853-1855, 19 items

Liquor Licenses, 1881, 18 items

List of Real Estate Sold for the Non-Payment of Taxes thereon and Purchased by Commonwealth, 1876-1926, 1 vol.

Lists of All Persons Assessed with a License Tax, 1881, 2 items

Ordinary Licenses, 1803-05, 1856, 4 items

Quit Claim, 1801, 1 item

Tax Receipts, 1880-96, 21 items

Tithables, 1752, 1778, 2 items

See also Court Records, County Court, Judgments.

Wills

Circuit Court Wills, 1833-71, .25 cu. ft.

Renunciation of Will, 1802, 1 item

Wills and related papers (including copies), 1777-1882 (broken series), ca. 75 items

Will Books Nos. 1-5, 1749-1804, 5 vols.

Index to Wills, 1749-1937, 1 vol.

See also Fiduciary Records, Inventories, Wills, and Deeds.

Miscellaneous Records

Accounts with J. W. Waller, 1884-85, 1887, 7 items

Article of Agreement for loan of goods, n. d., 1 item

Atlantic and Danville Railroad Company Papers, 1888-89, .1 cu. ft.

Certificates of Estray, 1785-1864 (broken series), ca. 50 items

Claims against the County, 1867, ca. 50 items

Claims Allowed, 1858-59, 1861-82, .15 cu. ft.

C. L. Borden's Pocketbook and Papers, ca. 1890-1900, ca. 40 items

Clerk's Correspondence, 1802, 1804-05, 1810, 1832-42, 1891, 1894-1907, .75 cu. ft.

County Expenses, 1792-1900 (broken series), 18 items

Estrays, 1836-64, 1 vol.

Inquisition for a mill, 1795, 1 item

Inquisitions, 1797-1875, 1877-80, .5 cu. ft.

Liquor Returns, 1878, .1 cu. ft.

List of Children to be Bound Out, 1795, 1 item

Lists of Allowances, 1807, 1853-56, 1859-60, 1863-64, 1866, 41 items

Lunacy Papers and Warrants, 1883, 1891, 3 items

Overseers of the Poor Report, 1825, 1 item

Patrol Returns and Lists (titles vary), 1802-04, 1808, 1810-16, 1859-61, ca. 75 items

Petition, 1761, 1 item
Petition for a mill, 1809, 1 item
Petitions of Infants, etc. for Support, 1866-68, .1 cu. ft.
Plans for construction and repair of the jail, courthouse and law office, 1760, 1803, 1823-24, 1884, n. d., 10 items
Proceedings of the Committee of Safety, 1775-76 (includes Minute Book, 1775-78), 1 vol.
Receipt, 1897, 1 item
Rejected Claims, 1858-59, 6 items
Reports on Insane Persons, 1903-21, .20 cu. ft.
Returns to Auditor, 1835-48, 1852-72, .15 cu. ft.
Small Pox Epidemic and Exposure Papers, 1812, 9 items
Statements of Aggregate Amount of Executions Stayed by General Order from Headquarters First Military District, 1868-69, 1 booklet

Sheriff

Sheriff's Reports [Process Book], 1875-1922, 1 vol.

Microfilm Records

Circuit Court Clerk
Court Records
County Court

Chancery Court Papers, 1750-1814, 10 reels
Minute Books, 1775-78, 1786-90, 1793-1807, 1809-70, 5 reels
Order Books 1749-63, 1768-89, 1802-05, 1807, 1811-12, 1814-24, 1835-49, 7 reels

Election Records

Poll Records, 1777, 1811-20, 1824-77, 7 reels

Fiduciary Records

Guardian Accounts, Nos. 1-4, 1751-79, 1810-67, 2 reels
See also Wills, Will Books.

Land Records

Deed Books Nos. 1-30, 1749-1870, 13 reels
Index to Deeds, 1749-1908 (Grantee and Grantor), 2 reels
Processioners' Plat Book, 1826-36, 1 reel (part)
Processioners' Returns, 1836-91, 1 reel (part)

Marriage Records and Vital Statistics

Marriage Bonds and Consents, 1750-1851, n.d., 19 reels
Marriage Consents, Licenses, 1851-64, 1 reel
Marriage Licenses, 1850-61, 1 reel (part)
Marriage Registers Nos. 1-9, 1750-1899, 6 reels
Index to Marriage Register, 1750-1853, 1 reel
Ministers' Returns, 1783-1851, 1 reel
Register of Births, 1853-70, 1 reel (part)
Register of Deaths, 1853-70, 1 reel (part)
Index to Registers of Births, Marriages, and Deaths, 1853-72, 1 reel (part)

Military and Pension Records

See Miscellaneous Records, Reel 45

Wills

Will Books Nos. 1-18 [No. 3 contains Guardians' Accounts, 1771-79], 1749-1867, 8 reels
General Index to Wills, Vol. 1, 1749-1937, 1 reel

Miscellaneous Records
Committee of Safety, Proceedings, 1775-76, 1 reel (part)
Miscellaneous Records, n. d., 1 reel (part)

SPOTSYLVANIA COUNTY

**Formed in 1720 from Essex, King William,
and King and Queen counties.**

Circuit Court Clerk
Bonds/Commissions/Oaths
Notary Bonds, 1897-1949, 1 vol.
Court Records
County Court
Minute Books, 1755-65, 1786-89, 1792-98, 3 vols.
Order Books, 1724-55, 1768-86, 9 vols.
See also Wills.
Circuit Court
Memorandum Book, 1868-88, 1 vol.
Election Records
Election Tickets, 1900-06, .45 cu. ft.
Poll Books, 1902-03, .395 cu. ft.
Fiduciary Records
Orphans' Accounts, 1759-77, 1 vol.
Land Records
Deed Books, A-F, H, J, N, Y, 1720-68, 1771-82, 1822-24, 15 vols.
Marriage Records and Vital Statistics
Marriage Register, 1795-1853, 1 vol.
Tax and Fiscal Records
Tax Accounts, 1775-76, 1 vol.
Wills
Will Books A, D, 1722-49, 1761-72, 2 vols.
Miscellaneous Records
Indentures of Apprenticeship, 1749-71, 1801-50, 84 items

Microfilm Records

Circuit Court Clerk
Court Records
County Court
Minutes 1755-65, 1774-82, 1785-88, 1792-95, 1799-1824, 1826-32, 4 reels
Orders 1724-55, 1764-74, 1782-92, 1795-98, 1824-26, 1832-71, 12 reels
Orders and Judgments, 1792-95, 1 reel
Record of Executions, 1756-71, 1 reel
See also Wills, Will Books.
Unidentified Court
Dockets, 1846-73, 1881-89, 1 reel (part)
Judgment Docket, 1843-82, 1 reel (part)

Land Records
>Deed Books A-SS, 1722-1922, 34 reels
>General Index to Deeds, 1722-1922, 2 reels
>[Embrey's] General Index, 1722-1917, 8 reels

Marriage Records and Vital Statistics
>Marriage Registers, 1795-1935, 2 reels

Wills
>Manuscript Loose Wills, ca. 1805-92, 4 reels
>Will Books A, B, D-K, N-Y, 1722-59, 1761-1824, 1830-76 (Will Book A contains Orders, 1722-24), 12 reels
>General Index to Wills, 1722-1947, 1 reel

STAFFORD COUNTY

Formed in 1664 from Westmoreland County.

Circuit Court Clerk
Court Records
County Court
>Court Records, 1664-68, 1689-93, 1 vol.
>Court Records, 1680, 1 booklet
>Loose Court Records (originals), 1671-1797, .1 cu. ft.; (photoprints), .1 cu. ft.
>Record Book, 1686-93, 1 vol.
>Scheme Book L-D (orders), 1790-1793, 1 vol.
>Writ, 1784, 1 item

Land Records
>Deed Books Liber P, [S] and unnumbered, 1686-93, 1755-65, 1780-86, 3 vols.
>[Old] General Index, 1721-1845, 1 vol.
>Rent Rolls, 1723, 1729, 1768, 1773, 40 items

Wills
>Deed Book [Wills] Liber O, 1748-63, 1 vol.
>Will Books, Liber Z and M, 1699-1709, 1729-48, 2 vols.
>See also Land Records, [Old] General Index.

Miscellaneous Records
>Manuscript of Grammar Rules, 1806, 1 booklet
>Miscellaneous Papers, 1664/5-1828, 1747-84, 28 items
>Proceedings of Trustees of Town of Falmouth, 1764-1868, 1 vol.

Microfilm Records

Circuit Court Clerk
Court Records
County Court
>Minute Books CC and unnumbered, 1830-35, 1852-67, 1 reel
>Order Books, 1664-68, 1689-93, 1790-93, 1806-09, 1825-27, 3 reels
>See also Land Records.

Fiduciary Records
>Estate Accounts, 1827-34, 1852-73, 1 reel

Land Records

 Deed Books Libers P, S, AA, GG, LL, MM, NN, OO, RR, TT, and unnumbered, 1722-28, 1755-64, 1780-89, 1809-13, 1825-27, 1837-48, 1854-57, 1861-73, 5 reels

 [Embrey's] Index of Records, 1664-1914, 4 reels

 <u>See also</u> Wills, Will Books Liber Z.

Marriage and Vital Statistics Records

 Marriage Register No. 1, 1854-1927, 1 reel (part)

 Register of Births, 1853-73, 1 reel (part)

 Register of Deaths, 1853-73, 1 reel (part)

Military and Pension Records

 Muster Roll, 1861-65, 1 reel (part)

Wills

 Will Books Liber, Z, M, O, 1699-1709, 1729-63, 1 reel

 <u>See also</u> Land Records, Deed Books.

SURRY COUNTY

Formed in 1652 from James City County.

Circuit Court Clerk

 Court Records

  County Court

   Order, 1681, 1 item

   Order Books, 1654-1718, 1743-49 (volume for 1654-72 contains deeds and wills), 8 vols.

  <u>See also</u> Land Records, Deed Books.

 Fiduciary Records

  Guardian Accounts, 1783-1804 (also includes Free Negro Register, 1795-1803), 1 vol.

  Orphan Accounts, 1744-62, 1 vol.

  <u>See also</u> Land Records, Deed Books.

 Free Negro and Slave Records

  <u>See</u> Fiduciary Records, Guardian Accounts

 Land Records

  Deed Books (titles vary), 1645-86, 1694-1715, 1730-54, 1783-87, 1792-99, (some volumes include wills and fiduciary records and volume for 1645-86 includes orders), 19 vols.

  <u>See also</u> Court Records, County Court, Order Books; Wills, Wills and Deeds.

 Marriage Records and Vital Statistics

  Bond, 1819, 1 item

  Marriage Register, 1768-1853, 1 vol.

  Index of Marriage Register, 1768-1853, 1 vol.

 Wills

  Unrecorded Wills, 1760-1847, 28 items

  Wills and Deeds, 1715-30, 3 vols.

  Wills, 1754-68, 2 vols.

  <u>See also</u> Court Records, County Court, Order Books; Land Records, Deed Books.

Microfilm Records

Circuit Court Clerk
  Court Records
    County Court
      Orders, 1671-1718, 1741-1826, 1829-77, 14 reels
    Superior and Circuit Courts
      Chancery Order Book, 1831-1874, 1 reel
  Fiduciary Records
    Administrators' Bonds, 1797-1891, 1 reel
    Executors' Bonds, 1798-1858, 1 reel
    Fiduciary Accounts, 1831-68, 1 reel
    Guardians' Accounts, 1672-1831, 1847-65, 3 reels
    Guardians' Bonds, 1797-1906, 1 reel
    See also Land Records.
  Free Negro and Slave Records
    Register of Free Negroes, 1795-1803, 1 reel (part)
  Land Records
    Deed Books, Nos. 4-8, 10, 12-13, 1741-78, 1783-92, 4 reels
    Deeds Nos. 1-9, 11-15, 1792-1834, 1839-73, 8 reels
    Deeds, Wills, Etc. Nos. 1-9, 1652-1754, 6 reels
    General Index to Deeds No. 1, 1848-98, 1 reel
    Plat Book 1, 1810-52 [1940], 1 reel
    Processioners Returns, 1796-1828, 1832-44, 1 reel
  Marriage Records and Vital Statistics
    Marriage Registers, 1768-1939, 2 reels
    Register of Births, 1853-96, 1 reel (part)
    Register of Deaths, 1853-96, 1 reel (part)
    Index to Births, Marriages and Deaths, 1853-1939, 1 reel
  Military and Pension Records
    Militia Records, 1840-61, 1 reel
  Wills
    Circuit Court Will Book, 1809-70, 1 reel
    Wills Books (titles vary) Nos. 10-12; 1-11, 1754-1875, 7 reels

SUSSEX COUNTY

Formed in 1753 from Surry County.

Original Records

Circuit Court Clerk
  Board of Supervisors Records
    Corrrespondence and Accounts, ca. 1869-75, .2 cu. ft.
    Receipts, 1874, .2 cu. ft.
    Warrants, 1888-90, 1 vol.
  Business Records/Charters/Partnerships
    Merchant's [Joseph A. Rogers?] Day Book, Mayesville/Henry, Virginia, 1845-47,
      1 vol.

Census Records

Population Schedules (includes Slave Schedules, 1850-60), 1850-80, .9 cu. ft.

Court Records

County Court

Alphabet [Index] to a Memorial for Judgments, 1773, and Alphabet [Index] to Execution Docket, 1773, 1 vol.

Chancery Docket, 1791-1873, 4 vols.

Docket Books, 1764-66, 1772-73, 1783-90, 1806-19, 1871-1903, 14 vols.

Docket of Executions on Warrants, 1825-39, 1 vol.

Execution Dockets, 1770-71, 1783-85, 1788-1869, 11 vols.

Fee Book of John J. Prince, Commissioner in Chancery, 1852-60, 1 vol.

Fee Books, 1754-1877, 1897-1905, 23 vols.

Issue Dockets, 1791-94, 1797-1826, 3 vols.

List of County Court and Justice of Peace Fines, 1894-1920, 2 vols.

Memorial of Judgments, 1773-74, 1784-1833, 1847-70, 9 vols.

Minute Books 1754-71, 1773, 1776-82, 1786-91, 1842-44, 24 vols.

Order Books, No. 2 and unnumbered, 1754-61, 1770-76, 3 vols.

Process Book, 1869-1904, 1 vol.

Process Book Index, 1869, 1 vol.

Reference Dockets, 1754-56, 1760-64, 1766-71, 1773-83, 11 vols.

Rule Dockets, 1785-1875, 8 vols.

Rules in Chancery, 1836-37, 1 vol.

Suits in Chancery, 1791, 1 item

Summons, 1873, .1 cu. ft.

Witness Attendance Books, 1807-48, 2 vols.

Circuit Court

Chancery Court Dockets, 1866-90, 2 vols.

Chancery Rules, 1866-1915, 1 vol.

Docket Books, 1891-1905, 2 vols.

Fee Books, 1902-1905, 1 vol.

Memorandum Book, 1866-1907, 1 vol.

Process Book, 1867-1934, 1 vol.

County and Circuit Courts

Witness Attendance Book, 1869-87, 1 vol.

Oyer and Terminer Court

Commission for Trial of slave Sinner, 1754, 2 items

Minute Book, 1756-71, 1 vol.

Unspecified Court

Fee Book, 1887-98, 1 vol.

Form Book, n. d., 1 vol.

Index to Order Book, 1835-42, 1 vol.

List of Fines, 1890-92, 1 vol.

Memorandum Books, 1816-24, 1866-91, 4 vols.

Office Judgments Docket, 1820-35, 1 vol.

Petitions, 1795-1808, 1817, 1820-21, 1 vol.

Election Records

Ballot, 1892, 1 item

Fiduciary Records

Guardians' Account Book, 1754-87, 1 vol.

Register of Administrators and Executors (titles vary), 1800-44, 2 vol.

Registry of Guardians, 1800-34, 1 vol.

See also Court Records, County Court, Order Book, 1754-87.

Free Negro and Slave Records

Lists of Free Negroes, 1801-03, 1805-12, 21 items

See also Census Records, Slave Schedules, 1850-60.

Justice of the Peace Records

See Court Records, County Court, List of County Court and Justice of Peace Fines

Land Records

Deed Books A-D, F, 1754-72, 1779-86, 7 vols.

Deeds, 1754-1826, 1828-30, 1833, 1835-37, 1839-40, 1842-44, 1846-49, 10.8 cu. ft.

General Index to Deeds, Vol. 3, 1878-1909, 1 vol.

Processioners' Book, 1874-99, 1 vol.

See also Miscellaneous Records, General Index.

Marriage Records and Vital Statistics

Marriage Register, 1754-1853, 2 vols. [2 copies]

Index to Marriage Register, 1754-1853, 2 vols. [2 copies]

Ministers' Returns, 1845-53, 1 vol.

Register of Births and Deaths, 1853-59, 1861-64, 1866, 1868-69, 1879, 1881-83, .52 cu. ft.

Register of Marriages, 1857, 1890, 2 items

Organization Records

Minutes and Roll of Confederate Veterans of Sussex County, Camp No. 100, 1902-05, 1 vol.

Road and Bridge Records

List of Roads and Surveyors, 1820-53, and Bridges, 1813-53, 1 vol.

Road Book, 1893, 1 vol.

Road Order Book, 1875-86, 1 vol.

Road Reports, 1875-76, 1889-91, .35 cu. ft.

Road Reports and Receipts, 1889, .1 cu. ft.

Road Surveyor and Processioner Warrants, 1877-81, ca. 100 items

Tax and Fiscal Records

Delinquent Capitation, School and County Levy List, 1872-73, 8 items

Delinquent Land and Personal Property, 1901-04, .15 cu. ft.

Fragments, n. d., 20 items

Improper Assessment of Land, 1873-1911, .1 cu. ft.

Insolvent Personal Property and Capitation Taxes, 1895-1911, 1 vol.

Land Tax Books, 1782-1904 (broken series), 3.8 cu. ft.

Personal Property Tax Books, 1850-1904 (broken series), 8.3 cu. ft.

Record of Taxes Collected or should have been collected, 1876, 1898-1907, 2 vols. and 2 items

Tax Receipts for 1904-05, paid in 1905-06, 1 cu. ft.

Tax Tickets, 1883, .1 cu. ft.

Tithable Lists, 1770, 1777, 1779-80, 1782, 20 items

Township Records

Henry Township Minutes, 1871-75; and Application for Purchase of Delinquent Land, 1898-1901, 1 vol.

Minutes of the Township Board of Newville, 1871-75, 1 vol.

Newville Township Warrants, 1872-78, 2 vols.

Stony Creek Township Warrants, 1872-75, 1882-85, 1 vol.

Sussex Court House Township Board Minutes, 1871-75, 1 vol.

Waverly Township Board Minutes, 1872-75 [and Register of Physicians and Surgeons, 1891-1908], 1 vol.

Waverly Township Warrants, 1872-75, 1 vol.

Wills

Alphabet [Index] of Wills [Will Book A, 1754-64], 1 item

Will Books A-E, 1754-96, 8 vols.

Miscellaneous Records

Aerial Photographs of Town of Woodstock, n. d., 9 items
Clerk's Correspondence, ca. 1870-1904, 1 cu. ft.
Contracts for Personal Property, 1890-1912, 1 vol.
General Index [to Deeds, Wills, Orders, Fiduciary], 1872-78, 1 vol.
Mechanics' Lien Record, 1893-1915, 1 vol.
Register of Letters [Postmaster], 1842-46, 1 vol.
[Unidentified] Index, n. d., 3 vols.
See also Township Records, Waverly Township Board Minutes.

Commissioner of Revenue

License Returns, 1873-76, .1 cu. ft.
License Tax on Dogs, 1872, ca. 50 items
License Tax Returns, 1868-74, .3 cu. ft.
Liquor License Returns, 1881-82, 3 items
Liquor Tax Returns, 1879-93, .1 cu. ft.
Lists of All Persons Paying License Tax, 1860, 1882, 2 items
Lists of Licenses, 1823-51 (broken series), 24 items
Lists of Liquor Licenses, 1884, 2 items
Personal Property Interrogatories, 1901-02, 3.7 cu. ft.
Receipts for Dog Licenses, 1902-03, .1 cu. ft.

Sheriff

Accounts of William Mitchell [Sheriff], 1869-70, .1 cu. ft.
Return of all who paid poll tax [and where lists were posted], 1904-18, 1 vol.
Sheriffs' and Jailors' Receipts, ca. 1875-85, .1 cu. ft.
Sheriff's Tax Book, 1807, 1 vol.

Treasurer

Accounts and Warrants, 1875, 1881-86, .4 cu. ft.
Accounts Current, 1871-1903, 1 vol.
Day Book, 1871-87, 1 vol.
Index to Accounts Allowed, n. d., 1 vol.
Journal [County, Road, School Fund], 1903-09, 1 vol.
Road Fund Ledger [and Railroad, Telegraph, Erroneous Assessments, 1900-11], 1900-08, 1910-11, 1 vol. and 3 items
See also Circuit Court Clerk, Township Records, Henry Township Minutes.

Microfilm Records

Circuit Court Clerk
Bonds/Commissions/Oaths
See Tax and Fiscal Records
Court Records
County Court
Court Papers, 1754-1838, 176 reels
Minute Books, 1818-27, 1 reel
Order Books, 1754-82, 1786-1864, 6 reels
Superior Court of Law
Order Book, 1812-31, 1 reel
Court of Oyer and Terminer
Order Book, 1754-1807, 1 reel (part)
Election Records
See Tax and Fiscal Records.

280

Fiduciary Records

Guardian Accounts, 1754-87, 1789-1866, 2 reels

See also Court Records, County Court Papers.

Land Records

Deed Books A-W, 1754-1864, 11 reels

General Index to Deeds, Vols. 1 and 2, 1754-1878, 1 reel

Survey Book, 1754-1827, 1 reel

See also Court Records, County Court Papers.

Marriage Records and Vital Statistics

Certificates of Marriage Licenses, 1850-1884, 1 reel (part)

Marriage Bonds, 1754-1850, 7 reels

Marriage Contracts and Agreements, 1746-1801, 1 reel (part)

Marriage Licenses, 1861-65, 1 reel (part)

Marriage Register, 1754-1853, 1866-1901, 2 reels

Index to Marriage Register, 1754-1853, 1 reel (part)

Ministers' Bonds, 1789-1833, 1 reel (part)

Ministers' Returns, 1781-1849, 1858, 1 reel (part)

Register of Births, 1853-69, 1 reel (part)

Register of Deaths, 1853-69, 1 reel (part)

Returns and Certificates, 1849-61, 1 reel (part)

Road and Bridge Records

See Tax and Fiscal Records

Tax and Fiscal Records

Tithables, Oaths of Allegiance, Bonds for bridge building and repair, and Polls, 1754-95, 2 reels

Wills

Will Books A-R, 1754-1864, 7 reels

Index to Wills, 1754-1948, 1 reel

TAZEWELL COUNTY

Formed in 1799 from Wythe and Russell counties. Parts of Logan, Russell, Wythe, and Washington counties were added later.

Original Records

Circuit Court Clerk

Board of Supervisors Records

Cancelled Vouchers (titles vary), 1887-94, .75 cu. ft.

See also Miscellaneous Records, Awards of Arbitrators on Line Fences.

Bonds/Commissions/Oaths

Commissioners' Bond Book, 1886-90, 1 vol.

Fidelity Docket [Bonds], 1901-1920, 1 vol.

See also Court Records, County Court.

Business Records/Corporations/Partnerships

Blacksmith's Account Book, 1890, 1 vol.

Dr. J. H. Crockett, Drug Book, 1895-96, 1 vol; Ledger, 1899-1909, 1 vol.

James Fulcher's Account Book, 1860-61, 1 vol.

R. D. Hufford, Doctor's Ledger, 1893-99, 1 vol.

Tazewell C. H. Imp. Co. Ledger, 1890-92, 1 vol.

Tazewell Electric Co. Ledger, 1898-1905, 1 vol.

Unidentified Merchants' Account Books, 1829-32, 1849-50, 1860-61, 1894-1905, 11 vols.

Unidentified store ledger, 1899-1900, 1 vol.

Court Records

County Court

Appeal Motion Docket, 1866-76, 1 vol.

Attorney's Receipt Book for Papers, 1872-87, 1 vol.

Call Court Papers, 1821-34, ca. 75 items

Chancery Papers, 1823, ca. 100 items

Chancery Rules Docket, 1826-32, 1 vol.

Commonwealth Causes, 1801-02, 1804, 1817-18, ca. 100 items

Commonwealth Executions and Capias pro fine, 1882-91, .1 cu. ft.

Commonwealth Papers, 1809-10, ca. 50 items

Court Docket, 1876-1901, 7 vols.

Court Minutes, Special Term, 1840-49, 1 vol.

Criminal Prosecutions, 1820-22, 10 items

Docket Book, 1876-82, 1 vol.

Execution Books, 1800-34, 2 vols.

Executions, 1801-10, 1813-62, 1866-75, 1880-1902, 3.05 cu. ft.

Fee Books, 1804-32, 1836-50, 1854-1903, 30 vols.

Felony and Motion Docket, 1901-03, 1 vol.

Issue Docket, 1866-73, 2 vols.

Judgments, 1800-62, 1865-98, 16 cu. ft.

Memorandum Books, 1873-80, 1887-94, 2 vols.

Order [Minute] Books, 1810-20, 2 vols.

Process Books, 1835-50, 1876-90, 5 vols.

Receipt Books, 1850-76, 4 vols.

Rough Minute Book, 1848-54, 1 vol.

Rule Dockets, 1855-73, 2 vols.

Witness Attendance Books, 1842-1904, 5 vols.

Superior Court of Law

Executions, 1822-28, ca. 100 items

Fee Book, 1810-32, 1 vol.

Judgments, 1810-31, (broken series), .4 cu. ft.

Circuit Superior Court of Law and Chancery

Chancery Fee Book, 1832-52, 1 vol.

Commonwealth Cases, 1834, ca. 50 items

Executions, 1832-41, 1846, .15 cu. ft.

Fee Books, 1832-52, 3 vols.

Judgments, 1832-50, .9 cu. ft.

Process Book, 1835-44, 1 vol.

Circuit Court

Abstract of Judgments, 1895-96, ca. 50 items

Attorney's Receipt Book for Papers, 1853-81, 1 vol.

Chancery Court Dockets, 1860-75, 1898-1903, 3 vols.

Chancery Execution Book, 1880-1913, 1 vol.

Chancery Fee Book, 1852-74, 1 vol.

Chancery Rules Dockets, 1858-1910, 3 vols.

Docket Books, 1876-98, 7 vols.

Executions, 1850-86, .65 cu. ft.

Fee Books, 1852-73, 1881-1903, 9 vols.

Index to Chancery Causes, 1895-1904, 2 vols.

Issue Dockets, 1854-75, 4 vols.
Judgments, 1853-54, 1856-58, 1875, 1891, 1 cu. ft.
Juror's Attendance Book, 1904-1925, 1 vol.
Law Dockets, 1873-90, 1898-1909, 3 vols.
Law Memorandum Books, 1855-73, 1880-89, 1894-1906, 3 vols.
Law Rules, 1891-1920, 2 vols.
Memorandum Books, 1873-1904, 7 vols.
Rough Minute Books, 1853-73, 1866-1907, 2 vols.
Receipt Book/Process Book, 1855-68, 1 vol.
Witness Attendance Books, 1853-70, 1886-1904, 3 vols.

County and Superior Courts
Abstract of Judgments, ca. 1840-90, .1 cu. ft.
Criminal Prosecutions, 1811-13, 1818, ca. 50 items
Judgments, 1814, 1816, 1819, .1 cu. ft.
Presentments, 1800-18, ca. 50 items

County, Superior, and Circuit Courts
Abstracts of Judgments, ca. 1890-1915, ca. 40 items

Superior and Circuit Courts
Book of Lost Records, 1837-1921, 1 vol.
Commonwealth Executions, 1849-74, ca. 40 items
Issue Docket, 1832-59, 1 vol.
Process Book, 1845-55, 1 vol.
Witness Attendance Book, 1810-53, 1 vol.

U. S. Circuit Court
U. S. Commissioner's Criminal Docket, 1894-1903, 1 vol.

Unspecified Court
Chancery Court Docket, 1832-58, 1 vol.
Chancery Execution Book, 1833-79, 1 vol.
Chancery Fee Book, 1893-1907, 1 vol.
Depositions, n. d., 2 items
Fee Books, 1843-98, 9 vols.
Index to Chancery Orders, 1886, 1 vol.
Law Memorandum Book, 1893-97, 1 vol.
Schedules, 1846-49, ca. 40 items
Witness Attendance Book, 1872-86, 1 vol.
Witness Summons Book, 1894-1904, 1 vol.

Election Records
List of Voters Registered, 1902-1924, 2 vols.
Poll Books, 1899, 1902, 1904, .5 cu. ft.

Fiduciary Records
Commissioner of Accounts, 1870-1909, 1 vol.
Estate and Guardian Accounts, 1894-98, 1900-02, .15 cu. ft.
List of Fiduciaries, 1850-70, 1 vol.

Justice of the Peace Records
Certificates of Justices of Causes Tried Before Them, 1882-88, 1 vol.
Civil Judgment and Execution Books, 1891-1917, 2 vols.
Dockets, 1837-50, 1860-80, 1883-89, 4 vols.
Executions 1800-40, 1842, 1844-1904, 1.5 cu. ft.
Judgments, 1841, 1843, 1845, 1850-53, .1 cu. ft.
Justices' Judgment and Execution Book, 1879-92, 1 vol.
Warrants, 1853-99, .9 cu. ft.

Land Records
Entry Book [for Buchanan County], 1786-1858 (transcript), 1 vol.
Index to Deeds, 1875-1917, n. d., 9 vols.

Land Office Caveat Book, 1853-62, 1 vol.

Map of Land in Controversy in Suit of Ejectment between W. W. Witten and Adam Sinkford, et. al., n. d., 1 item

Surveyor's Books, 1824-46, 1853-91, 3 vols.

Marriage Records and Vital Statistics

Marriage Bond, 1806, 1 item

Register of Births and Deaths, 1855-61, 1866, 1895 (broken series), .62 cu. ft.

Military and Pension Records

Confederate Pension Board Ledger, ca. 1900-10, 1 vol.

Confederate Pension List, 1902-12, 1 vol.

Road and Bridge Records

Jeffersonville and Maiden Spring Road Records, 1897-1901, 2 vols.

Map of the Change in Road Construction near Clinch River, n. d., 1 item

Plat of Road on Head of Mud Fork, n. d., 1 item

Road Warrants, 1892, ca. 100 items

Road Precincts Books, 1854-65, 1880-83, n. d., 3 vols.

School Records

Record of Board of Trustees for Maiden Spring School District, 1870-88, 1 vol.

Tax and Fiscal Records

Delinquent Tax Tickets, 1889-91, .25 cu. ft.

Land Tax Book, 1801-20, 1 vol.

Road Tax Books, 1871-74, 2 vols.

School Fund Warrant Book, 1871-91, 1 vol.

Township Records

Clear Fork Township Ledger, 1871-75, 1 vol.

Jeffersonville Township Ledger, 1870-74, 1 vol.

Minutes of Township Board of Jeffersonville, 1870-71, 1 vol.

Miscellaneous Records

Awards of Arbitrators on Line Fences, 1920 [includes Board of Supervisors's Warrants, 1870-75], 1 vol.

Book of Liens for Advancement, 1898-1910, 1 vol.

Clerk's Receipt Book, 1887-90, 1 vol.

Commissioner of Accounts Book, 1870-1906, 1 vol.

Estrays Book, 1801-66, 1 vol.

Medical Examiner's Book, 1891-1912, 1 vol.

Naturalization Petition and Record Books, 1904-1929, 3 vols.

Payments made to James R. Dills, 1856-58, 1 vol.

Receipt Book-County Warrants, 1896-1906, 1 vol.

Register of Estrays, 1882-1922, 1 vol.

Reservation of Title to Personalty, 1890-1915, 1 vol.

Specifications for Desks in Clerk's Office, n. d., 3 items

Stras Memorial Church Vestry Book, 1889, 1 vol.

Unidentified Indexes, n. d., 13 vols.

Unidentified List of Residents and Addresses, n. d., 2 vols.

Sheriff

Jail Register, 1872-1912, 1 vol.

Microfilm Records

Circuit Court Clerk
Court Records
County Court

Order Books, 1800-1817, 1820-71, 4 reels

Circuit Court
Chancery Orders, 1863-78, 1 reel (part)
Superior and Circuit Courts
Chancery Orders, 1832-63, 1 reel (part)
Unspecified Court
General Index to Law Order and Chancery Orders, 1832-1940, 1 reel
Land Records
Deed Books, Nos. 1-13, 1800-69, 6 reels
Index to Deeds No. 1, 1800-76, 1 reel
Surveyors Books Nos. 1-4, 1801-91, 2 reels
Index to Record of Surveys, 1801-1922, 1 reel (part)
Marriage Records and Vital Statistics
Marriage Registers Nos. 1-3, 1800-1920, 1 reel (part)
Index to Marriages, 1800-1939, 1 reel (part)
Register of Births, 1853-70, 1 reel (part)
Register of Deaths, 1853-71, 1 reel (part)
Wills
Will Books Nos. 1-3, 1800-66, 2 reels
Index to Wills No. 1, 1800-1908, 1 reel

WARREN COUNTY

Formed in 1836 from Shenandoah and Frederick counties.

Circuit Court Clerk
Board of Supervisors Records
Board of Supervisors Claims Allowed, 1870-1888, .35 cu. ft.
Board of Supervisors Papers, 1871-1919, .35 cu. ft.
Board of Supervisors Warrants, 1871-1903, 1 vol. and .2 cu. ft.
Bonds/Commissions/Oaths
Apprentice Bonds, 1888-98, 3 items
Attachment Bonds, ca. 1850-1904, 7 items
Bond Book, 1892-1901, 1 vol.
Bond Book, Special Commissioners and Trustees, 1901-18, 1 vol.
Bonds, 1898-1901, 50 items
County Officers Bonds, 1883-99, .2 cu. ft.
Deputy Sheriff's Bonds and Accounts, 1839-56, 30 items
Forthcoming Bonds, 1892, 3 items
Indemnity Bonds, 1892, 20 items
Injunction Bonds, 1892, 30 items
List of Officers Bonds, 1891-1904, 1 vol.
Liquor License Bonds, 1904-05, 3 items
Oaths of Allegiance for April-August 1861, 1865, 62 items
Oaths of County and Township Officers, 1879-81, 45 items
Oaths of Office, 1869-1910, .2 cu. ft.
Oaths of Office, Election Officials, 1885-1901, .1 cu. ft.
Oaths of Office, Justice of the Peace, 1899-1903, 30 items
Oaths of Office, School, etc., 1904-1919, .1 cu. ft.
Peace Bonds, 1902, 4 items
Recognizance Bonds, 1892, .1 cu. ft.

Record of County Officers Bonds, 1891-1904, 1 vol.

Registration Oath, Corporation of Front Royal, May 1886, 40 items

Business Records/Corporations/Partnerships

Lexington and Front Royal Inv. Co., Account Book of M. C. Richardson and W. E. Carson, Trustees, 1894-1903, 1 vol.

Luray and Front Royal Turnpike Co., Stockholders Minute Book and Ledger, 1851, 1 vol.

Census Records

Census Enumeration Sheets, 1880, 4 vols.

U. S. Census, 1840, 1 vol.

Court Records

County Court

Chancery Writ Docket, 1870-79, 1 vol.

Common Law Rules A-B, 1836-73, 2 vols.

Damages Allowed to Land Holders in Warren County from Manassas Gap Rail Road Co., 1852-55, .1 cu. ft.

Executions A-D, 1836-1903, 4 vols.

Executions Returned, 1836-92, 3.85 cu. ft.

Fee Books, 1847-68, 3 vols.

Index A [to Minute Books], 1836-ca. 1872, 1 vol.

Issue Docket, Chancery, 1871-73, 1 vol.

Issue Dockets, Common Law, 1850-62, 1871-73, 2 vols.

Memorandum Books, 1836-69, 4 vols.

Official Orders, 1840-41, .1 cu. ft.

Process Books A-B, 1836-94, 2 vols.

Record of Judgments, 1843-77, 1880-87, 2 vols.

Shenandoah Valley Rail Road, Commissions Reports &c. [Condemnations], 1872-82, .1 cu. ft.

Witness Attendance, 1836-88, 2 vols.

Writ Docket, 1836-49, 1 vol.

Circuit Superior Court of Law and Chancery

Memorandum, 1836-50, 1 vol.

Writ Docket, 1836-49, 1 vol.

Circuit Court

Chancery Dockets, 1873-99, 5 vols.

Chancery Rule Book B, 1879-1914, 1 vol.

Common Law Issues, 1880-99, 1 vol.

Executions B, 1883-1924, 1 vol.

Executions Returned, 1899-1909, .1 cu. ft.

Fee Books, 1854-81, 1883-89, 1893-99, 4 vols.

Issue Docket, 1852-80, 2 vols.

Pr(a)ecipes, 1886-97, .2 cu. ft.

Receivers' Books, 1851-96, 1898-1914, 3 vols.

Witness Attendance Book, 1871-87, 1 vol.

See also School Records, School Commissioners' and Other Records.

County and Circuit Court

Chancery Rules A, 1837-1913, 1 vol.

County, Superior, and Circuit Courts

Writ Docket, 1850-1903, 1 vol.

Circuit Superior Court of Law and Chancery and Circuit Court
 Chancery Executions A, 1839-1894, 1 vol. and .1 cu. ft.
 Chancery Process Book A, 1836-1933, 1 vol.
 Common Law Executions A, 1836-83, 1 vol.
 Common Law Rules A, 1836-1910, 1 vol.
 Issue Docket, 1836-52, 1 vol.
 Minutes, 1844-70, 1 vol.
 Orders of Attendance, 1837-84, 1 vol.
 Process Book A, 1836-94, 1 vol.
 Rule Book A, 1836-79, 1 vol.
Unidentified Court
 Chancery Fee Book, 1893-1899, 1 vol.
 Execution Book, 1869-82, 1 vol.
 Fee Books, 1836-53, 1868-71, 1881-83, 1899-1924, 5 vols.
 Index to Minute Books, 1898-1932, 1 vol.
 Index to Suits, 1845-1938, n. d., 2 vols.
Election Records
 Certificates and Polls of Elections, 1836-1903, 1.25 cu. ft.
 Election Records, 1860-1949, .45 cu. ft.
 Lists of Registered Voters, Colored, 1902-03, 36 vols.
 List of Registered Voters, White, 1902-03, 83 vols.
 Permanent Roll of Voters, 1902-03, 1 vol.
Fiduciary Records
 Administrators Bonds, 1850-71, 1891-1918, 2 vols.
 Executors' and Administrators' Bonds, 1852-1902, 1 vol.
 Executors' Bonds, 1850-1917, 2 vols.
 Executors' and Guardians' Bonds, 1836-47, .15 cu. ft.
 Guardians' Bonds, 1850-1918, 2 vols.
 Record of Fiduciaries, 1850-1938, 2 vols.
 Vouchers, 1835-41, ca. 50 items
Free Negro and Slave Records
 List of Free Negroes, 1855, 1 item
Justice of the Peace Records
 Cases Disposed of by Justices, 1888-1893, 1 vol.
 Constables' Executions Returned, 1882-1907, 2 vols.
 Executions Returned by Constables, 1872-92, .1 cu. ft.
 Justices' Executions Not Docketed, 1896-1910, .1 cu. ft.
 Magistrates' Executions, 1854-61, 1869-90, .35 cu. ft.
 Magistrates' Executions on which Ca Sa's have been issued, 1837-56, .1 cu. ft.
 Magistrates' Executions Returned by Constables, 1836-47, ca.60 items
 Magistrates' Executions Returned to Office, 1832-41, ca. 60 items
Land Records
 Conveyances, 1836-42, 1876-86, 3 vols.
 County Land Records A, 1842-46, 1 vol.
 Deeds, 1836-1905, 4.55 cu. ft.
 General Index to Deeds, 1839-1923, 1 vol.
 Index to Deeds A-Z, 1900, 4 vols.
 Deeds and related papers, 1891, 1899, 1904, 4 items
 F. R. & R. Improvement Co. to F. R. Investment Co., Deeds, ca. 1890, .1 cu. ft.
 List of Conveyances, 1863-74, 1 vol.
 Map of Shenandoah Valley Railroad, 1872, 1 item
 Old Deeds, Bills of Sale, Agreements, etc. Left in Office, 1795-1879, .1 cu. ft.
 Plats, 1875, 1880, 1882-84, 1890, 8 items
 Plats and Surveys Made by County Surveyor, 1837-78, 28 items

Records of Release No. 1, 1884-1909, 1 vol.
Releases, 1884-99, .1 cu. ft.
Marriage Records and Vital Statistics
Register of Marriages, 1850-1913, 1 vol.
Registers of Births and Deaths, 1854-61, 10 vols.
Registers of Births and Deaths, 1872-75, .35 cu. ft.
Military and Pension Records
See Tax and Fiscal Records, Tax on Deeds.
Road and Bridge Records
Descriptions of Roads in Front Royal District, 1883-90, 1 vol.
Road Contract Book, 1886-1905, 1 vol.
Road Contracts, 1902-03, 17 items
Road Papers and Orders, 1836-54, .1 cu. ft.
Road Warrants, 1889-1902, .55 cu. ft.
South River Township Accounts and Bonds of Road Commissioners, 1871-74, 1 vol.
School Records
Ledgers, State and County School Fund, 1887-94, 1 vol.
School Commissioners' Accounts and Drafts, 1836-57, 1859-61, 1.25 cu. ft.
School Commissioners' and Other Records, Circuit Court Minutes, 1836-65, 1 vol.
Tax and Fiscal Records
County Court Tax Book, 1898-99, 1 vol.
Fork Township Tax Bill Receipt Book, 1872-74, 1 vol.
Insolvent Debtors, 1827-59, .1 cu. ft.
Personal Property Tax Tickets, S. W. Pratt, 1845-50, 1 item
Tax on Deeds, 1889-1904 [includes Confederate pension certificates, 1888-91], 1 vol.
Warrant Book, 1900-12, 1 vol.
Township Records
Cedarville Township Board Account Book, 1871-75, 1 vol.
Cedarville Township Board Minutes of Meetings, 1871-75, 1 vol.
South River Township Minute Book, 1871-74, 1 vol.
Wills
General Index to Wills, 1836-1935, 1 vol.
Miscellaneous Records
Certificates from Board of Medical Examiners to Physicians and Surgeons, 1890, 1 vol.
Certificates of Board of Dental Examiners, 1890-1906, 1 vol.
Conditional Sales, 1902, 2 items
Contract Docket [Reservation of Title to Personalty No. 1], 1890-1916, 1 vol.
Crop Lien Docket No. 1, 1892-1938, 1 vol.
Estray Book, 1866-83, 1 vol.
Estray Warrants, 1836-85, .1 cu. ft.
Judgment Lien Dockets A-D, 1843-1913, 4 vols.
Mechanics Lien Docket, 1891-1914, 1 vol.
Overseers of the Poor Accounts, 1854-61, .2 cu. ft.
Overseers of the Poor Act, 1887, 4 items
Overseers of the Poor Indentures, 1839-78, .1 cu. ft.
Overseers of the Poor Papers and Vouchers, 1836-41, 1848-52, .25 cu. ft.
Parish Papers, 1855-57, 1870, .1 cu. ft.
Register of Descriptive Lists of Persons Convicted of Felony, 1867-1932, 1 vol.
Sheriff
Sheriff's Return of Voters Posted, 1904-64, 1 vol.

Treasurer

[Account Book] Treasurer, Corporation of Front Royal, 1881-1912, 1 vol.
Delinquent Lands Sold Lists, 1884-98, .1 cu. ft.
Delinquent Real Estate Lists, D-J, R-S, n. d., 2 vols. [notebooks]
Delinquent Real Estate Sold for Nonpayment of Taxes and Levies Lists, [1876-1901],
    1 vol.
Delinquent Tax Lists, 1846, 1850, 1853, 1874-1904, 2 cu. ft.
Record of Delinquent Lands, 1884-89, 1 vol.
Warrants Drawn on Treasurer, 1885-1902, 1.25 cu. ft.

Microfilm Records

Circuit Court Clerk
  Bonds/Commissions/Oaths
    Bond Book, 1850-91, 1 reel
  Court Records
    County Court
        Minute Books A-D, 1836-72, 2 reels
        Index to County Court Minute Books, 1836-1904, 1 reel
    Superior and Circuit Courts
        Chancery Order Book A, 1836-66, 1 reel (part)
        General Index to Chancery Orders, 1836-1951, 1 reel (part)
  Land Records
    Deed Books A-H, 1836-71, 3 reels
    General Index to Deeds, 1836-52 (Grantor/Grantee), 5 reels
    Land Record A, 1842-46, 1 reel (part)
  Marriage Records and Vital Statistics
    Marriage Registers, 1836-1913, 1 reel (part)
    General Index to Marriages, 1836-1952, 1 reel (part)
    Register of Births, 1853-1917, 1 reel (part)
    Index to Births, 1853-1917, 1 reel (part)
    Register of Deaths, 1853-74, 1 reel (part)
  Military and Pension Records
    Muster Roll, 1861-65, 1 reel (part)
  Wills
    Wills, Etc., A-C, 1836-66, 2 reels
    Wills, Etc., AA (Circuit Court), 1838-1904, 1 reel (part)
    General Index to Wills, 1836-1951 (Decedents/Heirs), 1 reel

WARWICK COUNTY

**Original shire established in 1634 as
Warwick River. Became Warwick in 1643, and
incorporated in 1952 as a city. It became
extinct in 1958 when it was consolidated
with Newport News.**

For listing of records, see A Preliminary Guide to Pre-1904 Municipal Records, City of
Newport News entry.

WASHINGTON COUNTY

Formed in 1776 from Fincastle County.
Part of Montgomery County was added later.

Original Records

Circuit Court Clerk
  Court Records
    County Court
      Minute Book No. 1, 1777-84, 1 vol.
  Fiduciary Records
    Orphans' Bonds, 1783, 1795, 3 items
  Land Records
    Records of Deeds No. 1, 1779-97, 1 vol.
  Tax and Fiscal Records
    List of Insolvents, 1783, 1 booklet
  Wills
    Will Books Nos. 1, 2, and 6, 1777-1806, 1824-84, 3 vols.
Sheriff
  Sheriff's Records, 1844-46, 8 items

Microfilm Records

Circuit Court Clerk
  Court Records
    County Court
      Minute Books Nos. 1-16, 1777-87, 1819-21, 1837-66, 5 reels
      General Index to Minutes Nos. 1-4, 1777-1872, 2 reels
    Superior and Circuit Courts
      Chancery Order Books A-C, 1831-70, 1 reel
  Fiduciary Records
    Guardian Accounts Nos. 1, 2, 1840-73, 1 reel
  Land Records
    Deed Books Nos. 1-26, 1778-1866, 12 reels
    District Court Deed Books A, B, 1789-1840, 1 reel (part)
    General Index to Deeds Nos. 1, 2, 1778-1877, 1 reel
    General Index to District Court Deeds A and B, 1789-1840, 1 reel (part)
    Surveyors' Records, 1781-1890, 1 reel
  Marriage Records and Vital Statistics
    Marriage Registers Nos. 1, 2, 1785-1902, 1 reel
    Register of Births, 1853-92, 1 reel (part)
    Register of Deaths, 1853-92, 1 reel (part)
  Military and Pension Records
    Muster Roll, 1861-65, 1 reel
  Wills
    Circuit Court Will Book C, 1840-1903, 1 reel
    Will Books Nos. 1-16, 1777-1866, 6 reels
    General Index to Will Books 1-37, 1777-1938, 1 reel
  Miscellaneous Records
    Overseers of Poor, Minutes, 1826-62, 1 reel

WESTMORELAND COUNTY

Formed in 1653 from Northumberland County.
Part of King George County was added later.

Circuit Court Clerk
  Board of Supervisors Records
    [Board of Supervisors's Account Record Book], 1871-74, 1 vol.
    Board of Supervisors Papers, 1890-95, .45 cu. ft.
    Board of Supervisors Warrant, 1896, 1 item
  Bonds/Commissions/Oaths
    Bond Books, 1826-32, 1851-1916, 4 vols.
    Bonds, 1759, 1781-83, 1785, 1787, .2 cu. ft.
    Clerks' Bonds, 1845-71, 24 items
    Liquor Bonds, 1878-1904, .45, cu. ft.
    Record of Bonds, 1850-1873, 1 vol.
    Supervision of Coming Bonds, 1815-14, 30 items
    See also Fiduciary Records, Administrators', Guardians', Executors', Officials',
      and Liquor License Bonds.
  Business Records/Corporations/Partnerships
    Tavern Keeper's Account Book, 1833-34, 1 vol.
  Court Records
    County Court
      Abatements, 1814-15, 1817-18, 1820-47, .58 cu. ft.
      Abatements, Discontinuances, 1788-1819, .1 cu. ft.
      Abatements, Dismissions, 1820-21, 1827-46, .35 cu. ft.
      Assignment, 1775, 1 item
      Capias, 1797, 1 item
      Chancery Causes, 1821, .1 cu. ft.
      Claims Levied, 1852, 1855, 1857-58, 1860-61, 1867, 1869, .55 cu. ft.
      Claims vs. H. G. Letuze, 1817-18, 45 items
      Confessions of Judgments, Abatements and Dismissions, 1852-68, .15 cu. ft.
      Court Papers, 1763-1894, 30.7 cu. ft.
      Depositions, 1753; 1760, 2 items
      Discontinuances, 1790, 20 items
      Discontinuances at Rules, 1803, .1 cu. ft.
      Dismissions, Abatements, Confessions, 1869-71, .1 cu. ft.
      Dismissions, Confessions, Abatements at Rules, 1846-52, .1 cu. ft.
      Docket Books, 1839-52, 1858-78, 1883-92, 3 vols.
      Execution Books, 1790-1903, 15 vols.
      Executions, 1763-74, 1784-1890, 8 cu. ft.
      Memorandum Book, 1827-28, 1 vol.
      Minute Book, Court of Oyer and Terminer and County Court, 1750-52, 1 vol.
      Minute Books, 1770-72, 1786-96, 1798-1808, 1815, 1818, 1827-28, 15 vols.
      Office Judgments, 1787-91, 1798-1828, 1830-73, 11.05 cu. ft. and 3 vols.
      Office Judgments Confirmed, 1796-98, .45 cu. ft.
      Order Books, 1662-64, 1675/6-1688/9, 1690-1746/7, 1750-64, 1776-95, 1797-
        1801, 1804-18, 23 vols.
      Promiscuous Papers, 1823-57, 1 cu. ft.
      Rule Book, 1842-57, 1 vol.
      Rule Book and Office Judgments, 1786-87, 1 vol.
      Thomas M. Carr v. The Council of Colonial Beach, suit papers, 1897, 3 items
      Writ, 1760, 1 item

Writs Ad quod damnum, 1792, 1795, 1797-99, 1804, 1814, 1817, 1826, 11 items

Writs of Habeas Corpus, 1853-1900, 12 items

See also Land Records, Deeds and Wills.

District Court

Court Papers, 1809, .1 cu. ft.

Superior Court of Law

Court Papers, 1810, 1817, 1820, 1822, .3 cu. ft.

Execution Book 1823-31, 1 vol.

Executions, 1810-16, 1819-31, 1.35 cu. ft.

Executions Returned, 1817-18, .1 cu. ft.

Judgments Confessed in Office, 1825-31, 6 items

Order Book 1809-23, 1 vol.

Orders at Law, 1823-30, 1 vol.

Records [Order Book] 1830-31, 1 vol.

Circuit Superior Court of Law and Chancery

Court Papers, 1832-33, 1835, .45 cu. ft.

Executions, 1832-50, 1.35 cu. ft.

Executions Returned, 1835, 1870, .1 cu. ft.

Office Judgments, 1831-45, 1849, 50 items and 1 vol.

Orders, 1831-34, 1 vol.

Records, 1831-41, 1 vol.

Circuit Court

Execution Books, 1857-66, 1870-1922, 2 vols.

Executions, 1851-53, 1855-60, .55 cu. ft.

Executions Returned, 1860-61, 1863, 1866-71, 1880-89, .45 cu. ft.

Extracts of Judgments, 1844-66, .2 cu. ft.

Memorandum Book, 1883-1901, 1 vol.

Office Judgments, 1853-55, 1857-59, 1861-62, 1866-69, 1.3 cu. ft.

Orders at Law, 1858-1911, 2 vols.

Orders of Court and Miscellaneous Court Notes, 1854-81, 1 vol.

Circuit and County Court

Court Papers, 1830, 1850-64, 1866-83, 1886-1904, 12.25 cu. ft.

Execution Book, Chancery Court, 1832-1915, 1 vol.

Extracts of Judgments, 1868-70, 1893-1901, .1 cu. ft.

Circuit and Superior Courts

Office Judgments, 1809-31, 1846-68, 2 vols.

Orders, 1839-57, 1 vol.

County and Superior Courts

Court Papers, 1831-52, 6.75 cu. ft.

Order Book, 1809-10, 1813-14, 1823-30, 1 vol.

Superior Court of Chancery at Fredericksburg

Webb v. Fauntleroy and Alderson v. Fauntleroy, suit paper, 1820, 1 item

Unidentified Court

Chancery Rule Docket, 1827-28, 1 vol.

Docket Books, 1843-69, 2 vols.

Fee Books, 1815-16, 1821-22, 1832-33, 1842-46, 1860-67, 1871-78, 6 vols.

Issue Docket, 1811-14, 1 vol.

Judgment Dockets, 1844-1919, 3 vols.

Law Docket Books, 1809-11, 1817-19, 2 vols.

Memorandum Books, 1833-37, 1839, 1841, 3 vols.

Minute Books, 1805-06, 1811, 1814, 1829-31, 4 vols.

Process Book, 1835-53, 1 vol.

Process Law Books, 1833-53, 2 vols.

Rule Docket, 1828-31, 1 vol.

Election Records

Abstract of Voters for Amended Constitution, 1862, 53 items
Colored Voters Poll Books and Registers, 1902-1949, 3 vols.
General Registration, 1902-03, 1 vol.
Lists of Voters, Black, 1902-54, 10 vols.
Lists of Voters, White, 1902-54, 18 vols.

Fiduciary Records

Administrators' Bonds, 1799-1800, 1832-50, 1872-73, .1 cu. ft. and 2 vols.
Administrators' and Executors' Bonds, 1832-50, 1 vol.
Administrators', Guardians', Executors', Officials, Committee, and Liquor
    License Bonds, (titles vary) 1761-1826, 1850-86, 1889-1906, 1.95 cu. ft.
Fiduciary Accounts, 1742-89, 1 vol.
Guardians' Bonds, 1832-50, 2 vols.
Inventories, 1664, 1853-98, 24 items
Inventories and Accounts, 1812-30, 1834-46, 1853-70, 1874-83, 1886-1906,
    5.85 cu. ft.
Records and Inventories Nos. [1]-8 (titles vary), 1723-1806, 8 vols.
Record of Fiduciaries, 1850-1916, 2 vols.

Free Negro and Slave Records

Free Negro Registers, 1817-26, 1828-61 (volume for 1828-49 includes estrays,
    1833-36), 3 vols.
Register of Slaves Held for Life, 1859, 1 vol.

Justice of the Peace Records

Cases Disposed of by Justices, 1883-1934, 1 vol.
Executions, 1894-1920, 1 vol.
Justices Executions, 1886-1902, 1 vol.
Justices Executions on Which Casas Have Been Issued, 1822-46, .2 cu. ft.
Justices Executions Returned, 1840-82, .4 cu. ft.

Land Records

Deeds, 1759, 1761, 1763, 1771-72, 1782 1784, 8 items
Deeds and Wills Nos. 1-20 (titles vary), 1653-71, 1691-99, 1701-09, 1717-1803
    (No. 19 includes orders), 21 vols.
Deeds, etc., Lodged for Recordation, Fees Not Paid, 1872-1910, 30 items
Deeds, Patents, etc. (includes wills) 1655-77, 1 vol.
Deed, Wills, etc., 1661-62, 1 vol.
Deeds, Wills, Patents, etc., 1653-59, 1 vol.
General Index to Deeds No. 3, n. d., 1 vol.
Index to Deeds and Wills Nos. 43-48, 50-53, 55-56, 61, 64-68, 70-79, n. d.,
    28 vols.
Old Deeds, Wills, Etc. Lodged for Recordation, 1892-98, 30 items
Record of Land Purchased by the Commonwealth, 1876-1905, 1 vol.

Marriage Records and Vital Statistics

Bride/Groom Index to Marriages 1772-1865, .1 cu. ft.
Marriage Bond Form, 1812, 1 item
Marriage Licenses and Ministers' Returns, 1840-41, 1843-45, 1849, 1853, 1855,
    13 items
Record of Marriages, 1826-1920, 2 vols.
See also Miscellaneous Records, Miscellaneous Paper.

Tax and Fiscal Records

Delinquent Land, 1898-1906, .35 cu. ft.
Delinquent Land List, 1832, .1 cu. ft.
Delinquent [Tax] Roll of Cople Parish, 1724, 2 items
Lists of Lands Returned Delinquent, 1832, .1 cu. ft.

Real Estate Delinquent For Non-Payment of Taxes Assessed for 1902-07 List, 1 vol.

Record of Delinquent Lands, 1884-89, 1897-1912, 3 vols.

Record of Insolvent Capitation and Property Tax, 1885-86, 1 vol.

Rent Roll, 1740, 8 items

Wills

Wills, 1664, 1710, 1716, 1720, 1724, 1736, 1754-63, 1766, 1774-79, 1781, 1783, 41 items

Liber S (includes deeds) 1747-53, 1 vol.

See also Land Records.

Miscellaneous Records

Appointment of Overseers of the Poor, 1801, 1 item

Conditional Sales, 1881-1916, 2 vols.

Conditional Sales Reservations of Title, 1899-1911, 25 items

Coroner's Inquest Papers, 1839-69, .1 cu. ft.

Index to National Farm Loan Mortgages No. 1, n. d., 1 vol.

Lunacy Papers 1903-1914, .1 cu. ft.

Mechanics Liens, 1894-1906, 8 items

Mechanics Liens Record, 1884-1920, 1 vol.

Miscellaneous Paper [Clerk's notations, includes marriage records], 1691-92, 1 item

Oyster Inspectors' Report No. 1, 1884-92, 1 vol.

Power of Attorney, 1768, 1 item

Proceedings of Committee of Safety, 1775-76, 28 items

Register of Convicts, 1871-1922, 1 vol.

Treasurer

Treasurer's Accounts, 1873-1917, 1 vol.

William Mayo's Treasurer Report, 1885, 7 items

Microfilm Records

Circuit Court Clerk

Court Records

County Court

Chancery Orders, 1851-73, 1 reel (part)

Order Books (titles vary), 1662-64, 1675-1764, 1776-95, 1797-1867, 20 reels

See also Land Records.

Superior Court of Law

Superior Court Orders, 1809-30, 1 reel

Superior Court Records, 1809-31, 1 reel (part)

Circuit Superior Court of Law and Chancery

Superior Court Orders, 1832-39, 1 reel (part)

Superior and Circuit Courts

Chancery Orders, 1831-56, 1 reel (part)

Superior Court Orders, 1839-57, 1 reel (part)

Fiduciary Records

Fiduciary Book, 1742-89, 1 reel (part)

General Index to Fiduciary Accounts, Etc., Vol. 1, 1723-1917, 1 reel

Records and Inventories Nos. 1-25, 1723-1867, 21 reels

Free Negro and Slave Records

Register of Free Negroes, Etc., 1828-49, 1 reel (part)

Land Records

Deeds, 1706-1804, 1 reel (part)

Deeds and Wills Nos. 1-37, 1653-71, 1691-99, 1701-09, 1712-1868, 25 reels
General Index to Deeds, Nos. 1, 2, 1653-1898, 1 reel
Deeds, Wills, Patents (titles vary), 1653-59, 1661-62, 1665-77, 1 reel
Land Causes, 1827-37, 1 reel (part)
Marriage Records and Vital Statistics
Marriage Bonds, 1772-1850, 3 reels
Marriage Bonds, Vols. 3-17, 1793-1865, 15 reels
Marriage Licenses, 1866-1912, 8 reels
Record of Marriages, 1826-50, 1 reel (part)
Register of Births 1858-95, 1 reel (part)
Register of Deaths, 1857-96, 1 reel (part)
Register of Marriages, 1854-1908, 1 reel (part)
Wills
Wills, 1755-1800, 1 reel (part)
See Land Records

WISE COUNTY

Formed in 1856 from Lee, Scott, and Russell counties.

Circuit Court Clerk
Board of Supervisors Records
Minutes, 1870-89, 1 vol.
See also Road and Bridge Papers, and Court Records, Unspecified Court.
Bonds
Bonds [various types], ca. 1856-1904, 1 cu. ft.
[County Court] Bond Books Nos. [1]-2, 1890-1911, 2 vols.
Circuit Court Bond Books Nos. [1]-2, 1892-1902, 1896-1907, 2 vols.
Hireling Bonds, 1880-1923, and Capias, ca. 1885-1900, 1 cu. ft.
Record of Forthcoming Bonds, 1899-1932, 1 vol.
Record of Title Bonds, 1889-1927, 1 vol.
Business and Organization Records
C[arbon], C[oal] and C[oke] Co. Ledger, 1903-13, 1 vol.
R. P. Hamilton's Fee Book No. 1 (lawyer?), 1898-1900, 1 vol.
Wise County Bank Debit Journal, 1904-05, 1 vol.; and, Deposit Ledger, 1901-05, 1 vol.
Court Papers
County Court
Bar and Reference Docket No. 5, 1893-97, 1 vol.
Cash Book, 1899-1904, 1 vol.
Common Law Order Books, 1870-83, 3 vols.
Dockets, 1889-96, 2 vols.
Execution Books Nos. [1], 3-4, 1857-84, 1893-1903, 3 vols.
Fee Books, 1867-77, 1896-1905, 7 vols.
General Index Key, 1858-1902, 1 vol.
Issue Dockets No. 1 and unnumbered, 1856-75, 1880-87, 2 vols.
Mechanics' Liens, 1891-1908, 1 vol.
Memorandum Books, 1868-79, 1892-1906, 4 vols.
Minute Books, 1886-92, 1894-98, 6 vols.
Order Books Nos. 2, 7-[16], 1862-67, 1885-1902, 11 vols.

Index to Order Books 7-18, n. d., 1 vol.

Process Books Nos. [1]-2, 1867-1903, 2 vols.

Rule Docket No. 1, 1856-71, 1 vol.; and, Chancery Court Rule Docket, 1856-87, 1 vol.

Witness Attendance Books Nos. 5, 7, and unnumbered, 1868-69, 1882-86, 1892-97, 1901-03, 6 vols.

County and Circuit Courts

Bar Docket, 1899-1901, 1 vol.

Judgment Lien Dockets Nos. 2-7, 1868-1906, 6 vols.

Direct Index to Judgment Lien Docket and Execution Books, 1856-1903, 3 vols.

General Index to Judgment Lien Docket and Execution Books, Plaintiffs A-Z, 1856-1927, 1 vol.; and, Defendants A-Z, 1856-1927, 2 vols.

Index to Judgment Lien Docket No. 4, 1890, 1 vol.

Tax Book, 1893-98, 1 vol.

Circuit Court

Chancery Court Issue Docket No. 1, 1857-82, 2 vols. (both labeled No. 1, same dates)

Chancery Court Rule Docket, 1856-87, 1 vol.

Chancery Fee Book No. 8, 1896-1900, 1 vol.

Chancery Papers, 556-610, 731-755, and unnumbered, ca. 1900-10, 2 cu. ft. (Notes, receipts, and return to sanity papers are mixed in with this series.)

Chancery Rule Books Nos. [1]-4, 1894, 2 vols.

Common Law and Chancery Court Reference Docket, 1881-91, 1883, 2 vols.; and, Washington [Wise] County Bar and Reference Docket, 1888-91, 1 vol.

Common Law Issue Docket, 1868-80, 1 vol.

Dockets Nos. 3-8, 1888-1906, 5 vols.

Execution Books Nos. [1]-5, 1858-1909 3 vols.

Fee Books, 1884-1908, 9 vols.

General Index to Chancery Record Book, 1904-25, 1 vol.

Index Vol. No. 1 to Court Orders, 1904-05, 1 vol.

Ledgerized Index to Judgment Lien Docket and Execution Books, 1903-11, 1 vol.

Memorandum Books, 1904-09, 1 vol.

Process Books Nos. [1]-2, 1856-1908, 2 vols.

Receipt Book, 1893, 1 vol.

W. E. Kilgore's Exhibit Books [Ledgers], 1895-1905, 5 vols.

Witness Attendance Books Nos. 20 and unnumbered, 1896-1900, n. d., 2 vols.

Unspecified Court

Civil Warrants, Abstracts of Judgments, Liquor Licenses, and Road Reports, ca. 1895, 1 cu. ft.

Commonwealth Cases and Civil Executions (some recorded deeds are mixed in with this series), ca. 1885-1900, 1 cu. ft.

Court Papers (contains some Board of Supervisors' papers), ca. 1899-1920, 8 cu. ft.

Court Receipt Books, 1893, 1896-97, 2 vols.

Direct Index to Docket Cases, 1856-1904, 1 vol.

Direct Index to General Orders, 1856-1905, 1 vol.

Executions A-Z, and Motions, ca. 1885-1900, 1 cu. ft.

Fee Books (includes Memoranda, 1900-02), 1887-92, 1899-1900, 5 vols.

Indictments (Fiduciary records, Commonwealth cases, bonds, deeds, J. P. reports, and suit papers are mixed in with these records), 1889-1904, 14 cu. ft.

Jury Attendance Books, 1891-92, 1897-1900, 2 vols.

Mossy Creek Woolen Mills Co. et al. v. T. R. Kyle et al.; and, Henry County Tobacco Company et al. v. T. R. Kyle et al., Exhibit Books, 1901, 2 vols.

Order Book, 1899-1900, 1 vol.

Register of Persons Convicted of Felony, n. d., 1 vol.

Rules, ca. 1895-1920, 1 cu. ft.

Suit Papers (Board of Supervisors' papers, election records, arrest warrants, and deeds are mixed in with this series), ca. 1870-1950, 11 cu. ft.

Warrants, ca. 1856-1904, 1 cu. ft.

See also Fiduciary Records, County Court Fiduciary Book and Fiduciary Records.

Election Records

General Registration, 1902-03, 1 vol.

Lists of Registered Voters, 1904-06, 1 vol.

See also Court Records, Unspecified Court, Suit Papers.

Fiduciary Records

County Court Fiduciary Book [includes Judgment and Execution Book, 1876-91], 1865-75, 1 vol.

Fiduciary Accounts, 1878-96, 1 vol.

Fiduciary Records, ca. 1885-1925, 2 cu. ft. (executions and licenses are mixed in with this series).

General Index to Fiduciary Accounts and Wills, n. d., 1 vol.

Record of Fiduciaries, Commissioner of Accounts, 1886-1952, 1 vol.

See also Court Records, Unspecified Court, Indictments.

Justice of the Peace Records

Justices' Civil Execution Book No. 3, 1899-1950, 1 vol.

Justices' Fines, 1888-93, 1 vol.

Justices' Judgment and Execution Books, 1884-1911, 45 vols.

Justice of the Peace Reports, 1900-20, 5 cu. ft. See also Court Records, Unspecified Court, Indictments.

Justices' Reports Nos. 4-5, 1900-07, 2 vols and .3 cu. ft.

Land Records

[Abstract of Deed Books 68-80], n. d., 1 vol. (Ts)

Deed Books [Record], 1874-82, 2 vols. (Ts)

Deed Receipt Book, 1896-97, 1 vol.

Direct Index to Deed Books Nos. 120-128, n. d., 1 vol.

Index to Deeds, 1857-87, 1 vol.

See also Court Records, Unspecified Court, Indictments and Suit Papers.

Marriage, Divorce, and Vital Statistics

Register of Marriages, 1856-1908, 1 vol.

Road and Bridge Papers

Road Books, 1881-91, [1896] 1897-1903, 1898-1907, 7 vols.

See also Court Records, Unspecified Court, Civil Warrants.

School Records

[Reports of School Superintendent] Judgment Lien Docket No. 1, 1858-60, 1 vol.

School Board Journals, 1885, 1 vol.

Tax and Fiscal Records

Delinquent Land Books, 1879-1903, 1895-1900, 2 vols.

Delinquent Land Book for Big Stone Gap, 1904-05, 1 vol.

Index to Delinquent Lands and Sales Book, 1865-1903, 1 vol.

Lands Improperly Assessed or not Ascertainable, 1884, 1 vol.

Miscellaneous Records

Conditional Sales Book, 1890-1905, 1 vol.

Miscellaneous Papers, 1883-1943, 2 cu. ft.

Record of Estrays, 1889-1911, 1 vol.
Record of Physicians' Certificates No. 1, 1893-1918, 1 vol.
Statements of Officers of Companies, 1903-12, .3 cu. ft.
Unidentified Day Books, 1892-94, 1892-96, 2 vols.
Unidentified Notebook, 1893-94, 1 vol.

Microfilm Records

Circuit Court Clerk
  Court Records
    County Court
      Order Book 1, 1856-61, 1 reel
  Land Records
    Deed Book 1, 1856-66, 1 reel (part)
    General Index to Deeds 1, 1856-88, 1 reel (part)
    Surveyors' Book, 1856-1924, 1 reel
  Marriage Records and Vital Statistics
    Register of Births, 1856-71, 1 reel (part)
    Register of Deaths, 1856-94, 1 reel (part)
    Register of Marriages, 1856-1908, 1 reel (part)
  Wills
    Will Books Nos. 1, 2, 1856-84, 1 reel
    General Index to Wills, 1856-1953, 1 reel

WYTHE COUNTY

**Formed in 1789 from Montgomery County.
Part of Grayson County was added later.**

Original Records

Circuit Court Clerk
  Land Records
    Deed Book 1, 1790-96, 1 vol.
Sheriff
  David A. Rich (deputy sheriff) Papers, 1879-95, .375 cu. ft.
  Tax and Receipt Book, 1805-07, 1 vol.

Microfilm Records

Circuit Court Clerk
  Court Records
    County Court
      Order Books, 1790, 1795-1865, 8 reels
    Circuit Superior Court of Law and Chancery
      Chancery Order Book 1, 1831-35, 1 reel (part)
      Complete Chancery Records Nos. 1-3, 1832-47, 1 reel
      Miscellaneous Records, 1832-45, 1 reel (part)

Superior and Circuit Courts
Chancery Order Book 2, 1835-53, 1 reel (part)
Circuit Court
Chancery Order Book 3, 1853-73, 1 reel
U. S. District Court
Miscellaneous Records, 1824-38, 1 reel (part)
Land Records
Deed Books Nos. 1-22, 1790-1867, 10 reels
General Index to Deeds, 1790-1907, Grantor-Grantee, 2 reels
Records of Surveys Nos. 1-4, 1790-1910, 2 reels
General Index to Surveys, 1790-1910, 1 reel
Marriage Records and Vital Statistics
Marriage Registers Nos. 1-3, 1790-1919, 1 reel (part)
Miscellaneous Marriage Records, 1790-1905, 1 reel (part)
Register of Births, 1853-72, 1 reel (part)
Register of Deaths, 1853-70, 1 reel (part)
Military and Pension Records
Confederate Veterans Records, 1861-65, 1 reel
Court Martial Records, 1797-1808, 1 reel (part)
Militia Rosters, 1813, 1 reel (part)
Wills
Circuit Court Will Book O, 1833-1903, 1 reel
Will Books Nos. 1-10, 1790-1865, 4 reels
General Index to Wills, 1790-1911, 1 reel

YORK COUNTY

**Original shire established in 1634.
Name changed from Charles River County in 1643.**

Circuit Court Clerk
Bonds/Commissions/Oaths
Bonds, etc., 1782-1860, .49 cu. ft.
Bonds for Oystering, 1821-23, ca. 100 items
Bonds of County Clerks [General Court], 1722-74, ca. 75 items
Bonds to Transport Oysters, 1821-27, 23 items
Executions Stay Bonds, 1808-10, ca. 100 items
Injunction Bonds, 1825-50, 8 items
Oaths of Allegiance, 1777-78, 2 items
Officials' Bonds, 1793-1889, .32 cu. ft.
Replevy Bonds, 1785-97, .35 cu. ft.
Court Records
County Court
Chancery Suit Papers, 1779, 1784-86, 1788-89, 1793, 1795, 1797-98, 1802, 1805-07, 1809-11, 1814-15, 1818, 1820-55, 1857-59, 1871, 1873, 1875, 1878-79, 2 cu. ft.
Common Law, Chancery, and Criminal Papers, 1762-1890, 15.3 cu. ft.
Declarations, 1776, 1782-86, 1820-50, .25 cu. ft.
Executions, 1760-75, 1783-1808, 1810, 1812-53, .91 cu. ft.
Fee Book, 1813, 1 vol.
Inquisitions and Commonwealth Cases, 1835-43, ca. 100 items

Judgments, 1766-74, 1824, 1826, 1837, .35 cu. ft.

Judgments and Dismissions, 1786-87, 1790, 1800-01, 1805, 1809-10, 1814-60, 1.75 cu. ft.

Judgments and Orders No. 3, 1759-63, 1 vol.

Orders, Wills, Records Nos. 14-17, 1709-32, 6 vols.

Presentments, 1856-60, 17 items

Subpoenas, 1835-55, ca. 100 items

Summons, 1820-60, .14 cu. ft.

Warrants, 1828-59, .1 cu. ft.

See also Land Records and Wills.

Superior Court of Chancery

Common Law Papers, 1817-30, .63 cu. ft.

Executions, 1819-22, .14 cu. ft.

Judgments and Dismissions, 1827, ca. 100 cu. ft.

Superior Court of Law

Common Law Papers, 1816-17, 1820, .14 cu. ft.

Executions, 1813-18, 1820-25, .1 cu. ft.

Circuit Superior Court of Law and Chancery

Chancery Suit Papers, 1833-50, 1853, 1.40 cu. ft.

Common Law Papers, 1831-51, .77 cu. ft.

Commonwealth Cases, 1834-48, ca. 50 items

Executions, 1841-51, .175 cu. ft.

Circuit Court

Chancery Suit Papers, 1853-61, 1866-67, 1869-74, 1877, 1881, 1884-85, 1887, 1.02 cu. ft.

Common Law Papers, 1852-80, .245 cu. ft.

Commonwealth Cases, 1872-1908, ca. 100 items

Executions, 1852-60, ca. 100 items

Judgments and Dismissions, 1852, ca. 100 items

Presentments, 1857-60, 18 items

Subpoenas, 1852-57, 1860, 1868-70, .1 cu. ft.

County and Superior Courts

Chancery Suit Papers, 1810-11, 1814-48, .35 cu. ft.

Common Law Papers, 1783-1871, 3.2 cu. ft.

Commonwealth Cases, 1826-57, ca. 100 items

Executions, 1824-39, ca. 100 items

Judgments, 1830-50, ca. 100 items

Miscellaneous Papers, 1783-1854, .1 cu. ft.

Subpoenas, 1825-50, ca. 100 items

Summons, 1805-60, .14 cu. ft.

County and Circuit Courts

Chancery Suit Papers, 1804-71, .14 cu. ft.

Common Law Papers, 1788, 1801-74, 1880-88, .56 cu. ft.

Executions, 1828-59, .1 cu. ft.

Presentments, 1822-59, ca. 50 items

Subpoenas, 1850-59, ca. 50 items

County, Superior, and Circuit Courts

Chancery Suit Papers, 1823-84, ca. 100 items

Common Law Papers, 1787-1889, 1.33 cu. ft.

Executions, 1825-55, ca. 100 items

Superior Courts

Common Law Papers, 1819-50, .45 cu. ft.

Commonwealth Cases, 1829-51, ca. 100 items

Judgments and Dismissions, 1820-50, ca. 100 items

Election Records

    List of Voters, 1858, 1 item

    Poll for Magistrates, 1844, 1 item

    Polls, 1825, 1847, 1851-59, .15 cu. ft.

Fiduciary Records

    Administrators' Bonds, 1782-1860, .56 cu. ft.

    Allen Chapman Estate Papers, 1855-57, ca. 30 items

    Appraisements and Settlements, 1777-1878, 1.47 cu. ft.

    Estate Accounts, 1812-78, ca. 100 items

    Estate Divisions and Receipts, 1800, 1810, 2 items

    Executors' Bonds, 1837, 1843, 2 items

    Guardians' Accounts, 1787-1860, .91 cu. ft.

    Guardians' Bonds, 1745-1859, .56 cu. ft.

    John R. Winston Estate Papers, 1860, 20 items

Free Negro and Slave Records

    Free Negro Certificates, 1811, 1817, 1833, 3 items

Justice of the Peace Records

    Summons and Warrants, 1850-60, ca. 100 items

    Warrants, 1820-59, .25 cu. ft.

Land Records

    Deeds, 1741-54, 1760-1880, 1.93 cu. ft. and 3 vols.

    Deeds and Bonds Nos. 1-3, 1694-1729, 3 vols.

    Deeds, Orders, Wills, Etc. Nos. 1-11, 13, 1633-62, 1665-1702, 1706-10, 25 vols.

    Land Causes, 1746-69, 1 vol.

    Procession Report of William C. Chisman and William S. Sclater, 1812, 1 item

    Processioners' Reports, 1795-1836, 6 items

    Processioners' Returns, 1800-40, 9 items

Marriage Records and Vital Statistics

    Certificates of Marriage, 1855-66, 20 items

    Certificates of Ministers of Marriages Solemnized, 1800-50, 15 items

    Marriage Bonds, 1828-49, 14 items

    Marriage Bonds and Consents, 1772-1849, 1 vol.

    Marriage Consent, 1828, 1 item

    Marriage Records, 1826-58, 3 items

    Ministers' Return, 1794-98, 1 item

    See also Bonds/ Commissions/ Oaths, Bonds, Etc.

Military and Pension Records

    List of pensioners, 1803, 1 item

Road and Bridge Records

    Petitions for Roads, 1848, 6 items

    Reports on Bridges, 1841, 1851, 3 items

    See also Court Records, County and Superior Courts, Miscellaneous Papers.

School Records

    Abstract of School Masters' Accounts for the Tuition of Poor Children, 1829, 2 items

    School Commissioners' Reports, 1830-59, 15 items

    School Masters' Accounts, 1835-37, 30 items

Tax and Fiscal Records

    County Levies and Vouchers, 1786-1800, 1807, 1810-24, 1829, .175 cu. ft.

    Land Tax Lists, 1783, 1786, 1788, 1793-97, 1801, 1809, 1812, 1840, 1846, 18 items

    List of Taxable Property in Town of York, 1792, 1 item

    List of Taxable Tithables in York County, 1794, 1 item

    List of Tithables belonging to York County in Williamsburg, n. d., 1 item

List of Tithables by Wm. Howard for the Upper Precinct in Charles Parish, n. d.,
1 item

List of Tithables in that part of City of Williamsburg lying in York County, 1792-96, 1801, 6 items

Personal Property Tax Lists, 1784, 1787-92, 1794-97, 1811, 1824, 1826, 1830, 1835-36, 1841-43, 1849, 25 items

Vouchers for County Levy, 1858, ca. 100 items

Vouchers for Levy, 1784-85, 1790-91, 1794, .175 cu. ft.

Wills

Wills, 1750, 1777-80, .52 cu. ft. See also Fiduciary Record, Appraisements and Settlements.

Wills and Inventories Nos. 18-20, 22, 23, 1732-59, 1771-1811, 6 vols.

See also Land Records and Court Records, County Court

Miscellaneous Records

H. H. Shield's receipt for mortgages due Overseers of Poor, 1820, 1 item

Inquisitions, 1845-56, ca. 100 items

Jail Keeper's Account, 1874, 1 item

Report of Clerk's Office of York County, 1843, 1 item

Report of Inspectors of Jail, 1842, 1853, 2 items

York County Agents Account and Commissioners Report, 1836, 1 item

Microfilm Records

Circuit Court Clerk
Bonds/Commissions/Oaths

See Land Records, Deeds and Bonds

Court Records
County Court

Judgments and Orders, 1746-54, 1759-65, 1770-74, 1803-14, 4 reels

Minute Book, 1851-59, 1 reel

Order Books Nos. 4-7, 9-14, 1765-70 [vols. unnumbered], 1774-1803, 1815-51, 7 reels

See also Land Records and Wills

Superior and Circuit Courts

Chancery Order Book, 1831-60, 1 reel

Hustings Court of Yorktown

Records, 1787-94, 1 reel

Fiduciary Records

Guardians' Accounts, 1736-1846, 1 reel

See also Wills.

Free Negro and Slave Records

See Fiduciary Records, Guardians' Accounts, 1823-46.

Land Records

Deed Books Nos. 1-16 (titles vary, Nos. 1-3 contain bonds), 1694-1866, 44 reels.

General Index to Deeds, 1777-1866, 1 reel

Deeds, Orders, Wills, Etc. Nos. 1-13, 1633-1710, 11 reels

Land Causes, 1746-69, 1795-1854, 1 reel

Marriage Records and Vital Statistics

Marriage Bonds and Consents, 1772-1849, 1 reel (part)

Marriage Register 1, 1854-1928, 1 reel (part)

Wills

Will Books Nos. 10-14, 1811-89, 3 reels

General Index to Wills, 1811-1942, 1 reel

Wills, Administrations, Etc. No. 3-A, 1831-58, 1 reel
Wills and Inventories Nos. 14-23 (titles vary), 1709-1811, 7 reels
Miscellaneous Records
Claims for Losses of Citizens of York County in the British Invasion of 1781, 1781, 1 reel
Sheriff
Execution Book, 1789-95, 1 reel

APPENDIX

Synopsis of "THE VIRGINIA STATE COURT SYSTEM, 1776-[THE PRESENT]," A Preliminary Survey of the Superior Courts of the Commonwealth with notes concerning the present location of the original Court Records and Published Decisions, by Thomas Jefferson Headlee, Jr. Virginia State Library, 1969.

General Court, 1777-1851

The General Court existed prior to the American Revolution as the principal court, and the only appeals court, in the colony. After statehood it was reestablished by an act passed in the 1777 session of the General Assembly.

Prior to the American Revolution the General Court had original jurisdiction in nearly all types of cases, and appellate jurisdiction from all of the lower courts. After the war its functions were reduced. When the district courts were established in 1789, they were given appellate jurisdiction over the county courts in common law cases, and the High Court of Chancery acquired similar jurisdiction in chancery cases. The General Court was therefore left with concurrent jurisdiction chiefly in civil cases connected with public debtors, probate of wills and granting of administrations, recordation of deeds, and appellate jurisdiction in criminal cases.

Since its judges were also judges of the district courts, they spent most of their time serving the lower courts; but in 1814 the General Court was made the sole supreme criminal tribunal in the state, and its business was increased. It continued to be the supreme criminal tribunal in Virginia until its abolition by the state constitution of 1851, which gave its appellate jurisdiction to the Supreme Court of Appeals. The General Court ceased to exist on 1 July 1852.

During its existence, the court sat at the state capital, with jurisdiction over the entire state. When it was abolished, all records relating to appellate cases still pending were transferred to the Supreme Court of Appeals in Richmond, and records of ended causes were transferred to the Circuit Court of the City of Richmond. Both were located in the State Court House; consequently, all records of the General Court, except for one order book dated 1670-76, were destroyed during the Confederate evacuation of the city. There are available, however, some published post-1788 decisions of the court.

[Supreme] Court of Appeals, 1779-[the present]

After an unsuccessful effort to create a supreme court of appeals in 1778, the court was established by the General Assembly in 1779 and continues to the present day. While the court has concurrent original jurisdiction in issuing and hearing writs of habeas corpus, mandamus, and prohibition (injunction), its jurisdiction is almost exclusively appellate. Since its creation it has had final jurisdiction in civil cases, and it has had criminal jurisdiction since abolition of the General Court in 1851. Since then it has been the state's only court of final appeals.

The Supreme Court of Appeals has always had jurisdiction over the entire state. Originally it met biannually at the state capital, but for the convenience of litigants it has since then met at other locations. Currently it meets at Staunton in September and in Richmond during the rest of the year. Original order books for the Richmond, Wytheville, and Staunton courts are available on microfilm, and numerous published decisions are available as well.

Special Court of Appeals, 1791-[the present]

As early as 1791 there was a Special Court of Appeals composed of judges of the General Court who heard cases pending before the Supreme Court of Appeals, but which the latter was unable to hear because its judges disqualified themselves, were sick, or otherwise were unable to sit. The special court gained importance in 1848 when it was authorized to receive cases pending on the Supreme Court of appeals docket in excess of two years. It was given constitutional status in 1850. Both microfilmed copies of original records and published decisions are available.

High Court of Chancery, 1777-1802

The High Court of Chancery was created by the General Assembly in 1777. It assumed all chancery suits then pending in the General Court and jurisdiction in all new chancery cases, whether brought before it by original process, by appeal from a lower court, or by other legal means. The court met at the state capital, with jurisdiction over the entire state.

It was at first composed of three judges who met biannually in April and September; in 1788 the number of judges was reduced to only one, who held court four times a year. In 1802 the General Assembly abolished the High Court of Chancery, replacing it with the Superior Courts of Chancery.

It is assumed that when the court was abolished its records passed into the custody of the Superior Court of Chancery at Richmond and its successor courts, which occupied the main floor of the old State Court House which was burned in 1865 during the Confederate evacuation of Richmond. Although the original records of the High Court of Chancery were apparently destroyed in that fire, there are surviving published decisions.

Superior Courts of Chancery, 1802-1831

The High Court of Chancery was replaced by three chancery districts, each with its own court, in order to expedite the hearing of chancery suits. The new superior courts of chancery were therefore sometimes called district courts of chancery. Each one heard cases from all the counties included in its district. They met in one place in each district, and records were kept at that location.

There were originally three courts, in Staunton, Richmond, and Williamsburg. In 1812 additional courts were established in Wythe County, Winchester, and Clarksburg; and in 1814 two more were added in Greenbrier County and Lynchburg. When the superior courts of chancery were abolished in 1831 the records of each one were removed to the nearest county's circuit superior court of law and chancery. Although many records have been lost or have not been located, some are available on microfilm. There are no published decisions.

Court of Admiralty, 1776–1789

The Court of Admiralty was created by an act passed at the October 1776 session of the General Assembly. It received all cases then pending before the colonial maritime commissioners and acquired jurisdiction in all new maritime cases except those in which the parties might be accused of capital offenses. The court sat at the state capital, hearing cases as required.

The Court of Admiralty was abolished after the United States Constitution assigned admiralty and maritime jurisdiction to the federal courts. Those few admiralty cases which were not subsequently passed to the federal court system went to the newly created state district courts.

District Courts, 1789–1808

The district courts, created by the General Assembly in 1788, were the first of a series of superior courts which met regularly in the localities rather than at the state capital. They were designed to alleviate congestion in the General Court which had caused long delays in adjudication of common law cases.

The state was divided into eighteen districts, each composed of several counties, plus the district of Kentucky. Courts were held biannually in each district, and always met at the same place in each district; records were kept at that location. Each district court was presided over by two General Court judges, each pair of whom had responsibility for three or four districts.

District courts met at the following locations:

Northumberland County Courthouse   Richmond
King and Queen County Courthouse   Williamsburg
Monongalia County Courthouse   Suffolk
Prince Edward County Courthouse   Winchester
Accomac County Courthouse   Staunton
Charlottesville   Dumfries
Brunswick County Courthouse   Petersburg
Fredericksburg
New London, or Franklin County Court House
Lewisburg or Botetourt County Court House
Montgomery County or Washington County Court House

The district courts were abolished in 1808 and were replaced by the superior courts of law. Many of their records have been lost, although some are available on microfilm. Original records of courts which met in counties now in West Virginia are either in the county courthouses or in the West Virginia Department of Archives and History, Science and Cultural Center, Capitol Complex, Charleston, West Virginia 25305.

Superior Courts of Law, 1808–1831

The superior courts of law were created in 1808, and met biannually in each county. A General Court judge rode a circuit throughout his district, and court records were filed with those of the county courts where the court met. Because of their structure, these courts were sometimes called circuit courts, circuit courts of law, or circuit superior courts.

Civil and criminal jurisdiction was the same as that of the old district courts which the superior courts of law replaced. They in turn were superseded in 1831 by the circuit superior courts of law and chancery. Records of the superior courts of law, if they survive, are filed with the records of the locality; some are also available on microfilm.

Circuit Superior Courts of Law and Chancery, 1831-1851

The organization of these courts was similar to that of the superior courts of law, in that sessions were held twice yearly in each county and their records were filed with those of the county court. Again, a General Court judge rode a circuit from county to county. There were originally twenty circuits which were grouped in pairs to make ten districts; additional circuits were added later.

These new courts assumed the functions of both the superior courts of law and the superior courts of chancery, both of which were abolished in 1831. They were, in their turn, abolished by the constitution of 1851, and were replaced by circuit courts. Surviving records are filed with the county court records, and many are available on microfilm.

Circuit Courts, 1852-[the present]

The circuit courts were authorized by the constitution of 1851, and were established by acts passed by the General Assembly in May 1852. Courts were held twice yearly in each county, and records were filed with those of the county court. There were originally twenty-one judges who rode circuits to preside over the courts in their districts.

These courts were granted original jurisdiction concurrent with that of the county courts. They also had appellate jurisdiction in all civil cases involving more than fifty dollars, and in criminal cases not "expressly cognizable in some other court" (of which there were few). Unlike the county courts, the circuit courts were also given jurisdiction in criminal cases involving loss of life. Since 1873 they have had exclusive jurisdiction in chancery cases.

The constitution of 1902 made no provision for continuing the county courts, and their original jurisdiction in all but petty suits and misdemeanors was given to the circuit courts effective 1 February 1904. At that time probate authority was transferred entirely to the circuit courts, which inherited all original wills and records pertaining to probate and fiduciary affairs. On 15 March 1904 the circuit courts were also given responsibility for recordation of deeds.

The circuit courts still exist today, and are now the only courts of record in Virginia localities. Those records which have survived are filed with the records of the county. Many are also available on microfilm.

District Courts, 1852-1870

In addition to the circuit courts, the constitution of 1851 established a second series of district courts. The state was divided into ten districts, with a court to be held at least once per year in each. The courts met in only one location in each district, but heard cases from each circuit court in that district. The ten judicial districts were:

Wood County Courthouse	Lynchburg
Marion County Courthouse	Fredericksburg
Albemarle County Courthouse	Winchester
Monroe County Courthouse	Petersburg
Washington County Court House	Williamsburg

These courts were abolished in 1870. Their loose suit papers were distributed to the circuit courts in each county, and volumes were turned over to the Supreme Court of Appeals in Richmond, Wytheville, or Staunton, whichever session had general jurisdiction over a particular district court's territory. Microfilm copies of the order books are available for some of the courts.

INDEX

Roman numerals refer to the Introduction; Arabic numerals refer to page numbers. County entries are in **boldface.**

A

Lunacy records. See heading "Mis-
 cellaneous Records" under
 individual entries
Lunenburg County, 181-184, 189
Luray, Va., 111
Luray and Front Royal Turnpike
 Company (firm)
  minutes, 285
[Lybrook, Beckley & Co.] (firm)
 day book, 45
Lynchburg, Va., 18
Lyon [Family]
 papers, 158

M

M. B. & E. (firm)
 journal and ledger, 73
[M. O. Lomenco], 218
M. P. Atkinson and Co. (firm)
 ledger, 218
Macon District, Powhatan County
 available funds, 220
 taxes collected, 223
Madison County, 184-186
Madison Court House, Va., 186
Madison District, Cumberland County
 road papers, 88
Madison Township, Cumberland County
 stub book, 88
Magett, Nicholas, 267
Magistrates, ix.
  See also heading
  "Justice of the Peace
  Records" under individual
  entries
Magow, Mrs. M. M., 232
Maiden Spring Road, Tazewell County
 road records, 283
Maiden Spring School District, Tazewell
  County
 trustees records, 283
Major, Barnard, 70
Manakin Iron Works
 records, 128
Manassas Gap Rail Road Co.
 damages allowed landowners, 285
Manchester, Va., 79
Mangorike Wharf Co. (firm)
 minutes, 237
 subscription book, 237

Mangorike Wharf Company v. Owners of
 Steamboat Wenonah and
 Matildal, 238
Manumissions. See heading "Free Negro
 and Slave Records" under
 individual entries
Marr, John, 98
Marriage banns, xix
Marriage bonds, xix
Marriage certificates, xix-xx
Marriage license, xx
Marriage records. See heading
 "Marriage Records and
 Vital Statistics" under
 individual entries
Marshall & Joseph Smith (firm)
 journal, 98
Marshall Township, Richmond County
 check book, 242
Marshall v. Keen et al., 125
Martin, William F., 119
Mason's Creek, Roanoke County, 245
Mason, Walker & Richardson (firm)
 day books and ledger, 103
Masonic lodges, 49, 65, 222
Massie & Co. (firm)
 day book, 23
Mathews County, 187-188, 195
Matoaca Township, Chesterfield County
 [minutes], 79
Matthews, Jonathan H., 158
Matthews, William B., 93
Maury ads. Grant, 146
Mayo, A. S., 219
Mayo, A. S., Clerk ads. Commonwealth,
 218
Mayo, William, 132, 293
McCall Dennistoun and Co. (firm)
 schedule of debts, 169
McCall suit papers, 93.
  See also Stewart-McCall
McClung, James, 248
McClung, James W., 248
McDowell, Jno., 45
McEndrus, John H., 111
McGarry, Earl A., 232
McGeorge, William, 168
McKee, A. R., 9
McKinney, John, 259
McKnight and Galbraith (firm)
 ledger, 45
McKnight et al. ads. Irwin et al., 27
McLaren ads. Commonwealth, 129
McMeechen v. Rumsey, 34

N

Namezine District, Dinwiddie County
  tax assessed, 91
Nansemond County, 200
National Express and Transportation Co.
  ads. Rash, 147
National Farm Loan Mortgages, 293
Naturalizations. See heading "Miscel-
  laneous Records" under
  individual entries
Negroes
  removed from Georgia & S.C., 215
Neill, Charles, 121
Nelson County, 18, **200–203**
Neston Store (firm)
  records, 68
New Glasgow, Amherst County, 18
New Kent County, 142, 168, **203–207**
New Market Precinct, Nelson County
  list of white voters, 201
New Mechanicsville Turnpike Co.
  [minutes], 149
New Norfolk County, 207
New Orleans, La., 87
Newport District, Giles County
  personal property book, 122
  treasurer's report book, 123
Newport News, 288
Newport Parish, Isle of Wight
  County, 164
Newport Township, Giles County
  minutes, 122
Newville Township, Sussex County
  minutes, 278
  warrants, 278
Next friend, xx
Nicholas v. Foster, 142
Nicholls v. Rudd et als. and Conquest Tie
  and Lumber Co., 220
Ninety-eighth Regiment [Civil War], 191
Ninety-third Regiment, 247
Noland, B. P., 99
Norfolk & Great Western Railroad
  bonds, 153
Norfolk and Western Railroad
  plats, 121
Norfolk County, 207
Northampton County, 208
Northern Neck Mutual Fire Assn.
  policies, 203
North Farnham Parish, Richmond County
  records, 244
North Frederick Turnpike Co.
  records, 116

North River Navigation Company (firm)
  receipts, 246
Northside District, Henrico County
  tax books, 150
Northumberland County, 209–210
Notaries public. See heading "Miscel-
  laneous Records" under
  individual entries
Nottoway County, 211
Nottoway Parish, Nottoway County
  marriage records, 211
Nulton, Joseph A., 111

O

Oak Forest, Cumberland County, 87
Oak Hill, Fauquier County, 98
Oakland School, Appomattox County
  register, 21
Oaths. See heading "Bonds/Com-
  missions/Oaths" under indi-
  vidual entries
Office judgment, xx
Old Dominion Bank
  letter books, 119
Oldham, (Mrs.) Nancy, 240, 243
[Old] Rappahannock County, 211
One hundred sixteenth Regiment
  (Virginia militia) 250
One hundred twenty-fourth Regiment
  (Virginia militia), 260
Opequan Township, Frederick County
  road record, 116
Orange County, 212–213
Orange County, N. C., 198
Orange Humane Society
  suits, 213
Orange Union Agricultural Society, 213
Orders, xx
Organization records. See heading
  "Organization Records"
  under individual entries
Orphans' accounts, xx
Orphans' Court
  records, 22, 25, 32, 55, 145, 152
Osborne's [Prince George County?]
  plat, 15, 230
Ostin, D., 191
Overseer(s) of the Poor, xx.
  See also heading
  "Miscellaneous Records"
  under individual entries
Owens ads. Washington, 96

Witt, Jesse, 131
Witten, W. W., 283
Wohlford's exrs. et al. ads.
                    Mitchell and wife, 120
Wohlford v. Mitchell et al., 120
Wolf suit papers, 261
Wood and Scull v. Labb, 125
Woods, W. J., 123
Woods & Co. (firm)
    order book, 6
Woodson, F., 84
Woodson, Mary ads. J. L. Hannah, 244
Woodson, Perkins & Co. (firm)
    daybook, 128
Woodstock, Virginia
    aerial photographs, 279
Woolwine, L., 119
Wythe County, 297–298

Y

Yager. See Collins and Yager estate
Yates, John, 181
Yerby ads. Downing, 237
Yerby v. Downing, 237
Yokum [Station District], Lee County
    road fund warrants, 175
York County, 298–302
Yorktown, Virginia
    tithables, 300

Z

Zimmerman and Thrasher (firm)
    account books, 45
Zimmerman et al. ads. Guggenheimer et
                    al., 47